Browns 5/18 £35.99

A Companion to Kan

D1766589

Do not W/D. On reading list - 2018-19

M

Learning Resources Centre

Class No .... 193 Bir

Accession 105166

Location ....

Blackwell Companions to Philosophy

This outstanding student reference series offers a comprehensive and authoritative survey of philosophy as a whole. Written by today's leading philosophers, each volume provides lucid and engaging coverage of the key figures, terms, topics and problems of the field. Taken together, the volumes provide the ideal basis for course use, representing an unparalleled work of reference for students and specialists alike.

A Companion to Kant

Edited by

Graham Bird

⊗**WILEY-BLACKWELL**

A John Wiley & Sons, Ltd., Publication

This edition first published 2010
© 2010 Blackwell Publishing Ltd except for editorial material and organization © 2010 Graham Bird

Edition history: Blackwell Publishing Ltd (hardback, 2006)

Chapter 1 is taken from "Life and Works," pp. 3–23 in Allen W. Wood, *Kant* (Blackwell, 2005).
© 2005 by Allen W. Wood. Reprinted by permission of the author and Blackwell Publishing Ltd.

Blackwell Publishing was acquired by John Wiley & Sons in February 2007. Blackwell's publishing
program has been merged with Wiley's global Scientific, Technical, and Medical business to form
Wiley-Blackwell.

Registered Office
John Wiley & Sons Ltd, The Atrium, Southern Gate, Chichester, West Sussex, PO19 8SQ, United Kingdom

Editorial Offices
350 Main Street, Malden, MA 02148-5020, USA
9600 Garsington Road, Oxford, OX4 2DQ, UK
The Atrium, Southern Gate, Chichester, West Sussex, PO19 8SQ, UK

For details of our global editorial offices, for customer services, and for information about how
to apply for permission to reuse the copyright material in this book please see our website at
www.wiley.com/wiley-blackwell.

The right of Graham Bird to be identified as the author of the editorial material in this work has been
asserted in accordance with the UK Copyright, Designs and Patents Act 1988.

Library of Congress Cataloging-in-Publication Data

A companion to Kant / edited by Graham Bird.
    p. cm. — (Blackwell companions to philosophy ; 36)
    Includes bibliographical references and index.
    ISBN: 978-1-4051-9759-5 (pbk : alk. paper)   1. Kant, Immanuel, 1724–1804.   I. Bird, Graham,
1930–   II. Series.
    B2798.C75   2006
    193—dc22

                                                                                    2006006916

A catalogue record for this book is available from the British Library.

Set in 10/12.5pt Photina by Graphicraft Limited, Hong Kong

1   2010

Contents

Notes on Contributors

Paul Abela is an Associate Professor of Philosophy at Acadia University, Nova Scotia. He is a graduate of the University of Toronto with postgraduate degrees from Queen's University and Oxford. His principal area of research is in Kant studies, and he has published articles on Kant's practical philosophy and a book on the theoretical philosophy, *Kant's Empirical Realism* (2002).

Henry E. Allison is Professor of Philosophy at the University of California at Davis and Professor Emeritus at Boston University and the University of California at San Diego. His numerous writings on Kant include *The Kant–Eberhard Controversy* (1973), *Kant's Transcendental Idealism: An Interpretation and Defense* (1983; new ed. 2005), *Kant's Theory of Freedom* (1990), *Idealism and Freedom: Essays on Kant's Theoretical and Practical Philosophy* (1996), and *Kant's Theory of Taste: A Reading of the Critique of Aesthetic Judgment* (2001). He has recently been awarded the International Kant prize 2005, given every five years for outstanding work on Kant.

Marcia Baron is Rudy Professor of Philosophy at Indiana University, where she teaches ethics, history of ethics, and philosophy of law. Her publications include *Kantian Ethics Almost Without Apology* (1995), *Three Methods of Ethics* (with P. Pettit and M. Slote) (1991), and articles on impartiality, friendship, justification and excuses, rape and sexual consent, the provocation defense, and patriotism and Kant's ethics.

Graham Bird is Emeritus Professor of Philosophy at Manchester University and Honorary Professor of the University of Wales. He has written many articles on Kant and on contemporary philosophy, and three principal books: *Kant's Theory of Knowledge* (1962), *William James* (1986), and *The Revolutionary Kant* (forthcoming). He is co-editor of *Kantian Review* and President of the UK Kant Society.

Gordon Brittan is Professor of Philosophy at Montana State University, and the author of *Kant's Theory of Science* (1974). He has written numerous articles on Kant's philosophy of mathematics and science.

Wolfgang Carl is Professor of Philosophy at the University of Göttingen, and has been Visiting Professor at Princeton and Florence Universities. He is the author of *Der Schweigende Kant* (1989), *Die Transcendentale Deduktion der Kategorien* (1992), and *Frege's Theory of Sense and Reference* (1994). He is currently working on persons and the first-person point of view.

Predrag Cicovacki is Associate Professor of Philosophy at the College of the Holy Cross, Worcester, MA, USA. He is author and editor of seven books, including *Anamorphosis: Kant on Knowledge and Ignorance* (1997), *Kant's Legacy: Essays in Honor of Lewis White Beck* (2001), and *Between Truth and Illusion: Kant at the Crossroads of Modernity* (2002). He was guest editor for a special double issue of the *Journal of Value Inquiry* on Kant's moral philosophy.

Lorne Falkenstein is Professor of Philosophy at the University of Western Ontario. He has published extensively on space and spatial representation in Kant, Hume, Reid, Condillac, and Berkeley. He published *Kant's Intuitionism* in 1998.

Katrin Flikschuh teaches political philosophy at the London School of Economics, specializing in Kant's political philosophy and contemporary liberalism. She has published articles in both major areas, and her book *Kant and Modern Political Philosophy* was published in 2000. Her current work is on Kant's philosophy of cosmopolitanism, and in contrast to currently dominant nonmetaphysical approaches she aims to defend a metaphysically informed conception of global justice.

Michael Friedman is Professor of Philosophy at Stanford University. He has written extensively on Kant, on philosophy of science, and on early twentieth-century philosophy. His books include *Kant and the Exact Sciences* (1992), and *A Parting of the Ways* (2003). He has edited and translated Kant's *Metaphysical Foundations of Natural Science* for the Cambridge edition of Kant's works.

Sebastian Gardner is Professor of Philosophy at University College London. He is the author of *Kant and the Critique of Pure Reason* (1999), and has principal interests in Kant, nineteenth century German philosophy, and phenomenology.

Hannah Ginsborg is Associate professor of Philosophy at the University of California, Berkeley. Her Harvard PhD thesis was published as *The Role of Taste in Kant's Theory of Cognition* (1990). She has written various articles on Kant and on issues in contemporary epistemology and philosophy of mind.

Michelle Grier is Professor of Philosophy at the University of San Diego. In addition to numerous articles and reviews on Kant's philosophy she is the author of *Kant's Doctrine of Transcendental Illusion* (2001). Her book was awarded an international Kant Society prize at the 2005 Sao Paolo Kant Congress.

Paul Guyer is the Florence R. C. Murray Professor in the Humanities at the University of Pennsylvania. He is the author of seven books on Kant, the editor of the new Cambridge Companion to Kant (forthcoming 2006), and the general co-editor of the Cambridge edition of Kant's works, for which he has co-translated Kant's first and third *Critiques* and *Notes and Fragments*.

Samuel J. Kerstein is Associate Professor of Philosophy at the University of Maryland, College Park. The author of *Kant's Search for the Supreme Principle of Morality* (2002), he is currently writing on Kant's injunction to treat persons as ends in themselves.

Alison Laywine is Associate Professor of Philosophy at McGill University, Montreal, Canada. Her research has been mainly directed towards understanding Kant's pre-Critical metaphysics, and she published *Kant's Early Metaphysics and the Origins of the Critical Philosophy* in 1993. Her most recent publications include "Kant on Sensibility and the Understanding in the 1770s," *Canadian Journal of Philosophy*, vol. 33 (2003), and "Kant on the Self as Model of Experience," *Kantian Review*, vol. 9 (2005).

Robert B. Louden is Professor of Philosophy at the University of Southern Maine. He is the author of *Kant's Impure Ethics: From Rational Beings to Human Beings* (2000) and *Morality and Moral Theory: A Reappraisal and Reaffirmation* (1992). He is also a translator and editor of Kant's *Anthropology from a Pragmatic Point of View* (2005), and co-editor and translator of two forthcoming volumes in the Cambridge edition of Kant's works.

Arthur Melnick is Professor of Philosophy at the University of Illinois. He is the author of *Kant's Analogies* (1974), *Space, Time, and Thought in Kant* (1989), *Representation of the World – A Naturalized Semantics* (1996), and *Themes in Kant's Metaphysics and Ethics* (2004).

James O'Shea has been a lecturer in the school of philosophy at University College, Dublin, since 1992, having completed his PhD on Hume and Kant on "substance" at the University of North Carolina at Chapel Hill. He has published articles on Hume, Kant, William James, Wilfred Sellars, and American philosophy. His book *Wilfred Sellars* will be published in 2006 by Polity/Blackwell Press, and he has a book on Kant forthcoming.

Derk Pereboom is Professor of Philosophy at the University of Vermont. He has published articles on Kant, philosophy of mind, philosophy of religion, and on free will and moral responsibility. His latest book on the latter topic is *Living Without Free Will* (2001).

Andrews Reath is Professor of Philosophy at the University of California, Riverside. He has written extensively on Kant's practical philosophy and is the author of *Agency and Autonomy in Kant's Moral Theory* (2006).

Anthony Savile is Professor of Philosophy at King's College London, and also teaches at Charles University, Prague. His interests are primarily in aesthetics and the history of philosophy. Among his most recent books are *Leibniz and the Monadology* (2000) and *Kant's Critique of Pure Reason* (2004).

Martin Schönfeld is Associate Professor of Philosophy and Environmental Studies at the University of Southern Florida. His interests are in Kant's philosophy of nature, the Enlightenment, and Eastern influences on early modern thought. He has edited and translated (with Jeffrey Edwards) Kant's first book, *A True Estimation of Living Forces* (1749) for the Cambridge edition of Kant's works. He published *The Philosophy of the Young Kant: The Pre-Critical Project* in 2000, *Kant's Philosophical Development* in the Stanford Encyclopedia of Philosophy (2003), and the entry for Christian Wolff in the Encyclopedia of Philosophy (2005). He is currently editing an issue of the *Journal for Chinese Philosophy* (no. 33, 2006) on Confucian influences on Leibniz and Kant.

Sally Sedgwick is Professor of Philosophy in the University of Illinois at Chicago. She is the author of numerous papers on Kant and Hegel and editor of *The Reception of*

Kant's Critical Philosophy: Fichte, Schelling and Hegel (2005). Current projects include a *Commentary on Kant's Groundwork of the Metaphysic of Morals* (forthcoming 2007) and *Hegel's Critique of Kant*.

Philip Stratton-Lake is Professor of Philosophy at the University of Reading. He is the author of *Kant, Duty, and Moral Worth* (2000), and the editor of *Ethical Intuitionism: Re-evaluations, On What We Owe to Each Other: Scanlon's Contractualism*, and the new edition of W. D. Ross's *The Right and the Good*.

Udo Thiel is Senior Lecturer in Philosophy at the Australian National University at Canberra. He has published widely in seventeenth- and eighteenth-century philosophy, and is currently writing a book on self-consciousness and personal identity in German, British, and French eighteenth-century philosophy.

Wayne Waxman is the author of *Kant and the Empiricists: Understanding Understanding* (2005), *Hume's Theory of Consciousness* (1994), and *Kant's Model of the Mind: A New interpretation of Transcendental Idealism* (1991).

Howard Williams is Professor of Political Theory in the Department of International Politics at the University of Wales, Aberystwyth. He has written many articles and written or edited eleven books, including *Kant's Political Philosophy* (1983), *International Relations in Political Theory* (1991), *International Relations and the Limits of Political Theory* (1996), and, most recently, *Kant's Critique of Hobbes: Sovereignty and Cosmopolitanism* (2003). He is co-editor of *Kantian Review* and was a Visiting Fellow at Stanford University and the Jagellonian University, Krakow, during 2004.

Allen W. Wood is Ward W. and Priscilla B. Woods Professor at Stanford University. He has also taught at Cornell and Yale Universities, with visiting appointments at the University of Michigan and the University of California at San Diego. He is the author of seven books, including *Kant's Ethical Thought* (1999), and editor or translator of eight others. He is a general co-editor of the Cambridge edition of Kant's works.

Acknowledgments

I would like to acknowledge the generous and friendly cooperation of the contributors, all of whom gave more to the project than merely their formal essays. I have been greatly helped and encouraged by Nick Bellorini, who initiated the work on behalf of Blackwell, and by the two editors Kelvin Matthews and Cameron Laux.

References to Kant's Works

1. References to the *Critique of Pure Reason* are given throughout to the first (A) and second (B) edition page numbers. Where a passage occurs in both editions only the B page number is given; A page numbers are given for passages which occur only in A. The A and B page numbers are provided in the margins of almost all the standard translations of the *Critique*, such as the following:

Guyer, P. and Wood, A. W., tr. (1998). *Critique of Pure Reason*. Cambridge: Cambridge University Press.
Kemp Smith, Norman, tr. (1929). *Immanuel Kant's Critique of Pure Reason*. London: Macmillan.
Pluhar, Werner, tr. (1996). *Immanuel Kant: Critique of Pure Reason*. Indianapolis: Hackett.

2. References to Kant's other works are given in the form volume/page no., e.g., (1.45) for volume 1, page 45; all of the "Akademie" edition (Berlin: Walter De Gruyter, 1902–; sometimes of course also referred to as the "Academy" edition). These are also routinely given in the margins of most translations, such as the Cambridge University Press edition of Kant's works listed below:

Theoretical Philosophy 1755–1770, eds. and tr. David Walford and Ralf Meerbote. Cambridge, 1992.
Lectures on Logic, ed. and tr. Michael Young. Cambridge, 1992.
Opus postumum, eds. and tr. Michael Rosen and Eckart Förster. Cambridge, 1993.
Practical Philosophy, ed. and tr. Mary Gregor. Cambridge, 1997.
Lectures on Ethics, eds. and tr. Peter Heath and Jerome Schneewind. Cambridge, 1997.
Prolegomena to any Future Metaphysics, ed. and tr. Gary Hatfield. Cambridge, 1997.
Lectures on Metaphysics, eds. and tr. Karl Ameriks and Steve Naragon. Cambridge, 1997.
Critique of Pure Reason, eds. and tr. Paul Guyer and Allen Wood. Cambridge, 1998.
Religion and Rational Theology, eds. and tr. Allen Wood and George Di Giovanni. Cambridge, 1996.
Critique of the Power of Judgment, eds. and tr. Paul Guyer and Eric Mathews. Cambridge, 2000.
Theoretical Philosophy after 1781, eds. and tr. Henry Allison and Peter Heath. Cambridge, 2002.

Metaphysical Foundations of Natural Science, ed. and tr. Michael Friedman. Cambridge, 2004.

Notes and Fragments, eds. and tr. Paul Guyer, Curtis Bowman, and Frederick Rauscher. Cambridge, 2005.

Anthropology, History, and Education, ed. and tr. Günter Zöller. Cambridge, forthcoming.

Natural Science, ed. Eric Watkins. Cambridge, forthcoming.

3. Other translations of Kant's principal works include:

Beck, L. W., tr. (1985). *Critique of Practical Reason*. London: Macmillan.

Greene, T. M. and Hudson, H. H., tr. (1960). *Religion Within the Limits of Reason Alone*. New York: Harper Torchbooks.

Paton, H. J., tr. (1964). *Groundwork of the Metaphysics of Morals*. New York: Harper Torchbooks.

Pluhar, Werner, tr. (1987). *Critique of Judgment*. Indianapolis: Hackett.

Reiss, Hans, ed., and Nisbet, H. B., tr. (1970). *Kant's Political Writings*. Cambridge: Cambridge University Press. (Does not provide *Akademie* edition pagination.)

4. Where it is useful to be explicit about the title of a work, references to the *Akademie* edition are sometimes supplemented with an abbreviated title reference, the key to which is given in the following list of works cited in the contributions:

APS	*Anthropology from a Pragmatic Standpoint*
CF	*Conflict of the Faculties*
CJ	*Critique of the Power of Judgment*
CPR	*Critique of Pure Reason*
CPrR	*Critique of Practical Reason*
DN	*Duisburg Nachlass*
FS	False Subtlety of the Four Syllogistic Figures
G	*Groundwork of the Metaphysics of Morals*
Geo.	*Physical Geography*
ID	*Inaugural Dissertation*
Idee.	*Idea of a Universal History for a Cosmopolitan Purpose*
JL	*Jäsche Logic*
JU	*The Joint Use of Metaphysics and Geometry in Natural Philosophy*
LB	*Loses Blatt Leningrad I*
MFNS	*Metaphysical Foundations of Natural Science*
MM	*Metaphysics of Morals*
NC	*Announcement of the Near Conclusion of a Treaty of Eternal Peace in Philosophy*
NE	*New Elucidation of the First Principles of Metaphysical Knowledge*
OD	*On a Discovery whereby any new Critique of pure reason is to be made superfluous by an older one*
OMF	*Outline of Meditation on Fire*
Op.	*Opus postumum*
OPG	*Only Possible Ground for a Proof of God's Existence*
OT	*What is it to Orient Oneself in Thinking?*
Päd.	*On Pedagogy*

PNTM	*Inquiry Concerning the Distinctness of Principles of Natural Theology and Morals*
PP	*Toward Perpetual Peace*
Prol.	*Prolegomena to any Future Metaphysics conceived as a Science*
R	*Reflexionen*
Racen.	*On the Different Races of Human Beings*
RBR	*Religion within the Bounds of Reason Alone*
RP	*What Real Progress has been made in Metaphysics in Germany since the Time of Leibniz and Wolff?*
SC	Spin Cycle Essay
TE	*True Estimation of the Living Forces of Matter*
TP	"On the Common Saying: That may be correct in theory, but it is of no use in practice"
UNH	*Universal Natural History and Theory of the Heavens*

Variant versions of Kant's reconstructed lectures on anthropology, metaphysics, and moral philosophy are abbreviated under their titles as "Busolt," "Collins," "Friedländer," "Menschenkunde," "Mrongovius (I and II)," "Parow," and "Powalski."

5. *Works by authors other than Kant*

These are given by reference to author and date. Some historical titles are abbreviated and so indicated in the contributions where they occur.

General Introduction

GRAHAM BIRD

1. Background to the Critical Philosophy

Kant's Critical philosophy, published in the three *Critiques*, of *Pure Reason, Practical Reason*, and *Judgment*, between 1781 and 1790, is the basis of his formidable reputation. His influence dominated Western philosophy throughout the nineteenth century and, after some neglect in the early twentieth century, has been more recently renewed. Only at the turn of the nineteenth and twentieth centuries did analytic philosophy, under the influence of Pragmatism, of Frege, Russell, and the Logical Positivists, develop an agenda which consciously rejected the grand metaphysical debates of the nineteenth century between idealism and realism, or monism and pluralism. Since Kant, seen through the eyes of the nineteenth-century commentators, was thought to have been a prime originator of those debates, his reputation suffered with their rejection.

Analytic philosophers in the early twentieth century, such as Carnap, Reichenbach, and Cassirer, were strongly influenced by aspects of the *Critique of Pure Reason*, but others, such as Kemp Smith, Paton, and Collingwood, retained an interest in Kant which was mainly historical. Later, from the 1960s, opposition from Wittgenstein and philosophers such as Ryle, Austin, Grice, and Strawson to the purely formal aspects of analytic philosophy encouraged a revival of interest in, and new interpretations of, Kant. That development began again to make Kant's project of live philosophical rather than merely historical interest. The renewed interest sometimes still insisted on the nineteenth-century idealist tradition of Kant interpretation, but it led also to accounts which set him at odds with that tradition. Some interpreters persisted in treating his philosophy as a version of the traditional idealism he claimed to reject, but others offered an account of his transcendental idealism consistent with that rejection. With new translations of, and greater access to, all his writing, including the unpublished *Nachlaß*, it has been possible to begin to correct earlier caricatures of his philosophy. Continuing interest in Kant as the basis for live philosophical enquiry continues in the twenty-first century. (See chapter 33 below.)

Such a thumbnail historical sketch already indicates some of the strong disagreements about Kant's position and its merits throughout the two centuries since 1781. From the first commentators on Kant in the late eighteenth and early nineteenth centuries to the present day, philosophers have disagreed radically about the nature

1

and value of his work. Kant himself responded to his earliest critics, such as Eberhard (*OD*) and Garve (*Prol.*, 4.372ff), but these often vehement rebuttals did not still the later criticisms of Hegel, Schopenhauer, and others after his death (see chapter 30 below). For the most part, nineteenth-century philosophers interpreted Kant as a thoroughgoing idealist, and criticized, or attempted to mitigate, the resulting conflicts in his views. Only occasionally, as in the polemic between Adolf Trendelenburg and Kuno Fischer in the 1860s, was there a clear suggestion that Kant had wanted not to revive a traditional idealism but to repudiate it and branch out in a new direction (see chapter 31 below). Later philosophers, such as Husserl and Heidegger, developed a phenomenological approach strongly influenced by their reading of Kant (see chapter 32 below). Throughout the nineteenth and twentieth centuries, from the polemics of the 1860s to the disagreements between Henry Allison (1983) and Paul Guyer (1987), commentators have continued to disagree radically about Kant's project, its alleged mistakes, and its fruitful points of development. These disagreements have arisen from almost every detail of Kant's work, but they indicate also a more general division.

One view is that although Kant aimed to transcend the metaphysical tradition he inherited and to point in a new direction for philosophy, his implicit commitment to that tradition meant that the project could not succeed. According to this view, despite his expressed intention to reject *all* previous philosophy (*Prol.*, Preface, 4.255), that underlying commitment to traditional idealism prevented him from achieving a stable, coherent outcome. Even though he qualified his own theory as a *transcendental* idealism in order to distance it from the tradition, the doctrine remains a *form* of idealism. To traditionalist commentators this marks an unstable adherence to a background which Kant had hoped to repudiate, and serves to explain the many blatant contradictions which they find in Kant's text.

An alternative view is that when his own conscious modifications to the tradition are adequately understood, Kant's doctrine can be seen to represent, as he explicitly claimed, a revolutionary rejection of the previous philosophical tradition. Transcendental idealism, according to this view, is not an incoherent acceptance and rejection of traditional idealism but a revolutionary attempt to dispense with its assumptions (see chapter 7 below). The uncertainty of Kant's repudiation of the tradition is then represented more as a function of the commentators' commitments than of Kant's. Throughout the nineteenth century most commentators accepted a traditional idealist background, but struggled and failed to make sense of Kant's position under those assumptions. In the twentieth century commentators who may not themselves have accepted traditional idealism nevertheless often regarded it as obligatory to ascribe such a doctrine to Kant. To distance Kant from that traditional view does not relieve him of all criticism, but it sets aside the gross inconsistencies he has sometimes been thought to commit through an ambiguous and confused adherence to both realism and idealism. It is a measure of Kant's stature, and of the intriguing elusiveness of his thought, that the lesser philosophers who have commented on, sometimes developing sometimes resisting, his work have not found it possible to agree at this general level about either its character or its merits.

It is inevitable that in this commissioned collection of essays on Kant there should be varied accounts of, even disagreements about, the Critical philosophy. The aim is nevertheless to provide a survey of the whole range of his work, to give some idea of its immense scope, its extraordinary achievement, and its continuing ability to generate philosophical interest. The contributions cannot deal with every aspect of his work, but the hope is that they will clarify its general structure and fill out many of its details. Nor can they be all of exactly the same kind. Some offer lucid exposition of Kant's claims while others take up historical, philosophical, scientific, moral, aesthetic, and social-political issues to which Kant made a contribution. They are designed to be relatively concise and sufficiently clear to be appreciated by anyone with an interest in philosophy and the history of philosophy. They cannot all be easy to read but their difficulties may encourage further exploration of Kant's own texts and of commentators' views about them.

Although the three *Critiques* represent the core of Kant's Critical philosophy, the full scope of his work in this collection covers more. Before 1781 Kant had written many smaller philosophical works in the so-called "pre-Critical" period. It is generally accepted that this phase terminated in the 1770 *Inaugural Dissertation* and was followed by a long period, the "silent decade," before 1781, during which no major work was published. Work done recently in Alison Laywine 2001, Martin Schönfeld 2000, and Wolfgang Carl 1989 – all authors represented in this volume – has thrown new light on that early period: Schönfeld 2000 provides an excellent survey of Kant's wavering commitments to rationalism, Newtonianism, and other doctrines during the pre-Critical period. (See chapters 2, 3, 4, and 12 below.)

But during the period of the three *Critiques* and afterwards Kant also published a wide range of works which variously fill out and apply the Critical principles. So the *Prolegomena* (1783) and the *Groundwork of the Metaphysics of Morals* (1785) offer a summary account, respectively, of the first *Critique* and of the moral philosophy in the second. *The Metaphysical Foundations of the Natural Sciences* (1786) and the *Metaphysics of Morals* (1797), with its Doctrines of Right and of Virtue, and *Religion within the Bounds of Reason Alone* (1793), apply the Critical principles, respectively, to natural science (that is, to Newtonian physics), to issues in law, morality, politics, and religious belief. The essays on *Perpetual Peace* (1795) and "Theory and Practice" (1793) pursue Kant's moral principles into the realms of political institutions and international politics (see chapters 24 and 25 below). Since the origins of the Critical philosophy lie in Kant's dissatisfaction with the methods and standards of traditional metaphysics it is not surprising that throughout his career he wrote further on the development of philosophy in such works as *On Progress in Philosophy* (1791) and *The Quarrel among Faculties* (1798). These aspects of Kant's philosophy have become more accessible with the publication and translation of smaller essays and lecture notes (see chapter 23 below).

At the very end of his life, between about 1786 and 1803, Kant worked on projects published only posthumously as the *Opus postumum*. The available text is not so much a philosophical work as a series of repetitive, often rambling, and frequently obscure, notes which offer hints of a seemingly ambitious plan to bring aspects of the Critical philosophy together in a synthesis of metaphysics and science. The text itself focuses on a more specific project of explaining the transition from an a priori metaphysics to the guiding principles of Newtonian physics. This project of bringing metaphysics and physics into harmony dominated also the pre-Critical writings, but Kant's conception of such a synthesis undoubtedly changed after the development of the Critical philosophy. Commentators consequently take different views of the *Opus postumum* and its achievement. To some it is the culmination of his philosophical system, but to others it is only an unfortunate reflection of Kant's declining intellectual powers. Despite a recent abbreviated, translated, and edited text for the *Opus postumum* (Förster and Rosen 1993), it remains an incomplete and dubious addition to Kant's central work. For that reason it is not specifically represented in this volume and finds no place in the following categories into which his central work is here divided:

1   Kant's life, the pre-Critical writings, and the empiricist and rationalist background. (Chs. 1–6.)
2   The metaphysical foundations of the Critical philosophy in the *Critique of Pure Reason* and *Prolegomena*. (Chs. 7–16.)
3   The transition to moral philosophy, pure and applied, in the *Grundlegung*, *Critique of Pure Practical Reason*, and *Metaphysics of Morals*; freedom, the character of the supreme principle of morality, and its uses. (Chs. 17–23.)
4   The applied philosophy, in science, morals, and politics. (Chs. 15–16, 19–27.)
5   The final *Critique of Judgment*; teleology, biology, aesthetics; beauty and morality. (Chs. 28–31.)
6   The aftermath of the Critical philosophy: Hegel, a neo-Kantian polemic, phenomenology, and the twentieth century. (Chs. 32–5.)

Brief editorial introductions to the issues in each of the three *Critiques* and the applied philosophy provide a background to the detailed discussions in these sections.

2. Foundations of the Critical Philosophy in the first *Critique* and *Prolegomena*

The outcome of Kant's decade of reflection after 1770 on the needed reform of philosophy is presented in the first *Critique* and *Prolegomena* in the form of two related enquiries. The first is to examine the distinction, and its consequences, between sciences which have established methods and metaphysics which so far lacks them. The consequence is, according to Kant, that metaphysics, lacking the clear and assured decision procedures of Newtonian physics or Euclidean geometry, goes endlessly in circles and produces only the pseudo-enquiries Kant describes as "bloodless mock battles." The circles characteristically take the form of alternate bouts of dogmatism and skepticism, of grossly optimistic claims about knowing a reality hidden behind ordinary experience, followed by a profound pessimism about our successfully achieving *any* knowledge even in ordinary experience or in science. Kant rejects the idea that these alternatives, associated respectively with rationalist extravagance and empiricist skepticism, are exhaustive.

Kant's central aim in the first *Critique* is to diagnose and cure the faults which lead to this endless oscillation of pseudo-issues, and to use the diagnosis as a guide to more "scientific" principles for metaphysics in a new direction for philosophy. Kant thinks of a scientific metaphysics as *different* from established sciences such as physics, mathematics, or logic, but he requires that it establishes its own clear and assured decision procedures. The *Critique* is consequently a "propaedeutic" or preparation for the substantive pursuit of metaphysics in its revolutionary, reformed, Critical form. The theme of diagnosing systematic errors in previous philosophy is extensively pursued only towards the end of the *Critique* in the penultimate section, the Dialectic and especially the Antinomies, but the theme is already identified from the start in the Prefaces. Kant later came to think that the diagnosis and therapy might usefully have been placed at the beginning of the work.

The second, related, enquiry, followed in the actual text of the first *Critique*, is to take our existing knowledge in ordinary experience and in science as a datum in order to uncover its structure, and to establish what *enables* us to achieve determinate knowledge. Kant believes that the disclosed structure reveals a necessary interplay between certain high-level, abstract principles and the lower-level presentation of specific experiences to the senses. Even that general description rules out the achievement of legitimate knowledge through either abstract principles *alone*, as rationalists might claim, or *solely* through the presentation of specific experiences, as empiricists thought. Although at this general level Kant rejects standard forms of both empiricism and rationalism, his own views owe debts to both (see chapters 5 and 6). More positively Kant claims to disclose principles, operating in experience, which function as "conditions" or "presuppositions" of that experience; that is, conditions without which experience would be impossible for us.

Three general aspects of this positive development deserve to be noted. First the discovered conditions are divided into those which govern or determine the operation of our fundamental cognitive powers, that is, the senses or sensibility, understanding, and reason. Later in the third *Critique* a parallel project deals with the principles of judgment and imagination. Sensibility has to do with the way in which items are presented to the senses; understanding deals with the discursive concepts with which those presentations are characterized; and reason is concerned with our powers of reasoning, especially in developing systems or theories in mathematics, natural science, and metaphysics itself. Kant explores the sensory conditions in the Aesthetic in a discussion of space and time, and the conditions of understanding in the Analytic's identification of the fundamental categories and their role in experience (see chapters 9 to 11).

The conclusions of the Aesthetic and Analytic are then used in the Dialectic to explain, criticize, and limit a range of comparable principles of reason. The general message is that principles of pure reason do *not* have the status or character of the other preconditions of experience. The "conflicts of reason with itself" which stimulated the need for reform in philosophy point to that conclusion, and the detailed arguments outline their legitimate role in experience and the illusory temptations they offer. They *have* a legitimate, limited, role, but they tempt us to make unwarranted claims that go beyond any experience into a supposed supersensible realm. Kant's technical contrast between "appearances" (or "phenomena"), tied to sense experience, and "things in themselves" (or "noumena"), supposedly independent of that experience, is required to separate what reason can and cannot legitimately do. Our immanent reality consists of appearances, but the Dialectic's antinomies may delude philosophers into thinking that they can establish truths about a transcendent pseudoreality of things in themselves. These limitations on the legitimacy of pure reason provide Kant with his title of a *Critique of Pure Reason*. (See chapter 13.)

Second, as preconditions of experience the discovered principles have priority in that experience. Kant believes that the prior conditions cannot provide experience on their own but need supplementation with what is materially given to the senses. Kant's technical distinction between the "a priori" and the "a posteriori" is designed to capture that appeal to the two separately necessary and jointly sufficient conditions for the full-blown experience which acts as a datum for the enquiry. In this part of the enquiry it is useful to distinguish claims about *priority relations* between items in experience and claims about some item's being a priori. Some contemporary philosophers would accept a legitimate enquiry into the relative *priorities* holding between items in experience, but reject Kant's idea that some items are prior conditions of *any* experience and so *a priori*. An underlying empiricism provides one motive for such a position, since Kant's conception of the a priori is incompatible with a standard empiricism. His conception of the a priori is the notion not just of logical or analytic truth, but of a substantial contribution to the character of experience, expressed in his classification of synthetic a priori judgments: Some synthetic a priori principles not only determine the nature of our experience but, according to Kant, are responsible for its objectivity. (See chapters 8 and 10 below.)

Third, the connected appeals to the a priori principles, and their necessary reference to our mental powers of sensibility and understanding, provide the basis for Kant's form of idealism. That form, heralded in the imagery of the Copernican experiment (B xx–xxiii), is contained in the supposition that objects conform to our knowledge (B xvi), and that we know a priori of things only what we put into them (B xviii). Kant's view is that *both* characteristics, being a priori and being dependent on those cognitive powers, make a necessary, ineliminable, reference to our minds as a contributory factor in that experience. Even empiricists hold that our minds, through such operations as Locke's "workmanship of the understanding," play a necessary part in developing our experience, but the previous paragraph and the Copernican imagery express a more substantial, distinctively non-empiricist, Kantian appeal to the mind's contribution. That contribution issues in those principles governing experience which are neither derived from experience nor analytically true but both synthetic and knowable a priori.

Commentators from Christian Garve's first review of the *Critique of Pure Reason* in 1782 to Strawson (1966) have expressed this Kantian commitment by talking of "the mind making nature," though Kant himself never uses that expression. It is dangerously naive since it encourages ascription to Kant of a literal project of psychological development, which he explicitly rejects, and it fails to distinguish, as he does, between purely "formal" and "material" nature. Despite what some commentators have claimed, Kant was concerned with the structure of *formal* nature and never thought that our minds literally constructed the material nature of such things as mountains in Africa (Stroud 1984). The doctrine of "the mind making nature" has been the basis for the ascription to Kant of the crudest, Berkeleian, form of traditional idealism, which Kant explicitly repudiates. It is time that that expression, and the thought behind it, vanished from the scene.

Kant's initial steps in the first *Critique* to provide a reformed metaphysics set the scene for the whole Critical philosophy. The later second and third *Critiques* can be properly understood only within the framework provided in the first, and that is why the largest single group of essays in this volume concerns the first *Critique*. There are serious dangers in working backwards from the third *Critique of Judgment* in order to interpret the framework of the first. Although Kant comments on that basic framework throughout his career, those first steps remain the fundamental reformed structure for all the subsequent developments. Kant undoubtedly changed his mind on some issues between the pre-Critical and Critical periods, and probably between the latter period and the *Opus postumum*, but in general his views show a remarkable consistency.

With that sketch of Kant's central, and basic, metaphysical goal, I now list five distinctive aspects of his discussion in the first *Critique*.

1. The whole Critical philosophy can be seen as an extended essay on *priority*, or *dependence*, relations among items in our experience. The preliminary, propaedeutic, framework in the first *Critique* and *Prolegomena* expresses the needed reform in philosophy and sets the course for the more detailed exploration of dependence relations in the subsequent works. It replaces a bogus transcendent metaphysics with an immanent, but transcendental, examination of the map of our experience within which each item has its proper location in relation to all others. Kant's "transcendental topic" is an explicit expression of that new, immanent, goal (B 324–5), as is his renunciation of "ontology" in favor of a "mere analytic of concepts" (B 303). Kant adds to that account a controversial step from mere "priority" to "a priority." The a priori elements in experience, which Kant claims to identify, are those which are prior to *all* other items in experience and not dependent on any others; they indicate a *fundamental* priority attached to elements without which experience would be impossible.

2. To identify and map that fundamental priority is, according to Kant, to uncover the normally hidden structure of experience in ordinary life, in science, in art, and in such special domains as morality, the law, religion, and politics among others. Kant notes, and decisively rejects, the temptation to construe that hidden structure as a realm of reality, of things in themselves. The structure is hidden only because in ordinary experience we are normally unaware of it, not because it designates a realm, accessible only to philosophers, which goes beyond that experience. It identifies the governing principles of our conceptual economy and not any cognitive access through pure reason to supersensible objects such as Leibnizian monads or Lockean primary qualities. It marks, again, a mere analytic of concepts rather than a "proud ontology." It differs substantially from a comparable empiricist map in virtue of its claim that the fundamental elements are independent of, and not reducible to, the simple a posteriori beginnings of our sense experience. It *answers* to our a posteriori experience but is not *derivable* from it.

3. The first *Critique* is primarily a "propaedeutic" because its enquiry is a necessary preliminary to the projected new direction of a reformed metaphysics. It consequently has a higher-order status than either science or traditional philosophy in questioning the methods and authority of the latter. Kant's project does not accept the authority of traditional philosophy in order to question or doubt experience, but accepts the authority of the sciences in order to question the methods of traditional metaphysics. The traditional authority which philosophy claimed for itself to question, and perhaps

reject, the results of the sciences gives way, under Kant's exploration of the structure of our cognitive economy, to an acceptance of science and a rejection of that traditional authority. Kant accepts as a datum for his cartographic enquiry the character of our experience, and of the sciences within it, and the outcome is a severe restriction of that traditional philosophical authority.

4. Kant's descriptive metaphysics, outlined in paragraph 3 above, does address *some* specific forms of skepticism head-on. Kant confronts an empiricist challenge to a belief in the necessity of causality, and more generally to a belief in synthetic a priori judgments and a substantive role for a priori elements in experience. The immediate task of the *Critique* is to establish against Hume that these challenges can be met; that our experience is governed by a range of a priori concepts whose role empiricism had overlooked or misunderstood. Beyond that, and as a somewhat peripheral further confrontation with *idealist* skepticism, Kant devises a new way of refuting the idealist doubt about the outer, physical, world in his Refutation of Idealism (B 274–9) (see chapter 12 below). In the moral philosophy of the second *Critique* and the *Groundwork* Kant has more to say of a skepticism which treats obligation and duty as fictions or delusions, but he adopts the same method of accepting experience as a datum from which to identify a priori elements in morality (see chapter 19 below).

5. Throughout Kant's project there is an essential, and characteristic, outcome to his discussion which marks a striking divergence from earlier philosophers. It is an explicit *reversal* of the traditional orders of priority attached to pairs of concepts. The Copernican "revolution," heralded in the Preface (B xxi–xxii), represents Kant's view against the empiricists that there are substantive a priori elements in our experience. It claims that sometimes our knowledge does not simply derive from objects presented to the senses, but actually contributes to their constitution. It thus *reverses* a priority attached to objects over our knowledge, and in the fundamental cases, such as the categories, gives a priority to our cognitive constitution over the objects of experience. In a similar way the Refutation of Idealism reverses the priority traditionally given in idealism to inner over outer objects of experience. For traditional idealists inner experience is immediate and certain, while outer experience rests on a mediate and dubious inference from that immediate certainty. The Refutation of Idealism argues that outer, spatial, experience has a priority over inner. Even more generally the first *Critique* reverses the skeptical authority attached traditionally to philosophy over science. In Kant's moral philosophy a central step is to reverse the priority attached, for example in Utilitarianism, to happiness over duty and obligation (see chapter 20 below). For Utilitarians, duty and obligation rest on the notions of welfare and happiness, but for Kant morality is not determined by welfare, and happiness is deserved only when the demands of morality are met (see chapter 21 below). At every stage in the discussion Kant's transcendental topic offers to redraw the map of priority and dependence relations among items in our experience. These reversals mark Kant's distance from the tradition; they underline his revolutionary goals and their considerable extent. They offer a major reform in philosophy comparable to that which occurred between the end of the nineteenth and the early twentieth century in Western philosophy.

References

Allison, Henry E. (1983). *Kant's Transcendental Idealism: An Interpretation and Defense*. New Haven: Yale University Press.

Carl, Wolfgang (1989). *Der schweigende Kant* [*The Silent Kant*]. Göttingen: Vandenhoek and Ruprecht.

Förster, Eckart and Rosen, Michael, tr. and ed. (1993). *Opus Postumum*. Cambridge: Cambridge University Press.

Garve, Christian (1782). Review of *Critique of Pure Reason*, in A. Landau (ed.), *Rezensionen zur kantischen Philosophie*, vol. 1, 1781–7. Bebra: Albert Landau Verlag.

Guyer, Paul (1987). *Kant and the Claims of Knowledge*. Cambridge: Cambridge University Press.

Laywine, Alison (2001). Kant in reply to Lambert on the disputed ancestry of general metaphysical concepts. *Kantian Review*, 4: 1–48.

Schönfeld, Martin (2000). *The Philosophy of the Young Kant*. Oxford: Oxford University Press

Stroud, Barry (1984). *The Significance of Philosophical Scepticism*. Oxford: Oxford University Press.

Strawson, P. F. (1966). *The Bounds of Sense*. London: Methuen.

1

Kant's Life and Works

ALLEN W. WOOD

Immanuel Kant was born April 22, 1724, in Königsberg, East Prussia, a seaport located where the River Pregel flows into the Baltic Sea. In Kant's time, the city was an isolated eastern outpost of German culture (though it was occupied by Russian troops for several years during Kant's lifetime). Most of the city was leveled by British and American bombing, or by Soviet artillery, prior to its invasion by the Soviet army in 1945. After the war it was ethnically cleansed of its German population, renamed Kaliningrad (after a thoroughly hateful Stalinist henchman), and became, what it still is, an isolated western outpost of Russian culture. For nearly 40 years of the twentieth century, as the headquarters of the Soviet Baltic fleet, it was entirely closed to foreigners and to most Russians as well.

The Lutheran cathedral at Königsberg, located on a large island in the middle of the Pregel, remained a bombed-out ruin until the Gorbachev era, but it was substantially rebuilt and renovated during the 1990s. In Kant's day, the main building of the University (no longer extant) was located nearby on the same island. Kant refused on principle to attend religious services at the cathedral, since he thought such exercises constitute "superstitious counterfeit service" of God, true service of whom consists only in good conduct of life, not in slavish praise or fetishistic rituals attempting to conjure up the divine presence. But Kant spent considerable time in the building, since the cathedral contained the University library, where Kant not only often studied, but also served for a time as librarian.

Kant's tomb, appropriately located *outside* the cathedral on the side (and to the left of the altar), is now pockmarked from wartime shrapnel, but it remains largely intact, never needing to be rebuilt. It somehow escaped demolition by allied bombs, and later also from the Russian invasion, reportedly because one Soviet general (having better than average education) ordered that it (together with a statue of Schiller that still stands elsewhere in the city) should be spared the destruction his troops were triumphantly wreaking on the rest of Königsberg. Since the war, the new Russian population of Kaliningrad has kept Kant's tomb constantly adorned with flowers. To this day it is customary for marrying couples to visit it. Apparently the austere rationalist philosopher Immanuel Kant – Lutheran by upbringing but in his maturity always deeply suspicious of popular religious superstition in all its forms – was the nearest imitation of a local Orthodox saint that this old German city had for the new population to venerate.

Early Years

Eighteenth-century Königsberg, at the Eastern corner of the Baltic, was connected to the rest of the world through its access to the sea, and boasted a rich and curiously varied intellectual culture. In that sense, it was not culturally isolated, and Kant was not the only Königsbergian to make important contributions to literature and philosophy in the late eighteenth and early nineteenth centuries. Nevertheless, Königsberg is hardly the place from which one might have expected the greatest revolution in modern philosophy to spring. Nor was Immanuel Kant, judging from his family or his social origins, the sort of person from whom one would have expected such a thing. He was the second son, and the sixth of nine children, born to Johann Georg Kant, a humble saddler (or leather-worker) of very modest means, and Anna Regina Reuter, daughter of a member of the same saddler's guild. Kant believed that his father's family had come from Scotland (and that the family name had been spelled "Cant"). He was proud to claim a heritage that would affiliate him with men he admired as much as he did Hutcheson, Hume, Lord Kames, and Adam Smith. More recent research has shown, however, that he was unfortunately mistaken on this point of his genealogy, probably misled by the fact that more than one of his great uncles had married recent Scottish immigrants. Kant's ancestors, for as far back as they can be traced, were entirely of German stock; his father's family came from Tilsit.

Kant's parents were devout Pietists. Pietism was a revivalist movement that arose in the seventeenth century and had a great impact on German culture throughout the eighteenth century. It is comparable to other contemporary religious movements, such as Quakerism or Methodism in England, or Hassidism among central European Jews. (We should never forget that the "age of reason" was also an age of religious enthusiasm.) Kant's family pastor, Franz Albert Schulz, was also rector of the newly founded Collegium Fredericianum. Noticing signs of exceptional intellect in the humble Kant family's second son, he arranged an educational opportunity for Immanuel that was surely rare for children of his parents' social class. At the Fredericianum Kant was taught Latin and enough else to enter the university at age 16. However, he found the atmosphere of religious zealotry, especially the intellectual tyranny of the catechism, insufferably stifling to both mind and spirit. In the course of a short treatise on meteorology, he later wrote about the catechisms that "in our childhood we memorized them down to the last hair and believed we understood them, but the older and more we reflective we become, the less we understand of them, and on this account we would deserve to be sent back to school once again, if only we could find someone there (besides ourselves) who understood them better" (8.323).[1]

Attempts are frequently made to identify Pietist influences in Kant's moral and religious thought. But virtually all explicit references to Pietism in his writings or lectures are openly hostile. He typically identifies Pietism either with a spirit of narrow sectarianism in religion or with a self-despising moral lethargy that does nothing to improve oneself or the world but waits passively for divine grace to do everything. Perhaps his mildest remark is one that defines a "Pietist" as someone who "tastelessly makes the idea of religion dominant in all conversation and discourse" (27.23). Kant's philosophy was in turn regarded with hostility by most of the influential Pietists in Königsberg.

Academic Career

Kant entered the University in 1740. This was the same year Frederick the Great became King of Prussia. The year is also significant in the intellectual life of Germany because one of Frederick's first acts was to recall Christian Wolff from exile in Marburg to his professorship at the University of Halle, thus offering symbolic support to the intellectual movement known as the *Aufklärung* (Enlightenment), of which Wolff was considered the father. Seventeen years earlier, Wolff had been summarily exiled by Frederick's father, Friedrich Wilhelm I, from Prussian territories under the influence of Pietists in the Prussian court. They objected to the way the enlightenment had made the German universities places of dry scholastic reasoning, rather than religious inspiration and moral exhortation. They also found objectionable Wolff's fascination with "pagan" thought (he was, for instance, one of the first Europeans to undertake the philosophical study of Confucian writings, which he treated in an alarmingly sympathetic spirit). They were equally horrified by some of his philosophical doctrines, such as that the human will is subject to causal determination under the principle of sufficient reason (though Wolff did not deny freedom of the will, but was what we would now call a "compatibilist" or "soft determinist"). The struggle, both within the universities and in intellectual life generally, between Wolffianism and Pietism was decisive for the intellectual environment in which Kant came of age.

The first study Kant took up at the University was Latin literature, which left its mark in the numerous quotations from Latin poets that constitute almost the only literary adornments in Kant's philosophical writings. But soon he came under the influence of those at the university who taught mathematics, metaphysics, and natural science. The best known of these was Martin Knutzen (1713–51), whose early death (it is sometimes speculated) might have deprived him of some of the philosophical influence that was later to be exercised by his most famous student. Knutzen is sometimes described as a Wolffian, but he was more a Pietist critic of Wolff than an adherent. Further, it is at best an oversimplification to think of Kant as "Knutzen's student." For one thing, Kant's talents were apparently not much appreciated by Knutzen. He never regarded Kant as among his better students, and this unfortunate fact was largely responsible for what, with hindsight, we now see as the extraordinarily slow development of Kant's academic career. Moreover, Kant's magisterial thesis was completed in 1746 under the direction of Johann Gottfried Teske (1704–72). This makes it more accurate to describe Kant as "Teske's student," though Teske was a natural scientist with few broader philosophical interests. The thesis itself was mainly an elaboration of Teske's researches on combustion and electricity. In fact, all the writings Kant published before the age of 30 were in natural science – on topics in Leibnizian physics, astronomy, geology, and chemistry.

Kant left the University in 1744, at the age of 20, to earn a living as a private tutor, which he did in various households in East Prussia for the next decade. The most influential of his employers was the Count von Kaiserlingk. Even in later years he maintained a social relationship with this family, especially with the Countess. During these years Kant was twice engaged to marry, but both times he postponed marriage on the ground that he was not financially solvent enough to support a family, and both times his fiancée tired of waiting and married someone else. By the time he was financially in a position to marry, he had come to appreciate – probably under the influence of his friend Joseph Green – the independence of a bachelor's life, and had resolved to do without a wife or family.

Kant returned to university life in 1755, receiving the degrees of Master and Doctor of Philosophy, and obtaining a position as *Privatdozent*. This means he was licensed to teach at the University, but was paid no salary, so that he had to earn his living from fees paid him by students for his lectures. Since his livelihood depended on teaching whatever students wanted to learn, he found himself lecturing not only on logic, metaphysics, ethics, natural theology, and the natural sciences – including physics, chemistry, and physical geography – but also on practical subjects that were related to them, such as military fortification and pyrotechnics. For a considerable time Kant devoted his intellectual labors mainly to questions of natural science: mathematical physics, chemistry, astronomy, and the discipline (of which he is now considered the founder) of "physical geography" – what we call "earth sciences." This work culminated in *Universal Natural History and Theory of the Heavens* (1755). In this essay Kant was the first to propound the nebular hypothesis of the origin of the solar system. But the financial failure of its publisher had the effect of almost totally suppressing it, and it remained virtually unknown for many years, until after Laplace had put forward essentially the same hypothesis with greater mathematical elaboration.

In the same year, however, Kant also began to engage in critical philosophical reflections on the foundations of knowledge and the first principles of Wolffian metaphysics, in a Latin treatise *New Elucidation of the First Principles of Metaphysical Cognition*. Here he subjected central propositions and arguments of the Wolffian metaphysics and theory of knowledge to searching criticism, and we find the earliest statement of some of Kant's characteristic thoughts about such topics as causality, mind–body interaction and the traditional metaphysical proofs for God's existence.

Many years later, in the Preface to his *Prolegomena to Any Future Metaphysics* (1783), Kant made the assertion that it was the recollection of David Hume that first awoke him from his "dogmatic slumbers." There is a literature in German that attempts (rather desperately, in my judgment) to give some sort of biographical substance to this remark.[2] Far more plausibly, Kant's point in making it was to invite his audience (assumed to have been taught Wolffian philosophy) to find its own path to his critical philosophy through reflection on Hume's skeptical challenges. The juxtaposition of Humean skepticism to Wolffian dogmatism may have been a striking way for Kant to raise the fundamental issue of the possibility of metaphysics, and is certainly indicative of Kant's lifelong admiration for Hume's philosophy. But it is most unfortunate that the remark has been taken as an authoritative autobiographical report about his own philosophical development. For when it is interpreted as saying that Kant began as an orthodox Wolffian metaphysician, only to be roused from complacent rationalism by Hume's skeptical doubts, the remark simply does not correspond at all to the facts of Kant's intellectual life. (As a statement about his own intellectual development, there is probably greater truth in Kant's later assertion that it was the problems of the four antinomies of reason, with which he became occupied in the 1770s, that "woke him from his dogmatic slumbers" (12.258).) A student of the development of Kant's philosophy finds that he was never an orthodox Wolffian, but from the very start took a critical stance toward some of the most basic tenets of Wolffian metaphysics. His rejection of the "dreams of metaphysics" was perhaps even more extreme in his satirical essay *Dreams of a Spirit-Seer* (1766) than it was later in the *Critique of Pure Reason* (1781). In that sense, there never was any "dogmatic slumber" from which to awaken: the long course of Kant's development toward the position of the *Critique of Pure Reason* (and just as significantly, beyond it) was always a restless searching that was terminated only by his eventual decrepitude and death.

A wider philosophical audience was first attracted to Kant's writings in 1762, when he entered a prize essay competition on the foundations of metaphysics. Moses Mendelssohn won the competition, but Kant's essay, *On the Distinctness of the Principles of Natural Theology and Morals*, won second prize, was published in 1764 along with Mendelssohn's winning essay, and received notable compliments from Mendelssohn (with whom Kant was always on terms of mutual admiration and respect).

Kant's interest in moral philosophy developed relatively late. In the prize essay, as well as his earliest lectures on ethics, he seems to have been attracted by the moral sense theory of Francis Hutcheson. But he was soon to become convinced that a theory based on feelings was inadequate to capture the universal validity and unconditional bindingness of a moral law that must often challenge and overrule corrupt human feelings and desires. His thinking about ethics was dramatically changed about 1762 by his acquaintance with the newly published writings of Jean-Jacques Rousseau: *Émile, Or on Education* and *Of the Social Contract*. Pietism had already taught him to believe in the equality of all human beings as children of God, and in the church universal, encompassing the priesthood of all believers, to be pursued as a moral ideal in a sinful world of spiritual division and unjust inequality. These convictions now took the more rationalistic form of Rousseau's vision of human beings, free and equal by nature, who find themselves in an unfree social world where the poor and weak are oppressed by the rich and powerful. Soon Kant began defining his own ethical position through emphasis on the sovereignty of reason, associating his moral philosophy with the title "metaphysics of morals." However, it was another 20 years before Kant brought his ethical theory to maturity. In the meantime, the task to which he devoted his principal labor was that of reforming the foundations of the sciences and discovering the proper relation within them between empirical science and the claims of *a priori* or metaphysical knowledge.

Kant's closest friend during his youth was Johann Daniel Funk (1721–64), a professor of law, who led a rather wild life and died at an early age. Like his friend Funk (and contrary to the grossly distorted traditional image of him), Kant was always a gregarious man, thought of by those who knew him as charming, witty, and even gallant. Compared to Funk, however, he was also much more self-controlled and prudent. His sociability included regular play at cards and billiards, which he did with notable shrewdness and skill. Kant's winnings often supplemented his meager academic income. After Funk's death, Kant made his longest and most intimate friendship, with the English businessman Joseph Green (1727–86). Green was an eccentric bachelor and a man of very strict and regular habits. It is probably through Green's influence that Kant acquired many of the characteristics pertaining to the (often highly distorted) picture that was later formed of him. From quite early on, Kant invested his savings in the mercantile ventures of the firm of Green & Motherby, which was profitable enough to provide Kant with a comfortable fortune by the time he gained his professorship in 1770.

The slow development of Kant's academic career corresponds to the long gestation period of the system of thoughts for which we now most remember him. Professorships in logic and metaphysics became open at the University of Königsberg in 1756 and 1758, but Kant did not even apply for the first, and with his still very limited qualifications he was routinely passed over for the second. After the recognition he received from Mendelssohn and the Prussian academy, he was offered a professorship of poetry at the university in 1764, but declined it because he wanted to continue devoting himself to natural science and philosophy. In 1766 he did accept a position as sublibrarian at the University, providing him with his first regular academic salary. But he declined opportunities for professorships in 1769, first at Erlangen and then at Jena, chiefly because of his reluctance to leave East Prussia, but also because he expected the professorship of logic at Königsberg would be available to him the following year. In subsequent years he had other opportunities (for instance, he was offered a professorship at Halle in 1778), but chose never to leave Königsberg. Just as Beethoven, the most revolutionary of all composers, wrote some of his most original music after he was totally deaf, so Kant, the most cosmopolitan of all philosophers, lived in an isolated province of northeastern Europe and never traveled farther than 30 miles from the place of his birth.

In the Latin inaugural dissertation he wrote on assuming his professorship at Königsberg, *On the Forms and Principles of the Sensible and Intelligible World*, Kant took several important steps in the direction we can now see eventually led him to the "critical philosophy" of the 1780s and 1790s. By 1772, Kant told his friend and former student Marcus Herz that he was at work on a major philosophical treatise, to be entitled *The Limits of Sensibility and Reason*, which he expected to finish within a year. But it was nearly a decade more before Kant published the *Critique of Pure Reason*. During the 1770s Kant wrote and published very little. Despite his elevation to a professorship, Kant continued to live in furnished rooms on the island in the Pregel on which stood both the University building and the cathedral in which its library was housed. It would be another 13 years before he was able to purchase a house of his own.

Early in this "silent decade," however, Kant began lecturing on the subject of "anthropology," stimulated (or provoked) by Ernst Platner's *Anthropology for Physicians and Philosophers* (1772). Kant rejected Platner's "physiological" reductivism in favor of an approach that emphasized the practical experience of human interaction and the historicity of human beings. Yet Kant was always deeply skeptical of the capacity of human beings to gain anything like a scientific knowledge of their own nature, and he was especially dissatisfied with the entire state of the study of human nature up to now, looking forward to a future scientific revolution in this area of study (which he himself did not pretend to be able to accomplish). He lectured on anthropology in a popular style for the next 25 years. These lectures were the most frequently given and the most well attended of any he gave during his teaching career. Kant's ideas about anthropology exercise a powerful but subtle influence on his treatment of epistemology, philosophy of mind, ethics, aesthetics, and the philosophy of history, but it is an influence difficult to assess because Kant never articulated a systematic theory of

15

anthropology, and his published writing on anthropology was limited to a popular textbook derived from his lectures, *Anthropology from a Pragmatic Standpoint* (1798), which he issued at the end of his teaching career.

Years of Academic Success

Kant was born poor, and he remained poor – an unsalaried, marginal academic – well into middle age. But his investments with Green and his appointment to a professorship finally gave him a comfortable living. And by the early 1790s his lately acquired fame had made him one of the highest paid professors in the Prussian educational system. During the late 1760s and for most of the 1770s he lived, along with many others from the University, in a large rooming house owned by the publisher and bookdealer Kanter. In 1783, at age 59, Kant finally bought a home of his own – a large, comfortable house on Prinzessinstraße in the center of town, almost in the shadow of the royal castle that gave the city its name.

The *Critique of Pure Reason* was finally published in the spring of 1781 (less than a month before Kant's 57th birthday). Although Kant brought his labors on it to a conclusion very rapidly, in the space of about four months in 1779–80, this book had been nearly 10 years in preparation. Once the *Critique* was published, the evident originality of the thoughts contained in it and the difficulty of his struggle to achieve them both led Kant to expect that it would attract immediate attention, at least among philosophers. He was therefore disappointed by the cool and uncomprehending reception it initially received. For the first year or two he received from those whom he most expected to give his book a sympathetic hearing only a bewildered silence.

Kant found especially frustrating the review of the *Critique* published in the *Göttingen Learned Notices* in January 1782. It was ostensibly written by Christian Garve (a man Kant respected) but had been heavily revised by the journal's editor, J. G. Feder, a popular Enlightenment philosopher of Lockean sympathies who had little patience for metaphysics in any form and no sympathy at all for the new and seemingly abstruse project of "transcendental philosophy" in which Kant was engaged. The review interpreted Kant's transcendental idealism as no more than a variation on Berkeley's idealism – a reduction of the real world to subjective representations, based on an elementary confusion between mental states and their objects. The review, together with the evident incomprehension of the *Critique* by most of its earliest readers, caused him to attempt a more accessible presentation of his ideas in *Prolegomena to Any Future Metaphysics* (1783). But Kant was not a good popularizer, and it would be several more years before the *Critique* began to get the kind of attention Kant had hoped for.

The first floor of Kant's house on Prinzessinstraße contained a hall in which he gave his lectures, and the kitchen where food was prepared by a female cook (he could now finally afford to hire one); on the second floor was a sitting room, a dining room, and Kant's study (where there reportedly hung over his writing desk the only decoration he permitted in the house – a portrait of Rousseau). Kant's bedroom was on the third floor. For many years, Kant had a personal servant, Lampe – who, however, was apparently given to drink, and was discharged in the late 1790s when he reportedly attacked his frail and aging master during a quarrel.

In the second-floor dining room Kant enjoyed his only real meal of the day, a dinner at which he usually entertained several guests. Königsberg was a seaport, and although Kant never himself ventured far from it, he took the opportunity to acquaint himself with many of the distinguished foreigners who passed through. By the time of these banquets (in the early afternoon), Kant had usually completed his main academic work. He rose regularly at 5 a.m., having only a cup of tea and a pipe of tobacco for breakfast. Then he prepared for his lectures, which he delivered five or six days a week, beginning at 7 or 8 in the morning. After them, he would go to his study and write until time for dinner. After his guests had departed, Kant would often take a nap in an easychair in his sitting room (sometimes a good friend, such as Green, would nap in the chair next to him). At 5 p.m. the philosopher would take his constitutional walk, whose timing, according to the famous legend, was so precise and unvarying that the housewives of Königsberg could set their clocks by the minute at which Professor Kant walked past their windows. Yet the regularity of Kant's schedule, as well as his crochets about his health and especially his diet (he believed in eating a lot of carrots, and drank wine daily, but never beer) probably resulted less from a compulsive personality than from the necessity of an aging man, who had never been in the best of health, to keep himself strong enough to complete philosophical labors which he had not been able properly to begin until he was far into middle age. Kant's evenings were often spent socializing, either at Green's house, or Hippel's, or with the Count and Countess Kaiserlingk.

Friendships

Kant's closest friend by far in his years of maturity was clearly Joseph Green, whose influence on him is hard to overestimate. Kant respected Green's judgment even in philosophical matters, to such an extent that it is reported he read every word of the *Critique of Pure Reason* to Green prior to its publication.

Another of Kant's friends was the mayor of Königsberg, Theodor Gottlieb von Hippel (1741–96), through whose help and influence he was able to purchase the house in Prinzessinstraße where he lived out his later years. Hippel was a remarkable man. He was not only active politically, but also intellectually. He was a learned and intelligent man, the author of whimsical, satirical plays and novels in the style of Laurence Sterne. He also wrote progressive political treatises defending the civil equality of Jews, and argued for a quite radical position on the social status of women, advocating the reform of marriage to ensure their equality with men in all spheres of life. Hippel's views on the emancipation of women were far in advance of Kant's own, even though at the time rumor had it that Kant shared in the authorship of these writings. Some of these rumors may have been benevolently intended toward Kant, but some surely were not, since like other defenders of women's rights in that time (such as William Godwin), Hippel was widely calumniated as an unprincipled sexual libertine. Kant refused to participate in these attacks on his friend's character, but he also publicly disavowed association with Hippel's "feminist" writings.

Another of Kant's notable friendships is even more curious – the one with J. G. Hamann (who was also a close friend of Green). Hamann was a thinker and writer of great brilliance, but his views – like his personality – could hardly have been more different from Kant's. Hamann was an eccentric religious thinker, who combined philosophical skepticism with fideist irrationalism. He had a troubled life-history, and lived an unconventional life (for instance, cohabiting with a woman he never married). Kant even seems to have helped him out financially for a time. Personally, Hamann was an imprudent, unstable, unhealthy man. Hamann's writings are terse, impressively learned, full of idiosyncrasies, ironies, and inventive allusions, always tantalizingly (or infuriatingly) cryptic. He was a trenchant critic of the Enlightenment, including Kant's philosophy, and a mentor of both the German counter-enlightenment and the *Sturm und Drang* literary movement. It says something very significant, and very favorable, about both men's characters and the largeness of both their minds, that they were genuinely friends, and that their profound differences in style and outlook apparently never led to any significant personal estrangement.

Kant's relation with other friends and acquaintances reveals a more ambiguous picture. During the 1760s he was close to the customs official Johann Konrad Jacobi and perhaps even more so to his wife Maria Charlotta.[3] But when she left her husband and took up with another acquaintance of Kant, master of the mint Johann Julius Göschel, after the divorce and remarriage Kant broke off relations with the adulteress and refused ever to see her or her new husband. He was not always so intolerant of sexual indiscretions, however. When his doctoral student F. V. L. Plessing[4] fathered an illegitimate child in 1784, Kant undertook the responsibility of conveying the necessary payments to the young woman, and may even have supplied some of the funds himself. Yet when in 1794 a troubled young woman, Maria von Herbert, sought the philosopher's advice and consolation in a time of inner anguish and despair, Kant showed remarkable insensitivity to her feelings and her situation, dismissing her to their mutual friend Elizabeth Motherby as "die kleine Schwärmerin" (the little enthusiast), and citing her as a sad example of what can happen to young women who do not control their fantasies. Some years later, Maria committed suicide.

Students whom Kant regarded as straying from the proper path were sometimes dealt with unkindly. When Kant's former student J. G. Herder criticized Kant in the first two volumes of his *Ideas for the Philosophy of History of Humanity* (1785–7), Kant wrote superficially laudatory but plainly condescending reviews of Herder's work, which infuriated his former student – who was himself a touchy and troubled person, all too easily offended. Despite a surprisingly warm tribute to Kant in Herder's *Letters on the Advancement of Humanity* (1793), Herder's last works were mainly devoted to anti-Kantian polemics. When Kant's work on the Critique of the Power of Judgment took too much time for him to review the third volume of Herder's *Ideas*, he tried to pass the dubious task of criticizing him along to another of his highly able students, Christian Jacob Kraus (who was the chief exponent of Adam Smith's economic theories in Germany). When Kraus refused to comply with Kant's wishes, they quarreled and their previously close friendship came to an end. Kant helped the young J. G. Fichte to begin his philosophical career by aiding him in the publication of his first work, *Attempt at a Critique of All Revelation* (1792). But in 1799, perhaps under the jealous influence of some of his students, Kant publicly denounced Fichte, disclaiming him as a follower of the Critical philosophy and citing the Italian proverb: "May God protect us from our friends, for we shall manage to watch out for our enemies ourselves" (12.371).

Kant's Character

The complexity of Kant's conduct toward particular people naturally raises questions about what sort of man he was. Today, of course, just as in eighteenth-century Königsberg, this is a matter that must be up to each of us to decide for ourselves. I think that on the whole, Kant seems to have been neither a particularly admirable nor a particularly unlikable human being. Rather, like most human beings, especially interesting ones, his character contained a rich mixture of attractive and unattractive traits. He was hard-working, patient and utterly devoted to his work as a scientist, scholar, and philosopher, but he was also both shrewd and ambitious, never missing out on the personal advantages he gained through the professional success and prosperity he eventually achieved. He was a gregarious, sociable man, but sometimes quarreled with his friends, and a number of his friendships came to an abrupt end. Though Kant believed above all in thinking for oneself, in his habits and lifestyle he seems at times to have been curiously open to the influence of certain friends – early in life, to Johann Daniel Funk, later in life to Joseph Green. He had a fierce love of the search for truth and of independent thinking, but he could also be jealous of his reputation, and mean-spirited toward students or followers he thought had personally betrayed him. He was not always above the intellectual cliquishness and academic backbiting characteristic of his time (and of many intellectuals and academics in any time).

Now that Kant has been dead for over 200 years, however, it is worth asking how far it should matter to us at all, as students of his philosophy, what kind of man he was. (We know all too little about Aristotle's personality, for example, a fact that perhaps mercifully saves us from many irrelevant thoughts about his philosophy.) Judgments about Kant's character, as we make them, are most often ancillary to – or rationalizations of – our reactions to his philosophy – especially those reactions (favorable or unfavorable) that exceed our ability to provide rational support for them. So it is worth asking how far judgments about Kant's character could possibly provide us with anything we can honestly make use of as critics or defenders of his ideas. Kant is sometimes either reviled or ridiculed by critics for the inflexibility of his mode of life and the alleged inhumanity of some of his moral opinions – as on the subjects of sex, suicide, the place of women in society, or the duty of truthfulness, capital punishment, or the wrongness of resistance to authority.

Of course it matters in evaluating Kant's views what conclusions they might lead to on these subjects. But often critics are less interested in this question (which may be difficult to decide) than in interpreting Kant's opinions as expressions of the kind of person he was, and in using our reactions to his character to color our reception of his philosophy. On some of these topics, the common image of Kant is all too accurate, while on others it is exaggerated and distorted. He was, however, an ardent supporter of the movement known as "Enlightenment" and his views on many subjects – politics, education, and especially religion – were on the whole quite progressive by the standards of the time. It is also remarkable that critics who typically attack others for failing to consider things in social and historical context often feel free to measure Kant's opinions by the same standards they would use to judge views voiced by someone living in our own day.

Kant is sometimes also criticized for the views on race that are expressed in some of his anthropology lectures and shorter essays. Here too there is sometimes distortion or exaggeration, since Kant had virtually no first-hand knowledge of non-Europeans and had to rely on travel reports (which he read avidly) for all his information about other peoples and cultures. Kant accepted some reports about nonwhite peoples that we would now regard as racist, but at times he also expressed skepticism about claims that nonwhites are intellectually inferior to Europeans, noting that the reports on this issue are contradictory (8.62). But on the subject of European colonialism in other parts of the world, Kant's opinion is consistent and (for its time) even extreme. Kant condemns without hesitation or qualification the injustice and hypocrisy of European imperialists who, he says, conquer other peoples in the name of visiting them and plunder and exploit them in the name of civilizing them (6.352–3, 8.357–60). Even if Kant accepted the racist view that nonwhites are intellectually inferior to Europeans, he definitely repudiated the practical corollaries of such a view for whose sake racists typically hold it.

It is a sometimes uncomfortable fact that the philosophers of the past whose thoughts we study with most profit were not especially fine human beings. The only way to deal with this fact is to face up squarely to the cognitive dissonance it occasions and then to resolve to set it aside as irrelevant to anything that could be of legitimate interest in deciding which philosophers to study. It displays a deplorable misunderstanding of what philosophy is – and what may be gained by studying it – to treat past philosophers as gurus at whose feet we are to sit in order to absorb their wisdom, or alternatively, to find in their unattractive personal traits and characteristics an excuse for not studying them at all. If a past philosopher, Kant for instance, was an admirable person, that still gives us no reason to study his philosophical thoughts if they were unoriginal or mediocre and do not repay our careful investigation and critical reflection. If the philosopher was a thoroughly unattractive character, or even if some of his opinions on morality or politics offend enlightened people today, it may still be true that his contributions to philosophy are indispensable to our understanding of philosophical problems and of the history of people's reflections on them. If we study the writings of the admirable philosopher in order to honor his virtuous character, then we are merely wasting time and effort that could have been better employed. By the same token, if we refuse to study the writings of the personally repulsive philosopher either because we think our neglect justly punishes him for his misdeeds or his evil opinions, or because we want to avoid being influenced by such a pernicious character, then all we accomplish by this foolish exercise in self-righteousness and closed-mindedness is to deprive ourselves of what we might have learned both from attaining to his insights and from exposing his errors. It is always sad to see philosophy students, and sometimes even professional philosophers, missing out on many things they might have learned on account of their moral or political approval or disapproval of the personality or opinions of some long-dead philosopher, who is far beyond their poor power to reward or punish. The only people we punish in this way are ourselves, and also those around us, or in the future, whom we might have influenced for the better if we had educated ourselves more wisely.

Enlightenment and Philosophy of History

In the middle of the 1780s, Kant laid the foundation for much of nineteenth-century philosophy of history in several brief occasional essays. To a significant degree, Kant's thinking about history was prompted by his reading of Herder's *Ideas*. Herder saw himself as a critic of the Enlightenment rationalism Kant defended, and Kant's contributions to the philosophy of history were in part an attempt to vindicate the cause of Enlightenment in that debate. In 1786 Kant added to these reviews a satirical essay, *Conjectural Beginning of Human History*, parodying Herder's use of the Genesis scriptures in Book 10 of the *Ideas* to support his anti-Enlightenment theory of human history. But the *Conjectural Beginning* also makes some serious points both about the use of imaginative conjectures in devising such narratives and about the role of reason and conflict in the progressive historical development of humanity's faculties.

Another important short essay displaying the historical conception of Kant's philosophy was prompted by the published remark of a conservative cleric, who dismissed the call for greater enlightenment in religious and political matters with the comment that no one had yet been able to say what was meant by the term "enlightenment." Kant's response was the short essay *Answer to the Question: What is Enlightenment?* (1784). Kant refuses to identify *enlightenment* with mere learning or the acquisition of knowledge (which he thinks is at most a consequence of that to which the term genuinely refers). Instead, Kant regards enlightenment as the act of leaving behind a condition of immaturity, in which a person's intelligence must be guided by another. Many people who are able to direct their own understandings, or would be able if they tried, nevertheless prefer to let others guide them, either because it is easy and comforting to live according to an established system of values and beliefs, or because they are anxious over the uncertainties they will bring upon themselves if they begin to question received beliefs or afraid of taking on the responsibility for governing their own lives. To be enlightened is therefore to have the courage and resolve to be self-directing in one's thinking, to *think for oneself*.

Kant also emphasizes that enlightenment must be regarded as a social and historical process. Throughout humanity's past, most people have been accustomed to having their thinking directed by others (by paternalistic governments, by the authority of old books, and most of all, and most degrading of all, in Kant's view, by the priestcraft of religious authorities who usurp the role of individual conscience). Becoming enlightened is virtually impossible for an isolated individual, but it becomes possible when the practice of thinking critically becomes prevalent in an entire public in which reigns a spirit of free and open communication between its members. Kant's proposals concerning freedom of communication in *What is Enlightenment?* are based not on any alleged individual right to freedom of expression, but are entirely consequentialist in their rationale and tailored to his time and place, designed to encourage the growth of an enlightened public under the historical circumstances in which he found himself.

One unjust calumny often directed against the Enlightenment is that it was a movement devoid of a sense of the historical or an awareness of the historical context of

21

human actions and endeavors. The charge is perniciously false, and especially so when directed toward Kant. What it often represents is a deceptive presentation of a different view of history from the Enlightenment's, or else an even shabbier attempt by nineteenth-century thinkers to pass off the Enlightenment's accomplishments in historical thinking as their own, or both of these at once. The *Critique of Pure Reason* (even its title) reflects a historical conception of Kant's task. Kant sees the "critique" as a metaphorical court before which the traditional claims of metaphysics are being brought to test their validity. His metaphor is drawn from the Enlightenment political idea that the traditional claims of monarchs and religious authorities must be brought before the bar of reason and nature, and henceforth the legitimacy of both should rest only on what reason freely recognizes. Kant's philosophy is self-consciously created for an age of enlightenment, in which individuals are beginning to think for themselves and all matters of common interest are to be decided by an enlightened public through free communication of thoughts and arguments.

For nearly 20 years, Kant had intended to develop a system of moral philosophy under the title "metaphysics of morals." It is probably no accident that he began to fulfill this intention only after he had been provoked into thinking about human history and the moral predicament in which the natural progress of the human species places its individual members. The *Groundwork for the Metaphysics of Morals* (1785) is one of the classic works in the history of ethics, and (as its title implies) it proposes to lay the ground for Kant's ethical system. But it never claims to do more than provide the fundamental principle of the system. It discusses the application of the moral principle only by way of selected illustrations, and does not provide us with a systematic theory of duties. During the next decade, Kant continued to reflect both on the foundations of ethics and on the application of his ethical principles to morality and politics. But he presented something like an ethical system only at the very end of his career, in the *Metaphysics of Morals* (1797–8). Kant's ethical thought, and even what is said in the *Groundwork* itself, is often misunderstood because these later works are not taken into account in reading it.

In 1786 Kant's philosophy was suddenly thrust into prominence by the favorable discussion of it presented in a series of articles in Christoph Wieland's widely read publication *Teutsche Merkur* (called "Letters on the Kantian Philosophy") by the Jena philosopher Karl Leonard Reinhold. Reinhold's presentations of Kant did very suddenly what Kant's own works had thus far failed to do – namely, to make the theories of the *Critique* into the principal focus of philosophical discussion in Germany. Soon the Critical philosophy came to be seen as a revolutionary new standpoint; the main philosophical questions to be answered were whether one should adopt the Kantian position, and if one did, exactly what version or interpretation of it one should adopt. Soon there also arose a new kind of *critic* of Kant's philosophy – an irrevocably "post-Kantian" philosopher, whose criticisms were motivated by alleged unclarities and tensions within Kant's philosophy itself. These critics sought to absorb the lessons of the Kantian philosophy and yet also to "go beyond" it.

For this reason, and because of the misunderstandings to which Kant had discovered his position was subject, he decided to produce a second edition of the *Critique*, in which he could present his position more clearly. At first he thought he would add a section on *practical* (or moral) reason, following up his treatment in the *Groundwork* (and also replying to critical discussions of that work that had appeared). In 1787 the new and improved version of the *Critique of Pure Reason* did appear, but by then Kant had decided that his discussion of practical reason would have to be too lengthy to be added to what was already a very long book, so he decided to publish it separately as a second "critique."

Within a short time, Kant was working on a third project that was to bear a parallel title. Kant conceived of philosophy as an architectonic system, but it was never part of his systematic project to write three "critiques." The *Critique of Practical Reason* grew opportunistically out of Kant's desire to respond to critics of his *Groundwork*, and also from his decision to revise the *Critique of Pure Reason* – he originally intended to include a "critique of practical reason" in this second edition, but wrote a separate book when he saw that the length of this new section was getting out of hand. Kant's reasons for writing the *Critique of the Power of Judgment* were complex, and a bit inscrutable, as is the work itself. Kant had been thinking for a long time about the topic of taste and judgments of taste, and wanted to come to terms with the modern tradition of thinking about these matters, found in such philosophers as Hutcheson, Baumgarten, Hume, and Mendelssohn. Judgments of taste, such as that something is beautiful or ugly, have the peculiarity that on the one hand they do not ascribe a determinate objective property to an object but report merely the subject's own pleasure or displeasure in it, and yet on the other hand they do claim a kind of quasi-objectivity, as though there are some things which *ought* to please or displease all subjects. Kant was dissatisfied with both Baumgarten's attempt to analyze beauty as perfection experienced by the senses rather than by the intellect and by Hume's view that taste is merely pleasure or displeasure in an object considered in relation to certain normative conditions of experiencing it, such as disinterestedness. He wanted to understand how the workings of our cognitive faculties themselves, especially the harmony between sensible imagination and understanding required for all cognition, might play a role in generating an experience that was at once subjective and yet normative for all. But to solve this problem is far from being the whole motivation behind the third *Critique*.

The two main themes dealt with in this work – aesthetic experience and natural teleology – were both preoccupations of the Enlightenment's critics, such as Herder. He also needed to clarify and explicate his own thinking about the status of teleological thinking in relation to natural science, a subject that had engaged him before both in essays about natural theology and the philosophy of history. But if we are to take him at his word, the main motive for writing the *Critique of the Power of Judgment* was to deal with the "immense gulf" that he saw between the theoretical use of reason in knowledge of the natural world and its practical use in morality and moral faith in God. It remains to this day a subject of controversy exactly how Kant hoped to bridge this gulf in the third *Critique* and how far he was successful. But the *Critique of the Power of Judgment* reveals Kant, now in his late sixties, as a philosopher who is still willing to question and even revise the fundamental tenets of his system. And to his idealist followers, Fichte, Schelling, and Hegel, it was the *Critique of the Power of Judgment* that seemed to them to show Kant as open to the kind of radical speculative philosophy in which they were interested.

23

A Decade of Struggle and Decline

The final decade of Kant's activity as a philosopher was one beset with conflict, and well before the end of it, Kant's health and even his mental powers were very much in decline. As the Critical philosophy became increasingly prominent in German intellectual life, and as it came to be variously interpreted by different proponents and would-be reformers of it, Kant found himself defending his position on several sides, against the attacks of Wolffians such as J. A. Eberhard, Lockeans such as J. G. Feder and C. G. Selle, popular Enlightenment rationalists such as Garve, religious fideists such as Wizenmann and Jacobi, or against a new kind of "Kantian" speculative philosopher, such as the brilliant Salomon Maimon. Kant's larger-scale published works during the 1790s, however, were devoted to applying the Critical philosophy to matters of general human concern, especially in the practical sphere – to religion, political philosophy, and to the completion of the ethical system he had for 30 years called the "metaphysics of morals."

Kant also came into conflict with the political authorities over his views on religion. From the beginning of Kant's academic career until 1786, the Prussian monarch had been Frederick the Great. Frederick may have been a military despot, but his views in matters of religion favored toleration and theological liberalism. Many considered him to be privately a "freethinker" or even an outright atheist. Frederick's death in 1786 brought to the throne a very different sort of monarch, his nephew Friedrich Wilhelm II, for whom religion was a very serious matter. The new king had long been shocked by the wide variety of unorthodoxy, skepticism, and irreligion that had been permitted under his uncle to flourish within the Prussian state and even within the Lutheran state church. Two years after coming to power, he removed Baron von Zedlitz (the man to whom Kant had dedicated the *Critique of Pure Reason*) from the position of Minister of Education, replacing him with J. C. Wöllner (whom Frederick the Great had described as a "deceitful, scheming parson"). Both the king and his new minister believed that the stability of the state depends directly on correct religious belief among its subjects, and hence that those who questioned Christian orthodoxy were directly threatening the foundations of civil peace. To them, Kant's attack on objective proofs for God's existence, and his denial of knowledge to make room for faith, seemed dangerously subversive. And his Enlightenment principles – that all individuals have not only a right but even a duty to think for themselves in religious matters, and that the state should encourage such free thought by protecting a "public" realm of discourse from all state interference – these seemed to the new King and his orthodox followers like recipes for civil anarchy.

Wöllner soon issued two religious edicts intended to reverse the effects of Enlightenment thinking on both the church and the universities, by subjecting clergy and academics to tests of religious orthodoxy concerning both what they published and what they taught from the pulpit or the lectern. The edicts put many liberal pastors in the position of choosing between maintaining their livelihood and teaching what they regarded as a set of outdated superstitions. Action was taken against some academics as well (especially critical biblical scholars), who were forced either to recant what they had said in their writings (which usually discredited them among their colleagues) or else to lose their university positions (and with them any opportunity to teach their views at all). Writings on religious topics were also to be submitted to a board of censorship, which had to approve the orthodoxy of what they taught before they could be published.

By 1791 Kant learned from his former student J. G. Kiesewetter, who was a royal tutor in Berlin, that the decision had been taken to forbid him to write anything further on religious subjects. But by this time Kant's prominence was such that this would not be an easy or a comfortable action for the reactionary ministers to take. Kant had planned to write a book on religion, and did not let word of these threats dissuade him. But he very much wanted to avoid confrontation with the authorities, both in order to protect himself and on sincerely held moral grounds.

Kant was far from being a political radical on matters such as this. His political thought is strongly influenced by the Hobbesian view that the state is needed to protect both individuals and the basic institutions of society against the human tendencies to violent infringement of rights, and that in order to prevent civil disorder, the state must have considerable power to regulate the lives of individuals. *What is Enlightenment?* teaches that it is entirely legitimate for freedom of communication to be regulated in matters that are "private," dealing with a person's professional responsibilities. This principle might have been used to justify the very actions that had been taken by the Prussian government against pastors and even professors, insofar as their unorthodox teachings were expressed in the course of discharging their clerical or academic duties. He deplored Wöllner's edicts, of course, and regarded their application to the clergy only as having the effect of making hypocrisy a necessary qualification for ecclesiastical office. But it is not at all clear whether he regarded these measures as anything worse than disastrously unwise abuses of the state's legitimate powers. Kant sincerely believed that it is morally wrong to disobey even the unjust commands of a legitimate authority, unless we are commanded to do something that is in itself wrong. Even before anything was done to him he had made the decision that he would comply with whatever commands were made of him. This is all quite clear in Kant's first extensive presentation of his philosophy of the state in the second part of the three-part essay he wrote on the common saying, "That may be correct in theory but it does not work in practice." There he defends (against Hobbes) the position that the subjects of a state have some rights against the state which are binding on the government but not enforceable against the head of state. This means that there can be no right of insurrection, and that even the unjust commands of a legitimate authority must be obeyed by its subjects (so long as these do not directly command the subject to do something that is in itself wrong or evil). The application of this last principle to Kant's own situation is obvious: He had decided that when the Prussian authorities commanded him to cease writing or teaching on religious subjects, he would obey them.

But of course Kant had no intention of anticipating such commands, or doing anything merely to please authorities he regarded as unenlightened, unwise, and unjust. And he was determined to make use of all the legal devices at his disposal to thwart their intentions. In 1792, when Kant gave his essay on radical evil (which later became Part I of the *Religion Within the Boundaries of Mere Reason*) to the *Berlin Monthly* for publication, he insisted on its being submitted to the censorship; when it was rejected, he submitted the entirety of the *Religion* to the academic faculty of philosophy in Jena, which under the law was an alternative to the official state censorship. A first edition appeared in 1793, and a second (expanded) edition in 1794. Kant's evasion angered the censors in Berlin, however, and led them finally to take the action against him they had been planning. In October, Wöllner sent Kant a letter expressing in the king's name the royal displeasure with his writings on religion, in which "you misuse your philosophy to distort and disparage many of the cardinal and basic teachings of the Holy Scriptures and of Christianity" (7.6). It commanded him neither to teach nor write on religious subjects until he was able to conform his opinions to the tenets of Christian orthodoxy. In his reply, Kant defended both his opinions and the legitimacy of his writing about them, but did solemnly promise to the king that he would obey the royal command (7.7–10). Even the title of the *Religion* was carefully crafted by Kant in light of what he took the legal situation to be. Kant regarded revealed theology (based on the authority of the Church and scripture) as a "private" province of those whose profession obliges them to accept that authority. But when an author writes on religion apart from appeal to such authorities, basing his assertions solely on reason unaided by any appeal to revelation, he is writing for the "public" sphere. In fact, Kant's *Religion* is an attempt to provide an interpretation, in terms of rational morality, of central parts of the Christian message – original sin, salvation through faith in Christ, the vocation of the Church. Its principal aim is to convince Christians that their own religious beliefs and experience are entirely suitable vehicles for expressing the moral life as an enlightened rationalist philosopher understands it. No doubt Kant's rationalistic reinterpretations were (and still are) apt to seem abstract and bloodless to many Christians. There is no role in Kant's account of salvation for vicarious atonement made by the historical person of Jesus Christ. His rational religious faith has no room for miracles, disapproves of religious practices such as petitionary prayer, and Kant regards religious rites as "superstitious pseudo-service of God" when they are presented as necessary for moral uprightness or justification of the sinner before God. He directly attacks the *Pfaffentum* ("priestcraft" or "clericalism") of a professional priesthood, looking forward to the day when the degrading distinction between clergy and laity will disappear from a more enlightened church than now exists. (As I have already mentioned, Kant's own conduct reflected his principles. He refused on principle to participate in religious liturgies. Even when his ceremonial position as rector of the University of Königsberg required him to attend religious services, he always declined, reporting that he was "indisposed.")

The *Religion* has much to tell students of Kant's ethical theory both about its moral psychology and about the application of moral principles to human life. The essay on radical evil makes it clear that for Kant moral evil does not consist merely in determination of the will by natural causes (as it may sometimes seem to do from what is said in the *Groundwork* or even the second *Critique*). Instead, the essay on radical evil insists that all moral choice consists in the adoption of a maxim (whether good or evil) by a free power of choice, and thus transcends the natural causality Kant takes to be incompatible with freedom. It also coheres with Kant's philosophy of history in presenting the social condition, and the natural propensity to competitiveness awakened in it, as the ground of all moral evil. Part III of the *Religion* argues that since the source of evil is social the moral progress of individuals cannot come from their isolated strivings for inner purity of will but can result only from their freely uniting themselves in the adoption of common ends. The ideal "realm of ends" is therefore to receive earthly reality in the form of a "people of God" under moral laws, who are to unite *freely* (not in the form of a coercive state) and *universally* (not as an ecclesiastical organization limited by creeds and scriptural traditions). The essence of religion for Kant consists in recognizing the duties of rational morality as commanded by God, and in joining with others to promote collectively the highest good for the world. It is in this free form of religious association, and not the coercive political state, that Kant ultimately places his hopes for the moral improvement of the human species in human history. The role of the state in history for Kant is not to provide the human species with its final aim, but rather to provide the necessary conditions of external freedom and justice in which the moral faculties of human beings may develop, and free (religious) forms of association may flourish in peace.

Kant had been forbidden by the authorities to write on religious topics, but he had no intention of keeping quiet on other matters of general human concern, even when his views were likely to be unpopular with the government. In March 1795 a period of war between the revolutionary French Republic and the First Coalition of monarchical states was brought to a close by the Peace of Basel between France and Prussia. Kant's essay *Toward Perpetual Peace* should be read as an expression of support not only for this treaty but also directly for the First French Republic itself, since here he declares that the constitution of every state should be republican and also conjectures that peace between nations might be furthered if one enlightened nation transformed itself into a republic and then through treaties became the focal point for a federal union between other states. Kant begins with four "preliminary articles" designed at promoting peace between nations through their conduct of themselves under the present condition of incipient warfare and the diplomatic conduct surrounding it. The essay then proceeds to three "definitive articles" defining a relationship between states that will lead to a condition of peace that is not merely a provisional and temporary interruption of the perpetual condition of war but constitutes a permanent or "eternal" condition of international peace. This is followed by two "additions" outlining the larger philosophical (historical and ethical) presuppositions of Kant's approach, and an appendix in which Kant discusses the manner in which politicians or rulers must conduct affairs of state if they are to be in conformity with rational principles of morality.

Toward Perpetual Peace is the chief statement authored by a major figure in the history of philosophy that addresses the issues of war, peace, and international relations that have been central concerns of humanity during the two centuries since it was written. Kant drew his inspiration from the *Project for Rendering Peace Perpetual in Europe* by the Abbé de Saint-Pierre (1712), and comments on it by Jean-Jacques Rousseau (1761). But his aims in *Toward Perpetual Peace* are much more ambitious in that their scope is not limited to the Christian nations of Europe but motivated by universal moral principles. His purpose is not merely to prevent the destruction and bloodshed of war, but even more to effect peace with justice between nations as an indispensable step toward the progressive development of human faculties in history, in accordance with the philosophy of history he projected over a decade earlier. *Toward Perpetual Peace* is perhaps Kant's most genuine attempt to address a universal

ALLEN W. WOOD

enlightened public concerning issues of importance not only to scientists and philosophers but vital to all humanity.

The history of Kant's conflict with, and for a time his submission to, the Prussian authorities regarding religion, has an unexpectedly happy ending. Friedrich Wilhelm II, typical of rulers in all ages who make a display of religious orthodoxy central to their conception of public life, permitted himself a private lifestyle that was morally unconventional, and the reverse of prudent, temperate, or healthy. When he died rather suddenly in 1797, Kant chose (in a spirit more wily than submissive) to interpret his earlier promise to abstain from writing on religion as a personal commitment to this individual monarch, and regarded the latter's death as freeing him from the obligation. The royal censors, who were always regarded within the hierarchy of Lutheran church as uncultured fanatics, probably never had the power to enforce their prohibitions against Kant anyway, and certainly lacked it once the king was dead. In the *Conflict of the Faculties* (1798), Kant had his final say on religious topics, framing his discussion in terms of an account of academic freedom within the state that vindicated his course of action in publishing the *Religion* several years earlier (the act that had provoked the royal reproof).

As for Kant's persecutor Wöllner, who had risen to the nobility from a rather lowly background on the strength of his devotion to the cause of religious conservatism, he had already been treated with conspicuous ingratitude by the fickle king whose religious prejudices he had done his best to serve. Soon after the death of Friedrich Wilhelm II, he lost whatever influence he ever had over Prussian educational and ecclesiastical policies, and eventually died in poverty.

Old Age and Death

Kant retired from university lecturing in 1796. He then devoted himself to three principal tasks. The first was the completion of his system of ethics, the *Metaphysics of Morals*, consisting of a Doctrine of Right (covering philosophy of law and the state) and a Doctrine of Virtue (dealing with the system of ethical duties of individuals). The first part was published in 1797 and the whole in 1798. Kant's second task was the publication of materials from the lectures he had given over many years. He himself published a text based on his popular lectures on anthropology in 1798. Declining powers led him to consign to others the task of publishing his lectures on logic, pedagogy, and physical geography that appeared during his lifetime.

Kant's third project after his retirement is the most extraordinary. He set out to write a new work centering on the transition between transcendental philosophy and empirical science. In it Kant was responding creatively both to recent developments in the sciences themselves (such as the revolution in chemistry initiated by Lavoisier's investigation of combustion) and to the work of younger philosophers who took their inspiration from the Kantian philosophy itself (such as the "philosophy of nature" of F. W. J. Schelling, who was still in his early twenties). Kant's failing powers prevented him from completing this work, but from the fragments he produced (that were first published in the early twentieth century under the title *Opus Postumum*), we can see that even in his late seventies, Kant still took a critical attitude toward every philosophical

28

question and especially toward his own thoughts. Even while struggling against the failure of his intellectual powers, he was also fighting to revise in fundamental ways the critical philosophical system whose construction had been the labor of his entire life. In this way, the next generation of German philosophers, who saw it as their task to "go beyond Kant," were thinking more fundamentally in Kant's own spirit than have been the generations of devoted Kantians since, who ever and again want to go "back to Kant" and who tirelessly attempt to defend the letter of the Kantian texts against the attempts of his first followers to extend and correct his philosophy. Kant died February 12, 1804, a month and a half short of his eightieth birthday.

Notes

1 Writings of Kant will be cited by volume/page number, in the form (v.p.), in the Akademie Ausgabe *Kant's Schriften* (Berlin: W. de Gruyter, 1902–).

2 For instance, see Hans Gawlick and Lothar Kriemendahl, *Hume in der deutschen Aufklärung: Umrisse der Rezeptionsgeschichte* (Stuttgart: Frommann-Holzboog, 1987).

3 One of Maria Charlotta's extant letters to Kant reads: "I lay claim to your society tomorrow afternoon. 'Yes, yes I will be there,' I hear you say. Good, then, I will expect you, and then my clock will be wound as well" (10.39). Much is read into this last figure of speech by a few Kant scholars who apparently want to entertain the desperate hope that Kant may not after all have been a lifelong celibate.

4 The troubled, romantic Plessing was also an acquaintance of Goethe, and is the subject of his poem "Harzreise im Winter," which later provided the text of Brahms's *Alto Rhapsody*, op. 53.

Further Reading

Beck, Lewis White (1969). *Early German Philosophy*. Cambridge, MA: Harvard University Press.

Beck, Lewis White (1995). *Mr. Boswell dines with Professor Kant*. Bristol, England: Thoemmes Press, 1995.

Beiser, Frederick (1987). *The Fate of Reason*. Cambridge, MA: Harvard University Press.

Cassirer Ernst (1981). *Kant's Life and Thought*, tr. James Haden. New Haven: Yale University Press.

Kuehn Manfred (2001). *Kant: A Biography*. Cambridge: Cambridge University Press.

Part I

Pre-Critical Issues

2

Kant's Early Dynamics

MARTIN SCHÖNFELD

1. Introduction: The Problem of Dynamics in the Enlightenment

Kant's reflections on dynamics form the starting point of his career. His first inquiries, in the 1740s, were about force, its activity and interplays. This research informed his subsequent examinations, in the 1750s and early 1760s, of nature, freedom, matter, and God. In the mid-1760s, Kant recognized that these examinations involved conjectural leaps, a recognition that prepared the critiques of speculation and reason of the 1780s. At this juncture, dynamic perspectives were fading into the background, but they did not entirely disappear. In the final two decades of his life, reminiscent of his pre-Critical project, Kant renewed his efforts at joining metaphysics and physics in the *Opus postumum* (1785–1802), and here dynamics returned to center stage. It guided his theory of a spatial force field (the ether), informed his energetic account of matter, and let him revisit Spinoza's ideas of a self-organizing nature – ideas Kant had explored from the beginning.

Scholarship has largely ignored the early dynamics, and for understandable reasons. Kant had formulated his views when he was very young (1744–7), and their publication, *Thoughts on the True Estimation of Living Forces* (1749), was full of errors, hard to read, and an academic failure. The flaws of his debut tempt one to ignore it. In addition, in Kant's lifetime, various factors undermined dynamic conjectures. By mid-century, a consensus emerged in Europe according to which there is only one good way of studying forces, Newton's way, which, incidentally, differed from Kant's own. The triumph of celestial mechanics – one of the engines of the Enlightenment – underscored the power of Newton's rigorous methods and sidelined conceptual speculations. Newton's famous dictum, "I feign no hypotheses," in the *Principia* (1686) discouraged speculation on the causes of gravity and on the puzzle of action at a distance (the puzzle of how gravity travels through empty space). For Newton and his followers, studies of force were to be restricted to what can be observed, quantified, and tested. Metaphysical studies of force, on the other hand, were conceptual and thus deemed unscientific and arbitrary by British Newtonians.

33

On the Continent, reflections on dynamics were not always welcome either. Calculating the momentum of projectiles or measuring the energy in collisions was acceptable if the conclusions concerned the details at hand, but wondering about the wider implications of such research was different. Inquiring too deeply about the forces of nature might eventually question religious authority and its doctrines. Hence academics and intellectuals, especially those schooled in theology, had problems with the philosophical upshot of dynamics.

The marginalization of the pioneers of dynamics was thus no surprise. Kepler's celestial dynamics had been integrated in Newtonian mechanics, and his ontological reflections on the light of nature, its celestial beat, and its cosmic music, had been dismissed or forgotten. Leibniz's metaphysical dynamics, however, was not yet forgotten, and the enduring interest in its claims worried Lutheran academics, who viewed Leibnizian dynamics as subversive and blasphemous. Theology departments often decided administrative matters at German universities, and their members had clout. Thinkers who pursued dynamic lines of thought were fired from their jobs and driven out of town – as befell the mathematician-turned-metaphysician Wolff in Halle (1723), his student Bilfinger in Tübingen (1725), or the Wolffian Fischer in Königsberg (1725).

Theologians of all stripes, but most of all the fundamentalist Pietists, were aghast at the wider implications of dynamic perspectives. Suppose there were a self-ordering natural energy at work and that such energy is constitutive of the world, then the world and everything in it would be a dynamically generated network or *nexus rerum*, as the young Wolff and his radical students had contended. How could such an evolving, self-organizing nature be God's complete, static creation? After all, the Bible says that God made the world and took a rest afterwards. Moreover God created bodies and souls, which are irreducibly different for theologians, but in the above claims matter and consciousness could *both* derive from a dynamic activity. Inspired by Leibnizian dynamics, the Wolffians argued that minds are energetic concentrations and that bodies are the lattices of such concentrations. But if matter and mind related to each other in this way, how could one uphold the boundary between mortal flesh and immortal souls? The Wolffians said that there are simple and complex substances; simple ones are souls, which cannot fall apart because of their simplicity and are thus immortal, while complex ones are bodies, which can fall apart (into simple substances) and die. But what are the consequences? Does Wolff not push matter and mind too close together, by explaining bodily aggregates in terms of elementary souls? Bodies and souls should remain different, and blurring their distinction creates problems. For instance, with ideas of this sort, how could Wolff and his students honestly respect the tenet that only humans have souls, in contrast to animals?

And if such threats to dogma were not bad enough, Wolff had even likened his dynamic ideas to those of the heathen Chinese. He argued that the normative thrust of moral action toward the good in the sphere of humans parallels the energetic thrust of natural processes toward harmony in the evolving cosmos. When he found the same view in the Confucian classics, he announced a match between his insights and those of Confucius (1721). Now the Christians had had enough. They went on the warpath, which resulted in a purge and Wolff's exile. The implications of dynamics were subversive. They were pagan threats in need of suppression.

2. Kant's Starting Point: The Ontology of Force

Kant turned to dynamics in his fourth year at Königsberg University. He wrote *Thoughts on the True Estimation of Living Forces* from 1745 to 1747. The book is a commentary on the debate on force. The controversy had begun in the 1680s between Leibniz and followers of Descartes; by Kant's time, it was a discussion among Cartesians, Leibnizians, and Newtonians. With over 250 pages in the printed edition of 1749, it was a good-sized work written towards the end of Kant's studies (he enrolled in 1740), and should have sufficed as a Master's thesis. The topic, a survey of the literature on force, was suited for a graduation piece, and its gist, a critique of Leibniz's dynamics, was something Kant's advisor Martin Knutzen (1713–51) would have been interested in reading. Knutzen, an associate professor of logic and metaphysics, had written on philosophical and scientific topics; he was an admirer of Newton, a devout Pietist, and a critic of Leibniz and Wolff.

Yet Kant failed to graduate. Whereas theses had to be written in Latin, which Kant knew well, the book is in German. After he finished it, he dropped out. He left town in summer 1748 without a degree. What happened? His father suffered a stroke in late 1744 and Kant took care of him in 1745, and buried him in spring 1746. Was Kant after the funeral perhaps too overcome by grief to finish his studies? This seems unlikely, for he completed the book in the first half of 1746, submitted it to the censor in mid-summer, and added the last revisions in spring 1747.

Could financial troubles have compelled the dropout? The father's disability and death certainly meant the loss of the family's income. After the burial in 1746, Kant began to disband the household (his mother had died in 1737), sold off what property remained, and found homes for his siblings. Poverty affected Kant's life, but did it cause a premature end to his education? The father's business had been declining years earlier; so badly, in fact, that the Kants had been registered as paupers in Königsberg since 1740. Thus the family was already destitute when Immanuel enrolled at the university, and the father's demise could not have made a big difference. The Kants were financially dependent on others, and Immanuel's support was taken care of. A maternal uncle, known only by his last name, Richter, had been paying the tuition. Even after Kant left town, Uncle Richter kept supporting the scholarly progress of his nephew. He paid for the printing of *Living Forces* in 1749 and financed Kant's second book, *Universal Natural History*, in 1755. Since this benefactor could apparently be counted on for academically related expenses, even for those incurred after the dropout, it seems unlikely that financial reasons forced Kant to leave school.

Instead, there are indications that Kant did not get along with his advisor. Knutzen was a respected thinker, who had written on the same topics that Kant explored in chapter 1 of *Living Forces*, such as nature's creation, substantial action, and the mind–body problem (1733–45). But Kant never mentions him, either here or in any other of his works. An implicit discussion of Knutzen's views in the book dismisses them as "confusions" of "some astute writer" (§6, 1.21). When the book was out Kant sent a copy with a very flattering letter to Leonard Euler (1707–83), who is today famous for Euler's number and the beta-function that triggered the superstring revolution, but who was then known as a critic of Knutzen. Kant's indifference towards his teacher appears to have been mirrored by Knutzen's impression of his student. Knutzen never mentions Kant when writing about students he was proud of, and the students he favored, Friedrich Buck (1722–86) and Johann Weitenkampf (b. 1726), were Kant's enemies.

Knutzen, a Pietist, was an opponent of Leibniz and Wolff. Kant, in his book, criticizes Leibniz and Wolff too, but in a way that sharpens their approach. Knutzen criticized Leibniz and Wolff for having been too radical, but Kant criticized Leibniz and Wolff for not having been radical enough. It seems that Knutzen rejected *Living Forces* as a thesis. And Kant flunked.

Living Forces contains three chapters. A metaphysical essay (chapter 1) is followed by an experimental review (chapter 2) and a theory of dynamics (chapter 3). The initial essay is on Leibniz's active force (*vis activa*). Kant announces he wants to determine "some metaphysical notions of force" (§1, 1.16), and what follows is a tersely stated ontology. The first paragraph is probably Kant's earliest known statement. He writes that the "whole lot of the scholastics prior to Leibniz" had failed to understand Aristotle's "dark entelechy." For Aristotle, entelechies are responsible for the development of objects such as organisms. The term means having (*echein*) a goal (*telos*) within (*en*), and modern examples of entelechies would be DNA or software. It was Leibniz who was the first to teach that bodies have essential forces – a force so fundamental that it is prior to extension itself (1.16). Leibniz's claim, which Kant states twice, is that force comes first in nature and even precedes extension (1.17). Examples of extension are matter and space – matter has volume, and space is volume. Since force is prior to extension, matter and space cannot be primitives. Before they emerged nature began with force.

For Kant, concurring with Leibniz, this ontological rock bottom should be called an *active* force. The aging Wolff, a metaphysician-turned-moderator in exile, had suggested another label, a "moving force" (*vis motrix*; §2, 1.18). For Pietist readers, Kant's support for Leibniz (at the expense of Wolff, who was trying to appease Christian critics) must have been irritating; it is one thing to make force only responsible for motion, but quite another to make it responsible for action in general. Still, the label "moving force" fails. Forces are so basic that motion is just one of their guises. Motion is not even a necessary condition of force, for motion, like rest, is a *state*, as Galileo found out, and it is changes of state, not states as such, that require application of force. Thus some bodies exert force at rest, while others fail to exert it when in motion (§3, 1.18).

So forces are primitive and are properly described as active. How do they act? At this point (§4), Kant breaks with Leibniz. He rejects the doctrine of preestablished harmony. Leibniz had assumed that interaction does not "really" occur, that it is an emergent property, observable among phenomena, without being part of the set-up of nature. But Kant takes interaction as a mark of substances and suggests that when substantial forces act, they do so by affecting others:

> Nothing is easier, however, than to derive the origin of what we call motion from the general concepts of active force. Substance *A*, whose force is determined to act externally (that is, to change the internal state of other substances), either immediately encounters an object that receives its entire force at the first moment of its endeavor, or it does not encounter such an object. (1.19) (Translations from Kant 1992 and Kant in press.)

While Leibniz's "monads have no windows," Kant's monads have them – they interact. In his *New Elucidation of the First Principles of Metaphysical Cognition* (1755) he would label his alternative as the theory of an "interactivity by truly efficient causes" (1.4).

Dynamic action is central to Kant's ontology. The sequence of claims – that there is force, that it acts, that it acts outwardly, and that it affects others – seems like a string of non-sequiturs. But a closer look reveals conceptual connections from present force to outward action and from outward action to foreign effects. In this account, force is the original presence, and it would not be so if it did not act (*wirken*). Force emerges by leaving marks, by having some effect (*Wirkung*), for an ineffectual power is not a power, but for any power, its effect or action (Kant's *Wirkung* means both) must be outbound to be noticed. A power failing to leave external marks would be hidden to any other point of observation. From anywhere in the world, such a sealed-off power would be a presence without a trace. Closed off from its environment, it would be invisible in it, ineffectual in it, and irrelevant for it. Thus a natural force must be a presence through outbound actions and reactions. Such activity, by definition, would affect something other than its source.

How do forces act externally? Suppose a power emerges, prior to anything else, as an unspecified presence. As long as it has not been modified, it will lack structure – it begins as unmitigated force. Such a presence acts by spreading itself. Kant describes this with terms such as *ausbreiten* (1.24, to "out-broaden" or radiate) and *Ausdehnung* (1.24; the "out-stretching," or extension). Force radiates by stretching itself out, and when it thus acts, it has effects.

Kant writes (§9):

> It is easy to show that there would be no space [*Raum*] and no extension [*Ausdehnung*], if substances had no force to act external to themselves [*ausser sich zu wirken*]. For without this force, there would be no connection [*Verbindung*]; without connection, there would be no order [*Ordnung*]; and without order, there would not even be space. (1.23)

Force extends space, and it does so by generating order and connection, hence structure. Thus force creates the universe and everything in it. But this does not mean that such a world-creating force creates all possible existence. The existences created by force, existences placed in an ordered context, are only one possible type. There may be others. Kant explains (§7):

> A substance is either in connection and relation [*Relation*] to other substances outside of it, or it is not. Because any independent being [*Wesen*] contains in itself the full source of all its determination [by definition], it is not necessary for its existence [*Dasein*] that it should stand in any connection with other things. That is why substances can exist and still have no outer bond [*Verknüpfung*] to other substances, or have no real connection with them. (1.21–2)

Outer bonds or real connections are not required for existence. Some substances may exist absolutely and without any ties, while other substances may exist relatively, hence with ties. The only difference that connections make is that they determine a thing as belonging to a world. Kant employs Wolff's concept of the world, as "the series of all simultaneously and successively existing contingent things that are connected

37

with each other" (1.23). The notion of world as a *nexus rerum* – a network or inter-connected whole – mirrors the modern sense of the term, as illustrated by the usage of "nature" in ecology and "universe" in physics. Kant goes a step further. Relations are constitutive of a referential frame. But places or positions presuppose a frame and hence relations; without connections weaving the world, there would be no location within it (§7):

> Now since there can be no place [*Ort*] without external bonds, contexts [*Lagen*], and relations, it is quite possible that a thing actually exists, yet is not present anywhere in the world. This paradoxical statement is a consequence . . . of the best-known truths, but as far as I know, it has not yet been noted by anyone. But other statements derive from the same source, and these are no less wondrous and invade the understanding, so to speak, against its will. (1.22)

One of the "wondrous statements" is the implication that parallel universes may exist and are theoretically admissible. Kant explains (§8):

> It is therefore not right to say, as is always taught in the philosophy classrooms, that not more than one world can metaphysically exist. For it is really possible, even in the strict metaphysical sense, that God may have created many millions of worlds. [In stating this] it remains undecided if they really exist or not. The error committed [in the classrooms] invariably arose because one did not pay close attention to the explanation of the world. For the definition counts as belonging to the world only what stands in a real connection with the other things, while the theorem [that only a single world can exist] forgets this qualification and refers to all existing things in general. (1.22–3)

Other universes, by definition, would be isolated from ours. Whatever exists in our world is connected with anything else. Nature's nexus is due to the external action of force, which generates location (§9; 1.23) – the spatial anchor of dynamic interconnections.

3. Relativistic Dynamics: The Force–Space Bond

How force determines location, and how force and space are specifically related, is what Kant examines in the next section (§10), arguably the heart of the metaphysical essay. Force spreads its effects outwardly (1.24; *ihre Wirkungen von sich ausbreiten*). The presence acts outwardly, on an absence or emptiness, and the action is the "broadening out" of the presence into the absence, thereby affecting and shaping it. When force spreads out, it radiates as a field. The field expands as a volume and extends as a space. Thus force transforms void into space, into the order of radiation. This deduction is remarkable enough as Kant's explication of Leibniz's dynamic plenum, but it is impressive today in light of the acceleration of cosmic expansion, whose rate supports the hypothesis of the void as quantum vacuum energy – that space is a plenum.

As soon as an extended field exists, the acting force is present *inside* its expansion. The created environment of force gives it context and is the frame in which force acquires its location. The field, as the spatial action of force, determines the dynamic source where force is now placed.

The placing of force within the field curdles the presence into parts. It acquires structure: there is an acting point source, and there is its sphere of radiating activity. In his professorial thesis or *Habilitationsschrift* (1756, *The Joint Use of Metaphysics and Geometry in Natural Philosophy, whose First Sample Contains the Physical Monadology*), Kant would apply this insight to matter. There he speculates that matter's elements must be force-points – points in a geometric sense, indivisible and non-extended – whose activity generates elementary continua, which he calls "activity bubbles" (*sphaerae* or *ambitae activates*; 1.481). Kant's claims about the dynamic makeup of matter agree with current physics. Superstring and M-theories assert concentrations of force that whip their outsides into order. The resulting dynamic spacelets – Kant's activity spheres or Calabi–Yau spaces – are stipulated as the smallest bubbles of matter. Likewise, Kant's claims about the dynamic makeup of space, in *Living Forces*, agree with current theory. Quantum loop gravity asserts that space is essentially granulated, not smooth, and that its elements are "quantum loops." Force extends space, and while doing so, curdles it.

From riverbeds to wings, structures order currents, and the spatial field is no exception. As force has ordered space, space now governs force. Space not only shapes the source to a point in the expansion, but also governs the *rate* of the flow from the well into the field. Echoing Kepler and Newton, though he mentions neither, Kant writes (§10):

> Everything found among the properties of a thing must be derivable from what contains within itself the complete ground of the thing as such. Thus the properties of extension, and hence also its three-dimensionality [*die dreifache Abmessung derselben*] must be based on the properties of the force that substances possess with respect to the things with which they are connected. The force by which any substance acts in union with others cannot be conceived without a certain law that manifests itself in its mode of action. The kind of law by which substances act on one another must also determine the kind of union and composition of many substances. Hence the law by which a whole collection of substances (that is, a space) is measured – or the dimension of extension – will derive from the laws by which substances seek to unite in virtue of their essential forces. . . . Thus I suggest that substances in the existing world, of which we are a part, have essential forces of such a kind that they propagate their actions in union with each other according to the inverse-square relation of distances. (1.24)

The order of currents reveals a rule: force spreads in inverse proportion to the square of distances. Kepler discovered this when studying light. In *Astronomia pars optica* (1604: prop. 9), Kepler showed that its brightness decreases with the square of the distance from the source. He suspected that gravity works the same way and applied the inverse-square rule to it (1605 and 1609). Almost a century later, Newton tied Kepler's discovery to Kepler's planetary laws in *De Motu* (1684), which allowed the derivation of the inverse-square rule for gravity in *Principia* (1687).

In *Living Forces*, Kant interprets the inverse-square rule as a law of the action of force. By doing so, he made a discovery of its own: he found the law of free-field radiation. Kant's law, in modern formulation, is that the pressure of any point source radiation in a free-field drops at a rate inversely proportional to the square of the propagated distance. It is the first generalization of the various and specific inverse-square laws in natural philosophy, uniting Kepler's law of photo measurement, Newton's law of universal gravitation, and Coulomb's later law of electrostatic force (1785). Kant's law is the shared pattern of their radiation, whether one thinks of light, gravity, electrostatic force, radioactivity, seismic forces, radio waves, or sound.

Kant's law expresses how force radiates in space, or, how space governs the rate of radiation. For Kant, force orders space, and space orders force. Without force, space would lack structure (*Abmessungen* or *Dimensionen*) and could not place a world (§9). And without space, force would lack a field, and its radiation would not have a rate (§10). That is, as soon as force creates space, force and space will interact – when space is forced, force is spaced. This interaction of force and space is fundamental, and with this insight, Kant anticipates general relativity, the idea that mass stretches spacetime and that spacetime grips mass (1915).

Since the interaction of force and space is fundamental, neither the particular rate of radiation nor the specific structure of space can be basic. The poles of interaction are not absolute, only their interactivity is. Whether radiation falls off in the inverse square to the distance, or at some other rate, is ultimately arbitrary. Likewise, that there must be three dimensions to space is not graven in stone either. In principle these things can vary, and they could play out differently in another universe. The one thing that would remain constant is their mutual determination – if the one pole was different, the other would be altered too. Kant writes (§10):

> Second, I think that the whole thus generated [by the propagation of essential forces] has the property of being three-dimensional on grounds of this [inverse-square] law. Third, I think that this law is arbitrary and that God could have chosen another, for example [a law of] the inverse-cube relation. Fourth and finally, I think that an extension with other properties and dimensions would have resulted from another law. (1.24)

Kant suspected the arbitrariness of three-dimensionality when he failed to deduce it. Until he tried to do so, the initial assumptions – that force precedes extension, and that substantial or placed forces interact – had smoothly spun out a series of implications. Forces are sources of action (§§2–3); they affect one another (§4); these reciprocal effects are illustrated by mind–body interaction (§5); mind–body interaction is an interplay of materially produced ideas and mentally intended actions (§5–6); and it occurs since substances, including the soul (1.21) are placed (§6). Place and relation are due to action (§7), as is the sum-total of both, the world (§8).

But when he examined three-dimensionality (§9), he found it "somewhat more difficult to see" how that plurality derives from the law that governs outward action (1.23). Leibniz had suggested a geometrical proof, but for Kant, this move begs the question: geometry presupposes three dimensions, so how could one prove them geometrically? He relates how he tried his hand at an arithmetical argument, hoping to link the dimensions of space to the powers of numbers. But he gave up on it, for the fourth power (corresponding to a fourth dimension) has no spatial equivalent (1.23). So the "necessity of three-dimensionality" remains inexplicable (1.23). Whether three dimensions are really necessary in nature is a question he cannot answer.

4. The True Estimation of Force: The Marriage
of Momentum and Energy

If one views the metaphysical essay from a distance, it becomes clearer how it failed and why Kant dropped out. Do forces stretch themselves as space; does space structure radiation? Does this "structuring" create substances? Do they create networks; and they the world? Is the world just one among many? Affirmative answers to such questions point to heresies – which a Pietist advisor would hardly tolerate in an academic thesis. Granted, when Kant mentions God, he says all the right things, characterizing him as maker of worlds (§8, 1.22; §11, 25.20–5) and as engineer of dimensions (§11; 1.25). But then he makes force responsible for these tasks (§§7–10). And he had already given the game away at the very start, with the praise for Leibniz and his explication of entelechies (§1). Kant's ambiguities – God here, force there – would have allowed only two readings to Knutzen: either God is the creative force, or God created this force. By the former, God would be immanent and a quantity. By the latter, God made force, and force made the world – God passed the torch to an energetic demiurge. However one interprets this text, one would be hard pressed to call the author a Christian. Academia had no place for such a rebel, at least as long as Knutzen was alive.

The reasons for Kant's larger professional failure concern the remainder of his book. The metaphysical essay is on active force. Kant turns to the topic of the title, living force, only toward the end of the first chapter (§18; 1.29) Living force (vis viva) is Leibniz's quantity of force. Kant discusses it in chapter 2, an experimental review, and chapter 3, a physical dynamics. It refers to a formula for falls, collisions, and the like. The need for a "true estimation" arose since this quantity was controversial – both Descartes and Newton had other ideas.

The controversy over living force, the vis viva debate, had begun in the previous century, when Leibniz attacked Cartesian philosophy. Descartes (dead then but defended by followers) had argued (1633 and 1644) that force is tied to matter and motion, and that it is the product of mass and velocity (mv). Descartes had also insisted that this quantity is conserved in the world, and that force is nothing but this quantity of motion. There is no "power" or "energy" as such; nature is matter in motion, and if one wants to examine nature in physical terms, then such an inquiry should be a kinematics, a study of moving masses. Leibniz objected to this (1686) that experiments with falling and rising bodies indicate force to be another quantity, the product of mass and velocity squared (mv^2), and it is this quantity that is conserved. Moreover, and contrary to Descartes' view, force is more than just a formula. It is describable as mv^2 or living force, but it is also the quality of nature, as an active force. "Mass," understood differently in Descartes' "quantité de la matière" and Leibniz's "magnitudo corporis," is now, following Newton (De Motu [1684] and Principia), determined by a body's resistance to acceleration to an applied force. For Leibniz, nature is essentially energy in motion. Hence the investigation of force must instead be a dynamics, a study of moving energy-packets.

Descartes' followers jumped to the defense of kinematics and cited cases in support of their mv-measure, but Leibniz, confident he was right, replied with Specimen

41

Dynamicum (1695). The exchange drew others in. Joining Leibniz were members of the Bernoulli family and their friends, like Hermann and Euler. Newton's *Principia* (1687) was gaining influence, and when the first philosophers had digested it, the dispute turned into a quarrel of three camps. While Descartes had argued for mv and Leibniz for mv^2, Newton suggested another concept of force, the product of mass and acceleration or $F = ma$. Newton's impact complicated things. The Cartesians first fought on two fronts and then sued for peace with the Newtonians. The Leibnizians split up; some negotiated (Wolff), while others deserted (Châtelet, Euler).

When Kant joined in, the debate was over, and *Principia* had won. Force was Newton's force (ma). Descartes' quantity (mv) and Leibniz's *vis viva* (adjusted to $^1/_2mv^2$) were found to be aspects of Newtonian force. Euler derived mv as its time integral and $^1/_2mv^2$ as its space integral (1737). D'Alembert (1743) and Boscovich (1745) proved that the two formulas denote different things – Descartes' quantity is what we now call momentum, and Leibniz's is kinetic energy.

Thus *Living Forces* has problems. Kant neither notes Euler's derivation nor remarks on d'Alembert's and Boscovich's proofs. It seems that he was not aware of them and their solutions to the debate. So he entered the debate over force when it was already settled.

And when he joined, he failed to side with the winner. He estimates force by reconciling Descartes and Leibniz, and only rarely mentions Newton. Kant's use of the inverse-square law (§10) suggests his familiarity with Newton's law of universal gravitation, but he does not take this law as basic. For Kant, it is a product of inter-action (1.24) that produces spatial structure (1.24). The action of force affects others that respond (§4), and thus interaction emerges (§§5–9) whose law "must determine" gravitation (§10). This makes Newton's law seem like a corollary of Kant's. Gravity, so conceived, has effects unlike those envisioned by Newton. For Kant, the "dimension of extension" will derive from gravitation. But if gravity generates the order of space, space will be different from Newton's conception. Instead of an absolute void in which forces act, as Newton had thought, space turns into a relational field, generated by the action of force. The force–space bond is basic for Kant, not universal gravitation.

Kant also doubts Newton's first law of motion (§51, 1.97–8), is unconvinced by Newton's concept of inertia (§§124–5, 132–3), and rejects Newton's claim that nature always loses some motion (§§48–50). And he never mentions $F = ma$ in the book, that force is Newton's product of mass and acceleration. While Newton and allies are mentioned perhaps five times, there are over a hundred references to Leibniz in the book and nearly as many to the Cartesians. Readers would have wondered whether Kant had grasped the extent of Newton's impact on philosophy.

Kant's last problem was that *Living Forces* contains mistakes. In chapter 2, he argues that Descartes' quantity is verifiable while Leibniz's is not (§§22–113a). Kant thinks force cannot be quantified as mv^2 and that all experiments support mv (which is false). In chapter 3 (§§114–63), he backtracks and admits mv^2 as a natural quantity (1.139–40). *Vis viva*, he says, is real but emerges over time. The force of a moving body changes from mv to mv^2 through a process of "vivification" (§§116–23) – which is false, too. His "new estimation" is the law that moving bodies have a force measured by the square of velocity (§124; 1.148). This living force originates in matter, is triggered by a stimulus that awakens a body's "inner natural force," and is created in time (1.148). This "law" will ground "true dynamics" (§125; 1.148).

Such problems doomed the book in its day. Any reader would have had questions. Why does Kant treat force as problem when it is already solved? Why does he talk so much of Leibniz and Descartes, and so little about Newton? Why does he read the experimental record as supporting only mv, and proposes a transition from mv to mv^2 without proof? It is this part of the book – chapters 2 and 3 – that reveal it as the work of a student who is on his own, without teachers willing or able to help, and without the quantitative skills required by the subject-matter.

Still, Kant was not on the wrong track. The questions asked then look different now, for the issue of force was certainly not settled with Newton. After Kant's day, science returned to dynamics with a vengeance, whether in chemistry (oxidization and molecular bonds) or physics (thermo- and electrodynamics). This return sparked a revision of Newtonian mechanics, and it was this revision (Einsteinian relativity or geometrodynamics) that led to our understanding of forces in space. Hence criticizing Newton for the sake of dynamic perspectives contributed to Kant's failure then, but highlights the soundness of his intuition now. Kant's central argument in a nutshell is this: The estimation of living force turns on the reconciliation of the warring parties; the truth must involve a synthesis of Descartes and Leibniz, with Leibniz being corrected by Descartes (ch. 2), and Descartes corrected by Leibniz (ch. 3), in a synthesis at Newton's expense. Today we know that Newtonian mechanics captures only certain aspects of forces, bodies, and motions. One and a half centuries after *Living Forces* Einstein found how Newton's laws must be adjusted and in hindsight vindicated Kant.

Einstein's discovery that mass and spacetime inform one another confirmed Kant's force–space bond. For Einstein, mass tells spacetime how to curve, spacetime tells mass how to move, and each is relative to the other. When Kant argued that interaction determines gravity, and that gravity determines structure, he put Newton on his Einsteinian head. "Relativity" means that mass (a gravity well) and structure (spatial curvature) depend on each other; neither is absolute.

Einstein's great idea, $E = mc^2$, involves the discovery that mass is convertible to energy. Descartes' quantity of motion we now call momentum ($p = mv$), the quantity of mass in motion. Leibniz's living force we now call kinetic energy ($K = {}^1\!/_2 mv^2$), the quantity of energy in motion. Since energy (E) is mass (m) times extreme velocity squared (c^2), mass and energy are tied together by motion. Momentum, mass in motion, and kinetic energy, energy in motion, must accordingly be connected, and in today's standard model, their very connection happens to be the invariant measure of mass. Any moving body has a momentum and some kinetic energy. If bodies collide, their values of momentum and kinetic energy differ before and after the collision. But their *sum* remains constant throughout. So Descartes' momentum and Leibniz's energy are essential to estimating matter's force, but only, as Kant argued, when combined. Momentum-energy is the measure of mass conserved in the universe, and it is the same in all relativistic floats. A synthesis of the warring parties is the Einsteinian heart of force. Momentum-energy is fundamental, indivisible, and contracts to *momenergy*, whose geometrical mirror is spacetime.

Historically, Kant was the first who had the momenergy hunch. His idea that mv and ${}^1\!/_2 mv^2$ must be combined is correct, although his specific explications of this idea – the one-sided experimental proof of Descartes' momentum (ch. 2) and the "vivification" of Leibniz's energy (ch. 3) – are spurious. Still, Kant's two insights, the momenergy hunch and the force–space bond, are deeper than the findings of Euler, d'Alembert, and Boscovich. Euler knew that momentum and kinetic energy are derivable from Newtonian force. D'Alembert and Boscovich knew they are real experimental quantities. But only Kant suspected that their marriage entails the true estimation of the force of moving bodies; and that the dynamic action of force points via gravity to the structure of space, even if that meant he had to distort Newton. Only Kant anticipated Einstein.

5. Conclusion – Kant's Unlikely Dialectical Inspiration

The irony of Kant's debut is that *Living Forces* was shrugged off as being behind its time, while its key claims were actually far ahead – so far, indeed, that they sounded obscure to Kant's contemporaries. What inspired this revolutionary approach? In chapter 2 (§20), Kant explains:

> In the treatise Bilfinger submitted to the Petersburg Academy, I find an idea I have always employed as a rule in investigating truths. If men of good sense, who can be suspected to be equally free or guilty of ulterior motives, advance diametrically opposite opinions, then it will accord to the logic of probabilities to direct one's focus mainly on some intermediate proposition that permits both parties, to a degree, to be right. (1.32)

If there are two conflicting views that keep each other in check – defended by experts with equal degrees of bias – then the truth of the matter will probably be somewhere in between. A middle way would cut through contradictions and be the best road to truth. Kant goes on (§21):

> I don't know if I have been lucky with this way of reasoning elsewhere, but in the dispute over living forces I hope to be so. Never before was the world more equally divided into certain opinions as in those about the dynamic measure of moving bodies. In all regards, the parties are equally strong and equally justified [*billig*]. Of course, ulterior motives can always enter [into a dispute], but of which party should one say that it be entirely free of this? Thus I choose the safest route, by adopting a view that accounts for either of the two great parties. (1.32)

This middle way reigns supreme in *Living Forces*. The Cartesians say one thing, the Leibnizians say another, and so the truth of the matter must be a synthesis. Here is momentum, there is kinetic energy; hence force is momentum-energy. Here is kinematic quantity, there is dynamic quality; hence force is number and nature, or formula and energy alike. The middle way guides Kant's estimation of force and is his schema for negotiating contradictions in general.

This heuristic strategy, the harmony of opposites, informs Kant's momenergy hunch as well as his force–space bond. From an ontological viewpoint, force and space are as distinct from one another as "cause–effect" or "inner–outer" are. Cosmologically, force was prior to anything else, and outside its presence there had been nothing, an absence. The absence or void was the original opposite to the presence or power, but force, which acts outwardly, structured the primal void into the present-day continuum. Dynamic action is cause and spatial structure is effect. Their harmony, the harmony of cause and effect, is reciprocal and is the interaction of dynamic interior and structural exterior. The harmony is thus dialectic: a constructive interplay of force and space, whereby force forms space as energy-field, while space places force as extended radiation – in short, space is forced as a field, and force is spaced as a radiation.

Granted, this is an unfamiliar way of reasoning. Although these lines of thinking are quite typical of German philosophy from Leibniz to Fichte, Hegel, Marx, and Engels, and although their employment – by German scientists such as Einstein and Heisenberg – has shed light on nature's constitution, they still strike us as exotic. And indeed they are, considering Kant's inspiration.

The inspiration Kant mentions for his method is Georg Bernhard Bilfinger (1694–1750). The tract Kant refers to is "On Forces in a Moving Body and Their Measure" (1728) in which Bilfinger asserts that a harmony of opposites is the path to truth in the *vis viva* dispute (§16). The treatise was published by the Russian Academy (*Commentarii Academiae Petropolitanae* vol. 1, 1728). Bilfinger was one of the dynamic thinkers who avoided persecution by joining the expatriate Leibnizian community in St. Petersburg in 1725, and had made his name as an expert on Chinese philosophy. His *Specimen of the Doctrine of the Ancient Chinese* (1724: esp. §§77–105) reveals Bilfinger's interest in natural harmony (lat. *consensum s. harmonia generalis*; chin. *ping*), and how natural harmony guides the humanity (*charitas universalis*; *ren*) of the Confucian gentleman (*perfectus vir*; *junzi*). Bilfinger's source, a canonical text of Confucianism available in translation (1687), was *Doctrine of the Mean*. This classic integrates Confucian ethics in Taoist metaphysics, and describes nature as a nexus of force-points and humans as nodes in the web. According to the classic, the goal of self-cultivation is to "follow the Way" – to harmonize one's life force (*xing*) with nature's essence, the Tao. Bilfinger explored the moral dimension of this harmony in *Specimen* and stressed its ontological role in his *Philosophical Elucidations* (1725, where he argues that nature's unfolding *possibilitas* forms a universal web, §139, uniting everything regardless of difference, §145, and that this harmonious order reveals nature's economy, the *oeconomia creationis*, §231). With "On Forces" Bilfinger reacted to the *vis viva* problem in the same vein and proposed that the nature of force must lie in the harmony of given opposites.

Kant's early dynamics is thus full of ironies. *Living Forces* anticipated general relativity – and caused Kant to flunk out. His starting point reveals an extraordinary thinker, who got publicity in *The Kingdom of Jokes* (1751) with a jingle by Lessing. And unbeknownst to Kant, the praised middle way derives from the Chinese – a culture he viewed throughout his life with contempt. In the end, the joke is on Kant, as it should be: it is an irony that one of the West's greatest thinkers was first inspired by the Tao of the East.

References

Kant, Immanuel (In press). *Gedanken zur wahren Schätzung der lebendigen Kräfte* [*Thoughts on the True Estimation of Living Forces*], tr. Martin Schönfeld and Jeffrey Edwards. In E. Watkins (ed.), *Natural Science*. The Cambridge Edition of the Works of Immanuel Kant. Cambridge: Cambridge University Press.

45

Kant, Immanuel (1992). *Principium primorum cognitionis metaphysicae nova dilucidatio* [*A New Elucidation of the First Principles of Metaphysical Cognition*]. In D. Walford and R. Meerbote (eds. and tr.), *Theoretical Philosophy, 1755–1770*. The Cambridge Edition of the Works of Immanuel Kant. Cambridge: Cambridge University Press. See Academy Edition, 1.369–84.

Further Reading

Adickes, Erich (1924). *Kant als Naturforscher* [*Kant as Investigator of Nature*]. 2 vols. Berlin: De Gruyter.

Beiser, Frederick C. (1992). Kant's intellectual development: 1746–1781. In Paul Guyer (ed.), *The Cambridge Companion to Kant* (pp. 26–61). New York: Cambridge University Press.

Canedo-Aguelle, Juan A. (1988). Comentario. In J. A. Canedo-Aguelle (ed. and tr.), *Kant: Pensiamentos sobre la verdadera estimacion de las fuerzas vivas* (pp. 189–476). Bern: Peter Lang.

Erdmann, Benno (1876). *Martin Knutzen und seine Zeit* [*Martin Knutzen and his Times*]. Leipzig: Voss.

Kühn, Manfred (2001). *Kant: A Biography*. Cambridge: Cambridge University Press.

Kühn, Manfred (2001). Kant's teachers in the exact sciences. In E. Watkins (ed.), *Kant and the Sciences* (pp. 11–30). Oxford: Oxford University Press.

Polonoff, Irving (1973). *Cosmos, Monads, and other Themes in Kant's early Thought*. Bonn: Bouvier.

Schönfeld, Martin (2000). *The Philosophy of the Young Kant*. Oxford: Oxford University Press.

Schönfeld, Martin (2003). Kant's philosophical development. In E. Zalta (ed.), *The Stanford Encyclopedia of Philosophy* (2003 ed.). http://plato.stanford.edu/archives/win2003/entries/kant-development/

Tonelli, Giorgio (1959). *Elementi metodologici e metafisici in Kant dal 1745 al 1768* [*Methodological and Metaphysical Elements in Kant from 1745 to 1768*]. Turin: Edizione di *Filosofia*.

3

Kant's Early Cosmology

MARTIN SCHÖNFELD

1. Introduction

Kant's cosmology has often been dismissed as a metaphysical jumble, but it is now rated by cosmologists as "the essence of modern models" (Coles 2001: 240). The praised "essence" is his pre-Laplacian model of system formation and environmental fate: Kant's Nebular Hypothesis. Sixty years ago, the astrophysicist Carl F. v. Weizsäcker (who learned from the quantum mechanic Max Born) built a new theory of nebular turbulences to explain the origin of the Sun and the Earth. He based his theory on Kant's model, anonymously published in Leipzig and Königsberg in 1755 as *Universal Natural History and Theory of Skies*, whose initially drafted title (1754) is *Cosmogony*. Kant's German title, *Allgemeine Naturgeschichte und Theorie des Himmels*, trades on the ambiguity of the German "*Himmel*" as both "heaven" and "sky," and the Spinozistic "God/Nature." It reflects the same ambiguity in the latin "caelum" and Chinese "tian" (Menge and Pertsch 1984; Beijing Foreign Language Inst., 1988).

Weizsäcker next wrote (2002: 181–203) that Born stressed the worth of Kant's scientific insights for quantum methods. The point of a "direct path from Kant to quantum theory" is now made by J. D. Barrow at Cambridge, UK (2000: 154). Stephen Hawking, in Newton's chair, sharpened it into a broad dismissal of all post-Kantian philosophy as a "comedown" (2003: 166). To him, Kant wrote the last philosophy in scientific top form. Like Aristotle, Kant was inspired by empirical findings and reasoned on in rigorous form. Because *Universal Natural History* partly anticipated and partly matches quantum cosmology, I shall read Kant in light of current science.

The Nebular Hypothesis grew into the knowledge of what happens in the solar system. In 1949 G. P. Kuiper found a remote ring orbiting the Sun behind Pluto, the Kuiper belt of gas, dust, asteroids, and planetoids. He used the Kant–Born–Weizsäcker ideas for tracing the belt's origin *inside* the solar system. The sight of an additional far-flung shell, the Oort cloud of comets, clinched the case for the nebular turbulence theory. Before this outer "cloud bank" was observed, it had been formally demonstrated by J. H. Oort (1927). Bank and belt behave as Kant had said. In this way, his pre-Critical *Universal Natural History* wound up informing twentieth-century astrophysics.

2. Kant's Universal Natural History: Fuzzy Wavefronts and the Dance of Comets

By our current physical knowledge of the development and growth of the solar system, the Sun, the planets, and everything else up to the outer banks spiraled up from an early tidal fog. The Oort cloud is the leftover outer margin of this old swirl and its gravitational glow deeper inside. Oort characterized his cloud as a "bank"; as a marina of comets gliding into irons to stay for awhile.

Comets cruise on sharp elliptic orbits. Their lanes go every which way, but the common engine driving them on is the Sun. They accelerate from the outer banks into the planetary rings. Incoming at maximum velocity, they race around their gravitational solar stake in a hairpin curve. The Sun tweaks them into escape velocity, throwing them around and out in explosive slingshots.

Boom – a comet: sharply coming about the solar weather, the Sun-tacked mass hardens leeward, shoots off, and races away, with the light storm astern zipping past its hull, out into the night. The farther the comet cruises the slower it sails, calming down and creeping into tribal glide zone. There it reaches for its negative climax and manages to deal its celestial lingering into slow jibes, around its individual rail outside and downwind from the busy well. The misty outer banks are the last reefs breaking the solar sea. They mark the boundary between solar system and open plane. The Oort barrier rings the inward pond as a concentric shell as seen from afar. On its field-stakes in the dark, the last gravity surf spilling on into the galactic ocean, the comets slowly turn back in.

Natural philosophy through Aristotle had argued for regular patterns of the environment which grow sensibly and individuate into locally divergent mirrors reflecting the cosmic blueprint. Copernicus tentatively suggested a better mathematical form of nature's visibly rolling sky-system. Galileo saw the Copernican blueprint and showed it. He identified the relativity of motion and rest (both are just dynamic equilibrium states in space) and deduced the cosmic laws of falling bodies. Kepler, trusting in Tycho's astronomical records, derived the drumbeat for the orbital sweeps and demonstrated the harmonic wave of rhythmically surging and ebbing field tides in solar spacetime. Kepler grounded optics on the inverse-square law of shining light – luminosity and brightness are exponentially inverted by space. He applied this musical form of astrophysical cognition to the pull of weights beating out the ringing notes of the Sun's planetary shells. The "celestial spheres," for Kepler, are sweeping, screeching, and ringing onward into a fateful energetic harmony along dimensional beats of their spinning masses. Listening to solar pitch, Kepler applied the light form of Sun flashes to fiery energy flows in general and inferred a mirror law of universal gravitation. Leibniz found him "peerless," Newton saw him as "a giant," and Halley could now explain comets.

Brilliant comets stunned the world in 451, 857, 1066, and struck fear again in 1456, 1531, 1607, and were explained as cruise-bys of one and the same solar windjammer by Halley in 1682. In 1755, three years before the comet's return was identified by a Saxon farmer, Kant modeled the system of comet world-lines in *Universal Natural History* II.3 and integrated it in successively larger systems of stellar, galactic, cosmic, and eternal world-lines. After Halley's great comet had slingshot from its

1758–9 perihelion (its period is 76 years; its next pass is 2062), Kant explained the same line of reasoning from comet to sun to planets once more (1763; 2.144–51).

Kant was 30 when he first worked this out. He had gained his naturalistic perspective and his cosmic appreciation from Aristotle, Lucretius, and Montaigne. He read Leibniz on energy, Descartes (of the Keplerian *dioptric*) on momentum, and Bilfinger (Wolff's orientalist) on dialectic. He also studied natural wave fronts – their binary patterns, their environmental destinies, and their fuzzy quanta ("nothing is exactly weighed out in the natural whole"; as his account begins, 1.246). Their quantitative blurriness had been studied by Leibniz's best friends, the Bernoullis in Basel. The Bernoullis were a generational thinktank on probability, statistics, calculus, thermo- and fluid-dynamics, heart rhythms, astronomy, and on the idea of nature's ubiquitous waveforms. This family of expert formal surfers impressed Kant with a fruitful expansion of Leibnizian thought.

In this way of looking at things, nature's stellar order is the logical reflection of its initial chaotic opposite in time. This opposite is some kind of energetic mist or smoke. Its dirty chaos of flow-vectors and explosive collisions is structurally a flip-flop of oscillating continuities and limits. Cosmic fog, to Kant (1.263; 1.264), is the ultimate key to unlocking nature's order. But such a key can be a mystical rival to religion, and if what it rationally unlocks is different from unexamined scripture, dogmatic flaws in the scripture will suddenly stand out as irrational defects.

In the eighteenth century, Christianity fought a series of rearguard actions against the pressures of new discoveries and events. The tension between religion and reason worsened through Newton's science, Jesuit editions of pagan Chinese thought, and the Wolffian cosmology based on logical form, conceptual analysis, and scientific finding. Pietist defenders of religion resolutely held out against the rising floods of naturalistic evidence that fueled the age of reason. By 1750 they still rejected Newton's *Principia* (1687) on epistemological and theological grounds. To maintain their hold, the churches had a vested interest in downplaying the power of reason and stressing the empirical limits of logical thought. Kant judged this attitude counterproductive. He worried that fundamentalist skeptics would make faith look uninformed in light of natural science. He asked "defenders of religion" to heed the facts for their own good, otherwise "naturalists" would win. And he called Christians out to a dare: give me matter, and I'll build you a world out of it! (1.229–30).

> I assume cosmic matter in a state of general dispersion and turn it into a perfect chaos. By proven attraction I see stuff forming itself; by [assumed] repulsion I see it modifying its motion. By the proven laws of motion and without relying on the help of willful fairytales, I enjoy the fun of seeing such a well-ordered whole self-organizing, which looks so like the cosmic system in front of us, that I can't resist identifying the two. (1.225–6; translations from Kant 1992)

As cocksure as Voltaire, Kant grounds his metaphysical provocation on empirical work. In college, he had learned Galileo's laws of fall and Newton's laws of motion and universal gravity. During his stint at the university, Leonard Euler was already famous for having joined energy, momentum, and Newtonian force in one analytic matrix, a mechanics of slow-motion interplays.

But at Königsberg, Kant risked a conflict with his Pietist teachers by taking Leibniz and the Bernoullis far more seriously than they did. His Christian professors preferred reading Locke, and some, like M. Knutzen, lectured on Newton. Knutzen's evangelical heirs (such as Hamann) liked Hume, not Kant. Another pantheist firebrand, a certain Fischer, had been kicked out not long ago. Kant made his case (1746) by broadening Kepler's inverse-square rule to the law of free-field radiation. He modeled radiation by systematizing reflections and absorptions among Leibniz's monadic mirrors into an interactive and progressively self-constructing system. In empirical terms, this first system was not quite up to par; he misunderstood experiments and scorned Newton as some evangelical British expert on the gravity-facet of Kepler's universal law.

After Kant had left school (1748), he found three different employments in the countryside, which kept his poverty at bay and protected him from homelessness. But in the big-sky coastland he was exposed to the elements. He tightened his naturalist model into environmental dynamics, by paying attention to wind and weather, cloud patterns and storm fronts, climate swings and farming seasons. Returning to the university (1754) he immediately called public attention to the rhythms of the coastal climate, the seesaw of tropical winds, and the drum-beat of the monsoon. In his time in the Baltic outback, it seems, the rational cosmologist had learnt to think like a cloud.

Rain clouds and sunshine, shadow and light, dark and bright, are the poles of all weather. Clouds form up through sunshine acting on water and inevitably blot out their interactive source through sheer growth. As they darken the sky, they reflect its energy and eventually tear apart. Sunshine will scatter cloud-mirrors to start the cycle anew. Cosmic weathers are no different.

In the solar system, sunshine is an incessant outbound weather front of particle winds that radiate into the hollow room of the system. Comets have gaseous tails that swing around their windswept hulls. Jibing from the Oort cloud, their glowing flags catch solar wind on the run. Like sailboats, comets speed up the closer they are gravitationally hauled into the wind, and as they dip deeper into the solar weather, their banners blaze up. The harder comets steer into the Sun, the more they come alive. The bows rock in explosions; pieces fall off, and the trails glow out along million-mile-long tails. Comet tails flutter freely leeward. Like weathervanes in a storm, these pivoting flags swing away from the solar wind. Returning to their cloud bank, comets are struck astern by sunshine that now sweeps their tails over the nose. As comets zip in and out of the solar well, their tails rhythmically brighten up whenever they cruise close to the Sun's shine.

In *Universal Natural History* II.3 Kant lays out the dance of the comets (1.277–83); there he also advances an "electric-geometrical" explanation of Northern Lights (1.283 and n.). In II.1 he sketches the assembly of the solar system from an energetic void (1.262 and n.). He draws from his studies of force, space, crashes, and "vivification" (1745–7), of tides, orbits, and environmental fate (1754–5), and of fire, clouds, weather, wind, and equilibrium (1755–8). Climate studies are a contemporary illustration of Kant's historically fertile naturalistic perspective. His cosmogony starts with outbound actions of force braiding into an organizing dynamic seesaw. This seesaw of interacting forces stakes out dimensional fields, whips up expanding clouds, and condenses into energetic showers, raining dewdrops of ever more complexly massive clusters.

3. Kant's Nebular Hypothesis:
Sun Clouds and Environmental Fate

A cloud, a fuzzily weaving smoke, is the source of the skies. The source is a disorder of such broad chaos that it follows a pattern: its blurry wavering seems like overlays of the same film. Tiny wisps of a cloud form big curvy shapes that dwindle into wisps of even bigger curvy shapes if seen over distance – which are again wisps from afar, growing mirrors of the tiniest curdles that first assembled into bigger curves. Chaos is an infinite mirror blinking the small into the large and the large into the small. Moving points in a cloud map out random curves, but their trajectories reflect across referential frames, always repeating the same random curdling over and over again. Today we would say that clouds are chaotic systems that obey a predictable reiterative structure.

Kant wrote centuries before chaos theory, fractal geometry, and Mandelbrot sets enabled the imaging of all conceivable shapes, whether global warming, beach erosion, or tree foliage (and, for that matter, velociraptor skin glistening in the rain). Kant grasped the outlines of chaos. Nature sometimes seems chaotic, sometimes ordered, but instead of reducing the one to the other (as Laplace would do), Kant accepts both: free chaos and lawful order hang together.

Kant's cosmos is essentially fuzzy; and no deduction can ever get rid of this blurriness and sharpen it into deterministic focus (1.246). A good account of cosmic structure cannot be geometrically "tight" or arithmetically "infallible" (1.235). Natural quantities are not exactly "weighed out"; and this applies to particle trajectories, planetary orbits, and cometary world-lines. In this way, Kant places Newtonian mechanics within its Keplerian energetic-musical roots. His cosmic theory owes more to German celestial dynamics than to English celestial mechanics.

Kepler discovered that the Copernican rings of the planets are fat ellipses and thus only roughly drawn circles. He could explain elliptic orbits by finding their dynamic interactive cause. To the Kepler-student Kant, orbital deviations from circularity come from mechanical seesaws of conflicting forces. The distinct rails of planetary and cometary orbits – rounded vs. elongated – turn on the "weights" (*Abwiegen*) of sideways and central pulls (1.245). Their ratio dictates circular deviation: the weaker centrifugal force is to centripetal force, the sharper is the ellipse. Planets and comets orbit differently since they are ruled by different dynamic balances (1.245–6).

This conclusion from empirical constants shows to Kant, as it did to Kepler, that the world, in all its fuzziness, obeys a "single universal rule" (1.306). Nature is blurry and yet it is precise. One cannot exactly point to the limits of pulses, but one can point to the form of any drumbeat with precision. Nature's form coheres across orders of magnitude; to Kant, the same beat rules all flows, big and small. Any system of flows, on any level, points to the systematic cosmic whole, and thus to *any other* system, on any other magnitude. Like a cloud, nature is an infinite mirror reiterating one and the same constant pattern. But this means that a theory of cosmic evolution turns on *analogies and accords*, "by the rules of plausibility and right logical form" (1.235).

Now the Nebular Hypothesis becomes all the more powerful: it explains the history of our solar system as it explains other solar systems – and the same analogy holds no matter the size: galactic systems such as the Milky Way and even cosmic systems such as our universe obey its regular, fateful, and dynamic way of structural evolution. Everything integrates in the same model.

Kant framed the Nebular Hypothesis during his isolation in the countryside 1748–54. First, it seems, he came across Euler (who hadn't yet figured in the dynamic theory) and wrote him a letter expressing his admiration (Aug. 23, 1749). Next he critically examined Huygens (in the drafts to *Spin Cycles*, 1753: 23.5–7); and by 1754 at the latest, he was floored by Newton's work.

He was all the more elated since Newton fit into what he had already figured out himself. Although a Leibnizian may enjoy the cosmic expanse as a field and its force-wells as smoky fires forming up into cities of light, Newton's viewpoint is a useful simplification: let's forget about foggy shines, blurry blobs, and celestial music, and concentrate on the formal centers of such activities. The centers can be modeled as points moving in space, and their forces act at regular distances.

If our world stems from a cloud, its primordial chaos will be a bunch of points randomly filling space. As particles, they have inertial and gravitational forces ordering lawful motions. Since particles have mass, and masses attract, collisions are inevitable. When they are elastic, particles will bounce off. From that event onward, motions are ruled by attraction *and* repulsion – the "single universal rule," outpouring "splendor and size in eternal and right order" (1.306).

Kant's universal rule of cosmic evolution is an attractive–repulsive seesaw. Nature's force, wielding the assembly of progressive frames, performs two actions, a pull and a push. Whatever else force may be in its various guises, at least in terms of its intelligible ontological identity, force has to be twinned into attractions trading repulsions. By a binary dialectic, Kant can "out-Newton" Newton and now explain the home system. Its evolution in spacetime develops like a movie – Sun, Planets, Kuiper Belt, and Oort cloud are current endings of an early, dense, and dusty space. Their historical beginning was an energetic mist, which was spinning up into an ancient fog bank. It clouded into central blaze, sheeted as orbital disk, and revolves in old shrouds at the very rim.

The movie starts. Seen from afar, the fog swirls into itself: a shroud blends with another, and as more come together, the bank thickens. Particles now fall toward drops which start pulling. The attractive drops run together, and the particles of the fog sink into a joint dimensional well: now the fog has evolved a center. There, the gravitational muscle flexes its wings, lifting more weights toward the inside. Lumps accelerate downtown. They open throttles on throughways and race at breakneck speed. *Boom* – an accident; and another; crashes occur left and right, up and down; fireworks of collisions bounce off from the incoming masses. Lethal crash-cones form ahead of the accelerating mass trains. The inbound lumps plough through dusty rainbows, which are sheeting off their noses. The fogbank, already centered, is evolving into a dynamic cloud.

The crashes flying off the massy nosecone spill away from the pull that hauls the traffic in. From afar, the fogbank ripples, lumps, and inwardly rains. The cloud accelerates internally into ever closer quarters and tightens to a cottony ball. Balls are round, which means that the conical currents swept sideways by the mass traffic will flow on and over to the far side to collide head-on. This rock "n" roll beats on; the lateral head-bangers surge to and fro; and deflected currents ripple the particle sheets into larger collective motions, in a swelling seesaw of growing, crashing waves. The dynamic cloud is evolving gravity tides.

The cloud pulses like a bellows; its particle sheets unfurl around an energetic inner tangle. In the drained outback only open fields and deserted lots remain. Outer space clears into a void by the suction of the cloud. The cloud tightens, thickens, and fights it out in crowded lanes inside. The tidal swells of sidelined particles crash into one another, surging toward towering wavefronts. The rising tsunamis run hither and yon but inexorably back into themselves on the spherical cloud, surging toward the ultimate tidal confrontation – the tsunamis collide into steeply angled tidal swell; the wave builds and peaks; and the crest tips and slides down one flank into a long dynamic rush. All lateral ripples now flow the same way, in one sideways sweep along the ball around the center. The gravity tides are evolving axial rotation.

The cloud completes a revolution and spins its ever faster rotation into rhythmic hum. The lanes go mad. Gravity rules, especially in the hotly happening downtown in the cloudy well. As the cloud tightens ever faster, spin and pull heat the crazy central traffic jams inexorably up. Energy surges; sparks fly; vibrations rise to infrared glow. Downtown is becoming so insane that its lanes oscillate to combustion. The traffic zips into bright light; downtown burns; a star is born. Now axial rotation has evolved the Sun.

The fiery Sun spins round its axis in tune with the tide of its orbiting shrouds and clouds. But no one likes to be taken for a ride: any mass spun around wants to escape. The faster any centripetal spin holds on to such mass, the harder the mass wants to peel off. New tides ripple, curl, and sweep out a centrifugal frame – as the bright cloud turns, the equatorial belt turns fastest, and puffs out. The middle belt bulges by draining the poles. The Sun squeezes its neighborhood into a spinning disk of revolving particle sheets. Now the Sun has evolved the ecliptic plane.

On the particle sheets of the baby system, revolving lumps plough into other drifts while particle snow sticks to their iron ploughshares. The ploughs gleam, harden, and sink into own wells. Lumps and snow rolls together along the well-dented spin-disk into harmoniously circling winners. Now the ecliptic plane has evolved the Planets.

But while Planets evolve only when the Sun is strong enough to create a plane for them, sunshine dims over distance. The farther out, the darker it gets and the iffier its pulls become. The system's insides have formed up into the Sun and the sun-warmed Planets, but the cold outback is slow to integrate into this order. Beyond the last lighthouse and the final beacon Pluto, the old-fashioned Kuiper Belt has ever so slowly evolved from the ancient shrouds of the fogbank. Even farther out, in the prehistoric Oort cloud, between solar somewhere and interstellar nowhere, a lazy lot of bodies is teaming up into periodic solar flybys, flaming downtown as the Comets.

In Kant's day, the stellar story of *Universal Natural History* II.1–6 sounded like a fairytale. But with the progress of last century's astrophysics, we know this is how solar systems form. Kant's Nebular Hypothesis is neither fantastic nor exceptional. What had been shrugged off as so much meaningless metaphysics was only too advanced – its reasons have been substantiated; and its assertions are now verified or will soon be testable. In II.3, Kant predicts,

> With the distances from the central point of the system, the lawless freedom of comets increases over their orbital deviation and eventually loses itself in total loss of turnabouts.

This sets the outermost forming bodies free from falling toward the Sun and thus spells out the ultimate boundaries of the systematic organization. (1.281)

Comets are accordingly the freest and wildest bodies that still belong to the solar system. Their bank is the limit; for the rational reasons stated by Kant (1.277–82), what is beyond comets would be interstellar space. We can expect data that clarify Kant's celestial metaphysics further from the 2006 *New Horizons* probe (NASA), which will provide information on the Kuiper belt and Oort cloud after its Pluto flyby in 2015. Given Kant's additional pre-Critical conjectures, this mission would be philosophically interesting.

4. Kant's Dare to Christianity: Joining Leibniz and Newton over Spacetime

Through waves, clouds, and comets, Kant extrapolates from the Nebular Hypothesis to a systematic cosmology. His extrapolation is optimistic, daring, and gutsy, not to say aggressive. He is convinced that nature, as cosmos, universe, or simply "the all" (*das All*, "everything") is fully explainable. In fact such an explanation is easy. Kant thinks that mapping out the mechanics of the ongoing cosmic creation is a far simpler project than, say, to understand the matter-weaving construction and creative generation of a caterpillar (1.230). Kepler, Leibniz, and Newton had charted the path for cosmology from their strict, shared, and incontrovertible Baconian basis. This empirical platform points in a rational direction that will be claimed by free-spirited naturalists, unless the soldiers of Christ get over their dogmas and start paying attention (1.222–3).

As mentioned above (section 2), Kant challenges all monotheist doctrine to a conceptual dare: just give me matter, he repeats in the preface of *Universal Natural History*, and I shall build you a world out of it! This dare he shall win, he confidently thinks, since he has two cards up his sleeve.

The one card is Kepler's and Leibniz's ontological dynamics. Kant uses their idea of the convertibility of matter and energy for his own theory of "living forces" (in the 1740s), which infers energetic space from dynamic action, as well as for his theory of "physical monads" (in the 1750s), which points from energetic space to a material foam (active bubbles or spheres; prop. 7, 1.481–2). The earliest known words of his career are his praise for Leibniz as the one who gets Aristotle's entelechy right (1746, §1, 1.17). Entelechies are blueprints of the self-organization of natural objects, like the DNA of a seed. (See Leibniz's *Discourse on Metaphysics* 1686: §19; *Nature and Grace* 1714: §§4–6, and *Monadology* 1714: §§73–6.) Under the right conditions, through its genetic information, the seed will germinate into a flower. For Kant, nature as such follows such informing blueprints that rule its organization in principle. These blueprints are energetic; force condensates to matter and leaves it with a potential that shapes all behavior of objects, whether bodies or minds. In his third book, *The Only Possible Ground for a Proof of God's Existence* (1763), he takes this potential as the "inner possibility" of things that governs self-realization (2.162–3). Matter grows from blueprints into the best forms sustained by a given environment, and energetic patterns of information rule the growth of flowers just as the history of the universe.

The other card is Newton's natural philosophy. The *Principia* is the rational role-model for figuring nature out. Its third book, System of the World, contains Newton's "rules of reasoning in philosophy." The first rule defends Ockham's razor: no more causes are admitted than are found to be true and sufficient for explaining observations. Rule II is on nature's constancy: same causes are held responsible for same effects. Rule III is on nature's uniformity: invariant features of bodies within the reach of experiments are to be taken as invariant features of all bodies. And Rule IV is on playing the scientific game: if good reasons point to a result, such result should be accepted until or unless qualified by more data. On nature's uniformity Newton says that we are not "to recede from the Analogy of Nature, which is wont to be simple and always consonant to itself" (Motte tr. 1739: 398–9). Newton's nature is regular, uniform, consistent, and harmonious.

To Kant reading this, invariant patterns in our neighborhood suggest analogues of such patterns elsewhere, at different times, and on orders of magnitude. As matter behaves locally, it will do so generally; and the cosmic blueprint informs an accessible historical mechanical order.

Kant's nature is a cosmos utterly in motion. It expands in space and evolves over time. Force, from which space and everything else starts, turns into seesaws of reciprocal oscillations. Attraction and repulsion create lingering energetic lattices in ongoing material self-organization and yield ever more structural order, organic diversity, and ultimately freely self-aware complexity. Things come about beat by Keplerian beat – the elements, stars, planets, life, and intelligence. His cosmology is a *cosmogony*: an account of nature's past, present, and future. A "theory of the skies" is a theory of nature's "history." The alternative, a cosmos just in space, misses time.

While Leibniz saw nature as a preestablished harmony of isolated units, of monads-without-windows, Kant transforms them into interacting units, as physical monads-with-windows. He views their "commerce" (1755; 1.415–16) as creating ever new harmonies in a dance of evolving poises. And while Newton saw nature as a system of bodies and motions, Kant changes the motion of bodies into a basic motion of nature. Creation is consequently a work-in-progress; and as this mechanical self-creation is not even done yet, Kant's cosmogony contradicts the Bible.

The authoritative cosmogony of Kant's day was Genesis. Newton did not challenge the creationist account; the *Principia* is celestial mechanics at present, which is mute on "causes of gravity" – on the issue of how things did get to this point, Newton did not feign any hypotheses. Leibniz, less timid than Newton, questioned religious authority with *Protogaea* (w. 1693; p. 1748), but limits his challenge to the geophysical development of the Earth after its original inception. Kant went farther than either of his predecessors. No one deviated from the theological standard as widely as he did, and it is no surprise that he published *Natural History* in 1755 anonymously.

Comparing Kant's with the then standard account shows how revolutionary his theory is. The Bible involves a distinction between God and cosmos. Creator and creation differ like artist and sculpture, or like author and book. And whereas God is supernatural, nature *à la* Augustine is "beneath" God. But Kant argues, to the extent that one can speak meaningfully of "god" at all, divinity is a telic possibility, the engine of progress. Kant's god is inside nature; it is cosmic DNA.

Furthermore, the Bible describes the act of creation as well as the completion of this act. On the seventh day, God is done; nature is fully set up after its divine initial creation. However, Kant argues for a universe always on the move, never done, and constantly evolving. Creation continues, and the vector of cosmic development, by *Living Forces* and *Universal Natural History*, points from chaos to order, from simplicity to complexity, and from primal matter to eventual life.

Of all life, only man is made in God's image according to the Biblical account of creation. Monotheist men rule life, females, as well as nonhumans (Gen. 1.26–8, 2.18–23). Kant dismisses this opinion in *Universal Natural History* and refutes anthropocentrism in *Only Possible Ground*. He relegates humans to a "middle rung" of the ladder of creatures (1.359), for presumably there exist other solar systems with planets supporting life, and given the vastness of the cosmos, some of its organisms would be dumber and others smarter than humans (1.355–60). Even on Earth, humans are not really unique, for souls are arguably of a "material nature" (*Prize Essay* 1764; 2.293), and animals clearly have souls as well (*Metaphysik L₁*; 28.275).

Kant's rejection of anthropocentrism goes hand in hand with a case for "cosmocentrism." According to the Bible, the world attests to God's magnificence, and miracles serve to further God's glory. Kant rejects miracles as incoherent and insists that the only purpose nature has is, well, nature. The universe serves its own end. To the extent teleological reasoning applies, it is internalized in the natural vector of cosmic development. The end, goal, or final cause is cosmic self-perfection: the incessant growth of ordered diversity. The means, tools, or telic vehicles that bring cosmic order, diversity, and fertility about, are for Kant merely physical forces and material elements. This entire self-perfecting cosmos is an ecological web of interacting elements. In its structure, the universe, to Kant, is a "*nexus rerum*" or *the natural chain* (1.22–3; 1.308; 1.365).

Finally, the defenders of religion see their anthropocentric world as a static creation that may come to an apocalyptic, absolute end. It is here that Kant's cosmology strikes the greatest contrast to the Western paradigm. In terms of nature's historical dynamics, Kant's cosmos is the current embodiment of an ever-changing "universal world soul" or of a "*Proteus* of nature" (1.211–12). While Kant in 1754 worries that this fluctuating will to power might eventually flag and weaken (1.212) – a view reminiscent of Newton's remark that "motion is much more apt to be lost than got, and is always upon the Decay" (cf. *Opticks*, 4th ed. 1730, query 31, p. 398) – he stops worrying about this rather pessimistic prospect on second thought. For if one dares to adopt a free-spirited and courageous perspective, nature's fate is just sublime. Even on the highest dimensional order of nature, Kant's cosmos remains in the grip of a "single universal rule" (1.306). This celestial rule, it seems, is that the universe is like a firebird.

> Is it so hard to believe that Nature, which can [rise] from chaos into regular order and settle into an elegant system, can just as well rejuvenate itself from new chaos into which it has fallen through the decay of its motions? Is it so hard to believe that nature will do it again, just as easily, and renew the first link? Can the springs [*Federn*; "feathers"] driving the stuff of scattered matter into motion and order, not again be put into work through expanded forces, even after the stopped machine had put them to rest? Can the springs not confine themselves by just the same universal rules to just the same agreement that had the primordial formation (*Bildung*) brought about? . . . Suppose we

follow this *phoenix of nature*, which burns itself up only for the sake of living it out again, rejuvenated, rising from its ash. Suppose we chase the phoenix through all infinity of times and spaces, and we see how nature (*sie*) does not exhaust itself in new performances even in places that decay and turn dated. If we see how nature proceeds at the other boundary of creation, in the void of unformed, raw matter; how it progresses with steady steps into extending the plan of divine revelation . . . then the mind . . . will want to know up close . . . this source of essential light radiating in nature as if from a central point. (1.320–1)

5. Kant's Cosmogony: Cyclic Universes and the Phoenix of Nature

Kant's cosmogony in *Universal Natural History* starts with a particle chaos; today we would say his account describes events since cosmic inflation (while his account of the initial dynamic action, in *Living Forces*, describes events up to cosmic inflation). Measured by science, his conceptual sketches roughly agree with the known series of events. By the standard model, nature started as an explosion of radiation at about 13.7 billion years ago. The length, width, and depth of space explosively untangled, the arrow of time flew away, and material foam spread out.

With time ticking a trillionth of a second since its start, cosmic inflation happened as a huge blowout. Expanse widened, self-seeding into blossoming quarks, and sub-atomic particles, all those made of quarks, zip up into protons and coalesce into other sets. With time ticking off one hundred thousandth of a second, a shining fog swirls, reflecting the glow. The fog thins and condenses; spinning masses curdle and try out other configurations, and when one hundred seconds have gone by, hydrogen and helium come into existence. Over the next 300,000 years, the mist precipitates as elementary pieces into ever-widening rooms, and the hot and smoky field darkens to transparency. 275 million years later the stars light up; their molecular ash is the star dust of the periodic table. With these new elements, modern stars shine in new colors and beats. One billion years after the Big Bang, stars grow new branches in spacetime; visible galaxies form.

10 billion years since Big Bang, life wiggled out in self-directed organization. 10.2 bio years since the start (3500 million years ago), plankton formed. 10.65 bio years since go (420 million years ago), plants and animals conquered the land. After the last wipeout (65 million years ago/13.635 bio years) all except dinosaurs bounced back. The survivors speciated and culminated in us, here and now.

How will things evolve from here? Kant argues that nature rises in a complex blaze, but such soaring into complexity cannot help but construct balance, level in equilibrium, and appease ever finer conflicts – and thus weaken the very polarity that sustains such a frame (II.7, 1.312–22). There is not a single instance in nature that would support the claim of an eternal stasis. It seems nothing lasts forever, and growth accordingly decays. Diversity will homogenize; the order will fray; and the frame will collapse. Energy, thus released, will rush back, down through the order of magnitudes, and swell once more as a fiery blaze: the very chaos of primal matter that allows rebirth. Consequently Kant's *phoenix of nature* (1.321) shall rise again from the ashes.

Kant's universe oscillates at the top order of spacetime. He reasons that Big Bang surfs into Big Crunch, surfing into another Big Bang. The wing flaps of the firebird (on whose pinions humans briefly ride) are the heartbeat of nature. Each beat echoes and informs the next beat. Since each rise of the firebird is a cosmos in a chain, in which each cosmos links to the next, any such oscillation owes its peak to the last trough – the more powerful a past down-stroke had been, the higher a current swing can rise. This pulse of outward evolutionary rises and inward entropic falls, of big bangs and big crunches, is to Kant the eternal dialectic chain of self-perfecting cosmoi.

This seal of the firebird, Kant's eternal wing stroke of mortal cosmoi, is not as unscientific as it may seem at first. Its conceptual elements are Big Bang, Big Crunch, and a cyclic universe. The Big Bang theory has been substantiated beyond all academic doubt, and its alternative, the so-called Steady State universe, was retired by countervailing data. A standard model of galactic, stellar, and planetary formations has come into view. This model relates to Kant's cosmogony like a photograph to a well-drawn cartoon; we know more than Kant did, but what we do know harmonizes with his claims, turning them into a recognizable sketch of our differentiated view.

The evolution of life is not conjectural anymore either; all known data tell the same story of progressively emerging, historically speciating, and increasingly complex organisms up to us. In cosmology, the qualified Anthropic Principle (the idea that the universe is tuned to generate life) is now integrated in the standard model: had the energetic and structural constants been different, stars and life would not have emerged – the cosmos would have stayed too hot, turned too cold, or been too short-lived; or hydrogen would not have transmuted to other elements such as carbon. As Kant suggests, there is a causal link from the cosmic conditions to their progressive unfolding; in a way, life is the historical result of a specific "tuning" of nature's cosmological constants.

Cosmic inflation and evolution remain problematic only in cultural contexts that oppose the scientific game and its rule-play by logic and evidence. Yet real problems remain. The model of the origin of nature and life has not grown into a model of their termination. Kant advanced four contentions in *Universal Natural History* that go beyond present knowledge. He argues that the cosmos will die in chaos (1.312–14); that this death is a new birth (1.314); that the universe is a cyclic chain of cosmoi (1.314–22); and that there is life elsewhere (1.351–66).

The discovery of cosmic acceleration (1998) has been taken as evidence for so-called dark energy or quantum vacuum energy – the wider an expanse unfurls, the more energetic a farther unfurling will be. This supports the idea of an energetic space, but it is unclear how accelerating expansion of the cosmic bubble will lead to a Big Rip or a Big Crunch. Several theories for such rips and crunches have been advanced, but none is as yet testable. Whether the universe is cyclic accordingly remains to be seen. There is also no proof of extraterrestrial life – no fossils in Martian ice, no fish in Titan's seas, and no SETI contact from afar. But Kant trusts that such life would have to be found eventually. Given how cosmically mediocre humans are (1.359; 1.365), it is plausible to assume better minds than ours in nature. In arguing so, he joins other Enlightenment thinkers. But as he admits (1.365) – who knows?

6. Conclusion

Kant first mentions his project of a history of the universe in a tract on the ultimate rotational fate of the Earth's rotation, the Spin Cycle Essay (1754). There he announces the planned work as,

> Cosmogony, or Essay of Deriving the Origin of the World System, the Formation of Celestial Bodies, and the Causes of their Motion, from the Universal Laws of Material Motion by Newton's Theory. (1.191)

A book with this title by Kant never came out. Instead a Leipzig publisher, Peterson, with a Königsberg store, released an anonymous treatise called *Universal Natural History and Theory of the Skies* a year later. By then, Kant was back in town, had re-enrolled and just earned his Master's degree. His advisor Johann Teske was a philosopher who experimented with electric shocks and lightning. Kant's thesis is on the fate of combusting material lattices and on the nature of light (cf. prop. 7; 1.376). He called it *Outline of Some Meditations on Fire* (1755).

Meanwhile advance copies of the anonymous book had been forwarded to a few journals, but a real publication never occurred. The publisher defaulted after the galleys had been typeset. The printed copies, Peterson's property, were locked up in a warehouse while the creditors were deciding what to do. We do not know what happened next. We just know that the building caught fire and burnt down.

This may have been just as well, because Kant was now earning his academic degrees and hoped to advance professionally. In 1755 he could not afford another confrontation with fundamentalists who, as he had learned the hard way, did not support free-spirited proposals. So the *Universal Natural History* vanished from sight. Kant earned his doctorate with arguments for the binary nature of identity (I.1–2), for a principle-pair of ontological cognition (III.12–13), and for his declared "universal system of the trade [*commercium*] of substances" (1.415–16).

After this second dissertation, *New Elucidation of the First Principles of Metaphysical Knowledge*, Kant prepared his next thesis in 1756. This third and professorial thesis has the unwieldy title, *The Use of Joining Metaphysics and Geometry in Natural Philosophy; First Sample: Physical Monadology*. He hoped this would get him Knutzen's chair, vacant since 1751. But after he successfully defended the thesis, and just when he was hoping to be appointed to this position, the anonymity of *Universal Natural History* was lifted and it was traced back to Kant.

A bookstore advertised in town the sale of the book "by Magister Kant" a month after he had won his last degree. Now his peers knew he was the culprit of a philosophy more scientific than Newton and disrespectful of Scripture. He had made himself academically impossible just when he hoped for promotion. For the next decade he worked as an adjunct and assistant.

The ill-fated *Universal Natural History* is central to Kant's pre-Critical project. His view turns on the material interplay of attraction and repulsion, allowing the evolution of cosmoi by ongoing "trade-ups" of binary forces. This idea is Kant's philosophical keystone, and it mirrors parallel arguments in his first book and his three theses. In *Living Forces* he had described the weaving of a world web through interacting radiations. In *Fire*, he studied how material webs collapse into radiated fate. In *Elucidation*, he split identity into plus/minus and interwove freedom and necessity as dual strands of ontological structures. The knot in his metaphysical web is the *potentia resistendi* of power-points that are autonomous in their context (cf. 1.402–4). In *Physical Monadology* he argued for an interweaving of space field and power-points, in that geometric continua oscillate in grids of dynamic "activity spheres"; the string-seeds of matter (cf. prop. 7, 1.481). While this third thesis is an account of how matter forms from fields, *Universal Natural History* is an account of how cosmic superstructure evolves on this basis.

In sum, Kant looks at nature as a cloth weaving itself and argues for the accessibility of the past, present, and future of this textile commerce. The endpoints and natural threads of fate matter, whether in the guise of the currently woven cosmos (1747), the spins of Earth and Moon (1754), the knitting of universes (1755), the tangle of light and matter (1755, MA), the patterns of the cosmic cloth and its willful ends (1755, doctor), or the material blossoms in the spatial field (1756, PhD).

The heuristic value of this philosophy of nature was first seen by Schopenhauer (1818). Schopenhauer defended Kant's Nebular Hypothesis as being superior to Laplace's later theory; Nietzsche (1873: in *Philosophy in the Tragic Era of the Greeks*, no. 17) found a Greek mirror of Kant's perspective in the presocratic thinker Anaxagoras, via "the type of vibration" (*eine Art der Schwingung*) and "the dancing mathematical form" (*eine bewegte mathematische Figur*) of this world-machine. To Nietzsche, Kant's world-machine looks like a God without being supernatural in any Christian sense. Heidegger, not a good Christian either, sharpened nature's will to power into the eternal-happening *Ereignis* (1940s); to him, being moves along a swinging fateful chain of dialectic, reciprocal, and appropriating events. If one wished to apply Heidegger to the early Kant, a rational ontology of *karma* would evidently emerge on the basis of the pre-Critical cosmogony. (See also chapter 32 below.)

Present-day cosmology is no longer the preserve of old physicists who might have done useful work in their youth but had turned into mystics in their dotage (Hawking and Penrose 1996: 75). The field is thriving, rigorous, and rests on an observational basis. Although models advanced remain open to revision (as any genuine scientific account must), findings in the field now carry a weight that cosmology did not have earlier in the past century. As a result, science is now catching up with Kant's philosophy of nature. We are elucidating the universe, and *Universal Natural History* is the mentioned essence of modern models. This worldwide project is fueled by what seems to be an increasingly realistic hope of understanding why nature exists. The philosophical stakes of this project are as high as it gets. If we can answer this question, it would be the ultimate triumph of reason, for then we would know "the mind of God" (Hawking 2003: 167). In light of a declared "final theory" as the emerging heuristic basis of physics, in light of the worsening weather-beats of climate dynamics, and in light of Kant's cosmological recognition in the twenty-first century, his ideas on nature's origin, evolution, and fate are inviting serious attention.

References

Kant, Immanuel (1754). *Untersuchung der Frage, ob die Erde in ihrer Umdrehung um die Achse . . . einige Veränderung seit den ersten Zeiten ihres Ursprungs erlitten habe . . .* [abbreviated title; *Investigation of the Question Whether the Earth in its Rotation on its Axis has Undergone any Alteration since the Earliest Times of its Origin*]. Published in two parts in *Wöchentlichen Königsberischen Frag- und Anzeigungsnachrichten* 23 (June 8, 1754) and 24 (June 15, 1754). Academy Edition 1.183–92.

Kant, Immanuel (1754). *Die Frage, ob die Erde veralte, physikalisch erwogen* [*The Question Whether the Earth is Aging considered from a Physicalistic Point of View*]. Published in six parts in *Wöchentlichen Königsbergischen Frag- und Anzeigungsnachrichten* 32 (Aug. 10, 1754) to 37 (Sept. 14, 1754). Academy Edition 1.193–214.

Kant, Immanuel (1755). *Allgemeine Naturgeschichte und Theorie des Himmels* [*Universal Natural History and Theory of the Skies*]. Königsberg and Leipzig: Petersen 1755. Academy Edition 1.215–368.

Kant, Immanuel (1992). *Theoretical Philosophy, 1755–1770*, eds. and tr. D. Walford and R. Meerbote. Cambridge: Cambridge University Press.

Further Reading

Adickes, Erich (1924). *Kant als Naturforscher* [Kant as Investigator of Nature]. 2 vols. Berlin: De Gruyter.

Barrow, John D. (2000). *The Universe that Discovered Itself.* Oxford: Oxford University Press.

Beijing Foreign Language Institute, ed. (1988). *Xin HanDe Cidian/Das Neue Chinesische–Deutsche Wörterbuch.* Nanwu Yin Shuguan: Beijing.

Coles, Peter (2001). *The Routledge Companion to the New Cosmology.* London: Routledge.

Hawking, Stephen W. (2003). *The Theory of Everything: The Origin and Fate of the Universe.* Beverly Hills: Millennium.

Hawking, Stephen W. and Penrose, Roger (1996). *The Nature of Space and Time.* Princeton: Princeton University Press.

Friedman, Michael (1992). *Kant and the Exact Sciences.* Cambridge, MA: Harvard University Press.

Krafft, Fritz (1971). *Analogie – Theodizee – Akualismus: Wissenschaftshistorische Einführung in Kants Kosmogonie.* In Krafft (ed.), *Allgemeine Naturgeschichte und Theorie des Himmels*, pp. 179–95. München: Kindler.

Lalla, Sebastian (2003). *Kants Allgemeine Naturgeschichte und Theorie des Himmels (1755).* Kant-Studien 94: 426–53.

Leibniz, Gottfried Wilhelm (1989). *Philosophical Essays*, eds. and tr. R. Ariew and D. Garber. Indianapolis: Hackett.

Newton, Isaac (1934). *Mathematical Principles of Natural Philosophy and System of the World*, tr. A. Motte, ed. F. Cajori. 2 vols. Berkeley: University of California Press.

Newton, Isaac (1931). *Opticks, or A Treatise of the Reflections, Refractions, Inflections & Colours of the Light.* 4th ed. [1730]. Eds. A. Einstein, I. B. Cohen, et al. London: Bell.

Menge, H. and Pertsch, E. (1984). *Lateinisch–Deutsch Taschenwörterbuch.* Munich: Langenscheidt.

Paneth, F. A. (1955). *Die Erkenntnis des Weltbaus durch Thomas Wright und Immanuel Kant.* Kant-Studien 47: 337–49.

Schönfeld, Martin (2000). *The Philosophy of the Young Kant.* Oxford: Oxford University Press.

Schönfeld, Martin (2003). Kant's philosophical development. In E. Zalta and P. Guyer, eds., *Stanford Encyclopedia of Philosophy* (winter 2003 online edition).

Schönfeld, Martin (In press). Pious Newton, pagan Kant: A parting of their ways. In M. Dickson and M. Domsky (eds.), *Synthesis: Festschrift for Michael Friedman*. La Salle, IL: Open Court.

Shea, William R. (1986). Filled with wonder: Kant's cosmological essay, the *Universal Natural History and Theory of the Heavens*. In R. Butts (ed.), *Kant's Theory of Physical Science*, pp. 95–124. Dordrecht: Reidel.

Weizsäcker, Carl Friedrich von (2002). Immanuel Kant. In Weizsäcker, *Grosse Physiker: von Aristoteles bis Werner Heisenberg* [*Great Physicists from Aristotle to Werner Heisenberg*], pp. 181–203. Munich: DTV.

4

Kant's Laboratory of Ideas in the 1770s

ALISON LAYWINE

The problem of reconstructing Kant's intellectual development in the 1770s is that he published nothing significant during this time. Our record of his thinking consists in spotty correspondence, lecture notes taken by students, and his own notes scribbled in the margins of books and on pieces of scrap paper. None of this material is as polished as anything that Kant ever finally published, and some of the personal notes or *Reflexionen* degenerate into total gobbledygook. Nevertheless, we can learn something important from it and use it to illuminate Kant's efforts to articulate what would later become his most significant philosophical ideas. But progress on this front requires that we learn how to interpret the available fragmentary evidence.

1. *Reflexionen* as Documentary Evidence for Kant's Philosophical Development

Kant habitually wrote down his thoughts, sometimes even before he really knew what they would look like on paper. This practice seems to have played an important role in his work as a philosopher; he can be understood to describe it explicitly in advice he gave his students in the lectures on anthropology from the winter semester 1772/3. First he warned them against slavishly consulting their notes and books, because this might block them from insight by "overtaxing the imagination" and thereby "restricting genius." He therefore recommended that they set aside their reference material after having fully immersed themselves in some subject and then give free play to their creative powers of invention: first by distracting the mind with pleasant conversation or perhaps fluffy reading, and then later by writing up spontaneously in one sitting everything on the subject that freely occurred to them (25[1].313).

> You have to continue writing in one go. Often you will get stuck, if you can't think of a word. But then it's better to leave gaps to write everything in one go. If a word occurs to you for later use, all you have to do is jot it in the margin. Then you read it through one more time and put it in order. (25[1].86; author's translations throughout)

Kant's advocacy of *"Reflexion-writing"* unexpectedly brings to mind André Breton, who called for automatic writing in the *Manifestes du surréalisme* as a means of freeing creative powers of the human imagination too easily stifled by conventional thinking. But automatic writing was supposed to set the imagination absolutely free of any and all constraints. That was certainly not the case for Kant, who assumed, by contrast with Breton, that the imagination would be exercising itself on some well-defined, predetermined subject and that reason would take over in the effort to tidy the results. For Kant, *Reflexion-writing* was not a vehicle of human liberation, as it would be for Breton, but a tool of discovery that he apparently used in his own philosophizing.

Parts of Kant's handwritten *Nachlaß* preserved on scrap paper seem to be exercises in *Reflexion-writing*. They show Kant struggling paradoxically not to overtax his imagination. Thus he puts down his ideas in the order that they come; he tries his best to get down everything he has to say. But, as he searches for the right words, he very frequently gets stuck and simply starts over again. It is clear in the passage quoted from the anthropology lectures that the material generated in this way was supposed to be revised. If it proved sufficiently promising, Kant would subsequently try to develop the revised *Reflexionen* into something readable that he hoped to revise further and integrate into proofs ready for the printer. This can be seen, as Eckart Förster points out, from the manuscript of the *Opus postumum*, which has material from every stage of this process except for final printer's copy (Förster 1993: xxiv–xxv). Hence, *Reflexionen* were the seeds of Kant's finished philosophical works. One would therefore expect them to give us a privileged glimpse into his ideas as they were developing and possibly into his thinking during the 1770s.

However, there is at least one serious problem in using *Reflexionen* to document any given period in Kant's development: their dating. We could search for points of agreement in their content with doctrines known from Kant's published works (Erdmann 1992). But taking these points of agreement to justify dating by the year of publication of the relevant work is to argue in a vicious circle, since the very thing at issue is when the relevant idea or doctrine began to play a role in Kant's thinking (Heinze 1894: 509ff). To avoid such a circle, we would have to look for objective criteria. Erich Adickes tried to show that such criteria could be found in dateable changes in Kant's handwriting (Adickes 1925, 1926). But Adickes's claims remain controversial; and, nobody has had the fortitude to try reproducing his results.

Fortunately for us, some of the *Reflexionen* have been preserved on the back of dated letters. Adickes thinks it was Kant's habit to use letters as scrap paper shortly after receiving them (Adickes 1925: xix). Since Kant could not have written up his own ideas before the letters themselves were written, the date of a given letter gives a pretty good date for the *Reflexion* itself. We happen to have one very significant set of *Reflexionen* that can be dated this way to the 1770s. The so-called *Duisburg Nachlaß* – R 4674 to R 4684, running from page 643 to 673 in volume 17 of the Academy edition – is a bundle of notes on scrap paper including a letter to Kant dated May 1775. It is widely accepted that the whole bundle was written at the same time, because the train of thought remains focused on the same set of issues and because Adickes reports that ink and handwriting were uniform throughout (many of the pages are now lost). We can think of the *Duisburg Nachlaß* as the documentary remains of a philosophical laboratory that Kant was running on paper in the mid-1770s. By supplementing it with selected correspondence and lecture transcripts of the time, we can use it to reconstruct a small but very significant part of a decade of thinking that would be completely lost to us otherwise.

2. Looking Ahead and Setting Things Up

Before examining this material in detail, let us jump ahead and announce what we may expect to find. The *Duisburg Nachlaß* is an extended reflection on human finitude as manifested in our understanding. As such, it addresses a significant problem that Kant himself found in the *Inaugural Dissertation* of 1770. He had argued there for the first time that sensibility and the understanding are two separate faculties governed by different principles. But in the famous letter to Marcus Herz of 1772, he acknowledged that his account of the understanding in the *Inaugural Dissertation* was undeveloped (10.129–35). He had argued, as he would later in the *Critique of Pure Reason*, that the principles of human sensibility are space and time taken to be pure intuitions. But all he had to say about the understanding was this: "intelligence (rationality) is the faculty of the subject through which he can represent those things that cannot, by their nature, meet with his senses" (§3, 2.392). The remark asserts that the understanding is not sensibility, but does nothing to specify the difference. Some of the most interesting work that Kant did in theoretical philosophy in the 1770s, as it has been preserved for us, was to remedy this deficit – an effort that culminated in the *Critique of Pure Reason* and more specifically the Analytic of Concepts: "the as yet infrequently attempted analysis of the faculty of the understanding itself" (B 90).

Already in the 1772 letter to Herz, Kant suggests a way of investigating the understanding in greater detail than he had in the *Inaugural Dissertation*, namely to contrast it as a finite faculty in created minds with the infinite faculty at the disposal of a divine mind. He characterizes the latter as an "intellectus archetypus" whose representations create their own objects and thereby relate to them in such a way as to yield knowledge. "We conceive of divine cognitions as the models [*Urbilder*] of things," he wrote, i.e., as a cognition "upon which the things themselves are grounded" (10.130). In this way, he went on, "we can see how there can be conformity of the same [sc. divine cognitions] with the objects" (10.130). God cannot fail to know his object as it is in itself: he creates it exactly as he conceives it to be; he conceives it exactly as he created it to be. But a finite understanding cannot create its objects and must therefore relate its representations to them in some other way. If it did so by being affected by objects, it would be indistinguishable from sensibility. Hence the problem is to characterize a finite understanding so that we learn more specifically how it differs not only from human sensibility, but also from the intellectus archetypus. This contrast will drive Kant's thinking in our dateable *Reflexionen*. Indeed, it will underlie the Analytic of Concepts in the first *Critique*, which is supposed to show us ultimately that our finite understanding is discursive and therefore incapable of intellectual intuition, i.e., some kind of direct, unmediated insight into the things themselves.

To see how Kant developed this issue, we have to consider first how he conceived it before 1770. One important assumption he apparently made almost from the beginning is that we cannot learn much about the nature of a divine intellect without taking into consideration the object to which it specially applies itself. For present purposes, this object is the universe as a whole. Kant did not mean by "universe as a whole" first and foremost the sum total of finite things God created, but rather the principles that cause them all to form a single world. A world is a whole that is not itself a part of another whole and that has unity because each of its parts somehow externally relates to all of the others. God's intellect takes as its object the principles that govern this unity (1.414), i.e., the "principles of the form of a world," as Kant would later call them (§13, 2.398). The question now is how such principles are to be specified. The quick and easy answer is that they have to be just the ones exhibiting the highest wisdom, since God most wisely picks them and no others to run the world. The harder problem is to say something meaningful about supreme wisdom.

Kant held that such wisdom consists in producing the greatest number of different results by the fewest possible means. Consequently, he attacked the view that the principles of the form of the world are specialized ends that God has set for different creatures and that he himself brings about by his frequent interventions. Since creation is as manifold as it is vast in extent, the view Kant attacked must multiply specialized ends and interventions accordingly. That was supposed to be the view's great attraction to those who propounded it: the sign of supreme wisdom is precisely that God is able to coordinate all of his specialized ends and interventions on their behalf in such a way that creatures relate to form a coherent world. Against this view, Kant argued that supreme wisdom minimizes the need for intervention by creating those things whose very nature is governed by universal laws that cause them to arrange themselves into a world on their own steam. Indeed, he argued that supreme wisdom would have required such economy and efficiency that God minimized the number of natural laws at work in the world: the natural phenomena we observe around us tend to follow from the same universal laws, no matter how different they seem to be. Thus the revolution of the planets around the sun, that of the moon around the earth, the motion of the tides and the fall of heavy bodies at the earth's surface are all the result of a single universal law at work in material nature: the law of universal gravitation (1.221–37; 2.93–151). (See also chapter 3 above.)

On Kant's early account, the human intellect can keep pace with its divine counterpart – if only by grasping the principles of the form of the world. It cannot create anything, but it can use these principles to do the next best thing: construct a world in thought by making certain assumptions about the matter of which it is composed and the universal laws to which it is subject. Kant himself had argued in 1755 that, if we suppose the nature of matter is to exercise a universal attractive force under the Newtonian laws of motion and that God created it in a state of initial chaos, then we can show that it would have organized itself into a physical universe with the same structure as our own (1.241–69). Large clumps of matter would have coalesced into stars, planets, and moons. All the planets in a given solar system would come to revolve in the same direction on the same plane around the centre of their sun; the planetary system as a whole would revolve with countless others in the same direction on the same plane around the centre of the galaxy; this galaxy would revolve with its sisters around the center of a system greater still.

The plausibility of this thought experiment depends on whether it succeeds in generating a physical universe that we can recognize as sufficiently like our own. It will succeed in this if it grasps the (physical) principles of the form of our world: the Newtonian laws of motion operating on an essential force of universal attraction in matter. But grasping these principles is possible just because the human intellect recognizes, as much as its divine counterpart, the supreme wisdom of maximizing the number of different results by the fewest possible means. Moreover, it quite reasonably expects to find such wisdom on display in the physical universe. This very expectation naturally leads it to the hypothetical cosmogony Kant tried to defend in 1755 and through the early 1760s – at least that is what Kant claimed on its behalf. The purported success of his cosmogony was supposed to meet the objections of those who argued that the human intellect is far too limited to learn how the universe came to be as it is and consequently that it cannot apply itself constructively to the special object of God's intellect (but see 2.115).

By 1770, Kant had to reconsider this optimism in light of his new distinction between sensibility and the understanding. In particular, he had to reconsider the claims he made in 1755 about the conjectural origin and structure of the physical universe. These claims did not concern a world as such, an object of pure understanding according to the *Inaugural Dissertation*, but a concrete one, the thought of which we build up successively through time by adding the thought of our local earth–moon system to the thought of our larger planetary system, to the thought of that system's place in the galaxy, to the thought of the galaxy's place with others like it in a still greater system, and so on (§1, 2.387). But if it is true, as Kant said in 1755, that the physical universe is infinite both in space and in time, the process of successively building up our thought of it can never be completed. In that case, such thought can never legitimately stake a claim to truth – at least not if it purports to say anything about the universe in its full extent. It cannot be "derived from an object" (§30, 2.417–18); hence it is more legitimately construed as an expression of hope: namely that the natural laws apparently unifying the part of the universe in our vicinity apply throughout the infinite in the same way always and everywhere. In the *Inaugural Dissertation*, Kant said that such a hope is a purely subjective "principle of convenience," grounded not on the "laws of sensitive knowledge," but rather on conditions of the intellect itself (§30, 2.417–18):

> we simply cannot renounce it without renouncing at the same time all rational motivation for investigating the world around us. If God rules the world by miraculous intervention we can only despair of making sense of it. (§30, 2.418)

But though the *Inaugural Dissertation* restricts us in this way, it does not take the further step of denying our intellect the concept of a world altogether. In particular, it holds out the possibility of the so-called "sensible world," i.e., the world considered as "phenomenon in relation to the sensibility of the human mind" (§13, 2.398). Still it does not explain how such a world can be possible except to say that all the things in it appear to us under the conditions of space and time taken to be pure intuitions. Hence, it leaves unanswered the question how the things that so appear to us, do so in such a way that we can think of them as parts of the same world (Laywine 2003).

Kant had a serious commitment to the sensible world. In the mid-1770s he made a concerted effort to supplement the story he had told about it in the *Inaugural Dissertation* and thereby get it to work for him. One reason for the effort is that he thought the

possibility of empirical thought depended on it. Empirical thought results from applying the human intellect to perceptions, i.e., to those appearances of which we are
conscious (*R*, 4679, 17.664). It consists in "perceptions that have been understood" –
that is to say, "experience" (*R*, 4679, 17.664). Kant took experience to have the structure of a sensibly given world insofar as the intellect represents appearances as universally related to each other in a spatiotemporal whole. This whole is never completed
once and for all: it will always be possible for the intellect to try representing it as
integrated into a still greater spatiotemporal whole. But however great or small
its scope, the intellect always understands this whole to be unified. In other words, it
understands the appearances that constitute it to be universally related to one another
in one and the same empirical context. You might well engage in empirical thought
about winter traffic conditions on the street outside your front window, without giving
any thought to the conditions at the same time of year in the alley beyond your back-
porch. But, under the principle of convenience, you may wish to see whether you can
connect these vital arteries in thought about your neighborhood as a whole. If you
succeed in making such a connection, your thinking will play itself out against a grid
of throughways laid out in one and the same space and persisting through one and the
same time as the seasons change. The spatial grid and its duration and position in time
exhibit unity, insofar as you can situate in space and time together each of its parts
relative to all of the others and, we hope, to the parts of neighborhoods beyond its
immediate confines. This unity gives experience or empirical thought spatiotemporal
coherence: it simply cannot be imagined, except perhaps by Hollywood script writers,
that crossing the street will lead you into a separate, parallel universe. Kant was
concerned in the 1770s with the intrinsically interesting question how experience –
understood as a unified spatiotemporal whole or universal system of relations – is
possible. This is a question of central importance to the *Duisburg Nachlaß*.

It is important to see, however, that precisely by couching his question in this very
peculiar way, Kant could investigate more fully than he had in the *Inaugural Dissertation* how the human intellect differs from its divine counterpart. Human intellectual
finitude manifests itself precisely in the fact that we engage in empirical thought: God
does not have experience. But as we saw earlier, the object to which God's intellect
specially applies itself is supposed to be a unified world-whole. Kant's reflections in the
1770s seem to have been guided by the question how the unified world-whole known
by God differs from the unified spatiotemporal world-in-the-making constructed by us
in empirical thought. This question seems to have pointed him towards a peculiar, yet
essential, notion in the *Duisburg Nachlaß*, the so-called "exposition of appearances."
This notion retains something from Kant's earlier cosmogony. But as an effort to
supplement the *Inaugural Dissertation*, it developed as the immediate ancestor to the
Transcendental Analytic familiar to us from the *Critique of Pure Reason* – with some
significant differences.

3. The "Exposition of Appearances" in the *Duisburg Nachlaß*

Kant characterizes the exposition of appearances in the *Duisburg Nachlaß* as a
"linking of representations" (*Verkettung der Vorstellungen*) and more specifically as "the

determination of the ground upon which rests the joining [*Zusammenhang*] of sensations in appearances" (*R*, 4674, 17.643). It is supposed to "[connect] representations . . . and thereby [make] a whole according to the matter (appearances)." "Here is thus unity," Kant writes, ". . . whereby the manifold is brought into one, thus universality" (*R*, 4674, 17.643, cf. 28.202). Exposition produces a unified whole by somehow determining the relations among appearances (*R*, 4674, 17.643). Every appearance has to relate, either directly or indirectly, to every other; an appearance isolated from all the others would disturb the unity Kant seeks. The exposition of appearances also has to render these relations necessary: they are not supposed to depend on our subjective perspective, i.e., on ways of regarding appearances that are merely convenient, interesting or pleasing to us. Rather, they are supposed in principle to be determined by universal laws. Now Kant says explicitly and repeatedly in the *Duisburg Nachlaß* that whatever can be determined in principle by universal laws is just what he means by "object" or "objective" (cf. *R*, 4675, 17.638; *R*, 4677, 17.658; *R*, 4681, 17.666–7). Thus an important part of the peculiar idea cluster that Kant associated with the exposition of appearances is summed up in the following passage: "The objective is the inner necessity of appearance, namely since appearance has been freed from anything subjective and is regarded as determinable through a universal rule (of appearances)" (*R*, 4675, 17.650). In keeping with this claim, Kant sometimes calls the exposition of appearances the operation for "making appearances objective" (*R*, 4677, 17.658) or converting them into experience (*R*, 4675, 17.648).

But we might well wonder why Kant thinks that the exposition of appearances is the necessary condition for both the objective in empirical thought, as he understands it, and the bringing together of appearances in a unified spatiotemporal whole. These seem to be two different, unrelated things. One way to get a start on an answer is to ask what Kant might have thought they have in common. An important clue is Kant's explicit claim in the *Duisburg Nachlaß* that an object, insofar as we think of it through "exposition," "can be represented only according to its relations" (*R*, 4674, 17.646). We cannot have empirical thought unless we represent the objects of our thought as related to one another in space and time. The other important clue is Kant's insistence that all thought of objects expresses universality. Empirical thought does not simply specify its objects as related to one another in space and time; it characterizes these relations as necessary, i.e., as determined by universal laws. Now Kant says explicitly in the *Duisburg Nachlaß* that representing appearances as necessarily related to one another according to such laws is just what it takes to bring them together in a unified spatiotemporal whole. Hence, any operation that makes it possible for us to think of appearances as related to one another in a unified spatiotemporal whole will make such thought objective in Kant's sense of the word. But while the text leaves no doubt that Kant was thinking in these terms, we can still wonder how he thought they were supposed to cash out.

One way to address this natural concern is to note how much of his earlier cosmogony seems to have been preserved and adapted in the *Duisburg Nachlaß*. The aim of the exposition of appearances is at once much more modest and more fundamental. But it is supposed to get us everything Kant wants through determinability by universal laws. The key move in the earlier cosmogony was likewise an appeal to universal laws. There is, to be sure, at least one important difference. The earlier cosmogony specified that a force of universal attraction operates on matter under the Newtonian laws of motion. In the *Duisburg Nachlaß*, Kant makes no mention of force (but cf. *R*, 40, 14.119), and he leaves open which laws are at work. Indeed, he can be understood to say that specifying which laws determine appearances is the separate task of empirical investigation (*R*, 4679, 17.663). Still, he claims that as long as some condition – which we have yet to sort out – enables the intellect to think of appearances as determined by universal laws, it will at the same time enable it to think of them as necessarily related to one another in space and time. If the intellect can thereby state as a law that water always freezes at zero degrees Celsius, it will also be able to think of a solid state of water succeeding a liquid state in time at a given position in space where the conditions are right. This is an echo of the earlier cosmogony, where the effect of subjecting matter to the relevant laws was at least in principle to set material particles in relations corresponding to the highly ordered structure of lunar, solar, and galactic systems embedded in heavenly systems greater still. Even when the exposition of appearances yields locally very modest systems, like that of ice-cubes forming in the tray of somebody's freezer, it does so – if at all – by means philosophically akin to those that yielded the cosmically vast systems of Kant's speculative cosmogony, namely the human intellect's presumed ability to state and apply universal laws.

The second point of contact is that the earlier cosmogony shows us very concretely how "objectivity" in the *Duisburg* sense neatly ties in with all this. By appealing to the relevant universal laws and thereby systematically relating the material particles God created in a state of initial chaos, the earlier cosmogony gave us an object of thought. Indeed, it gave us the special object of God's intellect: the physical universe as a whole. But it did so in just the way the *Duisburg Nachlaß* prescribes. In the first place, it enabled us to think this object in the only way possible, i.e., according to its relations. The thought of the physical universe, as spelled out in the earlier cosmogony, coincides precisely with the thought of those spatiotemporal relations that define the lunar, solar, and galactic systems of greater and greater scope. To get the thought of the physical universe, no further thought need, or can, be added to this one. Moreover, this thought, as it stands, presupposes the universal: it would not be possible to countenance the hierarchy of heavenly systems within systems, if we did not think of matter as governed in principle by universal laws, and in particular as subject to a force of universal attraction operating under the Newtonian laws of motion. (See also chapter 3 above.)

There may well be a third point of contact, if – as it seems – truth and objectivity were not the same thing for Kant in the mid-1770s. The earlier cosmogony was clearly objective in the *Duisburg* sense, but we could still ask if it is true or at least plausible. The answer to our question depended on whether the relations defining its object of thought were sufficiently like the structure of the world we actually live in – as far as we can determine. But the same further question arises for empirical thought as made possible by the exposition of appearances: though it must be objective in the *Duisburg* sense, if it is possible at all, it need not be true. It will prove true, one suspects, if we can recognize the relations that define its object as obtaining in the world around us.

If, then, we want to understand how to cash out the abstract pronouncements about the "exposition of appearances" in the *Duisburg Nachlaß*, we can do no better than to look back to Kant's early cosmogony, bearing in mind – of course – the restrictions we discussed earlier that have to come into play because of advances in the *Inaugural Dissertation*.

4. How to Get the "Exposition of Appearances" to Work?

Our problem now is to figure out how Kant thought the exposition of appearances was actually supposed to work. First of all he explicitly denies in the *Duisburg Nachlaß* that the pure intuitions of space and time are enough on their own to get it off the ground. Space and time make it possible in principle for us to represent appearances as externally related to one another in the so-called sensible world. But they cannot all by themselves determine for our thought which relations they will have, much less determine these relations as necessary. Thus Kant says that "relations among appearances do not rest on forms [sc. of sensibility]" (*R*, 4674, 17.643). The exposition of appearances will have to bring something else into play. His resources for filling out the picture will come from a theory of judgment supplemented by a metaphysical psychology.

From the theory of judgment, Kant drew a certain characterization of the understanding. He had said in an essay of 1762, "The False Subtlety of the Four Figures of the Syllogism," that the "higher power of knowledge" is nothing other than "the faculty of judging" (2.59). Judging is the act whereby a distinct concept becomes actual, i.e., when I clearly or explicitly recognize something as the mark of a thing. For example, I do not clearly recognize impenetrability to be the mark of bodies until I actually use the relevant concept and explicitly make the following judgment: bodies are impenetrable (2.58). In answer to the question at the end of the essay, "what sort of secret power makes judging possible?," Kant said that

[it] is nothing other than the faculty of inner sense, i.e., of taking your own representations as the objects of your thoughts. This faculty . . . can only be peculiar to rational beings. The whole higher power of knowledge rests upon it (2. 60).

The reflective aspect here suggests a passage in the first *Critique* (B 49) where he says that inner sense is "the intuition of our self and our inner state." But in the "False Subtlety," he associated inner sense not with sensibility, as he would later understand it, but rather with the "higher power of knowledge" and more specifically with the power of judging.

This association gets spelled out a little more fully in the transcript of a lecture on metaphysics – the so-called Pölitz lectures, or more elliptically L₁, believed to have been held between 1775/6 and 1779/80 (Heinze 1894: 516; Carl 1989: 117–19). Kant has been discussing the difference between men and beasts. He reportedly says that beasts have outer sense, but denies them inner sense. This is supposed to mean that they are incapable of "consciousness of self" and therefore lack the "concept of the I [*das Ich*]": "Hence they have neither understanding nor reason, for all operations of the understanding and reason are possible only insofar as one is conscious of oneself." He goes on to say that

> [Beasts] will have no universal knowledge through reflection, neither identity of representations, nor the connections of representations according to subject and predicate, or according to ground and consequence, or according to the whole and the parts: for all of these result from consciousness, lacking in beasts. (28.276)

This remark implies first that judging is supposed to require the ability to evaluate relations among concepts. Kant readily admits that animals recognize and act upon relations among images, as when a dog associates meal-time with the smell of sausages and steals some from the kitchen table. But he says that this will take place according to the laws of association and denies that these laws have to operate in inner sense: beasts have imagination, but not understanding. Kant's remarks in this passage imply, second, that the relations between concepts in a judgment will take different forms, namely the relation of subject and predicate, that of ground and consequence, and that of part and whole. Kant claims that these relations are somehow a feature or product of self-consciousness. He does not elaborate on this claim in our passage from L_1, but elsewhere in the lecture we learn that it is based on a metaphysical psychology.

Through inner sense, I immediately grasp the truth that I am: more specifically that I am an "intelligence" distinct from, but associated with, a body. Since I could lose parts of my body without suffering any loss of intelligence, my true self is unchanging. When I use the concept "I" in reference to myself, I therefore express the substantiality of my soul. L_1 reports Kant as saying this:

> Substance is the first subject of all inhering accidents. But this I is an absolute subject to which all accidents and predicates can be attributed and that can be the predicate of no other thing. Thus the I expresses the substantial. For the substratum that underlies all accidents is the substantial. This is the one case in which we can immediately intuit substance. We can intuit the substantial and the subject of no [sc. other] thing, but in me I intuit substance directly. Thus the I expresses not only substance, but also the substantial itself. Indeed, what is more, the concept that we have of any substance at all we borrow from this I. This is the original concept of substances. (28[1].225–6)

This passage makes a striking contrast with the position Kant will take in the *Critique of Pure Reason*. It asserts dogmatically and unequivocally that the soul is indeed a substance and that we know it to be so by some kind of direct and therefore intuitive insight. In context, this intuition can only come from inner sense. But precisely because inner sense is still explicitly associated with reason and understanding, it is impossible not to conclude that the direct intuitive insight I have of my soul as substance is some kind of intellectual intuition (but cf. 28.179).

Kant seems to have applied these ideas in his theory of judgment. As we saw earlier, the relation between concepts in a judgment can take different forms, one of which is the connection between subject and predicate. The implication of Kant's remarks in the two passages from L_1 quoted above is that the relation between my soul as first and only absolute subject and its accidents or predicates is somehow the source of this connection. When I judge that "Dogs are four-footed," I discursively treat "dog" as a subject and therefore as something substantial. I also treat "four-footed" as one of its attributes. But, according to L_1, dog is not a true subject. My thought of dog as a subject and four-footed as its attribute therefore depends somehow on the "original concept of substances," namely the intellectual intuition of myself as a thing that thinks. The nature of this dependence is unclear. A parallel passage we cannot date with certainty suggests that it is in the nature of an analogy (R, 3921). However the details are supposed to work out, the connection of subject and predicate in the judgment, "Dogs are four-footed," seems to be patterned on the relation between my soul as a thinking substance and the thoughts that inhere in it as accidents. There is no other way to account for this connection because no other model for the relation of substance to accident is available to us (Laywine 2005). Since I only know one true subject, namely myself, my judgments about dogs and everything else I treat discursively as subject must somehow be patterned on it if these judgments are to assume the form "S-is-P." It also looks as if the other two forms the relation between concepts in a judgment can take are somehow patterned on the other two relations that can obtain between the soul and its thoughts: i.e., the relation of ground and consequence, and that of part and whole.

We can now see a little more clearly why Kant thinks inner sense makes judging possible. This claim seems to rest on the following commitments. First, all judging involves a relation among concepts that has to take one of the three forms specified above. Second, these three forms are patterned on the three relations the thinking self can have to its own thoughts. Finally, these relations are given to us in inner sense. It is not clear how Kant would have spelled out these commitments more fully. But they do indicate that he already believed judgments have some kind of classifiable form or structure which we might as well call logical, since he explicitly ascribes it to judgments and distinguishes it from the association of images that goes on, for example, in beasts. By contrast with his position in the first *Critique*, however, he clearly took this logical structure to be grounded in the metaphysics of the thinking self. It would take the discovery of the Paralogisms to make him rethink all this and warn against the temptation to find any hint of a metaphysical psychology in the logical structure of judgment (B 406–10; Carl 1989: 101).

The three relations of the thinking self that determine the logical forms of judgment reappear in the *Duisburg Nachlaß*. Kant has new names for them: "exponents," "functions of apperception," "functions of self-perception"; very occasionally he calls them "categories," but usually he refers to them as "titles of the understanding." The capacity to take myself as an object of my thoughts he now sometimes calls "apprehension," but more usually "apperception." Thus we can find a passage in which he writes,

> Apperception is the consciousness of thought, i.e., of representations as they are set in the mind. Herewith are three exponents: 1. that of the relation [sc.? of my thoughts as accidents to myself as] subject, 2. of the relation of consequences with one another [sc.? as following from one another as ground to consequence], 2. that of the composition [sc.? of parts to whole]. (R, 4674, 17.647)

One would expect Kant to enlist this idea cluster for his theory of judgment – all the more so, since this theory confronts a new problem in the *Duisburg Nachlaß*, namely how to explain the difference between analytic and synthetic judgments. It seems pretty clear that the idea cluster of interest to us is meant to help solve this problem (R, 4676, 17.657). But for the most part Kant uses it to address the problem that has detained us all along, namely how empirical thought is possible. It is strange, and a little disappointing, that Kant develops the two problems on parallel tracks without ever trying to state explicitly how a solution to the one fits with, or contributes to, a solution to the other. Worse yet, the story about synthetic judgments simply fizzles out.

Nevertheless, Kant's appeal in the *Duisburg Nachlaß* to the three functions of apperception to explain how empirical thought is possible has a close family resemblance to the use he seemed to make of their counterparts in L_1 for the theory of judgment. This can help us get our bearings in the *Duisburg Nachlaß* when, for example, we read the following passage:

> There are these three functions of apperception that are found in [added: all] thought of our state as such and under which all appearances must conform, because no synthesis in itself lies within it [sc. in appearances], if the mind does not add such or make such out of the data of the same. The mind is thus itself the model [*das Urbild*] of [added: the possibility] of such a synthesis through original and not derived thought. (R, 4674, 17.646–7)

"Synthesis" is a new term for us, but it seems to mean whatever results in the relations among our perceptions needed for empirical thought (R, 4678, 17.661; R, 4681, 17.667). Our current passage indicates that synthesis is achieved through the functions of apperception. The idea seems to be something like this.

In order to engage in empirical thought at all, the mind has to be able to conceive of perceptions – those appearances of which it is conscious – as related to one another. But these relations are neither given to it with the appearances themselves, nor with the pure intuitions of space and time, the formal conditions of their possibility. Hence, the mind needs some sort of model or pattern to guide its thought of them, just as it needed a pattern to form "S-is-P judgments. The one and only pattern available to it in both cases is the same: the relations it has to its own thoughts as a thinking substance (R, 4676, 17.657). Just as these relations inform the way it relates concepts and thereby structures judgments, so they inform the way it relates perceptions and thereby engages in empirical thought. As Kant himself puts it,

> Every perception must stand under a title of the understanding [sc. a function of apperception], because otherwise it [sc. a perception] gives no concept and nothing is [sc. empirically] thought thereby. . . . [The functions of apperception] indicate the way we avail ourselves of appearances as matter for [sc. empirical] thought. (R, 4679, 17.664)

He uncharacteristically illustrates this claim with some examples: "Wax is soft"; "Gold is dense." As he construes them, both these thoughts or judgments rest on an assumption that the relevant accidents relate as parts in the relevant subject to form a composite whole with other accidents. For example, density is one accident in a composite whole including high malleability, resistance to tarnish, a certain color, etc., in gold treated discursively as the underlying subject. Kant's example judgments therefore rest on the intellect's capacity to grasp the part–whole relation (R, 4679, 17.664). But the pattern for such "connections" can only be found in the composite whole the thinking subject produces from its own thoughts as parts. Hence the example judgments depend on the relevant "function of apperception." Judgments that depend on the intellect's capacity to grasp the relation of ground and consequence or that of subject and accident take their pattern from the other two functions of apperception.

Kant spells out the implications of all this as we would expect. Immediately after commenting on the example judgments we were just considering, he concludes that the functions of apperception are the condition we have been seeking that makes it possible to relate appearances in some kind of unified whole. Thus he writes: "Without such concepts [sc. the functions of apperception], appearances would be altogether separate and would not belong with one another" (R, 4679, 17.664). But since we cannot get a whole of appearances unless the relations among them are necessary, it is also supposed to follow that the functions of apperception make it possible for us to think of them as determined by universal laws. Hence these functions make appearances objective. Kant explicitly draws these inferences in the following passage:

> Appearance is made objective by bringing it as contained under a title of self-perception [sc. a function of apperception]. Hence the original relations of apprehension [sc. the functions of apperception] are the conditions of perception of the [added: real] relation in appearance; and, precisely insofar as one says that an appearance belongs thereunder, it will be determined from the universal and will be represented objectively, i.e., it will be [sc. empirically] thought. (R, 4677, 17.658)

The functions of apperception are thus the intellectual condition, distinct from the formal conditions of sensibility, that are supposed to make empirical thought possible. They are the key to Kant's "exposition of appearances" which results from subjecting appearances to them.

5. Taking Stock

Now that we have fitted together as many pieces as have survived, we can try to take stock of the puzzle as a whole. The exposition of appearances gives us a portrait of human understanding – something missing, as Kant himself recognized, from the *Inaugural Dissertation*. We have spoken all along of apperception. But apperception is as closely identified with the understanding in the *Duisburg Nachlaß* as inner sense was in our passages from L$_1$. Now Kant recognized that there is a specifically logical use of the understanding whereby the metaphysical relations of the thinking subject to itself and its own thoughts determine the formal structure of all our judgments. He might have made this the focus of his portrait. Instead, he focuses on the use of the understanding in empirical thought. Thus the story in the *Duisburg Nachlaß* tries to account for how the understanding operates under constraints that are peculiar to us as finite sentient beings: the formal conditions of human sensibility. Kant makes this point explicit:

> If we had intellectual intuition, we would not need any title of apprehension [sc. function of apperception] in order to represent an object. For then the object would not appear.

Now appearance must be subordinated to a function whereby the mind disposes over it, and indeed to a universal condition, because otherwise there would be nothing universal in it [sc. and hence we could not represent it as an object at all]. (R. 4677, 17.658)

No doubt it will seem odd for Kant to deny that we have intellectual intuition, since some such direct grasping of our own nature as thinking selves is key to the whole story. But affirming that we have an intellectual intuition of ourselves is not obviously incompatible with denying that we can have it of outer appearances. Indeed, denying this should be just as crucial to the story Kant wants to tell about us as finite, human thinkers.

Our concepts cannot directly grasp what is given to us. If they could, the capacity to think and the capacity to sense would be identical, and thus the act of thinking would generate all by itself the matter of our thought. But precisely because the two capacities are distinct in human beings, the matter of our thought is not already thinkable, just by virtue of its having been given to us. The understanding must "dispose over it," i.e., take command of it for the purposes of thinking. This cannot be done immediately; it is the result of subjecting appearances to the functions of apperception. But thinking an object under the functions of apperception means thinking this object as determined at least in principle by universal laws and hence as embedded in a system of relations with other objects, i.e., in a unified whole of appearances. It follows, therefore, that Kant takes this business about unified wholes to be essential not simply to empirical thought as such, but more precisely to the work of our understanding insofar as it is finite in a peculiarly human way. The human understanding is not capable of constructing in thought an infinite universe such as God's intellect may have actually brought into being – as Kant had assumed in his early cosmogony. But it can build up in thought as much of a world as time allows – indeed, it must, because it is so constituted that it can apply itself to appearances in no other way.

In the letter to Marcus Herz of 1772, Kant set up the problem of positively characterizing human understanding as the question how purely intellectual concepts can relate to an object. As we saw earlier, this question derived some of its force precisely from the fact that human understanding cannot create its object, as God's intellectus archetypus can. But it derives the rest of its force from the fact that, unlike sensibility, it cannot be affected by its object either. We can now see that the portrait sketched in the *Duisburg Nachlaß* offers an answer to this famous question. The functions of apperception correspond to three purely intellectual concepts: substance and accident; ground and consequence, and composite whole. The understanding relates these concepts to itself by an intellectual intuition in which the act of thinking and the matter of thinking are identical, i.e., by making explicit the content of its self-awareness. But it also relates these concepts to appearances, not by an intellectual intuition, but rather by projecting the metaphysical structure of its self-awareness onto the sensible world.

The *Duisburg Nachlaß* would decisively inform the outcome of the Transcendental Deduction in the *Critique of Pure Reason* (see chapter 10 below). Kant winds up the argument in the first edition with the claim that the understanding is not best characterized as a faculty of thought or even judging, but rather as a faculty for giving laws to nature (A 126–7). This is supposed to mean that, though we discover the particular laws of nature through empirical investigation, our ability to recognize them comes from elsewhere, namely from the understanding itself. Hence, the understanding makes nature itself possible, since we cannot conceive it – i.e., a unified whole of appearances in the *Duisburg* sense – except as governed by universal laws. But if this claim can indeed be justified, it will establish what the Transcendental Deduction requires, namely that the pure concepts of the understanding relate a priori to all the objects of experience (A 128).

But while the Transcendental Deduction clearly draws on the *Duisburg Nachlaß*, it thoroughly revises the details of his story. The *Duisburg Nachlaß* plainly raises as many questions as it settles. This did not escape Kant. Once he had discovered the Paralogisms of Pure Reason, he called into question the metaphysical psychology underlying the whole story (see chapter 14 below). Hence he could no longer dogmatically characterize the understanding as proceeding from the self-awareness of our soul. Nor could he characterize the pure concepts as expressing the relation of the soul to itself and its own thoughts. Nevertheless, he needed to account for the structure appearances exhibit in our empirical thought of them. We cannot know for sure, because the documentary evidence is so fragmentary, but it is at least possible that the motivation for introducing the productive imagination – conspicuous by its absence from the *Duisburg Nachlaß* – may have been precisely to make up for this shortfall (Carl 1989: 139–45). Thus Kant would characterize the understanding anew in a fragment we can reasonably date to 1780 as "the unity of apperception in relation to the faculty of imagination" (B 12, 23.18). In the same fragment, he characterizes the categories as "nothing other than representations of something (appearance) as such insofar as it is represented through transcendental synthesis of the imagination" (B 12, 23.19). Whatever the motivation, Kant's mature portrait of human understanding will draw on the imagination and set aside the metaphysical psychology that played such a prominent role in his theoretical philosophy of the 1770s.

References and Further Reading

Adickes, Erich (1925). *Einleitung in die Abtheilung des handschriftlichen Nachlasses*. In *Kant's gesammelte Schriften*, Band XIV. Berlin & Leipzig: Walter de Gruyter.

Adickes, Erich (1926). *Vorwort*. In *Kant's gesammelte Schriften* (pp. v–xiv), Band XVII. Berlin & Leipzig: Walter de Gruyter.

Carl, Wolfgang (1989). *Der schweigende Kant* [*The Silent Kant*]. Göttingen: Vandenhoek & Ruprecht.

Erdmann, Benno (1992). *Reflexionen Kants zur kritischen Philosophie*, Neudruck der Ausgabe Leipzig 1882/1884, ed. Norbert Hinske. Stuttgart: Frommann-Holzboog, 1992.

Förster, Eckart (1993). Introduction. In Immanuel Kant, *Opus postumum*, eds. and tr. Eckart Förster and M. Rosen. Cambridge: Cambridge University Press.

Guyer, Paul (1987). *Kant and the Claims of Reason*. Cambridge: Cambridge University Press.

Haering, Theodor (1910). *Der Duisburg'sche Nachlaß und Kants Kritizismus um 1775* [*The Duisburg Nachlaß and Kant's Criticism around 1775*]. Tübingen: J. C. B. Mohr [Paul Siebeck].

Heinze, Max (1894). *Vorlesungen Kants über Metaphysik aus drei Semestern*. Band XIV, der *Abhandlungen der philologisch-historischen Classe der Königlichen Sächsischen Gesellschaft der Wissenschaft*, Nr. VI. Leipzig: S. Hirzel.

Klemme, Heiner (1996). *Kants Philosophie des Subjekts* [*Kant's Philosophy of the Subject*]. Hamburg: Felix Meiner Verlag.

Laywine, Alison (1993). *Kant's Early Metaphysics and the Origins of the Critical Philosophy.* Atascadero: Ridgeway Publishing Co.

Laywine, Alison (2001). Kant in reply to Lambert on the ancestry of metaphysical concepts. *Kantian Review,* 5: 1–48.

Laywine, Alison (2003). Kant on sensibility and the understanding in the 1770s. *Canadian Journal of Philosophy,* 33(4): 443–82.

Laywine, Alison (2005). Kant on the self as model of experience. *Kantian Review,* 9(1): 1–29.

5

Kant's Debt to Leibniz

PREDRAG CICOVACKI

I

It has become so customary to interpret Kant as working mostly on the problems that Hume presented to modern philosophy that his great indebtedness to Leibniz is easily overlooked. Kant's words from the *Prolegomena* about how Hume woke him up from his dogmatic slumber are quoted often (4.260; Kant 2002: 57), yet it is usually forgotten that Kant also maintained that "the *Critique of pure reason* might well be the true apology for Leibniz, even against those of his disciples who heap praises upon him that do him no honor" (20.250: translations from Kant 2002: 336).

This quotation comes from Kant's late work, *On a Discovery whereby any new Critique of pure reason is to be made superfluous by an older one* (1790), in which he defended himself against the charges brought by Johann August Eberhard (1739–1809). In the years of 1788–9, in the pages of *Philosophisches Magazin*, this Wolffian philosopher persistently argued that Leibniz's writings already contained everything that is true and noteworthy in Kant's Critical philosophy, and much else in addition (see Vleeschauwer 1962: 140–51; Allison 1973: 15–45). The gist of Kant's reply was to acknowledge his debt to Leibniz, but also to argue that the nature and scope of his indebtedness was misconstrued by Eberhard and like-minded Wolffians. They did not understand either the true spirit of Kant's philosophy, or that of Leibniz. It was not the Wolffians but he – Kant – who was the genuine philosophical heir of Leibniz.

Just as Kant's expressed sympathies for Hume must not deceive us into believing that he rejected Leibniz's philosophy altogether, his debate with Eberhard should not mislead us to believe that he accepted all the theories of Leibniz. Whether it was Leibniz, Hume, or any other of his great predecessors, Kant's attitude was never that of complete rejection or full acceptance, but always complex and nuanced. To mention a few examples, Kant was unequivocally critical of Leibniz's alleged proofs of God's existence, of his principle of indiscernibles, of his conception of space, of his lack of any sharp distinction between sensibility and understanding, and of his virtually unlimited optimism with regard to the power of reason. Nevertheless, in the debate between Locke and Leibniz on innate ideas, he was far closer to his countryman. Kant was also very supportive of Leibniz's dynamic conception of matter, of his insistence on the principle of sufficient reason and its separation from the principle of contradiction, and of Leibniz's unwavering commitment to the supersensible.

How then shall we interpret Kant's debt to Leibniz? If a downright denunciation and an uncritical acceptance are both rejected as too extreme and historically inaccurate, what exactly was Kant's relation to Leibniz? Kant himself made it difficult to find the right answers to these questions. In the concluding pages of *On a Discovery*, for example, Kant specified three points in which he regarded himself to be the true follower of Leibniz. He first set apart the principle of sufficient reason, which – Kant claimed – both Leibniz and he understood as a subjective, not an objective principle. Kant then brought up monads and their relation to material bodies, which even for Leibniz was not a relation of composition, but of condition. Leibniz was right in regarding the simple not as an element in the sensible, but as something supersensible, the ground of the sensible. Thirdly, Kant professed to follow Leibniz with regard to the principle of the preestablished harmony: not a harmony between independent substances, but a harmony between modes of knowing, between the senses and the understanding.

Kant appeared to have twisted Leibniz's terminology and views to suit his own purposes (see Allison 1973: 102; Vleeschauwer 1962: 151). Did not Leibniz, for instance, think that the principle of sufficient reason was an objective principle, a principle that reflects the very structure of being? Before we draw any definitive conclusion, we must remember that Kant was never interested in a historically accurate presentation of Leibniz, or of any other philosopher. The spirit of his approach was captured in his often quoted claim on Plato:

> it is not at all unusual to find that we understand him even better than he understood himself, since he may not have determined his concepts sufficiently and hence sometimes spoke, or even thought, contrary to his own intention. (B 370: Kant 1998: 396)

Kant's philosophical interest was clearly focused on leading the doctrines of previous philosophers to their ultimate conclusions, even when their authors were not fully aware of all the consequences of their thoughts themselves. To see what this means in our case, let us take a closer look at the three doctrines of Leibniz that Kant himself singled out. We will invert Kant's order of presentation, however, and begin with monadology, since it is the foundation of Leibniz's entire philosophical edifice.

II

The most inspiring but also most puzzling aspect of Leibniz's philosophical thought is his conception of substances as monads. Unfortunately, he never managed to offer its fully developed and systematic presentation. Leibniz had the main contours of this novel conception of substance in his early thirties, yet for a long time he could not find an appropriate terminology, and perhaps also the most adequate formulation, for his views. Although today it is universally associated with Leibniz, the term "monad" was actually used first by the English philosopher Henry More (1614–87). Leibniz probably learned of the term indirectly, through some of More's students, and started using it in his writings after 1695, when he was almost 50 years old. What we now take to be the most precise summary of Leibniz's system, his *Monadology*, was written when Leibniz was almost 70 years old.

The term "monad," which suited Leibniz's purposes extremely well, comes from the Greek word "monas," which can be translated as "one," "unit," or "unity." All of these translations were important to Leibniz in order to capture both the ideas of distinct individuality and of ultimate unity in his concept of substance. Thereby he hoped to correct the mistakes of his predecessors, but also to preserve their correct insights (see Dewey 1969: 291; Rutherford 1995: 129, 137). In opposition to Descartes and Locke, who both overstressed the individuality of substance, Leibniz wanted to uphold the principle of unity. By contrast, against Spinoza, who overemphasized unity, Leibniz wanted to safeguard the principles of individuality, diversity, and multiplicity. Thus the most basic message behind the word "monad" is the dual nature of simple substance: that of individuality without duplication, yet reflecting the order of the whole, or universal harmony (see Leibniz 1991: 15, 265; Beck 1969: 223).

Leibniz was involved in a debate concerning the nature of substance with the Cartesians far more than with Locke or Spinoza, and for the purpose of clarifying his views further it may be beneficial to compare his conception of monads with Descartes' conception of substance. Descartes understood the term "substance" in a traditional Aristotelian and scholastic sense, as that which sub-sists or stands-under. What characterized Descartes' own conception was a sharp separation of three kinds of substance: rex extensa, or the extended substance of material bodies, res cogitans, or thinking substance, and God as a unique kind of substance. Leibniz had a threefold categorization of substances of his own, yet the difference between them was that of degree, not of kind. On the lower level there are "bare monads," which have unconscious perception and lack memory and awareness. Then there are souls, or monads that have consciousness. On the highest level are spirits, which are conscious souls also capable of self-consciousness and reasoning (see Rescher 1991: 92).

To make the contrast between these philosophers clearer, let us consider some objections that Leibniz had against each of Descartes' three kinds of substance. It is easy to notice, for example, that in Leibniz's writings we do not find any extended discussion of Descartes' celebrated evil demon argument. The reason for this is that, unlike Descartes, Leibniz put priority on God's intellect rather than his will. The God of Leibniz is perfect intellect and his will is merely "a certain consequence of his intellect." God is envisioned as the "region of ideas," the inner necessity of whose perfection requires him to bring the best of all conceived possibilities into existence.

Even more instructive is Leibniz's disagreement with Descartes' conception of res cogitans. Although Descartes' thinking substance had served as an inspiration for Leibniz's notion of a monad, there are several discrepancies between the two (see Furth 1967: 170–3). (i) All events occurring in res cogitans must be conscious, while events occurring in monads need not. Leibniz accounted for the difference by distinguishing between perception and apperception, and also by famously postulating the possibility of unconscious perceptions, "petites perceptions." (ii) Thinking substances can differ from each other in nothing more than number, while numerical differences are not sufficient to distinguish two monads; monads are not individuated merely by their position in space and time, but by an internal principle. (iii) Res cogitans are capable of presenting only fragments of reality, while monads represent the entire universe, each monad from its own unique perspective. (iv) Res cogitans are for Descartes only the fractions of the entire universe, which also involves an incalculable multiplicity of extended bodies, while for Leibniz reality ultimately consists of monads, each of which is a simple immaterial and non-extended substance, a mere metaphysical point endowed with energy and a degree of consciousness.

Leibniz attacked the concept of extension and Descartes' conception of res extensa as well: the essence of body consists not in extension but in motion (see Loemker 1969: 338–48). To speak of something extended is to speak of an aggregate, which means a lack of unity. It also means a sheer plurality, continuity, and co-existence of parts. No substance can properly be called extended, since that predicate can be ascribed only to a class, and no substance is a class. An army of soldiers, or a heap of leaves, for example, is a class and an aggregate, but not a true unity and not a substance. The universe is not a mere aggregate of an infinite multiplicity of extended bodies independent from each other.

Leibniz wanted to preserve the unitary and universal aspects of monads – their interrelatedness to the whole universe. He compared monads to souls and claimed that every substance is either a soul or soul-like. In its relation to other monads and the universe as a whole, every monad is "pregnant with the future" and must be viewed in teleological terms: it must have what Aristotle and the Scholastics called a "form" toward which it strives. Thus, every individual substance not only receives the impressions from without but also determines itself from within, in accordance with its own internal entelechy. God alone is the ultimate unity or the original simple substance, of which all created or derived monads are the products. God alone is also the perfect entelechy, while created monads are what could be called *perfectibles*: "they are imitations approaching him in proportion to their perfection" (Leibniz 1991: 261).

III

What to make of this fascinating, yet barely comprehensible, theory of monads? Criticisms were coming from all sides, and even Wolff, the self-appointed official interpreter of Leibniz's philosophy, was uncomfortable with that aspect of the master's teaching. He interpreted monads against the spirit of Leibniz as spatial and temporal. Like many other contemporaries, Wolff ended up preferring the Cartesian mind–body dualism to the Leibnizian account of a living, spirited world, in which the role and function of matter was never made convincingly clear. Coming from another camp, scientists and philosophers of that time (Newton and Clarke included) criticized Leibniz for a revival of the Aristotelian and medieval concept of substance, which conflicted with the basic principles of the modern, mathematically and physically oriented mode of knowledge (see Cassirer 1981: 27).

Leibniz did not hide his affinity for Aristotle and the Scholastics, and some of his early definitions of substance are taken almost verbatim from Aristotle's *Categories* and *Metaphysics* (see Mates 1986: 190–5; Rutherford 1995: 125–6). To see how Leibniz defended himself, let us recall Aristotle's doctrine of four causes, all of which need to be known to gain a complete comprehension of our object of inquiry. (i) The formal cause roughly corresponds to the question: What a thing is? (ii) The final cause deals with the question: For what it is? (iii) The material cause addresses the question: From what it is made? (iv) The efficient cause discusses the question: How it came about?

Most modern scientists concentrated on material and efficient causality, and denied the relevance of formal and final causes for science. Leibniz, by contrast, thought that their material atoms have no internal and essential relation to other atoms and the world as a whole. Every variety and change in them is merely external; each atom is completely foreign to every other atom and they do not enter into the structure of a harmonious universe (see Dewey 1969: 294–5). Atoms are uniform and their behavior can be partially explained in terms of mechanical laws, but Leibniz held that they are neither individuated enough nor would they allow for a genuine unity of the world. For that we need formal and teleological causality, and both could be understood in a roughly Aristotelian way. Each substance has a form toward which it strives, and this form is its inner principle, its soul. This connection between form and soul is, again, Aristotelian: soul is the form of the body. The universe is full of life; it is full of inter-connected, living, and spirited organisms, which is a very different viewpoint from the mechanicism prevailing from the seventeenth century on, including our own time.

What did Kant have to say about monads and monadology? At the first glance, hardly anything, which may be very surprising considering the intellectual milieu in which he developed as a thinker. For this reason, Kant's most comprehensive comment on monadology deserves to be quoted at some length:

> [Monadology] has nothing at all to do with the explanation of natural appearances, but is rather an intrinsically correct *Platonic* concept of the world devised by *Leibniz*, insofar as it is considered, not at all as the object of the senses, but as a thing in itself, and is merely an object of the understanding, which, however, does indeed underlie the appearance of the senses. Now the *composite of things in themselves* must certainly consist of the simple, for the parts must here be given prior to all composition. But the *composite in the appearance* does not consist of the simple, because in the appearance, which can never be given otherwise than as composed (extended), the parts can only be given through division, and thus not prior to the composite, but only in it. Therefore, Leibniz's idea, so far as I comprehend it, was not to explicate space through the order of simple beings next to one another, but was rather to set this order alongside space as corresponding to it, but as belonging to a merely intelligible world (unknown to us). Thus he asserts nothing but what has been shown elsewhere: namely, that space, together with the matter of which it is the form, does not contain the world of things in themselves, but only their appearance, and is itself only the form of our outer sensible intuition. (*MFNS* 4.507–8; Kant 2002: 219)

This quote is from *Metaphysical Foundations of Natural Science*, published five years after the first edition of the *Critique of Pure Reason*, and we recognize a number of themes from that work compressed here in a single paragraph. The separation of appearances and things in themselves is important throughout the first *Critique*. The distinction between "the composite of things in themselves" and "the composite in appearance" echoes the discussion of the second (and partially also the first) antinomy (see *CPR* B 459, B 467–70). The idea that space is the form of outer intuition and does not contain the world of things in themselves is presented in the numerous sections of the *Critique*: Transcendental Aesthetic, Phenomena and Noumena, On the Amphiboly of Concepts of Reflection, and throughout Transcendental Dialectic.

The striking thing about the quoted passage is that Kant seems to be in fundamental agreement with Leibniz, although in the *Critique* he criticized him in all of the mentioned sections. To understand this difference in attitude, recall the word "Platonic" – underscored by Kant – which occurs in the first sentence, where he calls monadology "an intrinsically correct Platonic concept of the world." Everyone else was criticizing Leibniz's monadology for being Aristotelian (and scholastic), while Kant disagreed and considered it Platonic. Even if Kant's claim that things in themselves underlie appearances retains some echoes of the Aristotelian conception of substance, the overall tone of the quote makes it clear that he considered monadology correct only insofar as it was Platonic. There are several reasons for that. One is the Platonic two-world theory, about which there was, at least in broad contours, an essential agreement between Leibniz and Kant. Another reason can be seen if we recall Aristotle's four causes. Here, again, Kant may have had more sympathy for Leibniz's stance than for Newton's. He accepted efficient causality as indispensable for natural science and ordinary experience, but had a dynamic conception of matter that put emphasis on force rather than on particles of impenetrable mass. Furthermore, like Leibniz and unlike Newton, Kant was not ill-disposed toward formal and teleological causality.

Recall again Leibniz's idea of individuality without duplication, yet reflecting the order of the whole, or universal harmony. What is Aristotelian in this idea is the emphasis on the individuality of the monad: primary substance for Aristotle is individual substance. The Platonic aspect of Leibniz's conception deals with his emphasis on the unity and the order pervading the whole universe. A Platonic idea is a paradigmatic expression of that unity, yet void of any Aristotelian individuality. Individuality belongs only to concrete things, but not to an idea or a universal.

The central idea of Leibniz's monadology is to show that the monad captures both of these moments, individuality and universality. Kant's central criticism is that it cannot be done, at least not at the same epistemological and metaphysical level, without a Platonic two-world conception. If we separate the individual and the universal and give priority to the latter, then we have a truly Platonic reading of monadology, and Kant called this interpretation "an intrinsically correct Platonic concept of the world devised by Leibniz." In the next section we shall discuss why the universal should be primary, if not metaphysically then epistemologically. Let us consider here why it could not be the individual. The point that tied Kant's numerous criticisms of Leibniz throughout the *Critique* was that we do not have a way of individuating a monad or, in Kant's terminology, a thing in itself. He agreed with Leibniz that a noumenal entity, an object of the understanding, could not be individuated in terms of its matter. But Kant persistently denied – from his earliest writings, such as *Nova Dilucidatio*, to his latest, such as "What Real Progress has Metaphysics made in Germany since the time of Leibniz and Wolff?" – that an object of the understanding could be identified based on inner qualities: "we know of no internal real determinations which could be attributed to a simple, except for representations, and what depends on them" (20.284; Kant 2002: 375). Such representations, however, could only be attributed to bodies, and they are not only inner or conceptual, but also spatial and temporal. This was the ground of Kant's famous objection to the principle of indiscernibles, namely how Leibniz intellectualized phenomena: while Locke mistakenly assumed that there is no more in an object than what is presented in an intuition of that object, Leibniz took for granted that there is no more in an object than what is contained in the concept of the object (see B 326–7; Paton 1969: 75).

Thus, Kant did not reject Leibniz's theory of monads, but insisted on its radical transformation. He mostly abandoned Leibniz's terminology, but not all of his central views. On the one hand, the monad is not an individual substance for Kant, but rather the unanalyzable unity of which we are aware as the ultimate ground and condition of all other perceived reality. Insofar as monads are immaterial substances and objects of the understanding, Kant called them things in themselves and noumena. Since they are not spatially and temporally given, they cannot be individuated, and thus not known. On the other hand, Kant took seriously Leibniz's idea that a monad is a form, a unity of a kind. He did not consider the monad to be a substantial form, yet the idea of a spontaneous, formative activity of the self-conscious and rational monad became one of Kant's central preoccupations in the *Critique of Pure Reason*.

IV

The old scholastic ontology was based on the conviction that timeless, immaterial, and nonsensible universals and essences are the defining principles of perceivable things. If we could grasp these universals, these substantial forms of things, we would be able to understand the principles of their development and reasons for the changes they undergo. The methodological tool for their comprehension is the definition. This is the foundation for the deductive character of the old ontology: once human reason finds itself in the possession of the highest universals, it can then "derive" from them all that which it does not know how to extract from experience.

There is much that Leibniz inherited from this conception of ontology. Not only that he used the scholastic language of substantial forms and essences, but at various times tried to identify those highest universals and, starting with them, reconstruct the entire structure of being. He often mentioned the principles of contradiction, of sufficient reason, of indiscernibles, of plenitude, and of continuity as the highest principles that determine the structure and behavior of everything existing. The first two of these principles were by far the most important to him, yet there is a controversy concerning their exact relationship. In the famous essay on "First Truths," Leibniz tried to deduce a complete hierarchy of the rational principles, starting with the principle of contradiction. His most famous interpreter, Wolff, took this line of reasoning to be the master's official and definitive view. Other writings reveal, however, that Leibniz wavered in his conviction; he often held that the principle of sufficient reason cannot be derived from the principle of contradiction, and moreover, that the principle of sufficient reason may be the more important of the two.

The principle of sufficient reason plays diverse roles in Leibniz's *Weltanschauung*. Let us briefly point out five of them, although he himself did not always make any clear distinction between them. (i) While the principle of contradiction regulates our reasoning regarding necessary truths ("truths of reason"), the principle of sufficient reason seems to govern not only contingent truths ("truths of facts"), but necessary truths as well. All truths whatsoever must have a sufficient reason for being what they are, which in the case of necessary truths reduces to identity and non-contradiction (see Rescher 1991: 118–19). (ii) This principle provides a foundation for Leibniz's belief in the relevance of final causality: to say that everything has a reason is to say that a final cause exists for everything in this world as it was created. (iii) The principle of sufficient reason relates the world of the sensible and conditioned to something nonsensible and unconditioned: "the sufficient or final reason must lie outside of the sequence or series of this detail of contingencies, however infinite it may be" (Rescher 1991: 21–2). (iv) Leibniz also thought that, "were it not for this great principle we could never prove the existence of God" (Leibniz 1996: 179). (v) Finally, the principle of sufficient reason assures the rationality of the real. Events in the world are neither random nor arbitrary; as it is given to us, the world is rationally ordered (see Rescher 1991: 119).

Kant's quest for a new metaphysics was revolutionary insofar as he criticized the deductive procedure of the scholastic ontology, which Leibniz tried to modify for his purposes. Kant abandoned substantial forms and obliterated the whole doctrine of essences. Whether or not Leibniz intended to deduce all other principles from the principle of contradiction, Kant concluded that this program could not be carried out. If metaphysics is to be grounded on the secure foundations, a new kind of logic and a new kind of deduction had to be invented.

Although not often mentioned by its name in the *Critique of Pure Reason*, it would be hardly possible to overestimate the role that the principle of sufficient reason plays in Kant's new transcendental logic. That is why in acknowledging his debt to Leibniz in *On a Discovery* he mentioned this principle first. Even if not from Leibniz's point of view, Kant thought that the principle of sufficient reason was more important than monadology; it provided that backbone around which all the pieces of Kant's new metaphysics are gathered and in relation to which they obtained their meaning and validity.

This is not to say that in Kant's philosophy this principle is not modified, or that it served the same functions as it did in Leibniz. If we glance again at the list of five uses of this principle in Leibniz, it is not difficult to see that Kant did not tie it so closely to teleology, nor did he consider this principle as sufficient to prove the existence of God. Kant's most consequential novelty with regard to this principle was emphasized by Schopenhauer: neither the ancient nor modern philosophers, such as Descartes, Spinoza, or Leibniz, "reached a clear distinction between requiring a reason for knowledge in support of a judgment and requiring a cause for the occurrence of an actual event" (Schopenhauer 1974: 13). Under the influence of Hume, Kant came to realize that the general ground or reason for the occurrence of an event should not be confused with the epistemological ground or reason for believing something to be the case. "Cause" should not be confused with "because." This is presumably why in *On a Discovery* Kant claimed that Leibniz must have meant it as a subjective, not as an objective principle (8.247–8; Kant 2002). Kant should have added the following clarification: had Leibniz grasped clearly the distinction between "cause" and "because," he would have considered the principle of sufficient reason to be subjective.

In both *Critique of Pure Reason* and *On a Discovery*, Kant tied Leibniz's two most important principles to the distinction of analytic and synthetic judgments (see chapter 8 below). The principle of contradiction becomes the ground and the criterion of analytic judgments, while the principle of sufficient reason is the principle of synthetic judgments. Various forms of synthesis analyzed in the *Critique* are the various forms of sufficient reason. In Kant's own admission, this connection between the principle of sufficient reason and synthetic judgments "was certainly a new and noteworthy pointer to investigations that were yet to be instituted in metaphysics" (20.248; Kant 2002: 334). The task, however, was not carried out by Leibniz, but by Kant. While in Leibniz's philosophy the mind has to mirror the synthesis already created and given through the real essences and substantial forms, Kant's revolutionary turn consisted in ascribing the production of this synthetic unity to the spontaneous activity of the cognizing mind. The mind does not mirror the already existing order of the universe, but produces it in a synthetic combination of intuition and concept. The results of that synthetic activity are synthetic judgments.

Leibniz was seduced into various kinds of speculative deductions because he tended to blur the distinction between a concept of the thing and the thing itself, and also because he took for granted that the principle of sufficient reason is always a principle of determinative judgment (see Leibniz 1952: 44; Leibniz 1996: 179). As a result, he appropriated, as it were, God's point of view, while all that is available is our human perspective, our own discursive reason which depends on intuitions for direct contact with reality. We have no legitimate right to assume as the determinative principle of our cognition that nothing ever happens without the idea that an omniscient mind could give some reason why it should have happened rather than not. Such a position turns our allegedly rigid deductions into arbitrary speculations and constructions, as the antinomies and other dialectical illusions testify.

Kant did not blame the faculty of reason itself for these transcendental illusions. Very much in the spirit of Leibniz's understanding of the principle of sufficient reason, Kant formulated what he called the "principle of pure reason": If the conditioned is given, then the entire sum of conditions and hence the absolutely unconditioned is also given (B 364; Kant 1998: 392). What we experience is conditioned, and the possibility of our empirical cognition was explained by Kant in terms of cognitive synthesis. The proper task of metaphysics was – just as Leibniz held – to search for the unconditioned. Leibniz offered his monadology as a solution, but Kant found it unacceptable when he paired its claims to those advanced by skeptics and empiricists. The antinomial impasse between the dogmatic and rationalistic theses versus the skeptical and empiricist antitheses shows that both sides committed some common mistakes. The crucial one was a lack of the resolute distinction between appearances and things as they are in themselves, which then led both sides to further and more consequential mistakes. Since the chains of conditioned appearances are given, both sides uncritically assumed that the unconditioned itself must also be given, but then disagreed with respect to what it is.

Kant's revolutionary insight was that, for human beings, the unconditioned is cognitively inaccessible either through direct intuition, or through deductive reasoning, or through any symbolic or analogous representation. Since Kant was unwilling even to consider seriously the possibility that the task of metaphysics should not consist in the search for the unconditioned, he found an original solution: for us, with our discursive understanding, the unconditioned is not given but assigned. What we are truly concerned with is not the transcendent and unknown cause of our appearances, such as monads, substantial forms, real essences, God, or anything else traditionally proposed to solve this problem. Rather, what we are dealing with is the rule of the advance of the cognitive synthesis by means of which the sensible objects are experienced and cognized by us (B 526; Kant 1998: 514–15). (See also chapter 13 below.)

This restraint on the valid application of the principle of sufficient reason to the conditions of the possibility of experience does not show that metaphysical principles – such as the favorite of Leibniz: "Nature makes no leaps" – are false or meaningless. They could still be useful in guiding our empirical and scientific research. But we must realize that in imposing them we do not make any determinative judgment about the world as it is in itself, as Leibniz assumed. Without as yet having the benefit of the distinction between determinative and reflective judgments, which he later developed in the third *Critique*, the first *Critique* articulated the distinction in terms of "constitutive" and "regulative" use of reason. The former would enable us to expand concepts that are valid in the sensible world beyond the boundaries of possible experience, yet the antinomies revealed that any attempt to use the principle of pure reason in the constitutive way would lead to self-contradictions. In its regulative use, the principle of pure reason does not allow us to cognize what an object is as a thing in itself; nevertheless, it stimulates us to search for an ever more complete understanding of that object, insofar as it may be empirically given (*CPR* B 537, B 692; Kant 1998: 520–1, 602).

V

Underlying the seventeenth-century quarrels about the nature of substances was an always challenging problem concerning the relation of nature and reason, of the real and the rational. Most philosophers did not disagree so much with respect to whether a harmonious synthesis of the real and the rational exists, but with regard to how it could be explained and established. Locke, for instance, believed that everything that exists can, at least in principle, be rendered intelligible, but also subscribed to the view that the world is radically contingent. Hardly anyone was willing to follow him in endorsing both views. Leibniz gladly accepted the thesis of the intelligibility of the world but was uneasy about its radical contingency. If the world is indeed so contingent, would it not be the case that events occurring in it are arbitrary, and would not reality as a whole then be nonrational? Although Leibniz wanted to allow for contingency and individuality, his conception of rationality was too narrow to account for them. Many a reader has been baffled by his idea of a complete concept and wondered whether in the last account all truths, including truths of facts, do not turn out to be analytic for Leibniz. These exaggerations were due to his unshakable conviction that a complete explanation of anything that happens must be pursued to its farthest end, that it must touch the bottom. And that bottom could only be some metaphysical stopping point: substantial forms or essences, or – ultimately – God (see Lovejoy 1936: 148). Since the principle of sufficient reason, as the principle used to explain truths of facts, was interpreted by Leibniz in teleological terms, the combination of these assumptions led him to maintain that in the end even the seemingly most accidental happening must have a profound teleological explanation.

A paradoxical thing about rationality is that, when conceived as complete, as excluding all arbitrariness, it transforms itself into a kind of irrationality. Voltaire mocked Leibniz that, in his infinite wisdom and goodness, God must have created legs so that we can wear stockings on them. Clarke similarly reminded Leibniz of the celebrated ass of Buridan: having no sufficient reason to prefer either of the two equally large and appetizing balls of hay equidistant from his nose, this perfectly rational ass starved to death (see Lovejoy 1936: 331). Less humorous but more damaging for Leibniz was Hume's criticism of causality, which opened a huge gap between the real and the rational; it seemed to falsify rather than confirm the unity of nature and reason. Hume suspected that things in the world need not be what we think of them, that they may be untouched by the allegedly universal and necessary principles of reason. We are thus back to the Lockean thesis of the radical contingency of the world. This time, it was coupled with Humean skepticism not only with regard the world of our senses but the supersensible as well: Hume was ready to commit anything metaphysical to the flames.

A systematic examination of the nature and limitations of pure reason in the first *Critique* did not convince Kant that any metaphysical project is illegitimate, as Hume argued, but that it could not be carried out in way in which Leibniz and pre-Critical Kant assumed. Perhaps the *Critique* did not make sufficiently clear just how important this constructive – rather than merely negative – goal was for Kant, but the works written after 1781 leave very little doubt about that. In the first *Critique* the main objective was to show that metaphysics is possible as a rigorous intellectual discipline, rather than as an unrestrained dogmatic speculation. But after the publication of that work, which Kant himself considered a prolegomena, the emphasis shifted toward developing a full-blown metaphysics and showing what, as a science, it is about. Then the similarities with Leibniz became far more pronounced and Kant even used the old Leibnizian terminology to define metaphysics as the passage from the sensible to the supersensible (20.260 Kant 2002: 353).

In Leibniz, this ascent has two forms, which are really two aspects of the same process: cognitive and teleological. The principle of sufficient reason leads to a proof of the existence of God, and it simultaneously grounds a teleological account of the real; the universe is teleological both as a whole and in every one of its parts. The synthesis of the cognitive and the teleological moments is captured by the principle of preestablished harmony, by means of which Leibniz attempted to reconcile his conception of nature and his understanding of God.

Kant's first *Critique* demonstrated that there can be no cognitive access to the supersensible. The third *Critique* restrained the other aspect of Leibniz's doctrine, his teleology. To claim that God's intellect chooses among the infinite number of possible worlds and permits the actualization of the best of them, was for Kant yet another example of an amphiboly, an anthropomorphic attribution of the human concept of purpose to the absolute. The fact that for our intellect there must be a difference between the possible and the actual should not mislead us to take for granted that such a distinction must also exist for God's intellect. It is a peculiar limitation of the human mind that makes it possible, even indispensable, to use the concept of purpose to give teleological explanations. Kant agreed with Leibniz that the concept of purpose points toward the supersensible, but emphatically denied that it is sufficient to take us there since it ultimately reflects only how we are constrained to think about organisms and living nature (5.401–10; Kant 2000: 271–9). (See also chapters 26, 27, and 29.)

Despite such restraints, Kant rarely wavered in his belief that the gap between the sensible and the supersensible could be overcome. His critical stance was that this could be accomplished, if at all, only through the concept of freedom, only if the distinction between the actual and the possible is treated in terms of "is" and "ought."

That discussion, however, is out of our range, for it would take us to Kant's moral philosophy.

VI

When he wrote that "the *Critique of Pure Reason* may be the true apology for Leibniz," Kant earnestly spoke in his defense. Leibniz had to be defended not only from his disciples who misinterpreted him, but because there was much that was right and true in his philosophy. Kant grew up with that philosophy and it provided a standard against which he measured himself from his earliest writings to his latest. Although there was much in Leibniz that served as a stimulus – even a foundation – of his own thinking, Kant never tried to follow his exact footsteps. As was the case with Leibniz, Kant's only loyalty was to search for and serve the truth. His work was thus an apology for Leibniz in that other sense as well: it was an acknowledgment of the mistakes and oversights which his great predecessor committed and which needed to be corrected.

The fact that such corrections and deviations were numerous should not prevent us from recognizing that Leibniz and Kant not only took off from neighboring harbors, but also that their final destination was similar. For both thinkers metaphysics was the heart of philosophy, and for both it dealt with the passage from the sensible to the supersensible. Their disputes were not so much about the destination but about the journey. Kant was convinced that without his critique of pure reason the passage was not only unsafe but perhaps impossible. His Critical philosophy was to provide a compass needed to avoid the fog of metaphysical illusions into which all of previous metaphysical expeditions, Leibniz's included, got trapped.

Is it so clear, however, that Kant himself was always able to avoid all of these traps? Consider once more the relation of the real and the rational. Leibniz was firmly convinced of the complete overlap of the real and the rational in every aspect of being. If there is something that we do not yet know, the question is not whether it is knowable, but how it should be approached, so we could grasp and explain it fully. Kant demonstrated that things are far more complex. The real as such is not entirely transparent to our cognitive faculties, no matter how we approach it. Some aspects of the real simply cannot be known, due to no fault of our methods or cognitive abilities. Our knowledge is of appearances, not of the supersensible, not of things as they are in themselves. This, however, was not the end of the matter. When Kant used the phrase "things in themselves" interchangeably with "noumena," he clearly hinted that, like Leibniz, he also took the real to be ultimately rational: it may be unknowable but still rational. It is far from clear that Kant was entitled to such radical rationalism.

Things are similarly puzzling when we consider the relation between the rational and the ideal. Both philosophers took it for granted that there must be complete overlap between the rational and the ideal, without much of an argument and without considering any alternative. For Leibniz, God is the ultimate point in which all the arguments end and which guarantees the unity, order, and harmony of the entire creation. For Kant, the search for the unconditioned is the deepest need of reason, and it finds its expression in the "ideas of reason." Although the unconditioned is not accessible to us in knowing, it was considered by Kant as intelligible and accessible through acting. Upon what grounds it could be asserted that the unconditioned must be intelligible was not explained by either of the two philosophers. Nor did they question the search for the unconditioned: Why is it that the unity, order, and harmony of the world could not be explained in any other way, but by invoking the unknown yet intelligible unconditioned? Why must reason search for the unconditioned in the first place? Like Leibniz, Kant took the model of creation for granted: it is only when we think of the real as something created and conditioned that we expect that there must also be something not created and unconditioned, something that brought about the world in which we live. Almost the entire tradition of Western metaphysics developed in the thick shadow of God-Creator. Yet a truly critical metaphysics, which Kant's philosophy aspired to be, should not have left any assumption unchallenged, including these concerning the rationality of the noumenal and the ideal, as well as the model of creation.

There were indeed deep ties and similarities between the two great German philosophers. Not all of them should have been preserved by Kant.

References and Further Reading

Allison, Henry (1973). *The Kant–Eberhard Controversy*. Baltimore: Johns Hopkins University Press.

Beck, Lewis White (1969). *Early German Philosophy: Kant and his Predecessors*. Cambridge, MA: The Belknap Press.

Cassirer, Ernst (1981). *Kant's Life and Thought*, tr. James Haden. New Haven: Yale University Press. (Original work published 1918.)

Dewey, John (1969). Leibniz's new essays concerning human understanding. In John Dewey, *The Early Works, 1882–1898* (pp. 253–435). Carbondale, IL: Southern Illinois University Press. (Original work published 1888.)

Furth, Montgomery (1967). Monadology. *Philosophical Review*, 76: 169–200.

Kant, Immanuel (1992). *Theoretical Philosophy, 1755–1770*, tr. and ed. David Walford. New York: Cambridge University Press.

Kant, Immanuel (1998). *Critique of Pure Reason*, tr. and eds. Paul Guyer and Allen W. Wood. New York: Cambridge University Press. (Original work published 1781.)

Kant, Immanuel (2000). *Critique of the Power of Judgment*, tr. and eds. Paul Guyer and Eric Matthews. New York: Cambridge University Press. (Original work published 1790.)

Kant, Immanuel (2002). *Theoretical Philosophy after 1781*, tr. Henry Allison, Gary Hatfield, Peter Heath, and Michael Friedman. New York: Cambridge University Press.

Leibniz, Gottfried Wilhelm (1952). *Theodicy*, ed. Austin Farrer, tr. E. M. Huggard. New Haven: Yale University Press. (Original work published 1710.)

Leibniz, Gottfried Wilhelm (1991). *Discourse on Metaphysics. Correspondence with Arnauld. Monadology*. Tr. George Montgomery. La Salle: Open Court.

Leibniz, Gottfried Wilhelm (1996). *New Essays on Human Understanding*, tr. and eds. Peter Remnant and Jonathan Bennett. Cambridge: Cambridge University Press. (Original work published 1765.)

Loemker, L. E., ed. (1969). *G. W. Leibniz: Philosophical Papers and Letters*, 2nd ed. Dordrecht: Reidel.

Lovejoy, Arthur (1936). *The Great Chain of Being*. Cambridge, MA: Harvard University Press.

Mates, Benson (1986). *The Philosophy of Leibniz: Metaphysics and Language*. New York: Oxford University Press.

Paton, H. J. (1969). Kant on the errors of Leibniz. In Lewis White Beck (ed.), *Kant Studies Today*. La Salle: Open Court.

Rescher, Nicholas (1991). *G. W. Leibniz's Monadology*. Pittsburgh: University of Pittsburgh Press.

Rutherford, Donald (1995). Metaphysics: The late period. In Nicholas Jolley (ed.), *The Cambridge Companion to Leibniz* (pp. 124–75). Cambridge: Cambridge University Press.

Schopenhauer, Arthur (1974). *On the Fourfold Root of the Principle of Sufficient Reason*, tr. E. F. J. Payne. La Salle: Open Court. (Original work published 1813.)

Vleeschauwer, Herman-J. de (1962). *The Development of Kantian Thought: The History of a Doctrine*, tr. A. R. C. Duncan. London: Thomas Nelson and Sons. (Original work published 1939.)

6

Kant's Debt to the British Empiricists

WAYNE WAXMAN

The magnitude and principal focus of Kant's debt to empiricism are not in doubt. Kant credited Hume with rousing him from dogmatic slumbers and imparting a radically new direction to his investigations (*Prol.* 4.260). The alarm was sounded by the skeptical conclusion of Hume's investigations of the concept of cause and effect and the principle that every beginning of existence must have a cause. Once extended to all a priori concepts and cognition, the problem identified by Hume suffices, in Kant's view, to put into question the very possibility of metaphysics itself. He thus considered Hume's challenge to be of such urgency as to compel metaphysicians to set aside all other occupations until they could answer the question, how are synthetic a priori judgments possible? (*Prol.* 4.277–8).

Less widely appreciated than Kant's debt to Hume for the problem his philosophy is dedicated to solving is his debt to Hume for pointing the way to its solution:

> One cannot, without feeling a certain pain, behold how entirely every one of [Hume's] opponents – Reid, Oswald, Beattie, and lastly Priestley – missed the point of his problem [*Aufgabe*] . . . It was not the question whether the concept of cause is correct, serviceable, and in respect of the whole of our cognition of nature indispensable, for this Hume never doubted. Rather, it was the question whether the concept is thought through reason a priori and in this way has an inner truth independent of all experience and therefore also a far more extended employment, not limited to objects of experience: here is where Hume expected a breakthrough [*Eröffnung*]. It was indeed only the issue [*Rede*] of the origin of this concept, not of its indispensability in use: if only the former were ascertained, then everything concerning the conditions of its use and the sphere in which it can be valid would already of itself have been given. (*Prol.* 4.258–9) [Author's translations throughout]

Neither Hume nor Kant doubted the normative correctness and indispensability of concepts like cause and effect to objective representation. Yet, for them, this was quite beside the point philosophically. Their paramount concern was the origin of the concept as a representation in our mind: whether it is "thought through reason a priori" (*Prol.* 4.257), whether it is a mere "bastard of the imagination" (*Prol.* 4.258), or whether it arises from some other source. Hume pointed the way for Kant because he recognized that psychological accounts of the origin of the concepts at the heart of age-old philosophical disputes have the potential to do more than simply explain how these ideas are formed. Most notably, in his account of the origin of the idea of cause and effect, Hume contended that the operations whereby the mind forms the idea also contribute indispensable elements of its content as well. Why Kant viewed this as a "breakthrough" is not difficult to see: if a concept can be shown to be as bound up by content with conscious mind as pleasure and pain are, then any attempt to employ it in contexts in which abstraction is made from the mind and its representative constitution can result only in unintelligibility ("we either contradict ourselves, or talk without a meaning" [Hume 1978, *A Treatise of Human Nature (THN)*: 267]). Thus did Hume open Kant's eyes to the potential for psychological considerations to disclose inherent limitations on the scope of certain concepts that no amount of conceptual analysis is capable of revealing, particularly those concepts whose unrestricted scope seems a sine qua non of the possibility of metaphysics: space and time, substance, identity, reality, quantity, existence, and, of course, cause and effect.

Yet, the problem and method of solution Hume bequeathed to Kant did not emerge ex nihilo. In what follows, I examine the sources of Kant's endeavor to revolutionize metaphysics, beginning with Hume's most important empiricist predecessor, Locke, and concluding with Berkeley and Hume himself.

1. Locke: Sensibilism and Subjectivism

Locke was the first great philosopher to dedicate his magnum opus to the topic of human understanding. He did so in the belief that "we begin at the wrong end . . . [when] we let loose our Thoughts into the vast Ocean of Being, as if all that boundless Extent, were the natural, and undoubted Possession of our Understandings" (Locke 1975, *Essay Concerning Human Understanding* [*ECHU*]: I.i.7). To prove title to this possession, it is not enough to analyze and define our concepts. For if our understandings are acquainted with no object (notion, idea) capable of underwriting our discourse concerning reality, then no amount of clarification and disambiguation can make good this want. Instead, the philosopher's preeminent order of business must be to

> inquire into the original of those ideas, notions, or whatever else you please to call them, which a man observes, and is conscious to himself he has in his mind; and the ways whereby the understanding comes to be furnished with them. (*ECHU*: Intro. §3)

Only a psychological investigation of the sources of the materials available to our thought can reveal any limitations these origins may impose on their scope of application – limits on what is and is not possible to know by their means that inevitably remain hidden to any purely analytical approach to human understanding. Thus did Locke hope to employ the psychology of ideational origins to cut through the mists of language and safeguard himself against any temptation to claim knowledge where clear title to it is lacking.

Kant acknowledged his debt to Locke in this regard: "Locke's excellence was that since he did not cognize [*erkannte*] intellectualia as connata, he sought their origin"

(18. 4894, late 1770s). Why does the rejection of innate ideas (i.e. innate contents of thought, as distinct from innate faculties, propensities, etc.) confer such great importance on the psychological question of origins? Innatism is one explanation (Malebranchian illuminationism another) for what I shall term the intellectualist thesis that ideas preexist their presence to consciousness in sensation or reflexion (inner sense). If ideas preexist the sensory and reflexive operations whereby they are brought to consciousness in (clear or obscure, distinct or confused) perceptions, then these operations are incapable of contributing anything essential to the content of these ideas. For this reason, intellectualist philosophers relegated the psychological question concerning the origin of the perceptions in which ideas present themselves to the margins of the theory of understanding. Indeed, intellectualist reliance on ana-lytical methods to determine the contents of ideas stemmed in no small part from their utility in eliminating any and all sensory-psychological overlay imposed on ideas by the perceiving subject, thus leaving in their wake purely intellectual ("clear and distinct") perceptions, expressible in definitions confined to all and only what is essential to the idea.

Since for Locke, by contrast, "having Ideas, and Perception [are] the same thing" (*ECHU*: II.i.9), there are, and can be, no ideas prior to or independently of their presence to consciousness in sensation or reflexion. Once perceived, ideas may then be considered in new ways, "each of which Considerations is a new Idea" (xiv.14), by being combined, separated, related, abstracted, or otherwise acted upon by the understanding. Accordingly, to explicate an idea, rather than merely enumerating its constituents, we must first endeavor to discover which of the varied, often multiply complex psychological operations went into its formation; for only by distinguishing and comprehending these operations – their nature, workings, and inherent limitations – can we hope to demarcate the proper cognitive sphere of application of any of our ideas. The Lockean project of understanding understanding thus holds out the promise of enabling us to determine which cognitive applications of ideas are and which are not "the natural, and undoubted Possession of our Understandings."

To be sure, even while singling out Locke's theory of understanding as the one "most similar" to his own because it "concerns every employment of the understand-ing in general" (letter to Garve, Aug. 7, 1783), Kant rejected his predecessor's strictly empirical approach (B 118–19), charging him with "the error of taking the occasion for obtaining these concepts, namely experience, for their source" (18.4866, late 1770s). But this was not, as so often is supposed, because Kant, as transcendental philosopher, was in a different line of business from Locke:

> Logic begins from concepts and deals with their employment. The origin of concepts from sensible representations or the understanding belongs to psychology and transcendental philosophy. (15.1697, 1770s)

Kant, as transcendental philosopher, was just as committed as empiricist philosophical psychologists to tracing representations to their sources in the faculties of the mind in order thereby to determine their content. He was also just as committed to Locke's sensibilist principle that ideas (the contents of representation) are nothing prior to or independently of the senses and the psychological operations the mind performs on their data. He diverged only when it came to the question whether the senses are a source uniquely of empirical data. For Kant, though he seldom claimed complete originality, was saying nothing less than the truth when he averred that "it never occurred to anyone that the senses also may be supposed to intuit a priori" (*Prol.* 4.375n).

This was certainly true of Locke, who consequently overlooked the possibility of an a priori, yet still sensibilist, theory of understanding. For where the senses supply a manifold of a priori intuition, the potential is created for the understanding to act upon that manifold to generate further representations completely a priori, thereby opening the way to a theory of pure understanding, or transcendental logic (*CPR* B 79–80 and B 102), to complement and underpin the empirical logic of Locke and others:

> The logical system of intellectual cognitions is either empirical or transcendental. The first Aristotle and Locke, the second either epigenesis or involution, acquired or innate. The so-called sound understanding is asylum ignorantiæ. (18.5637, 1780s)

Transcendental logic is a system of epigenesis or involution because it focuses on the manifold furnished a priori by sense not as a source of objective content but as a raw material on which understanding can set to work to synthesize new representations that are equally a priori in origin. Nevertheless, the a priori manifold of sense is just as much its starting point as the a posteriori manifold of sensations and reflexions was for Locke, and their sensibilist accounts of the origin of the contents of objective representation parallel one another at every turn: Instead of a strictly empirical imagination, Kant's account postulates productive imagination responsible for synthesizing the a priori manifold of sense. Instead of a strictly empirical consciousness of the unity of the relation (synthesis) of the manifold in complex ideas, Kant posits a pure consciousness of the unity of pure synthesis of the pure manifold: first, in the form of pure apperception (pure self-consciousness); second, the universal representation in pure concepts of the understanding (categories) of the unity that results when pure synthesis in pure imagination of the pure manifold of sense is determined conformably to the pure logical functions of judgment; and third, the universal representation in transcendental schemata of the a priori determination of the pure sensible intuition of time conformably to the categories. And the collective consequence of the pure representations postulated in Kant's a priori sensibilism is the system of nature (natura formaliter spectata) comprising the synthetic a priori cognitions (principles of pure understanding) that result when appearances are subsumed under the categories by means of their schemata.

The great divergence between Kant's system and those of Locke and his empiricist successors cannot help but strike one. But it is no less important to recognize that virtually all of this divergence can be traced to a slight difference at their roots: whether or not the senses are a source exclusively of a posteriori representations. By comparison with the sensibilist principle that unites their systems in opposition to intellectualism, this is a point of detail, not of principle. In particular, Kant remained in fundamental agreement with Locke and his successors that (i) none of the contents of thought preexist the presence in us of sensation (B 349, B 400–1, B 422–3n, B 457n, and B 480n), so that all are acquired, none innate (8.221–3), (ii) that the explication of these contents is preeminently a matter of tracing them to their origins as representations in the mind, and (iii) that all representations originate directly from the (external or internal) senses or are synthesized from data of the senses.

Some interpreters will undoubtedly object that this unduly minimizes the difference between Kant's transcendental logic and Locke's empirical variety. They may point to the fact that Kant contrasted his treatment of the categories in the transcendental deduction with Locke's empirical deduction as investigations of two quite different types, the former dealing with the normative question of the origin of our title to apply the categories to objects of experience, the latter (taking such title for granted) concerned only with the factual question of the occasioning causes of their employment (B 118–19). Indeed, they regard the transformation of the Lockean search for origins from a psychological pursuit into an epistemological quest for justification to be among Kant's principal philosophical legacies. In confirmation, many would cite Kant's charge that Locke, in his treatment of the categories, sensibilized what are, in and of themselves, purely intellectual concepts, devoid of all sensible content, a priori no less than a posteriori (B 119–21 and B 327), and then compounded his error by employing these sensibilized concepts in transcendental contexts (Locke's "enthusiasm": B 127–8).

Kant's emphasis on proving the legitimacy of our title to employ the categories does express a normative concern, but we should not confuse the normative implications of a theory of understanding with the normative character of the theory itself. Hume traced the origin of the idea of necessary connection to the customary association in a non-normative psychology, but drew normative conclusions from it regarding cause and effect (e.g. "Rules by which to Judge of Causes and Effects" (title, *THN*: I.iii.15). These include a constraint on the scope of application of causal concepts quite similar to Kant's restriction of the categories to objects of possible experience:

> Such a discovery. . . . that this [causal] connexion, tie, or energy lies merely in ourselves, and . . . is acquir'd by custom . . . not only cuts off all hope of ever attaining satisfaction, but even prevents our very wishes; since it appears, that when we say we desire to know the ultimate and operating principle, as something, which resides in the external object, we either contradict ourselves, or talk without a meaning. (*THN*: 266–7)

Insofar as a psychological investigation of a concept's origin as a representation in the mind reveals that its application to objects under certain conditions is inconsistent with the general conditions of its applicability to anything at all, it can teach us something about the legitimacy and limitations of our title to employ the concept. And this holds true whether the psychological account of its origin concerns empirical or a priori data of sense, empirical or a priori syntheses of imagination, or an empirical or a priori unity of consciousness.

Certainly, Kant does not seem to be departing from a psychological focus on origins when, in criticism of both the analytic and the empiricist methods, he contended that

> It is not enough to know [*wissen*] what representations contain within them, nor to which occasioning causes and conditions they owe their origin, but in which faculties [*Vermögen*] and capacities [*Fähigkeiten*] they have their seat. (18.4917)

The moment we move from Kant's characterization of his investigation to what he actually does in it we find that the normative conclusions of the transcendental deduction invariably turn on considerations couched in terms of the different faculty origins of various representations and the psychological operations of unifying them (*Prol.* 4.258–9). The contrast Kant drew between transcendental and empirical deduction – quid juris vs. quid facti – may therefore have been intended merely to draw attention to the unique challenge of explaining how concepts whose origin in the psyche proved them to be both a priori and intellectual (in the Metaphysical Deduction, B 102–16) can apply to objects given only a posteriori whose possibility is conditioned by sensibility and not by intellect (B 122–4).

It is in the Metaphysical rather than the Transcendental Deduction that the account of their origin as pure concepts of the understanding is given (B 159). Although such concepts, unlike their schemata, are altogether devoid of sensible content, they become possible only when the synthesis in imagination of the pure manifold of sense is represented universally (B 103). The contribution of logical forms by the understanding is indeed crucial to their content, for they contribute the unity to this synthesis. But since the categories themselves consist "simply in the representation of necessary synthetic unity" (B 104) the contributions of sense (the a priori manifold) and imagination (pure synthesis) are no less essential ("The form of judgments transformed into a concept of the synthesis of intuitions produced categories," B 378). Thus neither the Metaphysical nor the Transcendental Deduction of the categories represents a break of any kind with the anti-intellectualist sensibilism of Locke and his successors.

A related comparison between Kant and Locke comes from what I shall term the latter's subjectivist conception of propositional thought. Where "having Ideas, and Perception [are] the same thing," the contents of any idea and the contents perceived in it – its reality and its appearance to (sensing, imagining, conceiving) consciousness – are indistinguishable (*ECHU*: II.xxix.5). Since their relational contents are no exception, this means that no idea can contain any relation it does not appear to contain, and that no two ideas are related unless and until they are sensibly perceived or imagined in that relation.

For the intellectualist, by contrast, ideas can contain many constituents that are not, and may never be, sensibly perceived or imagined. Our lack of a perfectly clear and distinct perception of the idea of a triangle obliges us to devise a proof in which we at last attain a clear and distinct perception of the quantitative equality between the sum of its angles and two right angles. Only the limitations native to human understanding prevent us from perceiving all the (potentially infinite) contents contained in the idea of a triangle with perfect clarity down to its least element – including those properties and relations yet or never to be discovered.

Against this, the sensibilist maintains that the idea of a triangle contains only those contents that the judging subject actually thinks in it. Some of these may be thought in it only confusedly so that a risk of confusing the idea with other ideas arises, and others may be so obscure as to escape attentive discernment completely. The rapidity of the actions of the mind and/or the concealing influence of custom may lead us to mistake the ideational products of complex cogitation for data passively received in perception (*ECHU*: II.ix.10). For the sensibilist the equality of the sum of its angles to two right angles is no more a constituent of the idea of a triangle than is its equality to the number of passengers on the 1:33 p.m. New York to Los Angeles flight on October 28, 1988. Neither is thought in the idea of a figure in a plane formed from three intersecting straight lines, even confusedly or obscurely. And, in general, propositional thought (mental, not verbal) has to be understood in terms of subjects and predicates that contain only so much content as the judging subject actually thinks in them.

It was Locke's espousal of a subjectivist conception of propositional thought that led him to regard mathematics as an instructive rather than a merely explicative science:

> we can know the Truth, and so may be certain in Propositions, which affirm something of another, which is a necessary consequence of its precise complex Idea, but not contained in it. As that the external Angle of all Triangles, is bigger than either of the opposite internal Angles; which relation of the outward Angle, to either of the opposite internal Angles, making no part of the complex Idea, signified by the name Triangle, this is a real Truth, and conveys with it instructive real Knowledge. (*ECHU*: IV.viii.8)

Since the idea of a triangle contains nothing – has no reality, meaning, content – other than that which appears immediately to our perception, geometrical demonstration does not so much clarify, and make distinct, relations already implicit in this idea as forge those relations itself. These relations are intrinsically bound up with the actions of the mind in comparing and considering the ideas, and are nothing prior to or independently of the sequence of propositions (comparisons of ideas) whereby we become sensible (perceive) that the ideas are necessarily conjoined in them. As Hume put the same point:

> the necessity, which makes two times two equal to four, or three angles of a triangle equal to two right ones, lies only in the act of the understanding, by which we consider and compare these ideas . . . rather than in the ideas themselves. (*THN*: 166)

For Locke and his successors from ideas alone, no matter how clear and distinct, not even the simplest mathematical equations could be known.

Kant's commitment to sensibilism is confirmed by the subjectivist conception of propositions evident in his distinction between analytic and synthetic judgments:

> whatever be the origin or their logical form, there is a distinction in judgments as to their content . . . Analytic judgments assert [*sagen*] nothing in the predicate but what has been already actually thought in the concept of the subject, though not so clearly and with the same consciousness. (*Prol.* 4.266)

That Kant meant it when he restricted analytic identities to what is actually thought in the concept of the subject seems clear:

> the question is not what we are supposed to join in thought to the given concept but what we actually think in it, if only obscurely. (B 17 and *Prol.* 4.269)

> that I am supposed to think 12 in the addition of 7 and 5 is here beside the point, for in analytic propositions the question is only whether I actually think the predicate in the representation of the subject. (B 205)

With analyticity strictly limited to what is actually thought in a concept, even if only obscurely, all relations – necessary or otherwise – between distinct representations must be considered synthetic rather than analytic, including even the simplest arithmetic equations. The operative criterion whereby synthetic judgments are distinguished from analytic is whether or not their component concepts are subjectively or objectively identical:

> I can form a concept of one and the same quantity by means of a multifarious mode [*mancherlei Art*] of composition and separation (though each, as well as addition and subtraction, is a synthesis), which is objectively identical (as in every equation) but subjectively, according to the mode of composition which I think in order to arrive at [*gelangen um*] the concept, is very different, so that the judgment must certainly go beyond the concept which I have from the synthesis, because it sets a different mode of composition (which is simpler and better suited to the construction) in place of the first, which nevertheless always determines the object in precisely the same way. (Letter to Schultz, Nov. 25, 1788)

These passages confirm Kant's anti-intellectualist sensibilism. And it is no accident that, of all his predecessors, Kant thought Locke came closest to recognizing the existence of synthetic a priori cognition (albeit without grasping the imperative need to comprehend its possibility).

2. Berkeley and Hume: The Separability Principle and the Paradox of Necessary Relations

Hume was a sensibilist theorist of human understanding who, like Locke, held that ideas are best explicated by tracing them to their origin rather than by defining them (*THN*: 157; Hume 1955, *Enquiry Concerning Human Understanding* [*EHU*]: VII.i.62). He concentrated on cause and effect because of its unique importance in the economy of human understanding, holding that, in the absence of this idea,

> Inference and reasoning concerning the operations of nature would, from that moment, be at an end; and the memory and senses remain the only canals, by which the knowledge of any real existence could possibly have access to the mind. (*EHU* VIII.i.82; also *THN* 73–4)

Attributing the preeminence of this idea to its principal constituent, the idea of necessary connection, Hume made it the principal focus of his inquiry. And it was Hume's analysis of this idea that Kant would consider a philosophical watershed.

The insight that led Kant to pronounce Hume's analysis of necessary connection the most decisive event in the history of metaphysics (*Prol.* 4.257) is that the kind of necessary connection concerned in it is restricted to existents distinct in the sense specified by the Berkeleyan separability principle which sets a limit to the abstractive powers of the mind. Locke, for example, supposed that our minds equip us to distinguish features in the objects (ideas) present to us that cannot exist independently of one another in perception or imagination. Even though the visible shape of a triangle and its particular light and color are inseparable in perception, he treated them as distinct ideas on the ground that we can immediately discriminate one from the other by an abstractive act of selective attention. According to Berkeley, however, the power to abstract "extends only to the conceiving separately such objects, as it is possible may really exist or be actually perceived asunder," and "does not extend beyond the possibility of real existence or perception" (Berkeley 1901, *A Treatise concerning the Principles of Human Knowledge* [PHK] I.5: 259–60); also Introduction: §10). Whereas the trunk of a human body and its limbs, or the rose and its scent, are pairs of distinct ideas because either can be met with in perception in the absence of the other, the visible shape and color of a triangle are not distinct visual ideas for Berkeley since shape is invisible in the absence of light and color.

Accordingly, to Berkeley, a distinction between visible shape and color reflects not a distinction between ideas but only between different significative uses of the same idea. Significative uses rest on different ways in which ideas can be found to resemble one another such as their sensible quality (the red of a tomato and the red of bell pepper), or the manner in which they are received (red and blue resemble not in quality but in being both sensed by the eyes) (Berkeley 1901, vol. 1, *A New Theory of Vision* [V], §128; and vol. 2, *The Theory of Vision or Visual Language Vindicated and Explained* [TV], §39). Visible shape and visible color differ in virtue of the various external relations of resemblance visual ideas have to other visual ideas. Such resemblances can then be put to a general significative use: one and the same visual idea can be used to denote *all* red things indifferently, *all* triangular things indifferently, and so on (*PHK*: Introduction, §§ 11, 12, 16, 18; and Berkeley 1975: 730). For Berkeley and his anti-abstractionist successors, the important thing philosophically is that a significative difference of denotations does not imply a real difference of ideas.

Because Berkeley shared Locke's sensibilism – the thesis that the contents of human understanding all originate in sensation and reflexion or the actions the understanding performs upon them – nearly all the differences between their theories of understanding can be traced to Berkeley's anti-abstractionist separability principle. The most important of these is the principle that the contents of thought have ontological (rather than merely significative) application only to such objects as they may originally have been acquired from: those derived from internal perception (ideas of reflexion) cannot be attributed to objects of external sense (ideas of sensation) or anything else, while those derived from external sense cannot be ascribed to the objects of internal perception or anything else. Because our notions of cause and effect have no source other than internally perceived volition and other actions of the understanding, the separability principle precludes the possibility of their application to objects of external sense (*PHK*: I.25–7 and Berkeley 1975: 217) or even to objects of a kind wholly unknown to us (Berkeley 1975: 239–40). This separability-principle restriction of application by *origin* pointed the way forward for Berkeley's successors. Indeed it was Hume who first explicitly formulated the restriction: "Ideas always represent the objects or impressions, from which they are deriv'd, and can never without a fiction represent or be apply'd to any other" (*THN*: 37).

Hume applied the separability principle to the idea of cause and effect with remarkable results. Cause and effect relations must always be between items recognized as distinct under this principle. Thus we cannot conceive mountains and valleys to be related as cause and effect because their necessary connection is purely conceptual, incorporated in the ideas themselves: valleys cannot be conceived to exist in the absence of mountains and vice versa. By contrast, fire and smoke can be conceived to be related as cause and effect precisely because we can conceive each to exist in the absence of the other. But there lies the rub: If to conceive cause and effect as distinct is to conceive the existence of the one to be possible even in the absence of the other, but to conceive them as necessarily connected is to conceive the existence of the effect to be impossible in the absence of the cause, the combination of these conceptions in a single idea seems self-contradictory. Forced to choose between incompatibles, Hume opted to supplant the genuine, but seemingly impossible, concept of cause and effect – an objectively real necessary connection between distinct existents – with a subjective psychological surrogate, customary association.

Having gone so far, Hume then undertook to show that all the purposes of empirical reasoning are served quite satisfactorily by an idea of necessary connection that has its source in the customary association we experience in imagination: ordinary and scientific, cognitive and moral, probabilistic and certain, situational and universal. Only philosophical speculation suffers for want of the kind of objective necessary connection Hume showed human understanding to be incapable of conceiving. For only on the supposition that chains of such connections exist prior to and independently of associative imagination could we hope to extend our knowledge of matters of fact and real existence beyond anything experience is capable of disclosing. Lacking even the ability to conceive such connections, however, Hume concluded that such speculation is not merely deficient but vacuous, or worse:

> When we run over libraries, persuaded of these principles, what havoc must we make? If we take in our hand any volume; of divinity or school metaphysics, for instance; let us ask, Does it contain any abstract reasoning concerning quantity or number? No. Does it contain any experimental reasoning concerning matter of fact and existence? No. Commit it then to the flames: for it can contain nothing but sophistry and illusion. (*EHU*: XII.iii.165)

In the course of questioning the very possibility of ideas of objective necessary connections between distinct existents, Hume also denied the intuitive certainty of the general causal principle that everything that begins to exist (object, action, state) must have a cause. To be sure, its problematic status is in the first instance simply a consequence of Hume's conceivability doubt, for, "If we really have no idea of a power or efficacy in any object, or of any real connexion betwixt causes and effects, 'twill be to little purpose to prove, that an efficacy is necessary in all operations" (*THN*: 168). But it is also something more: a skeptical challenge leveled at the epistemic thesis shared by virtually all of Hume's predecessors, empiricist no less than rationalist, that the general principle of causality is "one of those maxims, which tho' they may be deny'd with the lips, 'tis impossible for men in their hearts really to doubt of" (*THN*: 79): a principle whose truth is manifest to us in such a way as to make us sensible that its negation is a contradiction – unintelligible rather than merely false. Hume rejected this consensus: (i) On the ground that the only candidates for terms of causal relations are distinct ideas he argued that the possibility of conceiving "an object to be non-existent this moment, and existent the next, without conjoining to it the distinct idea of a cause or productive principle" is implicit in the very idea of such a relation. (ii) Given that ideas are nothing but copies of impressions originating in the senses (sensation or reflexion), from this conceptual possibility we can infer that it is possible in reality that something may begin to exist with a cause. And (iii) since all that is requisite to show that the general causal principle is neither intuitively nor demonstratively certain is evidence that their separation in reality implies no contradiction or absurdity, Hume boldly concluded that "'tis impossible to demonstrate the necessity of a cause."

Hume was nevertheless careful to emphasize that his conclusion does not imply that the general causal maxim is false, doubtful, or even dubitable. Quite the contrary, in endeavoring to show "Why a cause is always necessary" (Title, *THN*: I.iii.3), his purpose was not to challenge the certainty of the principle, but only the consensus assumption regarding the nature of its certainty. Hume broke new ground with his insistence that its certainty is not intuitive – not a purely intellectual affair of the relations of ideas alone – but rather something else entirely, involving the sensate, feeling part of our minds no less essentially than the conceiving part. Being a committed empiricist in his sensibilism, however, he saw no alternative but to trace its certainty to "observation and experience" (*THN*: 82), and ultimately to the very same source to which he traced ideas of necessary connection: customary association. Thus, the challenge Hume bequeathed to his successors was twofold: first to show that concepts of necessary relations between distinct existents are both possible and in our possession, and second to show that, as regards their existence, the objects of experience are subject a priori (necessarily and universally) to these concepts.

In taking up this challenge, Kant's first step was to determine whether its scope extends farther than Hume realized. One area in which he thought it did is that of necessary relations between distinct quantitative determinations, considered independently of matters of fact and real existence. Relations of equality and inequality are a case in point: although abstract and indifferent to matters of fact and real existence, they are distinct in the sense essential to Hume's skeptical reasoning regarding causal connections. For example, in equating 7 and 5 with 12, I conjoin quantitative determinations in a necessary relation that are conceptually as distinct as fire and smoke: I can think 12 without conceiving 5 and 7 just as easily I can think it without conceiving the difference between 31 and 19, the square root of 144, or the cube root of 1,728. Since this is just to say that the necessity of the relation cannot lie in the objects conceived in it, whence does it derive? In Kant's view, the same reasons that, in the case of causal understanding, led Hume to treat objective necessity as an illusion and set the subjective necessity of customary association in its stead apply with equal force to mathematical understanding (*CPrR* 5.52–3, *Prol.* 4.272–3). Of course, a foundation in experience and custom is inconsistent with the strict necessity Hume attributed to mathematics. In the belief that Hume's commitment to the a priori certainty of mathematics was unshakeable, Kant conjectured that the recognition of its vulnerability to this point would have led Hume to question the empiricist character of his sensibilism, and, probably for the first time, conceive the possibility of a priori sensible sources of concepts and cognition. He would thus have been led from transcendental realism "into considerations which must needs have been similar to those which now occupy us, while benefiting immeasurably from the beauty of his inimitable eloquence" (*Prol.* 4.273).

Kant also extended Hume's skepticism beyond cause and effect to the other fundamental concepts of metaphysics: substance, reciprocal determination, quality (reality, negation, limitation), quantity (unity, plurality, totality), and modality (possibility, existence, necessity). All, in his view, are concepts that stipulate necessary relations between objects (existents or determinations) presupposed as distinct. Applying Hume's reasoning, we thus obtain the same paradox met with in causal connections: to conceive the objects capable of entering into a necessary relation as distinct is to grant that it is always possible to posit one in the absence of the other, and so never contradictory to suppose a relation between them not to hold; whereas to conceive their relation as necessary is to deny that one can be posited independently of the other, and so in effect to deny their distinctness. Since the distinctness of the terms capable of entering into the necessary relation in question cannot be bargained away without changing the very meaning of the relational concept itself (e.g. substituting a merely conceptual relation such as that between mountains and valleys for one that, ostensibly at any rate, is objectively real), there seems no alternative but to settle for subjectively necessary psychological surrogates for all the fundamental concepts of metaphysics. And this of course is exactly what Hume did.

By extending Humean skepticism in these ways, Kant was able to distill it into a single, highly general question: how are synthetic a priori judgments possible? His entire Critical system, including the treatment of freedom (*CPrR* 5.54–7), should be regarded as a response to Hume ("my work in the *Critique of Pure Reason* was occasioned by Hume's skeptical doctrine," [*CPrR* 5.52]; also *Prol.*, Preface). To begin with, the metaphysical deduction of the categories not only provides a response to the initial phase of Humean skepticism, in which the very possibility of concepts of the objectively necessary relation between items presupposed as distinct is doubted, but does so in complete conformity to the Humean manner of tracing concepts to their origin as ideas in the mind with an eye to determining their content and delimiting their scope of application. For the origin of the categories in universal representations of the determinative relation in which the logical functions of judgment stand to the pure synthesis in imagination of the pure manifold of sense shows that they express precisely the kind of objective necessary relation Hume thought inconceivable (*CPR* B 104–5; B 377–8). The pure manifold corresponds to the distinct, its pure synthesis to the relation of the distinct, and the a priori determination of this synthesis in conformity with the logical functions to the necessary relation of the distinct. Of course, this content at the same time restricts the categories to objects constituted conformably to the pure manifold of sensibility (appearances in space and time). Yet, in contrast to the subjective connection of custom, the sensibly conditioned yet empirically objective connections thought in Kant's categories provide a means of forming "the concept of an empirically unconditioned causality," which, though "theoretically empty (in the absence of an intuition suited to it), . . . is given meaning in the moral law, and so in a practical relation" (*CPrR* 5.56).

Kant addressed the second, epistemic phase of Humean skepticism in the Analytic of Principles. For it was not enough to prove that the categories are applicable to objects of sensible intuition; he had also to show that they actually do apply to them, on a priori grounds alone, as the predicates of necessarily and universally valid synthetic a priori judgments. However, establishing the grounds requisite to this purpose obliged him to provide a transcendental deduction of the categories. There Kant contended that original apperception – the unity of the manifold in one consciousness – is the basis of every employment of the understanding, even the merely logical (B 131, B 133–4n), and so the supreme principle both of the possibility of discursive under-standing itself, as a faculty (A 117n, B 137, B 153), and of synthetic a priori judgments (B 136, B 197). Cognitive experience and its objects are no exception: if our perceptions were not subject a priori to the conditions requisite for unity of apperception, we would have as many-colored and diverse a self as we have perceptions (B 134), and the associ-ability of each perceived appearance with every other premised in all Hume's theorizing would be impossible (A 121–2). Finally, after showing that the categories are necessary conditions for unity of apperception in all combination of perceptions, Kant was at last in a position to turn the tables on Hume by arguing that the very possibility of an experience in which appearances are associable presupposes their conformity to concepts of the necessary relation of the distinct (determinations or existents):

> This complete . . . solution of the Humean problem thus rescues the a priori origin of the pure concepts of the understanding as well as the validity of the universal principles of nature as laws of the understanding, yet in such a way as to limit their use to experience, because their possibility depends solely on the relation of the understanding to experi-ence, but with a completely reversed kind of connection that never occurred to Hume: they are not derived from experience but rather experience is derived from them. (*Prol.* 4.313; also B 127–8, A 112–13, A 122, and B 810–11)

Although this was almost surely unknown to Kant, Hume himself came to appreciate he had a problem explaining how perceptions come to be united in one consciousness (*THN*: 635–6). On the one hand, he could not explain the unity of the manifold in one consciousness in terms of ideal relations in associative imagination since, in order for the imagination to associate distinct perceptions, they must already be present in one and the same consciousness. On the other hand, he could not explain it by reference to real relations of inherence or causal connection, since he was unable to renounce the fundamental principles of his philosophy, "that all our distinct percep-tions are distinct existences, and that the mind never perceives any real connexion among distinct existences" (*THN*: 636). Kant, however, had no need of real principles to explain how the distinct perceptions come to be found in one consciousness. Their unity in sensibility is guaranteed by their a priori conformity to a merely ideal space and time, and their unity in experience is ensured by their conformity a priori to equally ideal principles of the necessary relation of the distinct.

Yet, vast as is the gulf separating Kant's apriorist philosophy from Hume's empiri-cist one, it is, in my view, eclipsed by what unites them. For as we saw at the outset, Kant not only derived the problem he devised his philosophy to solve from Hume, but the basic approach to its solution as well. If, in tracing the concepts at the heart of age-old metaphysical disputes to their origin as representations in the mind, it is discovered that the operations of sensibility and understanding responsible for forming these representations also contribute indispensable elements of their content, then their scope of application is restricted, ontologically though not semantically, to the purview of suitably constituted conscious minds. The effect is to expose a hidden absurdity by converting it into a patent one. Hume, for instance, traced the idea of necessary connection – an essential ingredient in all concepts of cause and effect – to an origin in customary transitions of thought, and argued from this that any notion that causal relations might exist in mind-independent contexts is tantamount to supposing that customs of thought might exist in the absence of thought (*THN*: 266–7). Kant achieved a similar result with regard to space and time:

> space and time, including all the appearances in them, are nothing existent in themselves and outside my representations, but themselves only modes of representation, and it is obviously contradictory to say that a mere mode of representation also exists outside our representation. Thus the objects of the senses exist only in experience; whereas to accord to them a subsistent existence [*bestehendes Existenz*] apart from or prior to experience is as much as to represent the actuality of experience apart from or prior to experience. (*Prol.* 4.341–2)

However, to an extent not true of Hume, Kant's explications of the content of concepts in terms of psychological origin interlock. In the Transcendental Deduction he returned to the question of the origin of space and time and showed their unity as individuals that contain all their manifold to be bound up by content with synthesis in imagination and pure apperception (B 136n and B 160n; also A 99–100, A 107, and B 140). He also traced the necessary synthetic unity represented in the categories (B 104) to this same source, so that these concepts likewise prove to be bound up by content with unity of apperception (B 131; also B 399, B 401, and A 401). Even the logical functions of judgment (B 131) and discursive universality, the form of any *conceptus communis* (B 133–4n), have their source in, and are unrepresentable apart from, the unity of apperception. Despite what differentiates pure space and time, as sensible, individual, and given immediately in intuition, from discursive universality, logical functions, and pure concepts of the understanding, Kant's Humean method of tracing them to their origin revealed that there is, after all, a formal unity of consciousness common to them all. And it was by means of this common element that Kant was able to show how the sensible comes to be united with the intellectual to yield cognition without in any way compromising their radical heterogeneity.

References and Further Reading

Ayers, M. (2005). Was Berkeley an empiricist or a rationalist? In *The Cambridge Companion to Berkeley*. Cambridge, Cambridge University Press.

Berkeley, George (1901). *A Treatise Concerning the Principles of Human Knowledge. A New Theory of Vision. Theory of Vision Vindicated.* In *The Works of George Berkeley*, ed. Alexander Campbell Fraser. Vols. I and II. Oxford: Clarendon Press.

Berkeley, George (1975). *Philosophical Works*, ed. Michael Ayers. London: Everyman.

Hume, David (1955). *An Enquiry Concerning Human Understanding*, ed. Selby-Bigge. Oxford: Clarendon Press.

Hume, David (1978). *A Treatise of Human Nature*, ed. Selby-Bigge. Oxford: Clarendon Press.

Locke, John (1975). *Essay concerning Human Understanding*, ed. P. H. Nidditch. Oxford: Oxford University Press.

Waxman, W. (2000). Kant's refutation of Berkeleyan idealism. In *Idealismus als Theorie der Repräsentation* [*Idealism as a Theory of Representation*]. Paderborn: Mentis Verlag.

Waxman, W. (2005). *Kant and the Empiricists: Understanding Understanding*. Oxford: Oxford University Press.

Part II

Critique of Pure Reason

7

Kant's Transcendental Idealism

HENRY E. ALLISON

Kant defines transcendental idealism in two places in the *Critique of Pure Reason*, and in each case he contrasts it with transcendental realism. The first is in the first-edition version of the Fourth Paralogism, where his concern is to differentiate transcendental idealism from the "empirical idealism" associated with Descartes, which allegedly leads to a skepticism regarding an external world. In this context he writes:

> I understand by the *transcendental idealism* of all appearances the doctrine that they are all together to be regarded as mere representations and not things in themselves, and accordingly that time and space are only sensible forms of our intuition, but not determinations given for themselves or conditions of objects as things in themselves. To this idealism is opposed *transcendental realism*, which regards space and time as something given in themselves (independent of our sensibility). (*CPR*, A 369: translations from Kant 1996, 1998, 2002)

The second passage is from the Antinomy of Pure Reason, where Kant defines transcendental idealism as the doctrine that:

> all objects of an experience possible for us, are nothing but appearances, i.e., mere representations, which as they are represented, as extended beings or series of alterations, have outside our thoughts no existence grounded in itself.

In contrast to this, the transcendental realist is said to make "these modifications of our sensibility into things subsisting in themselves, and hence makes *mere representations* into things in themselves" (*CPR*, B 518–19; Kant 1998: 511). Although the first passage emphasizes the transcendental ideality of space and time, while the second focuses on that of the objects given in them, namely appearances, they really come to the same thing, since the ideality of the latter is entailed by that of the former.

At times, Kant also characterizes his idealism as "formal" or "critical," in order to distinguish it from the "dogmatic" or "material" idealism of Berkeley and the "skeptical" or "empirical" idealism of Descartes (Kant 2002: 87–8, 160–3; 1998: 511). As we shall see, this idealism is "formal" in the sense that it is a theory about the a priori "forms" or conditions under which objects can be cognized by the human mind. It is "critical" because it is grounded in a reflection on the conditions and limits of discursive cognition rather than one on the contents of consciousness or the nature of ultimate reality. In both respects it differs radically from what Kant terms idealisms of the "common sort," which include those of Berkeley and Descartes.

As the subsequent history of Kant interpretation indicates, however, this attempted clarification was of little avail, since critics up to the present day have continued to understand Kant's idealism in at least one of the manners he explicitly repudiated. The root of the problem lies in Kant's identification of appearances with "mere representations." Depending on how this identification is understood, it seems to suggest either a subjective idealism or phenomenalism, which is difficult to distinguish from the allegedly "dogmatic idealism" of Berkeley, a radical skepticism regarding empirical knowledge, which is not unlike the view Kant attributes to Descartes, since it denies the human mind any direct access to the "real," or some combination thereof. Consequently, any putative defender of transcendental idealism is confronted with the daunting task of providing an interpretation according to which it escapes these seemingly unappealing alternatives.

Unfortunately, neither of the two standard ways of interpreting transcendental idealism appear adequate to the task. One is the familiar "two-world" or "two-object" reading, which takes appearances and things in themselves to constitute two ontologically distinct realms of being. Although this may seem to be the more natural reading, it has at least two untoward consequences. First, it suggests that transcendental idealism is to be understood as a form of subjectivism, according to which the mind is acquainted only with its own contents (representations). Second, and perhaps even worse, it requires the postulation of a distinct set of entities (things in themselves) to which, according to the theory, the human mind can have no cognitive access. As one influential contemporary critic, who interprets Kant in this way, has put it, transcendental idealism is the doctrine that "reality is supersensible and . . . we can have no knowledge of it" (Strawson 1966: 16). On this "two-world" reading, then, it may truly be said that transcendental idealism gets the worst of both worlds!

The alternative "one-world" or "two-aspect" reading makes it possible to avoid saddling Kant with the excess baggage of an ontologically distinct, yet cognitively inaccessible, noumenal realm. It also finds strong textual support in the second of the above-cited characterizations of transcendental idealism, where Kant indicates that the identification of appearances with mere representations should be taken to mean that things as we represent them, that is, as spatiotemporal entities and events, have no mind-independent existence, not that the things we represent as spatiotemporal have no such existence at all. This locution implies that the intended contrast is between things as they appear and the same things as they are in themselves, rather than between two ontologically distinct sets of entities. Or, more precisely, the distinction pertains to two ways of considering things: as they appear to us in virtue of the spatiotemporal form of our intuition, and as they may be in themselves independently of our manner of intuiting them. On this reading, then, the distinction is adverbial rather than adjectival, since it characterizes the ways in which things can be considered in a reflection on the conditions of their cognition, not the kinds of thing being considered.

As has been often pointed out, however, the main problem with this interpretation of transcendental idealism is that it seemingly commits Kant to the view that objects only appear to us to be spatiotemporal, whereas in reality they are not, or at least that we have no way of knowing whether or not they are. But since by "knowledge" is usually understood the cognition of things as they truly are rather than as they may seem to us under certain conditions, this apparently implies that human knowledge is not really knowledge at all. The point is sometimes made by means of an analogy with the proverbial stick, which appears bent to an observer when reflected in the water, even though it really is straight. Clearly, if this is how the contrast between a thing as it appears and the same thing as it is in itself is to be understood, the distinction is ill equipped to explain the possibility of human knowledge, which is surely one of the essential tasks assigned to transcendental idealism.

Since the first of these ways of interpreting transcendental idealism obviously leads to a dead end, it is worthwhile considering whether the second, which appears to have better textual support, can be understood in a way that avoids the above-mentioned difficulty. One way of attempting such a rehabilitation of this reading is to view it in light of the contrast Kant draws between transcendental realism and transcendental idealism. However useful it may turn out to be, this strategy at least has the virtue of being based on the sound exegetical principle that often the best way to understand a philosophical doctrine is to see what it denies.

Although Kant never discusses transcendental realism in a systematic manner, his cryptic characterizations of it suggest that he understood it to cover any view which regards mere appearances as if they were things in themselves. As such, transcendental realism consists in what Kant considers to be a misinterpretation of appearances, understood as the proper objects of human cognition. In other words, a transcendental realist is someone who either ignores or denies the transcendental distinction between things as they appear and as they are in themselves. If, as the text suggests, this distinction is the defining feature of transcendental idealism, it follows that the epithet "transcendental realism" is applicable to every philosophy except transcendental idealism. Accordingly, the philosophical universe is divided into these two forms of transcendentalism, understood as competing global claims about the objects of human cognition.

At first glance, however, this does not appear to be a particularly promising strategy, since it seems highly implausible, if not artificial, to place all contrasting philosophies in the same bag. Consequently, if this is to prove useful, it must be shown that these philosophies share something in common beside their rejection of transcendental idealism. But, given the scope of transcendental realism, this common feature cannot be a shared metaphysical commitment, such as we usually associate with realism in its various forms. For if the philosophical universe is indeed divided in the way in which Kant suggests, then transcendental realism encompasses a wide variety of metaphysical and epistemological positions, including rationalism and empiricism, metaphysical realism, as ordinarily understood, and Berkeleian idealism, each of which may be said in one way or another to conflate appearances with things in themselves (see Allison 2004).

Nevertheless, there is another candidate for the requisite common feature, one which points to the essential difference between transcendental realism in all its forms and transcendental idealism. Rather than being straightforwardly metaphysical, or even epistemological, transcendental realism is perhaps best characterized as a metaphilosophical or meta-epistemological standpoint. Specifically, it consists in a commitment (either tacit or overt) to what is sometimes described as the "theocentric paradigm" or model of knowledge. In other words, the defining feature of transcendental realism is its underlying assumption that human knowledge is to be measured and evaluated in terms of its conformity (or lack thereof) to the norm of a putatively perfect divine knowledge. Although not of itself a straightforwardly epistemological thesis, insofar it determines the framework within which the first-order epistemological debate (between rationalism and empiricism) is typically conducted, it may be appropriately characterized as "meta-epistemological."

Moreover, it is precisely because transcendental realism (in all its forms) approaches cognition in light of this paradigm that it may be said to identify appearances (the actual objects of empirical cognition) with things in themselves (the putative objects of divine cognition). Consequently, what unites the various forms of transcendental realism is a normative commitment to a paradigm of knowledge rather than some shared metaphysical assumption.

This does not mean that Kant thought that all philosophies, apart from his own, maintain that the human mind is somehow capable of knowing things in the way in which God supposedly does, that is, nondiscursively by means of a nonsensible and, therefore, intellectual intuition. Although some of the classical rationalists, e.g., Spinoza, Malebranche, and Leibniz, come close to this view, insofar as they suggest that human cognition through "adequate ideas" may approximate and in some cases (typically in mathematics) even attain this ideal, this is not necessary to make one a transcendental realist. On the contrary, on this reading, even empiricists and skeptics such as Hume are dedicated transcendental realists. For while denying the possibility of the kind of knowledge to which the rationalist typically pretends, they share the underlying assumption that this is what genuine cognition would be like, if it were attainable by beings such as ourselves. In this methodological respect, then, they likewise adhere to the theocentric paradigm.

Given the way in which Kant draws the contrast between the two forms of transcendentalism, effectively viewing them as all-inclusive and mutually exclusive alternatives, it follows that transcendental idealism must likewise be seen as a meta-epistemological position, committed to an alternative model of cognition, and not as a competing metaphysical theory. Otherwise they would not conflict with one another in the way in which Kant clearly assumed that they do. Moreover, since the contrast is with the theocentric paradigm, the paradigm appealed to by transcendental idealism must be anthropocentric. In short, the conditions of human cognition, whatever they may turn out to be, rather than the unattainable ideal of a God's-eye view of things, determine the norms of our cognition.

This paradigm shift is equivalent to Kant's so-called "Copernican revolution in philosophy." As Kant famously puts it in what he initially describes as an experiment inspired by the "first thoughts of Copernicus,"

Up to now it has been assumed that all our cognition must conform to the objects; but all attempts to find out something about them apriori through concepts that would extend our cognition have, on this presupposition, come to nothing. Hence let us once try whether we do not get farther with the problems of metaphysics by assuming that the objects must conform to our cognition. (CPR, B xvi; Kant 1998: 110)

114

The assumption that all our cognition must conform to its object (in order to count as cognition) is not only the view of common sense, it also expresses the underlying presupposition of transcendental realism. And since it is further assumed that for our cognition to conform to its object is equivalent to its conforming (or at least approximating) to a putative God's-eye comprehension of it, this also amounts to a commitment to the theocentric paradigm.

Clearly, Kant was not the first philosopher to advocate something like an anthropological or subjectivist turn in epistemology. On the contrary, this is characteristic of the empiricists, who, reacting to the more or less overt theocentric paradigm of classical rationalism, insisted upon the importance of focusing on the "human understanding" (Locke), "the principles of human knowledge" (Berkeley), or "human nature" (Hume). Nevertheless, precisely because these philosophies remain committed to the normative status of this paradigm, it is a serious (albeit frequently made) mistake to interpret Kant's Copernican revolution along these lines. What distinguishes Kant's anthropological turn from that of empiricism and qualifies it as a genuine revolution is the explicit rejection of this paradigm, which is what also accounts for its *transcendental* character.

Kant's use of the term "transcendental" is notoriously confusing, since he construes it in a number of distinct ways, at least two of which involve a contrast with "empirical" (see chapter 8 below). One of these is the traditional sense in which it refers to things in general, that is, to all things indiscriminately, quite apart from the question of whether or not they can be objects of human experience. The illicit application of the categories to "objects in general," as opposed to objects of possible experience, is transcendental in this sense. The other, and distinctively "Critical" sense, refers to a second-order reflection on the conditions of the cognition of objects, particularly insofar as this cognition is deemed possible a priori (*CPR*, B 25; Kant 1998: 133).

Kant's idealism is transcendental in the sense that it is grounded in a reflection upon the conditions of the possibility of such cognition. What makes it a form of idealism is the thesis that these conditions, henceforth to be called "epistemic conditions," reflect the structure of the mind rather than the nature of a pregiven reality. Consequently, to assume that objects conform to our cognition is to assume that they conform to the (mind-imposed) conditions under which we can cognize them as objects. Conversely, what makes transcendental realism a form of realism is that, implicitly at least, it regards the conditions of human cognition as determined by the nature of a pregiven reality, which is equivalent to assuming that they reflect the ideal model of God's way of knowing. That is why, from Kant's point of view, transcendental realism cannot account for the possibility of a priori knowledge for beings like ourselves.

Since the notion of an epistemic condition is here intended to aid in understanding the distinctive thrust of Kantian idealism, it is essential to be clear about how it is construed. Put simply, by an epistemic condition is meant a necessary condition for the representation of objects, that is, a condition without which our representations would not relate to objects or, equivalently, possess objective reality. Assuming that there are such conditions, which it is the task of both the Transcendental Aesthetic and Transcendental Analytic to demonstrate, Kant has a ready explanation of the possibility of a priori knowledge, namely, we can know a priori that objects necessarily conform to the conditions under which we can alone cognize them. Otherwise they could not be objects for us.

As conditions of the possibility of representing objects, epistemic conditions (if there be any) may be distinguished from both psychological and ontological conditions. By the former is meant a propensity or mechanism of the mind, which governs belief and belief acquisition. Hume's custom or habit is a prime example of such a condition. By the latter is meant a condition of the possibility of the *existence* of things, which conditions these things quite independently of our cognitive access to them. Newton's absolute space and time are conditions in this sense. Epistemic conditions share with the former the property of being subjective in the sense that they reflect the structure and operations of the human mind. They differ from them with respect to their objectivating function. Correlatively, they share with the latter the property of being objective or objectivating. They differ in that they condition the objectivity of our representation of things rather than the very existence of the things themselves.

Clearly, not everything that one might regard as a condition of cognition counts as epistemic in the relevant sense. For example, critics intent on denying any link between conditions of cognition and idealism point to empirical illustrations, such as the fact that our eyes can perceive things only if they reflect light of a certain wavelength. As a fact about our visual capacities, which obviously has analogues in other sensory modalities, this is arguably a "condition" of a significant subset of the perceptual cognition of sighted human beings; but, as these critics note, this hardly has any idealistic implications (Hossenfelder 1990: 468–9).

Although true, this is beside the point. Conditions of this sort are not epistemic in the requisite sense because they have no objective validity or objectivating function. On the contrary, like the Humean psychological conditions, an appeal to them presupposes the existence of an objective spatiotemporal world, the representation of which is supposed to be explained. Accordingly, it hardly follows from the fact such conditions do not entail any sort of idealism that properly epistemic conditions do not do so either.

In fact, the concept of an epistemic condition brings with it an idealistic commitment of at least an indeterminate sort, because it involves the relativization of the concept of an object to human cognition and the conditions of its representation of objects. In other words, the claim is not that things transcending the conditions of human cognition cannot exist (this would make these conditions ontological), but merely that such transcendent things cannot be objects for us. Thus, epistemic conditions are by their very nature normative, since they determine what could count as an object.

Nevertheless, it has been pointed out by more sympathetic critics that this indeterminate concept of an epistemic condition is not of itself sufficient to capture what is distinctive in Kant's transcendental idealism (Ameriks 1992). The latter does not merely relativize the concept of an object to the conditions (whatever they may be) of the representation of objects, it relativizes them to the specific conditions of human cognition. And since Kant repeatedly insists that the distinguishing feature of our, indeed all finite, cognition lies in its discursive nature, it follows that a full understanding of transcendental idealism must await the determination of the unique conditions of such cognition.

Admittedly, it may seem strange to locate something so supposedly momentous as Kant's Copernican revolution in something so apparently noncontroversial as the discursive nature of human cognition. Insofar as such cognition consists in the application of general concepts to sensory data, this hardly seems to be a revolutionary proposal, involving something like a paradigm shift. Paradoxical as it may seem, however, when seen within the context of classical modern philosophy, this is precisely what it is.

In order fully to appreciate this, we must first stipulate that all cognition requires that its object in some way be given, otherwise it could not be known. This stipulation is noncontroversial because it is made by both transcendental realism and transcendental idealism. Moreover, given Kant's understanding of intuition as the means whereby objects are given, this means that *all* cognition rests ultimately on intuition. This applies even to God's, which is why it has traditionally been viewed as resting on a creative (nonsensible) intuition. But since a human or, more generally, a finite intellect cannot create its own data, it must receive them from without, which for Kant entails that it must be "affected" by its object. The product of such affection is what Kant understands by a sensible intuition.

Since this indicates that sensible intuition is a necessary condition of human cognition, the question becomes whether it is also sufficient. Kant's discursivity thesis denies that this is case. Also necessary (though not sufficient) are concepts through which the sensibly given is thought. This is what makes human cognition discursive as opposed to intuitive. In Kant's oft-cited dictum, "Thoughts without content are empty, intuitions without concepts are blind" (*CPR*, B 75; Kant 1998: 193–4).

In light of this conception of discursivity, it is illuminating to survey, however cursorily, the basic epistemological commitments of rationalism and empiricism. Although the former recognizes an important role for conceptual knowledge, that is, cognition through general concepts, which, as such, may be predicated of diverse particulars, it assigns to it a decidedly second class status. The basic idea, which goes back at least to Plato, is that to know something only in terms of features it shares with other objects is not to know its inherent nature. Consequently, the epistemological ideal for rationalism (as it was for Plato) is an immediate intellectual apprehension of an object in its full particularity, something which is unattainable through concepts. Moreover, since *all* cognition requires that its object be given and no object can be given in such a manner through sensibility, it follows that this rationalist ideal of cognition presupposes a nonsensible or intellectual intuition.

Empiricism, though committed to the same paradigm, is guilty of the opposite error. In other words, the problem with empiricism is not that it affirms the possibility of a kind of cognition that somehow transcends the conceptual variety, it is rather that it denies the very possibility of the latter, at least as such cognition is understood by Kant. Thus, if classical rationalism may be said to be "supraconceptional," classical empiricism is "subconceptual." This finds its overt expression in the empiricist's well known aversion to "abstract general ideas," which are just concepts as understood by Kant. But this aversion itself can be properly understood only in light of empiricism's equally well known tendency to regard what it terms "ideas" as images. In Hume's classical formulation, this means that ideas are pale copies of sensibly given impressions, which themselves provide all the requisite materials of thought. And this likewise rules out discursive cognition in anything like the Kantian sense.

At bottom, this denigration, if not outright rejection, of conceptual representation, which is common to both rationalism and empiricism, stems from the fact that each of them denies at least one of the two essential components of discursive cognition as understood by Kant, namely, concepts and sensible intuitions. Consequently, they both reject, albeit for quite different reasons, the discursivity thesis, which indicates that the latter is hardly noncontroversial.

Rationalism agrees with Kant that sensible intuition is not sufficient for cognition, but differs from him in also denying that it is necessary. This is not to say that rationalism rejects *any* dependence of human cognition on sensory input; it is rather that it typically limits this dependence to providing an "occasion" or stimulus for thought. Although clearly important, this does not amount to an *essential* dependence, since rationalism does not regard this input as part of the content of the non-empirical cognition at which it ultimately aims. In other words, sensible intuition, on the rationalist account, functions to start the cognitive process, but it does not help determine its outcome.

For present purposes, however, what is particularly noteworthy is that rationalism's assignment of a second-class status to conceptual representation is itself a consequence of its denial of an essential cognitive role for sensibility. Since the proper function of concepts is to bring the sensibly given under universal rules in virtue of which it may be viewed as the representation of a particular of one sort or another, that is, as betokening a type, a form of cognition that purports to dispense with the sensibly given is in a position to dispense with concepts as well. The two go hand in hand.

Conversely, empiricism rejects an *essential* cognitive function for concepts for precisely the opposite reason. Since for empiricism "experience" is not merely the starting point, but the unique source of all the materials of thought, it maintains that the ancestry of all concepts must somehow be traceable to it. For Locke, these materials took the form of "simple ideas," which are passively received "as they are in themselves" (in Kant's sense). Consequently, unlike Kant, Locke did not view conceptualization as itself a necessary condition of the possibility of experience. This does not rule out any role for concepts, but it limits it to a subordinate one, since it presupposes that experience is possible prior to, and independently of, their application.

On Locke's account, then, it is only subsequent to the reception of simple ideas, that is, to the commencement of experience as he understood it, that the understanding comes into play. Its function, which Locke termed the "workmanship of the under-standing" (Locke 1975: 415), is to combine the simple ideas into complex ones. Among the most important of the latter are sortal concepts produced by the understanding on the basis of observed similarities. Although hardly trivial, this function is far from the one Kant assigns to the understanding, when he claims that, through its categories, it prescribes laws to nature (Kant 1998: 261). An indication of the extent of this difference is Locke's insistence that these sortal concepts determine merely what he terms the "nominal essence" of things as distinguished from their "real essence." More-over, since the real essence is supposedly cognizable only by God (Locke 1975: 417, 439), this lends further support to the contention that Locke, like all empiricists, was committed to the theocentric paradigm.

The relevance of these epistemological reflections for the understanding of transcendental idealism may not be apparent, but it becomes so when considered in light of the analysis of transcendental realism and the associated conception of an epistemic condition. To begin with, as we have just seen, the denial of the inherently discursive nature of human cognition is already transcendentally realistic in Kant's sense, because it presupposes (perhaps unknowingly) the theocentric paradigm to which both rationalism and empiricism are committed.

Equally significant, it enables us to distinguish Kant's transcendental idealism not merely from the forms of idealism he explicitly rejects, but also from the indeterminate sort that is entailed by the conception of an epistemic condition. The point here is that, as discursive, human cognition must be seen as governed by two distinct kinds of epistemic condition, each of which plays a normative role. In other words, it is not merely that the human mind imposes its own (epistemic) conditions on what is cognizable, that is, on what can count as an object for it, but it does so through sensibility as well as through the understanding. Accordingly, even though it does not of itself yield cognition, as it does for empiricism, sensibility, for Kant, places its own conditions on the data for cognition, which precludes the kind of non-empirical cognition aimed at by rationalism.

Kant terms these sensible conditions "forms of sensibility," and the central task of the Transcendental Aesthetic is to demonstrate that, at least in the case of the human mind, space and time are such forms. This is to be contrasted with the traditional view, according to which they are either themselves self-subsisting things, properties of such things, or relations between things that hold independently of their epistemic relation to the human mind. Kant characterizes the demonstration of this thesis as a "direct proof" of transcendental idealism (*CPR*, B 534–5: Kant 1998: 519). In his analysis of the antinomies Kant also provides what he terms an "indirect proof" by arguing that the contradictions into which reason unavoidably falls when it endeavors to think the world as a whole stem from an implicit commitment to transcendental realism and do not arise for transcendental idealism (*CPR*, B 535: Kant 1998: 519).

Unfortunately, it is impossible to pursue here either of these arguments, which are among the most important and controversial in the *Critique of Pure Reason* (see Allison 2004). For present purposes, it must suffice to note that the key Kantian conception of appearance is to be understood in light of his attribution of a transcendental function to sensibility, something which no previous philosopher had done. Thus, even though Kant takes the term "appearance" in the traditional sense as referring to what appears, that is, what is given to the mind in sensory experience, he understands this givenness in a completely new way. Rather than being given as it is in itself (as it is for empiricism), what appears and provides the data for cognition is mediated by the mind's own forms of sensibility (space and time). Although these forms do not of themselves order the data, that being the work of the understanding, by giving these data a spatiotemporal form they ensure that the latter are orderable, that is, amenable to thought. That is what renders these forms epistemic conditions.

Given this conception of appearance, to claim that a discursive intellect cognizes things only as they appear, is to claim that it has access to objects only by way of its forms of sensibility. If the understanding could of itself cognize things, it would do so independently of these forms and, therefore, as they are in themselves. In fact, from Kant's standpoint, to consider things as they are in themselves just is to consider them as some pure understanding might think them, that is, in a way that bypasses the contribution of sensibility. Although the discursive nature of our cognition clearly rules out the possibility of fully *cognizing* objects in this manner, it allows for the possibility of so *thinking* them, because the conditions of thought (the pure concepts) are independent of, and more extensive than, the conditions of sensible intuition.

119

This also enables us to understand Kant's transcendental distinction in a way that underscores its difference from the traditional appearance–reality distinction with which it is frequently confused. Since the conditions of sensibility govern the way in which raw sensory data can be given to thought, they do not transform what might otherwise be genuine cognition into something less. On the contrary, these conditions make such cognition possible in the first place. Moreover, since the human understanding of itself cannot cognize things at all, it can hardly cognize them as they are in themselves. That would require that it be transformed from a faculty of concepts into a faculty of intellectual intuition.

The main lesson to be learned from this is that Kant's transcendental distinction, as well as the consequent limitation of human cognition to things as they appear, results from a reflection on the conditions of discursive knowing rather than on the ontological status of what is supposedly known. Consequently, it opens up the possibility of an essentially nonontological interpretation of transcendental idealism, one which allows it to be viewed as a true counterpart to transcendental realism. On this view, human cognition for Kant is not a pale copy or distorted, finitized version of the divine variety, but a genuine alternative to it. In fact it is precisely the latter that is problematic, not because we are unable to attain it, but because we cannot determine whether the putative epistemic condition of such cognition, namely, a nonsensible, intellectual mode of intuition, is even possible.

Thus, in sharp contrast to both the tradition he opposed and the views of many of his critics, Kant rejected the appropriateness of the theocentric paradigm in epistemology. Moreover, this rejection first makes possible a radically new kind of epistemology, one grounded in the revolutionary idea that human cognition is governed by its own autonomous set of norms. As already indicated, this is precisely how Kant's Copernican revolution is to be understood.

What makes this so puzzling and difficult to grasp is that the theocentric paradigm continues to have a strong hold on us. In an effort to loosen this hold, it may prove useful to examine a familiar metaphysical conundrum in light of it, namely, the problem of fatalism. Traditionally, this problem has been linked to the issue of divine foreknowledge. If God is omniscient he must know what I will do before I do it. But in that event the question naturally arises: How can I avoid doing it and, if not, how can I be held responsible for my deeds?

Typically, philosophical theologians attempt to deal with this problem by reinterpreting the concept of divine foreknowledge. Rather than knowing what I will do literally *before* I do it, which would entail fatalism, it is claimed that God grasps all things immediately in a timeless manner through a single intellectual intuition. Whether this provides an adequate basis for dealing with the problem, or even for interpreting omniscience, remains an open question. What is of interest here are the implications of such a move for understanding the nature of time.

To begin with, these implications cast grave doubt on the viability of a transcendentally realistic account of time, since they suggest that, insofar as transcendental realism affirms an atemporal conception of divine cognition (as it must, if it is to preserve omniscience), it is forced to conclude that time is not fully real, that objects and events only *appear* to be temporally successive. In other words, it is transcendental realism (not transcendental idealism) that is confronted with a dilemma: it must either deny divine omniscience, which is philosophically difficult (though not unheard of), or deny the reality of time, that is, it must admit that occurrences merely *seem* to be successive but in reality they are not, which is to reduce experience to illusion.

The problem does not arise for transcendental idealism because of its sharp distinction between empirical and transcendental reality. This enables Kant to preserve the empirical reality of time – its reality with respect to all human experience – at the modest cost of its transcendental ideality, that is, its lack of reality with respect to things when considered as they are in themselves. Otherwise expressed, by considering time as an epistemic rather than an ontological condition, transcendental idealism ensures the "objective reality" of time with respect to appearances, while also leaving conceptual space for a radically distinct atemporal perspective constituting the God's-eye view of things. Consequently, only transcendental idealism allows for the possibility of affirming both the essential temporality of human experience and the conceivability of an atemporal, eternalistic perspective on things.

Against this, however, it may be argued that whatever virtues such a version of idealism might possess, it cannot be attributed to Kant, because *his* idealism, whether construed in the "two-world" or "two-aspect" manner, is inherently metaphysical in nature. In the words of one recent critic, "On that [epistemic] reading there is still no reason to think the nonideal has a greater ontological status than the ideal." But this, it is further claimed, is incompatible with Kant's deepest philosophical commitments, which concern "the absolute reality of things in themselves with substantive nonspatiotemporal characteristics" (Ameriks 1992: 334).

Since the present account of transcendental idealism clearly entails the denial of a superior ontological status to the so-called "nonideal," this objection must be addressed. And having just discussed the issue of fatalism, it seems appropriate to consider the matter in light of the related problem of freedom, where the ontological question is most pressing. Given Kant's understanding of freedom as an independence from the causality of nature, an ontological reading is confronted with only two alternatives: either we really are free and only appear to be causally determined, or we really are causally determined and merely think (erroneously) that we are free. From a strictly ontological point of view, there simply is no way to claim that we are both at once – that is, there is no place for "compatibilism," as it is traditionally understood. Or, more precisely, there is no place for it if we wish to preserve the core Kantian conception of freedom. But neither remaining alternative is attractive: the former because it undermines Kant's empirical realism, and the latter because it effectively denies the reality of freedom. Consequently, the question is whether there is any viable alternative to the ontological reading, one which would allow for the possibility of affirming, as Kant clearly intended to do, both causal determinism and freedom.

What seems to foreclose the latter possibility is the difficulty of surrendering the assumption that there must be *some* context-independent "fact of the matter," a difficulty which may itself be seen as a consequence of the continued hold that the theocentric paradigm has on us. Again, it seems obvious that either we really are free or we are not. We may not be in a position to determine which alternative is correct, and in that case we remain agnostic about the free will problem, but that is beside the point.

Nevertheless it is precisely this assumption, which appears so obvious for a transcendental realist, that transcendental idealism calls into question. It does this by relativizing each of the claims to a point of view. For transcendental idealism there are only the opposing points of view and no higher, context-independent standpoint from which one might properly raise the seemingly unavoidable question: Are we *really* free? Moreover, since the assumption that there must be such a standpoint or point of view (the terms are here used interchangeably), even if we are incapable of attaining it, is a defining feature of transcendental realism, it follows that the ontological interpretation, which appears to make transcendental idealism so implausible, is a product of the very view to which Kant opposes his idealism. It is little wonder, then, that critics who approach transcendental idealism from a transcendentally realistic perspective find it so perplexing.

We can at least begin to understand this difficult notion of relativization to a point of view, if we consider it in light of Kant's conception of an "interest of reason." According to his analysis of the antinomial conflict, each of the parties to the dispute is motivated by a distinct interest, which may be termed an interest of reason because it represents some ultimate value or principle that is thought to be threatened by the opposing view (*CPR*, B 500–1; Kant 1998: 496–503). Kant characterizes these points of view as Epicureanism and Platonism (*CPR*, B 499; Kant 1998: 501). They represent respectively a radical empiricism and a kind of rationalism ("dogmatism"), which affirms the validity of non-empirical principles as requirements of pure thought.

In the case of the third antinomy (the conflict between freedom and causal determinism), the deterministic position, representing empiricism, is clearly *epistemologically* privileged in Kant's view, since it questions the legitimacy of claims that transcend the bounds of possible experience. But it is not thereby also *ontologically* privileged, as it must be for transcendental realism. Moreover, even though Kant clearly wished to salvage its conceivability, the indeterministic position is likewise not ontologically privileged either, since it rests upon an interest of reason rather than a presumed insight into the nature of ultimate reality.

What makes it possible for transcendental idealism to reconcile these competing interests is the division of labor between the two points of view. The empirical point of view is assumed for the purpose of explanation. Since the concern is to locate the motive causes of human actions, in terms of which they are alone explicable, there is clearly no room for freedom. By contrast, the main concern of the non-empirical (libertarian) point of view is the evaluation and imputation of human actions. Here Kant's claim, a deeply controversial one, is that from this point of view freedom (in an indeterminist sense) must be presupposed, even though its reality cannot be demonstrated or its possibility understood.

The basic point can also be made by noting that the difference between the two points of view is normative. As one would expect, the empirical point of view is governed by epistemic norms, that is, by what have here been termed epistemic conditions. Conversely, since the opposing point of view is concerned with evaluation and imputation, it is governed by practical norms, which stem ultimately from the nature of practical reason. And what allows the latter a place at the table is precisely the distinction between epistemic and ontological conditions. Given this distinction, which is essential to transcendental idealism, these two standpoints each retain their normative force, though neither is ontologically privileged. In fact, it is precisely because the latter is the case that the former is possible.

Against this, it might still be objected that Kant occasionally speaks in a Platonic fashion of the idea of freedom, or the consciousness of the moral law, as giving us *entrée* to an intelligible world or higher order of things, quite distinct from the sensible world of experience. Nevertheless, it is clear from the context of these remarks that the superiority of the former is to be construed in axiological rather than ontological terms. In other words, what we supposedly become aware of is a higher set of values and a vocation (*Bestimmung*) to pursue them, not of our membership in some higher order of being. Kant's insistence, in the *Critique of Practical Reason*, on the primacy of practical reason in relation to the speculative (*CPrR*, 5.119–21; Kant 1996: 236–8) is a case in point (see chapter 17 below). It must be understood as asserting that our practical interest, in morality and the conditions of its possibility, is entitled to override our speculative interest in avoiding ungrounded claims and that the latter must therefore submit to the former. Once again, then, there is no thought of any access (cognitive or otherwise) to an ontologically superior order of being. Consequently, transcendental idealism is best viewed as an alternative to *ontology*, rather than, as it usually is, as an alternative *ontology*. This is precisely what makes its interpretation and evaluation so difficult.

References and Further Reading

Allison, Henry E. (1990). *Kant's Theory of Freedom*. Cambridge: Cambridge University Press.

Allison, Henry E. (1996). *Idealism and Freedom: Essays on Kant's Theoretical and Practical Philosophy*. Cambridge: Cambridge University Press.

Allison, Henry E. (2004). *Kant's Transcendental Idealism: An Interpretation and Defense* (revised version). New Haven: Yale University Press.

Ameriks, Karl (1992). Kantian idealism today. *History of Philosophy Quarterly*, 9: 329–42.

Beck, Lewis White (1969). Kant's strategy. In T. Penelhum and J. J. MacIntosh (eds.), *The First Critique: Reflections on Kant's Critique of Pure Reason* (pp. 5–17). Belmont, CA: Wadsworth Publishing.

Beck, Lewis White (1975). *The Actor and the Spectator*. New Haven: Yale University Press.

Bird, Graham (1962). *Kant's Theory of Knowledge*. London: Routledge and Kegan Paul.

Falkenstein, Lorne (1995). *Kant's Intuitionism: A Commentary on the Transcendental Aesthetic*. Toronto: University of Toronto Press.

Glouberman, M. (1979). Conceptuality: An essay in retrieval. *Kant-Studien*, 70: 383–408.

Guyer, Paul (1987). *Kant and the Claims of Knowledge*. Cambridge: Cambridge University Press.

Guyer, Paul, ed. (1992). *The Cambridge Companion to Kant*. Cambridge: Cambridge University Press.

Hossenfelder, Malte (1990). Allison's defense of Kant's transcendental idealism. *Inquiry*, 33: 467–79.

Hudson, Hud (1994). *Kant's Compatibilism*. Ithaca and London: Cornell University Press.

Kant, Immanuel (1996). *Critique of Practical Reason*, ed. and tr. Mary Gregor. In *Practical Philosophy, The Cambridge Edition of the Works of Immanuel Kant*. Cambridge: Cambridge University Press.

Kant, Immanuel (1998). *Critique of Pure Reason*, eds. and tr. Paul Guyer and Allen Wood. *The Cambridge Edition of the Works of Immanuel Kant*. Cambridge: Cambridge University Press.

Kant, Immanuel (2002). *Prolegomena to any Future Metaphysics that will be able to Come Forward as Science*. In *Theoretical Philosophy after 1781, The Cambridge Edition of the Works of Immanuel Kant*, eds. Henry E. Allison and Peter Heath. Cambridge: Cambridge University Press.

Locke, John (1975). *An Essay Concerning Human Understanding*, ed. Peter H. Nidditch. Oxford: Clarendon Press.

Longuenesse, Béatrice (1998). *Kant and the Capacity to Judge*. Princeton: Princeton University Press.

Matthews, H. E. (1969). Strawson on transcendental idealism. *Philosophical Quarterly*, 19: 204–20.

Prauss, Gerold (1971). *Erscheinung bei Kant*. Berlin: de Gruyter.

Prichard, H. A. (1909). *Kant's Theory of Knowledge*. Oxford: Clarendon Press.

Putnam, Hilary (1981). *Reason, Truth, and History*. Cambridge: Cambridge University Press.

Robinson, Hoke (1994). Two perspectives on Kant's appearances and things in themselves. *Journal of the History of Philosophy*, 32.

Strawson, P. F. (1966). *The Bounds of Sense: An Essay on Kant's Critique of Pure Reason*. London: Methuen.

8

Kant's Analytic Apparatus

GRAHAM BIRD

Kant's analytic apparatus in the first *Critique* provides a framework for the whole Critical philosophy. The fundamental classification of synthetic a priori judgments or truths has been extensively discussed and criticized, but I shall suggest that the apparatus covers far more than that one item. The aim is to review the complexities of Kant's approach, to correct some misconceptions, and to offer some defensible versions of its features under the following headings:

1) The separate "analytic/synthetic" and "a posteriori/a priori" distinctions.
2) The consequent synthetic a priori classification of judgments, or truths.
3) The use of "a priori" to characterize subjudgmental elements such as intuitions and concepts.
4) The distinction between analytic and synthetic method.
5) The "empirical/transcendental" and "immanent/transcendent" distinctions.

The attention devoted to the synthetic a priori classification in (2), and its ground in the separate distinctions of (1), may suggest that these are regarded as the single most important items in the apparatus, but I shall claim that the related but different (3) has a stronger case. Certainly both (3) and (5) are essential in understanding Kant's philosophy and its procedures. It may be said that (4) and (5) involve Kant's *philosophical* doctrine rather than his *formal* apparatus, but even (1), (2), and (3) cannot be disconnected from the former. The headings differ with respect to the strength of their formal, rather than philosophical, character, but all of them *have* a philosophical significance. Kant's apparatus belongs to what he called a transcendental logic intimately linked to his philosophy and distinguished from formal general logic (*CPR*, B 75–9).

1. The "A Posteriori/A Priori" and "Analytic/Synthetic" Distinctions

Kant's predecessors in both the empiricist and rationalist traditions typically contrasted two types of judgment but gave them different labels. Locke distinguished "trifling," including "identical," and "instructive" propositions (Locke 1975: IV.viii); Leibniz separated "necessary truths of reasoning" and "contingent truths of fact" (Leibniz 1991: §§31–6); and Hume contrasted what he called "relations of ideas" with "matters of fact" (Hume 1902: §IV, part 1). More generally philosophers used a contrast between what is "a posteriori" and what is "a priori." Accounts of these contrasts were not all the same, but they all responded to a general distinction between the truths of formal disciplines, such as logic or mathematics, and those of informal experience and natural science. Truths of logic and mathematics, such as "2 + 2 = 4" or "If P then P," were intuitively recognized as different in character from those of natural science or ordinary experience, such as "The planets follow elliptical orbits round the sun," or "Aspirin relieves headaches." That motive continued in the twentieth century with a widely accepted contrast between what were variously described as logical, analytic, or a priori truths on one side and empirical, synthetic, or a posteriori truths on the other.

Kant's central goal of *separating* the "analytic/synthetic" and "a posteriori/a priori" distinctions attempted to refine the traditional classifications, and put him at odds with those historical and contemporary developments. His strategy is to characterize separately the two contrasts "a posteriori/a priori" and "synthetic/analytic," and to argue that the separation allows some judgments to be *both* synthetic *and* a priori (*CPR*, B 10–18). For anyone who holds that the two contrasts are just different verbal expressions of the *same* distinction, that conclusion will appear inconsistent.

The a posteriori/a priori distinction among judgments can be understood in terms of that intuitive contrast between disciplines such as logic or mathematics on one side and those of the natural sciences or ordinary experience on the other. The two kinds of judgment can be separated in terms of the different kinds of warrant on which they are based. Natural science and ordinary experience offer judgments warranted on empirical evidence, while logic and mathematics are grounded on proofs. The former rest typically on observation and on the supporting testimony of recurring cases of the same kind; the latter rest typically on formal proofs which require neither observation nor confirmation from repeated patterns of experience. Euclid's algorithm, "There is no largest prime number," seems wholly unlike such a claim as "Steel is a stronger material than iron." Both might be thought to achieve the appropriate standard of certainty in their respective contexts, but for Kant only the former has a strict or unrestricted generality and necessity. The strict universality and necessity achieved in valid proof are marks of a priori judgment and do not belong to a posteriori claims.

To understand the distinction in these terms is to deploy epistemic criteria concerning the way we can come to know the relevant judgments. For Kant a priori truths are those which *can* be known without empirical observation or evidence, while a posteriori truths *require* a warrant in terms of such observation and evidence. Whether the a posteriori/a priori distinction is attached to judgments or to subjudgmental constituents (as in (3) above), its *basic* sense distinguishes what is cognitively dependent on, or independent of, presented experience. Kant's view is that all cognitive disciplines, such as mathematics, natural science, and even metaphysics, contain a priori truths but only empirical natural science and ordinary experience contain a posteriori truths. Nothing in this account prohibits our coming to believe the truth of an a priori judgment on the basis of a posteriori evidence. I may come to believe in the truth of a judgment in mathematics or logic because expert mathematicians, or a trustworthy computer program, assure me that it is a theorem. What is required is only that a priori, but not a posteriori, judgments *can* be determined to be true (or false) without such evidence.

Kant's attempt to characterize the second distinction, between analytic and synthetic judgments, has been generally regarded as unsuccessful, but the familiar criticisms have often rested on a failure to distinguish between essential and peripheral criteria. Kant distinguishes, for example, between the "ampliative" character of synthetic judgments and the "explicative" character of analytic judgments. The latter's predicates add nothing to the concept of the subject in a subject–predicate proposition, while the former's go beyond that concept. It would be natural to understand this by saying, although Kant himself does not do so, that the former are informative while the latter are not. It is easy to object to this that even trivial analytic truths, such as "Bachelors are unmarried men," provide *some* information, namely information about the meaning of the subject term "bachelor." But if informativeness were to be used as a criterion it would require a *further* distinction between semantic and nonsemantic information, and that points to Kant's two more fundamental criteria, one of which turns on the strict meaning of a subject term.

That more fundamental criterion could be formulated as:

[1]   A subject–predicate judgment is analytic (synthetic) iff the meaning of its predicate is (is not) contained in the concept of the subject term.

Such a criterion is standardly criticized for its restriction to judgments of subject–predicate form, but the restriction, and other problems, can be remedied by reformulating [1] as:

[2]   A judgment is analytic (synthetic) iff its truth or falsity can (cannot) be determined solely by the meanings of its constituent terms.

That formulation reflects the intuitive idea that a judgment, such as "All bachelors are unmarried," can be determined as true solely by a proper understanding of its constituent terms, while this does not hold for such a judgment as "All bachelors are lonely." The former judgments can then be classified as "analytic" and the latter as "synthetic."

Kant also appeals to a "contradiction" test for analytic truths which can be formulated as:

[3]   A judgment is analytically (synthetically) true iff its denial yields (does not yield) a contradiction.

[3] reflects the intuitive idea that to deny a true analytic judgment such as "All bachelors are unmarried" yields the contradictory "Some bachelors are married," but that idea conceals a difficulty. It draws attention to, but does not resolve, a conflict between applying the classifications to "judgments," as in [2], or to "true judgments," as in [3]. We have to recognize that analytic judgments can also be false, as "Some bachelors are married" is. But plainly to deny that false analytic judgment will yield not a contradiction but the analytic *truth* "All bachelors are unmarried."

[3] can be amended by adding a formulation for analytic/synthetic *judgments* as well as *truths*:

[3a]   A judgment is analytic (synthetic) iff either it or its denial (neither it nor its denial) is a contradiction.

That problem is easy to remedy but a more serious difficulty arises. Even if [2] and [3] are accepted as separate fundamental criteria it is not obvious that they classify judgments (or truths) in the same way. A complex theorem in logic or mathematics may be proved by demonstrating that its denial is a contradiction, but that does not mean that its truth was determinable just by understanding its constituent terms. I may understand Euclid's algorithm without having the least idea whether its denial is a contradiction.

Characteristically such "indirect" proofs in logic or mathematics may be complex and involve a large range of other judgments and other concepts. It is tempting to say that the truth of such a theorem *must* be determinable through the meanings of all the constituents of all the judgments involved on the ground that if such truths are *not* established by empirical evidence then there is no alternative to their depending on meanings alone. But this begs the question against Kant's position whose central feature is that those two options are *not* exhaustive. Although it is widely accepted among empiricists that there is no third possibility – either truths are demonstrable through empirical evidence or through meaning alone – it is an essential part of Kant's anti-empiricism that this is an error. His classification is designed to mark that error by separating the criteria for "synthetic/analytic" and "a posteriori/a priori" in order to license the synthetic a priori classification.

That defense against an empiricist assumption nevertheless shows that [2] and [3] are not obviously equivalent. Some analytic truths, licensed as such by a contradiction test [3], may not be licensed in the same way by criterion [2]. It may be that satisfaction of criterion [2] entails satisfaction of criterion [3], but it is not obvious that the entailment works in the opposite direction. Just as [2] and [3] are evidently more fundamental for Kant than the "explicative/ampliative" criterion, so [3] is consequently more fundamental than [2]. [2] is a special case where analyticity can be determined immediately by consideration of a judgment's own constituents.

To make [3] Kant's fundamental criterion is to defuse part of Quine's influential criticism of the "analytic/synthetic" distinction (Quine 1980). Quine's primary objection is to a conception of "analytic truth" which requires reference to the meaning of constituents in a judgment, and so to criterion [2] rather than [3]. It rests on his belief that appeals to meanings, and more generally to intensional rather than extensional features of language, are inadequate, although he accepts a conception of logical truth determined by the formal features of an extensional logic. Kant's contradiction criterion is not explicitly restricted to any particular form of logic, or to any particular test procedure, and it is not explicitly restricted to Quine's preferred extensional logic, but that restriction is in any case questionable. Even the logical truths of Quine's preferred extensional, propositional and predicate, logic, in their intended interpretation, rest on the meanings of "formal" expressions such as "if . . . then . . . ," "either . . . or . . . ," "not," "all," and "some." Quine's objections are so far inconclusive.

2. Synthetic A Priori Judgments

Kant's novel synthetic a priori classification requires the establishment of the possibility that some judgments may be both a priori, knowable without appeal to empirical evidence, and yet fail to meet the contradiction criterion [3] for analyticity. Although it would be helpful to find *examples* of such judgments, I focus on the minimal requirement that such a classification is consistent. Kant's *proofs* of the transcendental synthetic a priori principles (*CPR*, B 187–294), which provide his most important examples, involve a complex and controversial *application* of the apparatus rather than its formal definition.

The new classification faces opposition from two quarters. On one side are those, influenced by Quine, who *reject* the distinction between analytic and synthetic judgments, and on the other those who *accept* the analytic/synthetic distinction but treat it as equivalent to the a priori/a posteriori contrast. The former objections have been already set aside as inconclusive, but the latter represent a typically empiricist doctrine radically at odds with Kant's anti-empiricism, and expressible in the following way:

> Twentieth century empiricists such as Ayer have maintained that a proposition can be known a priori only if it is analytic, i.e. true in virtue of the meanings of the words in it, rather than in virtue of the way the world is. On this account all a priori knowledge is of analytic truths; synthetic truths can be known only empirically. (Dancy 1989: 213–14)

The account effectively equates the analytic/synthetic and a priori/a posteriori distinctions. It is motivated by the natural and tempting assumption that there is an exhaustive and exclusive opposition between the way the world is, expressed only in synthetic propositions, known only through empirical procedures, and the analytic truths which merely reflect the meanings we attach to words. The assumption is tempting because we may think of "the way the world is" as wholly *independent* of our means of describing it. It may seem puzzling or absurd to say that the way the world is depends on us, on our language or our cognitive powers. Kant's claim that we can have a priori knowledge of the world, and not merely a priori knowledge of the meaning relations among our concepts, asserts a *dependence* between us, our cognitive powers or our language, and the world of our experience. Synthetic a priori truths are those which can be known a priori but are not analytic; they are not merely linguistic effects but purport to tell us something of the way the world is. Synthetic a priori *transcendental* principles express the governing rules of our experience; they make that experience and its objective standards possible. Kant claims that such principles stand apart from, and *constitute*, experience; without them our objective experience would be strictly impossible.

The position is succinctly expressed in the (B) Preface account of his "Copernican revolution" by contrasting the two, empiricist and Kantian, alternatives:

> Either I must assume that the concepts, by means of which I obtain this determination, conform to the object, or else I assume that the objects, or what is the same thing, that the *experience* in which alone . . . they can be known, conform to the concepts. In the former

case I am in the same perplexity as to how I can know anything a priori in regard to the objects. In the latter case the outlook is more hopeful. For experience is itself a species of knowledge which involves understanding; and understanding has rules which I must presuppose as being in me prior to objects being given to me, and therefore as being a priori. (*CPR*, B xvii; translations from Kant 1929, 1996)

The passage expresses Kant's anti-empiricist conviction that the world of our experience, the way the world is for us, *cannot* be totally divorced from the fundamental principles, neither merely analytic nor merely a posteriori, which govern it and make it intelligible.

Kant's novel classification questions Ayer's empiricist assumption of an exclusive and exhaustive opposition between the world and meanings, but to identify that dubious assumption may seem insufficient to support that classification more positively. Even the surrounding explanation of metaphysical principles governing experience may seem inadequate without the further detail provided in the proofs of the principles. But, with some provisos, Kant's formal position is further supported by a similar classification in Kripke 1972. There are significant differences between the two accounts, for Kripke has at his disposal a highly developed modal logic with a formal semantics, which Kant lacks. He also employs concepts in his apparatus, such as "rigid designation" and "necessity," which Kant either lacks or understands differently, and provides examples markedly different from those which Kant gives. Nevertheless on this central point, about an assumed exhaustive opposition between the way the world is and the meanings of words, Kant and Kripke are in agreement.

Kripke makes the point by asking why we should *assume* that anything knowable *a priori* must hold in *all* possible worlds. If Ayer takes analytic truths to hold in all possible worlds while synthetic truths hold only in some but not all possible worlds, then the assumption Kripke questions is Ayer's. It is the assumption that we cannot know anything a priori which holds only in some, but not all, possible worlds, and so is synthetic. Kripke puts the point thus:

> This assumption depends on the belief that there can't be a way of knowing about the actual world without looking, which wouldn't be a way of knowing the same thing about every possible world. (Kripke 1972: 262–3)

He consequently admits a classification of judgments as "contingent a priori" which opposes Ayer's view just as Kant's classification of "synthetic a priori" judgments does. Despite terminological differences Kripke and Kant accept the following:

Kripke: There are ways of knowing about the actual world without looking (a priori ways) which yield truths holding in some but not all possible worlds (i.e. are contingent).

Kant: There are ways the world actually is (i.e. reported in synthetic judgment) which can be known without presented experience (looking) (i.e. are a priori).

Although the examples offered by Kant and Kripke of these novel judgments are of different kinds, there is one point of contact in their explanations for such judgments. Kripke raises a question to which Kant's explanation provides an answer:

130

That means that in some sense it is possible . . . to know (something) independently of experience [a priori]. And possible for whom? For God? For the Martians? Or just for people with minds like ours. (Kripke 1972: 260)

It is a central part of Kant's positive metaphysics that some such judgments reflect a dependence on our cognitive powers. Kant's answer to Kripke's question is to reject any reference to God or to the Martians but to insist, for the reasons given, that what is known a priori, independent of experience, holds for subjects with *minds like ours*. It points to a formulation for synthetic a priori truth in which such judgments hold true in all possible worlds whose inhabitants have sufficiently similar cognitive powers to ours. They do not hold, as analytic truths do for Kant, in all possible worlds, but only in that limited subset whose subjects share with us those cognitive powers. Kant does not develop such a scheme in detail, but his primary point is formal and makes no immediate commitment to a traditional idealist account of the way we are supposed to "construct" or "make" the outer (external) world.

3. A Priori Elements

The quotation from B xvii makes clear that Kant talks not only of synthetic priori *judgments* but also of a priori *elements* with a distinctive governing role in our experience. The subjudgmental elements Kant identifies in the *Critique* are expressed in concepts whether formally classified as intuitions belonging to sensibility, such as space and time, or as categories belonging to understanding. But the criteria for synthetic a priori *judgments*, which make reference to their truth or falsity, cannot be carried over directly to identify those a priori, subjudgmental, *elements*, for the latter cannot be called true or false. In another use in the Dialectic of the first *Critique* and later in the third *Critique* Kant allows certain ideas of reason and their principles to be knowable a priori, but only as regulative injunctions and not as constitutive truths. (See the editorial introduction to Part IV, below; see also chapters 13 and 29 below.)

There is consequently no use for such expressions as "synthetic/analytic concept" or "synthetic a priori concept/intuition." One connection between the two aspects was already noted in the link between the formal characterization of the former and their metaphysical explanation. Synthetic a priori truths are those which hold in all possible worlds with similar cognitive powers to ours, and the cognitive powers are those associated with a priori intuitions (sensibility) and categories (understanding). It has been already noted that a priori concepts/intuitions are those claimed to be "independent" of presented experience, or not derivable from that experience. It is for this reason that the criterion of "independence from presented experience" is the more fundamental criterion for a priority.

That connection fills out the Kantian picture in his metaphysics, but it does not explain any formal link between synthetic a priori judgments and a priori elements. It would be an error to suppose that a priori elements can be identified because they alone occur in a priori, or even synthetic a priori, judgments. Analytic a priori truths may contain a posteriori concepts as subjects and predicates, so long as the connection between them is itself analytic. Synthetic a priori truths, such as those in mathematics, natural science, and metaphysics may also contain a posteriori concepts. Kant's Second Analogy principle that every event has, or presupposes, a cause uses "event" which Kant does not regard as an a priori concept.

A more adequate way of making the link indicates also another less noticed but important aspect of Kant's analytic apparatus. For it might be said that there is a possible way of "abstracting" from given judgments those elements, concepts, which are at least prima facie candidates for a priori status. The procedure requires that in any judgment that is already licensed as a priori, whether analytic or synthetic, the constituent concepts can be abstracted and considered separately for a priori status. We can first reject those judgments which are analytic a priori or synthetic a posteriori, and then, among synthetic a priori judgments, reject their constituent concepts which are clearly a posteriori, that is, derived from presented experience. Any remaining concepts will be *candidates* for a priori status. They will need a proof to be adequately validated as a priori, but Kant offers just such proofs in the Expositions of the Aesthetic, for a priori intuitions, and in the proofs of categories and their principles in the Analytic. Such an "abstraction" procedure is outlined at B 5–6.

> If we remove from our empirical concept of any object, corporeal or incorporeal, all properties which experience has taught us, we yet cannot take away that property through which the object is thought as a substance. Owing therefore to the necessity with which this concept . . . forces itself upon us we have no option but to admit that it has its seat in our faculty of a priori knowledge.

This "abstraction" or "separation" method is an important part of Kant's analytic apparatus throughout the Critical works. Kant's own preferred identification of categories, in the Metaphysical Deduction, by abstracting categories from *forms* of judgment is not the same as that outlined above, but it follows the same general procedure (see chapter 10 below). The view evidently is that a priori elements do not appear in their pure form in our experience, but have to be excavated, or disentangled, from that experience. Experience, in ordinary life or in science, does not come with its separate elements duly distinguished and labeled. The task of a reformed metaphysics is to accept that experience as a datum precisely in order to disentangle from its complex mixture of subjudgmental *elements* those which are a posteriori and those which are a priori, and among *judgments* those which are synthetic or analytic, a posteriori or a priori. We have to be content with a "modest analytic of concepts" rather than an ambitious "ontology" (B 303).

Whatever conclusions Kant may draw about the traditional philosophical theories he criticizes, such as idealism, realism, empiricism, rationalism, skepticism, and dogmatism, his approach is to provide a correct classification of those elements in experience which supports those criticisms. In the Amphiboly Kant speaks of this method as that of "transcendental reflection," and of its outcome as a "transcendental topic," that is, an accurate map in which the fundamental, structural, features of our experience are correctly located in relation to each other. The procedure is not confined to the first *Critique*, but is evident in the *Groundwork*'s "transitions" from "common rational to philosophical moral cognition" and from "popular moral philosophy to metaphysics of morals" (G 4.392) and elsewhere.

I have adopted in this work the method that is, I believe, most suitable if one wants to proceed analytically from common cognition to the determination of its supreme principle. (G 4.392; translation from Kant 1996)

An important corollary of this method is that those items, typically labeled "transcendental," which are finally isolated as "pure a priori," should be understood not as designating any *actual* items. Just as we may theoretically abstract and distinguish salient syntactic and semantic aspects from given utterances, so we may abstract and distinguish pure, a priori, elements from a given experience. Just as we cannot suppose that the former identify distinctly identifiable syntactic or semantic elements *divorced* from their respective semantic or syntactic accompaniments in speech, so we cannot identify a pure intuition of space or time as a *distinct* item in experience without reference to the presentation of a posteriori particulars located in space and time. The abstracted pure a priori elements of experience designate actual objects neither in our experience nor in any transcendent realm beyond it. In the *Groundwork* Kant talks of isolating the pure concepts of morality "in abstracto" and of the resulting metaphysics as "mixed with no anthropology, theology, physics, or hyperphysics, and still less with occult qualities (which could be called 'hypophysical')" (G, 4.409–10).

Kant has a particular reason to emphasize this lesson. For it is philosophically *tempting* to suppose that the pure elements identified in this abstraction procedure as "transcendental" designate items which because they cannot be found *in* experience *must* therefore exist beyond it. The temptation is to recognize the distinctive, abstract, nature of the fundamental elements of our experience but to think that they refer to items not in, but beyond, that experience, that is, to invest them with the ambitious ontological significance of B 303.

> But since it is very tempting to use these pure a priori modes of knowledge of the understanding . . . by themselves, and even beyond the limits of experience . . . the understanding is led to incur the risk of making, with a mere show of rationality, a material use of its pure and merely formal principles and of passing judgment on objects without distinction . . . which are not given to us and perhaps cannot be given. (*CPR*, B 87–8)

> The categories . . . without schemata are merely functions of the understanding for concepts; and represent no object. (*CPR*, B 186–7)

Such expressions as "transcendental synthesis" or "transcendental self" may, wrongly, be taken to signify some activity or thing quite independent of our *actual* experience of synthesizing or of selves. To understand Kant's abstraction method in that "hypostatizing" way is to confuse his terms "transcendental" and "transcendent" (*CPR*, B 370–1, B 610, B 647: see section 5 below). It is to subvert the basic lessons of Kant's philosophical therapy in the Dialectic which, typically, involve the unmasking of the "sophistical illusion" in just this error (*CPR*, B 88; see chapter 13 below). The abstracted pure forms of our experience *are* identified transcendentally but do *not* have for us transcendent, supersensible, referents.

4. Analytic and Synthetic Method

Kant also distinguishes in the *Prolegomena* between its "analytic" method (*Lehrart*) and the "synthetic method" of the *Critique*. The accounts given of this distinction (*Prol.*, 4.263–4; 4.274–5; A xxi) are puzzling and have been criticized, but they can be naturally and easily fitted into the account already given of Kant's project. Of the two passages from the *Prolegomena* the former rests on the more explicit and extensive later discussion.

> In the *Critique* my aim was to deal synthetically with the question: Is metaphysics in general possible? I therefore enquired into pure reason itself and looked in a principled way at that source for its elements and the laws of its pure use. Such a task is difficult and needs a determined reader who can gradually think himself into a system which has no ground but reason itself and which, without relying on any facts, seeks to develop [*entwickeln*] knowledge from its original seeds.
>
> The *Prolegomena* is, on the contrary, to be a preliminary exercise; to show what has to be done in order to realize a science rather than to prosecute it. Consequently it has to use something already known to be reliable from which one can confidently proceed to the sources which are not yet known, and whose elucidation will present not only what we know but also at the same time surrounding knowledge from those same sources. This method for the *Prolegomena*, which is to prepare for a future metaphysics, will consequently be "analytic." (*Prol.*, 4.274–5: author's translations)

The account has been criticized for failing to identify real differences between Kant's two works, and for a fundamental and unresolved ambivalence (Guyer 1987: 6–7). One way of characterizing that ambivalence is to regard the synthetic method as *assuming* certain universal and necessary truths while the analytic method is designed to *justify* them. That distinction is associated also with a suggested ambiguity in Kant according to whether he accepts or rejects our legitimate knowledge of reality. But I set that point aside with the claims that Kant evidently licenses immanent knowledge of *objects of experience* but rejects transcendent knowledge of *things in themselves* in both the *Prolegomena* and the *Critique of Pure Reason*.

Although the passage from the *Prolegomena* does not make a clear differentiation between the two works, it can be defended against some of these criticisms. In apparent conflict with the quoted passage Kant also represents the *Critique* as a preliminary exercise, as a "propaedeutic," to the development of a substantive metaphysics (*CPR*, A xx–xxi; B xliii–xlv; B 25). *Both* works are represented as *preparations* for the development of such a science. It is also true that Kant's conception of the two "methods" ambiguously represents them as methods of "discovery" or methods of "exposition," but I argue that this is not the central distinction at issue.

The primary difference between the procedures of the two works is that the *Prolegomena* takes the established sciences, mathematics and natural science, as data from which to identify their conditions, while the *Critique* does not. The *Prolegomena* examines in detail the articulation of those disciplines in order to make a comparison with the scientific aspirations of metaphysics. In the *Critique*, although references are made to the sciences (Introduction B 14–19, Transcendental Expositions [B 40–2,

B 48–9]) they do not provide the basic data for the enquiry. There the a priori structure for experience is identified, as Kant says, from abstract arguments in the Metaphysical Expositions of the Aesthetic and the Metaphysical Deduction. As he puts it: in the *Prolegomena* the established sciences are taken as data for the enquiry, but in the *Critique* the argument proceeds from an examination of reason itself, conceived as the supreme cognitive power overseeing our uses of sensibility and understanding in a general experience not restricted to the sciences. I suggest that the best way to understand this is to see the *Critique* as accepting that general experience in order to disclose its a priori structure, even in the sciences, through those metaphysical arguments, while the *Prolegomena* starts with acceptance of the established sciences. The procedure in the *Critique* is said to be "difficult" and "to require determination" because of its appeal to those abstract metaphysical arguments, but in some ways its data are even more readily available. For they amount to no more than our nonscientific experience including our fundamental psychology.

Nothing in such an account separates the ultimate goals of the two works. Both aim to identify the underlying preconditions of our experience, but one starts with established sciences as the data and the other starts more generally with our cognitive powers of sensibility and understanding beneath an overarching reason. These are merely different ways of arriving at the same terminus from different starting points. Nor can such a difference properly be characterized as a difference between methods of discovery and exposition. We might indifferently *both* discover *and* give an exposition of the underlying structure of experience in *either* way.

The significant distinction is not that between "discovery" and "exposition," but between "justification" on one side and both "exposition" and "discovery" on the other. Since Kant's project is patently *not* designed to justify knowledge of transcendent things in themselves, the crucial question is whether either method, so outlined, is designed to *justify* or only to *articulate* the structure of experience. The former is the traditional task of a normative philosophy which aims to justify our beliefs in the face of a skeptical challenge. The latter is the task of a descriptive metaphysics which aims to articulate accurately the structure of our experience without immediate prompting from skepticism. The aim is then to construct an accurate map, a transcendental topic, of our experience, and only then to consider how far its correction of earlier maps yields antiskeptical conclusions about that experience. If a skeptic's arguments are shown to be based on an inaccurate conception of experience, then those arguments can be set aside.

The earlier discussion (in section 3) showed that Kant's project has at its center the latter, descriptive, and not the former, normative, task, but the suggested ambivalence over methods then disappears. Kant's primary interest is in mapping the contours of appearances within our possible experience and in resisting the temptation to conjure up a realm of transcendent things in themselves beyond it. His secondary interest is to demonstrate that earlier doctrines such as idealism and realism, dogmatism and skepticism, committed those demonstrated inaccuracies. Typically Kant's demonstrations turn on revisions in the order of priorities given by earlier philosophers to elements in experience, such as his reversal of the priority accorded in traditional idealism to inner experience over outer in the Refutation of Idealism (B 274–9) (see chapter 12 below).

5. The Empirical/Transcendental Distinction

Just as the distinction between analytic and synthetic methods has seemed puzzling, so the distinction between empirical and transcendental enquiries, or claims, has also seemed mysterious and objectionable to some commentators. Despite its evident importance in outlining Kant's distinctively philosophical approach, it is defined casually in two early passages at B 25 and B 80–1.

> I entitle "transcendental" all knowledge which is occupied not so much with objects as with our mode of knowledge of objects insofar as this mode is to be possible a priori. (*CPR*, B 25)

> Here I make a remark which the reader must bear well in mind as it extends its influence over all that follows. Not every kind of knowledge a priori should be called "transcendental," but only that by which we know that – and how – certain representations (intuitions or concepts) . . . are possible a priori. The term "transcendental" signifies . . . such knowledge as concerns the a priori possibility of knowledge or its a priori employment. Neither space nor any a priori geometrical determination of it is a transcendental representation; what alone can be entitled transcendental is the knowledge that these representations are not of empirical origin, and the possibility that that they can yet relate a priori to objects of experience. . . . The distinction between the transcendental and the empirical belongs therefore only to the critique of knowledge; it does not concern the relation of that knowledge to its objects. (CPR, B 80–1)

Both passages indicate initially the importance of the distinction, and its higher-order status in identifying a priori knowledge and explaining its role and possibility in experience. The suggestion is that philosophy has that higher-order task of categorizing and explaining knowledge in science and more general experience rather than *adding* to our scientific knowledge of objects.

One difficulty in the passages results from an ambiguity in Kant's use of the term "empirical." There "empirical" is contrasted with "transcendental," although in other passages it is natural to equate it with "a posteriori" and contrast it with "a priori" knowledge. The quotations make clear that the "empirical/transcendental" contrast is not to be *equated* with the "a posteriori/a priori" distinction. For not *all* a priori knowledge, specifically not that in the sciences, is to be called "transcendental" or "philosophical." The difficulty is compounded by Kant's inclusion among the sciences of formal disciplines such as mathematics, whose judgments are *not* a posteriori but a priori. Commentators find it difficult to accept that Kant could use "empirical" to include those nonphilosophical but a priori judgments in such a science, but the correct response is to recognize that Kant uses the term in two distinct ways. "Empirical$_1$" *can* be equated with "a posteriori" and is then contrasted with "a priori"; "empirical$_2$" cannot be *equated* with "a posteriori" and is contrasted not with "a priori" but with "transcendental." A judgment that is a posteriori must be empirical$_2$, but some empirical$_2$ (nontranscendental) judgments are a priori.

Another difficulty arises from Kant's later elaboration of his apparatus in which the central "transcendental/empirical" distinction is associated with a contrast between what is "immanent" and what is "transcendent." Although the latter distinction is implicit throughout Kant's therapeutic exercise in the Dialectic it is formally introduced only at B 351–3:

> We shall entitle the principles whose application is confined entirely within the limits of possible experience, *immanent*; and those on the other hand which profess to pass beyond those limits, *transcendent*. . . . Thus *transcendental* and *transcendent* are not interchangeable terms. The principles of pure understanding . . . allow only of empirical and not transcendental employment, that is employment extending beyond the limits of experience. A principle . . . which takes away those limits or even commands us to transgress them, is called *transcendent*. If our criticism can succeed in disclosing the illusion in these alleged principles then those which are of merely empirical employment may be called *immanent* principles of pure understanding. (*CPR*, B 352–3)

Despite Kant's efforts to separate what is transcendental from what is transcendent commentators have thought his use of these terms inconsistent even in this passage where they are first introduced. Sometimes when he says "transcendental" it seems that he should have used "transcendent," but this handicap can also be remedied. What is needed is to recognize that "transcendental" and "transcendent" are not contradictories and that the former is the genus of which the transcendent and the immanent uses are, respectively, the illusory and genuine species. What is transcendent is the illusorily philosophical, and what is transcendental is the philosophically genuine use. The apparent inconsistencies in Kant's usage mostly stem from the mistaken belief that transcendental and transcendent are opposed coordinate species, but Kant's claim that they are "not interchangeable" is not committed to that view. The alternative is to recognize that they are not interchangeable and not equivalent, but that one is the genus of which the other is its illusory species. The *contradictory* opposition among *uses* of the relevant principles is "immanent/transcendent," and these terms characterize precisely the two kinds of metaphysics, one genuine one spurious, which Kant respectively advocates and rejects.

Earlier (in section 3) it was noted that one example of the temptation to illusory/spurious philosophy arose from a misunderstanding about a method of "abstraction." The general goal of the *Critique* is to identify, to abstract, those elements, concepts, in our experience which are a priori, but their abstract form makes it impossible for them to designate identifiable items *in* experience. The philosophical temptation is then to think that they must designate items *beyond* our experience, that is, items, objects, things in themselves, which belong to a supposed realm of reason and of which we can gain knowledge through pure reason. That would be to use them wrongly as if they designated that occult realm of supersensible things in themselves noted in the *Groundwork* (see section 3 above; and *G*, 4.409–10). The fundamental message of the *Critique* is that this belief is wholly spurious, and a perennial philosophical danger both in the speculative, theoretical and in the practical, moral, context. Kant's belief is that the endless disputes in metaphysics are characteristically the result of just such confusions, and to unmask those illusions is a central therapeutic task necessary for his proposed reform of philosophy as a science, that is, as a discipline properly regulated by objective standards and principles. (See chapter 13 below.)

Conclusion

Although Kant's distinctions have both formal and philosophical importance, each has its own distinctive mix of formal and philosophical aspects. The contrasts in (1) between synthetic and analytic judgments and the consequent synthetic a priori classification in (2) can be introduced in a relatively formal way, although they involve informal assumptions and have philosophical consequences. Kant's separate accounts of the synthetic/analytic and a posteriori/a priori distinctions involve informal assumptions about "meaning" and "contradiction," as well as commitment to conceptions of truth, necessity, and the warrant for universal claims. The synthetic a priori classification provides a contentious characterization of judgments in science, mathematics, and metaphysics, but the latter are provided, in the Analytic of Principles, with proofs supporting their Kantian classification. That classification, and particularly its metaphysical examples, marks a central, and more formal, part of Kant's fundamental disagreement with a standard empiricism, and that is even more true of the identification and characterization of a priori elements in experience. Kant's method of "abstraction," outlined in 3 and 4, is designed to isolate and identify those elusive a priori elements in immanent experience, but his primary task in the Transcendental Deduction and Analytic of Principles is to demonstrate and support their role in that experience.

Partly because of that link between the formal and philosophical aspects of Kant's transcendental logic, the formal characterization of his distinctions in (1), (2), and (3), is incomplete by contemporary standards. Kant appeals to meaning but provides little in the way of a theory of meaning for either formal or natural languages. His accounts of necessity and of synthetic a priori judgments appeal to a conception of possible worlds which is not supported by an adequate formal treatment. The Critical philosophy quite generally appeals at all its crucial points to dependence relations among concepts, but Kant offers no formal account of those relations. These are inevitable weaknesses of omission, but do not by themselves constitute objections. Serious objections to his apparatus would have to say that no formal or informal account of some distinctions can be coherently given, and commentators have variously claimed that the synthetic/analytic distinction and the synthetic a priori classification are incoherent. Some of those objections have been set aside in the discussion, but the best way of meeting them would be to supplement Kant's account with an adequate formal representation. The best that can be done here is to say that if these aspects of his apparatus are defensible in the suggested ways, then the further pursuit of that formal goal is not excluded by the standard objections.

The more philosophical, rather than formal, contrasts arise in (4) and (5). Given that Kant's primary aim is to outline the structure of our immanent experience, and its "fruitful bathos" (*Prol.*, 4.373), the distinction between analytic and synthetic methods is only between different ways of outlining, or coming to recognize, that structure. The two methods differ in their direction of interest, and in their accessibility to readers, but their upshot is exactly the same: they are different ways of arriving at the same destination by different routes. They point importantly to a Kantian "descriptive" metaphysics but they indicate only different ways of carrying out, or presenting, that project. More important to the substance of Kant's philosophy are his appeals to an "abstraction" method and to the distinctions between "empirical/transcendental" and "immanent/transcendent" claims. One central negative idea is that the a priori elements abstracted from a posteriori experience tempt us to think that they designate actual objects. In Kant's tradition that temptation is associated with the rationalist belief that pure reason alone provides access to such objects and to truths about them.

Because such supposed objects cannot be exemplified in immanent, sensory, experience the temptation is to conjure up an additional world of reason to which they belong.

> So [pure] concepts of understanding appear to have far more content and significance than their use in experience might provide, and understanding surreptitiously builds for itself next door to the house of experience a far larger edifice which it then fills with pure thought-entities. It fails to notice that with these otherwise legitimate concepts it has overstepped the bounds of their use. (*Prol.* §33, 4.315–16)

Kant's vehement belief that this is a central error throughout traditional philosophy is captured in his distinctions between the empirical and the transcendental, the immanent and the transcendent. These have also often been regarded as incoherent, but the suggestion is that they can be given a clear sense and express a fundamental criterion for philosophical legitimacy, namely that its claims are confined to immanent experience and do not "run riot" into the transcendent. Despite Kant's controversial defense of freedom against causal determinism that criterion still holds in Kant's moral philosophy (see *CPrR* 5.56–7; and chapter 18 below). The distinctions, and the restrictions they impose on a legitimate metaphysics, form an essential part of Kant's prescription for the reformed discipline. Although largely ignored or misunderstood throughout the nineteenth century they should have had as much of an impact on philosophy as the later revolutions of the Logical Positivists, or Russell, or Wittgenstein, which marked a transition from the nineteenth to the twentieth century (see chapter 33 below).

References and Further Reading

Ayer, A. J. (1936). *Language, Truth and Logic.* London: Gollancz.

Dancy, J. (1989). *Introduction to Epistemology.* Oxford: Blackwell.

Guyer, P. (1987). *Kant and the Claims of Knowledge.* Cambridge: Cambridge University Press.

Hume, D. (1902). *Enquiry concerning Human Understanding,* ed. L. A. Selby-Bigge. Oxford: Clarendon Press.

Kant, Immanuel (1929). *Critique of Pure Reason,* tr. N. Kemp Smith. London: Macmillan.

Kant, Immanuel (1996). *Groundwork of the Metaphysics of Morals.* In *Practical Philosophy,* tr. Mary J. Gregor. Cambridge: Cambridge University Press.

Kripke, S. (1972). Naming and necessity. In D. Davidson and G. Harman (eds.), *Semantics of Natural Language* (pp. 253–355). Dordrecht: D. Reidel.

Leibniz, G. W. (1991). *Monadology,* tr. G. Montgomery. La Salle, IL: Open Court.

Locke, John (1975). *An Essay Concerning Human Understanding,* ed. P. H. Nidditch. Oxford: Oxford University Press.

Quine, W. V. O. (1980). Two dogmas of empiricism. In *From a Logical Point of View,* 2nd ed. Cambridge, MA: Harvard University Press.

Strawson, P. F. (1966). *The Bounds of Sense.* London: Methuen.

9

Kant's Transcendental Aesthetic

LORNE FALKENSTEIN

Kant's Transcendental Aesthetic is a study of the human senses (B 35n). However, for reasons given below, it focuses on our representation of space and time. It can be divided into three main parts. Section 1 and the first paragraph of section 2 offer introductory comments on the human cognitive capacities and the purpose of the Aesthetic. The remainder of section 2, the first half of section 3, and sections 4–5 offer a number of brief demonstrations, called the "metaphysical" and "transcendental expositions." The second half of section 3 and sections 6–8 draw conclusions from these "expositions" and comment on these conclusions. The conclusions and comments comprise a preliminary statement and defense of the theory of transcendental idealism – an account of the nature of the objects of knowledge that is the central doctrine taught by the *Critique*.

The Introductory Sections

The Aesthetic opens with a capsule account of human cognition. As I have detailed (Falkenstein 1995: 17–142), this account ascribes two distinct cognitive capacities or "faculties" to human beings: a sensory faculty (*Sinnlichkeit*, often translated as "sensibility"), and an intellectual faculty (*Verstand*, often translated as "understanding"). Kant described the former as the capacity to receive representations (*Vorstellungen*), and the latter as the capacity to think, a capacity that he further described as involving concepts (*Begriffe*). He also claimed that only sense gives us intuitions (*Anschauungen*). Aside from a description of intuition as a representation that is immediately related to the object of knowledge, Kant did not define any of these terms. He would not have felt any need to. He used "representation" indiscriminately, to designate any kind of mental content, including purely subjective feelings (*CPR*, B 376). The terms "sensus," "intellectus," "intuitus," and "conceptus" (which Kant understood as the Latin equivalents of his German terms) are more specific. They have had a long history and Kant intended to both draw on this history (B 368–9) and resurrect its central feature (B 327). But while he did not define any of these terms, he did remark on how and why he meant to diverge from common ways of understanding them. If we are to understand him today, we must be aware of both the traditional meanings and his divergences.

As paradigmatically articulated by Aristotle (*De Anima* Books II and III), the sensory capacity is the capacity to perceive particulars. The intellectual capacity, in contrast, is the capacity to grasp universals. A concept is a grasp of a universal. For Aristotle, universals can only be grasped by inspecting previously sensed particulars, so that for him the intellect is dependent on the information supplied by the senses and directed to that information.

In the scholastic tradition, the term "intuitive" was used to refer to whatever is cognized immediately, that is, independently of any cognitive operation performed upon something previously cognized (Boler 1982). The contrasting term, "discursive," was used to refer to cognition that is obtained mediately, through relating previously cognized items to one another (paradigmatically, through joining subject concepts with predicate concepts to form propositions that figure in the internal mental "discourse" Kant labeled "thought"). The Aristotelian view that the intellect operates on what has previously been given by the senses entails that it must be a discursive capacity.

In conscious opposition to the dominant rationalist and empiricist tenets of his day, Kant agreed that human beings have distinct sensory and intellectual faculties (B 29, B 74, B 75–6, B 327). But in opposition to Aristotle and the Scholastics he insisted that neither can yield knowledge on its own. For Kant, our senses are insufficient for the perception of particular objects. Perception only occurs when the information acquired by the senses is recognized as an instance of an object of a certain kind. This necessarily involves a concept (the concept of a kind of object) as well as an act of judging that the sensory information falls under the concept. Apart from this characteristically discursive operation, which invokes concepts and hence involves the intellect, we can still be affected by objects and can still have sensory experiences (B 122), but insofar as we do not categorize these experiences we know nothing (B 74–6). Consequently, rather than identify the senses and the intellect as the capacities to know particulars and universals, Kant identified them by how they work. The senses are passive. They only supply us with representations insofar as they are affected. The intellect, in contrast, is active or "spontaneous" (B 92–3).

Kant nonetheless agreed that our intellectual faculty is discursive or dependent on the senses. But this is not because the intellect can only abstract universals from particulars previously grasped by the senses. He maintained that the intellect can spontaneously produce concepts (called "pure" concepts). But a spontaneously produced concept can only provide knowledge of an object if the act of producing the concept also brings objects instantiating that concept into being. Human intellects cannot do that. Because objects exist independently of our thought, we can know them only insofar as they make their presence felt by affecting us. This is why Kant declared that only our senses are intuitive. Our intellects can give us knowledge of particulars only through subsuming the representations supplied by the senses under concepts (B 135, B 138–9, B 145). Even pure concepts can only be applied in a discursive context to judge that a particular sensory experience is an instance of a certain type of experience. They cannot provide knowledge of an object apart from application to sensory experience (B 93).

Kant's use of the term "intuition" to refer to the representations supplied by the senses is idiosyncratic. Other early modern philosophers referred to the representations delivered by our senses as "sensations." However, Kant used the corresponding German term, *Empfindung*, in a more restrictive sense. He defined it as "the effect of an object on the representative capacity, insofar as we are affected by it" (B 34). But he also noted that

> it could well be that even what we recognize through experience is a composite of something that we sense as a consequence of impressions on our senses and something else that our cognitive capacity provides on its own on the occasion of such impressions. (B 1; translations from Kant 1998)

Insofar as sensation is a function of what objects happen to affect us, it constitutes the "properly empirical" or a posteriori component in intuitions – the component that can only be known after being affected (B 59–60). But if, as Kant speculated at B 1, our intuitions also contain something that our sensory faculty provides on its own on the occasion of sensory stimulation, then this component would be knowable a priori. Though we might not be able to identify it prior to some experience or other, its presence would be independent of what objects might happen to affect us. Our knowledge of it would therefore not depend on an encounter with any particular object.

One of the main projects of the *Critique of Pure Reason* is to establish that there are indeed such a priori components in our representations, and to show that they are contributed by both of the cognitive faculties. The Aesthetic is devoted to showing that this is the case with sense, and the Analytic that it is the case with the intellect. Indeed, the Aesthetic focuses on this task to the exclusion of the sort of study of our various sensations and the knowledge they enable us to obtain that had been previously undertaken in Condillac's *Traité des sensations* or Reid's *Inquiry into the Human Mind*. Kant's study of the senses is, as he qualified it, a transcendental Aesthetic, focused on demonstrating that there is an a priori component injected by the sensory faculty into experience and that this component serves as a basis for a priori knowledge. This is how it comes to devote so much attention to space, time, and mathematics and so little to an account of our various sensations and empirical knowledge.

Kant defined an "empirical intuition" as "an intuition that is related to its object through sensation" (B 34). Since intuitions are by definition immediately related to their objects, this makes sense only if sensations are taken to be components of intuitions. But Kant thought that empirical intuitions contain something more than just sensations. To make this point, he switched from speaking of empirical intuitions to ask us to consider the particular objects that we come to perceive through subsuming these intuitions under concepts – objects that he referred to as "appearances" (*Erscheinungen*). These objects contain some "matter" (*Materie*) that, he claimed, corresponds to sensation. But the various matters that make up an appearance, are also ordered in accord with certain relations – specifically, spatial and temporal relations. The "matters" have a spatial position relative to one another, and so are ordered in space, and the appearances have a history, consisting of a succession of states ordered in time. This suggests that, as the "matters" in the appearance correspond to sensation, so the spatial and temporal order of the matters corresponds to a spatial and temporal order among sensations, and Kant in fact proceeded to speak of sensations as being "ordered and set forth in a certain form" (B 34). He further claimed that this form is an a priori contribution of the mind that can be considered apart from all sensations, because "that in which sensations are ordered and set forth in a certain form cannot itself in turn be a sensation" (B 34). And he further claimed that this form is a characteristically spatial and temporal structure that is contributed by the sensory faculty to intuition so that even were everything that the intellect thinks through its concepts removed from appearances, and even were everything that belongs to sensation removed from intuition, extension and figure, and space and time, would still remain (B 34–5, B 36).

These claims are merely asserted in section 1 and need to be justified. Since perception cannot be divorced from intellectual acts of conception and judgment, some reason needs to be given for denying that the spatial and temporal orders of the "matters" of appearance arise by subsuming sensations under pure concepts. And some reason needs to be given for supposing that these orders are due to the constitution of our senses rather than to the objects that affect us. Kant's main project over the pages that follow was to prove that our representations of the spatial and temporal order of appearances originate neither from judgments nor from sensations.

Kant took the outcome of this project to have implications for our view of what space and time are. At the outset of section 2, he listed three alternative positions that might be taken on the ontological status of space and time:

i)   They are "actual beings" (*wirkliche Wesen*) that exist independently of the things in space and time, and so would continue to exist even were all other objects destroyed.

ii) They are properties or relations of the things in space and time (and so cannot exist apart from those things), though they belong to those things as they are in themselves.

iii) They are properties or relations that are ascribed to things only as a consequence of our cognitive constitution and that do not belong to those things as they are in themselves.

There had been considerable dispute over these options in the early modern period, particularly as concerns space. Newton (*Principia Mathematica*, def. 8 schol.) and Euler ("Réflexions sur l'espace et le temps") had argued that inertial motion presupposes an "absolute" space that serves as the ultimate reference frame for acceleration and hence that space must have some sort of existence independent of body. Descartes (*Principia Philosophiae*: pt. II, art. 16–18) and Berkeley (*De Motu*: §§54–5) had argued that, since all the properties of space are privative, it is tantamount to nothing, and all our concepts of space are in fact concepts of the extension and sequence of alterations in bodies. And Bayle (*Dictionnaire*, "Zeno," notes G and I) had invoked Zeno's paradoxes to argue that since space and extension cannot coherently be supposed to be either infinitely divisible or composed of atomic parts, our ideas of space and of spatially extended bodies cannot correspond to any actually existing thing.

Kant claimed that an analysis or "exposition" of our concepts of space and time could contribute something to this debate.

The Expositions

The Expositions are not identically numbered in the two editions or in the space and time sections of either edition, and they are distinguished as either "metaphysical" or "transcendental" in the second edition but not the first. But Kant at least made the same points in almost the same order. He appealed to the homogeneity, ubiquity, singularity, and unboundedness of space and time to draw the conclusions that our concepts of space and time are not concepts of the properties of the things in space and time, that they are concepts of a necessary feature of our experience, and that they cannot have originated from the intellect. Taken together, these points lead to the conclusion that our concepts of space and time must represent something originally given through sensory experience, rather than something contributed by the intellect to that experience, but that this thing must be a general "form," that all sensory experiences exhibit. An appeal to the special nature of our knowledge of geometrical and temporal principles proves that this form must be due to the constitution of the sensing subject rather than an effect of things as they are in themselves.

In more detail, Kant first claimed that referring sensations to objects at different places in space requires something more than is required for distinguishing those sensations from one another (B 38). Kant's point appears to be that if we take any two things that we experience as having a location in space, or any two arbitrarily small parts of such a thing and compare them with one another, we will discover nothing that tells us where they are located. The identical red color patch can occur anywhere on the visual field, for example. If we accept that all the parts of space are alike, then this makes sense: a change in place cannot be a change in any discernible feature. This means that our experience of the spatial order of things cannot be posterior to our experience of the things ordered in space. We do not first experience various objects, then compare them with one another, notice various ways in which they resemble one another, and finally deduce an order from these relations, as we do when we order colors by such features as hue, saturation, and brightness, or sensations of hardness, heat, or pain in terms of intensity. The same might be said of time. If we think that two objects are simultaneous it is not because, upon inspecting each of those objects in isolation, we discover some feature that both share in common. If we think that they are successive it is not because we discover that one has some feature to a greater degree than the other. (I argued for this interpretation in Falkenstein 1989. Warren [1998: 197–224] has independently argued for a variant on it.)

Kant proceeded to draw attention to a further difference between the spatiotemporal order and such qualitative orders as those of hues and color. He claimed that we can think of space and time as continuing to exist even were everything else in the world annihilated, but that nothing else can be represented without being located some-where in space, with the exception of my own mental states, which must occur at some time. From this he inferred that the representation of space and time is necessary for the representation of other things, but that the representation of other things is not reciprocally necessary for that of space and time.

Two main objections, classically stated by Kemp Smith (1923: 103–5), might be raised to this argument. One is that my inability to think something may not be a product of any deep-seated feature of either the external world or my cognitive consti-tution, but simply a temporary incapacity that could be rectified by further experience or effort. Someone who has not bitten into a pineapple cannot think what it tastes like, but subsequent experience will provide this ability. Someone who cannot think of the appearance of a chess board after the fifth move might be able, with some practice, to rectify this disability. The second objection is that the argument equivocates on the distinction between conceiving, forming a mental image, and perceiving. If the question is what we can conceive, then Kant himself allowed that we can conceive of objects that do not exist in space or time, such as spirits or freely acting minds. If the question is what we can image, then the point is trivial, since an image is by definition a spatially extended phenomenon. If the question is what we can perceive or know, then Kant himself was of the view that we are never in a position to perceive that any part of space is empty (B 261).

Some reply can be given to these objections if we consider that Kant asked us to imagine the result of removing something from what we have already experienced ("*in Ansehung* [*etwas*], [*etwas*] *aufheben*"; "[*etwas*] *aus* [*etwas*] *wegnehmen*"; B 46). My incapacity to imagine the taste of pineapple might be due to never having experienced a pineapple, or my incapacity to imagine the appearance of a chess board after the fifth move to not having practiced enough. If I now experience an object and am asked to imagine its appearance without one of its parts or properties (e.g., an apple without its taste or color, a currently seen hundred-sided figure without one of its sides), then my incapacity to perform the subtraction without losing the entire appearance in the process does argue for a connection between the two. That connection may not be logically necessary, but it is not merely a consequence of some temporary or idiosyncratic feature of my cognitive constitution.

Kant believed that we can think of aspatial objects and freely acting subjects, but argued throughout the Transcendental Dialectic that these thoughts do not arise from removing something from sensory experience, but from employing a pure intellectual concept without any reference to what is sensed. Conceptions of this sort are therefore not counterexamples to a claim that concerns what can be removed from what is sensed without destroying the entire appearance. And while Kant rejected appeals to empty space or time in physics, he did so because he believed that we could never be in a posi-tion to rule out the possibility that any given space is entirely filled with a repulsive force too weak to be detected by our senses (*MFNS*, 4.534–5). This is compatible with the space appearing to be empty, and if it can appear to be empty it can be imagined to be empty.

If we accept that space and time are necessary features of sensory experience, the next question is what accounts for this necessity. As a first step toward answering this question, Kant sought to rule out the possibility that spatial and temporal structure might arise from something due to the intellect. To establish this conclusion, he claimed that we believe particular spaces and times to be parts of a single, larger space and longer time. Moreover, he asserted, we do not conceive of these parts as individually given components that are subsequently assembled to form a larger space or longer time. Instead, we believe them to be delimited portions of a larger whole, originally given as having different locations within that whole.

Kant's background views on conception (*JL*, 9.91–100) – the operation characteristic of the intellect – help to show where he wanted to go with these claims. He accepted the traditional account of a concept as the thought of some "mark" or feature that a number of things can share in common, as well as the traditional account of genera and species, according to which concepts become more specific through the addition of "marks." He also believed that no list of "marks" could be known to apply to just one object. As he put it, there is no "lowest species." Even if a concept were in fact used to refer to just one object, we could never be certain that this one object does not possess further "marks" not contained in the concept – either because we have not noticed them or because we have deliberately disregarded them (*JL*, 9.97; cf. B 755–6). Consequently, there could be many objects that all exhibit the "marks" thought in any concept, but that differ from one another in "marks" not thought in the concept. Since we are never in a position to rule out this possibility, our concepts are inherently general. They can never be known to be more than "partial representations," that is, representations of a part of what we experience when we sense any particular object (B 48). Intuitions, in contrast, can never be known to be completely "bounded" by what is thought in concepts.

In light of the inherent generality of concepts, there would seem to be only two ways to account for the belief that a concept refers to just one object: either the concept refers to something originally given in sensory experience and our senses have only been able to discover one object that satisfies the concept; or even though the concept originates in the intellect, our intellect has imposed a singularity condition on its application. But the latter option does not sit well with the claim that particular spaces and times are conceived by drawing boundaries within a larger space and time. Since concepts are "partial representations," a cognition of space and time by means of imposed (intellectual) concepts should proceed from parts to whole. We should judge particular experiences to be instances of determinate shapes and intervals, judge these determinate shapes and intervals to have determinate relations to one another, and so construct a larger space and time by assembling individual spaces and times, under the guidance of a general intellectual demand that all spaces and times be integrated in a single whole. But if all our concepts of determinate spaces and times arise by drawing boundaries around shapes and intervals within surroundings that exceed those bounds, then the relation of any determinate part to its surroundings is already given. The fact that this network of already given relations turns out to constitute just one space and just one time is learned by what Kant called the progress of experience rather than imposed by the intellect.

Quinton (1962) famously claimed that it might be possible to have experience of two or more discrete spaces, but, a reference to the "essential unity" of space notwithstanding (B 39), Kant's argument is not especially invested in the singularity of space and time. The point is rather that, whether there is one space and time or more than one, that number is not determined by how the intellect subsumes experiences under concepts, but by what relations it finds between the spaces and times it subsumes under concepts and their surroundings. The unity of space and time may nonetheless be a condition of the intelligibility of experience (B 161n), but the fact that our experience is ultimately intelligible depends on what is given to the intellect to work with and not just on what it can do to it (B 122–3).

Kant invoked his views on the nature of concepts to offer a further argument for why our concept of space, in particular, must have been abstracted from something given in intuition. A concept can have an infinite extension (there can be infinitely many representations that fall under it or that share the marks it contains). But no concept, he claimed, can contain infinitely many representations. However, we believe that space contains infinitely many representations. This is supposed to prove that our concept of space must have been abstracted from something given in intuition. But, as Parsons (1964) has pointed out, it is hard to see how Kant could have felt entitled to claim that we intuit infinitely many simultaneously existing spaces.

If we grant Kant's arguments, they leave us with the conclusion that the ubiquity of spatiotemporal structure is not due to the fact that the human intellect is so constituted as to subsume all experiences under concepts of space and time. There remain two possibilities: that the necessity is grounded in the way that the world is, independently of us, or that it is grounded in the constitution of our senses. Some resolution of this question is suggested by Kant's remark that experience can only teach us that something *is* the case, not that it *must* be the case (B 1). Were the necessity of space and time grounded in the way the world is independently of us, we could only know of it through experience. But experience could only tell us that all objects that we have experienced so far have been in space and time, not that they must be. This might be taken to entail that the spatial and temporal features of our experience must be antecedently determined by features of our own constitution.

However Kant's argument for the necessity of space and time in the metaphysical expositions is not strong enough to support this inference. It only premises that we cannot imagine the removal of space and time from any of the objects we have so far experienced. That argument does not decide whether the necessity of space and time is strict or merely inductive. To further determine this question, Kant invoked the argument that in the second edition was entitled the "Transcendental Exposition."

The transcendental exposition focuses on what we know about space and time – knowledge that, in the case of space, is quite extensive and codified in the principles of geometry. Kant claimed that this knowledge does not follow from analysis of our concepts of space and time. It is not "analytic" that space has only three dimensions, that only a single straight line can be drawn between two points, or that two straight lines cannot enclose a space (B 41, A 24, B 65; see also chapter 8 above). But though such principles are not analytically true, they are nonetheless strictly necessary. We do not just think that no space we have so far experienced has proven to have more than three dimensions, but that no space we could possibly experience could have this feature. This means that the necessity of geometrical principles, and hence of the structure of space, which these principles describe, could not be grounded on the way the world is independently of us. Kant concluded that our representations of space and time must arise from the way our senses are constituted (B 41).

Since the function of the senses is to receive representations, and space and time are orders in which various elements can be disposed, it follows that our senses must be so constituted as to receive representations over space and time, and hence that space and time must be the "forms" of sensory experience. What items are disposed where is of course not something that can be anticipated (a priori). But that the space they are disposed in has a certain geometry and the time a certain topology is something that can be known, because to know that is simply to know how our own senses are constituted, not what things there are in the world outside of us.

Conclusions and Remarks

Kant claimed that it follows from the Expositions, that space and time are neither things in themselves, nor properties or relations of things as they are apart from all reference to human cognition (B 42, B 49). They figure in the world only insofar as it is represented by us or beings like us, and apart from us they are "nothing" (B 42[b], B 50–2, B 59).

But he immediately qualified this conclusion (B 42–5, B 51–3, B 59–60, B 62–3). He insisted that space and time are not ideal in the sense in which subjective states are ideal. Insofar as color, taste, and other sensations are viewed as phenomena that different people experience in different ways, even when in the presence of the same object, they are rightly considered to be alterations in the sensory state of perceiving subjects. But, Kant claimed, spatial and temporal properties and relations are rightly referred to objects, or, in the case of temporal properties and relations, rightly referred both to inner states and to other objects (B 49–51). Of course, Kant insisted, spatial and temporal properties and relations cannot be attributed to things as they are in themselves. But they can be attributed to the objects of our representations – objects that he appears to have considered to be distinct both from our representations, considered as subjective states, and from things in themselves. Moreover, they can be attributed to these objects in advance of experience or a priori, at least insofar as these objects are presumed to conform to geometrical axioms. The quality of sensory states, in contrast, can only be known a posteriori.

Kant cautioned that this position should not be identified with that taken by Leibniz and Wolff (B 60–2), or with the traditional distinction between primary and secondary qualities (B 62–4, B 69–71). As Kant represented their views, Leibniz and Wolff had maintained, like him, that space and time are not features of things as they really are, but only of things as they are represented through our senses. But unlike Kant, they had also maintained that our representations of the spatial and temporal properties of things correspond to certain other, real features of those things. These representations are, in effect, confused representations of the real features of things – ones that are therefore "well founded." Kant, in contrast, insisted that space and time do not reflect any feature of the world as it is apart from us, even confusedly. They are entirely due to the way our senses are constituted.

According to the traditional distinction between primary and secondary qualities, sensible qualities like color and taste are alterations of our own inner states. But as the consequence of a kind of illusion (Schein) we mistake these purely subjective modifications for properties of things as they are in themselves. Spatial and temporal properties and relations, in contrast, are correctly attributed to things in themselves. Kant was concerned that those wedded to this traditional distinction would misunderstand him. He meant to say that neither spatiotemporal properties nor sensible properties can be attributed to things in themselves, and that to make either of these attributions is to be misled by the same sort of illusion that leads people to think that Saturn has two handles (B 69–70n). But he also meant to draw a "transcendental distinction" (B 62) between what we attribute to the object in itself, what we attribute a priori to the object in relation to our senses, what we attribute a posteriori to the object in relation to our senses, and what we attribute merely to our own inner states and not to the object. There is no illusion in attributing either spatiotemporal properties or sensible qualities like color and scent to the objects of our representations. (Witness Kant's claim that "The predicates of appearance can be attributed to the object itself in relation to our senses, e.g., red color or scent to a rose . . ."; B 69–70n) But there is an illusion in neglecting the distinction between the a priori status of spatiotemporal properties and the a posteriori status of sensible qualities, or the distinction between either of these and the qualities of things in themselves, on the one hand, and merely subjective states, on the other.

This is what Kant meant by saying that space and time are "transcendentally ideal" but "empirically real." (See also chapter 31 below.)

Problems and Commentary

This "transcendental idealism" is a difficult doctrine to understand and accept (see chapter 7 above). One problem is that it is hard to see how the negative tenet that space and time are neither things in themselves nor properties or relations of things in themselves could be a *conclusion* from the Expositions. Another is that it is hard to make sense of Kant's claim that space and time are both subjective forms of sensory experience and objective features of things as they are represented by us.

Kant justified the claim that space and time could not be properties or relations of things in themselves by appeal to the a priori status of our knowledge of the principles of geometry (B 42, B 49, B 56–8). Were space and time properties or relations of things in themselves, the most we could say is that all the things we have so far experienced have exhibited spatial and temporal properties that conform to the principles of geometry and the recognized temporal axioms. But we could not rule out the possibility of a subsequent experience of things that occupy a radically different kind of space or time, or no space or time at all. The principles of geometry and the temporal axioms would be at best inductive generalizations and not absolutely necessary truths.

There has been a great deal of debate about this argument. The older Kant literature was critical, observing that the subsequent development of non-Euclidean geometries has forced us to recognize that it is an empirical question which of many alternative geometries actually describes the space of our world (for a summary presentation see Walker 1978: 60–73 – who, however, does not himself endorse this view). Strawson (1966: 281–92) attempted to defend a variant on Kant's position based on the notion that we are psychologically so constituted as to perceive objects as existing in a Euclidean space – a position that was ingeniously critiqued by Hopkins (1973) and even more ingeniously defended by Harper (1984). A different approach has been taken by Friedman (1992: 55–95), who has argued that, whatever questions subsequent developments may have raised for the validity of Kant's argument, it was based on a view that geometrical propositions can only be verified by ruler and compass constructions carried out on the backdrop of a "pure intuition" of space – a view that it was reasonable for Kant and others to have accepted at the time. This position has in turn been qualified by Parsons (1992: 78–9).

But even were we to grant the premises of Kant's argument from geometry, it is not clearly convincing. It only answers the "relationist" view that space and time are properties or relations of things in themselves, not the "substantivalist" view that they are containers that exist in themselves, independently of the objects they contain, and that constrain the objects that they do contain to possess a certain structure. Kant mentioned this possibility at B 49, but the reason he gave for rejecting it – that in that case time would be something that would still exist even in the absence of any existing object – is difficult to reconcile with the second of the Metaphysical Expositions, which claims that "one could quite well take appearances out of time" (B 46). If this does not mean that time could exist even in the absence of any object, then the argument of that earlier passage, which as interpreted above rests on an asymmetry in the dependence relations between time and the things in time, cannot be sustained.

Perhaps we could help Kant out by noting that were space a thing in itself, it would be a question whether it has uniformly the same geometry in all its parts, resurrecting the unacceptable implication that the principles of geometry are merely inductively valid. But there is a long-standing problem with this argument, nicely summarized by Allison (1983: 111–14) – who thinks he can resolve it. The argument neglects the alternative that space and time may be both forms of intuition and, coincidentally, things in themselves – things we know nothing of, but that just happen to possess the same geometry and topology as we find to be true of our experience.

The closest Kant came to addressing this "neglected alternative" is a discussion of the views of certain "mathematical natural scientists" (Newton and Euler) appended to section 7 (B 56–8). He there admitted that insofar as the mathematical natural scientists postulate an absolute, substantival, perfectly uniform space and time in which all things are contained, they leave the apodictic certainty of geometrical propositions unquestioned, but observed that this gain is made at the cost of postulating "two infinite and eternal, self-subsisting non-entities (space and time) that are present (without themselves being anything actual) only in order to contain everything that is actual." The problem with this postulate, Kant finally claimed, is that it puts the mathematical natural scientists in a position to extend the principles of mathematics to things as they are in themselves – an extension that leads them into errors. This is an allusion to the Second Antinomy (B 462–71), which argues that were things in themselves in space we would be compelled to accept the contradictory conclusions that they are both infinitely divisible and composed of simple, indivisible parts. A compelling discussion of Kant's grounds for this view has just been provided by Holden (2004).

As illustrated by the papers collected in Walker 1989, the question of how Kant could have taken space and time to be both subjective forms of sensory experience and objective features of things as they are represented by us also raises a nest of difficulties. The things that are represented as being in space and time cannot be things in themselves. Kant called them "appearances." One natural way to understand this term is as referring to some sort of effect that is brought about in perceiving subjects as a consequence of the action of external things on their sense organs. But this "idealist" understanding of Kant's notion of an appearance does not sit well with his attempt to distinguish the sense in which space and time are subjective from the sense in which sensations are subjective. It was also emphatically rejected by Kant himself. When he wrote the first edition of the *Critique* he assumed a realist stance, according to which there is an external world containing objects that somehow affect us and so cause us to experience sensations and eventually to cognize objects. He was dismayed when the first major review of his work, that published by Christian Garve in the January 19, 1782 *Göttingischen Anzeigen von gelehrten Sachen*, represented him as an idealist, who maintained that we only know our own inner states, and he furiously rejected that imputation (*Prol.*, 4.372–5) and thereafter devoted himself to demonstrating that, despite denying that we can have any knowledge of things in themselves, his account actually refutes idealism.

If Kant's "appearances" are neither subjective states nor things in themselves, then perhaps he intended them to be understood as things that are thought of or referred to by subjective states – as what are today called intentional objects. This has been endorsed by Parsons (1992) and Van Cleve (1999: 8–12), and some of Kant's passages (B 234–6, B 69–70) can readily be read as struggling to express such a notion. Be this as it may, it is important to stress that, unlike his contemporary, Reid, who supposed that we are innately so constituted as to reliably perceive things as they are in themselves (*Essays on the Intellectual Powers of Man* VI.5), Kant's view was that we are innately so constituted as to not perceive things as they are in themselves. For Kant we instead perceive things as possessing spatial and temporal properties and relations that they do not have in themselves and that do not even correspond to any of their features. This renews the question of what Kant can have meant by describing spatial and temporal determinations as objective.

An answer alluded to by Kant in such passages as *Prolegomena* 4.374–5 is that the a priori status of space and time for all human subjects ensures that the spatial and temporal features of objects will be judged by all subjects in the same way, and for this reason can be ascribed to the objects of a common human experience as opposed to the private states of an individual. Even though one subject might perceive a small, round array of color points, another a large square one, both judge themselves to be viewing the same, large, square tower situated at the same point in an ambient space that contains them both, because both subjects conceive the intentional object of their perceptions (in contrast to the perceptions themselves considered as private states) to be located outside of them in space and at different distances relative to each – a space that both describe using the same geometry (one that in this case entails that large square towers should project small round outlines at a distance). Something like this might be said of sensations of color and taste as well. Kant maintained that the intensity of sensation is indicative of a degree of force in the object of perception (B 209–10). This can be ascribed to "appearances," even if the qualia of color and taste are considered to be only subjective states. Our subjective states are similarly ascribed at least a "subjective" temporal order (and likely a spatial order as well in the case of colored and tangible points) distinct from the "objective" temporal and spatial order of states and parts judged to hold of appearances (B 234–8).

There remain two outstanding difficulties with this position. One was first pointed out by J. H. Lambert, Moses Mendelssohn, and Johann Schultz in correspondence with Kant, the other by F. H. Jacobi (*David Hume*, pp. 209–30, esp. 222–3). Both have

continued to bother Kant scholars down to the present day (among the most important recent discussions are Van Cleve 1999: 52–61, and Allison 1983: 247–54). The
first is that Kant's view that time is the form of inner sense, and hence of our experience
of our own representations, is inconsistent with his claim that things in themselves do
not have temporal features. For to say that my representations are successive in time
is to say that I myself pass through a temporal series of states – that I am first in one
representative state, then another. But then there is at least one thing in itself, namely
I myself as I am in myself, that is, in time.

The second difficulty arises from a claim only partially defended in the Aesthetic, the
claim that we can have no knowledge of things as they are in themselves either by
means of the senses, which only tell us about appearances, or the intellect, which can
only yield knowledge insofar is it is applied to the appearances the senses give us and
cannot legitimately extend beyond these bounds. That claim appears to undermine
the intelligibility of Kant's account of the senses. Kant declared that the senses give us
representations as a consequence of being affected by objects. But the notion of an
affecting object appears to defy analysis on Kantian terms. If affection is a causal
relation, involving a succession of events in time, and things in themselves are not in
time, then things in themselves cannot be the objects that affect the senses. If affection
is some sort of atemporal relation between things in themselves and human subjects,
then it is unknowable and the claims that the senses are affected by objects and that
sensations are specific effects resulting from that activity are unjustified. But there are
problems with taking affecting objects to be appearances as well. If appearances are in
space and time, and spatiotemporal relations can only be ascribed to objects as they
are in relation to our senses, then the nature of this relation needs to be very carefully
specified if we are both to preserve Kant's claims about the synthetic a priori status of
the propositions of geometry and avoid a vicious circle. Kant's claims about the synthetic a priori status of geometry would seem to imply that there is something in
appearances that is due to our own cognitive constitution, and it is not easy to see how
things that are determined by our cognitive constitution could be the things that affect
that constitution. Kant was aware of the first of these problems and attempted to
address it both in the Aesthetic (B 53–5 and B 67–9) and in a letter to Herz of February 21, 1772. His thought on both of them is further addressed in other chapters of
this volume (see chapters 7, 13, and 31). For other important recent work see Allison
1987, Ameriks 1992, Bird 2001, Guyer 1989, and Van Cleve 1999: 134–71.

References and Further Reading

Allison, H. (1983). *Kant's Transcendental Idealism*. New Haven: Yale University Press.
Allison, H. (1987). Transcendental idealism: The "two aspect" view. In B. den Ouden (ed.), *New Essays on Kant* (pp. 157–78). New York: Peter Lang.
Ameriks, K. (1992). Kantian idealism today. *History of Philosophy Quarterly*, 9: 329–42.
Bird, G. (2001). Lewis White Beck's account of Kant's strategy. In P. Cicovacki (ed.), *Kant's Legacy* (pp. 25–45). Rochester: University of Rochester Press.
Boler, J. F. (1982). Intuitive and abstractive cognition. In N. Kretzmann, A. Kenny, and J. Pinborg (eds.), *The Cambridge History of Later Medieval Philosophy* (pp. 460–78). Cambridge: Cambridge University Press.

Falkenstein, L. (1989). Kant's first argument in the metaphysical expositions. In G. Funke and T. M. Seebohm (eds.), *Proceedings of the Sixth International Kant Congress* (vol. II/1, pp. 219–27). Washington: University Press of America.

Falkenstein, L. (1995). *Kant's Intuitionism.* Toronto: University of Toronto Press.

Friedman, M. (1992). *Kant and the Exact Sciences.* Cambridge, MA: Harvard University Press.

Guyer, P. (1989). The rehabilitation of transcendental idealism? In E. Schaper and W. Vossenkuhl (eds.), *Reading Kant* (pp. 140–67). Oxford: Blackwell.

Harper, W. (1984). Kant on space, empirical realism, and the foundations of geometry. *Topoi,* 3: 143–61.

Holden, T. (2004). *The Architecture of Matter.* Oxford: Clarendon Press.

Hopkins, J. (1973). Visual geometry. *Philosophical Review,* 82: 3–34.

Jacobi, F. H. (1815). *David Hume. Werke,* vol. II. Leipzig: Gerhard Fleischer.

Kant, Immanuel (1998). *Critique of Pure Reason,* eds. and tr. Paul Guyer and Allen Wood. Cambridge: Cambridge University Press.

Kemp Smith, N. (1923). *A Commentary to Kant's Critique of Pure Reason,* 2nd ed. London: Macmillan.

Parsons, C. (1964). Infinity and Kant's conception of the "possibility of experience." *Philosophical Review,* 73: 182–97.

Parsons, C. (1992). The transcendental aesthetic. In P. Guyer (ed.), *The Cambridge Companion to Kant* (pp. 62–100). Cambridge: Cambridge University Press.

Quinton, A. (1962). Spaces and times. *Philosophy,* 37: 130–74.

Strawson, P. F. (1966). *The Bounds of Sense.* London: Methuen.

Van Cleve, J. (1999). *Problems from Kant.* New York: Oxford University Press.

Walker, R. C. S. (1978). *Kant.* London: Routledge.

Walker, R. C. S. (1989). *The Real in the Ideal.* New York: Garland.

Warren, D. (1998). Kant and the a priority of space. *Philosophical Review,* 107: 179–224.

153

10

Kant's Metaphysical and
Transcendental Deductions

DERK PEREBOOM

Introduction

The transcendental deduction (A 84–130, B 116–69) is Kant's attempt to demonstrate, against empiricist psychological theory, that a priori concepts correctly apply to objects in our experience. What makes a concept a priori is that its source is the understanding of the subject and not in sensory experience (B 106). Dieter Henrich (1968–9) points out that "*Deduktion*" is originally a legal term; it denotes an argument intended to provide a historical justification for the legitimacy of a property claim. In Kant's derivative epistemological sense, a deduction is an argument intended to provide a justification for the legitimacy of a concept, one that shows that the concept correctly applies to things.

David Hume attempts a deduction for various metaphysical ideas that he thinks are suspect – the idea of causal power, for example (2005: §7). In his view, a deduction will only be successful when a sensory experience, an impression, of causal power is found. Since the search for an impression of causal power is fruitless, Hume concludes that the idea does not truly apply to things. In Kantian language, Hume here attempts an empirical deduction (B 117), and from its failure he concludes that the concept of causal power has no objective validity, that is, it fails to apply to the objects of experience.

In the Transcendental Deduction, Kant develops a different sort of deduction for 12 concepts, one of which is the concept of cause, all of which he believes to be a priori. These a priori concepts are the categories. A transcendental deduction begins with a slender premise about any possible human experience, a premise to which reasonable participants in the debate can agree. Kant's argument attempts to establish a particular theory of mental processing by showing that its truth is a necessary condition for the truth of such a slender premise. As I shall contend his strategy involves employing two such premises; one concerns self-consciousness, the other certain characteristics of our representations of objective features of reality. Kant then aims to demonstrate that the categories have an essential role in this sort of mental processing. In his idealist view, the objects of experience result from this mental processing, and it is due to the role that the categories have in this processing that they correctly apply to these objects. Thus in the transcendental deduction he intends to secure a normative claim, that the categories correctly apply to the objects of our experience, by establishing a psychological theory (Kitcher 1990: 2–29). Kant's transcendental deduction presents general considerations supporting the applicability of categories to objects of experience; it does not concentrate on the applicability of specific individual categories (Bird 1962/1973: 112–15). That more focused task is taken up in the Analytic of Principles (B 169–287); see chapter 11 below.

In the Metaphysical Deduction (B 91–116) Kant sets out to derive the categories from what he calls the logical forms of judgment. The metaphysical deduction has a key role at a specific point in the transcendental deduction, and we will discuss its claims when we reach that point.

For Kant, the most important rival theory of mental processing is Hume's. Hume agrees that a theory of experience demands an account of the processing or ordering of mental states, but he does not believe that such an account requires a priori concepts. According to his theory, associationism, our mental repertoire consists solely of perceptions, all of which are sensory items – the more vivid impressions, and their less vivid copies, the ideas, which function in imagination, memory, and thought (Hume 2005: §§2 and 3). Association proper is the process by which these perceptions are ordered. The hallmark of this theory is that mental processing requires no resources beyond what perceptions provide; how perceptions are ordered is solely a function of the perceptions themselves. A subject that is distinct from these perceptions cannot have a role in Hume's picture, since for him the subject is merely a collection of perceptions (1978: I.IV.vi).

In Kant's theory, the ordering of mental states most prominently features the process of synthesis. Synthesis is "the act of putting different representations together, and grasping what is manifold in them in one cognition" (B 103); it is that which "gathers the elements for cognition, and unites them to form a certain content" (B 103). Synthesis is a process by which multiple representations – in Kant's term, a "manifold" – are connected with one another to form a single further representation with cognitive content. This process can employ concepts as modes of ordering representations. Crucial to the transcendental deduction is the claim that it is the categories by means of which our representations are synthesized. Since the understanding of the subject is the source of the categories, and also a faculty that produces synthesis, the subject has a central role in mental processing. For Kant this subject is distinct from its representations, as I shall argue.

This discussion will focus on the transcendental deduction in the second edition (1787) of the *Critique of Pure Reason* – the B-Deduction. I shall argue that in §§16–20 of the B-Deduction Kant employs a two-pronged strategy for defeating associationism and establishing synthesis. The first argument, contained in §16, is designed to show that association lacks adequate resources for explaining an aspect of self-consciousness, and that synthesis is required to provide this explanation. This type of argument is appropriately called an argument from above (A 119). Correlatively, in §§17–20 we find an argument from below, by which Kant aims to demonstrate that synthesis by means of the categories is needed to explain certain features of how we represent objects.

Apperception

The argument from above in §16 divides into two stages. The first aims to establish the various features of the principle of the necessary unity of apperception. The second advances to a priori synthesis by explaining how we might grasp an aspect of self-consciousness that this principle highlights. Apperception is the apprehension of a mental state, a representation, as one's own. In Kant's view, my apperception has necessary unity since all of my representations must be grounded "in pure apperception, that is, in the thoroughgoing identity of the self in all possible representations" (B 131–2). By this he means that:

(*The principle of the necessary unity of apperception*): It must be the case that each of my representations is such that I can attribute it to my self, a subject which is the same for all of my self-attributions, which is distinct from its representations, and which can be conscious of its representations. (A 116, B 131–2, B 134–5)

Consider three observations about the meaning of this principle.

i) Kant maintains that the apperceiving subject is not a collection of representations. In §16 he states: "through the 'I,' as simple representation, nothing manifold is given; only in intuition, which is distinct from the 'I,' can a manifold be given" (B 135). If intuition is distinct from the "I" in this sense, then intuitions will not be components of this subject. Furthermore, Kant would be implausibly interpreted as holding that the "I" consists merely of a collection of concepts. Supposing that all representations are either intuitions or concepts, it follows that the "I" does not consist merely of representations at all. Moreover, if this "I" were a collection of representations, Kant would not deny, as he does in the above passage, that anything manifold is given through the "I." In addition, he affirms that I have no inner intuition of the subject (e.g. B 157), and this claim would be at odds with the subject's being a collection of representations, since he maintains that I can intuit my representations by inner sense (e.g. B 49).

ii) The ability to attribute my representations to a subject is pure, rather than empirical, apperception. This means, in part, that I cannot attribute my representations to a single subject just in virtue of Humean inner perception, or Kantian empirical inner intuition. However, Kant repeatedly affirms that the purity of this apperception does not imply that the subject to which one's representations can be attributed is intuited – represented as an object – in a purely rational or a priori way (e.g. B 406–9).

iii) Kant also states that pure apperception is original, since "it is that self-consciousness which, while generating the representation 'I think' . . . cannot itself be accompanied by any further representation" (B 132). Pure apperception is original since I am not conscious of the self-consciousness, the apperceiving I that is the subject of apperceptive thoughts, in any manner independent of what is contained in these thoughts. I cannot have an intuition or any other type of representation of this subject other that by "I think . . ." – type thoughts, and thus, these thoughts are the original representations of this subject (e.g. A 350). Nevertheless, in virtue of my capacity for apperception, I can have a type of propositional grasp of the apperceiving subject; in apperception, I am conscious that I exist as subject (B 157).

Kant begins the first stage of the argument in §16 by saying:

It must be possible for the "I think" to accompany all my representations; for otherwise something would be represented in me which could not be thought at all, and that is equivalent to saying that the representation would be impossible, or at least would be nothing to me. (B 131–2; translations from Kant 1929 and Kant 1998)

On one reading, the sense in which a representation would be impossible or nothing to me if I could not attach the "I think" to it is just that I could not become conscious of it (Guyer 1987: 139–44). It might well be uncontroversial that for any representation of which I am conscious, I can attribute it to myself as subject, assuming my mental faculties are not defective, and as long as no particular account of the nature of the subject is presupposed. One might even understand why Kant would think a claim like this to be an analytic truth. But the assertion that, even supposing normal mental functioning, I can become conscious of each of my representations, and that I can thus attribute each of them to myself as subject, is not an analytic truth, and may well be false. Some of my representations are thoroughly subconscious, while they should still be classified as mine in virtue of the types of causal relations they bear to my perceptions, my behavior, and representations that are uncontroversially mine. But it is arguable that I cannot attribute each of these subconscious representations to myself, and it is certainly not an analytic truth that I can. As we shall see, however, the premise that each of my representations is such that I can attribute it to myself is not required for the first stage of the argument from above. Instead, the crucial claim here is for the identity or sameness of the subject of different self-attributions, and my being conscious of this identity.

Several commentators maintain that Kant's argument requires the unity of apperception to be a claim about simultaneous consciousness of representations, and that this undermines its soundness. For instance, one of Robert Howell's primary difficulties with the argument of §16 is that Kant does not establish what he considers to be a crucial premise:

> (S) All of the elements of the manifold of i (where i is some arbitrary intuition) are such that H is or can become conscious, in thought, that all of those elements, taken together, are accompanied by the I think.

This claims that all the individual elements of the intuition are such that the subject can become conscious of them simultaneously and contrasts with the weaker claim:

> (W) Each element of the manifold of i is such that H is or can become conscious, in thought, that the I think accompanies that element. (Howell 1992: 161)

This says that all the individual elements of the intuition are such that the subject can become conscious of each in turn. Howell supposes that if (S) cannot be established, the argument of the B-Deduction collapses, for only if Kant can show that the different elements of a manifold together and at the same time are accompanied by the same "I think" can he establish that H's mind must synthesize these elements (Howell 1992: 162). He contends that, by contrast, the unity expressed by (W) is insufficient to generate this need for synthesis. Howell goes on to argue that Kant cannot in fact demonstrate (S) – and it is indeed implausible that such co-consciousness for any arbitrary intuition is really possible for us – and that hence the argument of the B-Deduction falters.

But perhaps Kant does not require a premise as strong as (S) – as opposed to (W) – for the argument of §16. First of all, the co-consciousness claim is suggested, but not clearly stated, in §16 by the following sentence:

> That relation comes about, not simply through my accompanying each representation with consciousness, but only in so far as I *conjoin* one representation with another, and am conscious of the synthesis of them. (B 133)

By "am conscious of the synthesis of them," Kant might mean that I am conscious that these representations stand in a certain relation to one another, which need not involve actually my being conscious of them at the same time. I might be conscious that my representations are inferentially integrated with each other in a way distinct from how mine are integrated with yours, without being conscious of all of the representations that are so integrated at the same time. Moreover, perhaps Kant intends not that I am actually co-conscious of these representations, but that they could become co-conscious for me. This interpretation is suggested by Kant's assertion:

> For without such combination nothing can be thought or known, since the given representations would not have in common the act of apperception "I think," and so *could* not be apprehended together in one self-consciousness. (B 137, emphasis mine)

James van Cleve argues, however, that if the representations can only possibly become co-conscious, Kant can only conclude that they are possibly subject to the categories (Van Cleve 1999: 84). Is this a correct diagnosis?

At this point the argument of §16 features a subtlety that is often overlooked. In fact, the central feature of this argument is Kant's attempt to demonstrate that only a priori synthesis can explain how I might represent the identity of my apperceptive consciousness (B 133) or how I might represent the identity of the apperceiving subject (B 135) for different elements of the manifold of intuition to which I can attach the "I think." The difficulty Kant sees for "empirical consciousness," that is, for consciousness according to Humean psychological theory, is that "it is in itself dispersed [*an sich zerstreut*] and without relation to the identity of the subject [*und ohne Beziehung auf die Identität des Subjects*]" (B 133). One implication of this key passage is that Hume's theory lacks the resources required to explain how various of my representations can be attributed to a subject that is both conscious of them and the same subject for each act of self-attribution. This objection does not beg the question against Hume, for it assumes only a claim that one would not want to initially deny, that the conscious subject of different apperceptive self-attributions is the same. Hume's account cannot explain this identity, because Humean perceptions of perceptions are wholly distinct from one another; they are "dispersed" (B 133), and share no common element. Hume might propose to explain our sense that the conscious subject of different self-attributions is the same by the perceptions of perceptions being elements of a single causally coherent bundle. Still, the bundle is not conscious of perceptions; consciousness of perceptions would be a feature of individual perceptions. In Kant's view, explaining how the conscious subject of different self-attributions can be the same requires that this subject be distinct from its representations.

The second stage of the argument of §16 involves a further implication of the claim that "the empirical consciousness, which accompanies different representations, is dispersed and without relation to the identity of the subject" (B 133): that Hume's theory cannot account for my representation relation to the identity of the subject. It cannot explain how I can "represent to myself the identity of the consciousness in [i.e. throughout] these representations" (B 133). One might envision several types of explanation for my representation of this identity. One possibility is that inner sense enables me to represent this identity for each of my various self-attributions, and the way I represent the identity of the subject is similar to the way I typically represent the identity over time of ordinary objects – by noting similarities among the intrinsic properties represented. But Kant and Hume would agree that this is not the way I represent the identity of the apperceiving subject, since both would agree that by inner sense I do not represent any intrinsic properties of such a subject. The second type of explanation, which Kant endorses, is that I have a less direct way of representing this identity. As Henry Allison points out, this representation must instead depend on my apprehending a feature of my representations (Allison 1983: 142–4; Guyer 1987: 133–9). The relevant feature is some type of unity or ordering of these states. Kant's idea is that if the representations I can attribute to myself possess a unity of the appropriate type, and if I apprehend this unity, then I can represent the apperceiving subject of any one of them as identical with that of any other.

Thus my representation of the identity of the subject comes about "only in so far as I conjoin one representation with another, and am conscious of the synthesis of them" (B 133). What sort of unity must I recognize among my representations that would account for my representation of this identity? Need it be actual co-consciousness? Note that I represent the subject as identical for self-attributed representations that are not co-conscious, so actual co-consciousness could not explain generally how I represent this sort of identity. A plausible alternative is that the unity consists in certain intimate ways in which representations in a single subject are typically related. Perhaps the key aspect of this unity is that a single subject's representations are inferentially integrated to a high degree, by contrast with representations across discrete subjects. This integration might in turn be analyzed, at least in part, by the possibility of my representations becoming co-conscious. Memory and the capacity to become conscious of nonoccurrent states are means by which representations can become co-conscious.

Association and synthesis are possible explanations for the how this unity comes about or, less ambitiously, for my ability to recognize this unity. But, Kant seems to suppose, since we have already ruled out Hume's psychological theory, that synthesis is the only possible explanation. Consequently, in order to explain how I represent the identity of the subject of different self-attributions, I must produce or recognize a unity among these representations, and synthesis – indeed, a priori synthesis – must be adduced to explain this recognition. Kant argues that this combination "is an affair of the understanding alone, which itself is nothing but the faculty of combining a priori" (B 134–5). Since the understanding provides concepts for synthesis, and since for synthesis to be a priori in this context is, in part, for it to employ a priori concepts, Kant is contending here that synthesis by means of a priori concepts is required to account for my production of or recognition of the unity at issue.

As Paul Guyer contends, however, demonstrating the need for synthesis by means of a priori concepts would require ruling out the possibility that empirical information alone could account for the recognition of the unity among my representations (Guyer 1987: 146–7). It might be, for all Kant has shown, that this recognition requires awareness of information derived from inner experience. Kant does not at this point attempt to dislodge such rival empiricist hypotheses, and it seems he would need to do so to confirm the need for a priori synthesis. To advance his claims, he might try to point out features of this unity that would resist such an empiricist account. As we shall see, Kant employs this tactic in his account of our representations of objects.

Representations of Objects

One function of §17 is to provide a characterization of an object, or more significantly, of a representation of an object, that incorporates a challenge to Humean associationism. Kant's proposal is that an object is "that in the concept of which a manifold of a given intuition is united" (B 137). I think that here we should read "object" in the broad sense of "objective feature of reality" – a feature whose existence and nature is independent of how it is perceived (Bird 1962/1973: 130–1; Guyer 1987: 11–24). Such objective features might be physical, but could also be mental. According to Allison's interpretation §17 does not simply contain this challenge to Hume, but also a demonstration of our representation of objects on the basis of the claims about self-consciousness developed in §16. This reading is part of Allison's broader picture, in which Kant establishes that the unity of apperception entails the representation of objects, and, conversely, that the representation of objects entails the unity of apperception (Allison 1983: 144ff). The crucial claim for Allison's interpretation is that the unity of apperception is not only a necessary but also sufficient condition for the representation of objects. Other commentators, including Aquila (1989: 159) and Howell (1992: 227–8), agree. In my interpretation, by contrast, the unity of apperception, and more precisely, the synthesis that explains our consciousness of the identity of the subject, is only a necessary condition for the representation of objects, and, moreover, a condition which Kant proposes in §17, and only aims to demonstrate in §§18–20.

By Allison's reading, §§15–20 comprise a single argument whose only assumptions are premises about self-consciousness that Kant defends in §16. This interpretation of the B-Deduction is widespread. Demonstrating that we represent objects has a place in this schema, since then no mere assumption about the existence of representations of objects would be required for the stages of the argument that take place in §§18–20. However, there are reasons to be concerned about this interpretation. For instance, in §§18–20 Kant makes crucial assumptions about features of our representations of objects that exceed anything that he might be thought to have argued for in §17. In particular, he assumes that our representations of objects exhibit certain kinds of necessity and universality, and he never attempts to establish by argument that our representations of objects have such characteristics, either in §17 or elsewhere in the *Critique of Pure Reason*. Moreover, in the summary statement of the deduction in §20

Kant does not include premises from §§15–16. What we actually find in §20 provides evidence that Kant intends §§17–20, with some help from §13, to constitute a single, self-contained argument.

In Allison's view, the argument from the unity of apperception (or, equivalently, of consciousness) for the existence of representations of objects is found in the following passage:

> (A) Understanding is, to use general terms, the faculty of cognitions [*Erkenntnisse*]. They consist [*bestehen*] in the determinate relation of given representations to an object: and an object is that in the concept of which the manifold of a given intuition is united. Now all unification of representations demands unity of consciousness in the synthesis of them. Consequently it is the unity of consciousness that alone constitutes the relation of representations to an object, and therefore their objective validity and the fact that they are cognitions [*Erkenntnisse*]: and upon it therefore rests the very possibility of the understanding. (B 137)

Allison himself presents a problem for his interpretation of this passage. He argues, first of all, that the reciprocity thesis is encapsulated in this sentence:

> (1) it is the unity of consciousness that alone constitutes [*ausmacht*] the relation of representations to an object, and therefore their objective validity . . .

and Kant presents (1) as a direct consequence of the premise that

> (2) all unification of representations demands unity of consciousness in the synthesis of them.

But given this picture, Allison points out, Kant's reasoning seems to involve a gross non sequitur, since (2) would support only the claim that the unity of consciousness is a necessary condition for the representation of an object, and not that it is also a sufficient condition. Howell voices a similar worry: "In §17 Kant simply does not make this inference clear, and an air of blatant fallacy hovers over this part of his reasoning" (Howell 1992: 228).

Allison and Howell both venture that Kant's sentence in paragraph (A)

> (1) it is the unity of consciousness that alone constitutes the relation of representations to an object, and therefore their objective validity . . .

should be read as a statement of the sufficiency claim. In (A) Kant contends that cognitions of objects consist in some determinate relation of representations to objects, and as (1) indicates, this relation is constituted or produced by a synthesis that crucially involves the unity of consciousness. But (1) does not entail that the synthesis that involves unity of consciousness cannot take place without its resulting in a relation of a representations to an object. By analogy, the smelting and molding of steel are processes that constitute or produce steel girders, but it does not follow that the processes of smelting and molding steel cannot take place without the production of steel girders. Just as producing steel girders requires in addition moulds of particular shapes, so producing representations of objects could require particular concepts of objects in addition to the synthesis that involves the unity of consciousness.

How might §17 function in the argument absent the sufficiency claim? In my view, the main role of this section is to provide a characterization of an object that incorporates a challenge to Humean associationism and thereby initiates an argument from below. Kant proposes that an object is "that in the concept of which a manifold of a given intuition is united" (B 137). In his view, this unification of a manifold requires the unity of apperception together with synthesis, for immediately following the characterization of an object he claims that "all unification of representations demands unity of consciousness in the synthesis of them" (B 137). This depiction is designed to present his anti-Humean theory about the processing required for a represent ation of an object. This characterization does not set out a position that Kant expects his readers to accept without argument, but rather, one he intends to establish in §§18–20.

Universality and Necessity

In §18 Kant continues the argument *against* association and *for* synthesis by drawing our attention to certain features of our representations of objects:

> The transcendental unity of apperception is that unity through which all the manifold given in an intuition is united in a concept of the object. It is therefore entitled objective, and must be distinguished from the subjective unity of consciousness . . . Whether I can become empirically conscious of the manifold as simultaneous or as successive depends on circumstances and empirical conditions. Therefore, the empirical unity of consciousness, through association of representations, itself concerns an appearance, and is wholly contingent . . . Only the original unity is objectively valid: the empirical unity of apperception, . . . which . . . is merely derived from the former under given conditions in concreto, has only subjective validity. One person connects the representation of a certain word with one thing, the other [person] with another thing; the unity of consciousness in that which is empirical is not, as regards what is given, necessarily and universally valid. (B 139–40)

Here Kant characterizes the empirical unity of consciousness as non-universal, contingent, and subjectively valid, distinguishing it from the transcendental unity of apperception, which he describes as universal, necessary, and objectively valid. The empirical unity of consciousness is an ordering of representations produced by association. Hence, Kant is maintaining that association can achieve only an ordering that is nonuniversal, contingent, and lacks objective validity. The transcendental unity of apperception, by contrast, results in an ordering of representations produced by synthesis, and accordingly, Kant is claiming that synthesis can generate an organization that is universal, necessary, and objectively valid.

In this argument, a key feature of certain representations of objects is their objective validity. For a representation to be objectively valid it must be a representation of an objective feature of reality, that is, the existence and nature of the entity it represents must be independent of the way it is perceived (Guyer 1987: 11–24). In the argument of §§17–18, Kant assumes that the representations that make up experience are objectively valid. He then argues that association is inadequate because it can yield only representations that are not objectively valid, that is, whose existence and nature are not independent of how they are perceived (Guyer 1987: 11–24). In the argument of §§17–18 Kant assumes that the representations that make up experience are objectively valid. He then argues that association is inadequate because it can yield only representations that are not objectively valid.

The crucial premise in Kant's argument against the adequacy of association in the above passage is:

(3) Whether I can become empirically conscious of the manifold as simultaneous or as successive depends on circumstances or empirical conditions.

This leads him to conclude that "the empirical unity of consciousness, through association of representations, itself concerns an appearance, and is wholly contingent" (B 139–40). Kant here invokes considerations about the ordering of phenomena in time that foreshadow the discussion of the Second Analogy. There Kant argues that our representations, considered independently of their content, are always successive. What is represented by these successive representations, however, is not always itself successive. When viewing a boat floating downstream, its various positions are represented as successive, but in scanning the parts of a house from the roof to ground, these parts are represented not as successive but as simultaneous. The parts of the house are represented as objectively simultaneous, while the positions of the boat are represented as objectively successive. How do we account for this difference?

In §18, Kant implies that an important clue for answering this question is that these representations of objective simultaneity and succession are universal and necessary. A first approximation of the import of "universal" in this context is:

(4) Any human experience of the parts of the house is an experience of these parts as objectively simultaneous.

The addition of necessity has the following effect on (4):

(5) Necessarily, any human experience of the parts of the house is an experience of these parts as objectively simultaneous.

Now (5) can be denied by Hume, for example, if we take the necessity to range over all possible circumstances, because his theory can countenance the possibility of a deviant ordering in unusual empirical conditions. But (5) can be recast as

(5′) Necessarily, if empirical conditions are normal, any human experience of the parts of the house is an experience of these parts as objectively simultaneous.

Kant's view would then be that given only the resources of association, the truth of (5′) could not be explained, for "whether I can become empirically conscious of the manifold as simultaneous or as successive depends on circumstances or empirical conditions" and, therefore, "the empirical unity of consciousness . . . is wholly contingent" (B 139–40).

Guyer charges that at various places in the transcendental deduction Kant illegitimately assumes knowledge of necessity, and perhaps this argument falls to such a concern (Guyer 1987: 146–7). However, Hume might well not deny the necessity at issue. For example, he believes that it is impossible, in some sense, given an experience of constant conjunction, that the mind not be carried from the experience of the first conjunct to the thought of the next:

> having found, in many instances, that any two kinds of objects, flame and heat, snow and cold, have always been conjoined together; if flame or snow be presented anew to the senses, the mind is carried by custom to expect heat or cold, and to believe, that such a quality does exist, and will discover itself upon a nearer approach. This belief is the necessary result of placing the mind in such circumstances. It is an operation of the soul, when we are so situated, as unavoidable as to feel the passion of love, when we receive benefits; or hatred, when we meet with injuries. (Hume 2005: §5)

Thus Hume himself contends that given certain specific empirical circumstances, a particular type of ordering of perceptions necessarily or unavoidably comes about.

To forestall a further objection, asserting (5′) does not amount to presupposing that one of the categories, viz., necessity, correctly applies to the objects of experience. Although (5′) does make a claim to necessity or unavoidability, it does not presuppose that the "necessity" in the premise is an a priori concept. Moreover, the objection that no premise for the transcendental deduction may employ concepts whose applicability to experience Kant aims to establish is unreasonably demanding. "Existence" and "negation," for example, are among the categories, and to claim that the deduction may not employ premises involving these concepts is to submit to an impossible standard.

The argument also does not fall prey to a further concern of Guyer's, that Kant merely assumes that all knowledge of necessity is grounded in a priori concepts. One need not interpret him as arguing directly from (5′) to the claim that the categories correctly apply to objects in our experience. Rather, one should see him as advancing his claim for the applicability of the categories by ruling out association as an explanation for (5′). One might divide the next point he sets out to reach into three steps:

(**6**) To explain the truth of (5′), there must exist a mental faculty for ordering representations.
(**7**) This faculty does not consist solely of sensory items.
(**8**) This faculty must employ a priori concepts, the categories in particular.

Kant's challenge is to explain why, under normal conditions, the ordering in question is universal and necessary. Part of the best explanation, he believes, is (6), that there must exist a faculty for ordering the representations. Hume might agree with this conclusion, as long as a sufficiently thin conception of "faculty" is permitted. But he would deny (7), that this faculty does not consist solely of sensory items. Kant argues that the Humean proposal for a faculty that consists solely of sensory items, the faculty of association, cannot account for the truth of propositions such as (5′). He asks us to consider an activity, word association, which functions as a paradigm for association. Word association, familiarly, does not yield universal and necessary patterns; "one person connects the representation of a certain word with one thing, the other [person] with another thing . . ." (B 140). Hume's own paradigm for association is the relations among parts of a conversation (Hume 2005: §3). Kant's point is that in such conversations, people make different associations in the same circumstances. If the very paradigms for association fail to exhibit necessity and universality, then the hypothesis that association is powerful enough to yield such an ordering of representations – wherever we find it – is on insecure ground.

The associationist might argue that sensory experience is sufficiently uniform for association to produce the universalities and necessities at issue. Perhaps Kant was too quick to conclude that the argument from universality and necessity was decisive, for in addition, associationist objections of this sort must be answered – as contemporary discussions of proposals for innate concepts indicate (Pereboom 1995: 31–3). But this does not detract from the considerable anti-associationist force provided by the sorts of universalities and necessities Kant has in mind, and this fact is also recognized by the contemporary discussion.

Logical Forms of Judgment and Categories

In §§19–20, Kant argues that judgment is the medium that brings about synthesis, and that this medium employs certain forms of judgment, which are in turn appropriately connected to the 12 categories. By linking synthesis to judgment in this way, Kant aims to show that we use the categories in the synthesis of experience.

In §19, Kant suggests that there must be a certain way in which each of my representations is unified in the subject, and he identifies this way with judgment: "I find that a judgment is nothing but the manner in which given cognitions are brought to the objective unity of apperception" (B 141). Judgment, Kant claims, is objectively rather than subjectively valid, and hence exhibits the kind of universality and necessity that characterizes objective validity (B 142). He then claims that without synthesis and judgment as its vehicle, an ordering of representations might reflect what appears to be the case, but would not allow us to make distinctions between objects and the subjective states they induce.

In §20, Kant links this notion of judgment to the 12 forms of judgment presented in the metaphysical deduction (B 95), and he in turn ties these forms of judgment to the 12 categories (B 102–9). The claim has often been made that the connections he specifies between synthesis and judgment, judgment and the forms of judgment, the forms of judgment and the categories, are underargued. Guyer, for example, argues that Kant has not adequately established the last of these links, that although Kant asserts that the categories are simply the forms of judgment as they are employed in the synthesis of representations in an intuition (B 104 to B 105, B 143), he has failed to make this claim plausible (Guyer 1987: 94–102). It is fair to say that these concerns have merit. Kant's claims about these connections continue to be more obscure than the preceding part of the Transcendental Deduction, and it continues to be a serious challenge for interpreters to clarify and vindicate them.

Béatrice Longuenesse (1998), in her interpretation of the metaphysical deduction, has taken up this challenge. In her view, the faculty at issue in the production and use of concepts, the understanding, is the power to judge (*Vermögen zu Urteilen*), which is

165

ultimately a disposition or a conatus to make judgments and to shape what affects us so that we can make them (Longuenesse 1998: 208, 394). The logical forms of judgment are, most fundamentally, the forms of combination of concepts in judgments. One such form is the categorical, which is the form of subject–predicate judgments; another is the hypothetical, the form of "if–then" judgments. Kant maintains that the logical form of a judgment is what makes it capable of truth or falsity; it is that by which a judgment expresses the relation of a representations to an independently existing object (Longuenesse 2000: 93–4). He thinks, for instance, that by virtue of its categorical form the judgment "The boat is moving" (whether or not it is true) expresses the relation of my representations of a boat and motion to an objectively existing boat in motion.

One paradigmatic role of the logical forms of judgment is in the process of analysis, by which, for example, the objects we intuit are subsumed under concepts. What results from this process is a judgment that expresses an analytic unity – in this case the subsumption of objects under a single concept. But a logical form of judgment can also be called into service to perform a different function: namely the synthesis of a manifold of intuition, which now results in a synthetic unity. The understanding, as the power to judge, has both roles; "the same function that gives unity to concepts in judgment, also gives unity to the mere synthesis of representations in intuition" (B 104–5). When the logical form has the synthetic role, it is transformed or expressed as a category:

> The same understanding, and indeed by means of the very same actions through which it brings the logical form of judgment into concepts by means of the analytical unity, also brings a transcendental content into its representations by means of the synthetic unity of the manifold in intuition in general. (B 105)

The content added to the logical forms of judgment is some feature of intuition – more precisely, of the forms of intuition – that emerges when the power to judge sets out to unify a manifold of intuition (B 128–9). The categories are thus generated from the forms of judgment in the process of synthesizing intuitions. For example, what is generated from the categorical form of judgment is the category of substance, and from hypothetical form of judgment is the category of cause.

The Second Step of the B-Deduction

In §20 Kant concludes: "Consequently, the manifold in a given intuition is necessarily subject to the categories" (B 143). It is tempting to think that this is precisely what Kant intended to show in the transcendental deduction, and hence that the argument is completed in §20. However, in §21 Kant says: "Thus in the above proposition a beginning is made of a deduction of the pure concepts of understanding" (B 44). He goes on to explain:

> In what follows (cf. §26) it will be shown, from the mode in which the empirical intuition is given in sensibility, that its unity is no other than that which the category (according to

§20) prescribes to the manifold of a given intuition in general. Only thus, by demonstration of the a priori validity of the categories in respect of all objects of our senses, will the purpose of the deduction by fully attained. (B 144–5)

Here an old interpretive question arises: how should we conceive of the argument we find in §26, together with material from §24, which has become known as second step of the B-Deduction?

Erich Adickes (1889: 139–4) and H. J. Paton (1936: vol. II, p. 501) argue that while what precedes §21 is an objective deduction, what we find in §24 and §26 is a subjective deduction. This distinction has its source in the Preface to A, where Kant says:

> This enquiry, which is somewhat deeply grounded, has two sides. The one refers to the objects of pure understanding, and is intended to expound and render intelligible the objective validity of its a priori concepts. It is therefore essential to my purposes. The other seeks to investigate the pure understanding itself, its possibility and the cognitive faculties upon which it rests: and so deals with it in its subjective aspect. Although this latter exposition is of great importance for my chief purpose, it does not form an essential part of it. (A xvi–xvii)

Henrich (1968–9) rejects the Adickes/Paton proposal for the reason that in §21 Kant says that the demonstration of the validity of the categories is completed only in §26, and the passage from the A-Preface indicates that this is a task for the objective deduction. In defense of Adickes and Paton, in §20 Kant claims to have shown that the categories apply to the manifold in any given intuition, and says that he will now show that categories apply to any object that presents itself to the senses. In view of the aim of the objective deduction, this move would seem to require only a straightforward application of the result of §20 to any empirical intuition we might have.

Henrich points out that although in the B-Deduction Kant sought to avoid the problems of a subjective deduction, this "does not mean that he neglected the demand for an explanation of the possibility of relating the categories to intuitions." But by Kant's account, a subjective deduction contains not only an examination of cognitive faculties, but also an investigation of "the possibility of the pure understanding," which would include an investigation of precisely how the categories might be related to intuitions and to the objects of experience they represent. This is just the type of investigation that is to be found in §24 and §26 – and Henrich agrees. So in the last analysis, the views of Henrich, Paton, and Adickes can be reconciled; they can all concur that the second step is an attempt to show how the categories are related to objects of experience – in such a way as to show how the categories might correctly apply to them. Moreover this common ground provides a reasonable interpretation of the text. For in §26 Kant argues that our representations of space and time, because they themselves contain a manifold, must also be synthesized by the categories. Since all of the objects we experience are given to us in space and time, these objects too will be synthesized by the categories. Thus Kant provides an explanation of how the categories apply to the objects of our experience by way of the manner in which these objects are given to us (Longuenesse 1998: 211–33).

167

A Final Word

The legacy of the transcendental deduction includes not only the successes of Kant's actual argument, but also a number of influential philosophical strategies: the now-standard tactic of arguing for concepts, whose source is in the mind, from universal and necessary features of experience; the idea of drawing significant philosophical conclusions from premises about self-consciousness alone; and the notion of a transcendental argument, which from an uncontroversial premise about our thought, knowledge, or experience, reasons to a substantive and unobvious necessary condition of this claim.

References and Further Reading

Adickes, E. (1889). *Immanuel Kants Kritik der reinen Vernunft*. Berlin: Mayer & Müller.

Allison, H. (1983). *Kant's Transcendental Idealism*. New Haven: Yale University Press.

Aquila, R. (1989). *Matter and Mind*. Bloomington: Indiana University Press.

Bird, Graham (1962/1973). *Kant's Theory of Knowledge*. London: Routledge and Kegan Paul; rpt. New York: Humanities Press, 1973.

Guyer, P. (1987). *Kant and the Claims of Knowledge*. Cambridge: Cambridge University Press.

Henrich, D. (1968–9). The proof-structure of Kant's Transcendental Deduction. *Review of Metaphysics*, 22: 640–59.

Howell, R. (1992). *Kant's Transcendental Deduction*. Dordrecht: Kluwer.

Hume, D. (1978). *A Treatise of Human Nature*. Oxford: Oxford University Press.

Hume, D. (2005). *An Enquiry Concerning Human Understanding*. Oxford: Oxford University Press.

Kant, Immanuel (1929). *Critique of Pure Reason*, tr. Norman Kemp Smith. London: Macmillan.

Kant, Immanuel (1998). *Critique of Pure Reason*, eds. and tr. P. Guyer and A. Wood. Cambridge: Cambridge University Press.

Kitcher, P. (1990). *Kant's Transcendental Psychology*. Oxford: Oxford University Press.

Longuenesse, B. (1998). *Kant and the Capacity to Judge*. Princeton: Princeton University Press.

Longuenesse, B. (2000). Kant's categories and the capacity to judge: Responses to Henry Allison and Sally Sedgwick. *Inquiry*, 20: 91–110.

Paton, H. J. (1936). *Kant's Metaphysics of Experience*, 2 vols. London: Allen and Unwin.

Pereboom, D. (1995). Self-understanding in Kant's Transcendental Deduction. *Synthese* 103: 1–42.

Pereboom, D. (2000). Assessing Kant's master argument. *Kantian Review*, 5: 90–102.

Van Cleve, J. (1999). *Problems From Kant*. Oxford: Oxford University Press.

11

The Second Analogy

ARTHUR MELNICK

1. Hume's Threefold Challenge

Kant's account of causality in the Second Analogy is meant to address the central concerns Hume raises against the objective reality of causality. The first concern is over the nature of the causal relation itself. The cause doesn't just precede the effect, but determines it or necessitates it, makes it happen, produces it, etc. Equivalently, the effect is supposed not just to follow the cause but to emerge from it, derive from it, come out of it, etc. As Kant puts it, "the effect not only succeeds the cause, but . . . is posited *through* it and arises out of it" (B 124: translations from Kant 1965: 125). Hume contends that no objective account of this causal bond or nexus can be given. One task of the Second Analogy then is to explain how there can be necessary connections holding between events. We can label this the issue of singular causation, since for Kant as well as Hume, the causal bond is supposed to hold between particular events on particular occasions.

A second concern Hume raises is over the status of the law of causation itself; i.e., over the principle that every event has a cause. On what grounds does this hold as an objective truth of the world as opposed, say, to a merely regulative principle of inquiry? A third concern is over the nature and justification of causal reasoning. Hume argues against the reasonableness of extrapolating from experienced regularity to universal regularity encompassing the future and the unexperienced past. Suppose that a cause was not only necessarily connected to its effect, but was also universally so connected. In other words if A is the cause of B then there is a universal law of causation that A always causes B. If this were so (and known to be so a priori), and if it were also the case that every event had a cause, then it would follow, I now suggest, that an experienced regularity would constitute reasonable evidence for universal regularity. Let B be an event. We know that B has some cause and that it always follows its cause. If then B always follows A in our experience this is evidence that it is A which is the cause. The point is we know that something plays a certain role (of cause), and that whatever plays that role must have a certain characteristic (of always being followed by B). But then experiencing something as conformable to having that characteristic provides evidence that it is playing that role. The situation is somewhat similar to the following one. If we know that someone ate two pizza slices, then the sauce on Fido's nose is evidence he ate two slices, whereas just by itself the sauce on his nose is not evidence that he ate two slices. Kant indeed holds that causes come under universal laws. He says, for example that the concept of cause "makes strict demand that something, A, should be such that something else, B, follows from it *necessarily and in accordance with an absolutely universal rule*" (B 124; Kant 1965: 125; see also A 112; Kant 1965: 139, B 183 and 185). If he establishes this in the Second Analogy, then together with establishing that every event has a cause, he will have addressed Hume's third challenge that calls inductive reasoning into question.

In sum, in the Second Analogy Kant sets out to establish that every event has a cause in the sense of cause in which there is a singular bond or nexus between cause and effect and a universal law with the import that the same cause always leads to the same effect. This will be sufficient to answer the threefold challenge Hume presents to the objective validity of causation and causal reasoning (but see section 3 below).

2. Kant's Argument for Causation from the Nature of Time

Kant's argument for the sense and applicability of the concept of causation derives from the nature of time itself. According to Kant, "it is a necessary law of our sensibility . . . that the preceding times necessarily determine the succeeding" (B 244; Kant 1965: 225). What this means is that earlier times aren't just followed by later times, but necessarily give way to them, yield them, determine them, ensure them, etc. Equivalently, later times emerge from, arise out of, come from earlier times. The succession of times, or as Kant says the advance of time, is a necessary one. A particular time doesn't happen to give way to a succeeding time, but necessarily and inexorably gives way to it. If one holds an absolutist theory of time, this fact will be expressed as the fact that *moments* of time necessarily give way to later moments. If one holds a relational theory of time this fact will be expressed as a necessary advance in possible relations somewhat as follows: the possibility of there being occurrences 30 units earlier than a present occurrence necessarily gives way to the possibility of there being occurrences 29 units earlier. In this manner the possible relations defining earlier times necessarily give way to the possible relations defining later times. On both of these views the necessary advance is expressed as pertaining to *temporal* relations, either between moments or between possible occurrences.

Kant holds neither an absolutist nor a relational theory of time, both of which make time to be something objective. For Kant there simply isn't an objective series of temporal relations. Temporal relations for Kant exist only in time as a form of intuition. Without going into any detail, what is important for our purposes is that the succession represented in a formal intuiting doesn't necessarily advance from earlier intuiting or necessarily advance to later intuiting, since each intuition is properly independent (do-able on its own). Various extended processional intuitings do give temporal order to occurrences, but they provide no necessary connection between the temporal orders so as to form a single series of times that necessarily emerge from each other. It is for this reason that the necessary advance of the series must be found in something other than the temporal order.

170

Kant says that "it is an indispensable law of *empirical representation* of the time series that the appearances of past time determine all existence in the succeeding time" (B 244; Kant 1965: 225). In other words, it is earlier events (appearances) necessarily emerging into or determining later events that represents or constitutes the necessary advance of the time order. But now to say that *events* necessarily advance to later *events* is just to say there is a causal bond or nexus between the events. Indeed if it is the relationship of events themselves that constitutes the necessary advance of time (the later time arising out of or being determined by the earlier), then later events emerge from or are determined by earlier events. But this is just the notion of necessary connection that Hume couldn't account for between events. Kant "finds" this connection in the role that events have to play to represent or, indeed, to constitute the necessary advance of time. The necessity is "originally" not in the nature of transition-habits of mind, but in the nature of the advance of time itself.

Kant says at B 245 that "since absolute time is not an object of perception . . . appearances must determine for one another their position in time and make their time-order a necessary order." In this way, Kant goes on to say, "A series of appearances thus arises which makes necessary the same order and continuous connection in the series of possible perceptions as is met with a priori in time." Again, the nature of the time order (as a necessary order) is carried by the appearances via the understanding's application of the concept of causation (the concept of a necessary connection between appearances). Indeed it is the very function or role of the concept of causation to represent or constitute the necessary advance of time from the preceding to the succeeding, and in order to play this role it must be a concept of a *necessary emergence* of the later from the earlier. This then is Kant's answer to the first element of Hume's challenge regarding the nature of the causal bond or nexus itself. The necessary connection derives from the function causation plays in the constitution of time itself.

If the necessary advance from the earlier to the later is to be constituted by the advance of events, then every event at the later time must emerge from some event at the preceding time. The reason is that the emergence of later from earlier time is being understood as an abstract way of expressing that all events at the later time emerge from events at the earlier time. Events form equivalence classes under the relation of simultaneity and the relationship of times is expressed by the relationship of all members of the equivalence classes. In a similar vein, if relationships between cardinal numbers are represented or constituted by relations of members of equivalence classes of sets (under the relation of there being a one-to-one correspondence), then to say, for example, that 3 is less than 4 is to say that all members of the equivalence class for 3 are embeddable in all members of the equivalence class for 4. If only some events at the later time emerged from preceding events, then it wouldn't be the later time per se that emerged from the earlier time, but only the later time in regard to some events and not others, or only the later time in certain respects and not others. Times, however, do not emerge partially or in some respects, but simply emerge *tout court*. Hence all events at the later time must emerge or arise out of or derive from events that are earlier. In the paragraph at B 244 where Kant claims that it is appearances that constitute the representation of the time series, he says that because they do, "the appearances of past time determine *all* existences in the succeeding time" (italics mine). Since all events at later times emerge from (are determined by, arise from, etc.) preceding times, and every time is a later time (viz., no time is the first) it follows that every event whatsoever has a cause. Every event whatsoever, that is, is preceded by an earlier event that necessitates it. The causal bond or nexus holds for all events whatsoever. We thus have Kant's answer to the second element of Hume's challenge regarding the issue of why every event should have a cause. The universal law of causation follows from the function causation plays in the representation (or constitution) of time itself.

Again in the paragraph at B 245, where Kant says the appearances must "make their time-order a necessary order," Kant concludes that "that which follows or happens must follow in *conformity with a universal rule* upon that which was contained in the preceding states" (my emphasis). Kant is saying that the singular causal bond must also be in conformity with a universal rule; i.e., there must be a universal law that the particular cause always yields the effect. Now the necessary advance of time, I suggest, is homogeneous or uniform. The way or manner in which an earlier time gives way to or determines a later time is independent of which time it is. Equivalently, there is no respect specific to the time by which it determines or emerges into succeeding time. If the series of events, then, is to represent the necessary advance of time, now understood as also being a homogeneous necessity, then it cannot be that the same event at another time doesn't yield an effect that it (understood as a total cause) yields at one time. It follows then that any two events that are causally connected also come under absolutely universal laws. Equivalently, for all causes, the same cause always yields the same effect. But now recall that the fact that causes come under universal laws (together with the fact that every event has a cause) answers Hume's third concern regarding the cogency of causal reasoning (extrapolating from experienced regularity to unexperienced cases). Indeed these two facts together serve as the "uniformity of nature" principle that Hume demanded for the objective reasonableness of induction.

In sum, then, from the necessary advance of time and from time itself not "carrying" this advance, it follows that all events whatsoever are preceded by other events that determine or necessitate them and do so in accord with universal laws.

3. Specific Objections to Kant's Argument

The argument we have outlined depends on Kant's holding what we may call a partial causal theory of time. Unlike standard causal theories which attempt to define or constitute all temporal qualities and relations via causal relations, Kant's theory bases only the necessity of the advance or order of time on causality. In particular, the temporal relations of before and after or earlier and later are not based on causation. Succession, rather, derives from the pure intuition of the subject (Melnick 2000). Our interpretation of Kant's view then is not open to Suchting's objection (1969) that the causal theory derives the form of sensibility (time) from the form of the understanding (the concept of causation). Whereas Leibniz "well-founds" or grounds succession on the law of unfolding of the activity of substance (viz., on causation), Kant attributes succession and continuity to original intuition. Kant's partial causal theory of time then is not intellectualist or rationalist, but is in keeping with his explicit contention that time is an intuition (that sensibility is a factor distinct from understanding).

Further, Kant's partial causal theory of time is not an objectivist account. For Kant time does not exist objectively as either a series of moments or a series of temporal relations. Indeed as we have seen a key part of Kant's argument is that since there aren't any objective temporal relations it must be real (dynamical) relations among events that carry or bear the necessity of the advance from earlier to later. Although causal theories are classifiable with relational theories, perhaps, when the import is to contrast them with absolutist theories, they differ from relational theories precisely in refusing to countenance some or all specifically temporal relations. Time remains for Kant merely a form of intuition. Succession and magnitude is given only by the intuition of the subject (Melnick 2000). In the Second Analogy Kant is adding that it is only by such intuition governing or pertaining to events that are necessarily connected, that the order of time given by intuition becomes a necessary order via the events that intuited time encompasses. Holding either an absolutist or relational theory of time would contradict Kant's view that time is merely a form of intuition. However, holding that the succession of temporal intuition inherits necessity from the events it governs is consistent with time being nothing but a form of intuition. Hence, as against T. K. Swing (1969) and R. P. Wolff (1963), Kant's causal-dynamical theory of time in the Second Analogy is consistent with his view that there is no time apart from intuition.

Kant's argument turns essentially on there being an advance to time; viz., on times giving way or advancing or progressing (flowing) to other times. These characteristics pertain to what McTaggart (1927) called the A-series. McTaggart finds such characterizations problematic as they pertain to objective time, and Mellor (1995) goes so far as to say that accounts of causation which involve time's flow can be ignored. Now for Kant the flow or advance is not one of objective moments giving way or flowing into further moments. Rather it is the subject's intuition or time-construction (Melnick 2000) that is a flow (that advances). There is a flow to the motion of the subject that constitutes an advance. Kant says (B 153; 1965: 167) that time is represented by an act of the subject that determines succession, such as the drawing of a line. It is this act which literally flows or advances. This notion of time's flowing is not problematic. Further, as long as we remember that time exists only relatively to intuition (so that the advance of our time construction doesn't take place in relation to an objective time that flows) it doesn't lead to McTaggart's objections against an objective flow.

Kant himself raises a difficulty with his argument; namely, that most natural causes are simultaneous with their effects (B 248; Kant 1965: 228). If this is so then how can the causal relationship represent or constitute the necessary *succession* of time? Consider Kant's example of a ball on a cushion depressing it or hollowing it out. The necessary succession is in the states of the cushion from being fluffy to being hollowed out. That the continuing action of the ball is simultaneous with this succession is clearly consistent with the states of the cushion constituting a necessary advance. For Kant, indeed, it is states of substance which are the events or happenings that represent the necessary advance of time. The reason for this comes from the First Analogy where Kant defends what can be called a substance-based theory of time (Melnick 1989). Because substance represents or constitutes the ongoing-ness or lastingness of time itself, times exist basically in relation to each individual substance, and only secondarily are times coordinated into a universal time. Thus if events are to represent the necessary advance of ongoing time, the advance must be between events that are states of a substance. So far, this would be consistent with a Leibnizian view according to which the states of a substance unfold or necessarily give way to other states without any other conditions beyond the internal nature of the substance itself. I believe that from an a priori point of view, Kant's argument in the Second Analogy would permit this possibility. But it also allows (as with most natural causes) that the action, even the ongoing action, of other substances is involved in the necessary transition of states, so that the cushion goes from fluffy to hollow only with the impress of the ball. What the argument demands simply is that there be a necessary succession of states of substance, not that this transition be independent of any further simultaneous influence.

4. A General Objection to Kant's Argument

So far we have considered objections that are specific to the argument we set out in section 2. There are also objections directed not against that argument specifically, but against all arguments of that kind, and, indeed, against Kant's general method for establishing his results. One such influential objection is made by Stroud (1982) against transcendental arguments, that they only show what we must believe, not what is actually so. In regard to our present argument the objection would be that at best what it shows is that if we are to represent the necessary advance of time we must believe there are causes. If we take believing that there are causes to mean applying the concept of causation, the objection becomes that at most the argument shows that we must apply the concept, but not that it is truly applicable.

The concept of causality is a priori for Kant in that it goes beyond what can be given as an objective feature in the world. This is just Hume's point that the necessary bond is nowhere to be found in the objects. But this implies that applying the concept of a necessary bond cannot be mistaken because of a lack of correspondence to some feature in objects. Kant's basic employment of transcendental arguments is to deduce the necessity of applying a priori concepts, and thus to avoid skepticism regarding their objective employment. Now "skepticism" with regard to such concepts is not a doubt over whether they really correspond to what takes place in the object, since their being a priori exactly means that they don't apply by corresponding to features of the object. Rather, skepticism in regard to their application is that it is arbitrary, conventional, empty, or even meaningless. A similar issue of skepticism, I believe, arises in Quine's discussion of substance (1960) where he argues that the existence of substances is not given in possible sensory stimulation, but is part of an apparatus that is underdetermined by anything that could ever be given. In Kant's terms it is an a priori concept. But now the "skepticism" this leads to for Quine is in giving an account of how it is applicable. Quine wavers over whether its application is conventional, relative to background assumptions, arbitrary, or even whether it is meaningfully applicable at all or completely empty. A transcendental argument would show that the concept of substance must be applicable if cognition is to be possible. I believe Kant actually has such an argument in the First Analogy (Melnick 2001), but for now the important point is not the specific argument, but the fact that this type of argument with its conclusion effectively refutes the kind of skepticism that is relevant in regard to the application of a priori concepts. Once it is shown that they must be applicable and on what basis, there is no skepticism left as to whether they are applicable.

As an analogy, consider concepts of ordinal positions (first, second, third, etc.). These concepts are not found in features of things and so, in this sense, their application (via ordering procedures of the subject) is a priori But then it is also the case regarding four objects on my desk that the application of the concept of being the fourth one (by my giving an order to the objects) cannot fail for the object lacking a feature of fourth-ness that is supposed to belong to it on its own. Thus, an argument that established somehow the necessity of applying ordinal concepts to pluralities could not be criticized as still failing to show those concepts are applicable. In sum, the condition of the applicability of a priori concepts is their function in enabling cognition. The concept of a necessary bond is just a concept holding between events if the necessary advance of time (and so time per se, and so existence in time) is to be cognizable. This shows the concept must be applied, and it shows what the sense of necessity is (that pertaining to times inexorably giving way to or yielding other times). It refutes any contentions that the application is arbitrary, unfounded, or even empty and meaningless. In this manner it refutes skepticism with regard to a priori concepts and cannot be faulted for its leaving open any possibility that there might be a lack of this bond holding between the events themselves that would forge a distinction between our having to apply the concept and its being genuinely applicable.

We need to be somewhat more precise, at this point, as to what exactly is being deduced or established by transcendental arguments, since there seem to be empirical features, or features belonging to objects on their own, that are inextricably connected to the application of a priori concepts. In the case of causation, for example, the constant or universal conjunction of qualities of events (fire always followed by smoke) is an empirical factor. But now such universal conjunction is a condition of applying the concept of causation, or of a necessary bond, since this bond is also inherently universal (comes under universal laws of same cause always leading to same effect). Because this empirical factor is involved in the concept of causation, Kant avoids Maimon's objection (Thielke 2001) that a priori concepts have no empirical content and so nothing tying them specifically or differentially to objects. But now since there is this merely empirical element to the applicability of the concept of causation, we seem to be back into the problem of how transcendental arguments can establish the application of concepts *that include empirical elements* (Westphal 1997).

I do not believe that it is required to refute skepticism regarding a priori concepts that the empirical components of applicability be proven or established. Skepticism with regard to causation is that it is a concept that goes beyond constant conjunction, and hence is either empty or meaningless or subjective. To refute this one doesn't need to prove there are constant or regular conjunctions. It is enough to establish our right to apply to regular connections, *if there be any*, the concept that they are therefore connected by a necessary bond that comes under a universal law of such a bond. What needs to be deduced to avoid the skepticism specific to causation as an a priori concept is exactly that aspect of the concept of causation that goes beyond regularity or constant conjunction. Similarly, what is required to refute Quine's skepticism regarding substance is not to show that there is trackable reality (an empirical element) but that *if there is such trackable reality* we have a right to apply the concept of a single entity (rather than a series of entities) to such reality.

Suppose then that for every state whatsoever under certain further conditions there is a second preceding state that always is conjoined with it. What Kant is deducing is our right to hold that therefore all states have causes that necessitate them in accord with universal causal laws. What this means is that Kant is not deducing that there is cognizable reality (reality, say, existing in the necessary advance of time), since the existence of such cognizable reality depends on an empirical component (constant conjunction). Rather, he is deducing the a priori component or aspect of what is required for there to be cognizable reality. Once there is empirical regularity we are entitled to hold there are causal bonds between events, and there is no such thing as our merely believing there to be such bonds, since once the empirical conditions are met the applicability of the concept again becomes simply its required function in cognition. There is one respect, however, in which there being an empirical component to causation damages Kant's answer to Hume. If, as in section 1 above, the existence of universal laws of causation is to justify inductive reasoning, then we must *know* or have reason to believe that there are such laws. But whether there are such laws depends in part on there being universal conjunctions of qualities, so until these are known we do not know if there are universal laws of causation. But it seems that it is only by inductive reasoning from experienced regularities that we would know (empirically) that there are such conjunctions, and hence that there are universal causal laws.

According to our discussion, the concept of a necessary bond, though implicating empirical factors, is not an empirical concept. The notion of necessity is the notion of one element giving way to, yielding, or determining a second element. The notion gets its *sense*, for Kant, from the advance of time (that the earlier yields the later). Indeed the notion of causal necessitation is the application of *this* concept of necessary advance to events. The notion gets its *applicability* to events from the function events have to play in constituting the advance of time.

There will be such necessary connection in all possible worlds in which time necessarily advances. Since the uniformity of events is also implicated in this role or function and such uniformity is or involves an empirical factor, it is possible that different sorts of events play this role in different possible worlds. Thus, in our world it may be that transference of energy or momentum plays the role of what is universal or uniform in all transitions of events. This would mean that in our world the transference of momentum was the necessary bond or tie between events. This distinction between the a priori function that causation serves and the particular aspects of the world by which events fulfill this function, is one way of understanding the connection of the Second Analogy to the *Metaphysical Foundations of Natural Science*. (See also chapter 16 below.)

5. Other Interpretations of Kant's Argument

Kant says, "were I to posit the antecedent and the event were not to follow necessarily thereupon, I should have to regard the succession as a merely subjective play of my fancy" (B 247; Kant 1965: 227). Kant seems to be holding that the function of causality is to differentiate between what is merely subjective and what is objective. This is the view ultimately attributed to Kant by Lovejoy (1967), who notes that this would not distinguish Kant's defense of causation from that of many other philosophers who also held that causation (regularity, coherence) is the mark or criterion of objectivity. Another problem with this interpretation is that Kant discusses this function of causation in the Postulates, so this interpretation would make the Second Analogy somewhat redundant. Further, it is regularity or coherency or order that is usually taken to be the aspect of causation relevant to objectivity. But then this interpretation would provide no defense of a necessary bond between events, only their orderliness.

Further still, there seems to be no reason why causal coherency should go with objectivity. The idea is that those sensory states of ours that causally cohere among themselves are the objective ones pertaining to what goes on in the world. But if one looks at other machines their regular or coherent states derive from how they are built internally, whereas their irregular states are due to external disturbances or influences. This should lead us to believe that our coherent sensory states are due to the unfolding of our internal nature, and it is the irregular states that pertain to what is outside us. On our understanding of Kant's view, on the other hand, causal connections constitute the necessary advance of the time series. What this means is that if we took irregular experiences to be objective, we couldn't represent them taking place in a time that necessarily advances from earlier to later. It is this representation of time that requires us to take our regular (potentially causally coherent) experiences as the objective ones, or the ones that pertain to the unfolding of time. On our account then Kant has a reason for favoring regularity as a criterion of objectivity, unlike, perhaps, either Berkeley or Descartes. This doesn't mean that there cannot ultimately be irregular objective experiences, as in the detections of results in quantum-mechanical experiments. It only means there is a *prima facie* bias toward tying regularity apt for causality to objectivity.

The most serious objection to the first alternative interpretation is that it makes no connection at all between causation and time. Kant clearly holds that the Analogies deal with issues of existence in time. A second alternative interpretation that avoids this objection is that causality functions to give happenings determinate positions in time (see Guyer 1987; Melnick 1973). The determination of the times of occurrences, on this view, is in terms of causal laws. Thus Kant says in characterizing the Analogies, "What determines for each occurrence its position in time is the rule of the understanding through which alone the existence of appearances can acquire synthetic unity as regards relations of time" (B 262; Kant 1965: 237). One problem with this interpretation is that it is compatible with regularity accounts of causation. On such accounts, there are no singular necessary connections between events, but only events being instances of "law-like" generalizations, where the latter is defined independent of any conception of singular bonds. Now to begin with this is not Kant's account. His universal laws are of the form: Always events of type X *necessitate* (force, yield, determine) events of type Y (B 198; Kant 1965: 195). On the regularity account, on the other hand, the universal laws are of the form: Always, in some law defining manner, events of type X are followed by events of type Y. Now regularity accounts usually hold that the law-like regularities are the ones that allow of inductive generalization and hence allow for the determination of time position. In other words events are determined in time by our tracing back to them in terms of law-like connections.

A second problem with this interpretation is that it too, like the first alternative interpretation, seems to make the Second Analogy redundant in regard to the Postulates, since Kant there holds, "Our knowledge of the existence of things reaches ... so far as perception and its advance according to empirical laws can extend" (B 273; Kant 1965: 243).

A third problem with this interpretation is that it is perfectly compatible with an objectivist theory of time. Someone who holds either a relational or an absolutist theory of time (of what it is to have temporal position) can also hold that we determine the temporal position of occurrences via causal laws. On our interpretation, on the other hand, it is because there is no objective temporality (and the universal necessary advance is not to be found in the intuiting that generates time itself) that the necessary advance has to be found in the dynamical relations of appearances. Now the Second Analogy is supposed to be the deduction of an a priori concept, and hence an application of Kant's method for deducing a priori concepts set out in the Transcendental Deduction. However, it is clear that time as a form of intuition (as nonobjective) plays a key role in that method. It ought, therefore, to play a key role in the Second Analogy.

A final problem with this interpretation is that it depends on the knowability or verifiability of time positions. There must be causal laws, else we could not determine, verify, or know the positions of occurrences in time. However, Kant differentiates the categories of modality from the other categories by holding that the former "only express the relation of the concept to the faculty of knowledge" (B 266; Kant 1965: 239). This would seem to imply that the Second Analogy, by contrast, does not deal with *our* determining when things occurred. Rather it should be understood in a non-epistemological way as dealing with what it is for occurrences to *have* position in time. On our interpretation, what it is for occurrences to be in time is that they occur within the necessary advance of time from earlier to later which, independent of any determination of position in time, presupposes universal necessary connections between events.

A third interpretation, and the most common one perhaps, is that succession according to a rule is definitive of objective succession, as opposed to objective co-existence. This interpretation makes Kant's discussion of perceiving the successive states of a ship a opposed to perceiving the parts of a house the crux of his argument (Longuenesse 1998; Allison 1983). In the case of perceiving a succession as with the ship there is a rule of irreversibility governing the order of perceptions, whereas in the case of successively perceiving the parts of the house there is no such rule. Thus all perception of succession involves a rule governing the order of the perception. The first problem with this interpretation is that a rule of irreversible order is something different from a causal connection (Bennett 1966: 221). For example, in chess there is a rule of irreversible order according to which one must move at least one pawn before one moves a bishop. From this it does not follow that moving a pawn causes, necessitates, or forces moving a bishop. At best a rule of irreversibility expresses only a necessary condition for the second perception. This severs irreversibility from deterministic causation, since, for example, certain set-ups in quantum mechanics are necessary for particles to go through a potential barrier, but that set-up is compatible with the particle failing to penetrate the barrier. We have a succession from a particle projected to a particle going through barrier which is irreversible but not causal. The second problem with this interpretation is that it gives no reason for the same rule of irreversibility to hold on different occasions. Why shouldn't the rule on one occasion be that perceiving the ship upstream must precede perceiving it downstream, while on another occasion the rule is that one must first perceive upstream? This interpretation gives no defense of universal laws.

If this is not Kant's argument, the question remains why Kant discusses these examples at all. My suggestion is that Kant is not arguing for causation by these examples, but rather is setting up what the *relata* for causal relations are. Indeed Kant opens up the Second Analogy (B 235–6; Kant 1965: 219–20) with general remarks that reiterate his position in the Transcendental Deduction that the objects of our cognition are appearances (perceptions), not things in themselves, but that nevertheless we can represent objectively by rules (for perceptions) that constrain our actual perceptions. It is *proper* perceptions, that is, that constitute objectivity. Thus if I actually perceive X, that is nothing objective. It is this actual perception corresponding to how it is proper or correct to perceive that makes it objective. The objective truth, that is, is its being proper to perceive X. Now Kant has a minor problem when it comes to extending this account of objectivity to temporal succession. He cannot just say that perceiving X and then perceiving Y is an objective succession if it is proper to perceive X and then perceive Y. The reason is that in the case of a house it is perfectly proper to perceive the roof and then perceive the foundation in that order, but in that case there is no objective succession. Kant needs more than a rule that how I perceive is proper; he needs the rule to be that the order is not only proper, but is irreversible. Kant's discussion of irreversibility then is not to establish causation, but to extend his account of objectivity to temporal succession. In this way he then has objective temporal successions to which the concept of causation may then pertain. Causation, or necessary succession is supposed to hold between proper perceptions that pertain to a single substance. I claim that perceptions for Kant, unlike sensory states, are not mere monadic states of the subject, but are transactions. To signify this I shall call the perceptions *reactions*. Then the causal relation is expressible in terms of objective appearances (proper perceptions) as follows: With regard to a particular substance, the propriety of reacting fire necessitates or gives way to or yields the propriety of reacting smoke. It is this necessary connection between all possible appearances (proper reactions) that constitutes the necessary advance of time.

6. Concluding Textual Remarks

Kemp Smith (1918) recognizes the argument we have presented in section 2 as being the argument of the two paragraphs at B 244–5, but holds that this argument is distinct from the main line of argumentation in the Second Analogy. On our view the argument of these two paragraphs is the main line of argumentation. The first statement

ARTHUR MELNICK

of the argument in the A edition is from B 236, where Kant says, "Let us now proceed to our problem," to B 239 (Kant 1965: 221–2). Kant connects objective succession to irreversible order. He doesn't however just identify this rule of irreversibility with causality. Rather, he says that in conformity with such a rule there must be a causal connection (i.e., the preceding states together with some condition must necessitate the succeeding state). His defense of this claim is that "The advance . . . from a given time to the determinate time that follows is a necessary advance" (B 239; Kant 1965: 222). Although this paragraph is somewhat obscure, Kant clearly doesn't just derive causality from irreversibility alone, but somehow derives it from the necessary advance of time. This argument I believe can be reconstructed as follows. The rule of irreversibility cannot be arbitrary or made up like a rule in a child's game that you have to touch your nose before you touch your ear. The question then is what is the basis of the rule? It cannot be intrinsic objective states that the proper reactions correspond to, since there aren't such corresponding states for Kant. From what then do rules of irreversibility derive? Well Kant says that I cannot go back in time; time, that is, is necessarily irreversible. Not only is it irreversible, but more strongly the preceding necessarily determines the succeeding. If then events constituted this nature of time, there would be rules of necessary advance that a fortiori were also rules of irreversibility. In this way rules of irreversibility would be grounded or based in the nature of time. I believe an alternative way Kant could have argued is to say that succession to be objective requires not only a rule (irreversibility) that distinguishes it from co-existence, but also requires its taking place in an ongoing necessary advance of time, and the latter requires full causality.

The second statement of the argument is from B 239 ("Let us suppose there is nothing antecedent to an event") to B 241 (Kant 1965: 222–4). It ends with Kant saying the rule of causation "determines the series of events" and is "a condition of the unity of appearances in time." This at least allows that the function of causation is to generate a series of events that constitute the advance of time.

The third statement of the argument goes form B 242 to B 244 (Kant 1965: 224–5). The paragraph beginning "We have representations in us . . ." reiterates his general conception of objectivity. The next paragraph ("In the synthesis of appearances") applies it again to the special case of temporal relations. In that paragraph he claims that there is a twofold result. Firstly, there must be irreversible order, and secondly there must be a causal connection. Kant clearly then does not conflate irreversibility with causality. The causal or determining relation he holds connects an event "in necessary relation with itself in the time-series." Causation, then, for Kant is something more than irreversibility, and its role is to provide necessity in the time-series (and not just to constitute objective succession).

The fourth statement of the argument is just the two paragraphs at B 244 to B 245 (Kant 1965: 225–6) which we discussed in section 2 and which explicitly state that causation constitutes the necessary advance of time (or the time order being a necessary order). In each of these statements of the argument then there is explicit or implicit reference to the nature of the time-series itself as being a series in which the earlier time determines the later time, and so a connection of causation to the necessary advance of time. It is not true, then, that this connection of causation to time stands outside the main line of argumentation of the Second Analogy.

180

References and Further Reading

Allison, Henry (1983). *Kant's Transcendental Idealism*. New Haven: Yale University Press.

Bennett, Jonathan (1966). *Kant's Analytic*. Cambridge: Cambridge University Press.

Guyer, Paul (1987). *Kant and the Claims of Knowledge*. Cambridge: Cambridge University Press.

Hume, David (1978). *A Treatise on Human Nature*, ed. L. A. Selby-Bigge. Oxford: Oxford University Press.

Kant, Immanuel (1965). *Critique of Pure Reason*, tr. N. Kemp Smith. New York/London: St. Martin's/Macmillan.

Kant, Immanuel (1970). *Metaphysical Foundations of Natural Science*, tr. James Ellington. Indianapolis, NY: Bobbs-Merrill.

Kemp Smith, Norman (1918). *A Commentary to Kant's Critique Pure Reason*. London: Macmillan

Longuenesse, Béatrice (1998). *Kant and the Capacity to Judge*, tr. C. T. Wolfe. Princeton: Princeton University Press.

Lovejoy, A. I. (1967). On Kant's reply to Hume. In M. S. Gram (ed.), *Kant: Disputed Questions*. Chicago: University of Chicago Press.

McTaggart, J. M. E. (1927). *The Nature of Existence*. Cambridge: Cambridge University Press.

Mellor, D. H. (1995). *The Facts of Causation*. London and New York: Routledge.

Melnick, Arthur (1973). *Kant's Analogies of Experience*. Chicago: University of Chicago Press.

Melnick, Arthur (1989). *Space, Time, and Thought in Kant*. Dordrecht: D. Reidel.

Melnick, Arthur (2000). Kant vs. Lambert and Trendelenburg on the ideality of time. *History of Philosophy Quarterly*, 18(1).

Melnick, Arthur (2001). Categories, logical functions, and schemata in Kant. *Review of Metaphysics*, 54(3).

Quine, W. V. O. (1960). *Word and Object*. Cambridge, MA: MIT Press.

Stroud, Barry (1982). Transcendental arguments. In R. C. S. Walker (ed.), *Kant on Pure Reason*. Oxford: Oxford University Press.

Suchting, W. A. (1969). Kant's second analogy of experience. In Lewis White Beck (ed.), *Kant Studies Today* (pp. 322–40). LaSalle, IL: Open Court.

Swing, T. K. (1969). *Kant's Transcendental Logic*. New Haven: Yale University Press.

Thielke, Peter (2001). Discursivity and causality: Maimon's challenge to the second analogy. *Kant-Studien*, 92.

Westphal, Kenneth R. (1997). Affinity, idealism and naturalism: the stability of cinnabar and the possibility of experience. *Kant Studien*, 88.

Wolff, R. P. (1963). *Kant's Theory of Mental Activity*. Cambridge, MA: Harvard University Press.

12

Kant's Refutation of Problematic Idealism: Kantian Arguments and Kant's Arguments against Skepticism

WOLFGANG CARL

Since Strawson's book *The Bounds of Sense* (1966), many contemporary philosophers with some interest in Kant have been concerned with the question whether transcendental philosophy can provide a refutation of skepticism, and if so, how. But very often the discussion of this problem has focused not so much on Kant himself as on contemporary reconstructions of Kant, well-known under the title "transcendental arguments." It is not surprising, therefore, that a classic criticism of transcendental arguments was in fact directed not against Kant's own theory as such, but against the views of Strawson and company. The criticism I have in mind was raised by Barry Stroud in his paper "Transcendental Arguments" of 1968. Stroud concludes that a refutation of skepticism by means of a transcendental argument amounts to nothing more nor less than an application of some version of the verification principle. Stroud has more recently directed this criticism against Kant himself. In what follows I will discuss the validity of his criticism.

In his paper "Kantian Arguments, Conceptual Capacities and Invulnerability" (1994), Stroud characterizes Kant's transcendental philosophy by laying out the three things that such a theory must accomplish. They are the following:

1. The theory has to be an exhaustive investigation of the necessary condition of the possibility of knowledge.
2. It has to proceed a priori, independently of observation.
3. The conditions uncovered by transcendental philosophy have to concern not merely the ways we think about, or experience, the world, but also the ways things really are in the world.

According to Stroud, the third claim is "what is most striking and original about this radical Kantian turn in philosophy" (Stroud 1994: 231). For what is peculiar to this Kantian, or rather "Copernican," revolution is not quite captured by the general idea that the world has to behave in a certain way in order for us to think and experience things as we do. We know that the things around us must have certain characteristics and must affect us in certain ways, if we are going to experience them in the way we do. But this knowledge is empirical, while what is peculiar to transcendental philosophy is the fact, if indeed it is a fact at all, that the connection between the world and our thoughts must be uncovered by a priori reasoning. Moreover, the connection between world and thought sought after by transcendental philosophy is supposed to be a necessary one: that things are a certain way is a necessary condition of our thinking things as we do. Now given Stroud's characterization of what is peculiar to transcendental philosophy in the terms just indicated, a certain question comes immediately to mind, namely, as he puts it, how an inference from statements about how we *think* of the world to a statement about the way things *are* can ever be justified (Stroud 1968: 246).

According to Stroud we can give such a justification only by either presupposing a connection between the meaningful use of our language in our talk about the world and some kind of knowledge of its correct application, as Strawson did by calling on the "principle of significance" (a certain version of the verification principle), or by assuming some kind of idealism according to which the world depends in some way or other on our mind, as Kant is supposed to have done by calling on transcendental idealism. Thus we have to ask whether the project of a transcendental philosophy can be carried out without presupposing either an unsupported and controversial thesis about meaning, or a problematic idealistic interpretation of our notion of an external world. Stroud gives a negative answer to the question raised, while I want to show that there is a possibility of pursuing this project without accepting either horn of his dilemma.

Let's consider first what Kant himself has to say about the connection between necessary conditions of our empirical knowledge and certain "nonpsychological truths about the world," as Stroud would put it. In the *Critique of Pure Reason*, at B 124–5, Kant gives an analysis of the relation between "synthetic representations and their objects." He says to start out with that this relation can take two different forms. Either the representation is causally determined by the object; or the object is causally determined by the representation. The first case is supposed to hold true for all of our empirical representations. But how will Kant account for a priori representations, which – by definition – are not empirical and hence are not causally determined by their objects? It would seem that he has no choice but to invoke the second case of the sought after relation. But that would be to say that a representation can causally determine its object, and Kant explicitly denies that this can be the case with regard to the cognitive representations of finite beings such as we are (cf. Bird 1996: 232). Thus he proposes a third kind of relation between an a priori representation and its object: "the representation is thus determinant of the object a priori, if it is possible through it alone *to cognize something as an object*" (B 124–5; author's translations throughout). What does he have in mind, and how can the third kind of relation be established?

As to the first question, there is no denying that Kant's talk about determination of an object is not very perspicuous, but it is obvious from the passage I just quoted that he wants to exclude a causal dependency. Thus the widespread idea of a constitution or generation of the world we talk about by means of the conditions of our thinking is plainly excluded; the model "mind makes nature" – or that our "beliefs are 'made true' by believing them" (Stroud 2000: 200) – doesn't fit the picture Kant wants to give. But that said, it remains for me to give a positive account of what is going on here. Kant's claim has the form of an implication and states that a representation is determinant of an object a priori, if the representation is a condition of the possibility of our knowledge of the object. Given the propositional nature of our knowledge, the idea of an object has to be cashed out in terms analogous to Stroud's talk of "nonpsychological truths about the world." How is it possible that nonpsychological truths about a world independent of our thought and experience can be determined by the conditions of our knowledge?

At the end of the paragraph from the first *Critique* we were just considering, Kant claims that the conditions of knowledge "refer necessarily and a priori to objects of experience, since only by means of them can any object of experience ever be thought" (B 126). This claim states that conditions, which Stroud calls "psychological truths," are satisfied by – or, as Kant says, refer to – the objects of our knowledge, if these conditions make knowledge of objects possible in the first place. Given the propositional nature of our knowledge, these objects have to be taken as whatever it is that makes our statements true or false. Kant claims, therefore, that the conditions of our knowledge of the truth-value of a given statement refer to whatever it is in virtue of which the statement has its truth-value. The meaning of Kant's claim is determined by what the claim excludes. At a minimum, the claim excludes the possibility that the conditions of knowledge of the truth-value of a statement, that is the conditions of its verification or its falsification, have nothing to do with whatever is responsible for the truth-value we ascribe to the statement. To admit the excluded possibility would be to allow that the conditions of verification might be satisfied, without our being able to determine what makes the statement true or false. In other words: what is excluded by Kant's claim is the possibility that our knowledge of the truth-values of our statements about the world has nothing to do with the existence of the world and the way the world is. If this possibility were not excluded, the world would be "nothing for us," as Kant sometimes puts it (*R* 4634, 28.87). The world would be epistemically inaccessible to us, and the notion of knowledge of objects would make no sense at all. On the other hand, Kant's claim does not exclude the possibility that the world extends beyond the reach of our mind; but it does entail that we cannot divorce the notion of being verified from the notion of being true, for those things that are not beyond the mind's reach. In his *Lectures on Metaphysics*, Kant claims: "The objects must conform to the conditions according to which they can be known; this is the nature of human understanding" (28.239). For Kant, the nature of human understanding is captured by the conceptual truth that we do not have any notion of knowledge of the world separate from our notion of the world itself. This claim does not imply that the world depends on our knowledge of it, nor does it identify the world with our actual or possible knowledge of it.

At this point Stroud might object to Kant that truths about an external and independent world cannot follow from truths concerned with our ways of thinking, that there is a gap between statements about an external world and statements about our thoughts and experiences – a gap which cannot be bridged. But according to Stroud Kant does not deny the semantic distinction between these two kinds of statement – a distinction to be explained by the different truth conditions these statements are assumed to have. Instead Kant allegedly tries to undercut the semantic distinction by giving an idealistic reinterpretation of the statements which are supposed to describe an external and independent world. But what is the relation between Kant's claim about the conformity of objects with the conditions of their knowledge and the semantic distinction pointed out by Stroud? And is it true that Kant's claim has to be understood in terms of such an idealistic reinterpretation? In order to answer these questions one must attend to two peculiar features of Kant's claim.

First of all, the claim is concerned with the non-empirical conditions of knowledge and, therefore, not quite generally with what Stroud calls "psychological truths," but rather with *a priori truths* with regard to whatever "is necessary for the synthetic unity of experience" (B 197). Because experience is for Kant the only way of having any access at all to truths about the world, the a priori or formal conditions of experience have to be in conformity somehow with whatever can be given in experience, i.e., with whatever can be said truly about the world. For example: if a temporal or spatial order of our representations belongs to the formal conditions of our knowledge of the world, whatever can be said truly about it has to include reference to some temporal or spatial location. Thus Kant's famous claim that "the conditions of the possibility of experience in general are at the same time conditions of the possibility of the objects of experience" (B 197) has to be understood in light of the conformity thesis just invoked. The conditions referred to are a priori or formal conditions, and Kant is claiming in effect that there is a correspondence between the formal conditions of our knowledge and those of a true description of the world. One can perfectly well hold to this restriction with regard to a priori conditions, without thereby giving an idealistic reinterpretation of our talk about an external and independent world, contrary to what Stroud supposes. Restricting oneself to the conformity between the a priori conditions of our knowledge and the formal conditions of a correct description of the world is perfectly harmless: it does not commit us to saying that what is, or can be, described is constituted by, or dependent on, our ways of thinking.

Given the restricted scope of Kant's conformity thesis, it follows that the thesis does not license any "idealistic" reinterpretation of our talk about the world. Nor does it lead to the "horrors of transcendental idealism" (Stroud 1994: 236). But how can the thesis account for the semantic difference between statements about an external and independent world and statements about our thoughts? In order to answer this question, one must attend to the second peculiar feature of Kant's claim, namely that it is not as general in scope as Stroud assumes when he invokes the semantic distinction. Kant himself is interested only in conditions of knowledge, while Stroud's so-called "psychological facts" include only our beliefs, thoughts, and representations, excluding those very psychological facts which are picked out by our epistemic vocabulary: the language we use to talk about knowledge. What is peculiar about the justified use of our epistemic vocabulary is that it bridges the gap between what we take to be true and what really is true. But it is not difficult to understand why Stroud excludes talk about knowledge: if one takes for granted that transcendental philosophy aims at a refutation of skepticism, one cannot assume from the outset that any justified use of our epistemic vocabulary is possible. In this way we come to realize what is the basic issue for Stroud's criticism of transcendental reasoning, and so we will be able to point out the real difference between him and Kant.

Any philosophical investigation of human knowledge has to take account of the possibility of error. By distinguishing between "psychological facts" and "truths about the world" (Stroud 1994: 232), and by insisting upon the gap between them, Stroud certainly makes room for the independence of truth from what we take to be true, but he does so in such a radical way that the possibility of knowledge cannot be explained

185

any more. Stroud interprets the said distinction in the spirit of "strong realism," as von Kutschera calls it, according to which a statement P is objective, if and only if its meaning is independent of the meaning of statements about psychological facts, that is, if and only if neither P nor its negation follows from a consistent set of psychological statements. In other words: if and only if nothing about the world itself follows from anything we think about the world. But notice that the semantic distinction between psychological truths about our thoughts and nonpsychological truths about the world does not entail that the latter must be objective in the sense defined. For the distinction is compatible with the uncontroverted assumption that nonpsychological truths about the world are, or can be, empirical, i.e. with the assumption that the truth-values of nonpsychological statements about the world can be established (at least in part) by observation (cf. Kutschera 1981: 396ff). When we merely state the truth conditions of such statements, we make no reference to any observation or to anything mental; such reference comes into play only when we give the conditions of the statement's verification. But to say that a statement's conditions of verification have been satisfied is to imply that the statement is true. Therefore empirically verified statements about an external, mind-independent world cannot be objective in the sense of strong realism.

The distinction between a statement's truth conditions and the conditions of its verification doesn't deny the difference between psychological and nonpsychological truths. Quite the contrary: it does justice to this difference by distinguishing between what a statement means and the way we establish the statement's truth-value. A key thing about this distinction is that it also points to an intimate connection between the two: when we can show that a statement's conditions of verification have been satisfied, we have shown at the same time that the truth conditions of the statement have also been satisfied. For the satisfaction of the former implies that the truth conditions of statements about the external world have been satisfied, i.e., that such statements are true. Hence, nonpsychological truths are necessary conditions of psychological truths, because knowledge implies truth. But the semantic distinction between psychological and nonpsychological truths, which underlies Stroud's criticism of transcendental arguments, is compatible with such a claim. Nor does the claim amount to an "idealistic" reinterpretation of our talk about the world. Thus, what Stroud takes to be the "most striking and original" thing about the "radical Kantian turn in philosophy" (Stroud 1994: 231) is neither striking, nor radical, nor perhaps even all that original. In any case, the "Kantian turn in philosophy" is untouched by Stroud's criticism of transcendental arguments.

I think Stroud's misapprehension of what is really going on in Kant stems from the assumption that Kant's transcendental philosophy is designed *tout court* to face "the threat of general skepticism" (Stroud 1994: 234). It is this assumption that governs Stroud's characterization of the semantic distinction between psychological and nonpsychological truths. The same assumption explains why Stroud excludes from consideration those psychological truths which are picked out by an epistemic vocabulary. While Kant's concern is the connection of knowledge with its object, as far as the a priori conditions of knowledge go, Stroud's concern is more generally with truths about our thought, belief, and experience on the one hand and truths about an external, mind-independent world on the other. It is therefore quite characteristic of Stroud that he should explain the "most ambitious form of transcendental arguments" in the following way: they demonstrate "of some of the things we believe that their truth is a necessary condition of our thinking and believing them" (Stroud 1994: 241). But remember that Kant was not concerned with the necessary conditions of our believing something or other; rather his concern was with the necessary conditions of our *knowledge*. If his reflections were supposed to refute skepticism, he would have been well advised to raise the question whether we have any knowledge at all – instead of taking on the connection between knowledge and its object.

At this point, one might wonder how Kant himself faces the skeptical challenge. The first thing to notice is that Kant's answer to skepticism differs a lot from that given by philosophers in this century, such as Carnap, Wittgenstein, and Heidegger (cf. Bird 1989: 34ff). They all try to "neutralize" that challenge, although it goes without saying that these different philosophers are doing it in different ways. One of the most subtle ways of performing this task is to be found in the writings of Stroud.

What I mean by "neutralizing the skeptical challenge" can be explained as follows. The skeptic is concerned with the beliefs about an external world we ascribe to ourselves and to others. We cannot attribute beliefs unless we understand them, which presupposes in turn that we share many of the beliefs with those to whom we ascribe them. Given Davidson's idea that interpretation should be governed by the rule of maximizing agreement between the interpreter's beliefs and those of the person to be interpreted, it follows that there are limits on the extent and kind of error we can attribute to those whom we are interpreting. It goes without saying that we can assume that this person might be wrong with regard to a particular case, or even with regard to a whole class of cases, and that we therefore disagree with him or her. But disagreement no longer makes much sense if we come to more general, or to more abstractly formulated, beliefs: the belief, for example, that there is an external world, that there are spatiotemporal objects existing independently of us, etc. The skeptic is concerned with beliefs of this kind.

The skeptic entertains the possibility that we believe many things about an external, mind-independent world, but that all these beliefs are false. To entertain this possibility is to assume two things: (1) that there are such beliefs and (2) that they are all false. It is the complexity of this twofold assumption which makes life hard for the skeptic. The real difficulty is not that the assumption of these beliefs is incompatible with the assumption that they are all false: that we have beliefs about an external, mind-independent world does not imply that they are true. The two sides of the possibility entertained by the skeptic are compatible with each other. The real difficulty is rather that you yourself can't believe many things about an external, mind-independent world, and yet assume that your own beliefs about this world are false. We must therefore distinguish between what is impossible as such and what is impossible to believe. The possibility entertained by the skeptic is of the latter kind: it is not inconsistent as such, but it is inconsistent to believe it. Hence, what the skeptic wants to doubt cannot be doubted after all. This holds true of certain very general beliefs which are indispensable for any conception of an independent world. What is shown in this way is not the truth of those beliefs, but rather that they are invulnerable against any skeptical attack. Indispensability implies invulnerability (Stroud 1999: 166).

Now let's have a look at Kant's way of facing the idealist skeptical challenge. His discussion of skepticism has no well-defined place within the overall architecture of the *Critique of Pure Reason*; it differs quite a bit in both editions of the first *Critique*, and even after 1787 it underwent revisions. It is not my concern here to explore Kant's different arguments against skepticism and to determine whether they hold water. Rather I am interested in considering what they are supposed to prove and their general proof-strategy. What Kant aims to prove is defined in the first *Critique* as follows (B 275): "even our inner experience, undoubted by Descartes, is possible only under the presupposition of outer experience." In *R* 6313, written in 1790, he claims: "even inner experience can be understood only by the relation between our sense and an object outside me." Inner experience is the way we get knowledge about our mental states, activities, etc. – an idea taken over by Kant from Locke. A constitutive part of such knowledge is the awareness of someone who is in such a state or performs such an activity. This awareness, described by Kant as "empirical consciousness of one's own existence in time" (*R* 6313, 18.613), presupposes the notion of something persisting in change; and this notion is available to us only by means of the notion of a spatial object and of outer sense.

Such a consideration has to be seen within the framework of Strawson's "only connect" – analysis in *Skepticism and Naturalism*, which connects the meaningful use of certain concepts with that of certain others. But I don't think that this fits Kant's way of proceeding. Kant doesn't aim at the availability of certain concepts, but rather at the knowledge one must have, if one is to have beliefs, to evaluate them and to correct them in the light of others. It is a kind of knowledge entailed by the very possibility of ascribing beliefs to oneself. Even the skeptic has to grant such a knowledge of his own mind, if his project of a critical scrutiny of our beliefs about an external, mind-independent world is to make any sense at all. Kant's refutation of skepticism consists in exploring what is required for having this kind of knowledge. My account is based on his posthumous writings, because they are more explicit and more revealing than anything he published.

For pursuing the project of a critical scrutiny of one's beliefs one has to know that at different times one might have the same or different beliefs, or "representations," as Kant would have put it. This knowledge presupposes that one knows oneself as being the same subject of different belief states at different times. One can explain this point by giving an example: I can't pursue the project of a critical scrutiny of my beliefs, if I am not able to recognize some error or other of mine. But being able to do that requires an ability to correct one's earlier beliefs within the context of present beliefs and to come to believe that some of one's earlier beliefs are wrong. Having this belief presupposes that one knows in some way or other that one is the same person having different beliefs at different times. But how can I know that I am the same person and, therefore, something persistent for different belief states? Kant's answer to this question mentions that I have to know my "place in the world," because "the soul as an object of the inner sense cannot perceive her place in the body, but she is at that place where there is the human being" (*R* 6315, 18.619). This claim has to be understood in the following way: In order to know something about me considered as being a soul, i.e. as a diachronic subject of different mental states, I have to know something about me here, about my "place in the world." But why do I have to know something about the place "in which my soul is" and, therefore, something about me as a human being, i.e. as "an object of outer sense," and about "my place in the world" (loc. cit. 18.620)?

Let's suppose that all my perception of spatial objects, including myself, and all my beliefs about them are illusions, "a play of imagination." However, having those perceptions and beliefs at all, entails that "one is conscious of being affected by external objects" (*R* 6312, 18.613). Why? It is the content of my beliefs which requires a certain kind of causal interaction between my beliefs and external objects: "There would be no material for external representations in the imagination, if there were no outer sense" (*R* 6313, 18.613). Even if all my perceptions and beliefs about outer objects are wrong, these mental states must have some content or other for being wrong about anything at all. Thus, these perceptions might be fictions or, as Kant puts it, "*Dichtungen*," but this possibility "does not concern that they do not have outer objects at all" (*R* 6315, 18.619). It is this assumption of content which cannot be avoided even in a counterfactual situation like a complete dream or an unlimited madness and which leads to the view of "a realist of outer intuition" (*R* 6315, 18.620), who claims that the content of our outer representations *guarantees* that we as subjects of such mental states are themselves in space, and that these states are causally related to what happens to occur in space. This argument has to be considered as a piece of an "externalist theory" of mental content: Given the fact that we know that we do have representations of spatial objects, it concludes that we know that we are somewhere in space. But we can't know that without knowing that we are spatially related to other objects in space (cf. Burge 1986: 125ff). Thus the skeptical claim that we don't have any knowledge of external objects is wrong.

Another attempt to refute the skeptical claim is based upon the reference of what is called "pure indexicals" to be found in a very late manuscript – the so-called "*Loses Blatt Leningrad 1 (LB),*" only recently discovered in a public library in St. Petersburg. Kant begins with the idea of a subject who makes an attempt to scrutinize his beliefs. Such a subject is called "empirical apperceptio percipientis," who "says I was, I am, I will be, that means: I am something past, present and future" (*LB* I.22–4). What Kant has in mind can be stated in the following way: the idea of a subject of beliefs is connected with using indexicals like "I," "now," "before," and "later" for self-ascribing the same or different belief states at different times. However, given the use of these indexicals you are not able to say or to think that something is at the same time as something else ("*zugleich sein*" – *LB* I.27). Kant argues that the content of this thought requires a representation of something in space, because the sequence of datable mental occurrences is only successive (cf. *R* 6312). In this way he wants to make room for the idea that I am here, somewhere in space. I am not convinced by this argument. Perhaps there is another way of establishing his point.

We have to distinguish between different representations occurring at the same times and presentations of different things existing at the same time. Kant refers to a particular case of the latter kind by mentioning perceptions of different objects in space existing simultaneously which you can't see at once (cf. B 257). Thus, although there is a temporal succession in perceiving them, this order can always be reversed. You see first the tree and then the house, or the other way round. In such a case the temporal sequence of your mental representations has nothing to do with the temporal sequence of the existence or occurrence of what is represented. That there is no such correlation has to be explained by reference to the facts that you need a point of view for perceiving, and that not everything existing simultaneously at a given place can be perceived

189

simultaneously. These facts seem to be rather basic for understanding the very notion of perceptions of objects in space (see chapters 10 and 11 above).

One can understand the possibility of there being no correspondence between the temporal order of perceptions and the temporal order of what is perceived without having any veridical perception at all. Because we have perceptions of outer sense which are representations of things existing simultaneously, but not perceived simultaneously, we have to think that we are somewhere, and that, given our present perceptions, we are here. The content of those perceptions has to be explained by our point of view which provides only a limited accessibility to what simultaneously exists and, thus, by the place where we are. One has to conceive one's perception of an outer object, veridical or otherwise, therefore, not only as something occurring right now, but as well as occurring right here. Thus, you have to conceive yourself as a "*Weltwesen*" (*LB* II.4) – as a being that is somewhere at a given time.

The general strategy behind Kant's considerations can be described in the following way: You need all the "pure indexicals" together for making sense of any of them. There is no doubt, as we know from Descartes, that the skeptic needs the indexical "I." Kant reminds us that we need the temporal indexical, as well, which in turn has to be supplemented by the use of the spatial indexical "here." But the truth of my belief that I am now here gives me all that I need for knowing that there is at least one external object, namely myself. Thus, the skeptic's claim that we don't have any knowledge of external objects is wrong.

I think that these sketchy remarks may be sufficient to point out the peculiarity of Kant's way of facing the skeptical challenge. Strawson and Stroud show that the skeptical challenge can be rebutted because the possibility entertained by the skeptic cannot be held to be true. They differ from Davidson, because they do not presume to have shown that this possibility cannot obtain. Hence they do not offer a refutation of skepticism, but rather a way of neutralizing it: the skeptical doubt is "idle." However, Kant does make an attempt to refute skepticism, namely by considering the kind of knowledge that even the skeptic has to make room for in order to establish his doubt. This knowledge concerns our beliefs, and the identity of the people having beliefs, and is required for any scrutiny of our beliefs, because otherwise we wouldn't know which beliefs we are examining, or whose. I stressed two particular features of his considerations concerning such knowledge: his externalist point of view with regard to the mental content of empirical representations of outer sense and his concern with indexicals. These two considerations converge: they attempt to prove that there is no knowledge of my mental states without knowledge that I am an object in space and spatially related to other objects. Thus they amount to a direct and definite refutation of idealist skepticism.

There is a further difference which I believe is even more important. Kant's reply to the skeptical challenge consists in arguing that a certain kind of knowledge called "inner experience" depends on another kind of knowledge called "outer experience." It is the systematic nature of knowledge itself which is supposed to refute skepticism. Knowledge of spatial objects is required for any empirical knowledge about my mental states. His refutation, if it succeeds, has to be achieved within a general theory of knowledge according to which there can be no knowledge of one's own mental states without some knowledge of outer objects. Because the converse holds as well, Kant wants to establish a mutual dependence between both kinds of knowledge and thus to reject the *autonomy* of knowledge of one's own mental states. The success of this strategy does not depend on the assumption that it is possible to identify a certain piece of outer knowledge as error-proof, as it did for Moore; and the strategy itself is completely different from the attempts of philosophers in this century to refute skepticism by testing its consistency and its semantic or *"lebensweltliche"* presuppositions. Such strategies reject skepticism by pointing out that the skeptical doubt doesn't make sense, because of the conditions under which the doubt can be raised. It is an internal way of facing the skeptical challenge, quite independent of any systematic theory of knowledge. In other words: the idealist skeptical challenge is not taken as an attempt to question our conception of knowledge, and in particular the fundamental role which the possibility of an empirical knowledge of an external, mind-independent world has within that conception. What is most striking about Kant's reply to skepticism is that it faces the skeptical challenge by establishing and defending such a conception.

References and Further Reading

Bird, G. (1989). Kant's transcendental arguments. In E. Schaper and W. Vossenkuhl (eds.), *Reading Kant* (pp. 21–39). Oxford: Blackwell.

Bird, G. (1996). McDowell's Kant: Mind and world. *Philosophy*, 71: 219–43.

Burge, T. (1986). Cartesian error and the objectivity of perception. In P. Pettit and J. McDowell (eds.), *Subject, Thought, and Context* (pp. 117–36). Oxford: Oxford University Press.

Kant, Immanuel (1928). *Reflexionen zur Metaphysik*. In *Kant's Gesammelte Schriften*, hrsg. v. d. Preußischen Akademie der Wissenschaften. Band 18: Handschriftlicher Nachlaß, Band V. Berlin und Leipzig: Walter de Gruyter & Co.

Kant, Immanuel (1968). *Vorlesungen über Metaphysik* [*Lectures on Metaphysics*]. In *Kant's Gesammelte Schriften*, hrsg. v. d. Deutschen Akademie der Wissenschaften zu Berlin. Band 28: Vorlesungen, Band V.1. Berlin: Walter de Gruyter & Co.

Kant, Immanuel (1987). *Loses Blatt Leningrad 1: Eine neu aufgefundene Reflexion Kants "Vom inneren Sinne"* [*Loses Blatt Leningrad 1: A Recently Discovered Reflexion of Kant's "Of Inner Sense"*]. In R. Brandt and W. Stark (eds.), *Kant-Forschungen 1. Neue Autographen und Dokumente zu Kants Leben, Schriften und Vorlesungen*. Hamburg: Felix Meiner Verlag.

Kutschera, F. v. (1981). *Grundfragen der Erkenntnistheorie* [*Fundamental Problems in the Theory of Knowledge*]. Berlin, New York: Walter de Gruyter.

Strawson, P. F. (1985). *Skepticism and Naturalism*. London: Methuen.

Stroud, B. (1968). Transcendental arguments. *Journal of Philosophy*, 65: 241–56.

Stroud, B. (1994). Kantian arguments, conceptual capacities and invulnerability. In P. Parrini (ed.), *Kant and Contemporary Epistemology* (pp. 231–51). Dordrecht: Kluwer Academic.

Stroud, B. (1999). The goal of transcendental arguments. In R. Stern (ed.), *Transcendental Arguments: Problems and Prospects* (pp. 155–72). Oxford: Oxford University Press.

Stroud, B. (2000). *The Quest for Reality: Subjectivism and the Metaphysics of Colour*. New York, Oxford: Oxford University Press.

13

The Logic of Illusion and the Antinomies

MICHELLE GRIER

Kant's *Critique of Pure Reason* is astonishing in the complexity as well as the subtlety of its progressive arguments, and unique, too, in its many but intricately interwoven distinctions and conceptions. Yet despite the philosophical density of this long work, it remains guided by the thesis that propels Kant's efforts from the title to its closing passages. That thesis concerns itself with the power and the limits of human reason. Curiously enough, it is the latter, the limitations of reason, that absorb Kant (and the reader) most. In the Preface to the first edition, Kant remarks on the perplexity into which reason is thrown by its being enticed into questions that it cannot answer:

> But by this procedure human reason precipitates itself into darkness and contradictions; and while it may indeed conjecture that these must be in some way due to concealed errors, it is not in a position to be able to detect them. (A viii; translations from Kant 1929 and 2002)

Rather than be cast into the despair of utter skepticism, the *Critique* throws a new light into the darkness and provides a revelatory analysis of the contradictions. The errors to which reason is prone are open to scrutiny and therefore to correction. We suffer inescapably from the illusions of reason, to be sure, but they are mitigated and redirected when we grasp the logic of illusion, a logic we can master (by transcendental reflection and transcendental criticism), and for which philosophy as well as the cherished sciences of mathematics and physics may acquire a secure foundation. There is, however, something more to our transcendental illusions than their mischief: they give direction to our thought that would in no other way be received.

In the Introduction to the Transcendental Logic, Kant distinguishes between general and transcendental logics. Whereas the rules of general logic concern only the form of thought in general, without any regard to the relation between such thought and any object, transcendental logic is a science that concerns the formal rules for thinking objects in general (cf. B 80–2). Kant declares that neither the rules of general logic nor those of transcendental logic (the unschematized categories) can, by themselves alone (a priori), yield any knowledge of objects. The attempt to deduce knowledge of objects from the rules of either general or transcendental logic is thus held by Kant to be "dialectical." Accordingly, the second part of Kant's Transcendental

Logic, the Transcendental Dialectic, is devoted to exposing and criticizing those faulty inferences in accordance with which knowledge of objects is alleged to follow simply from thought alone.

Kant generally defines "dialectic" as a "logic of illusion" (B 86–7; B 249). At first, in the Introduction to the Transcendental Logic, Kant suggests that dialectical forms of thought are generated simply by the above-noted and faulty assumption that the disciplines of general or transcendental logic can be used as organons (B 86). Certainly, one aim of the Transcendental Analytic is to disabuse us of this view. As a first step towards understanding Kant's Dialectic, therefore, it is important to consider what follows from the Transcendental Analytic with regard to attempts in metaphysics.

The Critique of Ontology and Transcendental Realism

Kant's criticism of general metaphysics (ontology) in the Analytic clearly turns on his rejection of the "transcendental employment of the understanding." Kant tells us that the "transcendental employment of a concept in any principle" involves its application both to "things in general and things in themselves" (B 178). That such an employment is inadmissible, for Kant, follows straightforwardly from the fact that the pure concepts of the understanding (the categories) can only yield knowledge when applied to the contents of sensibility. More specifically, the pure unschematized categories, which is to say the categories viewed in abstraction from the conditions of sensibility (space and time), are held by Kant to be nothing but formal rules for thinking possible objects that must be given to us in experience. This fundamental Kantian claim is most famously articulated in the familiar pronouncement that "concepts without intuitions are empty" (B 76). It seems to follow directly from this that the hope of acquiring metaphysical knowledge is already undermined rather early on, in Kant's Transcendental Analytic. In short, the attempt to engage in metaphysical speculations, the attempt to acquire knowledge of "objects" through "pure concepts" alone, is precluded by Kant's transcendental epistemology. Such a procedure, which erroneously deploys unschematized forms of thought as principles yielding material knowledge, leads to the mere semblance of knowledge. With this conclusion comes the downfall of traditional ontology, the discipline in which we seek to acquire knowledge of "objects in general" simply from concepts alone, a practice which characterizes, for example, the metaphysical arguments of the rationalists (B 303). A classic example of such an argument can be found in the writings of Spinoza, who for the most part deduces his monistic metaphysical system simply from the very general and abstract definition of a substance as "that which exists in itself and is conceived through itself."

The critique of ontology, in turn, is linked up with Kant's rejection of the infamous "transcendental realism," the defining characteristic of which is the conflation of appearances and things in themselves (Allison 2004; Bird 1962). For in taking the formal concepts and principles of transcendental logic to yield knowledge of objects directly, and independently of any application to the conditions of sensibility (that is, to yield knowledge of objects in general), we are effectively taking them to hold of objects regardless of whether or not they are considered in connection with the conditions of space and time. In Kantian terms, this practice involves the conflation of

193

appearances with things considered as they are in themselves (see chapter 7 above). Kant's reasoning is fairly simple: objects of human knowledge must be given to us under the conditions of space and time. The thought of an object in general has no correlate in experience, it being rather a general mode for thinking possible objects. To attempt to acquire knowledge of things through the pure unschematized concepts (as concepts of objects in general) is therefore to assume that we can access objects independently of their being given to us under the conditions of sensibility, and that we can therefore deduce knowledge about them without considering them in their necessary connection to the specifically human standpoint.

Having said this, it should be admitted that Kant's criticisms of transcendental realism are somewhat opaque. As has frequently been noted, Kant refers to transcendental realism on only a few occasions (Allison 2004: 21; Guyer 1987: 413). At A 369–70, he identifies transcendental realism with the view that space and time are "something given in themselves (independently of our sensibility)." As a result of taking space and time to be things in themselves, the transcendental realist "represents outer appearances . . . as things in themselves, which would exist independently of us and our sensibility" (cf. B 518). Kant's basic charge is that the transcendental realist, in taking space and time to hold of things considered independently of our particular mode of sensibility (things in general), thereby takes appearances (objects as experienced by us) to have absolute mind independence. In such a case, presumably, the spatiotemporal properties of objects are also taken to hold independently of any human standpoint, something tantamount to taking them to be things in themselves.

It is nevertheless clear that Kant is interested in detailing different forms of transcendental realism and, in conjunction with this, different ways in which the failure to draw the transcendental distinction between appearances and things in themselves generates ways of applying concepts "transcendentally" (see chapter 8 above). As above, Kant rejects the assumption that space and time hold of "objects in general or objects in themselves," for he maintains that these lie "in us," as forms of human sensibility. In accordance with this, Kant frequently stresses the need to "curb the pretensions of sensibility" so that we do not misemploy the concepts of space and time by extending them to everything in general, independently of human minds. But we have also seen that Kant is equally concerned to curb the pretensions of the intellect, which may be understood to involve the faulty assumption that whatever formally holds of the thought of objects in general also directly yields material claims about spatiotemporal objects (appearances). Indeed, it is precisely the assumption, that we can deduce truths about appearances simply from the pure concepts of the understanding, that characterizes the field of ontology. These different errors are distinguished by the "directions" in which we seek to apply concepts. Regardless of this, Kant's view is that we can neither take sensible conditions to apply to objects in general, nor general conceptual conditions to yield immediate knowledge of appearances. Both the pretensions of sensibility and those of the understanding, in other words, share the transcendentally realistic failure to draw the Kantian distinction between appearances and things in themselves.

Kant explicitly criticizes both of these forms of transcendental realism in the Amphiboly of Concepts of Reflection. There he argues that examining the possibility of knowledge of objects through concepts requires first that we become clear about whether the objects in question are objects of thought (noumena) or real objects given to us under the conditions of sensibility (phenomena):

> The concepts can be compared logically without worrying about where their objects belong, whether as noumena to the understanding or as phenomena to sensibility. But if we would get to the objects with these concepts, then transcendental reflection about which cognitive power they are objects for, whether for the pure understanding or for sensibility, is necessary first of all. Without this reflection I can make only a very insecure use of these concepts, and there arise allegedly synthetic principles, which critical reason cannot acknowledge and that are grounded solely on a transcendental amphiboly, i.e., a confusion of the pure object of the understanding with the appearance. (B 325)

In accordance with this, Kant criticizes both what he refers to as the Leibnizian tendency to deduce alleged knowledge about phenomena simply from the pure concepts, by themselves alone, as well as the "Lockean" project of extending the conditions of sensibility to all objects in general:

> Leibniz intellectualized the appearances, just as Locke totally sensitivized the concepts of the understanding . . . Instead of seeking two entirely different sources of representation in understanding and the sensibility, . . . each of these great men holds on only to one of them . . . (B 327)

Kant thus takes himself to be providing a corrective to transcendental realism, which systematically conflates appearances and things in themselves. One result, once again, is that concepts of objects in general are thought to yield knowledge that would apply indiscriminately both to appearances and things in themselves. Another is that the concepts of space and time are taken to hold of objects in general and things in themselves. Moreover, as we shall see, these two ways of (mis)employing concepts will provide the basis for Kant's criticisms of the antinomial conflicts, for each side to the dispute operates in accordance with one of these two strategies. It might seem, then, that establishing transcendental idealism is sufficient to undermine the "logic of illusion" long before we have reached the Transcendental Dialectic.

Later, in the Introduction to the Dialectic, however, Kant deepens his view. The so-called logic of illusion is, it turns out, itself driven by reason, and its propensity to demand knowledge which goes beyond any possible experience. Kant calls such alleged knowledge "transcendent" (as opposed to transcendental), and the purpose of the Dialectic is to "expose the illusion in transcendent judgments" (B 355). The problem, we now see, is not simply that the concepts and principles of the understanding or the conditions of sensibility are inappropriately subject to a transcendental use, but that reason contains within it unique principles which seem, unavoidably, to demand such use. And the problem is that in the process reason catapults us even beyond the general field of ontology, into the specific disciplines of "special metaphysics" (Ameriks 1992). Kant repeatedly tells us, in this regard, that the antinomies alerted him to the way in which reason comes into conflict with itself and generates error by falling victim to reason's inherent illusion. In the Dialectic, Kant thus turns his attention to the ultimate source of metaphysical error, transcendental illusion. To understand why dialectic is a "logic of illusion" one must attend to Kant's doctrine of transcendental illusion.

Transcendental Illusion

The doctrine of transcendental illusion is clearly central to Kant's critique of metaphysics, and it plays an especially important role in his diagnosis of the errors of the antinomies. Transcendental illusion is essentially characterized by Kant as the tendency, presumably characteristic of reason, to take *subjective* demands for unification of thought to be *objective* characteristics of things. More formally, Kant takes transcendental illusion to be grounded in reason's tendency to take "a subjective necessity in the connection of our concepts" to be "an objective necessity in the determination of things in themselves" (B 353). The subjective necessity about which Kant speaks is the rational demand for a complete, systematic, unity of thought or explanation. Although Kant, as we shall see, in no way wants to jettison the rational demand for complete and systematically unified knowledge, he does argue that reason is subject to an illusion that posits such systematic unity as already holding objectively, of "things themselves." Kant formulates the problem of reason by introducing two formulations of the demand for systematicity and completeness. First, he identifies the maxim that defines reason in its logical use:

P$_1$: Find for the conditioned knowledge given through the understanding the unconditioned whereby its unity is brought to completion. (B 364)

The above maxim is essentially a prescription to seek systematic unity of knowledge. Taken thus, and from the standpoint of the understanding, the maxim is satisfactory as far as it goes. The problem, according to Kant, is that from the standpoint of reason (which is defined by the requirement to think beyond all standards of sensibility) the prescription to seek unity and completeness of knowledge presents itself as a principle for the real use of the intellect. More specifically, reason posits the following:

P$_2$: If the conditioned is given . . . the complete series of conditions, a series which is itself therefore unconditioned, is also given. (B 364)

P$_2$ goes well beyond the prescriptive P$_1$. It does not simply enjoin us to seek to extend our knowledge; it decrees that the series of objects we seek to know is already given in its absolute completeness, that nature itself already conforms to our demand. This assumption, however, is according to Kant "illusory" in the sense that the unconditioned is never actually "given" to us in anything other than our thought. Although it might seem that Kant's aim is to reject P$_2$ altogether, he nevertheless argues for what I have elsewhere referred to as an "inevitability thesis," that P$_2$'s assumption, and, as we shall see, the metaphysical ideas generated by it, are somehow "inevitable, unavoidable, and subjectively necessary" (Grier 2001). The allegedly unavoidable nature of this transcendental illusion is captured by Kant's repeated analogies to optical illusion:

Transcendental illusion [Schein] . . . does not cease even after it has been detected and its invalidity revealed by transcendental criticism . . . This is an illusion [*Illusion*] which can no more be prevented than we can prevent the sea from appearing higher at the horizon than at the shore; . . . or to cite a still better example, than the astronomer can prevent the moon from appearing larger at its rising, although he is not deceived [*betrogen*] by this illusion. (B 354)

And again:

That the illusion should . . . actually disappear and cease to be an illusion [*Schein*], is something which a transcendental dialectic can never be in a position to achieve. For here we have to do with a natural and inevitable illusion [*Illusion*], which rests on subjective principles, and foists them upon us as objective. (B 355)

As the quotations indicate, despite the unavoidable and inevitable nature of transcendental illusion, Kant does not think that we are necessarily deceived by it (Grier 2001). Indeed, the Dialectic is devoted to demonstrating the way in which we can avoid the judgmental errors drawn on the basis of this illusion, errors that characterize the metaphysical arguments under Kant's scrutiny in the Dialectic. Although these have often been conflated, it is important to note that transcendental illusion is to be distinguished from the position discussed above that Kant refers to as "transcendental realism." Although transcendental illusion is, according to Kant, unavoidable, transcendental realism is a presumption that not only can, but on Kant's account must, be abandoned. It is thus that Kant thinks that establishing his own transcendental idealism can provide a corrective to the pretensions and errors generated by transcendental realism without, however, "ridding ourselves of the illusion which unceasingly mocks and torments us."

This account of reason and its inevitable illusion provides the basis for Kant's sustained criticisms of rational cosmology, the metaphysical discipline in which we are allegedly concerned to secure "the unconditioned unity of the objective conditions in the field of appearance" (B 433). The Antinomy of Pure Reason thus yields insight not only into Kant's diagnosis of Dialectic as the logic of illusion; it also illuminates Kant's efforts to show incontestably and fully the errors of transcendental realism and the corrective benefits of transcendental idealism with which it is to be replaced. In an effort to clarify the connection between these, I shall for the most part focus in what follows on the mathematical antinomies, which are held by Kant to provide an "indirect argument" for transcendental idealism. Before turning to the specific conflicts, however, some general comments about the antinomies are in order.

Transcendental Illusion and Transcendental Realism in the Antinomy of Pure Reason

Kant is quite clear that the antinomial conflicts are generated by reason's illusory assumption that the unconditioned is already "given." He thus insists that the cosmological arguments:

involve no mere artificial illusion such as at once vanishes upon detection, but a natural and unavoidable illusion [*einen natürlichen und unvermeidlichen Schein*], which even

197

after it has ceased to beguile still continues to delude [*tauscht*], though not to deceive [*betrügt*] us, and which though capable of being rendered harmless can never be eradicated. (B 449–50)

That this natural and inevitable illusion refers to P_2 (the assumption that because the conditioned is given, the unconditioned is also given) is clear from Kant's claim that the each of the antinomies expresses a very general form of dialectical reasoning which runs as follows:

1. If the conditioned is given, the entire series of all conditions [the unconditioned] is likewise given.
2. Objects of the senses are given as conditioned.
3. Therefore, the entire series of all conditions of objects of the senses is already given. (B 526)

There are, for Kant, a number of problems with this syllogism, one of which is that it commits the fallacy of equivocation. Simply put, Kant's claim is that there is an equivocation in the use of the term "the conditioned." Whereas the major premise deploys the term "transcendentally" (it makes a claim that allegedly applies to objects in general), the minor premise refers to objects specifically under the sensible conditions of knowledge (appearances). The problem, of course, is that the conclusion (that the entire series of all conditions of appearances is actually given) would only follow if we were justified in drawing conclusions about appearances from conceptual considerations about objects in general. Kant's rejection of the transcendental employment of the understanding precludes this application of thought. In attempting to deduce knowledge about appearances from the major premise, the rational cosmologist is thus implicitly assuming a transcendentally realistic position. It would thus seem that the dialectical nature of the argument follows rather straightforwardly from the transcendental misapplication of thought.

There is another, deeper, problem with the syllogism, however, and this is that the major premise is illusory. Kant's complaint here is more subtle. On the one hand, he repeatedly tells us that we are not entitled to assume that the totality of conditions is actually given, that this assumption expresses reason's illusion, and its demand for the absolutely unconditioned. Whereas one might therefore expect that the major premise should be dismissed outright, we have already seen that Kant takes P_2 to be an unavoidable and inevitable product of our reason. Rather than rejecting the major premise, then, Kant basically criticizes its inappropriate ("constitutive") use as a principle of material knowledge. More specifically, in the Antinomies, the problem centers on the dialectical attempt to deduce knowledge about appearances (objects of experience) from the transcendental and illusory principle.

No transcendental employment can be made of the pure concepts either of the understanding or reason; . . . the [assertion of] absolute totality of the series of conditions in the sensible world rests on a transcendental employment of reason in which reason demands this unconditioned completeness from what it assumes to be a thing in itself. (B 543–4)

This complaint illuminates Kant's view that in failing to distinguish appearances from things in themselves, the rational cosmologist is seduced into trying to determine appearances independently of the subjective conditions of sensibility by subsuming them under the transcendental principle of reason. Since the failure to distinguish appearances from things in themselves is precisely the hallmark of the transcendental realist, Kant's view is that the transcendental illusion expressed in the major premise only yields the fallacious inference given the rational cosmologist's transcendental realism. Indeed, in his discussion of the antinomies, Kant remarks that if appearances were things in themselves, then we would be justified in applying this principle (B 527). As we shall see, this is why Kant thinks that his own transcendental idealism resolves the metaphysical disputes in rational cosmology without eliminating the unavoidable, albeit illusory, P_2.

This also sheds light on Kant's treatment of the idea of the "world" that motivates the antinomial conflicts. Recall that the dialectical conclusion in the above syllogism involves asserting that the entire series of all conditions of objects of the senses is already given (B 526). Put more succinctly, the conclusion is that there is a world, understood as the sum total of all appearances and their conditions (cf. B 448). The idea of the world is said by Kant to be generated by a subjectively necessary syllogism; because of reason's inherent and unavoidable demand for the unconditioned, that is, Kant contends that we are inevitably led to the idea of the unconditioned as it relates to the field of appearances (the world). The problem, of course, is that the idea suffers from an internal inconsistency: it purports to refer to a supersensible (unconditioned) but still somehow empirical object (B 509). In contrast to the other ideas of reason (the soul and God), the world is supposed to present us with the idea of a totality of empirical conditions, despite the fact that reason has produced the idea by expanding the "connection of the conditioned with its condition" so extensively that it transcends all possible experience. In short, the problem is that the idea of the world is supposed to be a representation of the sensible world as an empirically given whole in itself (B 448).

This accounts in turn for the fact that rational cosmology is characterized by sets of opposing arguments (the thesis and antithesis arguments, respectively). It is precisely because the idea both purports to refer to a sensible object and that it involves thinking that object as already given in its totality, that it generates these opposing sets of arguments. For one can either think the totality of appearances as having an unconditioned ground (as in the thesis arguments) or as the total (even if infinite) set of all appearances (the antitheses). Unfortunately, both strategies fail. Although the thesis positions satisfy reason's demand for the unconditioned, they do so by providing explanations that go well beyond that which is or could ever be given in any spatiotemporal experience. Such efforts problematically assume that whatever can be thought in general holds for appearances. On the other hand, the antithesis arguments, which allegedly restrict themselves to the sensible conditions of space and time, fail to satisfy reason, which is defined by its capacity to think beyond all standards of sensibility and by its demand for intelligible explanation. Moreover, in this case, the efforts assume that whatever holds within space and time also holds generally (of objects in general). Both of these assumptions characterize the standpoint Kant refers to as transcendental realism, and fuel Kant's claim that the antinomies provide an "indirect" argument for transcendental idealism.

The Antinomial Conflicts

The so-called logic of illusion is perhaps most dramatically exhibited in the conflicts in cosmology, and among these, Kant takes the first two (mathematical) antinomies to be particularly important for showing the way in which illusion generates error on the assumption of any transcendentally realistic standpoint. Each of these conflicts centers on the relation between what are presumed to be sensible objects and space and time. The first antinomy pits arguments for the finitude of the world in space and time against those for its infinitude. The second antinomy centers on the conflict generated by opposed views on the divisibility of composites given in the world, with the thesis argument maintaining that such composites must be reducible to ultimately simple substances. The antithesis position counters that any such composite must be infinitely divisible. In both cases, according to Kant, the conflicts are irresolvable so long as one adopts the standpoint of transcendental realism. So long, that is, as one continues to take both appearances and space and time to be "things in themselves," the antinomies "allow of no solution." Kant's own transcendental idealism, therefore, is supposed to rescue us from the conflict by demonstrating that the two opposing sets of arguments are actually guided by norms that cannot legitimately compete in the same domain. At the heart of Kant's solution, then, is the view that it is only by recognizing the transcendental ideality of space and time (and hence appearances) that one can disentangle the various methodological demands that lead to apparently irresolvable conflict.

One way to clarify this last point is to recall that Kant takes the thesis and antithesis positions to reflect seemingly legitimate, albeit competing, strategies for thinking the unconditioned totality demanded by reason and its illusory principle, P_2. The thesis positions adopt a broadly Platonic ("dogmatic") view of the relation between the sensible world and space and time. Here, the proponent of the arguments sees the ultimate ground or explanation of phenomena in noumenal (nonspatiotemporal) terms. As above, this position presupposes the legitimacy of arguing from purely conceptual (general) requirements to conclusions that allegedly hold for appearances. In Kantian terms, the thesis arguments demand "intelligible beginnings" (B 494). The antithesis positions, by contrast, are said to adopt a broadly Epicurean ("empiricist") standpoint, and to take reality as that which is given to sensation, in space and time. Although this allows the antithesis positions to avoid flights into intelligible (noumenal) explanations, it also leads to the extension of spatiotemporal predicates to "objects in general," and thus suffers from its own transcendentally realistic position and a transcendental application of concepts (Grier 2001).

That this is Kant's view can be seen from looking more closely at the conflicts themselves. In the first antinomy, the thesis argument essentially argues from a conception of the sensible world in general, whereas the antithesis begins with the conception of the world as co-extensive with space and time. The argument for the finitude of the world in space and time (the thesis argument) proceeds by demonstrating the impossibility of an infinite regress of states. Confining ourselves to the temporal portion of the argument, we see that the thesis deduces a "first beginning" both of and as part of the temporal series from the purely conceptual impossibility of taking any infinite series in general to be already given in its totality or completeness. The series of past (already elapsed) events cannot be infinite, the argument contends, for an infinite series is by definition a series that has no completion ("the infinity of a series can never be completed through a successive synthesis," B 455). Any allegedly past series that is infinite, then, cannot coherently be thought as having "already elapsed." Therefore, it is concluded, the past series is finite (the world has a beginning in time) (B 454).

What is of present concern is the fact that the thesis argument seeks to draw conclusions about the world in space and time from very general intellectual considerations. Thus, in taking the "world" to be given, the thesis argument conflates a sensible object with an object in general. Thinking through the pure understanding, the thesis argument contends that the entire series of past events (the world) must have some first beginning. According to Kant:

> if we represent everything exclusively through pure concepts of the understanding, and apart from the conditions of sensible intuition, we can indeed at once assert that for a given conditioned, the whole series of conditions subordinated to each other is likewise given. The former is only given through the latter. (B 444)

The problem is that such a principle (P_2) only yields conclusions about the sensible world on the assumption that appearances are things in themselves.

The antithesis to the first antinomy attacks the presumption that there can be any coherent conception of the sensible world that abstracts from the spatiotemporal framework. Essentially, the strategy of the antithesis argument amounts to pointing out that the postulation of a finite cosmos requires positing a premundane empty time and space. The temporal portion of the argument, for example, notes that if the world has a beginning then its existence is preceded by a time in which the world is not, which is tantamount to claiming that the world comes to be in empty time. The latter option, however, makes no sense, for the "nothing" in empty time would then contain no antecedent condition "out of which" an event or beginning (a change in state) could possibly take place; in an empty time, there would be no "distinguishing condition of existence" that could explain the beginning (cf. B 456). Simply put, there must be an antecedent state that provides the condition for any coming to be in time. In such a case, however, we are forced to conclude that the world-series is co-extensive with (infinite) past time. Indeed, according to Kant, the only way to avoid this conclusion is to cling (as the thesis argument does) to a conception of the world as altogether nonspatiotemporal (cf. B 459). Unfortunately, this violates the conception of the sensible world that both parties accept.

Although it might seem that Kant is siding with the antithesis, it is clear that the antithesis is plagued by its own version of transcendental realism. In arguing that there could be no determinate beginning in time, the proponent of the argument takes himself to be demonstrating that there can be no limit to the world at all. Such a conclusion is only legitimate if space and time are taken to be universal ontological conditions. Thus, whereas the thesis argument erroneously transmutes the demand for a limit to the world in general into the claim that the spatiotemporal world must have a determinate beginning in time, the antithesis argument demonstrates that there are no such limits by showing that they could never be satisfied by any spatiotemporal object or events. This last effort involves extending spatiotemporal considerations to the "world in general." Kant famously rejects both procedures.

201

It is clear that both sides to the dispute succeed only because appearances are not clearly distinguished from "things in themselves." That this is the problem is demonstrated by the conflict in the second antinomy as well. Here the thesis position maintains that there must be some ultimately simple substance that grounds any composite, whereas the antithesis asserts the infinite divisibility of material substance. As in the first antinomy, Kant pits the transcendental misapplication of pure concepts of the understanding (thesis) against the transcendental misapplication of spatiotemporal predicates (antithesis). More specifically, the thesis argument operates with a conception of composite substance in general, whereas the antithesis assumes a composite that necessarily occupies and is conditioned by space.

The argument of the thesis concludes that all things in the world are ultimately simple beings, and composition is merely an external state of these (B 462–4). The assumption that there are no simple substances is incoherent, it is contended, because by definition "composition" is an accidental and external relation that holds between and presupposes self-subsistent substances (B 470). The real crux of the argument turns on the incoherence of the notion of an irreducibly composite substance. The standard conception of substance as "that which exists in such a way that it needs nothing else in order to exist" is used to draw the conclusion. Because substance is understood to be self-subsistent being, it follows that any composite is reducible to the individual parts that collectively make it up and persist throughout changes in composition. Kant accordingly remarks that the thesis is concerned with composita, or wholes, "the possibility of which is grounded in the existence of self-subsisting parts" (cf. B 466–8).

It is obvious that the argument draws a metaphysical conclusion that allegedly applies to appearances from a fairly general concept of "composite substance," one which abstracts from any necessary connection to space. The problem, Kant tells us, is that when we are concerned with appearances, "it is not sufficient to find for the pure concept of the composite formed by the understanding the concept of the simple" (B 469). In this, the thesis argument falls victim to transcendental realism, and conflates appearances with things in themselves. Indeed, it is exactly this presumption, that the very abstract and general concept of substance directly yields conclusions that apply to appearances, that is attacked by the antithesis, for the argument against infinite divisibility is said to follow from the failure to see that space is the condition of the possibility of objects of the senses, or "bodies" (B 470).

The antithesis argument emphasizes that "everything real which occupies space" is extended and, therefore, composite. The postulation of a simple, then, is said to be incoherent, for such a simple would have to occupy space. The upshot is that the simple would, on such an account, itself be extended and, therefore composite. Because this is palpably absurd, it is concluded that there are no simples whatsoever, i.e. that composite objects (appearances) are infinitely divisible. Although Kant agrees that appearances are subject to the truths established for pure intuition in geometry (infinite divisibility) (B 207), he does not side with the antithesis over the thesis. Indeed, Kant argues elsewhere that "reason requires the simple as the foundation of all composites," even despite the fact that he denies that any simple can be taken to be a part of bodies (Ameriks 1992). The problem with the antithesis is thus not that it maintains the infinite divisibility of bodies, but rather that it concludes that there are no simples whatsoever merely by arguing from space, as the condition of matter. In this regard, the antithesis establishes a general metaphysical claim by appealing to what are from a Kantian standpoint mere forms of human sensibility. More specifically, because space is thought to apply to objects independently of the human mind, the antithesis takes the subjective forms of our intuition to be universal ontological conditions.

On the interpretation offered here, what characterizes the antinomial conflicts is the clash between different norms or criteria for thinking the unconditioned demanded by reason (P_2). Whereas the thesis positions seek to argue from pure concepts of the understanding to conclusions about appearances in the transcendental sense, the antitheses argue from spatiotemporal considerations (forms of sensibility) to broad claims about objects in general. Although I shall not consider the arguments for the dynamical antinomies in detail, it is worth noting that the same general conflict between competing norms plays out in these arguments as well.

The third antinomy expresses the conflict between the argument for an absolute, spontaneous first cause of the world (transcendental freedom) and the demand for a thoroughgoing mechanistic causality (see chapter 18 below). Here, the thesis demands a first causal beginning (transcendental freedom) to the world, but it achieves this only by adopting a conception of causality that is abstracted from the spatiotemporal framework. Hence, according to Kant, the "absolutely first beginning of which we are here speaking is a beginning not in time, but in causality" (B 479). The antithesis argument counters that such transcendental freedom can only be defended by abstracting from "nature's own resources" (B 479–80). In refusing to go beyond nature's "resources," however, the antithesis extends the laws governing events in space and time (here, the law of causality) to objects considered in abstraction from their connection to the human mind. Once again, then, it is the transcendentally realistic conflation of appearances and things in themselves which governs each of the two strategies. Kant's resolution to this conflict therefore again involves appealing to his own transcendental idealism (Allison 2004). Doing so allows him to claim that the thesis argument for an absolute (nontemporal) causal beginning is acceptable, but cannot be held to account for appearances in nature. Similarly, the antithesis demand for the universality of the causal law holds, but only in relation to objects of human experience. Similar considerations apply to the arguments for and against a necessary being in the fourth antinomy. There, the demand for a necessary being is allowed to stand, so long as the being in question is not taken to be part of nature (that is, such a being would have to be an intelligible ground altogether outside the spatiotemporal series, cf. B 592). The denial of any such necessary being is also legitimate, so long as we understand that we are limited in this locution to the spatiotemporal series.

The essential point is that each side to these disputes arrives at conclusions only by a dialectical inference that involves a transcendental misemployment of concepts. Moreover, it is the underlying ontological commitments of both parties that fuels the conflict. The theses take pure concepts to apply directly to objects in general, and so assume a purely intellectual access to reality, whereas the antitheses take subjective forms of sensibility to be universal ontological conditions. This clarifies the sense in which the antinomies are said to provide an "indirect argument" for transcendental idealism. In effect, by insisting on the transcendental distinction between things considered as appearances and things considered as they are "in themselves," transcendental idealism defuses the strong ontological commitments of both sides, and asserts that the different norms for thinking objects need to be limited to their proper domains. What transcendental idealism does, in other words, is to insist on the methodological principle that concepts be deployed relative to the specific conditions under which they can legitimately apply to their alleged objects (cf. Bird 1982).

What is of present interest, however, is Kant's view that what motivates all of these dialectical inferences is the illusory P_2 and the idea of the world that is generated in accordance with it. In short, the "logic," or the rule for thinking, which motivates these inferences is in each case the illusory P_2. It is only because both parties assume that the "unconditioned" is given that they attempt to satisfy reason by appeal to these competing norms. It is thus that Kant can continue to argue that transcendental idealism allows us to resolve the traditional disputes in cosmology without vanquishing the "supreme principle" of pure reason, that the "unconditioned" is given. It thus seems clear that Kant's claim that dialectic is a "logic of illusion" ultimately refers to the view that the dialectical inferences are guided by the illusory postulations of reason.

The Regulative Use of Reason

Although Kant claims that adopting his own transcendental idealism allows us to avoid drawing the fallacious inferences in rational cosmology, he nowhere claims that the illusory nature of reason either can, or should, be overcome. In fact, exposing the errors generated by transcendental realism makes it possible for Kant to defend the positive, narrowed to the merely regulative, use of reason's illusory principles and ideas. For his view is that without reason's ideas, projected as "imaginary focal points" (B 672) the understanding would be bereft of any guiding principle in its theoretical efforts. Without the assumption that nature itself (objectively) conformed to our subjective demand for a systematic completeness of knowledge, that the ultimate truth was "out there," our investigations into nature would lack grounding. Thus, according to Kant, not only is transcendental illusion (as we have seen) unavoidable, it is (construed properly) subjectively necessary, and even indispensable to the "project" of knowledge acquisition. Indeed, Kant repeatedly tells us that the "supreme principle of pure reason" (P_2) is crucial for theoretical investigations into nature. In the Appendix to the Transcendental Dialectic, for example, Kant defends the retention of the principle as a subjectively necessary, regulative, principle:

> For the law of reason to seek unity is necessary, since without it we would have no reason, and without that, no coherent use of the understanding, and, lacking that, no sufficient mark of empirical truth; thus in regard to the latter we simply have to presuppose the systematic unity of nature as objectively valid and necessary. (B 679)

Kant's point seems to be that the assumption of P_2 is unavoidable since it is, as it were, logically presupposed by any application of the prescriptive P_1, for in seeking to bring our knowledge closer and closer to completion and systematic unity, we are assuming that nature conforms to our demand. In a very real sense, then, what we find is the claim that the general project of knowledge acquisition is itself grounded in the adoption of another, a rational, standpoint.

204

This illusion [*Illusion*] (which need not, however, be allowed to deceive us) is indispensably necessary if we are to direct the understanding beyond every given experience. (B 673)

As with the principle that motivates it (P₂), Kant also takes the idea of the world to be subjectively necessary. Given the demand for the unconditioned (P_2), reason is inevitably led to infer the unconditioned as it relates to the set of all empirical conditions (appearances). Thus, after arguing in the Appendix to the Transcendental Dialectic that the transcendental P_2 is "indispensably necessary" for scientific pursuits, he also argues for the regulative necessity of the idea of the world in guiding our theoretical investigations into nature (cf. B 697; B 699). At this point, one might ask how the idea of the "world," understood as the totality of conditions of all appearances, guides empirical investigations into nature. Surely, it seems, a theoretical physicist might undertake his pursuits without accepting the admittedly idiosyncratic account Kant gives of the "world," as the thought of the absolutely unconditioned. Indeed, it seems that many investigations into nature are conducted at rather specific levels, none of which explicitly assume Kant's idea of the "world."

Although this might seem to be a good counter to Kant's strong claim, it entirely misses the point, which is that the idea of the world is implicit in the general human project of natural science. Here one might simply ask what sense it would make to investigate nature in the sciences in the absence of any assumption that the series of empirical conditions is given in its entirety. In the absence of the assumption that there is a truth of the matter independent of us, one that is complete and explicable, one that lies there as an object to be known, our theoretical investigations would lack purpose. And although individuals may not operate with this explicit conception, Kant is certainly right that the "project," as he calls it, of knowledge acquisition is grounded in this implicit rational assumption, that nature itself conforms to our goals, that it provides an objective correlate to our subjective demands for a completeness and systematic unity of knowledge.

Human reason may be the "seat of illusion," but it is precisely the capacity to project the ideal goal of a complete and unified science that stimulates the ongoing project of knowledge acquisition. In a very real sense, the point of Kant's "critique" of pure reason is to show that reason's principles and demands are illusory, that the transcendent principles and ideas that define it do not yield metaphysical knowledge of nonsensible objects. But knowledge is nevertheless obtained only under the regulative guidance of reason's legislations. In Kantian terms, the assumption that nature conforms to our demands for unity takes the form of a rational decree, and "here reason does not beg, it commands" (B 681). Such a view goes hand in hand with Kant's view that knowledge must conform to various conditions of the specifically human mind. Dialectic may be a "logic of illusion," but illusion, as it turns out, has a logic of its own.

References and Further Reading

Al-Azm, Sadik (1972). *The Origins of Kant's Argument in the Antinomies*. Oxford: Oxford University Press.
Allison, H. E. (2004). *Kant's Transcendental Idealism*, rev. and enl. ed. New Haven and London: Yale University Press.

Ameriks, Karl (1992). The critique of metaphysics: Kant and traditional ontology. In P. Guyer (ed.), *The Cambridge Companion to Kant* (pp. 249–79). Cambridge: Cambridge University Press.

Bennett, J. (1974). *Kant's Dialectic*. Cambridge: Cambridge University Press.

Bird, Graham (1962). *Kant's Theory of Knowledge*. London: Routledge and Kegan Paul.

Bird, Graham (1982). Kant's transcendental idealism. In G. Vesey (ed.), *Idealism – Past and Present*. Royal Institute of Philosophy Lecture Series 13 (pp. 71–92). Cambridge: Cambridge University Press.

Butts, Robert (1997). Kant's dialectic and the logic of illusion. In P. Easton (ed.), *Logic and the Workings of the Mind: The Logic of Ideas and Faculty Psychology in Early Modern Philosophy*. Atascadero: Ridgeview Publishing.

Grier, Michelle (2001). *Kant's Doctrine of Transcendental Illusion*. Cambridge: Cambridge University Press.

Guyer, P. (1987). *Kant and the Claims of Knowledge*. Cambridge: Cambridge University Press.

Kant, Immanuel (1929). *Critique of Pure Reason*, tr. Norman Kemp Smith. London: Macmillan.

Kant, Immanuel (2002). *Critique of Pure Reason*, eds. and tr. Paul Guyer and Allen Wood. *The Cambridge Edition to the Works of Immanuel Kant*. Cambridge: Cambridge University Press.

Strawson, P. F. (1968). *The Bounds of Sense: An Essay on Kant's Critique of Pure Reason*. London: Methuen.

Walsh, W. H. (1975). *Kant's Criticism of Metaphysics*. Chicago: University of Chicago Press.

Wood, Allen (2005). *Kant*. Oxford: Blackwell. (Blackwell Great Minds Series.)

14

The Critique of Rational Psychology

UDO THIEL

Kant's critique of rational psychology forms the first substantive part in the Transcendental Dialectic of the *Critique of Pure Reason*, where it appears as the first chapter of Book II, The Paralogisms of Pure Reason. Like the other two main chapters of the Transcendental Dialectic, which deal with rational cosmology and rational theology, this chapter presupposes the results of both the Transcendental Analytic and the Transcendental Aesthetic. Its subject-matter, the soul and the nature of self-consciousness, is closely related to the Transcendental Deduction of the Categories, and, importantly, the chapter's significance is not restricted to its critical treatment of rational psychology. Together with the Transcendental Deduction it contains elements of a philosophy of the subject, and is relevant to aspects of Kant's moral philosophy as well as his conception of empirical psychology. Moreover, some writers have emphasized the importance of Kant's arguments here to present-day debates relating, for example, to reductionist theories of the mind (Sturma 1998: 408–10).

Kant's Target

Kant's critique here, as elsewhere, is not directed at particular historical "books and systems" (A xii). Rather, it is meant to be a systematic critique of the nature of speculative reason itself. Nevertheless, it is plain that the metaphysical treatises of Christian Wolff (1679–1754) and his followers such as Alexander Baumgarten (1714–62) form the background to Kant's discussion. Kant used the fourth edition of Baumgarten's *Metaphysica* (1757) as a textbook for his lectures (1.503), and although he mentions neither Wolff nor Baumgarten in this chapter, Baumgarten's psychology (Baumgarten 1757: §§501–799) is of particular importance to Kant's treatment of the topic (Ameriks 1998: 373). Also, Kant refers variously to Descartes and the Cartesian cogito (A 367–8, A 370, B 405, B 422n), which plays a central role in the rationalist metaphysics of the soul.

According to Kant, self-consciousness, apperception, or the "I think" is "the sole text of rational psychology, from which it is to develop its entire wisdom" (B 401). Thus, "the expression 'I,' as a thinking being, already signifies the object of a psychology that could be called the rational doctrine of the soul" (B 400). Kant argues that for the rational psychologist the "I think" or apperception not only assures us of our own existence, but can also be used to prove a priori what the nature of our self or soul is.

In Kantian terminology, rational psychology claims to be able to make valid synthetic a priori judgments about the nature of the human soul (B 416). More specifically, according to Kant, it aims to show by way of a priori reasoning that (1) the soul is a substance (2) which is simple, (3) numerically identical at different points of time, and (4) exists detached from "possible objects in space" (B 402). These four are the main, fundamental knowledge claims of rational psychology. Kant states that "all the concepts of the pure doctrine of the soul," such as the soul's immateriality, spirituality, and immortality, are derived directly from these four "elements" (B 403). However, Kant argues that rational psychology's four fundamental theses are based on fallacies or paralogisms.

These fallacies are not merely formal ones, as they have, Kant claims, a "transcendental ground" (B 399), leading to a transcendental "illusion" (A 396) (see chapter 13 above). The claims of rational psychology are based on syllogisms in which the ambiguity of the middle term leads to an illicit move from logical considerations about the self to a priori knowledge claims about the self as object. Kant emphasizes that, although this mistake of rational psychology can be identified and corrected, the transcendental illusion is unavoidable and even natural to human reason (A 396, A 402). He argues that there are four paralogisms corresponding to the four fundamental knowledge claims of rational psychology, listed above. Hence the title of the chapter: The Paralogisms of Pure Reason.

The First and Second Edition Versions of the Paralogisms

In an attempt to respond to criticisms and misinterpretations (B xxxviii) Kant changed the chapter considerably for the second edition of the *Critique of Pure Reason* (1787). However, although the second-edition version is much more concise, there is no difference as far as the main result of Kant's analysis is concerned, with both versions concluding that rational psychology fails to prove its knowledge claims about the nature of the human soul.

With regard to the changes, there is some scholarly disagreement about their significance, and many ingenious hypotheses have been proposed which cannot be rehearsed here (see Sturma 1998: 393). It is plain, as Kant himself suggests, that the changes do not concern merely the "mode of presentation" (B xxxix) and nor were they made merely "for the sake of brevity" as Kant himself suggests (B 406). On the other hand, it is not plausible either that they effect a radical change in content, so that, for example, in the first edition Kant does not wish to reject completely the rationalist tradition while in the second edition he does. Rather, it appears that the changes, apart from the individual points listed below, amount mainly to a difference in method outlined in the discussion of point (6) below.

In addition to several subtle terminological changes, the following are the most obvious differences between the two editions.

1) The paralogisms are treated more extensively in the first edition.
2) Kant adds to the second edition a brief discussion of an argument for immortality that he found in the "rational psychologist" Moses Mendelssohn (1729–85).
3) The discussion of the fourth paralogism in the first edition contains a detailed critique of the view that the existence of the external world is doubtful. That material is revised and moved to the Transcendental Analytic to form the new, separate, section, The Refutation of Idealism (B 273–9; see Gäbe 1954: 111ff).
4) The first, but not the second edition has an extensive discussion of the problem of the mind–body relationship (A 381–96; cf. B 427–8).
5) Kant emphasizes the importance of this chapter to issues in moral philosophy more strongly in the second edition; there are only hints at such a connection in the first edition (A 365). This is not surprising, as he developed the fundamentals of his moral philosophy in the years between the first and second editions of the *Critique of Pure Reason*.
6) Kant's main focus in the second edition shifts to the first paralogism, which concerns the substantiality of the soul. This change is perhaps the most significant, as it points to a different method of critique.

Kant states in both editions that in analyzing the four basic theses of rational psychology, "we have merely to follow the guide of the categories." "We will begin here," he says, "with the category of substance" (under the heading of relation), moving on to simplicity (quality), identity (quantity), and ideality in regard to outer relation (modality) (A 344, B 402). In the second edition, however, the discussion is not only much briefer, but is also different in kind. First, the four mistakes of rational psychology are briefly presented in terms of the distinction between analytic and synthetic judgments. Rational psychology treats analytic propositions about the thinking I as synthetic a priori propositions (B 416–17). This mistake is summed up in Kant's statement that "the logical exposition of thinking in general is falsely held to be a metaphysical determination of the object" (B 409). Then, second, only the first claim of rational psychology which concerns the substantiality of the soul is examined in terms of a paralogism. The reason for this is, as Kant suggests, that the first paralogism is fundamental. "The procedure of rational psychology is governed," he says, by the substance paralogism (B 410). And indeed, if it can be shown that we cannot prove a priori that the soul is a substance, then it is also clear that we cannot prove a priori that the soul is a simple, identical substance that exists detached from objects in space (B 409). The critique of the first paralogism undermines rational psychology as a whole.

It appears that this shift in focus to the substance paralogism was inspired by critics who maintained that Kant's notion of the I of pure apperception contradicts his claim that we cannot know noumena or things in themselves, because we have entered the sphere of noumena already when we think of ourselves as pure subjects (Erdmann 1878: 110, 227; Gäbe 1954). Kant concedes that, if this were right, it would "put an end to this whole critique and would bid us to leave things the same old way they were before" (B 410). Thus, he sees the need to focus on the substance paralogism and show that his arguments concerning the I of pure apperception do not amount to synthetic a priori propositions about the soul, as noumenal substance. Indeed, more fundamentally, he argues that no synthetic or informative knowledge about the I as an object can be derived from the I of pure apperception.

Logical Subject versus Substantial Subject

According to Kant, the project of rational psychology is based on "the I of apperception" (B 407). Its aim is to arrive at synthetic knowledge of the soul that "independently of all experience . . . can be inferred from this concept **I**" (B 400). But what is this "I of apperception"? Kant introduces this notion in the Transcendental Deduction of the Categories by way of distinguishing between empirical and pure apperception. Empirical consciousness or apperception is the actual awareness of particular mental states, "it accompanies different representations" (B 133). "Pure apperception," by contrast, is "that self-consciousness which . . . produces the representation 'I think'" (B 132). This is an "act of **spontaneity**," and that is to say that it "cannot be regarded as belonging to sensibility" (B 132). About the "I think" Kant famously says that it "must **be able** to accompany all my representations" (B 131). In other words, there is a necessary connection between the I and its thoughts or representations. According to Kant, the statement, that the "I think" must be able to accompany all my representations, is analytic (B 135; B 407). Every consciousness of a representation involves self-consciousness or apperception, i.e. the consciousness that the representation belongs to me (A 117). This does not mean that there are no unconscious representations, but if I were not able to become conscious of them, there would be no reason to say they are "my" representations (cf. Baum 1986: 93–4).

Kant argues further that pure apperception is a necessary condition of "thinking in general" (B 423). Thinking consists in combining representations; and this combination would not be possible without pure apperception. Representations a and b could not be combined if they did not belong to one and the same consciousness or the same I. The "I" in the proposition "I think" is a "purely intellectual" representation precisely because it necessarily "occurs in all thinking" (B 400). For that reason it is logically prior to the latter, it "precedes a priori all **my** determinate thinking" (B 134). That is why in contrast to the I of empirical apperception, which is called "the psychological self," the I of pure apperception is called "the logical self" (20.270). Now Kant argues that rational psychology illicitly infers the substantiality of the soul from this "constant logical subject of thinking" (A 350). This invalid inference is made in the first paralogism of pure reason. In the second edition he presents this paralogism as follows:

> What cannot be thought otherwise than as subject does not exist otherwise than as subject, and is therefore substance.

> Now a thinking being, considered merely as such, cannot be thought otherwise than as subject.

> Therefore it also exists only as such a thing, i.e. as substance. (B 410–11; translations from Kant 1998 throughout)

This syllogism attempts to connect "substance" and "thinking being" in such a way that we arrive at the conclusion that a thinking being exists only as substance. But

Kant argues that the middle term that is meant to connect the two terms ("substance" and "thinking being") does not mean the same thing in the major and minor premises. He says that in the major premise the expression "cannot be thought otherwise than as subject" refers to something that might be given in intuition, but that in the minor premise it refers to the pure subject (B 411; compare A 402–3). The conclusion of the rational psychologist, then, is drawn "by means of a deceptive inference" (B 411).

We cannot apply the category of substance to the pure subject of apperception of the minor premise because the categories are restricted in their application to experience, and there is no sensible intuition for the pure subject of apperception (B 413), since it is only of "logical significance" (A 350). The I of pure apperception is a necessary condition of all thought, and thus it is a necessary condition also of any knowledge of objects. But this means that it is not itself "determinable" as an object (B 407). "I cannot cognize as an object itself that which I must presuppose in order to cognize an object at all" (A 402). As Kant puts it, the I of pure apperception is the "determining self," but not a "determinable self" (B 407). Rational psychology, however, treats the logical I of apperception as an object that exists as "a self-subsisting being or substance" (B 407). Thus, the transcendental ground of this core paralogism is that the logical unity of consciousness "is here taken for an intuition of the subject as an object, and the category of substance is applied to it" (B 421). An analytic truth about the I as subject of thoughts is illicitly used to extend our synthetic knowledge about the I as an object.

Logical versus Substantial Simplicity of the Subject

The second paralogism concerns the simplicity of the soul. Now, several times Kant characterizes the I of pure apperception as "simple" (B 135, B 404, B 419, B 420). This means that in all thought it "is a **single thing** that cannot be resolved into a plurality of subjects" (B 407). The I of apperception must be one because otherwise a multiplicity of representations could not be combined into the unity of a thought. That the I of apperception is such "a logically simple subject, lies already in the concept of thinking, and is consequently an analytic proposition" (B 407–8; cf. A 355). Moreover, simplicity here means that the I of pure apperception is empty of content (B 404; cf. B 135, A 381). Kant explains this in terms of the notion of logical *unity*. "*I* **am simple** signifies no more than that this representation 'I' encompasses not the least manifoldness within itself, and that it is an absolute (though merely logical) unity" (A 355; cf. A 356). The logical subject is simple "just because one determines nothing at all about it" (A 355).

Since simplicity in this logical sense is analytically contained in the notion of the I of pure apperception and even functions as a necessary condition of thought, Kant has no problem with it. But he argues that rational psychology illicitly infers the simplicity of the soul, as substance, from the logical simplicity of the I. Kant's critique here is similar to his argument against the first paralogism. He claims that the rational psychologist misreads the analytic truth about logical simplicity as a synthetic truth about the simple nature of the self as substance (B 408). But, as Kant points out, "the simplicity of consciousness is . . . no acquaintance with the simple nature of our subject" (A 360).

211

UDO THIEL

The rationalists's argument for the simplicity of the soul, then, is just as invalid as their argument for the soul's substantiality.

The first-edition discussion of the simplicity argument contains a detailed discussion of the related issue of thinking matter which survives in briefer comments about materialism and spiritualism in the second edition. According to Kant, the rational psychologist maintains that, by proving that the soul is of a simple nature, he has thereby distinguished it "from matter as a composite being" (A 360). Indeed, the real motive behind the fundamental arguments of rational psychology is "the intent of securing our thinking Self from the danger of materialism" (A 383). And having shown that the soul is not a composite, material being, the rationalist thinks that therefore we can "except it from the perishability to which matter is always subjected" (A 356) and demonstrate its immortality.

As Kant indicates, traditionally the immateriality of the soul (and therefore also its simplicity) is considered to be at least a necessary condition of immortality. And one central argument for the simplicity and immateriality of the soul is derived from the nature of thought. It is argued that the very nature of thought is such that it requires the thinking subject or soul to be a simple and immaterial substance. If the soul were composed of a multiplicity of material parts, it was held, thought could not occur at all, as the parts of a thought would exist in separate material beings, each with its separate consciousness, and so the parts could not be combined into one consciousness to constitute the whole thought (cf. A 352). In other words, the soul's materiality, that is, its being composed of parts, is inconsistent with the unity of consciousness required for thought to be possible. As Kant says, "the *nervus probandi* of this argument lies in the proposition that many representations have to be contained in the *absolute unity* of the thinking subject in order to constitute one thought" (A 352; second emphasis mine). But he argues that this proposition can be proved neither through reason nor through experience. His argument consists of three parts. (1) Since it does not concern the mere logical simplicity of the I of apperception, it is not an analytic truth. The thought that a multiplicity of beings can cooperate to produce a thought involves no contradiction (A 353). (2) It is not a synthetic a priori truth because it lacks the relation to possible experience required for such truths (A 353). (3) It is not a synthetic a posteriori truth, i.e., one that is derived from experience. "For experience gives us cognition of no necessity, to say nothing of the fact that the concept of absolute unity is far above its sphere" (A 353).

In order further to undermine the rationalist theory, Kant argues that there is a sense in which the thesis about the simple nature of the soul may be conceded, but that even this concession could not be used to demonstrate the soul's "dissimilarity to or affinity with matter" (A 357). Kant appeals here to his transcendental idealism and its distinction between appearances and things in themselves. Bodies, or matter in general, Kant emphasizes, are appearances of outer sense, not things in themselves (A 357). Now thoughts are not objects of outer sense, but only of inner sense; we do not and cannot intuit "thoughts, feelings, inclinations or decisions" externally (A 358). Therefore it is possible to say that in one sense at least "the thinking subject is not corporeal," simply because it is not "an appearance in space" (A 357). But, Kant argues, nothing follows from this for the nature of the soul in itself. The transcendental ground of both inner and outer appearances is entirely unknown to us. And it is at

212

least possible (i.e. the thought involves no contradiction) that inner and outer appearances have the same transcendental ground, that the "same Something that grounds outer appearances" be also "the subject of thoughts" (A 358; cf. B 427–8). Contrary to the claims of rational psychology, then, it cannot be shown that that "substratum" which grounds matter as appearance cannot think. As Kant puts it, even if we concede the simplicity of the soul, the latter "is not at all sufficiently distinguished from matter in regard to its substratum" (A 359). Lastly, Kant emphasizes that the initial concession to the rational psychologist concerning simplicity need not and indeed should not be made in the first place. For the very notion of a simple nature "is of such a kind as cannot be encountered anywhere in experience, and hence there is thus no path at all by which to reach it as an objectively valid concept" (A 361). Thus the concession violates Kant's overall argument about what is required for the objective reality of concepts.

Materialism, Spiritualism, Immaterialism

As far as the "danger of materialism" is concerned, Kant argues that rational psychology is not needed to avoid it. His own account of the logical subject of pure apperception is sufficient for this purpose. The fact that the notion of the I of pure apperception is essential to an understanding of the thinking self makes it clear that any attempt to account for thought entirely in physicalist terms cannot work (B 419–20). But since the I of pure apperception concerns only the logical "form of consciousness" (A 382), Kant's rejection of materialism here does not constitute a concession to rational psychology and its spiritualist knowledge claims. As far as knowledge of the nature of the soul in itself is concerned, the materialist is no worse (and no better) off than the spiritualist (A 380; B 417–18n).

So Kant rejects both materialism and spiritualism. But he suggests a distinction between spiritualism and immaterialism (A 345/B 403). Spiritualism can be said to be the view that the thinking being is not merely immaterial but also "has the property of being in its existence necessarily independent of material beings" (Ameriks 2000: 305). Thus Kant's rejection of materialism and spiritualism seems to leave open the possibility of a "rationalist commitment" to an "immaterialist metaphysics" about the soul in itself, as has been claimed (Ameriks 2000: xvi, 303, 312). However, such a commitment would be inconsistent with Kant's view that the transcendental ground of inner and outer experience is entirely unknown to us. And indeed, there is no need to ascribe such an inconsistency to Kant. It is true that immateriality does not entail spirituality (Ameriks 2000: 36) and that in this sense Kant's rejection of spiritualism would seem to leave room for a commitment to immaterialism. But there is no such commitment in Kant. For while it may be true that immateriality does not entail spirituality, it is certainly required for spirituality. Immateriality concerns the possibility of spirituality. Now Kant, having rejected both spiritualism and materialism, adds, "the conclusion is that in no way whatsoever *can we cognize anything* about the constitution of our soul that in any way at all concerns *the possibility* of its separate existence" (B 420; my emphases). But if we knew that the soul in itself is of an immaterial nature we would know something about its constitution that "concerns the possibility of its separate

213

existence." Clearly, then, Kant consistently remains committed to an agnostic position about the nature of the soul or mind *in itself*, that is, as a noumenon.

Logical versus Substantial Identity of the Subject

The logical subject of pure apperception, Kant argues, is characterized not only by simplicity but also by identity (A 362–3). If the I of pure apperception were not numerically identical through time, then it would be impossible to combine thoughts even from one moment to the next. Therefore, "the identity of the consciousness of myself in different times is . . . a *formal condition of my thoughts and their connection*" (A 363; my emphasis). This "logical identity of the I" (A 363) must be presupposed as a necessary, a priori condition of thought and knowledge (cf. Allison 1983: 140).

Rational psychology attempts, however, to go beyond the logical identity of the subject and prove the real identity of the soul as a substance. This argument contains the third paralogism of rational psychology, according to Kant. In the second edition Kant deals briefly with this paralogism, arguing that rational psychology's move from the identity of the I as logical subject (which is an analytic truth) to the claim that the I, as thinking substance, is identical through time (which would be a synthetic truth) is not permissible. For the identity of the logical subject "does not concern the intuition" of the subject. To prove the identity of the soul, as a substance, "what would be demanded is not a mere analysis of the proposition 'I think,' but rather various synthetic judgments grounded on the given intuition" (B 408).

In the first edition the third paralogism receives a separate and detailed treatment and is called the "paralogism of personality." Kant formulates it thus: "What is conscious of the numerical identity of its Self in different times, is to that extent a **person**. Now the soul is . . . etc. Thus it is a **person**" (A 361). Note that here the very notion of a person or of personality is tied to that of numerical identity through time (cf. Ameriks 2000: 129). This differs from Kant's account of the notion of person in the moral-practical context, as we shall see. Kant's main argument against the rationalist claim here is the same as in the second edition. He points out that nothing can be inferred from "the logical identity of the I" (A 363) regarding the real identity of the subject "in which . . . a change can go on that does not allow it to keep its identity" (A 363).

But Kant begins his discussion here with a brief comment on how we can know the identity of an external object. Such knowledge can be obtained through experience, he says, if we "attend to what is persisting" in the appearance of an object while its determinations change (A 362). As an appearance of outer sense the external object has something "abiding in it, which supplies a substratum grounding the transitory determinations" (A 381). Now Kant points out that inner experience by contrast does not provide any evidence of something "persisting and abiding" (A 364). Rather, inner experience "gives cognition only of a change of determinations" (A 381). And since Kant's discussion of the first paralogism has demonstrated that the substantiality of the soul cannot be proved a priori, there is no justification at all for the assumption that the soul is a substance. If we were entitled to that assumption then the possibility of a continuing consciousness in an abiding subject would follow because persistence through time is an essential characteristic of substances (A 364–5). As rational psychology cannot assume the substantiality of the soul it must attempt to prove the identity of the soul from the logical identity of consciousness (A 365).

But Kant argues that rational psychology fails in this attempt. And it makes no difference whether we consider the soul from the standpoint "of our own consciousness" or "from the standpoint of someone else" (A 364). An external observer would recognize the identity of my consciousness but would not "infer the objective persistence of my Self" because the identity of my consciousness is not "combined with his consciousness, i.e. with the outer intuition of my subject" (A 363). Thus he "cannot make out whether this I (a mere thought) does not flow as well as all the other thoughts that are linked to one another through it" (A 364). If the external observer did infer my objective persistence he would be guilty of illicitly turning an analytic truth into a synthetic one. From the standpoint of "our own consciousness" we are able to "ascribe to our identical Self only that of which we are conscious; and so we must necessarily judge that we are the very same in the whole of the time of which we are conscious" (A 364). In this sense, then, the identity of myself is "inevitably to be encountered in my consciousness" and is "valid a priori" (A 362). But this a priori validity concerns merely an analytic truth. We cannot judge from this "whether as soul we are persisting or not" (A 364). Thus the "identity of person in no way follows from the identity of the I in the consciousness of all the time in which I cognize myself" (A 365). And so the attempt of the rational psychologist to prove the "absolute persistence of the soul," and to do so "from mere concepts" fails. In fact the persistence of the soul, Kant concludes, "remains unproved and even unprovable" (B 415). And since its persistence is unprovable it follows that its immortality is unprovable as well.

As indicated above, in the second edition Kant adds a brief discussion of Moses Mendelssohn in order to show that, even if we concede the simplicity of the soul, its immortality does not follow (B 413–15). Mendelssohn argued that a simple being such as the soul cannot cease to exist because "it cannot be diminished and thus lose more and more of its existence" (B 413–14). But Kant objects that, even if we allow the soul to have no parts or no "extensive magnitude," it would still have an "intensive magnitude, i.e. a degree of reality in regard to all its faculties." And this "might diminish . . . and thus the supposed substance . . . could be transformed into nothing" (B 414).

The Thinking Subject and the Existence of External Objects

The fourth paralogism concerns the doctrine that "the existence of all objects of outer sense is doubtful" (A 367). Kant calls this doctrine "problematic idealism" (B 418). It is based on the rationalist claim that thinking substances do not require external things for the determination of their own existence in time. For once that is admitted, "such things are only assumed, entirely gratuitously, without a proof of them being able to be given" (B 418). Kant's critique in the second edition is brief and focuses again on the distinction between analytic and synthetic judgments. "[That] I distinguish my own existence, that of a thinking being, from other beings outside me (to which my body also belongs) – this is . . . an analytic proposition" (B 409). It follows from a mere analysis of the "I think." But it does not follow from such an analysis that I thereby know "whether I could *exist* merely as a thinking being (without being a human being)," i.e. without being at the same time a bodily being (B 409; my emphasis). The latter is a synthetic proposition and would require intuitions for its objective validity.

In the first edition Kant examines the fourth paralogism in detail. The problem is, again, that rational psychology does not distinguish between appearances and things in themselves. Rather, it is committed to what Kant calls "transcendental realism" and "represents outer appearances (if their reality is conceded) as things in themselves, which would exist independently of us" (A 369) (see above, chs. 7 and 13). The transcendental realist can then "play" the problematic idealist because if external things are conceived of as existing in themselves, "even apart from sense," he can argue that sense perception "is insufficient to make their reality certain" (A 369). Kant, as a transcendental idealist, by contrast, "is an empirical realist, and grants to matter, as appearance, a reality which need not be inferred, but is immediately perceived" (A 371). This is so because transcendental idealism considers bodies as only "empirically external," that is to say, they are considered as "things *that are to be encountered in space*" (A 373). But space is the a priori form of our sensibility, and so "every outer perception . . . immediately proves something real in space" (A 375). For Kant, therefore, the existence of matter or objects in space is as certain as is "the existence of myself as a thinking being" (A 370).

Kant holds that transcendental realism is the source also of the wrong-headed debates within rationalism about the problem of the mind–body relationship (A 381–96; cf. B 427–8). This problem is a "self-made difficulty" (A 387) of rational psychology. For the latter's transcendental realism implies a "transcendental dualism" (A 389) which assumes that thinking subjects and their bodies are beings entirely different in kind. And once we have assumed that mind and body belong to two different worlds, we have created the problem of how the two can relate to one another (A 391). Kant undermines the whole debate by questioning its fundamental assumption, "transcendental dualism." The mind–body difference should be understood not in a transcendental sense but in an empirical sense; it signifies "only the heterogeneity of . . . appearances" (A 385). Understood in this way, both body and mind are possible objects of empirical study and knowledge. Here the question is not about two entirely different substances, but merely about the conjunction of the objects of inner and outer experience, and about "how these may be conjoined with one another according to constant laws, so that they are connected in one experience" (A 385–6).

From Rational Psychology to Empirical Psychology

Since the rationalist program "collapses" into paralogisms, Kant argues that "nothing is left except to study our soul following the guideline of experience" (A 382). The distinction between rational and empirical psychology goes back to Christian Wolff. In Wolff the two disciplines are two parts of metaphysics complementing each other. For Kant, however, rational psychology has only "an important negative utility" in that it allows for "a critical treatment of our dialectical inferences" (A 382); and empirical psychology is dealt with by him in the context of a "pragmatic" anthropology. It is not, then, part of philosophy (B 876–7; cf. Bird 2000: 145), but nevertheless in the Paralogisms and elsewhere Kant does comment on the possibility and nature of empirical psychology.

According to Kant, empirical psychology seeks to make knowledge claims about the self as an object of inner experience. Kant envisages empirical psychology as not only a descriptive, but also an explanatory enterprise; he notes that it "would be a species of the *physiology* of inner sense, which would perhaps *explain* the appearances of inner sense" (B 405; second emphasis mine). However, it is this understanding of empirical psychology as a purely introspective inquiry that leads to problems (cf. Sturm 2001). Kant states that empirical psychology cannot become a science in the strict of sense of the term. This is so because, for Kant, science requires the application of mathematics, but mathematics is not applicable to inner sense (*MFNS*, 4.471), for in "that which we call the soul everything is in continual flux" (A 381). It has been pointed out variously that Kant's mathematical restriction on empirical science is rather problematic (Hatfield 1992: 219–22), but Kant also and more convincingly argues that introspective empirical psychology cannot be properly "experimental" because the objects of inner observation cannot be easily retained and connected. Moreover, our "experiments" cannot be applied to subjects other than ourselves, and our observations here can alter and distort the state of the observed object (*MFNS*, 4.471). Nevertheless, although Kant holds that empirical psychology cannot be turned into a science in the strict sense of the term, he suggests it is possible and useful as a methodical and even explanatory "natural history" of inner sense (*MFNS*, 4.471).

Perhaps the most problematic aspect of Kant's conception of empirical psychology is his claim that the latter requires the idea of the soul as simple substance as its guiding principle or "regulative" idea. In the Paralogisms Kant argues that in empirical psychology "nothing at all can be cognized a priori from the concept of a thinking being" (A 381). How is it, then, that empirical psychology needs the idea of the soul as simple substance as its guiding principle? Kant's answer is that this idea is required for the systematic unity of our study of "the appearances of inner sense" (B 710). Experience provides us only with fragments of knowledge. It is the idea of the soul as simple substance that provides the required "principles of systematic unity in explaining the appearances of the soul" (B 711). This means that in empirical psychology we "connect all appearances, actions, and receptivity of our mind to the guiding thread of inner experience *as if* the mind were a simple substance that (at least in this life) persists in existence with personal identity" (B 700; cf. B 711). The "as if" is emphasized by Kant to indicate that the rational idea of the soul functions only as a "heuristic" concept here. Thus, Kant's account of the regulative use of this idea is no concession to rational psychology and is consistent with his critique of the latter, as he continues to hold that any knowledge claims about the properties of the soul must be based on experience. The problem is, however, that Kant has not shown in the first place that the idea of the soul as simple substance has indeed "an excellent and indispensably necessary regulative use in directing the understanding" (B 672). Occasionally, even Kant himself expresses doubts about the status of these considerations on the regulative use of transcendental ideas (*MFNS*, 4.362–3; cf. Horstmann 1998: 540ff).

From Logical Subject to Moral Subject

In the concluding sections of the second-edition version of the Paralogisms Kant reflects on the notion of self-determination, a central concept of his moral philosophy. How are these reflections related to Kant's critique of rational psychology? We saw that Kant distinguishes between the "logical self" of pure apperception, the self as appearance, and the self as thing in itself or noumenon. He argues that we can have no knowledge whatsoever of the self as noumenon – indeed "we can have nothing more than merely the general concept of it" (B 569). What we can do, however, is analyze the *concept*. And what is the result of such an analysis? If I think of myself as a *noumenon*, I think of myself as existing independently of the conditions of our experience (space and time), and, consequently, I think of myself as not being affected by spatiotemporal determinations and in this sense as "free" (B 567–9).

Importantly, Kant emphasizes that "the objective reality" of this concept "can in no way be cognized" (B 310). This means that I can make no synthetic judgments about the question of the reality of my freedom (B 586). Nevertheless, this notion of myself as a noumenon "contains no contradiction" (B 310). And the fact that the analysis of the concept of the self as noumenon leads to the idea of the self as a free being makes it possible for Kant to develop the notion of practical freedom in his moral philosophy. He argues that I acquire a moral personality not through empirical self-consciousness, but only by thinking of myself as a rational and free being. I am a moral being only in virtue of considering myself "as a *person*, that is as a subject of moral-practical reason" (*MM*, 6.434). And that is what it means to consider the self, in the moral-practical context, as homo noumenon (*MM*, 6.239; cf. 6.223, 6.418, 6.429).

Kant's reflections on self-determination in the Paralogisms must be read in light of this notion of the self as "a subject of moral-practical reason." He argues here that if we think of ourselves as free, we can think of ourselves as being "**legislative** fully a priori in regard to our own **existence**, and as self-determining in this existence" (B 430). The a priori or "purely intellectual" principle of this self-determination is "the moral law" (B 431). Importantly, Kant emphasizes that these considerations relate only to the practical sphere and do not amount to a concession to the rationalist metaphysician of the soul (B 431).

One notorious feature of Kant's moral philosophy, however, seems to be inconsistent with his critique of rational psychology, at least on the face of it. This is the immortality of the soul as a "postulate of pure practical reason" (*CPrR*, 5.122). Kant's (problematic) reasons for introducing this postulate need not concern us here. But given that he rejects rationalist arguments for immortality in the Paralogisms, is he at all entitled to introduce immortality as a postulate in his moral philosophy? The answer is a clear yes, and for the following reasons. (1) Kant emphasizes that by arguing for the postulate of immortality he does not thereby claim that we can acquire a priori theoretical or speculative knowledge about the nature of the soul. The postulate is not a theoretical dogma but merely a presupposition of practical reason (*CPrR*, 5.134ff). (2) In the Paralogisms Kant argues that there can be no a priori speculative proof for the immortality of the soul; but he does not, and does not intend to, disprove immortality there

(A 393–4; cf. B 424). Indeed he argues that we can no more prove the mortality of the soul than its immortality. Since we cannot know what the appearances of inner and outer sense rest on in a transcendental sense, we "also cannot claim to know that the condition of all outer intuition, or even of the thinking subject itself, will cease after this state (after death)" (A 394–5; cf. A 383–4). Thus, the critique of speculative or rational psychology leaves room "for the assumption of a future life in accordance with principles of the practical use of reason" (B 424; cf. B 425). That critique does not preclude belief in immortality on other than speculative grounds.

Conclusion

On the whole, then, Kant's critique of rational psychology would seem to be consistent both in itself and with other parts of his philosophy. It can also be said to be convincing overall, but this would obviously depend on whether or not we accept central doctrines of the *Critique*, such as transcendental idealism and the account of pure apperception in the Transcendental Deduction. There can be no doubt, however, that Kant's discussion constitutes a considerable advance over traditional treatments of the soul from both rationalist and empiricist perspectives. Certainly it has proved to be successful in the sense that Wolffian rational psychology did not survive Kant's attack in mainstream philosophy. As far as his conception of empirical psychology is concerned, we saw that there are problems, for example with his idea of empirical psychology as a purely introspective inquiry. But at least Kant saw that the project of empirical psychology needs to be informed by epistemological considerations that are not themselves of an empirical nature. And the fact that he removes empirical psychology from metaphysics should not be read in a negative way. Rather, he thereby assigns it a distinct place in theoretical inquiry and provides a positive revaluation of it.

Moreover, the theme of the Paralogisms relates to what is called today "philosophy of mind" in analytical philosophy or a theory of "subjectivity" in the Continental tradition. But Kant does not develop a comprehensive philosophy of the subject here. Nor should we expect Kant to do such a thing in the *Critique of Pure Reason*. The aims of the relevant chapters, the Transcendental Deduction and the Paralogisms, are quite different; the former attempts to prove the objective validity of the categories, the latter is part of a critique of traditional special metaphysics. It is true, however, that in the process of attempting to achieve his stated aims in those chapters, Kant sees it as necessary to reflect deeply on issues such as self-consciousness and self-knowledge. But what we have there is the *basis* of a Kantian philosophy of the subject. Kant's distinction between the logical self of apperception, the phenomenal self of inner experience, and the noumenal self as an idea of reason would obviously be an essential part of such a philosophy. Crucially, we have argued above that the temptation to read Kant's rejection of materialism as a commitment to an immaterialist metaphysics must be resisted. It is precisely the fact that Kant does not, and does not need to, commit himself to views about the metaphysical nature of the soul as a thing in itself that highlights the contemporary relevance of his discussion of self-consciousness. Some may consider as problematic the very notion of a noumenal ground of inner and outer experience. But that notion is part of the doctrine of transcendental idealism as a whole, and the extent to which it is or is not problematic would depend on our reading of transcendental idealism. What is clearly lacking in Kant's conception of the subject, however, is an account of the relationship between the logical self and empirical self. This is a gap that would need to be bridged in a Kantian philosophy of the subject, but Kant does not, and does not need to, reflect on this in the context of his project in the *Critique of Pure Reason*.

References and Further Reading

Allison, Henry (1983). *Kant's Transcendental Idealism: An Interpretation and Defense*. New Haven: Yale University Press.

Ameriks, Karl (1998). The paralogisms of pure reason in the first edition. In G. Mohr and M. Willaschek (eds.), *Immanuel Kant. Kritik der reinen Vernunft* (pp. 371–90). Berlin: Akademie Verlag.

Ameriks, Karl (2000). *Kant's Theory of Mind: An Analysis of the Paralogisms of Pure Reason*. New edition. Oxford: Clarendon Press.

Baum, Manfred (1986). *Deduktion und Beweis in Kants Transzendentalphilosophie* [*Deduction and Proof in Kant's Transcendental Philosophy*]. Königstein: Hain bei Athenäum.

Baumgarten, Alexander (1757). *Metaphysica*. Halle: Hemmerde.

Bennett, Jonathan (1974). *Kant's Dialectic*. Cambridge: Cambridge University Press.

Bird, Graham (2000). The paralogisms and Kant's account of psychology. *Kant-Studien*, 91: 129–45.

Brook, Andrew (1994). *Kant and the Mind*. Cambridge: Cambridge University Press.

Erdmann, Benno (1878). *Kant's Kriticismus in der ersten und in der zweiten Auflage der Kritik der reinen Vernunft* [*Kant's Critical Philosophy in the First and Second Editions of the Critique of Pure Reason*]. Leipzig: Voss.

Evans, J. D. G. (1999). Kant's analysis of the paralogism of rational psychology in the Critique of Pure Reason edition B. *Kantian Review*, 3: 99–105.

Gäbe, Lüder (1954). *Die Paralogismen der reinen Vernunft in der ersten und zweiten Auflage der Kritik der reinen Vernunft* [*The Paralogisms in the First and Second Edition of the Critique of Pure Reason*]. Marburg: Dissertation.

Hatfield, Gary (1992). Empirical, rational, and transcendental psychology: Psychology as science and as philosophy. In P. Guyer (ed.), *The Cambridge Companion to Kant* (pp. 200–27). Cambridge: Cambridge University Press.

Horstmann, Rolf-Peter (1993). Kants Paralogismen. *Kant-Studien*, 83: 408–25.

Horstmann, Rolf-Peter (1998). Der Anhang zur transzendentalen Dialektik [The appendix to the transcendental dialectic]. In G. Mohr and M. Willaschek (eds.), *Immanuel Kant. Kritik der reinen Vernunft* (pp. 525–45). Berlin: Akademie Verlag.

Kant, Immanuel (1998). *The Critique of Pure Reason*, ed. and tr. P. Guyer and A. Wood. Cambridge: Cambridge University Press.

Keller, Pierre (1998). *Kant and the Demands of Self-Consciousness*. Cambridge: Cambridge University Press.

Kitcher, Patricia (1990). *Kant's Transcendental Psychology*. Oxford: University Press.

Klemme, Heiner F. (1996). *Kant's Philosophie des Subjekts* [*Kant's Philosophy of the Subject*]. Hamburg: Meiner.

Strawson, Peter F. (1966). *The Bounds of Sense: An Essay on Kant's Critique of Pure Reason*. London: Methuen.

Strawson, Peter F. (1987). Kant's paralogisms: Self-consciousness and the outside observer. In K. Cramer et al. (eds.), *Theorie der Subjektivität* (pp. 203–19). Frankfurt/Main: Suhrkamp.

Sturm, Thomas (2001). Kant on empirical psychology: How not to investigate the human mind. In E. Watkins (ed.), *Kant and the Sciences* (pp. 163–84). Oxford: Oxford University Press.

Sturma, Dieter (1998). Die Paralogismen der reinen Vernunft in der zweiten Auflage. In G. Mohr and M. Willaschek (eds.), *Immanuel Kant. Kritik der reinen Vernunft* (pp. 391–411). Berlin: Akademie Verlag.

Thiel, Udo (1996). Between Wolff and Kant: Merian's theory of apperception. *Journal of the History of Philosophy*, 34: 213–32.

Thiel, Udo (2001). Kant's notion of self-consciousness in context. In V. Gerhardt et al. (eds.), *Kant und die Berliner Aufklärung* (vol. 2, pp. 468–76). Berlin: de Gruyter.

Wunderlich, Falk (2001). Kant's second paralogism in context. In W. Lefèvre (ed.), *Between Leibniz, Newton, and Kant: Philosophy and Science in the Eighteenth Century* (pp. 175–88). Boston, Dordrecht, London: Kluwer.

221

15

Kant's Philosophy of Mathematics

GORDON BRITTAN

It is not too much to say that Kant's views on mathematics have had as much influence on mathematicians as on philosophers, and in both cases have provided the motive for creative and important work. One has only to think of Gauss, Riemann, Poincaré, Frege, Russell, Hilbert, and Brouwer. It comes as a surprise, then, that Kant wrote comparatively little about mathematics, and then almost always by way of a comparison between mathematics and philosophy. He was certainly familiar with the history of mathematics and the main developments of his time, and remarks about both, sometimes extensive, are scattered through his writings. Yet in the *Critique of Pure Reason*, the only extended discussions of mathematics come near the beginning, in the Introduction, and towards the end, in the Transcendental Doctrine of Method. Later commentators on his work have had to do a great deal of reconstruction.

Moreover, almost all who have followed him have tried to show that Kant was wrong; wrong about the synthetic and a priori character of arithmetic and geometry, wrong about what could, or could not, be "proved," and wrong about the necessity of what he called "intuitions" in mathematics.

Kant's critics as well as his supporters have for the most part embraced what might broadly be called an "evidentialist" interpretation of his views. On this interpretation, intuitions provide indispensable evidence for the truths of mathematics. The critics try to show that this is not the case. The supporters, whose position I will emphasize in what follows, think to the contrary that there is something to it.

In my view the "evidentialist" interpretation is itself mistaken. I want to develop it in more detail and show precisely how it is mistaken, and put a more adequate semantic, or "objectivist," interpretation in its place. This will involve indicating the roles the notion of an intuition plays within his philosophy of mathematics and the philosophy of mathematics, in turn, plays within the context of his general philosophical position. Along the way I will have something to say about the synthetic and a priori character of mathematical propositions and the nature of mathematical proof.

1.

In fact, there are two main contemporary lines of "evidentialist" interpretation current among Kant's supporters.

On one (see Brittan 1978: chs. 2 and 3), our attention is drawn to the premises of mathematical inferences – the axioms, basic propositions, or principles of arithmetic or geometry. This interpretation has its source in reflection on the position of Frege (1950), who maintains that arithmetic is "analytic" in the sense that one can derive all of its truths in a logically rigorous fashion from the definitions of "zero" and "is the successor of" and the basic laws of logic, here taken to include the axioms of set theory. According to the first line of interpretation, Frege was wrong in taking these axioms as analytic; they can be denied without contradiction, as can the postulates of Euclidean geometry. It follows that conceptual analysis alone cannot establish their truth. An appeal to "intuition" must also be made.

On the other line of interpretation, we are to concentrate not on the premises of mathematical inferences, but on the proof procedures used to demonstrate their conclusions (see Friedman 1992: chs. 1 and 2; and Friedman 2000). This second line of interpretation has its source in Russell (1919: 145). Those who follow him maintain that the proof procedures furnished by monadic quantification theory (Aristotle's theory of the syllogism) which were available in Kant's time are not capable of establishing all of the conclusions demanded by mathematics, and in particular those having to do with infinite series and the notion of continuity. It was for this reason that Kant was able to make reference to "extralogical" or "intuitive" considerations in mathematics, although the development of a more adequate conception of logic, in a general quantification theory, and of infinite series has since shown how such reference can be avoided.

According to the two schools of interpretation, then, the establishment of the premises of mathematical inferences or of their conclusions requires "intuition," in a sense of the word not yet made clear. According to the first, "logic," the principle of contradiction and its corollaries proves too much: there are several systems of geometry which are consistent, and intuition is necessary to determine which one among them is true.

According to the second, "logic," monadic quantification theory, does not prove enough; intuition is necessary in order to obtain all the classical (Euclidean) geometrical results.

The first line of interpretation is strongly suggested by the following passage from the *Critique of Pure Reason*:

> For since one found that the inferences of the mathematicians all proceed in accordance with the principle of contradiction (which is required by the nature of any apodictic certainty), one was persuaded that the principles could also be cognized from the principle of contradiction, in which, however, they erred; for a synthetic proposition can of course be comprehended in accordance with the principle of contradiction, but only insofar as another synthetic proposition is presupposed from which it can be deduced, never in itself. (B 14; translations from Kant 1998)

The evident implication of this passage is that those (before Kant, Leibniz and his disciples; after Kant, Frege and his) who have remarked correctly that the inference from the axioms to the theorems is valid, were mistaken in believing that the axioms are themselves conceptual truths. That they are not such truths follows, once again, from the fact that they can be denied without contradiction. Systems of non-Euclidean geometry, in which at least some of the axioms of Euclidean geometry are denied, are logically consistent. As Kant puts it (B 268): "Thus there is no contradiction in the concept of a figure which is enclosed within two straight lines, since the concepts of two straight lines and of their coming together contain no negation of a figure."

But if one cannot determine the truth of the axioms of Euclidean geometry in a conceptual fashion, then, if one supposes that the axioms are true and the "concept"/ "intuition" disjunction is exhaustive, one must appeal to intuition in order to determine this truth. Only intuition serves to pick the "true" from among the diverse consistent geometries.

It's worth mentioning here a variation on this line of interpretation. Some of the axioms, or "postulates" in Euclid's sense, necessary in order to establish the conclusions of geometry and arithmetic are "existential" in character ("At least two points exist," for example; or "There exist a denumerable number of objects"). According to Kant, one cannot demonstrate the existence of an object by way of an analysis of its concept. This is one of the principal points in his rejection of the ontological proof for the existence of God. One can always deny an existential judgment, even insofar as it concerns God, without any contradiction. But if one cannot demonstrate the existence of objects required by mathematical theories by way of an analysis of their concepts, one must, once again, appeal to intuition.

The other interpretation of Kant's conception of mathematics does not concentrate on the premises and first principles, but on the proof procedures utilized. There are, in fact, a good number of passages in which Kant insists on the reasoning employed by the mathematician and ties it directly to the synthetic a priori status of mathematical propositions. For example, at *Critique of Pure Reason* B 744:

> Give a philosopher the concept of a triangle, and let him try to find out in his way how the sum of its angles might be related to a right angle. He has nothing but the concept of a figure enclosed by three straight lines, and in it the concept of equally many angles. Now he may reflect on the concept as long as he wants, yet he will never produce anything new. He can analyze and make distinct the concept of a straight line, or of an angle, or of the number three, but he will not come upon any other properties that do not already lie in these concepts. Now let the geometer take up this question. He begins at once to construct a triangle. Since he knows that two right angles together are exactly equal to all the adjacent angles that can be drawn from one point on a straight line, he extends one side of his triangle, and obtains two adjacent angles that together are equal to two right ones. Now he divides the external one of these angles by drawing a line parallel to the opposite side of the triangle, and sees that here there arises an external adjacent angle which is equal to an internal angle, etc. In such a way, *through a chain of inferences that is always guided by intuition*, he arrives at a fully illuminating and at the same time general solution of the question. (My emphasis)

It is explicit in this passage that it is the *inference*, and not the *axioms*, that demand intuition.

But in what respect is the mathematical reasoning intuitive? One answer, more obvious perhaps in the case of arithmetic and analysis than in geometry, is that it involves calculation. Consider the method of calculating continuous quantities, the infinitesimal calculus. Kant's conception of "logic" was thoroughly Aristotelian and roughly similar to monadic quantification theory. What is especially noteworthy about this theory is that monadic formulas always have finite realizations or models. This fact is linked closely to the decidability of these formulas so that one can, in a finite number of steps, determine whether they are true or false. Polyadic formulas, to the contrary, sometimes have only denumerable models, when, for example, existential quantifiers depend on universal, as in the simplest case (x)(Ey)(Fxy). But mathematical reasoning often has need of a denumerable number of individuals, in order to guarantee the closure of certain arithmetical operations, say, or in proofs which demand the density of the Euclidean straight line. With its essentially finite character monadic quantification theory does not have the resources to represent, still less to demonstrate, all of the classical mathematical theorems of which polyadic quantification is capable. In identifying conceptual determination with monadic provability, Kant was conscious of the fact that the proof of many theorems demanded "intuition," calculations which take time, often depend on representations of objects in space, and are irreducible to the laws of logic (as he understood it).

Michael Friedman, on whose discussion I draw, rejects an "evidentialist" interpretation of Kant's position. But his point of departure is Russell's and lends itself without much difficulty to such an interpretation. According to Russell, Kant, lacking a procedure for representing continuity and irrational numbers, called on intuition to represent the motion of a point (following Newton and his notion of a "fluxion"). But Weierstrass, Dedekind, Cantor, et al. have succeeded in accounting for continuity and irrational numbers, and so on, on the basis of the whole numbers alone, without any appeal to motions or other spatial-temporal intuitions. "It is this result, still more than non-Euclidean geometry, which is fatal to the Kantian theory of a priori intuition as the basis of mathematics" (Russell 1937).

Often the calculation is symbolic in character. When the magnitudes are much larger than the number of our fingers and toes, we count on the familiar properties of the base-ten system of their representation. This calculation by means of numerals not only abridges the otherwise laborious procedure of adding and subtracting numbers unit by unit, but also supplies us with the means to verify the results (see Young 1992).

There is much to be said in support of these two lines of interpretation, particularly from the vantage-point provided by Frege and Russell. There is also much to criticize in them individually considered. But what is crucial is the common theme they share. Despite the fact that they underline different aspects of the synthetic character of mathematical propositions, the two interpretations are agreed that intuition plays an *evidential* role in Kant's conception of mathematics. Conceptual analysis alone does not suffice to establish mathematical truths; one must therefore appeal to intuition in order to verify and confirm both the premises of the inferences and the conclusions that result from them. Intuition furnishes us with the necessary evidence. As one of the most astute of contemporary commentators, Charles Parsons, has it, "a mathematical proposition cannot be *verified* except on the basis of a proof or calculation, that which is, in fact, a construction in intuition" (1983: 138; my emphasis).

This notion, that intuition in some way provides the evidence that verifies or confirms mathematical truths extends beyond the interpretations just examined. Let me cite several passages from recent Anglo-Saxon Kant commentary to indicate its extent.

> Although the mathematician complains that a premise required in all rigour by a demonstration or a construction is missing, it is probably the case that the pictured meanings of the relevant expressions [i.e., intuitions] eliminate every alternative to the missing premise [i.e. falsify every alternative]. (Strawson 1996: 383–4)
>
> Kant cites as an example of what he has in mind the propositions "Two straight lines cannot enclose a space, and with them alone no figure is possible" (B 65). Then he provides his explanation that these propositions, because they are synthetic, that is to say are not derived from the concepts of the objects mentioned, require intuition for their confirmation. (Guyer 1987: 364)
>
> How does one know that the proposition ["Every cube has twelve edges"] is true? The majority of people verify it by evoking the image of a cube and counting the edges – an example of what Kant calls "pure intuition." (van Cleve 1999: 25)

Carl Posy, than whom no one on Kant's philosophy of mathematics is more expert, expresses the same thought in a very direct way: "Mathematics is, in fact, Kant's paradigm of synthetic a priori knowledge. And so he must define 'intuition' in a way that includes the evidence for mathematical judgments" (Posy 1992: 3).

But there is a major difficulty with the evidential interpretation. Intuition *cannot* constitute evidence. In falling back on intuition, we verify nothing. There are three things to note.

First, whatever constitutes "evidence" is necessarily propositional. The notion of evidence is a relation, be it deductive or inductive, which holds between the propositions which compose an inference. But intuition is not propositional. Only by way of a concept is a proposition possible. This is one of the most important aspects of the distinction that Kant makes between concept and intuition. If one *sees that* 5 and 7 make 12, for example, one has evidence in support of the proposition. But "see that" is propositional (i.e., the indirect object of the verb is a proposition).

Second, Kant insists on the concept/intuition distinction in order to illuminate and criticize the epistemological positions of his empiricist and rationalist predecessors. The empiricists erase the difference between "Graham sees a red balloon" and "Graham sees that the balloon is red." They want to establish a foundation for knowledge in what is immediately given to the senses, the indubitable. But that which is immediately given is only a sense impression and is perfectly extensional. Graham might see the balloon without noticing that it is red, but if he does not notice that it is red, he has no evidence that it is red. Once again, "notice that . . ." is intensional. The empiricists wanted to assimilate the intensional to the extensional and in this way furnish us with a firm foundation for knowledge but in so doing, according to Kant, they made a very bad mistake. In the same way, the rationalists assimilated the extensional to the intensional, they reduced, so to speak, "Graham sees the red ball" to "Graham sees that the ball is red." Evidently, they chose more basic propositions than these examples but the effect is the same, namely to confuse that which is immediately given to the senses with that which can serve as evidence. In distinguishing sharply between concept and intuition, Kant wants to expose and avoid this confusion. Yes, something is given immediately to our senses, but that which is given has no logical consequences.

In fact, Kant rejects explicitly the idea that unaided intuition is able to furnish us with evidence. Rather, it is concepts which are the source of our mathematical knowledge. Is there another plausible interpretation of this important passage from the Preface to the second edition of the *Critique?*

> A new light broke upon the first person who demonstrated the isosceles triangle. For he found that what he had to do was not to trace what he saw in this figure, or even trace its mere concept, and read off, as it were, from the properties of the figure; but rather that he had to produce the latter from what he himself thought into the object and presented (through construction) according to *a priori* concepts, and that in order to know something securely *a priori* he had to ascribe to the thing nothing except what followed necessarily from what he himself had put into it in accordance with its concept. (B xi–xii)

One must not inspect what is discerned in the figure, that construction in intuition so favored by "evidentialists." Instead of that, it is necessary to draw consequences from the concept.

There is an additional difficulty in this connection with the idea that pure spatial intuition is evidence for, or "grounds," the propositions of Euclidean geometry. It is that the pure intuition of space, as Kant characterizes it in that section of the first *Critique* entitled the Metaphysical Foundations of the Concept of Space, has only some very general topological properties. There is not enough there to induce any sort of metric, a "determinate" space, let alone a specifically Euclidean distance function, a point on which Kant insists in §38 of the *Prolegomena*: "Space is something so uniform and so indeterminate with respect to all specific properties that certainly no one will look for a stock of natural laws within it." In fact, "the metricization" of space comes only much later, in the Analytic, with the application of the principles of understanding. It is not "given" in the pure intuition of space. From a slightly different perspective, the "pure intuition of space" is not able to distinguish between the various geometries, except insofar as we attribute to it, in a question-begging sort of way, just those properties needed to "ground" Euclid." It is at this point, of course, that an unhelpful appeal is often made to what can and cannot be "visualized."

Further, Kant rejects totally the idea that mathematics needs a foundation, a "verification." As he tells us in the (A) Preface of the *Critique*: mathematics "merits its old reputation for solidity." His problem has to do with metaphysics, which was for the most part denigrated. The search for a foundation for empirical and mathematical knowledge is untoward. Still less could intuition furnish it, in regard to either the premises of our mathematical inferences or the procedures invoked to demonstrate the truth of mathematical propositions.

I don't think, in any case, that the evidential interpretation responds very well to the question why Kant placed the discussion of mathematics at the very beginning of the *Critique of Pure Reason* in the Introduction? This question apparently unsettles commentators, even the greatest. Strawson has something to say on the subject of mathematics, but not until an appendix to his book, and in connection with the maligned thesis of transcendental idealism. Henry Allison (1983) and Graham Bird (1962) ignore it. I will suggest shortly a more extended interpretation of the remarks Kant makes in the Introduction. For the moment, it suffices to note that he there draws a parallel between mathematics and metaphysics and in the process hopes to shed light on the latter. Since mathematics and metaphysics are alike a priori, in the initially uncontroversial sense that the concepts of each are "pure," Kant focuses on the synthetic character of mathematics and links it to the use of intuitions in a way that suggests the second line of evidential interpretation.

> The concept of twelve is by no means already thought merely by my thinking of that unification of seven and five; and no matter how long I analyze my concept of such a possible sum I will not find twelve in it. One must go beyond these concepts, seeking assistance in the intuition that corresponds to one of the two, one's five fingers, say, or, five points, and one after another add the units of the five given in intuition to the concept of seven. For I take first the number 7, and, as I take the fingers of my hand as an intuition for assistance with the concept of 5, to that image of mine I now add the units that I have previously taken together in order to constitute the number 5 one after another to the number 7, and thus see the number 12 arise. (B 15)

I "see the number arise" certainly suggests that by this dactylic procedure I verify the sum at the same time that I establish its existence. Fingers furnish me with the evidence; "intuition is necessary to see that $7 + 5 = 12$" (Parsons 1983: 133). But there are at least two problems that prevent us from embracing too quickly an evidential reading of this text.

One problem concerns the passage which comes soon after that which I have just cited, at B 16:

> To be sure, a few principles that the geometers presuppose are actually analytic and rest on the principle of contradiction; But . . . they only serve for the chain of method and not as principles, for instance a = a, the whole is equal to itself, or $(a + b) \geq a$, the whole is greater than the part. And yet even these, although they are valid in accordance with mere concepts, are admitted in mathematics only because they can be exhibited in intuition.

It is not possible that intuition plays an evidential role here; we already know that the propositions are "valid" on the basis of an analysis of their concepts alone. There is thus no question of "verifying" them. If one assumes that intuition plays the *same* role *throughout* the Introduction, then it is not able to play an evidential role in the preceding paragraphs either.

The other of the two troubling aspects of an evidential reading of the passage at B 15 concerns a point already alluded to. It is clear in the Introduction that Kant wants to establish a rather close parallel between metaphysics and mathematics. It is one cornerstone of his critique of Hume. But if this parallel is close, and if mathematics is synthetic in virtue of the fact that intuition must be used to establish or verify its several truths, it follows that metaphysics too will need intuition to verify its own propositions. But intuition does not verify a single metaphysical proposition. One must conclude, I think, either that the parallel between mathematics and metaphysics isn't very close, in which case Kant's use of the former to support his claim that the latter is both synthetic and a priori has little force, or that the role played by intuition in the Introduction is not "evidential."

2.

One cannot understand "intuition" as "evidence," despite the great number of commentators who do so. The fundamental issue for Kant has little to do with "proof." It is, rather, whether one can "determine" the object of singular reference in mathematics in a purely conceptual or descriptive fashion. That is to say that Kant's motives are primarily semantic, even if they also entail some important epistemic consequences. On my interpretation of his position, singular reference, on which the objectivity and not the truth of mathematics depends, requires intuition. It is not a matter of "verifying" mathematical propositions, but of showing how they are "possible," that is of providing an account of how their subject terms manage to refer.

In this respect, Kant's philosophy of mathematics is of a piece with the rest of the Critical project. That project is defined by the question which he raised in the famous letter to Marcus Herz of 1772: "on what basis [does] that in us which is called 'representation' refer to an object?" – a question we might rephrase in a more linguistic mode as: How is it that singular terms, particularly those that have no empirical elements, manage to refer to objects? What Kant comes to realize is that such reference requires intuitions as well as concepts. A merely conceptual determination of its objects is never adequate, a point made explicit in the *Jäsche Logic* (9.99 and B 340).

In my view, Kant's strategy is to begin with what might appear to be the most difficult case for his thesis, the case of mathematics. For pure mathematics seems to turn entirely on the manipulation and analysis of concepts, a fact often underlined by calling it a purely "formal" discipline. If he can show that this is not true, that even pure mathematics requires the use of intuitions, then he will have gone some way in the direction of persuading us of the general thesis that there is no determination of any object whatsoever without recourse to intuition. This is to say that the case of mathematics illustrates the general thesis, and for this reason is placed in the Introduction of the *Critique*.

Allow me to approach the issue from a slightly different direction. If we were to schematize Kant's general position, it could be seen to turn on three crucial claims: there is no objectivity without objects, there are no objects without reference, there is no reference without intuition. Since he thinks that mathematical propositions are in the intended sense "objective," it follows for him that that reference of the singular terms in these propositions requires intuition. Of course, all of this needs to be spelled out.

We can begin with the claim that mathematics is "objective." On my reading, this comes down to saying that mathematical propositions have knowable truth values. In this respect, they contrast with merely analytic propositions. On the face of it, this claim seems mistaken. Kant says, for example, that the truth of analytic judgments "must always be able to be cognized sufficiently in accordance with the principle of contradiction" (B 190). But this saying does not cohere very well with Kant's views that "truth . . . is the agreement of cognition with its object" (B 82), and that

> an analytic [judgment] takes the understanding no further, and since it is occupied only with that which is already thought in the concept, it leaves it undecided whether the concept even has any relation to objects . . . what the concept might pertain to is indifferent. (B 190)

229

It is for this reason, of course, that in the passage already cited at B 16, Kant insists that analytic propositions are admitted into mathematics only on condition that their terms refer. What we have to say, I think, is that for Kant an analytic proposition if true is necessarily true, that is, if its terms refer to objects then the truth of the proposition can be determined by inspection.

This point has an important corollary, that truth cannot be reduced to proof (as several variations in the evidentialist interpretation assume), for every analytic proposition can be "proved" (from a zero premise set and the law of contradiction), and yet no analytic proposition per se is true. The proof of a mathematical proposition might in this sense be said to demonstrate its "certainty" without at the same time demonstrating its "objectivity." But what Kant mainly wants to show is not that mathematical propositions are *certain*, that is, derivable from self-evident premises using rigorous modes of proof, but that they are *objective*.

Kant goes on to equate "objectivity" (in his chosen vocabulary, "objective validity") with meaningfulness:

> If a cognition is to have objective reality, i.e., to be related to an object, and is to have significance and sense in that object, the object must be able to be given in some way. Without that, the concepts are empty, and through them one has, to be sure, thought but not cognized anything through this thinking, but merely played with representation. (B 194)

If the propositions of pure mathematics are meaningful, and Kant simply assumes that they are, then, once again, their terms must manage to refer. In this respect they cannot be, for the reason just given, merely analytic.

Two conditions of such "objective reference" suggest themselves. One of these is that the objects of reference be independent of my *conception* of them. It is necessary that the *same* object be conceivable or representable in different ways. I will call this the "uniqueness condition."

A second condition on objective reference is that the objects to which reference is made are distinct from my perception of them. We could call this in what is perhaps a somewhat misleading way the "existence condition."

Kant's view, as I understand it, is that purely descriptive theories of reference do not satisfy these conditions, from which it follows that intuition must also be invoked. General representations or concepts alone can never completely determine an object, or *guarantee* reference. Only singular representations of objects, "intuitions," can do so. So far as mathematics is concerned, we can "indicate" the object in a variety of ways, by drawing or imagining certain figures, for example, though what is crucial is not the existence of the object per se but of its formal properties (those implicit in the concept of the object under consideration). Moreover, that an object can be intuited in this way demonstrates that it can be given in, and conforms to, the "formal determinations" of space and time.

My approach to Kant's view will be by way of Leibniz, for here as elsewhere it can scarcely be understood apart from the Leibnizian context in which it was developed. Let me sketch this context briefly. First, Leibniz holds that:

> It is in the nature of an individual substance or of a complete being to furnish us a conception so complete that the concept alone suffices to understand and to deduce all

of the predicates of which the substance is or will become the subject. (*Discours de métaphysique* VIII)

Leibniz calls these conceptions "complete individual concepts."

Second, complete individual concepts identify a unique individual. This is simply a trivial consequence of their characterization. The converse is true as well: every term which picks out a unique individual will be a complete individual concept. For this reason, we can call them genuine singular terms. Any predication in which such a singular term is subject will be a genuine predication.

Third, it follows that every genuine predication is necessary ("analytic") in the familiar Leibnizian sense that it must be true in all possible worlds Suppose that a genuine predication, "Adam ate the apple," is true in or of our world. If this predication were not necessary, that is to say, if it were not true in or of all possible worlds which contained Adam, there would be a world in which it was false. But if there were a world in which it was false, "Adam" would no longer be a genuine singular term. For in that world, "Adam" would refer to a different individual, the individual who lacked the property "ate the apple" which Adam possesses in our world. Given that we supposed from the outset that "Adam ate the apple" was a genuine predication, it follows that "Adam" is a genuine singular term. That is, it is necessary that "Adam" refers to the same individual in all the possible worlds that contain him. Thus, "Adam ate the apple" is necessary.

But Kant rejects all of this. With the sole (partial) exception of "the thing in general," there are no complete individual concepts in a decisive sense (which the results of Gödel and Skolem only underline), semantics surpasses syntax, with us if not also with God. However extensive *our* description of the object, it is always possible that this description refers to distinct individuals, which differ one from another with respect to a property which has not yet been mentioned, or, in the case of "incongruent counterparts," which are distinct even if all of their intrinsic properties are in common. We must pass from concept to intuition – show, exhibit, point to the object – if our reference to the object is to be objective. In this sense of the word, our reference must be demonstrative.

Thus in the Amphiboly of Concepts, Kant insists on the fact that "even if there is no difference whatever as regards the concepts," that is to say, even if their descriptions are identical, "it is still possible that at least two distinct objects satisfy them." Our individuation of objects, in a paradigm case spatial objects which are described by all and only the same concepts, is by way of the fact that they occupy different locations at the same time. Singularity is not possible without immediacy. Kant expresses this insight by saying that the determination of the object requires (sensible) intuition as well as concepts, which means, at least in large part, that intuitions as well as concepts are necessary to designate or refer to unique individuals.

I suggested earlier that Kant uses mathematics as an example to illustrate his general thesis that there is no determination of the object without intuition, and that without intuition there is no objectivity. In other words, he wants to show that even in mathematics, despite its a priori or "pure" character, there are no complete individual concepts. Even in mathematics we must indicate the object if the conditions of singular reference are to be satisfied.

From this point of view the intuitive character of such elementary arithmetical truths as "7 + 5 = 12" is to be understood as follows. On the one hand the concepts of "seven" and "five" do not determine what "that *single* number may be which combines both" (B 15; my emphasis), that is to say that they do not determine the unique reference of "twelve." But on the other hand, although this is true and serves to make Kant's point it is also misleading. For the concepts of "five" and "twelve," considered separately, do not serve to "determine" their objects either; here too we must engage (demonstrative) reference. It then follows that, the reference of "five" and "twelve" having been determined (the use of the fingers to make this reference precise is but an example of the means by which its "demonstration" is possible), the reference of "twelve" is determined as well. When Kant adds that his point is "more evident if we take larger numbers," I take him to mean that the particular number which is their sum is even less obviously "determined" by their concepts. Similarly, the concept of a straight line does not by itself pick out or designate the shortest line between two points. To do this, intuition is also required.

The majority of commentators on Kant's philosophy of mathematics give intuition specific, more restricted, evidential roles to play. We have already looked at some of their suggestions. But the great variety of these suggestions itself makes clear that there is no one special evidential role that it plays, there is no one criterion with regard to which figures or numbers are or are not "constructible," over and above the fact that their exemplification makes "genuine" singular reference possible, and with it the complete determination of every mathematical object.

What Kant does is to illustrate this fact with a great number of examples, and there is no common thread which runs through them all other than the one I've just stated. Thus, when Kant claims in his letter to K. L. Reinhold of May 19, 1789, that "the mathematician can make no claim about an object without first pointing it out in intuition," the point is that the mathematician must first assure himself of the reference of his concepts by showing (constructing) them in intuition. The specific content of the intuition remains open. Kant's goal is always the same, to show that Leibniz is mistaken about the possibility of guaranteeing the reference of singular terms (especially when the concepts at stake are a priori) using conceptual methods alone.

A second letter, this time to A. W. Rehberg (before September 25, 1790), supports and clarifies my position. Rehberg asks Kant the following question: "Given that the understanding can create numbers at will, why is it not capable of thinking $\sqrt{2}$ in numbers"! Kant's response is complex, and I want only to bring out two aspects of it.

One: The objective reality of the concept of the square root of two is given by its construction in intuition, that is, by its geometrical representation – the square root of two can be represented by the diagonal of a unit square. This representation indicates that there is one quantity to which the expression "$\sqrt{2}$" refers even if one is not able to think it in numbers, that is, to provide it with a precise numerical determination. It does not furnish us with "evidence" in support of any arithmetical proposition.

Two: At the same time, one can "determine" the number that corresponds to $\sqrt{2}$ by a series of successive approximations. This succession never terminates. But we have a rule for rendering it more and more precise. That is to say, one can "calculate" the number, and in this sense "determine" it. It is in this same sense that one can "verify" that such and such a number in a more and more well-defined interval corresponds to $\sqrt{2}$.

Two corollaries follow from these observations. On the one hand, in establishing the objective reality of the concept, one does not "verify" a number which corresponds to it. On the other hand the "verification" of this number, by way of algebraic procedures, does not establish its objective reality; given that the procedure used in its "determination" never terminates, *the* reference of √2 is not guaranteed. One can admit that the calculation of this number is "intuitive" in the senses already mentioned, but it is the primary role of intuition to make reference, or semantic determination, possible, and not to make possible arithmetical or geometrical results (what might be called "epistemological determination").

3.

I want finally to elaborate three claims implicit in my discussion, in the attempt both to clarify and defend them. First, Kant says that a proposition is synthetic just in case its predicate "cannot be derived from its subject by way of the principle of contradiction" (B 16). This suggests that in a synthetic proposition the predicate is derived from the subject by way of an intuition. But as we have seen, nothing can be "derived from" or with the help of an intuition. The role of intuition, rather, is to fix the reference of the subject and in the process to provide a semantic tie to its predicate. In other words, the role of intuition is to establish the "objective reality" of propositions. Mathematics is unique in this respect, that its concepts furnish us with rules for their construction, that is, for the production of intuitions, or ostensible objects in a very wide sense of the word "object," corresponding to them. Which is to say that the intuitions establishing the objective reality of mathematics are invariably a priori. When in a synthetic proposition we "go beyond" the subject concept, it is not in the first instance to another predicate concept, but to an object – the main point made in his comments on the Greek geometer Apollonius in the polemic against the Leibnizian Eberhard (Allison 1973: 110).

Second, Kant is clear that while non-Euclidean figures are "thinkable," that is, their concepts are consistent, they cannot be "constructed," that is, they cannot be given a priori in intuition. It is precisely at this point that the evidentialist interpretation is often invoked, to the effect that, for Kant, only Euclidean figures can be "visualized" or otherwise congruent with the data given to the senses.

I think, in fact, that Kant's commitment to Euclidean geometry is rather minimal, or rather, that his commitment derives from various causal considerations that come well after the exposition of the doctrine of pure intuition. In the Transcendental Exposition of space, which argues from the alleged fact that geometry "determines the properties of space synthetically, and yet a priori," to the conclusion that space is "the form of outer sense in general," the only propositions for which arguments are made is that the intuition of space is of an infinite whole and (only very indirectly) that it has only three dimensions, a proposition consistent with Euclidean and non-Euclidean geometries alike. Indeed, Kant says that the conclusion of the Transcendental Exposition of Space is the only way in which the "possibility" of geometry, as a body of synthetic a priori knowledge, can be explained. There is no suggestion here that Euclidean geometry is uniquely "possible," or that its necessity derives from our insight into the form of outer sense.

Otherwise, there are no more than scattered references to Euclidean examples. I have already cited one of the most celebrated, at B 268, where Kant says that the concept of a figure enclosed by two straight lines is both consistent and "impossible." But he goes on to say that "the impossibility rests not on the concept in itself, but on its construction in space, i.e. on the conditions of space and its determinations."

More light is shed on what Kant means here by the proof that J. H. Lambert, Kant's friend and frequent philosophical correspondent, gives of the "impossibility" of elliptic space in his *Theorie der Parallellinien* (1766). The crucial fact about the proof that he gives is that it depends on the axiom of Archimedes, an axiom that says (in one of its many equivalent formulations) "that if one magnitude is less than another, there is an integer by which the first can be multiplied so that the result is larger than the second." To put it very simply, the figure proposed is incompatible with this axiom (see Bonola 1912: 37, 46).

Now what Kant says at B 268 is that the figure cannot be "constructed," a fact which rests in turn on the conditions of space and its determinations. In a number of passages Kant makes clear that "only the concept of magnitudes [for which there exists an appropriate additive operation] can be constructed, i.e. exhibited a priori in intuition" (B 742). This is, of course, closely connected with the fact that space is "determined" only to the extent that it has magnitude, i.e. only to the extent that it is measurable precisely. If we add, what is in fact the case, that a condition on measurement is that the axiom of Archimedes holds, then a figure enclosed by two straight lines is "impossible" in the precise sense that it is incompatible with the determination of space.

There are three points I would emphasize in connection with this example. First, Kant simply follows Lambert's lead here. He assumes that the latter has shown the impossibility of the figure; it remains to draw some philosophical consequences. Kant does not think it is his task to show that particular mathematical propositions are true or false or to provide a explanation of how we know this. Still less it is his task to show how the propositions of Euclidean geometry in particular are knowably true.

Second, it is not the case that Lambert's proof turns on any "intuitive" considerations, concerning what we visualize in connection with the concept of a "straight" line, for example. If there are difficulties with the proof, they have little to do with appeals to what is "given" to the senses.

Third, Kant makes explicit at the end of his discussion at B 268 that the point has to do with the "objective reality" of geometrical figures, and not with their "necessity." While there is the suggestion that only Euclidean figures are "objectively real," there is nothing to indicate that intuition provides the evidence on the basis of which the propositions describing them can be known to be true. Once again, the main point is that even in mathematics one cannot go from the consistency of a concept to its "objective reality," a lesson that, as against Leibniz, we are now to apply to metaphysics.

References and Further Reading

Allison, H. (1973). *The Kant–Eberhard Controversy*. Baltimore: Johns Hopkins UniversityPress.
Allison, H. (1983). *Kant's Transcendental Idealism*. New Haven: Yale University Press.

Benacerraf, P. and Putnam, H., eds. (1964). *Philosophy of Mathematics: Selected Readings*. Oxford: Blackwell.

Bird, G. (1962). *Kant's Theory of Knowledge*. London: Routledge & Kegan Paul.

Bonola, R. (1912). *Non-Euclidean Geometry*. LaSalle, IL: Open Court.

Brittan, G. (1978). *Kant's Theory of Science*. Princeton: Princeton University Press.

Friedman, M. (1992). *Kant and the Exact Sciences*. Cambridge, MA: Harvard University Press.

Friedman, M. (2000). Geometry, construction, and intuition in Kant and his successors. In *Between Logic and Intuition: Essays in Honor of Charles Parsons*. Cambridge: Cambridge University Press.

Frege, G. (1950). *The Foundations of Arithmetic*, tr. J. Austin. Oxford: Oxford University Press.

Guyer, P. (1987). *Kant and the Claims of Knowledge*. Cambridge: Cambridge University Press.

Kant, Immanuel (1998). *The Critique of Pure Reason*, eds. and tr. P. Guyer and A. Wood. Cambridge: Cambridge University Press.

Parsons, C. (1983). *Mathematics in Philosophy*. Ithaca, NY: Cornell University Press.

Posy, C. (1992). *Kant's Philosophy of Mathematics*. Dordrecht: Kluwer Academic.

Russell, B. (1919). *Introduction to Mathematical Philosophy*. London: Allen & Unwin.

Russell, B. (1937). *The Principles of Mathematics*, 2nd ed. New York, W. W. Norton.

Strawson, P. F. (1966). *The Bounds of Sense*. London: Methuen.

Van Cleve, J. (1999). *Problems from Kant*. Oxford: Oxford University Press.

Young, J. M. (1992). Construction, schematism, and imagination. In Posy 1992.

16

Metaphysical Foundations of
Natural Science

MICHAEL FRIEDMAN

Kant's *Metaphysical Foundations of Natural Science* appeared in 1786, at the height of his mature or "Critical" period and, in particular, between the first (1781) and second (1787) editions of the *Critique of Pure Reason*. Not surprisingly, then, Kant's treatise on natural science exhibits an explicit and systematic correspondence with the structure and content of the first *Critique*: for example, the three "laws of mechanics" derived in the former correspond to the three Analogies of Experience derived in the latter. Moreover, with respect to natural science proper, Kant's treatise also exhibits a systematic correspondence with some of the main elements of Newton's *Principia* (1687): for example, the same laws of mechanics correspond (at least approximately – see below) with the Laws of Motion Newton takes as the axiomatic basis of his mathematical system. These specific correspondences with the "transcendental philosophy" of the first *Critique*, on the one side, and Newtonian mathematical physics, on the other, are relatively straightforward and clear. But what, more generally, does Kant mean by the idea of metaphysical foundations of natural science; and how does this idea then frame the radical transformation of the very meaning of "metaphysics" Kant takes to be one of the main achievements of his Critical philosophy?

The relationship between "metaphysics" or "first philosophy" and "physics" or "natural philosophy" was a prominent theme in the most important early modern discussions of the new mathematical science – paradigmatically, for example, in Descartes, Leibniz, and Newton. For all of these thinkers, physics or natural philosophy dealt with the sensible or corporeal part of the universe, spatiotemporally distributed matter in motion, whereas metaphysics or first philosophy dealt with the supersensible or incorporeal part, namely, God and the soul. Moreover, the relationship between these two disciplines was now especially problematic precisely because the new mathematical science initiated by the scientific revolution of the sixteenth and seventeenth centuries took its starting point from a rejection of the Aristotelian-Scholastic system of natural philosophy and metaphysics which had dominated the high Middle Ages and was now being seriously threatened by the work of Copernicus, Kepler, and Galileo. The relationship between metaphysics and physics – first philosophy and natural philosophy – had now to be radically rethought.

In particular, the condemnation of Galileo in 1633 for defending the Copernican conception of the mobility of the earth had a decisive effect on Descartes' work in metaphysics. Descartes was just about to publish his first major work, *The World*, a comprehensive exposition of his physics – wherein all phenomena in the sensible or corporeal part of the universe were to be accounted for in terms of the motions and interactions of tiny parts of matter or corpuscles, which, in turn, possess only the purely geometrical properties (later called "primary qualities") of extension, figure, and motion, and interact with one another (and thereby change their speeds and directions) only by impact. Thus, according to Descartes' theory of planetary motion (and of light), the planets are carried along in a rotating vortex of invisible fluid matter with the sun (more generally a star) at the center (where the light associated with the star consists of a centrifugal pressure propagated rectilinearly from this center). Even in this early work physics was supposed to have a metaphysical foundation, for the basic law of nature governing all changes of motion of matter – the conservation of what Descartes called the total "quantity of motion" ("size" multiplied by speed) – was ultimately grounded in the unity and simplicity of God, whereby God continually recreates the entire material universe at each instant while constantly expressing the very same divine essence. But Descartes did not undertake a systematic development of metaphysics in *The World*. All of this changed with the condemnation of Galileo; for, immediately upon learning of this event in 1633, Descartes resolved not to publish his work in physics (based, as it was, on his essentially Copernican vortex theory), and he devoted himself, instead, to a more systematic presentation of "method" and metaphysics: first in the *Discourse on Method* of 1637 and then in the *Meditations on First Philosophy* of 1641 – whose subtitle, we should recall, was "in which are demonstrated the existence of God and the immortality of the soul" (changed in the second edition to "in which are demonstrated the existence of God and the distinction between the human soul and the body"). Only after this properly metaphysical work was completed did Descartes finally return to physics with the *Principles of Philosophy* of 1644, where the physical system of *The World* is now depicted as deductively derived from the metaphysics of God and the soul most fully articulated in the *Meditations*. It is not too much to say, therefore, that the most fundamental task of the scientific and philosophical revolution initiated by Descartes was precisely to show how the new mathematical physics is, after all, fully compatible with (and in fact best adapted to) both the spirit and the letter of the Christian religion.

From the point of view of most later thinkers, however, the Cartesian system turned out not to be fully satisfactory, and it failed to solve, in particular, two fundamental problems. In the first place, Descartes had failed to formulate the basic laws of motion in an adequate way; and, in fact, it appeared that an additional dynamical quantity (which we now take to be the quantity of mass, together with the closely related quantity of momentum) – one that is not reducible to the purely geometrical properties of extension, figure, and motion – is actually required. In the second place, although the Cartesian system had indeed instituted an essential relationship between God and nature, it appeared that nature might still not be related to God in the right way. For, given the basic laws of motion, all changes in the sensible or material world then proceed purely mechanically, with no reference whatsoever to purpose, value, intention, or choice. What room was left, therefore, for moral or spiritual values within extended nature? What room was left, more specifically, for the exercise of human moral freedom of choice? Although Descartes himself had a very strong conception of the absolute

237

MICHAEL FRIEDMAN

(infinite) freedom of the human will, it remained quite unclear how this could be reconciled with the thoroughgoing determinism of the physical world. And this problem was exacerbated, for most subsequent thinkers, by the intervening philosophy of Spinoza, who explicitly argued (approvingly) that the purely geometrical or mechanical character of Cartesian physics entails not only the complete elimination of Aristotelian teleology but also that of human freedom of the will.

From our point of view, the most important post-Cartesian thinker to react to these problems was Leibniz. Leibniz began, in fact, by reacting to the first problem: Descartes' failure adequately to formulate the basic laws of motion and interaction which were supposed to govern, according to the then dominant paradigm of the "mechanical natural philosophy," all phenomena in the material or corporeal world. Leibniz responded to this problem, in his "Brief Demonstration of a Notable Error of Descartes and Others Concerning a Natural Law" (1686), by emphasizing the importance of a new, essentially dynamical quantity, which he called *vis viva* or living force (mass times the square of the velocity), where the basic law of motion is now formulated as the conservation of the total quantity of vis viva. Beginning with his *Discourse on Metaphysics* (published in the same year), Leibniz also strongly emphasized that living force is not purely geometrical or mechanical, so that, in particular, this quantity (unlike Descartes' purely mechanical "quantity of motion") reintroduces an element of Aristotelian teleology into the mechanical philosophy. For vis viva, on Leibniz's view, is the counterpart of the Aristotelian notion of entelechy: namely, that internal (nonspatial) principle by which an ultimate simple substance or monad determines (by a kind of "appetition") the entire future development of its own internal state. In this way, an element of intention or value was reintroduced into the mechanical worldview quite generally; and Leibniz then articulated a doctrine of divine creation in terms of God's choice of the best among all merely logically possible worlds. The distinction between what is logically possible and what is actual – between all merely thinkable worlds available to the divine intellect and the best and most perfect of these worlds as determined by the divine will – thereby corresponds to the distinction between principles of pure mathematics (including geometry) and principles of natural science or physics (the laws of motion). In particular, the laws of motion, unlike the merely mathematical laws of pure geometry, precisely express the divine wisdom in actualizing or creating the best and most perfect of all possible worlds.

Leibniz's system was thus a major improvement on Descartes' with respect to both of the two problems sketched above. First, Leibniz succeeded in formulating the basic laws of motion of the mechanical philosophy – the laws of impact – in a much more adequate way; and, second, Leibniz thereby also established a more satisfactory relationship between God and nature, whereby divine wisdom and value are clearly and explicitly reintroduced within the divine creation. Once again, however, from the point of view of most later thinkers, Leibniz had still not solved either problem completely. In the first place, Newton soon formulated the basic laws of motion in a way that generalizes and extends the mechanical philosophy in a quite essential (and also quite controversial) way. For Newton, the fundamental dynamical quantity governing all changes of motion was momentum (mass times velocity), and the fundamental dynamical quantity causally responsible for such changes was "impressed force" – where this refers to any action of a second body on the body in question by which a change of

238

momentum of the first body is produced. Force, in the Newtonian sense, is thus an external action of one body on another, not an internal principle like Leibnizean *vis viva*; and, what is worse, it is an action not intrinsically limited to the condition of contact. On the contrary, the principal instantiation of this concept, in Newton's *Principia*, was precisely the force of universal gravitation, whereby one body attracts another immediately and at a distance (as in the sun's gravitational attraction of the earth). In the second place, however, and going beyond all such details of specifically Newtonian physics, it seemed that Leibniz had still not made sufficient room for human moral freedom of choice. To be sure, God in some sense freely chooses (in a way that exceeds the bounds of purely geometrical necessity) the best of all possible worlds. But what is the sense in which we human creatures – whose lives, in particular, are apparently completely determined by God's prior choice – are similarly morally free? Leibniz struggled mightily with this remaining moral and theological problem, but no fully satisfactory solution (from the point of view of most later thinkers) was in fact ever achieved.

That Descartes and Leibniz were centrally concerned with the metaphysical foundations of physics in this sense – with the relationship between the supersensible realm of God and the soul and the sensible realm of corporeal nature – is relatively well known. But Newton was centrally concerned with fundamental metaphysical issues in precisely the same sense. Newton touched on these questions in some of his published writings, for example, in the General Scholium to the *Principia* and the Queries to the *Optics*. However, his clearest and most developed treatment occurs in the unpublished *De Gravitatione*, which was framed as an explicit rejection of Descartes' system of metaphysics and physics in the *Principles of Philosophy*. What was most important for Newton was decisively to reject Descartes' identification of matter with extension and to defend, accordingly, the concept(s) of absolute (empty) space (and time) existing independently of matter – and hence the concept of absolute motion. Thus, for example, the concepts of absolute space and absolute motion are necessary because without them the basic idea of Descartes' own vortex theory cannot even be coherently formulated. According to Newton, absolute rotation (defined relative to space itself rather than other matter) must be assumed by Descartes' theory, and this concept is also centrally present, now quite explicitly, in Newton's planetary theory based on universal gravitation. Yet absolute space is neither a substance nor an accident, for Newton, but what he calls "an emanative effect of God and an affection of every kind of being" (Newton 2004: 21). In particular, absolute space or pure extension is even an affection of God himself, since God is omnipresent or everywhere. God can thereby create matter or body (as something quite distinct from pure extension) by endowing certain determined regions of space with the conditions of mobility, impenetrability, and obedience to the laws of motion: God can do this anywhere in space, in virtue of his omnipresence, by his immediate thought and will, just as our souls can move our bodies by our immediate thought and will. Thus, Newton's metaphysics of divine creation was a striking alternative to the conceptions articulated by Descartes and Leibniz, respectively, where Newton's primary emphasis (even more, if possible, than for his two great philosophical adversaries) was on the absolute power and freedom of God *vis-à-vis* the material world.

The early eighteenth century witnessed a great stage-setting intellectual debate, the famous correspondence between Leibniz and Clarke of 1715–17, which sharply focused attention on the opposition between the Leibnizean and Newtonian philosophies. This debate paid equal attention to both technical problems in physics and natural science (such as the laws of impact and the nature of matter) and very general issues within metaphysics and theology (such as the principle of sufficient reason and God's choice to create our world). Leibniz objected to the Newtonian doctrine of direct divine intervention in the phenomena of the material universe – such as specially adjusting the orbits in the solar system, for example, so as to ensure that they all lie in approximately the same plane – and defended his own version of the principle of sufficient reason, whereby God's creative activity is exercised only in his initial choice of the best of all possible worlds. Clarke (representing Newton) replied that this would entail an unacceptable limitation on God's freedom of action, and, in particular, he defended Newtonian absolute space against Leibniz's use of the principle of sufficient reason to argue that such a space is impossible because God would then have no reason to place the material universe in one position rather than another within absolute space. In mid-eighteenth-century Germany this great debate between Leibnizeans and Newtonians dominated the intellectual agenda within both natural science and metaphysics, and Kant himself was no exception. Indeed, Kant's earlier pre-Critical writings were overwhelmingly concerned with problems of natural philosophy in general and the project of reconciling Leibniz and Newton in particular.

Two of Kant's most important pre-Critical works were the *Universal Natural History and Theory of the Heavens* (1755) and the *Physical Monadology* (1756). In the first work Kant developed one of the earliest versions of the nebular hypothesis. He formulated the idea that the band of stars visible as the Milky Way consists of a rotating galaxy containing our solar system and that other visible clusters of stars also consist of such galaxies. Moreover, according to the hypothesis in question, all such galaxies originally arose from rotating clouds of gas or nebulae whose centrifugal force of rotation caused a gradual flattening out in a plane perpendicular to the axis of rotation as they cooled and formed individual stars and planets. The laws of such galaxy formation, for Kant, proceed entirely in accordance with "Newtonian principles." At the same time, however, since our solar system has the same nebular origin as all other galactic structures, we are able to explain one important feature of this system for which the Newtonians had invoked direct divine intervention – the fact that all the planets in our system orbit in approximately the same plane – from purely mechanical natural laws after all, precisely as the Leibnizeans had maintained. (See also chapters 2 and 3 above.)

The question dominating the *Physical Monadology* concerned a specific metaphysical problem arising in the debate between Leibnizeans and Newtonians. If the ultimate constituents of matter are absolutely simple elementary substances or monads, as the Leibnizeans contend, how can this be reconciled with the geometrical infinite divisibility of space? It would appear that by dividing the space filled or occupied by any given piece of matter, however small, we would also eventually divide the elementary material substances found there as well – contrary to the assumed absolute simplicity of such substances. So how can an elementary constituent of matter or "physical monad" possibly fill the space it occupies, without being infinitely divisible in turn? Kant's answer (in 1756) is that physical monads do not fill the space they occupy by being immediately present in all parts of this space; they are not to be conceived, for example, as bodies that are solid through and through. Physical monads are rather to be conceived as point-like centers of attractive and repulsive forces, where the repulsive force, in particular, generates a region of solidity or impenetrability in the form of a tiny "sphere of activity" emanating from a central point. Geometrically dividing this region of impenetrability in no way divides the actual substance of the monad, but merely the "sphere of activity" in which the point-like central source manifests its repulsive capacity to exclude other monads from the region in question. So the Leibnizean commitment to ultimate simple substances or monads is perfectly consistent with the infinite divisibility of space after all – but (and here is Kant's characteristic twist) it can only be maintained by explicitly adopting the Newtonian conception of forces acting at a distance (in this case a short-range repulsive force acting at a very small distance given by the radius of its "sphere of activity").

Kant's conception in the *Physical Monadology* is thus an early example of what came to be called a dynamical theory of matter, according to which the basic properties of solidity and impenetrability are not taken as primitive and self-explanatory but are rather viewed as derived from an interplay of forces. Although this kind of theory exerted a powerful influence on the development of natural philosophy in the later part of the eighteenth century (in the work of such thinkers as Boscovich and Priestley, for example), Kant's own original motivations, in the *Physical Monadology*, were in fact primarily metaphysical. In particular, Kant's incorporation of Newtonian action-at-a-distance forces within the framework of a Leibnizean monadology served to unify the intrinsically nonspatial (and thus essentially mental or spiritual) realm of ultimate simple substances lying at the basis of corporeal nature with what was now generally believed to be the correct Newtonian formulation of the laws of motion. As Kant makes clear in the complementary metaphysical treatise framing the *Physical Monadology*, the *New Elucidation of the First Principles of Metaphysical Cognition* (1755), the primary motivation for creating his dynamical theory was to accept the Leibnizean doctrine of the fundamentally internal intrinsic natures of the ultimate simple substances themselves, while simultaneously granting that they have essentially external or relational determinations as well. It is precisely these external determinations, by which the monads are first set into genuine relation with one another, that are now phenomenally manifested as the fundamental forces of repulsion and attraction, and Newtonian absolute space, in particular, is nothing but the phenomenal expression of these relations. Moreover, since Newtonian absolute space is thus the phenomenal expression of the divinely ordained laws of interaction in virtue of which the originally nonspatial monads co-exist together in a common world, we can thereby vindicate a version of the Newtonian doctrine of divine omnipresence as well. We can accept the Newtonian formulation of the laws of motion (and we can accept universal gravitation as a genuine action at a distance through empty space) while also retaining the Leibnizean reconciliation of the corporeal and spiritual realms – which Leibniz himself termed the realms of nature and of grace.

Kant reconsiders the dynamical theory of matter in the *Metaphysical Foundations*, which appeared, as already noted, at the height of Kant's Critical period. Nevertheless, the fundamental questions in both natural science and metaphysics characteristic of the pre-Critical period were also very salient here. In particular, the *Metaphysical Foundations* continues, and also attempts to integrate, two separate lines of thought from the pre-Critical period: the extension of Newtonian gravitational astronomy to cosmology

241

first suggested in the *Theory of the Heavens*, and the further development of a dynamical theory of matter as first sketched in the *Physical Monadology*. At the same time, however, Kant now frames both developments within the radically new context of his Critical philosophy. Indeed, it is not too much to say that the *Critique of Pure Reason* stands to the *Metaphysical Foundations* as the pre-Critical *New Elucidation* stands to the *Physical Monadology*: the former presents the more general philosophical-metaphysical framework within which the latter, more specifically natural-philosophical work is formulated. And, whereas the pre-Critical metaphysical framework, as we have seen, is a mixture of Leibnizean and Newtonian elements, the Critical framework radically transforms these elements so as thereby completely to revolutionize the discipline of metaphysics itself.

The Critical version of the dynamical theory of matter is developed in the longest and most complicated part of the *Metaphysical Foundations*, the second chapter or Dynamics (see chapter 2 above). Here, as in the *Physical Monadology*, Kant views the basic properties of matter – impenetrability, solidity, hardness, density, and so on – as arising from an interplay of the two fundamental forces of attraction and repulsion. In sharp contrast to the *Physical Monadology*, however, Kant abandons the idea of smallest elementary parts of matter or physical monads, and argues instead that all parts of matter or material substances, just like the space they occupy, must be infinitely divisible. Indeed, in the course of developing this argument, Kant explicitly rejects the very theory of physical monads he had himself earlier defended (in 1756). A space filled with matter or material substance, Kant now argues, necessarily consists of an infinity or continuum of material points, each of which exerts the two fundamental forces of attraction and repulsion. The "balancing" of the two fundamental forces which had earlier determined a tiny (but finite) volume representing a "sphere of activity" of impenetrability around a single point-like central source now determines a definite density of matter at each point in the space in question effected by the mutual interaction of attraction and repulsion.

Thus, in the *Metaphysical Foundations*, as in the first *Critique*, material or phenomenal substance is no longer viewed as simple and indivisible, but is instead a genuine continuum occupying all the (geometrical) points of the space it fills. Accordingly, the problem posed by the infinite divisibility of space that the *Physical Monadology* had attempted to solve by invoking finite "spheres of activity" is now addressed, in the Dynamics of the *Metaphysical Foundations*, by invoking the transcendental idealism articulated in the Antinomy of Pure Reason of the first *Critique*. According to that view all objects of human knowledge are necessarily spatiotemporal phenomena or appearances and thus cannot include nonspatiotemporal noumena or things in themselves (where such noumena, for Kant, are modelled on precisely the Leibnizean monads). More specifically, Kant now invokes the argument of the Second Antinomy resolving the apparent incompatibility between the infinite divisibility of space and the presumed absolute simplicity of the material or phenomenal substances found in space. Matter or material substance is infinitely divisible in space but never, in experience, ever infinitely divided; hence, since matter is a mere appearance or phenomenon in space and is thus given only in a spatiotemporal "progress of experience," it consists neither in ultimate simple elements nor in an actual or completed infinity of ever smaller spatial parts. Therefore, it is only by viewing matter as a thing in itself or noumenal

242

substance (which would be necessarily simple or monadic) that we obtain a genuine contradiction or antinomy; and so, by an indirect proof or reductio ad absurdum, we have a further argument in support of Kant's characteristically Critical doctrine of transcendental idealism.

The cosmological conception presented in the *Theory of the Heavens* had also included a striking vision of how the various galactic structures are distributed throughout the universe. The smallest such structure (due to nebular formation) is our own solar system, consisting of the sun surrounded by the six then known planets. The next larger structure is the Milky Way galaxy, in which our solar system as a whole orbits around a larger center together with a host of other stars and (possible) planetary systems. But the Milky Way galaxy itself, for Kant, is then part of an even larger rotating system consisting of a number of such galaxies; this system is part of a still larger rotating system; and so on ad infinitum. The universe as a whole therefore consists of an indefinitely extended sequence of ever larger rotating galactic structures, working its way out from our solar system orbiting around its central sun, through the Milky Way galaxy in which our solar system is itself orbiting around a galactic center, then through a rotating system of such galaxies, and so on. Moreover, this indefinitely extended sequence of galactic structures reflects a parallel indefinitely extended sequence of nebular galactic formation, as the structures in question precipitate out from an initial uniform distribution of gaseous material sequentially starting from the center.

The *Metaphysical Foundations*, unlike the *Theory of the Heavens*, is not a work of cosmology. But the cosmological vision of the Theory of the Heavens is still centrally present there, transposed, as it were, into a more epistemological key. The very first explication of the *Metaphysical Foundations*, in the first chapter or Phoronomy, defines matter as the movable in space; and, as Kant immediately points out, this inevitably raises the difficult question of relative versus absolute motion, relative versus absolute space. Kant firmly rejects the Newtonian conception of absolute space as an actual "object of experience," and he suggests, instead, that it can be conceived along the lines of what he himself calls an "idea of reason." In this sense, "absolute space" signifies nothing but an indefinitely extended sequence of ever larger "relative spaces," such that any given relative space in the sequence, viewed initially as at rest, can be then viewed as moving with respect to a still larger relative space found later in the sequence. In the fourth (and final) chapter or Phenomenology, which concerns the question of how matter, as movable, is possible as an object of experience, Kant returns to this theme and develops it more concretely. He characterizes absolute space explicitly as an "idea of reason" and, in this context, describes a procedure for "reducing all motion and rest to absolute space" (*MFNS* 4.558–63). This procedure then generates a determinate distinction between true and merely apparent motion – despite the acknowledged relativity of all motion as such to some given empirically specified relative space. The procedure begins by considering our position on the earth, indicates how the earth's state of true rotation can nonetheless be empirically determined, and concludes by considering the cosmos as a whole, together with the "common center of gravity of all matter," as the ultimate relative space for correctly determining all true motion and rest.

What Kant appears to be envisioning, then, is an epistemological translation of the cosmological conception of the *Theory of the Heavens*. In order to determine the true motions in the material, and thus empirically accessible universe, we begin with our parochial perspective here on earth, quickly move to the point of view of our solar system (where the earth is now seen to be really in a state of motion), then move to the perspective of the Milky Way galaxy (where the solar system, in turn, is itself seen to be in motion), and so on ad infinitum through an ever widening sequence of ever larger galactic structures serving as ever more expansive relative spaces. What Kant calls the "common center of gravity of all matter," relative to which all the motions in the cosmos as a whole can now be determinately considered, is never actually reached in this sequence; it is rather to be viewed as a forever unattainable regulative idea of reason towards which our sequence of (always empirically accessible) relative spaces is converging. In this way, in particular, we obtain an empirically meaningful surrogate for Newtonian absolute space using precisely the methods used by Newton himself (in determining the true motions in the solar system in the *Principia*, for example). At the same time, we preserve the fundamental Leibnizean insight that any position in space, and therefore all motion and rest, must ultimately be determined, in experience, from empirically accessible spatiotemporal relations between bodies.

Kant's conception of absolute space in the *Metaphysical Foundations* therefore corresponds – in the more specific context of a consideration of matter as the movable in space – to his famous attempt in the *Critique of Pure Reason* to depict his own doctrine of the transcendental ideality of space as the only possible middle ground between the two untenable extreme positions of Newtonian "absolutism" and Leibnizean "relationalism." It also corresponds, even more directly, to Kant's conception of the extent of the material or empirical world in space articulated in the First Antinomy, according to which there is indeed no limit to this extent at any particular finite boundary, but, at the same time, the world cannot be conceived as an actually infinite completed totality either. In the end, there is only the purely regulative requirement or demand that, in the "progress of experience," we must always seek for further matter beyond any given finite limit and, accordingly, accept no given such boundary as definitive. We must seek, in the terminology of the *Metaphysical Foundations*, for ever larger relative spaces encompassing any given relative space; and, in this way, Kant's conception of absolute space as an idea of reason is the complement, from the point of view of the Critical doctrine of transcendental idealism, of his new version of the dynamical theory of matter as consisting of a potential (but not actual) infinity of ever smaller spatial parts. Both are thereby firmly embedded within the radically new Critical perspective of "transcendental philosophy" (see chapter 8 above).

But it is in Kant's third chapter or Mechanics, as already suggested at the beginning, that we find the most developed and explicit correspondence between the pure natural science of the *Metaphysical Foundations* and the transcendental philosophy of the first *Critique*. The main business of this chapter is establishing what Kant calls the three "laws of mechanics." These are, first, a principle of the conservation of the total quantity of matter in the universe; second, a version of the law of inertia; and third, the law of the equality of action and reaction. We find a very explicit correspondence, in particular, between these three laws of mechanics and the central Kantian pure concepts of the understanding or categories – the concepts of substance, causality, and community – which, along with the pure forms of intuition or sensibility, space, and time, constitute the a priori "transcendental" framework underlying all human experience and knowledge of the phenomenal world (see chapter 7 above). The principle of the conservation of the total quantity of matter corresponds to the more general transcendental principle established in the first *Critique* – the permanence of substance in all changes in the (phenomenal) world; the law of inertia corresponds to the category, and accompanying principle, of causality; and the law of the equality of action and reaction corresponds to the category, and accompanying principle, of thoroughgoing dynamical interaction or community. Thus, in considering material substances or bodies as interacting with one another through their fundamental forces and, as a result, thereby standing in relation to one another in a community of what Kant calls their inherent motions (that is, momenta), we are, at the same time, applying the categories or pure concepts of substance, causality, and community to these same bodies.

More specifically, it is precisely by applying Kant's three laws of mechanics that we are then able, in the Phenomenology, to implement the procedure of "reducing all motion and rest to absolute space" sketched above. In particular, the most important step in this procedure depends on Kant's proof of the equality of action and reaction in the Mechanics. Kant there explicitly chides Newton for attempting to derive this law from experience, and what Kant proposes instead is an a priori proof from the concepts of absolute motion and rest. In any interaction between two bodies whereby they stand in a community of their fundamental forces (repulsion in impact or attraction in gravitation), there is a privileged relative space or reference frame for considering the resulting changes of motion: namely, the center of mass frame of the two bodies, in which the two corresponding momenta (and their changes) are necessarily equal and opposite. The principle of the conservation of momentum therefore necessarily holds in this frame (where the total momentum in question is always identically zero), together with the equality of action and reaction. We then implement the procedure described in the Phenomenology by a kind of successive iteration of this argument to wider and wider systems of bodies: we move from the center of mass of the solar system, to the center of mass of the Milky Way galaxy, to the center of mass of a system of such galaxies, and so on ad infinitum. Absolute space, as we have seen, is thus no actual space at all but rather a forever unattainable regulative idea of reason – given, in the end, by the "common center of gravity of all matter" – towards which our procedure is converging.

Kant's proof of his second law of mechanics, a version of the law of inertia, marks a further fundamental break with the pre-Critical conception of the *Physical Monadology*. For Kant now formulates the law of inertia as the proposition that "every change of matter has an *external* cause" (my emphasis), where the ground of proof of this proposition is precisely that "matter has no essentially internal determinations or grounds of determination" (*MFNS*, 4.543–4). But the whole point of the *Physical Monadology*, as we have seen, was to combine a Leibnizean insistence on the essentially internal intrinsic natures of the ultimate simple substances lying at the basis of corporeal reality (the physical monads) with a Newtonian physical description of this same reality. Indeed, in the pre-Critical period, Kant went so far as explicitly to associate the internal or intrinsic determinations of the ultimate simple substances with the Newtonian force of inertia or *vis insita*. Now, in the *Metaphysical Foundations*, Kant decisively rejects this force of inertia, and he decisively rejects, at the same time, the understanding of vis viva or living force characteristic of Leibnizean natural philosophy. Just as, in the

Critical period, there is no longer any room for the simplicity of phenomenal substance, there is similarly no longer any room for attributing a purely internal (and thus mental or spiritual) nature to such a substance. Kant's earlier attempt to combine the Leibnizean realms of nature and grace within a single metaphysical description of the corporeal or material universe must now be seen as a failure.

Indeed, according to the transcendental idealism characteristic of the Critical philosophy, no reconciliation or unification of these two realms (which Kant now calls the realm of nature and the realm of freedom) within a single picture of reality is possible at all, at least from a purely theoretical point of view. For this would involve our having theoretical knowledge of the nonspatiotemporal – and thus supersensible – noumenal realm, contrary to the most fundamental claim of the first *Critique*. Moreover, it is further reflection on the problem of human moral freedom (as expressed, for example, in the Third Antinomy of Pure Reason) that primarily drives Kant to this conclusion. What Kant now proposes, in particular, is that we must sharply distinguish between theoretical and practical reason, where the former is confined to knowledge of spatiotemporal phenomena and only the latter can meaningfully grasp the supersensible. But practical reason "grasps" the supersensible solely from an essentially practical point of view, in terms of directives regulating our conduct. In the end, the three most fundamental ideas of reason – the ideas of God, Freedom, and Immortality – function as the ultimate and most general regulative principles guiding and framing all human conduct whatsoever, including the conduct of theoretical natural science itself (see chapter 13 above). The indefinitely extended sequence of stages of inquiry governing our progressive investigation into both smaller and smaller parts of matter (in accordance with Kant's critical version of the dynamical theory of matter) and larger and larger regions of space (in accordance with Kant's Critical conception of absolute space) must in turn be entirely subordinated, by what Kant now calls the primacy of pure practical reason, to humanity's morally necessary progression towards the Highest Good. (The doctrines of the primacy of pure practical reason and the Highest Good are developed in the second *Critique*, published in 1788; the subordination of all regulative teleology to what Kant calls "ethico-theology" is developed in the third, published in 1790 – which also emphasizes the distinction between the realm of nature and the realm of freedom: see chapter 17 below.)

Kant's Critical philosophy, as the counterpart to the more specific philosophy of natural science developed in the *Metaphysical Foundations*, thus completes the metaphysical project begun by Descartes in response to the scientific revolution – the project of showing how the new mathematical physics is fully compatible with (and indeed best adapted to) both the spirit and the letter of morality and religion – just as Newton's *Principia* completes the scientific revolution itself (Kant gives a detailed morally-rational reinterpretation of Christianity in *Religion within the Limits of Reason Alone*, published in 1793). Kant completes this metaphysical project, as we have seen, precisely by transforming the Leibnizean attempted solution of the problem (which is a transformation, in turn, of Descartes' original attempt) in light of the mathematical physics and natural philosophy of Newton. In particular, Kant's transcendental idealism replaces Newtonian absolute space with a regulative idea of reason governing our progressive investigation of larger and larger regions of space, and it replaces the Leibnizean ultimate simple substances or monads with a parallel "progress of experience" governing our successive investigation into smaller and smaller parts of matter. Scientific inquiry thereby takes the form of an indefinitely extended sequence of stages that is itself governed, in the end, by the three most fundamental regulative ideas of reason, namely, God, Freedom, and Immortality; and, in this way, the entire progress of our theoretical knowledge of nature (the entire progress of natural science) is subordinated to the higher demands of morality and religion. But these demands, as we have seen, have no properly theoretical cognitive meaning at all: there is no theoretical knowledge of the supersensible. The proper objective meaning and function of these ideas is purely practical, as directives regulating our conduct (including our conduct of scientific inquiry) in accordance with the moral law. This is what Kant means by his famous statement, in the Preface to the second edition of the first *Critique*, that he had to deny knowledge (*Wissen*) in order to make room for faith (*Glauben*) (B xxx): transcendental idealism had to deny theoretical knowledge of the supersensible in order to allow the idea of the supersensible properly to guide us.

The full extent of Kant's radical transformation of the very meaning of "metaphysics," in the context of his metaphysical foundations of natural science, is now clear. For Kant's early modern predecessors – and, in particular, for Descartes, Leibniz, and Newton – metaphysics was a theoretical investigation of the supersensible or incorporeal part of the universe (God and the soul) just as physics was a theoretical investigation of the sensible or corporeal part (spatiotemporally distributed matter in motion). Such a dual investigation was especially urgent because the deeply interwoven philosophical, theological, and religious culture of the high Middle Ages was now being seriously threatened by the scientific revolution initiated by Copernicus, Kepler, and Galileo. By the late eighteenth century, however, this scientific revolution was an already accomplished fact, and Newtonian mathematical physics, more specifically, was now completely triumphant. Newton had formulated the universally accepted laws of motion, but there remained serious unclarities surrounding the Newtonian concept(s) of absolute space (and time) and the idea of action at a distance through empty space – which, as we have seen, were in turn closely connected, for Newton himself, with his own novel attempt to rethink the relationship between space, God, and matter. Kant's project then took the form of a reconceptualization of precisely these fundamental Newtonian concepts, against the background of the Leibnizean metaphysical framework within which he had been trained. Whereas, in the pre-Critical period, Kant combines elements of Leibniz and Newton in a way that preserves the possibility of theoretical knowledge of the supersensible, in the Critical period he pushes his reconsideration of space and matter ever further, and he simultaneously develops a radically new approach to the foundations of morality and religion. In the end, the resulting philosophical doctrines of transcendental idealism and the primacy of practical reason institute a fundamentally humanistic conception of the demands of morality and religion in relation to the entirely open-ended progress of theoretical scientific investigation.

It is striking, then, that Kant explicitly reconsiders the meaning of "metaphysics" towards the end of his Preface to the *Metaphysical Foundations*. In the course of sharply distinguishing between general metaphysics or transcendental philosophy and the special metaphysics of corporeal nature (that is, the metaphysical foundations of natural science), Kant explains that an

247

important reason for detaching [the metaphysics of corporeal nature] from the general system of metaphysics, and presenting it systematically as a special whole . . . [is that general] metaphysics has busied so many heads until now, and will continue to do so, not in order thereby to extend natural knowledge (which takes place much more easily and surely through observation, experiment, and the application of mathematics to outer appearances), but rather so as to attain cognition of that which lies wholly beyond all boundaries of experience, of God, Freedom, and Immortality. (4.477; translations from Kant 1992 and 2004).

The general metaphysics or transcendental philosophy advanced in the first *Critique* (and then further articulated in the second and third) portrays nature in general and human experience as a whole as necessarily framed by a priori principles of reason extending far beyond the boundaries of all theoretical science of the natural world. This world is thereby seen to be much more than a theater for objective human experience and knowledge; it is also, and primarily, a vehicle for the realization of the moral law.

References and Further Reading

Adams, R. (1994). *Leibniz: Determinist, Theist, Idealist*. Oxford: Oxford University Press.

Alexander, H., ed. (1957). *The Leibniz–Clarke Correspondence*. Manchester: Manchester University Press.

Buchdahl, G. (1969). *Metaphysics and the Philosophy of Science*. Oxford: Oxford University Press.

Descartes, R. (1984). *The Philosophical Writings of Descartes*, eds. J. Cottingham, R. Stoothof, and D. Murdoch. 3 vols. Cambridge: Cambridge University Press.

Friedman, M. (1992). *Kant and the Exact Sciences*. Cambridge, MA: Harvard University Press.

Garber, G. (1992). *Descartes Metaphysical Physics*. Chicago: University of Chicago Press.

Gaukroger, S. (1995). *Descartes: An Intellectual Biography*. Oxford: Oxford University Press.

Kant, I. (1969). *Universal Natural History and Theory of the Heavens*, ed. M. Munitz. Ann Arbor: University of Michigan Press.

Kant, I. (1992). *Theoretical Philosophy, 1755–1770*, ed. D. Walford. Cambridge: Cambridge University Press.

Kant, I. (2004). *Metaphysical Foundations of Natural Science*, ed. M. Friedman. Cambridge: Cambridge University Press.

Laywine, A. (1993). *Kant's Early Metaphysics and the Origins of the Critical Philosophy*. Atascadero, CA: Ridgeview.

Leibniz, G. (1989). *Philosophical Essays*, eds. R. Ariew and D. Garber. Indianapolis and Cambridge: Hackett.

Loemker, L., ed. (1969). *Leibniz: Philosophical Papers and Letters*. Dordrecht: Reidel.

Newton, I. (1999). *Mathematical Principles of Natural Philosophy*, tr. I. Bernard Cohen and A. Whitman. Berkeley: University of California Press.

Newton, I. (2004). *Philosophical Writings*, ed. A. Janiak. Cambridge: Cambridge University Press.

Schönfeld, M. (2000). *The Philosophy of the Young Kant*. Oxford: Oxford University Press.

Warren, D. (2001). *Reality and Impenetrability in Kant's Philosophy of Nature*. New York and London: Routledge.

Watkins, E., ed. (2001). *Kant and the Sciences*. Oxford: Oxford University Press.

Wood, A. (1970). *Kant's Moral Religion*. Ithaca, NY: Cornell University Press.

Part III

The Moral Philosophy: Pure and Applied

Introduction

GRAHAM BIRD

Kant's Critical account of our speculative, theoretical, experience in the first *Critique of Pure Reason* is continued in the *Groundwork* and second *Critique of Pure Practical Reason* with his account of our practical, moral, experience. What Kant calls speculative, theoretical, knowledge concerns our cognitive experience in mathematics, natural science, metaphysics, and everyday life; it is contrasted with the "practical" context which includes morality, politics, and the law. The two accounts share many of the same assumptions and the discussion of the pure moral philosophy takes similar forms to that of the theoretical. The former, as I shall suggest, cannot be understood without the background from the first *Critique*, and many of Kant's substantive practical views are anticipated in that work. In the two central works of pure moral philosophy, the second *Critique* and the *Groundwork*, Kant outlines an a priori structure for our practical experience, just as he had outlined such a structure for the theoretical sphere.

Kant consciously follows a strategy of first isolating and characterizing the a priori elements in moral experience, and then returning to apply the consequent a priori moral principles to specific issues in those practical contexts (*Groundwork*, 4.392). These are the same procedures exemplified in the theoretical context in which a priori principles are abstracted from ordinary and scientific experience, in the first *Critique* and *Prolegomena*, and then applied to specific issues in the *Metaphysical Foundations of the Natural Sciences*, and later in the *Opus postumum*. The central ideas of pure moral philosophy in the *Groundwork* and second *Critique* are similarly applied to a posteriori circumstances in such works as the *Metaphysics of Morals* and "On a Supposed Right to Lie." The outcome is similar in both speculative and practical contexts. The pure moral philosophy offers an abstract, formal, account of a supreme moral law, supplements this with a complex moral psychology, and yields similar reversals of previous philosophy. Priorities accorded among earlier philosophers to happiness over morality, to consequences over intentions, and to the good over the right, are either modified or reversed in Kant's account.

In the works of applied practical philosophy, such as the *Metaphysics of Morals*, the essays on "Perpetual Peace," "On a Supposed Right to Lie," and "Theory and Practice," Kant considers more specific applications of the pure moral theory to moral, legal, and political circumstances. The two parts of the *Metaphysics of Morals*, the Doctrine of Right and the Doctrine of Virtue, deal respectively with the application of the pure theory to issues in the law and in morality. The Doctrine of Right deals with a wide range of issues such as those we would associate with property, family, and international law. The Doctrine of Virtue and other works, such as "On a Supposed Right to Lie," similarly explore a wide range of often controversial moral issues. Kant distinguishes between duties of wide and narrow scope, and discusses ends, happiness, duties to oneself, and a large number of commonly recognized virtues and vices, such as love, beneficence, arrogance, and ridicule. In a concluding section he considers ways of teaching ethics and so underlines a more general interest in educational methods (Louden 2000; see chapter 23 below).

Many of the later developments in Kant's applied practical philosophy are present in earlier works such as the first *Critique*. Even there he identified a role for political philosophy in formulating the a priori principles governing the promulgation of constitutions, and noted the requirements for philosophy that it should be communicable to, and arguable among, members of an informed citizenry (B 358, B 372, B 767, B 859). In *Perpetual Peace* and the Doctrine of Right he considers wider issues arising not from relations between citizens and institutions *within* states but from relations *between* states and their citizens. His discussion offers views about cosmopolitan rights and about the legitimate authority and powers of an international organization that might regulate international affairs (see chapters 24 and 25 below). Many of these ideas are still debated and supported among political theorists (Rawls 2000), but some of Kant's applied moral verdicts are notoriously ill-judged. His remarks on other cultures and other religions and especially his views about the role of women in society are simply unacceptable today (Louden 2000). These prejudices cannot be defended, but their failings do not necessarily impugn the pure moral theory. Officially the applied views are derived both from the theory and the a posteriori historical circumstances; if the views are rejected the pure theory may be at fault, but it does not follow that it is.

Throughout these applied comments Kant in this way both uses the results of his pure theory and also to some extent modifies its abstract character. With an increasing emphasis on the works dealing with specific issues in morality, politics, and the law it has become clear that the charge of rigorism, commonly attached in the past to Kant's pure theory, is little more than a misunderstanding. It failed to recognize the consciously abstract, a priori, character of the pure theory which needed supplementation with a posteriori material in order to provide specific guidance on practical moral issues. Kant likened his own metaphysical a priori structure for experience to Euclid's a priori geometrical structure for space. Just as Euclid's geometry offers such an a priori structure for space in our experience so Kant's Critical philosophy offers an a priori structure for the whole of our theoretical and practical experience. Nobody would think of complaining that Euclid's account of points, lines, and planes was too rigorous and unrealistic. Kant represented a reviewer's complaint about his needlessly technical a priori structure for experience as similarly irrelevant (*Prolegomena* 4.374).

1. Freewill and Causality

One central topic, that of freedom, links the first two *Critiques* and provides a transitional bridge from the speculative to the practical philosophy. The concept of freedom is said to be "the keystone of the whole structure of a system of pure reason, even speculative reason" (*CPrR*, 5.3–4). The immediate connection, exemplified in the Third Antinomy of the first *Critique*, addresses the traditional threat to freedom, human agency, and responsibility from a belief in causal determinism. The traditional issue, variously outlined, saw a direct threat to our belief in freedom from the equally natural and compelling belief in a strict determination of every event through necessary causal laws. If such strict causal laws necessitate the sequence of events, including human actions, there may seem to be no room for an ascription of freedom. At least part of that conception of freedom takes human agents to be able to act otherwise than they did, and to have responsibility for the actions they choose to perform. The immediate conflict can be represented as one between saying of such actions both that they were *necessitated* by causal laws and yet that they could have been different. For this may seem to entail that it was both possible and impossible for those events not to have occurred.

Kant's philosophy has a powerful stake in the issue since his own account in the second Analogy of causality as a priori and necessary may seem to reinforce the threat to freedom and morality. Kant's motive, consequently, is to maintain both his view of causal necessity against Hume's empiricist account and his belief in freedom and morality against determinism. The Critical account of causal necessity is taken to represent natural science's investigation of causal relations more accurately than Hume's, but Kant cannot accept that it decisively threatens our conception of freedom. The resulting traditional conflict outlined in the Third Antinomy gives way, in Kant's discussion, to his resolution of the dispute by means of the metaphysical apparatus of the first *Critique*. The relevant part of that apparatus, heralded in the first *Critique*'s Preface (B xxvi–xxx), is the distinction between appearances (phenomena) and things in themselves (noumena). The resolution of the antinomy depends on the claim that freedom and causality can be assigned to different realms, so that transcendental freedom is attached to noumena while causality is assigned to phenomena. The suggestion is that without such a distinction there is no prospect of defending either causality or freedom (B 571).

Commentators have recognized Kant's motive in attempting to reconcile moral freedom and causal necessity but have, even now, found it virtually impossible to accept or even to understand. The primary texts are in the first *Critique* (B 556–86), the *Groundwork* (section III, 4.446–63), and the second *Critique* (5.5–10; 5.50–65). My aim here is not to show that the reconciliation is either comprehensible, acceptable, or impossibly flawed, but only to summarize its main outlines and to underline its evident difficulties. (See also chapter 18 below.)

The important first step is to recognize Kant's distinction between what he calls "transcendental" and "practical" freedom. Its importance is made clear in two ways. First Kant underlines repeatedly that the issue, as he understands and discusses it in the antinomy, concerns *transcendental* and not *practical* freedom. The second point confirms this by claiming that the latter, practical freedom, can be "proved through experience" (B 830). Plainly if the antinomy concerned only *practical* freedom then its recognition requires experience rather than philosophical argument. Since Kant insists, on the contrary, that the traditional conflict requires argument of a peculiarly subtle and complex kind (B 565), this can be only in relation to *transcendental* freedom.

That first step avoids one evident misunderstanding of Kant's position, but it may seem to make that position less, not more, comprehensible. It requires that we distinguish clearly between the two, transcendental and practical (or empirical), conceptions of freedom, and Kant's efforts in this direction have been generally regarded as at best inadequate and at worst a failure. Commentators may stumble at the first hurdle by finding the general distinction between the "empirical" and the "transcendental" mysterious (see chapter 8 above). But even if that general distinction is accepted Kant's further steps have been thought unacceptable and even inconsistent. The difference between transcendental and practical freedom is that the former is a "spontaneous initiation" of a sequence of events, and the latter an action unconstrained by "sensuous impulses." A "spontaneous initiation" is understood to be in some way exempt from causal determination even though it is effective in initiating a sequence of events; it is a cause but apparently not an immanent effect. Practical freedom, "proved through experience," is negatively a resistance to "sensuous impulses" and positively a determination to act through reason.

Kant evidently believes that our experience enables human agents, with an arbitrium liberum, to go beyond the lures of sensory pleasure and respond to reason in a way in which animal arbitrium brutum does not. It might be questioned whether arbitrium brutum covers both a response to the prospect of immediate gratification and a reasoned preference for prudence in maximizing long-term pleasure or happiness. The latter is not characteristic of many animals, even primates, but Kant distinguishes in his moral philosophy between reason's role in moral and prudential motivation. For him the latter yields only a hypothetical imperative, while the former provides a categorical imperative. Reason's role in the former is only to find the best technical means of achieving a desired end; in the latter it has the more elevated role of formulating and applying a supreme moral law. These aspects of the pure moral philosophy are further outlined in section 2 below.

Queries over making the threefold distinction between a compulsive desire satisfaction, a longer-term prudential strategy for maximizing happiness, and a distinctively moral use of reason, are not the most serious obstacle to understanding Kant's reconciliation. That arises from his final step of associating transcendental freedom with noumena despite his speculative insistence in the first *Critique* that we can have no *knowledge* of such things. Kant's undoubted view is that human agents can be said to be transcendentally free in virtue of their moral use of reason as noumenal beings. As noumena agents exist in a timeless or atemporal realm which exempts them from causality and yet enables them to initiate sequences of events in the phenomenal world. It is not hard to see why this form of reconciliation between freedom and causality looks unpromising to the point of hopelessness. It is not easy to understand how we can be nonphenomenal, timeless, agents, or how we can act in such a realm. Even if that were a barely comprehensible fiction, as Kant indicates (B 573), it is hard to see how it can be exemplified in our experience, or how it can reconcile freedom and causality in the same agent and same act. If the claim is that we can conceive of an atemporal, noncausal, realm of reason associated with phenomenal conduct which obeys the necessary laws of causality, why should we think of both aspects as exemplified in the same agent? The noumenal agent has characteristics essentially different from its phenomenal aspect. Even if we accept that this allows us to conceive of two distinct, causal and noncausal, worlds, it does not explain how such distinct factors can be combined in one and the same phenomenal agent.

254

If these difficulties were not enough it has to be finally recalled that for Kant we can have no knowledge of noumena in principle. This motivates Kant's suggestion that the noncausal, atemporal, story is a fiction, but it makes its use as part of an *argument* hard to follow. The account is difficult to grasp at almost every stage of its development, and in addition seems inconsistent with Kant's own speculative insistence that we can have no knowledge of the acausal, atemporal, realm of noumena. It is of no use to suggest that Kant restricts the ban on knowledge of noumena to the speculative realm alone but allows it in the practical. The reconciliation is said to be itself essentially a *speculative*, not practical, matter; and in the *Groundwork* and second *Critique* Kant insists as strongly as ever that the resolution allows us no more latitude to "fly into the transcendent" (*CPrR*, 5.57).

These difficulties have eroded confidence in Kant's resolution of the antinomy and attempted reconciliation of causality and freedom, but the argument is supplemented with further material from the side of moral philosophy. In the *Groundwork* and the second *Critique* Kant claims that the analysis of moral experience, especially the recognition of the moral law and the place of reason in determining our moral responses, provides a "fact" which confirms the reconciliation. Kant has consequently two supporting lines of argument for his resolution, even though he insists that the Third Antinomy is itself concerned only with the speculative issue. In one the argument responds to pressure from the determinist and offers to show that the determinist can be forced to admit an intelligible freedom. In the other it responds to pressure from Kant's moral philosophy and claims to show how the "fact" of reason in our moral experience establishes the propriety of ascribing freedom to human agents (Allison 1990; Bird 2006).

2. Outline of the Pure Moral Philosophy

The pure moral philosophy, like the pure theoretical, outlines the general structure of the relevant part of our experience. In both cases that general structure discloses fundamental concepts and principles presupposed in that experience. In the moral philosophy more emphasis is placed on principles rather than elements (*CPrR*, 5.16), and this reflects the fact that the structure has at its centre a supreme moral law. The discussion formulates that moral law in various ways claimed to be equivalent, explores its a priori ground in reason, and surveys the psychology in which it functions.

The moral law is connected to the defense of transcendental freedom in the following way: If transcendental freedom could not be defended against causal determinism then there would be no room for morality (or for causality). That speculative defense indicates only how transcendental freedom can co-exist with causality; it does not indicate more particularly how moral experience functions under that presupposition. Kant believes that the examination of common moral experience and the subsequent abstraction of its a priori rational elements allows us to see free agents, with arbitrium liberum, as belonging to an order, a rational, moral order, quite different from that of animal nature's arbitrium brutum. That is the cash value of regarding agents as noumena and of subsequent references to noumena in the practical realm, such as the Doctrine of Right's account of "possessio noumenon" (*MM*, 6.268). But Kant remains adamant that none of these claims licenses any *knowledge* of noumena or encourages any "flying into the transcendent." The a priori analysis of moral experience with its account of pure and empirical determinations of reason supports that limited speculative defense of transcendental freedom from the practical side. Together the speculative defense and the practical analysis set aside a determinist threat to freedom and morality, and explain how their function supports a distinctive, rational, a priori, order in our practical experience. These considerations do not allow us to claim that we *know* human agents to be atemporal noumena, but they entitle us to continue to deal with that distinctive order in morality, politics and the law unencumbered by determinism.

At the head of Kant's account is an appeal to morality's overriding demands in the shape of a supreme moral law. The supreme moral law is associated with Kant's distinctions between hypothetical and categorical imperatives, and between autonomy and heteronomy. Hypothetical imperatives are those injunctions of technique or skill which prescribe how best to achieve some desired goal. They indicate what to do *if* such a goal is aimed at, and are associated with specific desires which Kant would classify as "sensuous." Desire, not reason, sets the goals, and reason's role is only to indicate how best to achieve the satisfaction implicit in those desired goals. Categorical imperatives by contrast are not of this kind. They do not advise but command (*CPrR*, 5.36); they do not rest on sensuous desires or impulses; and they do not require a posteriori knowledge of techniques or skill. The claim is that they are a priori requirements of morality which rest on pure practical reason. Hypothetical imperatives aiming at desire satisfaction are classed by Kant as "heteronomous"; that is, they respond to pressures placed on the self by a sensuous character. They reflect a self, or agent, in the grip of feelings and desires which naturally impel courses of action towards a material goal. Categorical imperatives are by contrast dependent on reason, not the senses; they are a priori and unconditional in a way in which achieving satisfaction is not, and their imperatives are for that reason categorical. They mark an agent's autonomy, that is, a freedom from sensuous impulses, an ability to choose among alternatives guided by reason, and an appeal to an overriding morality.

Kant's aim is to identify and support the general form of such categorical imperatives, and he claims to do this in the various formulations of the supreme moral law in the *Groundwork*. One initial formulation requires an agent to act only in ways which could be willed as a universal law (FUL); another subsequent formulation enjoins the treatment of other agents not merely as means, but as ends in themselves (*G*, 4.429) (see chapters 19 and 20 below). Informally these requirements express an impartiality in moral responses which rejects special pleading on one's own behalf, and a recognition of parity of status between such free moral agents. The latter formulation is linked to Kant's imagery of a "kingdom of ends," that is, a community of free agents all of whom treat others with the respect and consideration that morality demands. In the political sphere that conception allows infringement of others' liberty only insofar as one's own liberty can be similarly restricted. The variant formulations are important not only in disclosing Kant's fundamental conception of morality, but also in raising questions about the consistency and clarity of that conception.

Reason comes into this picture of morality in diverse ways. It provides access in metaphysics to the a priori elements in practical experience, but is then not of concern to ordinary folk (*CPrR*, 5.163). The suggestion is that ordinary people respond to the demands of morality in an intuitive way; the philosophical exploration of an intuitive morality's presuppositions prevents that intuitive response from being arbitrary. It underpins moral behavior philosophically but does not need to be recognized in order to fulfill moral demands. Reason, through its connection with logic, also offers guidance in moral conduct by way of a contradiction test for separating moral and immoral acts. Kant holds that mere conformity to moral law is not sufficient for strict moral worth. What is additionally needed is conformity *for the sake of duty or morality*. The shopkeeper who fails to cheat his customers merely from fear of the consequences, or even from a general benevolence, does not reach the strictest moral standard. In the *Groundwork* Kant offers many examples of cases where the crucial test for the morality of an action lies in an agent's being able consistently to will a universalization of his action, and this is linked to Kant's initial conception of a supreme moral law as a possible universal legislation (FUL). There is some inconsistency in deliberately cheating or not fulfilling promises when, if that policy is generally followed, it will damage or destroy the institutions of trading or promising themselves. According to Kant if it is irrational in that way to take advantage of the institution then that application of reason points to immoral conduct.

In all these cases the distinctive feature of Kantian morality is its emphasis on the agent's willing or intentions. That emphasis is related to a wide range of Kant's vocabulary, including his account of "maxims" as the driving motives for action, his distinction between "*Wille*" and "*Willkür*," and recognition of both transcendental and empirical influences from the will. That emphasis and its associated moral psychology point to an agent's deliberation about acting and to the distinctive motives which drive moral considerations, and it puts the primary weight in moral evaluation on the agent's maxims or intentions. It marks more of Kant's great reversals of previous philosophy in which moral worth has priority over happiness or pleasure; reason has priority over sensuous desire; the right has priority over the good; and principled intentions in acting have a priority over consequences. In all these Kant distances himself from other moral philosophies, in which the consequences of acts have primary importance, or in which pleasure or happiness is the overriding goal and criterion of moral action, or where what is right depends on a prior conception of what is good. Kant rejects Utilitarianism as "heteronomous," rejects Hume's view of reason as providing no goals of its own and operative only in hypothetical imperatives, and rejects the idea that the outcome, or consequences of acts alone determine their moral status.

Each of these distinctive priorities is interesting, subtle, and arguable, but the picture Kant gives of morality has been extensively criticized. Among its primary stress points are the appeal to reason and the contradiction test; the formality of the supreme moral law; its rigid appeal to a morality apparently divorced from sentiment; and its revival of a notional reference to noumena.

The contradiction test does not involve a strict logical inconsistency. The free rider who takes advantage, by cheating, of others' adherence to the institutional rules may be thought a paradigm of immorality or unfairness, but is not obviously committing a logical error. There is some inconsistency in playing chess, with an acceptance of its rules, and cheating in order to win which violates those rules, but more explanation is needed to identify the kind of inconsistency involved (O'Neill 1989; Korsgaard 1996: ch. 3). The formality of the supreme moral law can be partially defended by recognizing

Kant's aim to provide an abstract, formal, representation of moral experience, much as Euclid provided an abstract representation of our spatial experience. But at a crucial point in Kant's argument (G, 4.420–2) that formality is linked necessarily to the universalizability criterion, and it remains uncertain why that connection should be accepted (see chapter 20 below). Kant has also been criticized for emphasizing the strict demands of morality as if they had to be met without sentiment or pleasure, or as if one who conformed to such moral demands out of an immediate sympathy for someone in need deserved less moral credit (see chapter 21 below). Finally he has been criticized for inconsistency in appealing to the realm of noumena in the practical sphere when that appeal was so severely restricted in the speculative philosophy.

References

Allison, Henry E. (1990). *Kant's Theory of Freedom.* Cambridge: Cambridge University Press.

Bird, Graham (2006). *The Revolutionary Kant.* Chicago: Open Court.

Korsgaard, Christine (1996). *Creating the Kingdom of Ends.* Cambridge: Cambridge University Press.

Louden, Robert (2000). *Kant's Impure Ethics: From Rational Beings to Human Beings.* Cambridge: Cambridge University Press.

O'Neill, Onora (1989). *Constructions of Reason.* Cambridge: Cambridge University Press.

Rawls, John (2000). *Lectures on The History of Moral Philosophy,* ed. Barbara Herman. Cambridge, MA: Harvard University Press.

17

The Primacy of Practical Reason

SEBASTIAN GARDNER

1.

Kant's conception of the primacy of practical reason is set forth in a short, pregnant section of the Dialectic of the *Critique of Practical Reason*, entitled "On the Primacy of the Pure Practical Reason in its Association with Speculative Reason" (5.119–21; all translations from Kant 1996a, 1996b, 1998, 1999, 2000, 2002). Other passages in Kant's writings – in particular, the "Canon of the Doctrine of Method" in the *Critique of Pure Reason*, the "Orientation" essay of 1786 (Kant 1996b), and the essay "Proclamation of a treaty" (Kant 2002) published 10 years later – are closely relevant, as are numerous shorter discussions scattered over Kant's corpus; but interpretation of Kant's conception must concentrate on "On the Primacy."

It is helpful to distinguish two senses that the term "primacy of practical reason" carries in Kant's philosophy. They may be regarded as two expressions or dimensions, one narrow and one broad, of a single conception. Both are visible and argued for in "On the Primacy." First, the term refers to a philosophical principle that is formulated and defended at a key juncture in Kant's exposition of his argument for what he calls moral theology, in the Dialectic of the *Critique of Practical Reason*. Second, the primacy of practical reason refers to an overarching conception of the nature and method of Critical philosophy, which may be argued to characterize Kant's system at its very deepest level. The first, narrower sense of the primacy of practical reason is that of a rule of inference or of justification in philosophical reasoning, while the second and broader sense is that of a conception of the nature and structure of reason, a meta-philosophical conception expressed by Kant in the language of faculties. The former is connected closely with Kant's concept of a postulate of pure practical reason, and thereby crucial for Kant's account of God's existence, while the latter points to Kant's concepts of the unity, "interest," and teleology of reason as a whole. The interconnection of all these elements, along with the relation between the two senses of the primacy of practical reason and the question of what grounds and justifies the total conception, are complex matters which touch on some of the deepest nerves in Kant's philosophical project.

In what follows, "PPR" is used to refer to Kant's conception of the primacy of practical reason as a whole, inclusive of its two senses; where only one sense is in question,

I shall make this explicit by talking either of "the principle of PPR" or of "PPR in the broader sense."

2. Kant's Statement of the Principle of the Primacy of Practical Reason, and its Role in Kant's Moral Theology

Primacy is defined by Kant as "the prerogative of one [thing] to be the first determining ground of the connection with all the rest" (*CPrR*, 5.119). *Practical primacy* refers to the prerogative of the interest of one thing by virtue of which others are subordinated to it (*CPrR*, 5.119). To assert the primacy of practical reason with respect to speculative reason is, therefore, to assert that propositions on which the interest of practical reason depends necessarily, so long as they are not contradicted by theoretical reason, must be accepted by theoretical reason. Their acceptance involves, Kant adds, their being integrated by theoretical reason with the rest of its cognition.

The principle of PPR is thus easily stated, and its immediate role in the context of the Dialectic's moral theology is relatively straightforward. The argument of the Dialectic, sketched in the Preface (*CPrR*, 5.4–5), turns on Kant's conception of what he calls the "highest good," which has two components: (1) complete virtue, where virtue constitutes worthiness to be happy, and (2) happiness proportional to virtue (*CPrR*, 5.108–11; see also *CPrR*, 5.145–6). The highest good is a "necessary object" of a moral will, Kant claims: without hope of being able to achieve it, practical reason would be caught in an antinomy – the thesis of which is represented by the desire for happiness, and the antithesis by the demands of virtue (*CPrR*, 5. 113–14) – and the moral law would thereby generate a practical absurdity and forsake its validity (*CPrR*, 5.111–14). Now the conditions of each part of the highest good are, respectively, immortality (to make it possible for us to progress to the morally required condition of complete virtue, as our finite empirical existence does not) and the existence of God (to distribute happiness proportionately to virtue, as nature does not) (*CPrR*, 5.122–5). Since the moral law commands unconditionally, and hope of attaining the highest good is necessary in order for us to fulfill its command, practical reason is warranted in enjoining our assent to belief in God and immortality. God and immortality are "postulates" of pure practical reason (Kant borrows the term from geometry, while modifying its meaning): "by which I understand a *theoretical* proposition, though one not demonstrable as such, insofar as it is attached inseparably to an a priori unconditionally valid *practical* law" (*CPrR*, 5.122; see also the explication at *CPrR*, 5.11n). Other definitions are given by Kant elsewhere: *NC* 8.418n, *OT* 8.141, and *JL* §38.

"On the Primacy" is located mid-way through this argument, between the argument for the highest good as necessary to resolve the antinomy of pure reason, and the further argument for God and immortality as necessary conditions for the realization of the highest good: PPR is intended to legitimate our assent to the postulates, our attitude towards which Kant describes as "pure rational belief [or faith: *Glaube*]" (*CprR*, 5.126).

Other statements of the moral argument for God include the Second Section of the Canon of the first *Critique* (B 832–47), §§88–91 of the Critique of Teleological Judgment in the third *Critique*, and the First Preface to *Religion within the Bounds of*

Reason Alone (Kant 1996b, 6.3–8). There are important differences between them, and arguably Kant's view of the argument changed over time; Förster (2000: ch. 5) argues that the *Opus postumum* shows Kant to have finally abandoned the moral argument for God. The best study in English of Kant's moral theology remains Wood (1970).

3. The Primacy of Practical Reason in the Broader Sense

PPR in the broader sense consists in the thesis that the use of our reason in general, inclusive of its philosophical use, is fundamentally practical rather than theoretical: that is to say, practical reason has superiority over theoretical reason, not just from its own point of view, but also from that of theoretical reason.

Since it is morality that constitutes the truest, most rational expression of practical reason, PPR in the broader sense entails that philosophy finds its ultimate ground, purpose, and guiding norm in moral consciousness, as befits it as the activity of a being whose true vocation is morality. Kant puts this in various ways: "the entire armament of reason" is directed to "**what is to be done** if the will is free" (*CPR*, B 828); "What sort of use can we make of our understanding, even in regard to experience, if we do not set ends before ourselves? The highest ends, however, are those of morality" (*CPR*, B 844–5); the interest "of speculative reason is only conditional and is complete in practical use alone" (*CPrR*, 5.121); "theology and morality were the two incentives, or better, the points of reference [*Beziehungspunkte*] for all the abstract inquiries of reason to which we have always been devoted" (*CPR*, B 881); "*God, freedom and immortality of the soul* are the three problems whose solution all the apparatus of metaphysics aims at as its ultimate and sole purpose" (*CJ*, 5.473); "in the end all the effort of our faculties is directed to what is practical and must be united in it as their goal" (*CJ*, 5.206).

This conception is evident in the construction of the Critical system as a whole, in the teleological ordering of its parts, whereby theoretical philosophy's proof of idealism regarding space and time, its restriction of knowledge to appearances and demonstration that the ideas of reason must be *thought* even if they cannot be *known*, serve to prepare the way for moral philosophy and "make room for faith" (*CPR*, B xxx). The teleological ordering within the Critical system, Kant argues in the concluding section of the Dialectic of Pure Practical Reason (*CPrR*, 5.146–8), mirrors the teleological order which we must think of as obtaining in our rational faculties.

PPR in the broader sense has a general implication for how Kant's theoretical philosophy should be regarded. Though Kant's argumentation in the *Critique of Pure Reason* is not itself moral reasoning, there are respects in which a practical conception of the task of Critical philosophy may be regarded as expressed even in Kant's theoretical philosophy. The critique of theoretical reason is undertaken, Kant tells us in the Discipline of Pure Reason and in many other places, with a view to bringing order to reason, "disciplining" it, correcting its tendency to waywardness, ending its quarrels and so on. The ultimate point of this normative labor, and indeed of the whole history of rational enquiry, is moral: "the transcendental improvement of our rational cognition is not the cause but rather merely the effect of the practical purposiveness which pure reason imposes on us" (*CPR*, B 845; see also *CPR*, B 880–1).

261

PPR in the broader sense is thus equivalent to the thesis of the unity of reason as a whole, a unity which goes beyond and encompasses the internal unities which Kant shows must be possessed by the individual forms of reason: it tells us both that there is a deep unity to our rational powers, which therefore compose more than a mere aggregate, and what this unity *consists in*. Exhibiting this unity of reason has for Kant a philosophical importance that is independent of his moral theology.

Regarded historically, PPR is situated at the exact meeting point of the several, conflicting philosophical and cultural currents which Kant's philosophical project is designed to bring into equilibrium. On the one hand, PPR involves a fundamental correction to the prevailing assumption of modern philosophy that matters of morality and religion are properly determined by theoretical reflection. In this it shows the influence of Rousseau's *Émile*, and it concedes to the critics of Enlightenment thought that their worries about its atheistical, fatalistic, naturalistic trajectory have not been entirely without ground. On the other hand, as Kant's "Orientation" essay makes clear, the intention of Kant's moral theology is to side firmly with the *Aufklärung* in matters of religion, against Friedrich Heinrich Jacobi and the sentimentalism of *Sturm und Drang*: acceptance that the grounds of faith are (and in natural consciousness always have been) practical rather than theoretical involves, if Kant is right, no trace of a qualification of their rationality. This gives PPR an enormous importance which is not reflected in the relatively little discussion which it has received as a topic in Kant's philosophy. Velkley (1989) and Neiman (1994: esp. pp. 129–34 and ch. 4) are important correctives to the common view of PPR as a merely subsidiary topic in Kant's philosophy. Other important discussions of PPR and the associated topic of the unity of reason include Beck 1960: pt. III, Guyer 2000: chs. 2 and 10, Henrich 1994: ch. 1, Sullivan 1989: ch. 8, and Yovel 1980: pp. 287ff. Timm 1974 is a very fine account of Kant's historical situation.

4. The Primacy of Practical Reason and the Assumption of Freedom: Their Relation

One important preliminary issue that arises in getting to grips with Kant's conception of PPR concerns its scope. Is the principle of PPR necessary only for the theological postulates, or is it necessary also for freedom? The latter may seem the case, for freedom (in the transcendental, positive, noumena-involving sense) is described by Kant as a postulate (e.g. *CPrR*, 5.132, 5.134; *JL* §38), and the concept of a postulate is linked intimately with that of PPR. Furthermore, the principle of PPR has clear application to the claim that we possess transcendental freedom: PPR is designed to authorize the use by practical reason of ideas that are for theoretical reason only problematic, and exactly this is involved in the assumption of transcendental freedom.

From this, however, it does not follow that PPR is necessary for the legitimation of the claim that we are transcendentally free, and there are considerations that lead one to think that this is not, or not straightforwardly, Kant's view.

In the first place, there is no statement of the principle of PPR in the *Groundwork*'s justification of morality through freedom. This may be thought to be due to a change in Kant's views between the earlier and the later work, in particular to Kant's having been brought to appreciate the need for a more extended defense than is provided in the *Groundwork* of the claim that practical reason can give application to concepts that for theoretical reason remain merely problematic. It may also be conjectured that the principle of PPR is implicit in the *Groundwork*'s statement that the laws of freedom are valid for any being "that cannot act otherwise than under the idea of its own freedom" (*G*, 4.448n).

However, the second *Critique* itself appears to present a justification of the claim to freedom for which PPR seems not to be required: in "On the Deduction of the Principles of Pure Practical Reason" (*CPrR*, 5.42–50), the section on the "fact of reason" which comes in the Analytic, well before "On the Primacy," Kant appears to complete to his own satisfaction his argument that morality provides sufficient assurance of the objective reality of freedom without appealing to PPR. In the section that follows the Deduction, "Of the Warrant" (*CPrR*, 5.50–7), where Kant addresses the question of how our cognition can be extended to the intelligible world, his answer consists chiefly in a restatement of his demonstration of the apriority of the concepts employed in such cognition; the significance of the point that the context in question is practical is identified simply with the fact that practical "dispositions or maxims" provide objects which allow the concepts to have "real application" (CPrR, 5.56); PPR is not adverted to. That the exposition of PPR comes in the Dialectic, mid-way through the presentation of the theological postulates, provides a further strong textual indication that it is specifically for the defense of the theological postulates that PPR is required.

The following account of Kant's reasoning clarifies matters. The assumption that we are free is on Kant's account validated sufficiently by direct reference to moral consciousness – our pure awareness of moral obligation, of having to do such-and-such on grounds not drawn from experience. The theological postulates cannot receive a similarly direct validation, for they are not in the same sense contents of moral consciousness; they are not engaged in the very act or state of moral willing. Kant himself underlines the difference in epistemology of the two kinds of practical postulate: we have immediate cognition of freedom but only mediate cognition of the objects of the theological postulates (*CPrR*, 5.4). The indirectness of the relation of the theological postulates to moral consciousness is what makes the enabling role of PPR necessary. However, once the principle of PPR has been formulated at the behest of the theological postulates, it then *becomes available* for application also to the assumption of freedom, since this too, like the propositions that God exists and that we possess immortal souls, is a theoretical proposition concerning the supersensible. The assumption of freedom thus figures twice in Kant's theory: initially as a fact of reason, where it is considered exclusively from the angle of practical reason; and later, when it is considered from the point of view of reason as a whole, it returns as a postulate. Freedom thus has a double, two-stage validation: originally, on purely practical apodictic grounds, and then, at a higher level of reflection, it is confirmed on grounds that reflect also the perspective of theoretical reason (see chapter 18 below).

Taking Kant's initial justification of freedom to be independent of PPR carries an advantage. It has yet to be seen how Kant proposes to ground PPR, but if freedom can be defended on the basis of moral consciousness alone, this suggests a possible route to the defense of PPR: the consideration that pure practical reason can achieve what is impossible for theoretical reason may be claimed to support Kant's claim that practical reason is preeminent among our faculties. If on the contrary Kant's defense of freedom were to presuppose PPR, then this line of argument would not be unavailable.

5. The Primacy of Practical Reason in Relation to the Theological Postulates

While the remote aim of PPR in Kant's system is to demonstrate the unity of reason, its immediate function, if the above is correct, is to justify the theological postulates, and for this purpose it takes the narrow form of a principle of philosophical inference.

It is important to clarify in what ways Kant's conception of PPR is, and is not, bound up with the fate of the theological postulates. In order for Kant's conception of PPR to be vindicated, it is not necessary for Kant's moral theology to succeed: PPR is not intended to be sufficient for the moral theology, which may fail for reasons that have nothing to do with PPR. In particular, it may be, as alleged by many of Kant's contemporaries (in particular, Gottlob Ernst Schulze and Friedrich Schleiermacher), that the introduction of happiness as an object of concern for practical reason whose claim competes with that of morality, contradicts Kant's basic principle concerning the sufficiency and independence from inclination of the motive of duty; and without the formulation of a highest good distinct from and necessary for the good will, the antinomy of practical reason vanishes and the theological postulates lose their warrant. If the moral theology fails in this way, then PPR is not impugned. The principle of PPR is directed at overcoming a specific obstacle in Kant's construction of his moral theology, and so long as it is successful there, Kant will have given grounds for PPR in the broader sense. It should be noted also that, even if the principle of PPR has no utility in relation to theology, there may well be other contexts in which it can be employed fruitfully; for instance, in Kant's political philosophy and philosophy of history, with respect to the ideas of property, perpetual peace, and historical progress.

The specific difficulty which PPR is designed to solve concerns Kant's *reasoning to the objective reality of ideas of reason on the basis of a practical need*. The question is whether a coherent account can be given of how theoretical reason is to relate itself to the judgments which issue from practical reason, and it presents Kant with a serious challenge, arguably more difficult to meet than the other major issues – concerning the deduction of the moral law, and the application of the categories to supersensible objects – addressed in the *Critique of Practical Reason*. The objection was made several times by Kant's contemporaries that practical reason is circumscribed by and conditional upon theoretical reason in ways that conflict with Kant's argument. In general, Kant's critics argued, it is rational to allow a need or interest to play a determining role only if the need is *well-founded*, and this requires the fulfillment of appropriate *theoretical* cognitive conditions. In the case of the theological postulates, since what is held to be determined by moral need is a *belief*, it must be shown that it is possible for me to *form* the belief in question, and this I can do only if there are theoretical reasons for holding it *true*. So morality can ground the theological postulates only if they are already theoretically grounded, or capable of being theoretically grounded – contrary to what Kant claims, and in any case making their practical justification redundant. (Contemporaries of Kant's who pressed this point in some form or other include Johann

Georg Feder, Johann Friedrich Flatt, Schulze, Thomas Wizenmann, and Schelling.) Kant's annihilation of theoretical reason's knowledge of God makes impossible, his critics alleged, the indirect restoration of theology along a practical route.

What Kant must show, then, is that the intersection of theoretical and practical reason required by the theological postulates is intelligible. If it is not, then the moral theology collapses, and in addition, PPR in the broader sense must be admitted to lack grounds, with the consequence that, while Kant would still be left with the claim that morality affords cognition of supersensibly grounded freedom, no unity of reason would have been brought into view by his moral philosophy.

6. Kant's Argument in "On the Primacy"

The justification of PPR offered by Kant in "On the Primacy" presents a set of considerations as rich and complex as anything in Kant's philosophy, and it requires close analysis.

A preliminary matter consists in clarifying the difference between an argument based on pure, and one based on inclination-governed, practical reason. Kant argues that PPR remains indefensible so long as the pure form of practical reason is unrecognized, since it is patently irrational to ground beliefs on practical need when the latter is "pathologically conditioned" (*CPrR*, 5.120–1, at the beginning of the third paragraph of the section; and at *CPrR*, 5.143n).

This is, however, obviously not a full solution. The fact that it is not irrational to claim cognitivity for pure practical reason in the same way that it would be to claim cognitivity for empirical practical reason, does not show that it is rational to claim cognitivity for pure practical reason. Three arguments designed to secure this further claim may be discerned in "On the Primacy":

1) First, Kant argues (in the first full sentence of *CPrR*, 5.121) that since (1a) "pure reason of itself can be and really is practical," and (1b) "it is still only one and the same reason which, whether from a theoretical or a practical perspective, judges according to a priori principles," it follows that (1c) theoretical reason "must accept" propositions which "*belong inseparably to practical interest.*"

2) Second, Kant argues (*CPrR*, 5.121, in the fourth paragraph of "On the Primacy") that without the proposed subordination of theoretical to practical reason, (2a) theoretical reason "would of itself close its boundaries" and "admit nothing from" practical reason, (2b) practical reason would then "extend its boundaries over everything and, when its need required, would try to include" theoretical reason within them. Thus (2c) "a conflict of reason with itself would arise." With an implicit premise, (2d) that reason must not contradict itself, (2e) the proposed subordination of theoretical to practical reason is inferred.

3) Third, Kant argues (*CPrR*, 5.121, in the final sentence of "On the Primacy") that (3a) "all interest is ultimately practical" and that (3b) "even that of speculative reason is only conditional and is complete in practical use alone," such that (3c) "one cannot require pure practical reason to be subordinated to speculative reason"; and since (3d) one must be subordinated to the other, (3e) theoretical reason must be subordinated to practical reason.

Note that, as in (3d), Kant sets up the issue in terms of two exclusive possibilities, that is, he rules it out that neither theoretical nor practical reason has primacy over the other. As he explains, to conceive of them in that way – as "merely juxtaposed (coordinate)" (*CPrR*, 5.121) – just is to grant primacy to theoretical reason. This is because the situation of reason is such as to present only two possibilities: that theoretical reason either accepts or rejects practical reason's propositions. Strictly there is a third possibility, viz. that reason be left in conflict with itself, but this Kant rules out, as in (2d). I return to this below.

Kant is entirely clear, then, that theoretical reason cannot be indifferent to practical reason; it cannot turn a blind eye to the postulates. If the propositions in question were imperatival, this would not be the case, for imperatives as such are incapable of either truth or falsity and theoretical reason is concerned only with matters of truth. The postulates are, however, assertoric. As Kant makes clear in the *Jäsche Logic*, the postulates are, according to his definitions, *both* practical and theoretical: they are "practical" because (even though they are not themselves imperatives) they contain "*the grounds for possible imperatives*," and they are "theoretical" because they (unlike imperatives) "have as their object not an *acting* but rather a *being*" (*JL*, 86–7: Introduction, Appendix; see also *CPR*, B 833). So even though the function that the propositions are to perform concerns practical reason alone, this requires the sanction – the permission or assent – of theoretical reason, which in turn requires that they be accepted by theoretical reason as *true*. Again Kant, in the first Critique, makes it clear that our attitude to the postulates is a case of "*Fürwahrhalten*," holding-to-be-true (in the Third Section of the Canon of Pure Reason) (*CPR*, B 850ff). Judgments about the supersensible made on practical grounds are not instances of knowledge (*Wissen*), since they lack sufficient "objective" grounds, but they are, in virtue of having sufficient "subjective" grounds, instances of belief (*Glauben*), rather than of mere opining (*Meinen*). Kant calls this attitude "not logical but moral certainty" (*CPR*, A828–9/B856–7). (The same set of distinctions returns in *CJ*, §91, 5.467ff, and appears in *JL*, 65–74: Introduction, sect. IX.)

The three arguments appear to be, at least at first sight, independent of one another. The second and third have clearly identifiable weaknesses.

The difficulty of the second argument is that the nature of the catastrophe, which Kant pretends can only be avoided through PPR, is obscure. Suppose theoretical reason rejects the postulates. Since practical reason, as a faculty concerned with what ought to be done rather than what is the case, cannot itself affirm the truth of the propositions that it conceives, reason is not put in the position of violating the principle of noncontradiction. Consequently Kant's argument cannot be a strict reductio ad absurdum, and PPR cannot be grounded on the principles of general logic alone (as Kant makes clear in *G*, 4.460n: "the logical interest of reason (to further its insights) . . . presupposes purposes for its use"). The conflict generated in reason by the rejection of the postulates would be a matter only of theoretical reason's denying that we can *know* to be the case what *needs* to be (known to be) the case in order for practical reason to achieve its necessary end, i.e. a "contradiction" of practical reason only in the sense of frustrating its volition. But practical reason would still be able to *hope* for God and immortality, and it could entertain the postulates as regulative principles, along the lines of "let me regulate my will and act in light of the *hope* that God exists and my soul is immortal; or, *as if* this were the case." (Kant says in *NC* 8.419

that "merely the hope" is insufficient and that morally necessary presupposition is required, but the assertion is not explained or justified.) The moral law need not, it seems, collapse, and it is significant that the account Kant later gives in *RBR* 6.3–8 of what is lost if the highest good cannot be an object for me is more circumscribed and does not take the form of a contradiction: our moral resolve would, Kant says, encounter a "hindrance" (*RBR*, 6.5) and "obtain no satisfaction" (*RBR*, 6.4), but the moral law would not cease to bind (*RBR*, 6.3–4). The first argument boils down, it would thus appear, to a claim about the rational supremacy of the telos of pure practical reason, but without an appropriate explanation of this alleged supremacy the first argument merely reasserts PPR without justifying it.

Suggested by Kant in the third argument is a very plain and direct inference from the fact that theoretical cognizing is itself an activity, an instance of doing something, to PPR. This seems too quick. It may be agreed that necessarily all instances of the employment of theoretical reason are practical in the sense of being also, and primordially, instances of doings, not merely in the empty sense that epistemic descriptions involve verbs, "knowing," "believing," "hypothesizing," etc., but in the substantial sense that cognition, like action, rests on and is guided by the principles to which it gives application: theoretical judgment belongs to the order of reasons, not that of nature, and so has some relation to freedom; there is a spontaneity in the theoretical employment of reason, as there is in the practical. Still, it is not clear what follows from this. Kant's account of each faculty as having a priori grounds creates a space for practical reason to play a role in the constitution and operation of theoretical reason, but it does not follow from the consideration that theoretical reasoning is a case of doing something, that the conditions (principles, ends, etc.) of practical reason are what explain, or what should determine, theoretical reasoning in any important or interesting sense. If Kant's thesis of the primacy of practical reason has a deeper meaning – if practical reason is explanatory of the constitution of theoretical reason, and/or properly determinative of its operations – then more must go into the idea, and it is natural to think that this must have to do with Kant's claim about the telos of reason. Again, this is what the first argument leans on.

It is therefore the first argument that carries the weight, and its key lies with Kant's suggestion that the authority of practical reason is due to theoretical reason's recognition of their *shared nature* or *essence*: "it is still only *one and the same reason* which, whether from a theoretical or a practical perspective, judges according to a priori principles" (*CPrR*, 5.121; emphasis added). The claim is also made earlier in the *Groundwork*: "there can, in the end, be only one and the same reason, which must be distinguished merely in its application" (*G*, 4.391). An enormous amount is staked on this claim: not just the moral theology, but also the systematic completion of the Critical philosophy; in particular, the fuller unity of reason which Kant goes on to construct in the third *Critique* is dependent on PPR (see *CJ* Introduction, sect. III, 5.177–9).

Now Kant does not pretend to derive PPR analytically from the concept of reason as such, and he also denies that we can have cognition of the underlying ground(s) of our faculties (e.g. *CPR*, B 29). Yet the onus is on Kant to give some account, for he himself says that the theological postulates are "not grown on its [theoretical reason's] own land" (*CPrR*, 5.121) but are "handed over to it," "as a foreign possession" (*CPrR*, 5.120). That it is "one and the same reason" which judges both theoretically and practically can be taken to mean that theoretical reason recognizes practical reason as pursuing its very own interest. But to the extent that theoretical reason has an interest *of its own* in the postulates, due to their giving application to its own highest but problematic ideas, this interest lies in its *being true* that there is a God, etc.: and the postulates can serve this interest only if theoretical reason can be assured that it is indeed true that there is a God, etc.; with which the original problem returns.

Alternatively, Kant might be thought to be appealing to the interest of reason as a whole in some way that is *anterior* to its differentiation into theoretical and practical employments and purposes, as a ground for obliging theoretical reason to recognize in practical reason a higher form of itself. This would require Kant to specify the task or purpose of reason as a whole, and to do so without invoking the very sense of the unity of reason that stands in need of justification. The only candidate for this role appears to be systematicity: theoretical and practical reason share an interest, not just in their own systematic form, but in systematic form in general. The relevant, teleological sense of unity is defined at *CPR* B xxiii: "a unity entirely separate and subsisting for itself, in which, as in an organized body, every part exists for the sake of all the others as all the others exist for its sake." Also important here is Kant's view regarding "the undeniable need of human reason" "to derive everything from one principle" (*CPrR*, 5.91).

Yet again the argument, which Kant does seem tempted to make, comes to a halt prematurely: the unity of reason supplied by PPR may be necessary in order for reason to fulfill its teleological self-expectations, but the architectonic and systematic desirability of a comprehensive unity of reason does not entail its actuality. In Kant's terms: the sense in which it is true that "reason itself (subjectively) is a system" (*CPR*, A 738/B 766) and that "[t]he unity of reason is the unity of a system" (*CPR* B 708) is (self-)regulative, not constitutive, of reason. Thus for Kant to argue "Reason is systematic; systematicity is unity; therefore, there exists a unity of reason," would be to exploit an equivocation in "reason is systematic" (see also chapter 26 below).

It is also possible to attribute to Kant, on the basis of this and other passages in his writings, a conception of theoretical reason as having not one but two points of view: an initial, undeveloped point of view, which it has *prior* to its encounter with the postulates, and then another, more comprehensive view, which *emerges* from the encounter. Kant's idea, it may be thought, is that theoretical reason *evolves in its self-understanding*, and only thereby comes to identify itself with pure practical reason. This would explain why Kant should not have provided at the outset an overarching description of the task of reason – if reason has to *learn* what its unity consists in, then the interest of reason as a whole cannot be stated in advance of its full development. But the hypothesis of an evolving reason does not, as it stands, suffice for the purpose at hand. In order to explain and justify this step in reason's self-development, it would be necessary to establish first of all the rationality of theoretical reason's new self-identification: Kant would need to tell us what it is that allows theoretical reason to discover itself in practical reason, and this crucial element is missing from his account.

There is an important dimension of Kant's argumentation in "On the Primacy" that has yet to be considered, but so far, on the basis of what is explicit in the text, it would seem that a clear justification for PPR has not been provided. At bottom, the foregoing suggests, this is because Kant is reliant in his defense of PPR on a unity of reason which is under construction and yet for the construction of which PPR is itself necessary.

This would explain the peculiar elusiveness of the argument in "On the Primacy," where Kant seems on the one hand to be targeting for justification the principle of PPR as a point of entry to the broader idea of PPR, and on the other, to be appealing to PPR in the broader sense, as if it were a result already established, in his attempt to show the reasonableness of the principle of PPR. Now, if it were a given that reason *must have* unity in a strong sense, then it could be inferred, from the capacity of practical reason to supply this unity and the absence of any other candidates, that the unity of reason is practico-moral; PPR in the broader sense would then be established, and it would in turn ground the principle of PPR. But the major premise here is undersupported, for reasons that have been given.

7. Other Texts

That the explicit case made in "On the Primacy" is unconvincing suggests that other texts of Kant's be scrutinized, in particular "Orientation" (*OT*). There Kant speaks of "reason's feeling of its own need [*das Gefühl des der Vernunft eigenen Bedürfnisses*]" (*OT*, 8.136) conjoined with "*the right of* reason's *need* [*das Recht des Bedürfnisses der Vernunft*]" (*OT*, 8.137) as a rational determinant of belief. Need is a "subjective determination," Kant says, which provides reason with the "orientation" that it requires when it strives to fill up the "space for intuition" which lies beyond the bounds of theoretical reason, on the analogy with the way that the sense of left and right provides a sense of direction.

Kant's ingenious analogy does not, however, show the postulates to be unproblematic for theoretical reason. The subjective determinations which our sense of left and right provides us with are indices of objective states of affairs, and nothing besides that. That reason's *need* or the feeling thereof has the same status as the sense of left and right, i.e. is an index of anything objective, is not what may be assumed but what needs to be *established* as more than a mere logical possibility. Kant may be justified in speaking of a "right of need" insofar as this means simply that it is *right* of practical reason, given its interest, to formulate the theological postulates, and arguably reason is also *right to demand* that extrarepresentational reality *be* as the theological postulates represent it (that reason is right to require of reality that it include God's existence). But in the absence of an account showing reason's needs to be necessarily more than problems for itself, it seems that this is as far as the "right of need" can extend; in which case the "Orientation" essay cannot be said to have provided a more conclusive argument for the coherence of the theological postulates than "On the Primacy."

No other extended defense of PPR is offered by Kant. Instead we find Kant emphasizing repeatedly the significance of the fact that pure practical reason succeeds, through its validation of the assumption of freedom in the fact of reason, in determining the supersensible which is inaccessible to theoretical reason (this is the argument referred to above at the end of section 3): e.g., "the concept of freedom . . . proved by an apodictic law of practical reason, constitutes the keystone of the whole structure of a system of pure reason" (*CPrR*, 5.4). This approach is particularly prominent in the third *Critique*'s exposition of the moral theology, and several commentators follow Kant's lead in attributing practical reason's primacy directly to its superiority in respect to our supersensible freedom, or alternatively to its ability to secure reason's autonomy through the moral law and to make a real, not merely logical, use of pure concepts independently of intuition (see Wundt 1984: ch. 6, and Sullivan 1989: 98).

It may be doubted, however, that this sort of strategy can yield the desired result. If PPR is to be derived directly from the primacy of morality – if practical reason is to be shown to be related to theoretical reason in the way that pure practical reason is related to empirically conditioned practical reason – then Kant needs to show, not just that there is some rational or cognitive virtue possessed by practical reason and lacked by theoretical reason, but that it is one that obliges theoretical reason to credit practical reason with greater cognitive power than it itself possesses. Theoretical reason must be brought to see not merely the necessity of the *representations* of God and immortality for the purposes of practical reason, but that there are grounds for thinking that these representations have *objects* (ones which are, unlike freedom, trans-subjective). This is the stumbling block: for the only way of doing this, of getting theoretical reason to agree to cross the representation/object divide, is, it seems, to ascribe to pure practical reason a sheer cognitive power of insight that goes beyond what may be claimed for it on the basis of the fact of reason; and while such an assumption may not be strictly inconsistent with any of the central tenets of Kant's philosophy, its effect is undoubtedly to give a very peculiar, convoluted look to the Critical system. This is an important part of the reason why post-Kantian philosophers felt licensed to distinguish the "spirit" from the "letter" of Kant's philosophy, and claimed to be seeking a more adequate form for expressing Kant's insights. It also explains why theists such as Jacobi, who took religious consciousness to be immediate and primitive, found it baffling and disingenuous of Kant to claim, in "Orientation," that his rational faith has nothing in common with their intuitive epistemologies.

8. Kant's Copernicanism and the Concept of Practical Cognition in the Context of the Postulates

Kant's use of PPR to legitimate the theological postulates raises a broad question, which has far-reaching implications, concerning the scope of Kant's philosophical Copernicanism. Again this issue was highlighted in the earliest responses of Kant's contemporaries to his moral theology, and it plays a key role in the development of German idealism. Suppose the difficulties detailed above are waived and the cognitive authority of pure practical reason is accepted. It must then be asked, What sort of philosophical results can be grounded by appeal to PPR?

Recall Kant's claim in "On the Primacy" that reason cannot be left in conflict with itself. This echoes his claim that all of the problems set for reason by its ideas must have solutions within reason itself (*CPR*, B 791; *Prol.*, 4.349). Now it may be asked why this should be assumed, or, if it must be assumed, how it should be understood. It may be agreed that, insofar as reason is concerned simply with its own structure, it is justified in employing whatever means are necessary to eliminate conflict from itself. This is not, however, to provide reassurance that whatever reason does in order to harmonize with itself will lead it also to harmonize with reality: it may be that judgments which reason needs to form in order to free itself from conflict are ones that detach it from reality (in a transcendental analogue of the way in which, according to Freud, neurotic solutions to psychic conflict produce a loss of reality). Unless Kant has shown that the structure of our reason is necessarily also that of reality, the self-harmony of reason may not be isomorphic with, and the pursuit of reason's interests may not provide a route to knowledge of, reality.

Now, to the extent that Kant may be thought to claim only *Copernican* status for his philosophical conclusions – i.e. to the extent that he directs us to measure philosophical solutions by the criterion of how much satisfaction they give, in terms of making us transparent and unproblematic to ourselves, allowing us to fulfill our vocation and so on, and to the extent that things are considered as objects of our knowledge only *insofar as* they conform to our mode of cognition – this is no objection. This would in fact explain much of Kant's reasoning. For, if the only conclusions that Kant aims to establish are Copernican ones, then he can argue for PPR in the way indicated earlier, directly from the necessity that reason have unity and that its problems be solved (see Wundt 1984: 414ff). And it would then be explained why Kant should express the principle of PPR in exclusively intrarepresentational terms, i.e. of relations between judgments, saying nothing at all about their relations to objects, and why Kant should regard reason's *need* as convertible immediately into its *right*. The prospect thus opens up of salvaging the arguments of "On the Primacy" and "Orientation" by making explicit their implicit Copernican premise.

But what now appears puzzling is that Kant, on the most natural reading, seems to acknowledge that our reason contains an aspiration to reach a reality that is not in this way merely transcendentally ideal, i.e. a reality which is (and is known to be) the way it is, independently of our subjectivity and its representations, an aspiration which, Kant seems to claim, morality fulfills. The whole point, one might think, of Critical philosophy's restriction of theoretical knowledge to appearances, to the transcendentally ideal, is that it allows us to claim knowledge of things in themselves, of the transcendentally real, in the sphere where such a claim truly matters, that of morality. Yet, if the ground supplied by practical reason, through PPR, for attributing objective reality to the ideas of reason is also purely subject-orientated and Copernican, then this is not the case: we may know that our representations of God and immortality are not subjective in the same sense as our cognition of empirical objects, since they are not conditioned by our forms of sensibility, but we still do not know that they match transcendental reality. PPR in the broader sense, as a metaphilosophical conception, thus seems an affirmation of unrestricted Copernicanism, i.e. of the view that all objects without qualification are to be considered as having to "conform to our cognition" (*CPR*, B xvi).

Does Kant intend this? Commentators divide on this point, and with reason, for the uncertainty appears to lie deep in Kant. Kant's use of the concept of practical cognition in the context of the postulates manifests the ambiguity very clearly. Kant claims that we have "practical cognition" of God and our immortality. Is this genuine cognition, to be understood wholly realistically? On the one hand, Kant affirms that the ideas of freedom, God, and the soul are given "objective reality" (*CPrR*, 5.54–5, 5.135). And yet, at the same time the practical cognition expressed in the postulates is, Kant emphasizes again and again, *merely* practical (*CPrR*, 5.103, 5.133; *CJ*, 5.174–5, 5.484–5; *NC*, 8.416).

The equivocation surrounding Kant's concept of practical cognition in its application to the postulates is related to the difficulty of grasping the intersection of practical and theoretical reason in the theological postulates. A nonrealist reading of practical cognition makes it intelligible that theoretical reason should accept the postulates: it simply need not take their claim with full cognitive seriousness. However, a nonrealist interpretation makes it hard to see what value the theological postulates could be thought to have and all too easy to understand why Kant's rational faith should have been attacked by his contemporaries as mere ersatz religion: what use are God and immortality as mere "as-if" representations, mere "*Fictionen*," as Jacobi put it? There is pressure, therefore, to interpret practical cognition realistically, yet this interpretation confronts the problem discussed at length above, which, it seems, only unrestricted Copernicanism can solve. In sum, if Kant's defense of PPR is staked on unrestricted Copernicanism, then it is saved from incoherence, but its philosophical power is reduced below the level required for its designated task of validating the theological postulates.

To the extent that Kant is thought to have no other option but to endorse the realist reading of practical cognition, and to claim PPR as sufficient for philosophical results whose status is not merely Copernican, he must, as it was concluded earlier, ascribe to pure practical reason a sheer cognitive power of insight. If so, then we are led to a somewhat startling realization: namely that what Kant calls theoretical cognition in fact represents only the lowest grade of our knowledge, and that practical cognition of the supersensible, though not on a level with the intellectual intuition of an infinite being, is the highest form of human cognition. It may then be wondered why pure practical reason should not be reconceived and redeployed as a general philosophical foundation – and the limiting qualification "practical" removed. In this way a direct avenue to German idealism is opened up by PPR and Kant's postulates.

The text which shows most clearly and forcefully how the difficulties of Kant's strategy of practical postulation can seem to simultaneously demand and enable a fundamental transformation of Kant's philosophical system is Schelling's early *Philosophical Letters on Dogmatism and Criticism*. Schelling presents Kant with a dilemma: either reason must be expanded in the manner of German idealism, or the notion of practical cognition remains empty and incoherent.

9. Influence

Kant's conception of the primacy of the practical has been influential in the history of philosophy to a degree that it is hard to exaggerate. Beginning with Fichte in the closing years of the eighteenth century, numerous strands of nineteenth-century philosophy, in which ideas of human will, agency, and practice become ascendant, have firm connections to Kant's conception. An understanding of the historical unfolding of Kant's conception is an important and necessary part of grasping critically the conception itself, for the post-Kantian development of the idea of the primacy of practical reason, far from being uniform, reflects the great, abiding uncertainty surrounding the ultimate import of Kant's philosophical endeavor: Does Critical philosophy signal (i) the end of metaphysics altogether, (ii) the provision of a new ground for a marginally revised version of the old, rationalist metaphysics, or perhaps (iii) the birth of a new form of metaphysics?

What I have suggested above tends to support the second, conservative, interpretation, in favor of which there is much to be said. (See Kant's letter to A. G. Kästner, August 5[?], 1790, *Corr.*, 11.186, no. 112, p. 355), and the Kant interpretations of Ameriks 2003, Krüger 1967, and Wundt 1984.)

But it is not hard to see how Kant's thesis of PPR may be thought to require logically either a clear rejection of metaphysics, or a much fuller metaphysical grounding than Kant provides it with, and on that account, to suppose that Kant's true intention must have been either (i) or (iii). For it may be held that PPR implies that metaphysical concepts have objective validity *only* insofar as they are correlates of practice, and that a "merely practical" grounding for metaphysics implies that they are to be denied realistic status. On this (postmetaphysical) view, the consistent Kantian position is either to *reduce* metaphysics to practical contents or to regard metaphysics as a fiction that has value only insofar as it serves practice. On the opposing view exemplified by the German idealists, the reasoning runs in reverse: it is argued that PPR, or rather the profound truth concerning the unity and power of reason contained in this notion of Kant's, requires a more substantial metaphysics than Kant provides.

Whatever view is taken of Kant's intentions, it is important to keep in focus the difference of Kant's conception of PPR from neighboring conceptions in post-Kantian philosophy, which Kant in part helped to sponsor, but which are better described as different versions of the general idea of the primacy of the practical in which either (a) the practical is not identified with practical *reason*, or (b) practical reason is not identified with *pure* practical reason. For Kant, the primacy of the practical is staked entirely upon the existence of pure practical reason, and notions such as Schopenhauer's primacy of the will over the intellect, Nietzsche's conception of cognitive perspectives as expressions of will to power, or William James's will to believe, count for Kant either as claims of theoretical reason regarding the causation of belief, or as claims that reduce theoretical reason (unintelligibly and at the cost of its destruction) to an instrument of inclination. A conception of the primacy of the practical which in some respects remains closer to Kant than nineteenth-century irrationalism or classical pragmatism is found in the Frankfurt School: the idea of critical theory formulated by Max Horkheimer, reworked in Jürgen Habermas's early writings, retains Kant's idea of granting the practical rights or authority over the theoretical, by grounding certain spheres of theoretical reflection on a conception of human interest; but it departs from Kant in demoralizing this interest and in denying all connection of PPR with supersensible metaphysics. Neokantianism in contemporary anglophone moral and political philosophy dispenses more thoroughly with PPR. While theorists such as Rawls follow Kant in maintaining that practical thinking originates and supports itself independently from theoretical reason, they discard Kant's idea of the intelligible as the ground of the empirical, insulating the basics of practical philosophy from metaphysics and obviating the need for PPR. (See Rawls 1993: Lecture III, esp. p. 100; Scanlon 1998: Introduction; and Korsgaard's 1996 appeal to "practical identity.")

References and Further Reading

Ameriks, Karl (2003). *Interpreting Kant's Critiques.* Oxford: Clarendon Press.

Beck, Lewis White (1960). *A Commentary on Kant's Critique of Practical Reason.* Chicago: University of Chicago Press.

Förster, Eckart (2000). *Kant's Final Synthesis: An Essay on the Opus Postumum.* Cambridge, MA: Harvard University Press.

Guyer, Paul (2000). *Kant on Freedom, Law, and Happiness.* Cambridge: Cambridge University Press.

Henrich, Dieter (1994). *The Unity of Reason: Essays on Kant's Philosophy,* ed. Richard Velkley, tr. Jeffrey Edwards. Cambridge, MA: Harvard University Press.

Kant, Immanuel (1992). *Lectures on Logic,* ed. and tr. J. Michael Young. Cambridge: Cambridge University Press.

Kant, Immanuel (1996a). *Practical Philosophy,* ed. Mary J. Gregor. Cambridge: Cambridge University Press.

Kant, Immanuel (1996b). *Religion and Rational Theology,* ed. and tr. Allen W. Wood and George di Giovanni. Cambridge: Cambridge University Press.

Kant, Immanuel (1998). *Critique of Pure Reason,* eds. and tr. Paul Guyer and Allen W. Wood. Cambridge: Cambridge University Press.

Kant, Immanuel (1999). *Correspondence,* ed. and tr. Arnulf Zweig. Cambridge: Cambridge University Press.

Kant, Immanuel (2000). *Critique of the Power of Judgement,* tr. Paul Guyer and Eric Matthews. Cambridge: Cambridge University Press, 2000.

Kant, Immanuel (2002). *Theoretical Philosophy After 1781,* eds. and tr. Henry Allison, Gary Hatfield, Michael Friedman, and Peter Heath. Cambridge: Cambridge University Press.

Korsgaard, Christine (1996). *The Sources of Normativity.* Cambridge: Cambridge University Press.

Krüger, Gerhard (1967). *Philosophie und Moral in der Kantischen Kritik [Philosophy and Morality in Kant's Critical Philosophy].* Tübingen: Mohr.

Neiman, Susan (1994). *The Unity of Reason: Rereading Kant.* Oxford: Oxford University Press.

Rawls, John (1993). *Political Liberalism.* New York: Columbia University Press.

Scanlon, Thomas (1998). *What We Owe to Each Other.* Cambridge, MA: Harvard University Press.

Schelling, F. W. J. (1980). *Philosophical Letters on Dogmatism and Criticism.* In *The Unconditional in Human Knowledge: Four Early Essays 1794–1796,* tr. Fritz Marti. Lewisburg: Bucknell University Press. Originally published in 1795.

Sullivan, Roger (1989). *Immanuel Kant's Moral Theory.* Cambridge: Cambridge University Press.

Timm, Hermann (1974). *Gott und die Freiheit: Studien zur Religionsphilosophie der Goethezeit [God and Freedom: Studies in the Philosophy of Religion in Goethe's Time].* Frankfurt am Main: Vittorio Klostermann.

Velkley, Richard (1989). *Freedom and the End of Reason: On the Moral Foundation of Kant's Critical Philosophy.* Chicago: University of Chicago Press.

Wood, Allen (1970). *Kant's Moral Religion.* Ithaca, NY: Cornell University Press.

Wundt, Max (1984). *Kant als Metaphysiker: ein Beitrag zur Geschichte der deutschen Philosophie im 18. Jahrhundert [Kant as a Metaphysician: A Report on the History of 18th Century German Philosophy].* Hildesheim: Olms. Originally published in 1924.

Yovel, Yirmiyahu (1980). *Kant and the Philosophy of History.* Princeton: Princeton University Press.

18

Kant's Critical Account of Freedom

ANDREWS REATH

I. Introduction

Kant's treatment of free will is one of the most intriguing, as well as most perplexing, elements of his philosophical system. His Critical account of free will is given mainly in the Resolution of the Third Antinomy of the *Critique of Pure Reason* (B 559–86) and the Analytic of the *Critique of Practical Reason*, but important components are found in the third section of the *Groundwork of the Metaphysics of Morals*, the *Metaphysics of Morals*, and Book I of *Religion within the Boundaries of Mere Reason*. It draws on and requires some understanding of several aspects of his system, but principally his transcendental idealism and its distinction between phenomena and noumena, or appearances and things in themselves, and his account of the moral law as a principle of autonomy that gives reasons for action that are independent of and take priority over reasons based on desire. The former is developed in the first *Critique*, and the latter in the *Groundwork* and the second *Critique*.

Kant defends what at first might seem to be an impossible position. Having established the principle of causality by arguing that it is a necessary condition of possible experience, Kant accepts a strict form of causal determinism for the natural world, according to which every event follows necessarily from prior events according to empirical laws. At the same time he argues that we are warranted in ascribing to ourselves a strong libertarian form of free will, according to which rational agents have the capacity to choose courses of action independently of determination by antecedent conditions, and that, accordingly, alternate possibilities are open to them at the time of action. In particular, in a situation where an agent fails to do what she ought to have done, she could have chosen what she had most reason to choose. Kant thinks that moral responsibility requires no less.

What allows Kant to avoid outright contradiction in accepting both strict causal determinism and libertarian free will is the distinction between phenomena and noumena, and it will be helpful to begin with some background on that distinction. Kant's transcendental idealism holds that space and time are the "forms of intuition"; they are not mind-independent features of reality, but structural features of experience specific to human cognition (see chapter 7 above). The properties of objects and events as they are given in space and time, including their causal relations to prior events, are not properties of things as they are in themselves but of objects as they appear to us. By claiming that spatiotemporal properties are features of objects as they appear to us, transcendental idealism creates the possibility of thinking about objects under two aspects, both as phenomena and as noumena. Since knowledge requires grounding in intuition and things in themselves are not given in intuition, knowledge is limited to objects as they appear to us. But while there is no knowledge of noumena, there is still room for thought about noumena. For example, we can coherently entertain the thought of objects as they are in themselves. That is just the thought of ordinary objects apart from the conditions under which they appear to us – though for that reason, interactions between things in themselves (or between things in themselves and our minds) cannot be characterized. As we will see, Kant thinks that we can make warranted assertions about noumena if we have grounds for thinking of entities that are governed by laws different in kind from the causal laws governing the occurrence of events in space and time. Such assertions would be a way of conceiving of such entities, but are not *knowledge* claims. Noumena are entities that can be thought though not known, but warranted assertions about noumena are possible if they can be grounded in something other than intuition or the conditions of possible experience.

The distinction between phenomena and noumena opens up the possibility of viewing human actions under two different aspects or from two different standpoints. When we view human beings as phenomena, we treat their actions as events in the natural world that are causally determined by facts about their psychology and their circumstances. So regarded, actions are to be explained by a person's desires and interests, and by the psychological traits that Kant terms a person's "empirical character." Likewise a person's empirical character can be causally explained in terms of formative influences such as the person's environment, native temperament, and so on. But Kant argues that our possession of various rational capacities, including the capacity to guide our activity by various rational norms, warrants ascribing to ourselves the power to choose independently of determination by antecedent conditions. When we think of ourselves as exercising this kind of causality, namely free agency, we regard ourselves as noumena. A person's "intelligible character" is the set of fundamental principles and value priorities that guide an agent's choices. We think of the intelligible character as under a person's control, and it is by seeing a person's actions as manifestations of his intelligible character that we trace them back to his activity. By this route, Kant's transcendental idealism permits him to argue that strict determinism in the natural world does not rule out the possibility of free will. As phenomena, human actions are causally determined by antecedent conditions that extend back in time. But when we think of ourselves as noumena, we ascribe free agency to ourselves, and the same actions may be thought of as flowing from an agent's free choices.

The intuitive appeal of Kant's theory is that we do adopt different standpoints on human action, both of which seem deeply rooted in our thought. We believe that human actions are parts of the natural world and can be explained by tracing them back to prior conditions. In this context, understanding takes the form of seeing how an action results from a person's psychological states and character traits, which in turn result from past influences according to psychological laws. This is sometimes called the "third person" or "theoretical" standpoint. But as rational agents who think and act, we take up a very different standpoint towards ourselves, a "first person" or "practical" standpoint. As thinkers and agents we face the practical or deliberative tasks of determining what we have reason to believe or what we have reason to choose in various situations. Engaging in these practical tasks appears to carry certain presuppositions. We are aware of the capacity to guide our activity and choices by a wide range of rational principles, such as norms that govern inference and the formation of belief or principles of rational choice that determine how we ought to act. We suppose that our choices and decisions are settled by our judgments of what we have reason to believe or to do. In that sense they are up to us. This is a capacity for self-determination that is independent of certain kinds of causal determination, because the idea of a reason introduces a *different* kind of connecting ground from that seen in causal connections between events. The connections between a set of premises and the conclusion that follows, between a body of evidence and a belief, between a set of justifying reasons and a choice, and so on, are normative rather than causal connections. Reasoning and judgment thus appear to involve a capacity for self-determination and, when they guide choice, a capacity to initiate courses of action that is not governed by causal laws.

Arguably this is how we conceive of ourselves when we engage in reasoning and deliberation, and how we conceive of others when we regard them as responsible agents. But can this conception of ourselves be sustained in the face of causal determinism? Kant aims to show that it can be. His account of free will unfolds in different stages. In the first *Critique*, he argues that libertarian free will is not ruled out even if one accepts strict determinism, as he does. He tries to establish the possibility of free will through the distinction between phenomena and noumena and the idea that normative principles that are essential to rational activity are different in kind from causal laws. Some passages in the first *Critique* and in the *Groundwork* appear to suggest that our rational capacities of understanding and theoretical reason warrant ascribing freedom to ourselves. But Kant's final view, seen in the second *Critique*, is that the reality of freedom is established through our moral consciousness.

Sections II and III of this essay will concentrate on Kant's claims in the first *Critique* that transcendental idealism creates room for the possibility of free will. The final section touches briefly on Kant's claim in the second *Critique* that our consciousness of the authority of the moral law establishes its reality. Kant's attempt to establish the possibility of free will is often dismissed because it is thought to rely on a very strong and implausible metaphysical conception – that the acting self exists in a noumenal realm outside of time, free from causal determination, and that its free choices are the ground of its actions in the phenomenal world. There is certainly textual material that suggests such a conception, but I develop a different reading. I treat the phenomenal and the noumenal as two different standpoints that we adopt toward action in different contexts. To regard human beings as noumena is simply to take up the practical standpoint and regard ourselves as agents who act for reasons. Likewise Kant's view that reason, or the noumenal self, is not subject to the conditions of time may be understood in terms of the idea that rational activity is guided by normative principles, which are essentially different in kind from empirical laws that determine how events follow from temporally prior conditions.

II. Transcendental Freedom and Practical Freedom

The Resolution of the Third Antinomy has three sections. The first distinguishes different notions of freedom that shape Kant's understanding of the free will problem (B 560–5). The second gives what he terms "a silhouette of a solution" (B 570), that sketches how transcendental idealism might preserve the notion of free agency required for moral responsibility (B 566–9). The third is a "Clarification" of how free agency in human beings can be consistent with causal determinism (B 570–85). In this section, I discuss Kant's distinction between "transcendental freedom" and "practical freedom," and in the next section outline his account in the first *Critique* of the possibility of freedom (supplemented with material from other important texts).

"Transcendental freedom" is the cosmological idea of a spontaneous first cause. Kant defines it as a form of causality "through which something happens without its cause being further determined by another previous cause, i.e., an absolute causal spontaneity beginning from itself" (B 474). Or as he says elsewhere, it is "the faculty of beginning a state from itself, the causality of which does not stand in turn under another cause determining it in time in accordance with the law of nature" (B 561). It is the capacity to initiate a series of events without being determined by temporally prior causes. It is important to note that transcendental freedom is a form of causality – a way of making things happen – though one that differs from natural causality. In contemporary terms, natural causation is event causation. Transcendental freedom, however, is not a form of event causation, since the activity of a transcendentally free cause is not determined by temporally prior events or conditions. However, to say that transcendental freedom is not determined by prior causes does not imply that it is undetermined. Throughout the Critical philosophy Kant makes clear that any cause must be governed by some law which connects the cause or its activity to its effects, and the same holds for freedom as a causality "of a special kind" (G, 4.446). Transcendental freedom must therefore be a form of causality that operates on principles *different in kind* from empirical laws of nature, though he does not specify what these principles are when he first defines this idea.

While transcendental freedom is an abstract idea that arises in cosmological contexts, "practical freedom" is the form of free agency that seems to be supported by our first-person experience of ourselves as agents. Kant writes: "*Freedom in the practical sense* is the independence of the power of choice from *necessitation* by impulses of sensibility" (B 562). The human power of choice is "pathologically affected" but not "pathologically necessitated." To explain, we are moved by sensible desires and interests, but they do not directly cause our actions. The human power of choice appears to be free "because sensibility does not render its action necessary, but in the human being there is a faculty of determining oneself from oneself, independently of necessitation by sensible impulses" (B 562). Elsewhere Kant says that a power of choice "which can be determined independently of sensory impulses, thus through motives that can only be represented through reason, is called *free choice* (arbitrium liberum), and everything that is connected with this . . . is called *practical*" (B 830; cf. also *MM*, 6.213). In these passages Kant defines practical freedom as the power to act on principles of reason, independently of causal determination by sensible motives. It is a power of self-determination, because it involves the power to determine oneself to action through one's application of rational principles, both principles of instrumental and prudential rationality and moral principles.

The idea that practical freedom involves independence of determination by sensible motives contains different elements worth distinguishing. In these passages, Kant certainly says that sensible desires do not directly cause our actions, and that we can set aside even powerful desires when they conflict with our judgments (both prudential and moral) of what we ought to do. This dimension of practical freedom is developed further in an important passage from the *Religion* that has come to be known, following Henry Allison (1990), as "The Incorporation Thesis":

> The freedom of the power of choice has this characteristic, entirely peculiar to it, that it cannot be determined to action though any incentive, *except so far as the human being has incorporated it into his maxim* (has made it into a universal rule for himself, according to which he wills to conduct himself); only in this way can an incentive, whatever it may be, coexist with the absolute spontaneity of the power of choice (of freedom). (*RBR*, 6.23–4; translations from Kant 1996 and 1998)

It is a feature of free agency that a desire or motive can influence choice and lead to action only when the agent "incorporates it into his maxim" – roughly, when the agent takes the motive to give him a good reason for action and adopts the subjective principle of acting on that motive. The "incorporation" of an incentive is an agent's spontaneous act of taking it to be a good reason, judging that it is worth acting on, or in some way endorsing it. It is important to note that the Incorporation Thesis is a claim about the influence of *any* incentive on choice, including rational motives and considerations. It claims that the influence of any incentive on choice always passes through a spontaneous act or judgment on the part of the agent; roughly, motives of all sorts lead to action only when we choose to act on them. But Kant's discussions also suggest that we are not bound to take our sensible desires as reason-giving. We can, for example, judge that acting on a certain desire would be injurious, unworthy, or morally wrong, and that it provides no reason for action. As is clear from his moral theory, Kant believes that we have the capacity to act from reasons that make no reference to our sensible desires.

Implicit in the Incorporation Thesis is a further sense of "independence of determination by sensibility" that is central to Kant's account of free will. The very idea of rational judgment (e.g., a judgment about reasons) rules out causal influence. Kant claims that a rational agent necessarily "acts under the idea of freedom," and says that reason cannot "receive direction from any other quarter" since the resulting judgment would then be determined not by "reason" but by an "impulse" (*G*, 4.448). Judgments understood as caused according to psychological laws cannot be regarded as a rational. More generally rational activity is "independent of determination by sensibility" in the sense that it does not operate according to empirical laws, but is guided by normative principles, which are essentially different in kind.

Another important feature of practical freedom appears in Kant's claim that practical freedom presupposes that although something has not happened, it nevertheless *ought* to have happened, and its cause in appearance was thus not so determining that there is not a causality in our power of choice such that, independently of those natural causes and even opposed to their influence, it might produce something determined in the temporal order in accord with empirical laws, and hence begin a series of occurrences *entirely from itself*. (B 562; see also B 583)

Often we fail to act as we ought to. For example, I might be inclined to act in a certain way, decide that it would be imprudent or wrong, but nonetheless choose that action. It is part of our ordinary conception of our agency that we can do what we judge that we ought to do, or what we have reason to do. That means that in situations like these, we believe that we could have acted otherwise – that alternative possibilities were open to us. In this example I acted on a sensible motive, contrary to my judgment of what I had most reason to do, but that motive "was not so determining" as to close off the possibility of having acted differently. I could have set that motive aside and done what I had most reason to do.

In sum, the practical freedom that we ascribe to ourselves is a capacity for self-determination, or a capacity to initiate action through one's judgments about reasons. It is a form of agent causation that is guided by an agent's reasoning. There are different senses in which this capacity is not sensibly determined. Motives do not directly cause action, but rather influence choice through a spontaneous act or judgment by the agent; and we are not bound to take sensible motives as reasons, but can set them aside or oppose them. Further, practical freedom involves the possibility of acting otherwise, since in cases where we act against reason, we suppose that we could have done what we judged we had reason to do. Finally, it is independent of sensible determination in the sense that it does not operate according to empirical causal laws, but rather according to normative principles. Since this practical freedom appears to be a power to initiate actions that is not determined by temporally prior causes, it seems to be an instance of transcendental freedom, and therein lies the problem. Since nature is a deterministic system, there is no room in nature for transcendental freedom. That raises the question whether the practical freedom that we ascribe to ourselves is illusory. Since "the practical concept of freedom is grounded" on the transcendental idea, "the abolition of transcendental freedom would also simultaneously eliminate all practical freedom" (B 561, B 562).

Kant rejects compatibilist solutions to the free will problem as "a wretched subterfuge" (*CPrR*, 5.96). Compatibilists adopt what Kant calls a "comparative concept of freedom." They hold that human actions are free when "caused from within, by representations produced by our own powers, whereby desires are evoked on occasion of circumstances and hence actions are produced at our own discretion" (*CPrR*, 5.96). In other words, actions are free when caused by an agent's internal psychological states, such as beliefs, desires, and intentions. Kant argues that this conception of freedom falls short of the practical concept outlined above. The psychological states that compatibilists identify as causes of action are still events that follow causally from prior events, in this case according to psychological laws. Since psychological causation is still natural causation, the compatibilist solution does not give the agent any real control at the time of action. Their conception of freedom is "nothing better than the freedom of the turnspit, which, when once it is wound up, also accomplishes its movements by itself" (*CPrR*, 5.97).

How then does Kant establish that the free will required for agency and responsibility is possible? Since Kant holds that the law of causality applies to all events in the natural world, and since human actions are such events, free agency is possible only if actions may be viewed under different aspects as the effects of both natural causation and free agency. This is not an option for the transcendental realist: if spatiotemporal determinations are properties of things in themselves, then descriptions of events in terms of such properties and deterministic causal laws are exhaustive. But the distinction between appearances, phenomena, and noumena may enable the transcendental idealist to view human action in these two different ways.

III. The Possibility of Freedom of the Will

The following passage articulates a principle that guides Kant's solution to the free will problem:

> I call *intelligible* that in an object of sense which is not itself appearance. Accordingly, if that which must be regarded as an appearance in the world of sense has in itself a faculty which is not an object of intuition through which it can be the cause of appearances, then one can consider the *causality* of this being in two aspects, as *intelligible* in its *action* as a thing in itself, and as *sensible* in the *effects* of that action as an appearance in the world of sense. (B 566)

Here Kant claims that if an entity in the natural world has a capacity to bring about changes in the world that is "intelligible" and "not an object of intuition," then its causal powers and relations may be considered under two aspects. As noumenon it would have a capacity for activity that is "intelligible" – presumably a capacity to guide its actions by normative principles – while as phenomenon its actions would be causally determined events in the natural world. Kant goes on to claim that such an entity would have both an empirical character, which determines how its actions follow from temporally prior conditions, and an intelligible character, which guides its rational activity as noumenon. In its intelligible character it "would not stand under the conditions of time" (B 567), which is to say that its actions would not follow causally from temporally prior conditions according to empirical laws. Since it has the power to initiate actions without being determined by temporally prior conditions, this entity would satisfy the definition of transcendental freedom.

Relying on this principle, Kant constructs roughly the following argument in the Clarification:

1) Since the principle of natural causality holds without exception of all events, free will is possible only if human actions can be regarded, under different aspects, as effects of both natural causation and free agency.
2) If an entity in the natural world has a capacity to effect changes that is intelligible and not an object of intuition, its causal powers may be viewed under two aspects and will have both an empirical character and an intelligible character. As phenomenon its actions would be explainable in terms of its empirical character. But

as noumenon, its activity will be guided by intelligible (i.e. normative) principles, according to its intelligible character.

3) In its intelligible character, this entity will have a capacity to initiate actions independently of determination by temporally prior conditions, and thus will be transcendentally free.

4) Human beings possess rational capacities that are intelligible and not objects of intuition. These appear to include the capacity to guide their choices and actions by rational principles – that is, it appears that "reason has causality" (B 575) and is a power to effect changes in the world. If so, human beings have a causal power that is intelligible and they satisfy the principle in (2) above: their causal powers and relations may be viewed under two aspects and would have both an empirical and an intelligible character.

5) Assuming that reason is a causal power that can lead to action (as in (4) above), human beings are transcendentally free in their intelligible character. They have a capacity to initiate actions through the exercise of their rational capacities, even though these same actions can also be given empirical explanations in terms of psychological facts about the agent.

Initially this argument raises more questions than it answers, and there is much that needs explaining. I shall focus on three general questions: (a) why does the possession of rational capacities require that we view the causal powers of human beings under different aspects and what does it mean to say that rational capacities are "intelligible" and "not objects of intuition"? (b) What is the relation of the empirical character to the intelligible character? And (c) what does it mean to say that "the acting subject, in its intelligible character, would not stand under any conditions of time," and how would that support the claim that human beings, considered as noumena, are transcendentally free?

To begin with the first question, Kant draws on the fundamental insight that rational activity is guided by normative principles, which are different in kind from causal laws, and that it cannot be understood in terms of empirical causal principles. Accordingly, when we ascribe rational capacities to ourselves, as we do in taking up the practical perspective, we regard our activity differently than when we think of human actions as events in the natural world subject to causal determination; we view our powers and activity "under a different aspect" because we understand it in terms of normative principles. To see this, consider what goes on in a chain of reasoning when a person draws a conclusion from an argument. The person draws normative connections between the steps of the argument, judging that one step follows from another and that the conclusion follows from the entire argument. She comes to accept the conclusion because she judges that the argument provides rational grounds for accepting it. In valid reasoning, the conclusion does not follow from its rational ground (i.e., from the supporting argument) in the way that an effect follows from its cause according to empirical laws. In this case, the conclusion follows from the argument via the relevant principles of inference, and her judgment that it follows is the reason why she accepts the conclusion. The connections here – the logical or rational connection between premises and conclusion, and the connection between the person's going through the argument and her accepting the conclusion – are normative not causal, because they are given by norms of inference and rationality.

The same things can be said about an agent who judges that she has a sufficient reason to choose a particular action, forms the relevant intention and acts accordingly; in Kant's terms, she "incorporates" an incentive into a maxim of action. Her judgment about what she has reason to do is the rational ground of her action, and her action does not follow from its rational ground in the way that an effect follows from its cause according to empirical laws. In this case, the action follows from the judgment through the norm of rationality to the effect that someone who judges that he has most overall reason to perform a certain action in a given situation rationally ought to perform that action. (Someone who makes this judgment but for no good reason fails to perform the action displays a form of irrationality.) The agent is exercising a form of causality since he acts and brings about changes in the world on the basis of his rational judgment. But it is not empirical causality, since it is not governed by empirical causal laws. It is the kind of causality involved in rational agency.

If we do try to understand a rational process in terms of empirical causal laws, we lose the sense of it as rational. For example, consider trying to understand the reasoning in the above two cases as a causal process in which one psychological state or set of states (rehearsing steps of the argument, the judgment about what one has reason to do) causes subsequent psychological states (accepting the conclusion, the motivation or intention to act) according to psychological laws. We would be thinking of the relevant psychological states simply as events in the person that follow causally from prior events. But once we think of the process in these terms, we lose the sense that there is *an agent* who is *drawing normative connections* between the relevant items (from premises to conclusion, or from a judgment about reasons to action). These notions need to be in play if we are to think of the process as rational activity.

Normative principles tell us what we ought to think or do, and Kant says that "ought expresses a species of necessity and a connection with grounds which does not occur anywhere else in the whole of nature" (B 575). In addition to providing a ground of action that differs from empirical causal grounds, they introduce a possibility that does not apply to events that are part of the natural causal order, namely the possibility of actions other than those that actually occurred. We assume that rational agents can do what they judge they ought to do. Thus when agents act contrary to reason we assume that they could have acted otherwise. They could have done what they had reason to do.

We can now explain why rational capacities are "intelligible" and "not given in intuition." A capacity is "intelligible" if it is conceived through concepts and principles that originate in understanding or reason. Rational activities such as reasoning and judgment are intelligible in this sense because in order to understand them in their distinctive character as rationally guided, we must bring them under normative concepts and principles, as explained above, and such concepts and principles have an a priori origin in understanding and reason. Neither our possession of rational capacities nor particular exercises of rationality are given in sensible intuition (e.g., as items or events in the natural world) because they are not objects of observation in the normal sense, to be understood by bringing them under empirical causal principles. One feature of Kant's epistemology is that objects of sensible intuition are brought to the unity of consciousness by bringing them under empirical concepts whose form is given by the categories of the understanding, and any event given in intuition must follow from temporally prior conditions according to empirical laws. For something to be a possible object of intuition, it must be amenable to this form of understanding. But as we have seen, rational activity cannot be understood in this way, because it loses its character as rational if we try to bring it under empirical causal laws. In that specific sense, neither rational capacities nor instances of their exercise (such as acts of reasoning, judgment, choice, and so on) are given in intuition.

Turn now to the distinction between empirical and intelligible character, which is simply a consequence of the idea that our causal powers may be viewed under two aspects. Kant writes that every cause "must have a character, i.e., a law of its causality, without which it would not be a cause" (B 567). The "character" of a form of causality would be the principle according to which it operates. A person's empirical character would be the principles that connect his actions with temporally prior conditions, while the intelligible character would be the set of basic (normative) principles that determine how one exercises one's practical reason. Starting with the latter, two features of the intelligible character are worth noting. First, one's intelligible character is the set of basic principles, value commitments and priorities, and maxims that guide one's choices by determining what one sees reason to do in various circumstances. Second, it will be these basic principles, understood as originating in that person's rational agency – that is, as principles and values that one has in some sense adopted or endorsed, and for which one is responsible. The intelligible character is intended to capture the notion of a person's moral character since it includes a person's basic principles and values, thought of as adopted or endorsed by the person.

The empirical character will have two corresponding features. First, Kant understands a person's empirical character as a set of rules or laws that specify how his actions follow from temporally prior conditions and that may be inferred from the person's observed actions (cf. B 567, B 577). Since it involves rules or laws, it includes facts about the person's psychology such as standing desires and dispositions or motivational tendencies that determine, and may be cited to explain, how the person acts in various circumstances. Second, it treats these standing dispositions and motivational tendencies as themselves subject to empirical causal explanation. Presumably the dispositions that make up the person's empirical character follow from such temporally prior conditions as the person's upbringing and social environment, native temperament, past experiences, and other formative influences, according to psychological laws or generalizations. In this respect, empirical character is a naturalistic explanatory notion that locates human actions in a temporally extended causal process.

Matters are complicated somewhat by the fact that a person's reason exhibits an empirical character. Kant writes:

> every human being has an empirical character for his power of choice, which is nothing other than a certain causality of his reason, insofar as in its effects in appearance this reason exhibits a rule, in accordance with which one could derive the rational grounds and the actions themselves . . . and estimate the subjective principles of the power of choice. (B 577)

The implication here is that a person's empirical character includes a person's reasons (the "rational grounds" of action) and subjective principles, in other words, the maxims from which the person acts. If so, it is natural to include such items as a person's observed value commitments, tendencies to take certain considerations as reason-giving, or even tendencies to reason in certain ways. One might think that these are normative dispositions that belong to the intelligible character, but the puzzle can be resolved in this way. We may assume that the empirical character includes basic principles, value priorities, tendencies to reason in certain ways, and so on, viewed simply as psychological facts about the person that can be inferred from observing a person's choices, and that are susceptible to empirical explanation in terms of past influence. The empirical character takes a purely descriptive approach to these disposi-tions, focusing on the principles that the person actually accepts and treating them simply as dispositions and motivational tendencies that can be cited in empirical explanations of actions.

Kant holds that the intelligible character may be regarded as the ground of the empirical character, and this idea is crucial to making sense of the idea that human actions may be viewed as resulting both from natural causation and free agency. As phenomena, actions are causally explainable in terms of the dispositions and motiva-tional tendencies that comprise the empirical character. But Kant says that it is possible that this "empirical causality" has an intelligible ground in the person's intel-ligible character (B 572). What is possible, in other words, is that the dispositions observable in a person's actions are grounded in the person's basic principles and value commitments. Since commitments to principles, judgments about reasons, acts of "incorporating incentives" into maxims, and so on, are not given in intuition (in their character as rational), they are not items in our empirical understanding of action, but are introduced only when we ascribe rational capacities to human beings.

Two ideas may be at work in the thought that the intelligible character is the ground of the empirical character. First, the motivational tendencies that go into the empirical character may reflect principles and value commitments that are their ground. Someone who thinks that honesty is important unless it requires personal sacrifice will display a certain pattern of motive, feeling, and action. Likewise someone who judges that on balance he ought to be honest in a particular situation will be motivated to act honestly. When their actions are regarded as phenomena, the selective disposition to act honestly, or the motivation to be honest in a particular situation, will figure in a causal explanation of the action, and, as psychological states of the agent, will be explainable in terms of antecedent conditions. But these empirically given motivations also reflect the agent's acceptance of a principle, or his assessment of the reasons in those circum-stances; thus the motivations that appear as the empirical cause have an "intelligible ground" in the rational activity of the agent. Second, according to Kant's Incorpora-tion Thesis, even desires or motivational tendencies that are best understood simply as causal products of past influence only lead to choice when the agent incorporates them into a maxim; their efficacy as motives is grounded in an act of the agent. Here consider a person in a situation that elicits a strong inclination to act dishonestly who acts on that inclination; assume further that the inclination is explainable in terms of a disposition that can be traced to facts about his upbringing. This inclination and its causal antecedents will figure in an empirical explanation of the action as phenomenon. But when we view the person as an agent who acts for reasons, we introduce an additional item into our understanding of the action that does not show up, as it were, when the action is regarded as phenomenon – namely, the "incorporation" of the incentive of dishonesty into a maxim of action. It is through a spontaneous act of the agent that the inclination to dishonesty becomes the operative incentive that leads to action. That is, the motivational state that we might identify as an empirical cause of the action becomes efficacious through a spontaneous act, and thus its "empirical causality" is grounded in the agent's intelligible character.

The thesis that the intelligible character is the ground of the empirical character expands our conception of the grounds of human action. When we limit ourselves to the material given in intuition, empirical explanations are adequate for certain purposes and complete as far as they go. Successful empirical explanations provide an understanding of actions by showing how they follow from temporally prior conditions. But taking up the practical perspective and thinking of ourselves as rational agents introduces additional items such as commitment to principles, reasoning, judgment – in a word, elements of normative guidance – that do not show up in the empirical standpoint since they are not given in intuition. These elements enlarge our conception of the causality underlying human action. As we have seen, they permit the thought that an intelligible act (such as the adoption of a maxim, the application of a principle, or a judgment about reasons) is the ultimate ground of the action because it is the ground of the motivational state that appears as the empirical cause of the action – that is, that empirical causal factors have a further ground in the activity of an agent that enables us to see the agent as the source of his or her actions. Furthermore, because rational choice is guided by "ought" judgments, the elements of normative guidance introduce the possibility of acting otherwise in circumstances in which an agent acts contrary to reason.

Once such concepts are on board, it is clear that empirical explanations do not complete the story of human action because they omit one of its essential features, namely the rational activity of the agent. Presumably Kant needs to hold that the empirical understanding of action is incomplete in order to deal with a looming problem. He wants to say that actions as phenomena are causally determined and follow with necessity. But as noumena they are the results of free agency, which involves the possibility of acting otherwise. But isn't it just an outright contradiction to hold both that actions follow with necessity and that agents have the possibility of acting otherwise? The fact that the possibility of acting otherwise is only introduced by taking up the practical perspective and thinking of ourselves as rational agents may help with this problem. When we view actions as phenomena they do indeed follow from prior events that are, based on what is given in intuition, sufficient to bring them about. From that perspective, we cannot give any content to the idea that actions could have occurred differently. But thinking of ourselves as rational agents introduces further items into our conception of the causality underlying action that are not part of our understanding of actions as phenomena. Among other things, it allows us to say that the agent could have chosen differently (in situations where he or she chose contrary to reason). The possibility of acting otherwise is only introduced when we think of actions as noumena. But once we have a way to give content to that possibility, we see that our understanding of action based on what is given in sensible intuition is limited, though empirical explanations remain adequate for certain purposes.

One of the most perplexing features of Kant's account of free will is the idea that reason in its intelligible character does not "stand under any conditions of time"

(B 567). This idea is part of his argument that human beings, considered in terms of their intelligible character, act freely, and is seen in the following representative passages:

> Pure reason, as a merely intelligible faculty, is not subject to the form of time, and hence not subject to the conditions of the temporal sequence. The causality of reason in the intelligible character *does not arise* or start working at a certain time in producing an effect. For then it would itself be subject to the natural law of appearances, to the extent that this law determines causal series in time, and its causality would then be nature and not freedom. (B 579–80)

> But of reason one cannot say that before the state in which it determines the power of choice, another state precedes in which this state itself is determined. For since reason itself is not an appearance and is not subject to any conditions of sensibility, no temporal sequence takes place in it even as to its causality, and thus the dynamical law of nature, which determines the temporal sequence according to rules, cannot be applied to it. (B 581)

> In regard to the intelligible character . . . no *before* or *after* applies, and every action, irrespective of the temporal relation in which it stands to other appearances, is the immediate effect of the intelligible character of pure reason; reason therefore acts freely, without being determined dynamically by external or internal grounds temporally preceding it in the chain of natural causes, and this freedom of reason can not only be regarded negatively, as independence from empirical conditions . . . but also indicated positively by a faculty of beginning a series of occurrences from itself . . . (B 581)

According to a common reading of such passages, Kant secures free will by placing the noumenal self outside of time, thereby freeing it from causal determination. Actions as phenomena are then somehow grounded in the atemporal and therefore free choices of the noumenal self. This conception is indeed suggested by these and other passages. But if Kant's resolution of the free will problem depends on such strong and, to most philosophers, dubious, metaphysical assumptions, its philosophical interest will be limited. We do better to look for a more innocuous reading of such passages, and I shall. (Allen Wood (1984) defends the "strong," "timeless agency" reading, while Henry Allison (1990) develops a metaphysically more "innocent" interpretation.)

The idea that reason, or agents considered in terms of their intelligible character, are not subject to temporal conditions may be understood through what we earlier identified as the distinctive feature of rational activity – that it is guided by normative principles, which are different in kind from empirical causal laws. We can put it this way: to say that reason is not subject to temporal conditions is just to say that the relation "is the rational ground of " is not the temporal relation "is the empirical cause of," since that relation is understood through normative principles rather than causal laws. Thus when Kant says that "no temporal sequence takes place in [reason] even as to its causality," he need not deny that actual reasoning takes place in time. The point is rather that the sequence in a rational process is not a causal sequence in which one state or event arises from preceding events according to empirical laws. The rational grounds of an action (or of a judgment, or an the agent's drawing a conclusion) are not its "antecedent conditions" in the way that an empirical cause is an antecedent condition of an effect – because to be an antecedent condition in that sense just means one from which the subsequent occurrence follows according to empirical laws. And actions (or judgments, conclusions, and so on) do not follow from their rational grounds in that way since their connection to their grounds is normative. Likewise, in saying that "the causality of reason in the intelligible character does not arise or start working at a certain time in producing an effect," he means that reasoning is not understood in its character as rational or normatively guided through the kinds of laws that govern the occurrence of events in time.

We saw in the last section that Kant defines transcendental freedom as the capacity to initiate a series of events without being determined by temporally prior causes, and he claims that practical freedom – the form of free agency implicit in the practical perspective – presupposes transcendental freedom. Our ascription of rational capacities to ourselves and the conception of an intelligible character support the idea that human agents are transcendentally free by supplying both the negative and the positive components of transcendental freedom. First, since rational activity is normatively governed, the elements of a rational process do not follow from temporally prior states according to empirical laws. ("[T]his freedom of reason can not only be regarded negatively, as independence from empirical conditions . . .") Second, normative guidance introduces the idea of spontaneous acts of an agent, such as an agent's judging that a conclusion follows from an argument, judging that there is reason to act in a certain way, applying a principle to a situation, and so on. When acts of this sort lead to action, we would have an instance of an agent initiating an event in the world. This is the positive component of transcendental freedom (The "freedom of reason" is "also indicated positively by a faculty of beginning a series of occurrences from itself . . .") Thus, in virtue of having a capacity to initiate events without being determined by temporally prior causes, human beings would satisfy the definition of transcendental freedom.

Kant gives an example of a person who tells a malicious lie that illustrates how we move between the empirical character and the intelligible character. Kant supposes that we can give an empirical explanation of the action in terms of "the sources of the person's empirical character," such as his upbringing, social environment, and native temperament. Such factors and the resulting motivational state would be the "occasioning causes" of the action as phenomenon. However, we might still blame the agent, and if so, we regard the agent's "reason as a cause that, regardless of all the empirical conditions just named, could have and ought to have determined the conduct of the person to be other than it is" (B 583). If we blame the agent, we think of his agency in a certain way. For example, though the agent may have been strongly inclined to lie (due to past formative influences), we suppose that this incentive leads to action through the agent's judgment that the benefits achievable by lying were a sufficient reason to lie. In that way we trace the action back to the agent. Further, we suppose that the agent could have refrained from lying. He had reason not to lie, had access to that reason, and could have done what he judged he ought to have done. It is worth noting that Kant's claim here is conditional: *if* we blame the agent despite our belief that the action has empirical causes, then we are supposing that the agent initiated the action without being determined by antecedent circumstances, and that he could have chosen as he ought to have. The distinction between phenomena and noumena, between the empirical and the intelligible character, is intended to show how we can ascribe free agency even though we believe that the action is empirically caused.

288

IV. The Reality of Freedom of the Will

The Resolution of the Third Antinomy only shows that the possibility of free will is not ruled out by causal determinism. To establish that human beings actually have free will, Kant needs to show that we can be motivated to act by principles of reason, in which case, reason is a "form of causality." We would then be entitled to employ the conception of intelligible character and ascribe transcendental freedom to ourselves – entitled in the sense that our awareness of these rational capacities is a ground for ascribing such capacities and doing so is consistent with causal determinism.

The argument that we can be motivated to act by reason in the requisite way comes in Kant's moral theory. In *Groundwork* III Kant demonstrates a conceptual connection between the moral law as a principle of reason and free will. He then argues from the possession of theoretical reason to the existence of free will, and from there to the authority of the moral law. (See Hill 1992.) In the *Critique of Practical Reason* Kant relies on the same conceptual connection between morality and free will, but *reverses* the order of argument, moving *from* the authority of the moral law as a "fact of reason" *to* the reality of free will. I sketch the latter argument.

It is part of our ordinary concept of duty or moral requirement that if an action is your duty, you ought to do it regardless of your desire-based interests. We take duties to apply with special normative necessity: they give us reasons for action that do not depend on desires and that limit the force of desire-based reasons that are inconsistent with duty. In this way, moral requirements are "unconditional practical laws" that are reason-giving in virtue of their "legislative form" (*CPrR*, 5.27). An agent who acts from duty is motivated by the legislative form of the maxim: her reason for acting is the fact that the action is morally required. This analysis leads to the thesis that "freedom and unconditional practical law reciprocally imply each other," which consists of two claims: (1) If an agent is subject to the moral law, that agent is transcendentally free; and (2) If an agent is transcendentally free, that agent is subject to the moral law (*CPrR*, 5.28–9). The first is needed to establish free will, and the argument for this claim is simple. An agent subject to the moral law can act from the moral law – that is, can set aside desire-based reasons and take the legislative form of a maxim (the fact that an action is required) as a sufficient reason for action. Desire-based reasons can ultimately be traced back to empirical conditions that produce the relevant desires and interests. Thus, an agent who can base her reasons for action simply on the legislative form of her maxim can act independently of determination by empirical conditions. An agent who can act on this kind of reason satisfies the definition of transcendental freedom.

Are we such agents? Kant claims that the moral law is given as a "fact of reason" (*CPrR*, 5.31). In ordinary practical reasoning we acknowledge the authority of moral requirements and are conscious of our capacity to act from the moral law. Its authority is reflected in the standards to which we hold ourselves and in the workings of conscience and the moral emotions. By establishing that we are subject to and can act from moral law, the fact of reason establishes that we are free. Indeed, our recognition of the authority of the moral law is at the same time an awareness of freedom: "this fact is . . . indeed identical with consciousness of freedom of the will" (*CPrR*, 5.42).

Two comments on this way of establishing free will. First, in addition to showing that reason is a causal power in us, Kant's moral theory specifies the normative principle that governs that power. Moral consciousness gives us a determinate positive conception of our free agency: it is the capacity to act from the moral law (cf. *MM*, 6.213–14, 6.224–5). Second, to defend moral responsibility as he understands it, Kant must hold that we act freely even when we do not act from moral reasons. His view is that we have this capacity even when we fail to exercise it. Thus he can say that an action is freely chosen if performed by an agent with the capacity to act from the moral law, whether or not that agent acts from moral reasons.

In order to respect the limits on knowledge established by the first *Critique*, Kant stresses that the reality of free will is not an object of theoretical knowledge, but has "objective though only practical reality" (*CPrR*, 5.48, 5.49). Kant has not given a theoretical proof that we are free, nor is free will given in intuition. Rather the warrant for ascribing free will is our consciousness of the authority of the moral law. The assertion that we have free will is rationally based, but not in the way that knowledge claims are. Because the reality of free will is not established theoretically, it does not expand theoretical knowledge and, for example, it cannot enter into empirical explanations of events. Finally, the capacity with which free agency is identified is specified through moral consciousness – as the capacity to act from the moral law. In sum, both the grounds for ascribing free will to ourselves and our determinate understanding of what free will is are given by moral consciousness, and this idea can only be used from the practical perspective, as part of our self-conception as agents.

References and Further Reading

Allison, Henry (1990). *Kant's Theory of Freedom*. Cambridge: Cambridge University Press.

Hill, Thomas, E., Jr. (1992). Kant's argument for the rationality of moral conduct. In *Dignity and Practical reason*. Ithaca, NY: Cornell University Press.

Kant, Immanuel (1996). *The Metaphysics of Morals, Groundwork of the Metaphysics of Morals*, and *Critique of Practical Reason*. In *Practical Philosophy*, ed. and tr. Mary J. Gregor. Cambridge: Cambridge University Press.

Kant, Immanuel (1998). *Religion Within the Boundaries of Mere Reason*. In *Religion and Rational Theology*, eds. and tr. Allen W. Wood and George Di Giovanni. Cambridge: Cambridge University Press.

Korsgaard, Christine M. (1996). Morality as freedom. In *Creating the Kingdom of Ends*. Cambridge: Cambridge University Press.

Reath, Andrews (1997). Introduction to *Critique of Practical Reason*. In Immanuel Kant, *Critique of Practical Reason*, ed. and tr. Mary J. Gregor. Cambridge: Cambridge University Press.

Rawls, John (2000). *Lectures on the History of Moral Philosophy*. Cambridge, MA: Harvard University Press.

Wood, Allen, W., ed. (1984). *Self and Nature in Kant's Philosophy*. Ithaca, NY: Cornell University Press.

19

Kant's Formulations of the Moral Law

ALLEN W. WOOD

Kant's project in the *Groundwork* is "the search for and establishment *of the supreme principle of morality*" (G, 4.392). He does this by formulating the principle in three ways, of which two have significant variants that are supposed to bring the moral principle "closer to intuition" and thereby "provide entry and durability for its precepts" by relating it more intimately to human experience and human feelings (G, 4.405, 4.436). His *establishment* of the moral principle apparently relates to only one of these formulations, but it is the formulation that he says follows from the other two and in which, I will argue, the other two are combined.

The *search* for the principle, by contrast, leads through a progressive development first (in Section I of the *Groundwork*) of the concept of acting from duty, and then (in Section II) of the concept of a categorical imperative. Section I, beginning from moral common sense (or "common rational moral cognition") arrives only at the first formulation of the law, while Section II (proceeding more philosophically from an account of the will) develops all of them. For this reason, we should focus here on this later development. First, let us look at the different formulations of the moral law as Kant presents them:

FIRST FORMULA:

FUL *The Formula of Universal Law*: "Act only in accordance with that maxim through which you at the same time can will that it become a universal law" (G, 4.421; cf. G, 4.402); with its variant,

FLN *The Formula of the Law of Nature*: "So act, as if the maxim of your action were to become through your will a *universal law of nature*" (G, 4.421; cf. 4.436).

SECOND FORMULA:

FH *The Formula of Humanity as End in Itself*: "So act that you use humanity, as much in your own person as in the person of every other, always at the same time as an end and never merely as a means" (G, 4.429; cf. 4.436).

THIRD FORMULA:

FA *Formula of Autonomy*: "the idea *of the will of every rational being as a will giving universal law*" (G, 4.431; cf. G, 4.432), or "Not to choose otherwise than so

291

that the maxims of one's choice are at the same time comprehended with it in the same volition as universal law" (*G*, 4.440; cf. 4.432, 4.434, 4.438), with its variant,

FRE *The Formula of the Realm of Ends*: "Act in accordance with maxims of a universally legislative member for a merely possible realm of ends" (*G*, 4.439; cf. 4.433, 4.437, 4.438).

FU "*Universal Formula*": Act in accordance with that maxim which can at the same time make itself into a universal law (*G*, 4.436–7). Compare:

FK "So act that the maxim of your action could always at the same time hold as a principle of universal legislation" (*CPrR*, 5.30);

FM "Act upon a maxim that can also hold as a universal law" (*MM*, 6.225; translations from Kant 1996 throughout.)

FU is presented at the end of the development, as part of the systematization. It bears a close resemblance to the general formulation of the moral law presented in the *Critique of Practical Reason* (FK) and the *Metaphysics of Morals* (FM). Below, at the proper time, we will consider the relationship of these formulas to one another and to the three main formulas Kant distinguishes in the *Groundwork*.

The Concept of a Categorical Imperative

Kant proposes to derive FUL, FH, and FA (as well as their "intuitive" variants, FLN and FRE) from the concept of a categorical imperative, which (he argues) is the form all properly moral principles must take. It is with this concept, therefore, that it makes sense to begin.

Kant's theory of the will takes us to be agents who are self-directing in the sense that we have the capacity to step back from our natural desires, reflect on them, consider whether and how we should satisfy them, and to be moved by them only on the basis of such reflections. An inclination (that is, a habitual empirical desire, such as hunger) moves us to act only when we choose to set its object as an end for ourselves, and this choice then sets us the task of selecting or devising a means to that end. If I see an apple up in a tree and a desire to eat it occurs to me, then I will eat it only if I first decide to make eating it my *end*, and then devise a *means* (such as climbing the tree, or reaching for the apple with a stick, or knocking it to the ground by throwing something at it) to achieve the end. In acting on my inclination, I thus make a series of decisions and create in myself a set of new desires (to climb the tree, or find a suitable stick) whose source is not merely the original desire I am trying to satisfy, but even more the exercise of my own capacities to set ends, devise means, and hold myself to some self-chosen plan for applying the means. Our inclinations, then, do not simply push us around like the levers and pulleys of a machine. Instead, they rather provide inputs into a rational process of self-direction involving our adoption and recognition of rational norms, and the ultimate decision to follow (or not follow) the norms we recognize.

Setting an end is the most basic normative act, since (Kant holds) there is no action without an end to be produced by it. This act involves the concept of an object (or state of affairs) to be produced and also the concept of some means needed to produce it.

Setting an end thus subjects me to a normative principle commanding me to perform the action required as a means to the end. Kant calls this principle a "hypothetical imperative." It is called an "imperative" because it is a command of reason requiring the agent to do something; it is "hypothetical" because the command governs our action only on the condition that we will the end in question. By contrast, an imperative that has no such condition would be called a "categorical imperative."

Categorical imperatives are categorical because their validity is not conditional on some *prior* end. "If you make a promise, keep it" is a conditional imperative in the grammatical sense, but it is not a "hypothetical imperative" in Kant's sense because the "if"-clause does not refer to an end that conditions the validity of the imperative. A moral imperative, in Kant's view, is categorical because its function is to tell us not how to reach some prior end of ours based on what we happen to want, but rather commands us irrespective of our wants or our contingent ends, and is therefore not conditional on any of them. A categorical imperative may be conditional in other ways, however – for instance, there may be implied conditions that release us from a promise, in which case there is no categorical imperative at all to keep it under those conditions.

The words "prior" and "contingent" are crucial here, since categorical imperatives, in commanding us to act, also thereby always command us to set ends (according to Kant's theory in the *Metaphysics of Morals*, our own perfection and the happiness of others are the kinds of ends that are also duties, *MM*, 6.385–8, cf. *G*, 4.422–3). These ends, like the end of our own happiness, are not *contingently* set, but are ends reason *requires* us to set. In the case of our own happiness, it is *prudential* reason that requires the end of us; in the case of our perfection and the happiness of others, the command comes from *moral* reason. In relation to the actions we take toward our own happiness, it counts as a prior end conditioning the rational requirement that we perform them, so the prudential imperative is not categorical. By contrast, the act of keeping a promise is not merely a way of achieving some prior end (such as benefiting the person to whom the promise was made) but is morally required of us irrespective of any prior end.

Since in Kant's view every action has an end to be produced, following a moral principle will always involve setting and achieving some end – for instance, fulfilling a promise will involve setting further ends involved in accomplishing the thing you promised to do. More generally, since every action has an end to be produced, it is essential to categorical imperatives that they should command us to set certain ends, such as our own perfection and the happiness of others. The thought that categorical imperatives do (or even might) command us to act without our having any end at all is a false (and even a nonsensical) thought.

The First Formula: FUL and FLN

As Kant later informs us (*G*, 4.436), his development of the supreme principle of morality considers the concept of a categorical imperative from three different points of view: "form," "matter" and "complete determination." This triad is drawn from Kant's theory of concept formation. Every concept has a "form," provided by the understanding, and the role of the concept in judgments and inferences. It also has a "matter" or condition of cognitive application, consisting in a possible intuition through which an instance of the concept might be given in experience. Every concept also "determines" the subject to which it is applied as a predicate in a judgment. Following Leibniz, Kant thinks of universal concepts (such as "human") as universal because they are not "completely determined" (the concept "human" is undetermined relative to such pairs of opposites as, "male–female," "young–old," and so forth). By contrast, a fully individual concept (such as the concept of Alexander the Great) would be "completely determined" with respect to every pair of contradictories.

It is not entirely clear why Kant chooses this triad as the vehicle for developing the moral principle, and the elements of the triad themselves are certainly used in extended (or even metaphorical) senses. I will have some further things to say about this topic as we go along (see Wood 2001). But Kant's systematization of his formulas at G 4.436 suggests several points that his readers ought to keep in mind as they consider his development of the formulas themselves in the Second Section. Kant says that all three are formulations of "the very same law," but differ both "subjectively" (in the way the law is presented to an agent) and also in the aspect of the law that they present. This suggests that we need all the formulas in order to have a complete account of the content of the supreme principle. But Kant also says that there is a "progression" among them, analogous to the categories of quantity (unity, plurality, totality) (G, 4.436; cf. CPR, B 106). Since Kant thinks about each triad of categories (including the categories of quantity) that they represent a progression, in which the first member leads to the second, and third member of the triad is generated by combining the first two, this implies that FUL (FLN) is a preliminary (or provisional) formulation of the moral law, a stepping stone to FH (which is an intermediate formulation), and that FA (FRE), which somehow combines FUL and FH, represents the fullest development of the principle. As we proceed, I think we will see that these suggestions are borne out.

FUL corresponds to the category of unity by bringing to expression the unity of form that maxims must have in order to be compatible with the moral law. By the "form" of a categorical imperative, Kant appears to mean a formal property of maxims (or normative principles contingently adopted by a will) such that having this property makes the maxim consistent with a categorical imperative (that is, morally permissible). This property, according to FUL, is that the agent could, without contradiction or conflicting volitions, will the maxim to be a universal law; according to FLN, it is that the agent could, without contradiction or conflicting volitions, will the maxim to be a universal law of nature. In FUL, the term "universal law" appears to be meant normatively. That is, the test is whether you could will it to be *permissible* for everyone (presumably, everyone in relevantly similar circumstances) to act on the maxim. In FLN, the test is whether you could will that everyone, with the regularity of a law of nature, should actually follow on the maxim. Thus in Section I, where Kant derives only FUL, he asks: "Would I be able to say that anyone may make an untruthful promise when he finds himself in embarrassment which they cannot get out of in any other way?" (G, 4.403). In Section II, where FLN is applied to the same maxim, the question is whether you could will that everyone, as a law of nature, actually make false promises when they find themselves in financial difficulty (G, 4.422).

There has been much dispute in the literature about what these universalizability tests amount to, and how they are supposed to work. There are many common misunderstandings about them abroad among philosophers, especially among critics of Kant. But I think a large part of the interest in these issues is due to some even more fundamental misunderstandings of Kant's use of these formulas in the *Groundwork*, and their role in Kant's ethical theory, that are extremely common among Kant's sympathizers and critics alike. It is commonly thought, namely, that the universalizability tests involved in FUL and FLN are supposed to constitute a universal moral criterion applicable to any maxim that might be proposed, a method for grounding all moral duties, or even a universal rational procedure for constructing the content of all morality. As such, FUL and FLN (which are seldom clearly distinguished from each other) are thought to constitute the foundation of Kantian ethics, and even Kant's chief (or perhaps his only significant) contribution to moral reasoning.

On the basis of these thoughts, Kant's critics think that Kantian ethics as a whole can be discredited by showing that the universalizability tests do not yield the right results for some maxims, while his defenders seek to devise an interpretation of the universalizability criteria that enable them to serve as a universal method of moral reasoning and get the right results in the difficult cases. Both sides, however, seem to me guilty of serious misunderstandings of Kant's first formula both in relation to the foundations of ethics generally and to the four famous examples he uses to illustrate FLN. Once we rid ourselves of these misunderstandings, I think the subject matter of their quarrels will be seen to have little relevance to Kant's ethical theory or our estimation of it.

The first point to be clear about is that if the right question to raise about Kantian ethics were the one they are arguing about, then Kant's critics would be right, and Kantian ethical theory would be a hopeless enterprise. To begin with, the universalizability test as Kant uses it is never more than a permissibility test for maxims. As such, it cannot be used to ground any positive moral injunctions or any classes of moral duties. The most the test could show, for instance, is that it is wrong to commit suicide or make false promises *on the specific maxims under consideration*. To show this is not to show that there are not other maxims that pass the universalizability test that might involve committing suicide or making a false promise to repay money one has borrowed. In order to show that suicide and false promising are wrong in general using these tests, one would have to show that there is no possible maxim involving these kinds of acts that could be willed as universal laws (or laws of nature). Kant never attempts to do this, nor is there any clear way in which anything of the kind might be done.

Even regarded as a universal criterion of permissibility for any and all maxims, the universalizability tests are systematically subject to counterexamples – not only false positives (maxims that look morally wrong but are able to pass the tests) but also false negatives (morally innocent maxims that cannot pass them). The recipe for a false negative is to formulate any maxim that could not itself without contradiction be a universal law (or law of nature) but which clearly does not violate any universal moral laws on any reasonable construal of what these might be. (Example: "I will give a larger percentage of my income to charity than the average person does.") The recipe for producing a false positive is to formulate a maxim involving a kind of action that is intuitively immoral but specifying the action in terms so specific that even if the maxim were a universal law of nature, that law would very likely have no instances

ALLEN W. WOOD

other than the present (intuitively immoral) action, so that it would be no more difficult for the agent to will the maxim as a universal law than to will this (immoral, but self-serving) action itself.

Self-appointed Kantians strive valiantly to answer these objections, and their stubborn perseverance is such that it would not be possible, especially in the space available here, to answer all the sophistries they have invented in their attempts (pointless as well as fruitless, since what they are defending is not authentic Kantian doctrine anyway) to respond to them. To the problem of false negatives there seems to me no plausible reply at all, since there simply is a whole class of maxims that we must count as permissible that could not themselves be (or be willed as) universal laws. It is hard to believe that Kant was even worried about such maxims when he put forward FUL or FLN, and hence it is only through a strained interpretation of these formulas (motivated by some common but misguided ideas about what a moral principle is for) that one could attribute to him any intention to rule them impermissible. Rather, FUL and FLN are intended, as Kant himself says (G, 4.424), to apply to cases where we want to make exceptions of ourselves, for our own advantage, to moral principles we hope others will follow. None of the false negatives present us with cases of this kind. On the contrary, if I ask myself whether my maxim of giving more of my income to charity than the average person is consistent with a system of universal legislation, and whether in following this maxim I am trying to take advantage of the compliance of others in order to gain special advantages for myself, the answer to the first question is obviously Yes and to the second question it is obviously No. The right conclusion is that if we interpret Kant in such a way that we think any of this makes trouble for him, then we have obviously interpreted him wrongly. It is not that philosophers never make unintended mistakes, but that when an interpretation, not explicit in Kant's text, leads to transparent difficulties, it is a sound hermeneutical practice to reconsider that interpretation.

To the problem of false positives, the obvious remedy would be to specify in some way the kinds of action-descriptions (and the right level of generality) to be used in formulating maxims that are suitable for morally evaluating the actions that fall under them. In order to use FUL and FLN, in other words, we must be careful how we formulate the maxims to be tested, so as to guarantee that the maxim's formulation raises a genuine moral issue. No doubt there are many ways of providing such specifications, but the fact is that FUL and FLN do not provide them, and so they cannot without further ado be employed as universal criteria for the moral permissibility of maxims. (See Wood 1999: 102–7.)

If we look more closely than is customary at Kant's own use of FLN in his four famous examples (G, 4.421–3), we will see that (whatever shortcomings we might find in his discussion) he has carefully avoided both the problems we have just been talking about. He begins: "Now we will enumerate some duties, in accordance with their usual division into duties toward ourselves and toward other human beings, and into perfect and imperfect duties." Since we are focusing on maxims that violate determinate duties, there is no occasion for us to consider any of the maxims that generate the problem of false negatives. The maxims he considers are patently intended to represent typical examples of maxims on which someone might be tempted, quite knowingly, to violate a duty that Kant assumes we will recognize, and recognize to be

296

of a certain kind. This more or less guarantees that the problem of false positives will be avoided, since the duty in question in effect represents a determinate moral principle, which as moral beings we rationally will to hold universally, and the maxim under consideration is formulated so as to represent a determinate principle of action that stands opposed to this moral principle.

Kant even says all this quite explicitly immediately after his discussion of the examples:

> Now if we attend to ourselves in every transgression of a duty, then we find that we do not actually will that our maxim should become a universal law, for that is impossible for us, but rather will that its opposite should remain a law generally; yet we take the liberty of making an exception for ourselves, or (even only for this once) for the advantage of our inclination. (G, 4.424)

The only question is whether these restrictions that Kant intentionally places on his use of FLN are part of his intention in formulating and employing this principle, or rather *ad hoc* and illegitimate. One reason to think they are the former is Kant's own explicit statement, just quoted, in which he describes his purpose in presenting these examples, and with it his understanding of the intended scope of FUL and FLN. To think they are the latter, you need to bring to the text the idea that Kant intends to formulate a universal moral criterion to be used to test the morality of any and all maxims. But some readers think they see an expression of such an intention in the following passage from Section I:

> Thus I need no well-informed shrewdness to know what I have to do in order to make my volition morally good. Inexperienced in regard to the course of the world, incapable of being prepared for all occurrences that might eventuate in it, I ask myself only: Can you will also that your maxim should become a universal law? (G, 4.403)

However, we need to consider carefully the context and aim of this remark. Kant's sole aim in this passage is to draw a clear distinction between the prudential question whether it is safe to make a false promise for immediate gain and the moral question whether it is permissible to do so. He has just been observing that whether it is in our long-term self-interest to make a false promise is often a nice question, hard to decide on account of the conflicting considerations of momentary advantage and possible long-term risk. His point in this remark is that the same subtleties do not afflict the question whether it is morally right to make a false promise, since he thinks it is obvious that we could not rationally will that others should be allowed to perpetrate such deceptions on us, or fail to believe our promises – as they obviously would if everyone were permitted to adopt the policy of making any promise they liked with no intention of keeping it. It is not at all clear, however, that the obvious generalization suggested by Kant's remark is true, or is anything he would want to support. About many decisions made every day in the business world, for example, (in particular, decisions about how far to be wholly frank with people and when to let them act on false beliefs) it is easy to see that these decisions are both safe and profitable, but a subtle and difficult question whether they are morally right. We would seriously misunderstand Kant's ethics if we concluded from this passage that he has some deep theoretical reason for wanting to deny this obvious fact. The fact even further supports his main conclusion by showing another way moral questions can be easily distinguished from prudential questions.

Once we understand Kant's aim in the passage, we can see that it is a serious error to read the remark "I ask myself only: Can you will also that your maxim should become a universal law?" as implying that the criterion implied in this question is intended to be suitable as a universal moral test for all maxims – as if Kant had meant to say instead: "No matter what moral question may come before me, and no matter what possible maxim should cross my mind, all I ever need to do is ask: 'Can I will this maxim to be a universal law?'" Of course Kant never says anything remotely like that, and those who attribute such claims to him, and then seek to evaluate his moral philosophy based on whether they can be sustained, are engaged in an inquiry that is irrelevant to any thoughts Kant himself ever had or expressed.

As I read him, then, Kant intends his four illustrations of FLN to be understood against a background of commonly accepted moral duties, and its universalizability tests to be restricted to maxims formulated in terms that reflect the intentions, and relevant action-descriptions that those duties, and our commonly intelligible motives for violating them, bring readily into view. Of course, even then there may be problems with his reasoning about the particular examples, since the reasoning in each example depends on empirical assumptions (about the natural purpose of self-love, about what people would become aware of, and would consequently do, if they became aware that people would always make false promises to escape pecuniary distress, about our need for the voluntary beneficence of others, and so on), that may be controversial. But to point out that he might rely on dubious empirical assumptions in order to derive practical conclusions from his principle in no way constitutes any challenge to the principle itself. It would be an elementary mistake to think that pure moral principles need no further empirical information for their application. What Kant calls "moral anthropology" treats that empirical discipline as a necessary part of moral philosophy (see chapter 23 below).

We will find further reasons for taking Kant's aims in presenting the four illustrations of FLN to be limited in the ways I have described when we gain a better understanding of the determinate and limited role FUL and FLN are intended to play in Kant's larger search for the supreme principle of morality. To that end, we need to leave FUL behind and move along to FH.

The Second Formula: FH

One of the commonest objections to Kantian ethics is that it is too "formalistic," that its moral principle misguidedly attempts to dispense with all substantive values. A corresponding objection is made to the very idea of a categorical imperative – such a concept is either unintelligible or offensive because it is the notion of a principle that we ought to obey just because we ought, thus a principle with which we could in principle have no reason or motive to comply. It is true, as we have seen, that Kant begins his exposition of the moral principle by considering it from the side of "form." But those who raise the objections just described behave as though they had not read past *G* 4.425. For as soon as he moves beyond his discussion of FUL and FLN, Kant turns from the "form" of the moral principle to its "matter," and in so doing he sets about answering their objections in the most direct manner imaginable. Kant's "formalism" applies only to the first stage of his development of the principle; it is complemented immediately by considering the principle from the opposite "material" point of view, in which Kant inquires after our rational motive for obeying a categorical imperative, and locates this motive in the distinctive value that grounds morality, which he identifies with a kind of *end.* (The "matter" of a concept is its conditions of application to what is given in sensible intuition; the "matter" of a maxim is the end contained in it.)

Yet Kant uses the term "end" broadly in this context, meaning by it any value for the sake of which one acts, or whatever provides the reason or motive for acting. Traditionally, the end of an action is taken to be some object or state of affairs that is to be brought about by the action. Kant follows the tradition in holding that every action must have such an end to be produced. But he departs from it by thinking quite differently about the fundamental end that motivates obedience to a categorical imperative. For if this were an end to be produced, then the bindingness of the imperative on us would be conditional on the desirability for us of that end – which would render the imperative hypothetical. Therefore, the end that grounds a categorical imperative must be of a different kind altogether. Kant first describes such an end by way of mere supposition:

> But suppose there were something *whose existence in itself* had an absolute worth, something that, as an *end in itself,* could be a ground of determinate laws; then in it and only in it alone would lie the ground of a possible categorical imperative, i.e. of a practical law. (G, 4.428)

In other words, the substantive value grounding a categorical imperative cannot be the value of something future to be brought about as a consequence of our obeying it, but rather the value of something already in existence, which grounds our obedience to the imperative because such obedience serves to manifest or express our recognition of that value. Such an existent value is an end in the sense that it is that *for the sake of which* it is rational for us to act.

Kant next presents his thesis in the form of an *assertion*: "Now I say that the human being, and in general every rational being, exists as an end in itself" (G, 4.428). He then proceeds immediately to support the assertion by presenting, first, in a series of arguments eliminating other possible candidates for what might exist as an end in itself: the objects of empirical desires or inclinations, the inclinations themselves, nonrational beings (G, 4.428). He follows this up with a brief, obscure, but crucial positive argument that only "humanity" understood in the technical Kantian sense of rational nature regarded as the capacity to set ends, can qualify as an end in itself: we value our own existence as an end in itself, but we do so *rationally* only insofar as we value the existence of other rational beings in precisely the same way (see Wood 1999: 124–32, and Korsgaard 1996: 106–33). These considerations lead to the second main formulation of the moral law, FH: "*Act so that you use humanity, as much in your own person as in the person of every other, always at the same time as an end, never merely as a means*" (G, 4.429).

Rational nature as an end in itself stands in a determinate relation to all ends to be produced that might fall under the principle of morality. All ends to be produced are set as ends by rational beings, since only rational nature has the capacity to regulate itself by rational norms, the most basic of which is the setting of ends and the selection of means to them (G, 4.437). Morality therefore commands us to seek those ends to be produced the pursuit of which expresses proper respect or esteem for rational nature in the person of some human being or human beings. There are, in Kant's theory, two basic kinds of ends that meet this condition: our own perfection and the happiness of others (MM, 6.386–8, 6.391–4; cf. G, 4.423, 4.430). FH is the formula of the moral law to which Kant most consistently appeals when he derives the duties belonging to the system he expounds in the *Metaphysics of Morals*.

FH also tells us that the motive of duty (discussed only abstractly in Section I of the *Groundwork*) consists in acting out of respect for the worth of rational nature as an end in itself, as it is found in some person or persons. FH is also overwhelmingly the formula appealed to most often when Kant constructs his system of duties in the *Metaphysics of Morals*. In the *Groundwork*, Kant illustrates FH using the same four examples he used to illustrate FLN. I submit that in every case the discussion under FH gives us a clearer and more comprehensive understanding of the duty involved and why the selected maxim violates it. It is therefore indefensible to treat the discussion of the four examples under FLN as definitive of Kant's account of moral reasoning, and this further confirms our assertion that FUL (FLN) are not the definitive forms of the moral law, and they do not provide any sort of basis on which the content of morality is to be constructed.

Further: If the motive to follow the law consists in the worth of rational nature as end in itself, then this, and not the unconditioned goodness of the good will, is the fundamental value on which Kantian ethics rests. Even if the value of the ends we pursue is derived from or conferred on them by our setting them as ends, if this conferred value depends on the objective value of the rational nature that set them, then that value is not conferred by or constructed out of anything, but must be regarded as possessed really and originally by rational nature. Kant does not explicitly address the issues of twentieth century meta-ethics, but the value claims made by FH make it most natural to interpret him as a moral realist, for whom rational nature as end itself is the fundamental value in the world. The unconditional and unlimited value of the good will is in fact best understood in terms of this value, since rational nature actualizes itself as will, and thus the good will is the thing in which the value of rational nature as end in itself is most fully realized.

Third Formula: FA (and FRE)

Kant has now derived two distinct formulas of the supreme principle of morality, both from the concept of a categorical imperative. The first was derived from the concept of a maxim that is compatible with this kind of imperative, and the general form that such a maxim would have to have. The second was derived from the concept of the substantive value (or the end) that could give us a rational ground to follow a categorical imperative. These two lines of argument from the concept of a categorical imperative are quite independent of each other, and lead to distinct formulations of the moral principle, even if (as Kant thinks) there is no conflict between these distinct formulas, and they can be treated as merely different ways of expressing "precisely the same law" (G, 4.436). Kant's next step, however, is to combine the two ideas behind these first two formulas to derive a third formula:

> The ground of all practical legislation, namely, lies *objectively in the rule* and the form of universality, which makes it capable of being a law (at least a law of nature) (in accordance with the first principle), but *subjectively* it lies in the *end*; but the subject of all ends is every rational being as an end in itself (in accordance with the second principle): from this now follows the third practical principle of the will, as the supreme condition of its harmony with universal practical reason, the idea of the *will of every rational being as a will giving universal law.* (G, 4.431)

The third formula combines the conception of a law valid universally for all rational beings (in FUL) with the conception of every rational nature as having absolute worth, to get the idea of the will of every rational being as the source of a universally valid legislation. The term "idea" used in this formulation should be understood in Kant's technical sense: an "idea" (*Idee*) is a concept of reason to which no empirical object can ever correspond, but which we use regulatively in arranging our cognitions in a system (*CPR*, B 368–77, B 670–732). Thus to regard the legislator of the moral law as the *idea* of the will of every rational being is not to say that the law is given by your arbitrary will or mine (for our wills are corrupt and fallible), but rather that the law is regarded as having been legislated by each of our wills insofar as it corresponds to an ideal rational concept of what it ought to be (but always falls short of being).

FA is also stated this way: "Do not choose otherwise than so that the maxims of one's choice are at the same time comprehended with it in the same volition as universal law" (G, 4.440). Or again: "Act in accordance with maxims that can at the same time have themselves as universal laws of nature for their object" (G, 4.437). In these formulations, FA may sound superficially like FUL (or FLN), but in fact it is a formula quite distinct from either of them, making a much stronger demand on maxims and yielding much stronger conclusions about what we ought to do. Where FUL and FLN provide a mere condition of permissibility for maxims, consisting in its being *possible* (without contradiction or conflicting volitions) for you to will the maxim as a universal law, FA tells you *positively to follow* those maxims which *actually contain in themselves the volition* that they should be universal laws. FUL (or respectively, FLN) counts a maxim as permissible if there would be no contradiction or conflicting volitions in willing it to be a universal law (or law of nature); but a maxim might pass this purely negative test without containing in itself the volition that it should actually be a universal law (or law of nature). So the criterion on maxims proposed in FA is significantly stronger than the criteria of universalizability proposed in either FUL or FLN. And it justifies a correspondingly stronger conclusion about maxims, telling us not merely which ones are permissible and which not, but also which ones we have a positive duty to adopt because they are part of a system of universal moral legislation given by our own rational will.

Of course FA does not pretend to offer us any *test* to discriminate maxims that have this property from maxims that do not. But as I have already said, it would be error to think that the universalizability tests present in FUL or FLN are intended (even as permissibility tests) to apply to all conceivable maxims, so there is really nothing they can do that FA cannot. Both FUL and FA, rather, should be seen as indicating the spirit of a universal moral principle, and defining a task for reasoning: namely, in the case of FUL, that of deciding which maxims are compatible with a system of universal law (which maxims do not violate the laws of such a system), or, in the case of FA, which ones belong to that system as part of its actual legislation as given by the idea of the will of every rational being.

FA is arrived at by combining FUL with FH: The idea of universal law is combined with the value of a rational will that is suitable for legislating such a law. Kant writes:

> The three ways mentioned of representing the principle of morality are, however, fundamentally only so many formulas of precisely the same law, one of which unites the other two in itself [*deren die eine die anderen zwei von selbst in sich vereinigt*]. (G, 4.436)

This is often mistranslated so that it is read as suggesting something like a demonstrable equivalence among the duties imposed by the three formulas, or even that each must somehow be deducible from one or both of the other two. Not only would it be futile to attempt such deductions or equivalence proofs, but even tolerating the demand for them involves a basic misunderstanding of what Kant is saying. For it is only of FA that Kant ever explicitly claims that it unites the other two in itself; no such claim is ever made about FUL or FH. Consequently, I think we should regard FA as having a special status among the three formulas: FA is the formula that unites and sums up the others. It should be regarded as the definitive formulation of the principle of morality, insofar as there is one. FA is the formula in which Kant's search for the moral law culminates, and which serves to summarize the system of all the formulas.

Just as Kant earlier provided a more "intuitive" version of FUL in the form of FLN, so here he also provides a more intuitive variant of FA, the Formula of the Realm of Ends (FRE): "Act in accordance with maxims of a universally legislative member for a merely possible realm of ends" (G, 4.439). FRE provides a new characterization of the system of legislation referred to in FA, by describing the nature of the community that is to result from it. It calls this community a "realm of ends" (*Reich der Zwecke*). By a "realm" Kant means "a systematic combination of various rational beings through communal laws," or again, "a whole of all ends in systematic connection" (G, 4.433). In other words, a collection of ends constitutes a "realm" if these ends are not in conflict or competition with one another, but are combined into a mutually supporting system. The laws of a realm of ends are those which, if followed, would bring the ends of rational beings (both the existent ends which are the rational beings themselves according to FH, and the ends set in the maxims chosen by those rational beings) into a mutually supporting harmony with each other. FRE commands us to follow maxims involving ends that belong to this mutually supporting system, and forbids us to adopt ends that fall outside it.

Kant sometimes looks upon this system (or "realm") of ends as something like a single over-arching end, and thinks of following the principle of morality (as formulated in FRE) as joining with others in the shared pursuit of this collective end (or system of ends). The key terms Kant uses to express this idea are "system" (*System*) and "combination" (*Verbindung*). Thus at the conclusion of the *Anthropology*, he speaks of human progress from evil towards good as achievable only "through progressive organization of citizens of the earth in and to the species as one system, cosmopolitically combined" (*APS*, 7.333). Kant's two main conceptions of what it is to act empirically according to the idea of a realm of ends are the relation of friendship, in which the happiness of both friends is "swallowed up" in a common end which includes the good of both, and the religious community, which in Kant's view should be bound together fundamentally not by creeds or scriptural traditions but by the shared pursuit of the highest good as a common end. In this way FRE gives absolute priority to the notion of community and corrects a common view of Kant's ethics as essentially individualistic (see Wood 1999: 274–82, 309–20).

FRE also gives priority to securing human community or harmony over maximizing human welfare or satisfaction. We should avoid all patterns of end-setting that involve fundamentally competitive relations between different rational beings, and we are forbidden to engage with others in ways that require the frustration of some people's deepest ends. Conflict or competition between human ends is permissible only if it is in service of a deeper systematic unity among all human ends, a system in which no member of the realm of ends is left out. The moral law commands us, in other words, to seek only that degree and kind of welfare for ourselves, and for others, that can be made to cohere with and support everyone's pursuit of the common welfare of all. If this means less total welfare than could be gotten by permitting fundamental conflicts between the ends of different rational beings, then lesser, not greater, total welfare is what the moral law commands us to seek.

The System of Formulas and the "Universal" Formula

At *Groundwork* 4.436 Kant presents the three formulas as a "system," organized by the triad "form," "matter," "complete determination." The "complete determination" of a concept consists in its containing one member of every pair of contradictories, which makes it (according to Leibnizian doctrine) the concept of an individual thing rather than the abstract concept of a universal. I suggest that the analogy to this in the formulation of the moral law is the completeness of an entire system of legislation. FUL provides the common "form" of any maxim that makes it compatible with the laws of this system, FH specifies the "matter" or end for the sake of which we act in following these moral laws; FA now represents the moral law *as* a universal system of legislation, specifying its source in every rational will as self-legislative, and also (through FRE) its result: a systematic harmony between all the morally legitimate aims of rational beings, who are conceived of as combined into an ideal self-legislating community. The system also proceeds, as Kant says, in a manner analogous to the progression of the categories of quantity. For with FUL it begins with the *unity* of form possessed by all morally permissible maxims, proceeds from there to the *plurality* of ends in themselves (or rational beings), and then (by combining these two, as the concepts of unity and plurality are combined in the concept of totality) culminates in the idea of the rational will as self-legislative and the idea of the *totality* of moral laws in the system of legislation that proceeds from this ideal will.

In presenting the formulas systematically, Kant chooses the more "intuitive" variants of the first and third formulas (FLN and FRE) over the more abstract ones. He does this, he says, because "if one wants to obtain access for the moral law, then it is very useful to take one and the same action through the three named concepts and, as far as may be done, to bring the action nearer to intuition" (G, 4.436–7). However, one does better in moral judging always to proceed in accordance with the strict method and take as a ground the universal formula of the categorical imperative: "*Act in accordance with that maxim which can at the same time make itself into universal law*" (G, 4.436).

The main point Kant is making here is that the way of thinking (closer to "intuition") that is best for animating human hearts and actions on behalf of morality is not the same as the way of thinking that is best when it comes time to pass critical judgment either on the actions we have performed or on the maxims we are proposing to adopt. For this latter task, a more austere and abstract principle is better, because, corrupt human nature being what it is, the same feelings and intuitions that make us enthusiastic friends of virtue also make us more susceptible to self-deception and more likely to pass off corrupt actions and maxims to ourselves as morally commendable ones. (In other words, those sentimentalists who think that what satisfies the heart, but not the head, represents greater moral purity, have things exactly wrong: where the head has been corrupted, it was the heart that corrupted it; and the first remedy for the corruption of our hearts is to learn to think in an enlightened way, with our heads, about what to do, and which feelings we should allow to influence us.)

But what are we to make of his reference here to "the universal formula of the categorical imperative"? Many scholars suppose, almost without thinking, that the "universal formula" is to be identified with FUL (see Paton 1947: 130; O'Neill 1989: 127; Guyer 1998: 216.) Henry Allison claims (in Guyer 1998) that at this point "The categorical imperative is thus only a single one and specifically [FUL]," but this is massively contradicted by Kant's going on to formulate the principle in four other ways. It seems more reasonable to take Kant to mean that the categorical imperative is that "precisely same law" which receives variant formulations in the ensuing pages. Which formulation deserves to be considered the "universal formula" has surely not been decided at this point.

In an article in *Mind* written over 60 years ago, Klaus Reich made the interesting suggestion that this is none of the three (or five) "particular" formulas derived so far, but is a distinct sixth formula (Reich 1939: 452–3). Above we have followed Reich provisionally to the extent of stating this formula separately as "FU." But Reich's suggestion raises the question where this new formula is supposed to have come from, and in what way it is more "general" (or "universal") than the formulas that have already been derived and explained. Surely it is more natural to suppose, as the most common interpretation does, that FU is one of the formulas already derived. The question is: Which one?

Since, as we have seen, the system of formulas as a whole culminates in FA, and since it is the one in which the other two are combined, I suggest that FA is the most natural candidate for FU. For one thing, the "universal" formula occurs in the same paragraph devoted to FRE (which is the more "intuitive" version of FA). Then too, as we have seen, FA is the formula that combines the other two in itself, and in which, in that sense, the search for the supreme principle of morality culminates. But the best reason is found simply in what the "universal formula" *says*: It tells us to act on that maxim that can *make itself* into a universal law. If a maxim "can make itself into a universal law" by "containing in itself the volition that it should be a universal law," then this makes the "universal formula" equivalent to FA in several of its formulations.

FU bears a distinct resemblance to the definitive formulations of the moral law that are presented (as already having been derived) in the *Critique of Practical Reason* (FK) and the *Metaphysics of Morals* (FM). These two formulas are also best understood as formulas of FA. They are equivalent to it if what it takes for a maxim to be able to hold or be valid (*gelten*) as a universal law is that it should contain in itself the volition that it be a universal law. Further, FK in the *Critique of Practical Reason* is said reciprocally to imply freedom of the will (*CPrR*, 5.28–30), but FA is the only formula in the *Groundwork* about which this claim is made (*G*, 4.446–9). So that is another reason for thinking that FU is FA.

Conclusion

Our main conclusions, then, can be summarized as follows:

1. FUL (FLN) is *not* the definitive statement of the moral law. These formulas could not in any case serve as a general moral criterion for the permissibility of maxims, still less could the content of morality be "constructed" using some "categorical imperative (CI-)procedure" conceived in terms of them. If we are to understand anything at all about Kantian ethics, we must unlearn the false idea that Kant's principle of morality should be associated with anything like the universalizability tests or the thought that what is right in every situation can be determined by asking "What if everybody did that?"

2. Kant's own favored formula when he derives specific duties in the *Metaphysics of Morals* is not FUL but FH. However, it also provides no general test of maxims, but only identifies the fundamental value for the sake of which we act in obeying a categorical imperative. If, again, we are to understand the first thing about Kantian ethics, we must unlearn the false idea that a categorical imperative is a principle which is to be obeyed just because it is to be obeyed, and not because of any substantive value. On the contrary, the categorical imperative is grounded on the absolute worth of rational nature as an end in itself, and the dignity of the rational will as self-legislating.

3. If there is such a thing as a definitive statement of the moral law, it is FA (FRE). But neither FA nor FRE provide us with anything resembling a general test of maxims that could be used in the way that FUL (FLN) are frequently thought to do. Kantian ethics does not provide, and does not even try to provide, any such test or criterion. On the contrary, Kant's ethical theory in the *Metaphysics of Morals* rests on a taxonomy of duties: juridical and ethical, perfect (or narrow, or strictly owed) and imperfect (or wide, or meritorious), to oneself and to others. The system of duties leaves a good deal of latitude to individual agents in choosing the ends on which they will base their lives, but it underwrites the pursuit of ends that involve one's own perfection and the happiness of others.

If we are to understand properly the spirit of Kantian ethics, and the aim of his formulations of the moral law, then in one respect we must learn to ask far less of a "supreme principle of morality" than moral philosophers often assume we must ask. The function of a supreme principle of morality, then, is *not* to tell us directly, from day to day and minute to minute, through some uniform canonical process of moral reasoning to be applied in exactly the same way to all situations, exactly which actions we should (and should not) be performing and precisely how we should be spending our time.

On the other hand, if we are to follow the spirit of Kantian ethics, we must also learn in another respect to ask a lot more of the supreme principle of morality than moral philosophers often do. Analytical philosophers often aim at producing moral principles that may be very complex in structure, full of sub-clauses and qualifications, because these principles enable them to capture "our moral intuitions" and the precisely worded epicyclical subclauses enable us to deal cleverly with threatened counterexamples of various kinds. (Kant's Formulas of Universal Law and the Law of Nature, when subjected to sophisticated interpretations that are intended to deal with all the trouble-some counterexamples, are easily perverted into principles of this kind.) The resulting principles, however, often do more to disguise than to clarify the fundamental value basis on which moral decisions are to be made.

Kant's own formulations of the moral law aim, by contrast, at precisely that sort of clarification. The correct interpretation of Kant's formulation of the supreme principle of morality exhibits the principle as concerned not with devising a "CI" decision proce-dure, or a ravishingly subtle and clever calculus leading to the choices that agree with our "intuitions," but rather with stating the ultimate value on which moral rules and duties may be grounded. If those values have been convincingly displayed and argued for, and what they dictate comes into conflict with what we euphemistically call our moral "intuitions," then a proper exposition and defense of the supreme principle of morality ought to give us reason to abandon or revise our moral tradition, education and prejudice and turn it into something sounder and more rational.

References and Further Reading

Aune, Bruce (1979). *Kant's Theory of Morals*. Princeton: Princeton University Press. (See esp. chs. 2–4.)

Duncan, A. R. C. (1957). *Practical Reason and Morality*. London: Thomas Nelson and Sons. (see esp. chs. 7, 8, 10, and 11.)

Guyer, Paul (2000). *Kant on Freedom, Law and Happiness*. Cambridge: Cambridge University Press. (See esp. chs. 5 and 6.)

Guyer, Paul, ed. (1998). *Groundwork of the Metaphysics of Morals: Critical Essays*. Lanham, MD: Rowman and Littlefield.

Herman, Barbara (1993). *The Practice of Moral Judgment*. Cambridge, MA: Harvard University Press. (See esp. chs. 4–7.)

Hill, Thomas E., Jr. (1992). *Dignity and Practical Reason*. Ithaca, NY: Cornell University Press. (See esp. chs. 2, 3, and 5.)

Höffe, Otfried, ed. (1989). *Grundlegung zur Metaphysik der Sitten: Ein kooperativer Kommentar* [*Groundwork of the Metaphysics of Morals*: A Co-operative Commentary]. Frankfurt: Vittorio Klostermann. (See esp. the essays by Pogge and Rossvaer.)

Kagan, Shelly (2002). Kantianism for consequentialists. In Immanuel Kant, *Groundwork for the Metaphysics of Morals*, ed. and tr. Allen W. Wood. New Haven: Yale University Press.

Kant, Immanuel (1996). *Critique of Practical Reason. Groundwork of the Metaphysics of Morals. Metaphysics of Morals.* In *Practical Philosophy*, ed. and tr. Mary J. Gregor. Cambridge: Cambridge University Press.

Korsgaard, Christine M. (1996). *Creating the Kingdom of Ends.* Cambridge: Cambridge University Press. (See esp. chs. 2, 3, 4, 6, and 7.)

Nell (O'Neill), Onora (1975). *Acting on Principle.* New York: Columbia University Press. (See esp. ch. 5.)

O'Neill, Onora (1989). *Constructions of Reason.* Cambridge: Cambridge University Press.

Paton, H. J. (1947). *The Categorical Imperative.* London: Hutchison & Co. (See esp. chs. 13–18.)

Rawls, John (2000). *Lectures on the History of Moral Philosophy*, ed. Barbara Herman. Cambridge: Harvard University Press. (See esp. lectures II–IV and VI.)

Reich, Klaus (1939). Kant and Greek ethics. (Tr. W. H. Walsh.) *Mind*, 48.

Schneewind, J. B. (1992). Autonomy, obligation and virtue: An overview of Kant's moral philosophy. In P. Guyer (ed.), *The Cambridge Companion to Kant*, 1st ed. (pp. 309–41). New York: Cambridge University Press.

Sullivan, Roger (1989). *Immanuel Kant's Moral Theory.* Cambridge: Cambridge University Press. (See esp. chs. 11–15.)

Wood, Allen W. (1999). *Kant's Ethical Thought.* New York: Cambridge University Press. (See esp. chs. 2–5.)

Wood, Allen W. (2001). The moral law as a system of formulas. In H. Stolzenberg and H. F. Fulda (eds.), *Architektur und System in der Philosophie Kants.* Hamburg: Felix Meiner Verlag.

Wood, Allen W. (2004). The supreme principle of morality. In P. Guyer (ed.), *The Cambridge Companion to Kant*, 2nd ed. (pp. 394–416). New York: Cambridge University Press.

20

Deriving the Formula of Universal Law

SAMUEL J. KERSTEIN

In the *Groundwork of the Metaphysics of Morals*, Kant strives to locate and to establish the supreme principle of morality (G, 4.392). He devotes Sections I–II largely to the first goal. Working under the assumption that there is a supreme principle of morality, he tries to locate it in the sense of specifying its content. Kant attempts to find the supreme principle that, on reflection, we hold to be at work in our moral practice. This principle, Kant believes, is the categorical imperative. In *Groundwork* I–II, Kant tries to show that if there is a supreme principle of morality, then it is this imperative, or something equivalent. Not until *Groundwork* III does he try to establish the categorical imperative, that is, to prove that we are all rationally compelled to conform to it.

This chapter focuses on Kant's *Groundwork* I attempt to locate the categorical imperative, and does not address a parallel effort Kant makes in *Groundwork* II (G, 4.420–1). In the idiom of contemporary Kant scholarship such an attempt is called a "derivation" of the categorical imperative. In *Groundwork* I Kant derives one particular formulation of the categorical imperative, namely a version of his famous Formula of Universal Law (FUL): "act only on that maxim through which you can at the same time will that it become a universal law" (G, 4.420–1). According to the reading dominant in contemporary Anglo-American Kant scholarship, this derivation contains an obvious and obviously significant gap, and therefore fails miserably. This chapter contains a different reading of the derivation, one according to which it turns out to be a stronger and more philosophically interesting argument than the dominant interpretation implies.

I

Kant's *Groundwork* I derivation of the FUL culminates in the following passage:

> But what kind of law can that be, the representation of which must determine the will, even without regard for the effect expected from it, in order for the will to be called good absolutely and without limitation? Since I have deprived the will of every impulse that could arise for it from obeying some law, nothing is left but the conformity of actions to universal law as such, which alone is to serve the will as its principle, that is, I *ought never*

to act except in such a way that I could also will that my maxim *should become a universal law*. (*G*, 4.402; translations from Kant 1996a and 1996b)

According to the received view, this derivation contains a fatal gap. Kant embraces a principle that is, for practical purposes, rather empty. Without argument, he then jumps from this principle to a version of the FUL as the only viable candidate for the supreme principle of morality.

Bruce Aune has offered an influential expression of the dominant view. In the very sentence in which Kant sets out for the first time the FUL, he says that "nothing is left but the conformity of actions to universal law as such, which alone is to serve the will as its principle" (*G*, 4.402). According to Aune this amounts to Kant's embracing the principle L: Conform your actions to universal law (Aune 1979: 28–9). Kant, Aune says, jumps directly from L to the FUL: "act only on that maxim through which you can at the same time will that it should become a universal law." Kant assumes that "we conform to universal law (and so satisfy L) just when we obey [the FUL] and act only on maxims that we can will to be universal laws" (Aune 1979: 30; see also 32 and 86–7).

Yet, notes Aune, this assumption is highly questionable, as it is easy to illustrate. Kant holds that in acting on a maxim of nonbeneficence, for example, "In order to maximize my happiness, I will refrain from helping others in need," I would be violating the FUL (*G*, 4.423). Suppose Kant is right about this. According to the assumption in question, then, in acting on this maxim, I would not be conforming to universal law: to a principle that is necessarily binding on all of us. But it is unclear why I would not be. For all Kant has shown thus far, it could be that a principle necessarily binding on all of us is: "Always do what you believe will maximize your own happiness." In acting on my maxim of nonbeneficence, I could be conforming to this universal law. Kant, Aune suggests, embraces L as the basic requirement of moral action, and so affirms that if there is such a thing as moral action, then it is action conforming to universal law. But then, without argument, Kant jumps to the conclusion that the only way for an action to conform to universal law is for it to conform to the FUL. The gap Aune finds in Kant's *Groundwork* I derivation is between the, for practical purposes, rather uninformative principle L and the FUL (Aune 1979: 34).

Aune is far from alone. Several other philosophers, even some sympathetic to a Kantian approach in ethics, have claimed to find a gap of this sort. (See, for example, Allison 1996: 144, 150; Hill 1992: 121–2; Wood 1999: 47–9, 81–2.)

II

According to the reading I wish to defend, Kant's *Groundwork* I derivation of the FUL takes place in three main steps. First, he tries to pinpoint criteria that we, on reflection, believe that the supreme principle of morality must fulfill. Second, Kant attempts to establish that no possible rival to the FUL fulfills all of these criteria. Third, at least implicitly, Kant argues that the FUL remains as a viable candidate for a principle that fulfills all of them. With these three steps, Kant strives to prove that if there is a supreme principle of morality, then it is this formula. In short, Kant argues by elimination.

When we have before us a clear notion of the characteristics the supreme principle of morality must possess, Kant suggests, we are able to eliminate every candidate for this principle except the FUL or equivalent principles. I call this interpretation of Kant's derivation the "criterial reading," since it emphasizes that Kant develops criteria that any viable candidate for the supreme principle of morality must fulfill.

From the very outset of the *Groundwork*, Kant suggests that the supreme principle of morality would have to fulfill *four* criteria. According to what I call Kant's basic concept, the supreme principle of morality must be practical, absolutely necessary, binding on all rational agents, and serve as the supreme norm for the moral evaluation of action. I call this concept of the supreme principle of morality basic because Kant suggests it in the *Groundwork*'s Preface.

To say that a principle must be the supreme norm for the moral assessment of action suggests several things. The principle would obviously distinguish between morally permissible and morally impermissible actions as well as specify which actions are morally required. In addition, whether an action was morally good would depend on how it related to this principle. Kant implies, for example, that no action that violated the principle would count as morally valuable (G, 4.390). Finally, as the supreme norm for the moral assessment of action, the supreme principle of morality would be such that all genuine duties would ultimately be derived from it (see G, 4.421, 4.424, 4.425). The supreme principle would justify these duties' status as such.

Kant says that the supreme principle of morality "must hold not only for human beings but for all *rational beings as such*" (G, 4.408; see also G, 4.389, CPrR, 5.32). This principle would have an extremely wide scope: one that extended not only to all rational human beings, but to all other rational beings, if any others exist, for example, to God, angels, and intelligent extraterrestrials.

A third feature the supreme principle of morality would have to possess is that of absolute necessity (G, 4.389). For every agent within its scope, that is for Kant every rational agent, the principle would hold without exception (G, 4.408). For us, human agents, the supreme principle of morality would be an unconditional command, that is, a categorical imperative in one sense of the term. That we were obligated to perform the action it specified would not be conditional on our having any particular set of desires.

Finally, for Kant the supreme principle of morality must be practical, that is, a rule on account of which agents can act. Kant implies this in the *Groundwork* Preface by specifying that morally good actions involve an agent's acting for the sake of the moral law, that is, the supreme principle of morality (G, 4.390). For Kant the supreme principle must be able to figure directly in an agent's practical deliberations.

Central to the criterial reading is the idea that in *Groundwork* I Kant sets out further criteria for the supreme principle of morality. In order for this reading to constitute a successful alternative to the dominant one, this idea needs to be grounded in the text. In section III, below, I therefore explore at length the three "propositions" Kant there develops. I try to show that each of them contains a criterion for the supreme principle of morality.

Anchoring the criterial reading in the text also involves offering an alternative to the received interpretation's construal of the statement that immediately precedes the introduction of the FUL. Kant says:

Since I have deprived the will of every impulse that could arise for it from obeying some law, nothing is left but the conformity of actions to universal law as such, which alone is to serve the will as its principle. (*G*, 4.402)

In section IV I make a brief attempt to demonstrate that, contrary to the received view, Kant's text does not require us to interpret him here to be embracing the relatively empty principle "Conform your actions to universal law."

While sections III–IV aim to show that the criterial reading is textually plausible, the last two sections of this chapter probe the strength of the derivation, as the criterial reading interprets it. Section V attempts to illustrate that this reading renders Kant's derivation more philosophically forceful than does the received interpretation. On the latter interpretation, the derivation does nothing to eliminate consequentialist rivals; on the former it suggests a simple but forceful argument against them. But as I point out in section VI, the derivation nevertheless suffers from a serious shortcoming. It fails to eliminate some striking rivals to the FUL. Following a suggestion by Kant, we might mitigate this shortcoming by adding a criterion for the supreme principle of morality to those implicit in Kant's propositions. Unfortunately, as section VI concludes, it is far from clear that FUL itself fulfills this additional criterion.

III

In his *Groundwork* I derivation of the FUL, Kant develops three propositions, each of which in my view contains a criterion for the supreme principle of morality. The best way to shed light on the plausibility of this view is to examine what the propositions mean and how Kant arrives at them.

It makes sense to begin with Kant's first proposition. It is not explicitly stated but is widely, and I believe correctly, taken to be the following: An action has moral worth if and only if it is done from duty.

As a first step towards understanding this proposition we need to delve briefly into Kant's famous discussion of a good will. Kant tells us that the concept of duty "contains that of a good will though under certain subjective limitations and hindrances" (*G*, 4.397). Let us focus on Kant's discussion of the good will as it relates to us, agents who can indulge their inclinations and thereby act contrary to what morality requires. In this context, Kant seems to use the notion of a good will in two ways. According to the first usage, a good will is a particular sort of willing or, what for him amounts to the same thing, of acting. Kant writes of "the unqualified [*uneingeschränkten*] worth of actions" (*G*, 4.411). These are presumably actions done from duty; for he has earlier stated that actions from duty have "unconditional and moral worth" (*G*, 4.400). Since, according to Kant, the good will is good without qualification [*ohne Einschränkung*], it appears that sometimes "good will" refers to a certain kind of action, that is, action done from duty.

According to a second usage of "good will," it refers not to a particular kind of action an agent might perform but rather to a kind of character she might have. An agent has a good will on this usage, I believe, just in case she is committed to doing what duty requires, not just in this or that particular action but overall. If an agent

311

has this commitment, then she will presumably sometimes act from duty. She will for example invoke duty as her incentive to do what is morally required in cases in which she is tempted by her inclinations to act contrary to what morality demands. Kant intimates that having a good will amounts to having a certain kind of character in the first paragraph of *Groundwork* I (*G*, 4.393; see also *G*, 4.398–9).

Kant's "particular action" conception of a good will is more important for our purposes. Kant suggests that a good will in the sense of good willing is equivalent to acting from duty. And, according to "common understanding" (*G*, 4.394), this willing, or acting, has a special, moral worth. First, it is unconditionally good. In all possible circumstances in which it appears, a good will is not only good, but also has the same level of goodness. Even if a good will

> should wholly lack the capacity to carry out its purpose – if with its greatest efforts it should yet achieve nothing and only the good will were left . . . then, like a jewel, it would still shine by itself, as something that has its full worth in itself. (*G*, 4.394)

Second, according to ordinary moral thinking, the worth of a good will is especially high. We take a good will to be preeminently valuable (see *G*, 4.394 and 4.401). That presumably implies that no particular action that is not done from duty is as valuable as any action that is done from duty.

Let us now return to Kant's first proposition. It states that an action has moral worth if and only if it is done from duty or, equivalently, that all and only actions done from duty have moral worth. The two key concepts in this proposition are obviously those of moral worth and of acting from duty. Moral worth, as we just noted, is unconditional and preeminent worth. At this stage in his argument, Kant does not explain precisely what acting from duty amounts to. But from the *Groundwork*'s Preface, it is easy to discern the basic idea he, and presumably his readers, have in mind. Acting from duty is doing something "for the sake of" the moral law (*G*, 4.390). In other words, to act from duty is to do something because a valid moral principle, or at least a principle one takes to be valid, prescribes that one do it. A more rigorous account of acting from duty emerges from Kant's discussion of his third proposition.

In the *Groundwork*, Kant apparently finds it unnecessary to argue that all actions done from duty possess moral worth. But he thinks we need help in order to discern that only actions from duty have moral worth. He highlights two conditions on actions with such worth, both of which he takes to be accepted by common rational moral cognition. He then intimates that no action from inclination could meet these conditions.

Kant introduces the first condition in the *Groundwork* Preface:

> in the case of what is to be morally good, it is not enough that it *conform* with the moral law; but it must also be done *for the sake of the law*; without this, that conformity is only very contingent and precarious, since a ground that is not moral will indeed now and then produce actions in conformity with the law, but it will also often produce actions contrary to the law. (*G*, 4.390)

The claim is that morally valuable action is action done from a motive that will not produce actions contrary to duty. Kant maintains that acting "for the sake of the law," that is, doing something because it is required by moral principle, meets this condition, while acting from inclination does not. Kant invokes this condition in his famous discussion of the "philanthropist" (or "friend of humanity") (G, 4.398). The philanthropist has an inclination to promote the well-being of others. But, according to Kant, acting from this inclination is like acting from the inclination to honor, "which, if it fortunately lights upon what is in fact in the common interest and in conformity with duty and hence honourable, deserves praise and encouragement but not esteem . . ." (G, 4.398, see also RBR, 6.30–1). Here Kant suggests the possibility that in acting from an inclination to help others, that is, from sympathy, an agent might do something that conflicts with duty.

In his discussion of the philanthropist Kant points to a further condition he places on an action's having moral worth (Herman 1993: 5–6). Kant says that the maxim on which the philanthropist acts "lacks moral content, namely that of doing such actions not from inclination but from duty" (G, 4.398). Kant does not tell us explicitly what the philanthropist's maxim is, but we can assume that it is something like the following: "Because I want to help others, I will promote their happiness." This maxim, says Kant, lacks moral content, and it is not hard to pinpoint a reason why. The maxim reflects no commitment to the action's being morally permissible, that is, in accordance with what moral principle requires. According to Kant's view of ordinary moral understanding the grounds of a morally valuable action, that is, its motive, must express an interest in the action's moral rightness. This is the second condition that any action having moral worth must fulfill. Kant holds that actions done from duty fulfill both this condition and the previous one, while actions from inclination do not.

Kant's first proposition and his defense of it have attracted ample critical attention. Kant is perhaps too quick to conclude that, according to common rational moral cognition, an action has moral worth only if it fulfills his two conditions and thus only if it is done from duty. He might also be precipitate in assuming widespread endorsement of the notion that all actions from duty have moral worth. My own view (Kerstein 2002: 114–38) is that Kant is on much stronger ground in claiming that, according to common rational moral cognition, *all* actions from duty have moral worth than he is in claiming that *only* actions from duty have moral worth.

The arguments Kant suggests for the second and third propositions are far less directly tied to intuitive moral judgments than his arguments for the first. In his "second proposition," Kant says that

> an action from duty has its moral worth *not in the purpose* to be attained by it but in the maxim in accordance with which it is decided upon, and therefore does not depend upon the realization of the object of the action but merely upon the *principle of volition* in accordance with which the action is done . . . (G, 4.399–400)

Later Kant says that "the moral worth of an action does not lie in the effect expected from it" (G, 4.401; see also G, 4.435).

Kant here invokes the notion of a principle of volition or maxim. We have already made use of this notion, but it makes sense to pause here to get a more precise idea of what a maxim is. The brief account of maxims that follows is certainly not the only plausible one, but it will serve to fix ideas. A maxim is a "subjective principle of acting"

(G, 4.421n; see also G, 4.400n). It is a subjective principle in that it is held by some agent, it can be freely adopted or discarded by her, and it applies only to her own actions. An agent's maxims are principles of acting in that they play a role in the generation of her actions. An agent acts on maxims. When fully specified, a maxim includes a description of a kind of action to be performed in a kind of situation, as well as a specification of the agent's end and his incentive in performing it. An example of a fully specified maxim is the following: "From self-love, during my free time I exercise in order to stay in shape." Self-love is the agent's incentive; staying in shape is her end. According to Kant, whenever an agent acts, she does so on some maxim, even though she might not have it explicitly in view.

Kant's second proposition says essentially that an action done from duty derives its moral worth from its maxim rather than from its effects. The proposition relies on a distinction between an action, always done on some maxim, and its effects. For Kant, to act is to exercise one's will (Kerstein 2002: 20–1). It is to try, based on some principle of volition, to realize a state of affairs (an object or end). This state of affairs, or whatever actually results from the action, is an effect of the willing. Acting consists in the willing itself, not in its effects (see G, 4.400). According to the second proposition, it is the maxim behind an action done from duty that gives it moral value, rather than the action's results.

Implicit in Groundwork I is a straightforward argument for the second proposition. Suppose that, contrary to it, the moral worth of an action from duty did stem from its effects. There would, then, be possible circumstances in which an action from duty did not have moral worth, namely ones in which the action failed to produce certain effects. For Kant, however, if an action is done from duty, then it has moral worth no matter what the circumstances may be. His first proposition incorporates this view. Moral worth is, for Kant, "unconditional" (G, 4.400). Therefore, as the second proposition indicates, the moral worth of an action from duty does not stem from its effects.

According to Kant's third proposition, "duty is the necessity of an action from respect for law" (G, 4.400, emphasis omitted). This proposition fills in some details regarding what it means for an action to be done from duty. According to the proposition, if an action is done from duty, then what determines it is "objectively the law and subjectively pure respect for this practical law, and so the maxim of complying with such a law even if it infringes upon all my inclinations" (G, 4.400–1). By "law" here, Kant means a universally binding and absolutely necessary practical principle. When an agent acts from duty, Kant here suggests, his action stems from the notion, incorporated into his maxim, that a practical law requires it. Kant even says that "an action from duty is to put aside entirely the influence of inclination" (G, 4.400). So, in his view, an agent who needs to rely on an inclination in order to get something done fails to act from duty. If an agent acts from duty, the notion that a law requires her action itself generates enough motivation for her to do it. It generates this motivation at least in part by producing in her a feeling of respect for the law. Kant develops his complex concept of respect in detail in the Critique of Practical Reason (CPrR, 5.71–89) and we have no need to explore it here. But we do need to hold in view that, according to Kant's third proposition, when an agent acts from duty, her notion that her action is required by a practical law provides her with sufficient motive for doing it. In other words, this notion gives her a ground sufficient to determine her will.

314

How does Kant defend this proposition? In my view he suggests, but does not explicitly offer, the following argument (see G, 4.401). Suppose that in an action done from duty the notion that the action was required by a practical law did not give an agent sufficient motive to perform it. In that case, Kant suggests, the additional motive necessary for the agent to perform the action would have to be the agent's expectation that her action would bring about certain effects (G, 4.401). But now further suppose that the action did not produce the expected effects. In that case, the agent would be rationally compelled to agree that the action had less value than it would have had if the expected effects had occurred. After all, if, in the agent's view, the action's value was not at all contingent on the effects being produced, then why would she need to acquire part of her motivation for doing it from the prospect that the effects would be produced? But if an action done from duty has less value than it otherwise would have as a result of its not producing certain effects, then its value is not unconditional. And this result conflicts with Kant's first proposition, according to which all actions have moral worth, that is, the same high degree of value in every possible situation in which they occur. The result also conflicts with his second proposition, since according to it the moral worth of an action does not depend at all on the action's effects. So it makes sense for Kant to suggest, as he does (G, 4.400), that his third proposition follows from the previous two.

In discussing Kant's propositions, philosophers have focused so much on his views on the value of acting from duty that it is easy to fall into the assumption that his foremost interest in developing them is to specify necessary and sufficient conditions for an action's having moral worth. But Kant's main aim in articulating his three propositions is to derive the supreme principle of morality, that is, to show that if there is such a principle, then it is the FUL. And Kant derives it with the help of criteria implicit in his propositions. According to the criterion implicit in the first proposition, the supreme principle of morality must be such that all and only actions conforming to it because the principle requires it, that is, all and only actions done from duty, have moral worth. The second proposition implies that whatever the supreme principle of morality is, the moral worth of conforming to it from duty must stem from the maxim of the action, not from its effects. According to the criterion implicit in the third proposition, the supreme principle of morality must be such that an agent's notion that it is a practical law and that it requires her to do something gives her sufficient motive to do it.

Why should we take Kant's propositions to contain criteria for the supreme principle of morality? In the sentence preceding his initial presentation of the FUL, Kant asks:

> But what kind of law can that be, the representation of which must determine the will, even without regard for the effect expected from it, in order for the will to be called good absolutely and without limitation? (G, 4.402)

He is, in effect, asking what law, or principle, can fulfill each of these three criteria for the supreme principle of morality: the third, which invokes an agent's representation of a law as a sufficient motive for her action; the second, which incorporates the notion that the moral worth of an action does not stem from its effects; and finally the first, which specifies when an action, that is, an instance of willing, has moral and thus unconditional worth. If we can show that a particular principle is unable to fulfill

315

any one of these criteria, then we can, Kant suggests, eliminate it as a viable candidate for the supreme principle of morality. If Kant's derivation of the categorical imperative is successful, then we should be able to see that the only principle that remains as a viable candidate for satisfying all three of these criteria, plus those implicit in Kant's basic concept of the supreme principle of morality, is the FUL or an equivalent principle.

Let me close this section by contrasting the basic structure of the received reading with that of the criterial reading. According to the former, Kant develops his propositions in order to establish that upon reflection we recognize L ("Conform your actions to universal law") as the basic moral requirement. Once L has been located Kant makes no further appeal to the propositions. Kant simply assumes that the only way we can conform to universal law is to conform to the FUL. On the criterial reading, Kant's argument unfolds differently. Kant's propositions contain criteria that, upon reflection, we see must be fulfilled by any viable candidate for the supreme principle of morality. These criteria supplement those with which Kant begins, that is, the ones that are contained in his basic concept of the supreme principle of morality. At least implicitly, Kant relies on the full set of these criteria to eliminate rivals to the FUL, so that only this formula and its equivalents remain as viable candidates for meeting the full set. Whether or not Kant adequately defends this claim, on the criterial reading the *Groundwork* I derivation contains no obvious gap between a practically uninformative principle and the FUL.

IV

But what might Kant mean when he says that "nothing is left but the conformity of actions to universal law as such, which alone is to serve the will as its principle"? Is there a plausible alternative to the notion, incorporated into the received interpretation, that he is embracing the imperative "Conform your actions to universal law" as the basic moral requirement? I believe that there is. However, the obscurity of Kant's remarks does render it very difficult to arrive at a definitive interpretation. Kant writes:

> But what kind of law can that be, the representation of which must determine the will, even without regard for the effect expected from it, in order for the will to be called good absolutely and without limitation? Since I have deprived the will of every impulse that could arise for it from obeying some law, nothing is left but the conformity of actions to universal law as such, which alone is to serve the will as its principle, that is, *I ought never to act* except in such a way that I could also will that my maxim *should become a universal law*. (G, 4.402)

In the first sentence Kant implicitly invokes criteria for the supreme principle of morality. In the second, before he introduces the FUL, Kant is, I believe, briefly restating these criteria. In effect he is saying that since the supreme principle of morality must meet all of them, the only viable candidate for this principle is the FUL or something equivalent.

It is not difficult to defend this view. Immediately prior to the cited passage, Kant distinguishes between two basic ways we can be motivated to conform to a principle.

Kant contrasts cases in which the representation of a principle in itself constitutes the determining ground of the will from ones in which some expected effect constitutes this ground. Moreover, he suggests that only cases of the former sort are cases of good willing. Thus he says

> nothing other than the *representation of the law* in itself . . . insofar as it and not the hoped-for effect is the determining ground of the will, can constitute the preeminent good we call moral, which is already present in the person himself who acts on this representation. (G, 4.401)

Returning to G 4.402, Kant is concerned with the kind of willing that is absolutely good, willing that he has identified earlier, in connection with his first proposition, with acting from duty. Kant specifies here that what determines absolutely good willing is not the effects one expects to result from the willing. He has "deprived the will of every impulse that could arise for it from obeying some law" in the following sense. In his defense of the second proposition he has shown that absolutely good willing is not at all motivated by some "impulse," such as the sensation of pleasure that one believes will result from obeying some principle. It is rather motivated by the representation of the law. What determines absolutely good willing is the "conformity of actions to universal law as such." In other words, the motive for absolutely good willing is the notion that it conforms to a universally and unconditionally binding practical principle. Here Kant is invoking the core of his third proposition, according to which when an agent acts from duty, her notion that her action is required by a practical law provides her with sufficient motive for doing it.

Kant's claim that "nothing is left but the conformity of actions to universal law as such, which alone is to serve the will as its principle" need not be interpreted as an endorsement of "Conform your actions to universal law" as the basic moral requirement. There is room for another reading, namely that Kant is here invoking a criterion for the supreme principle of morality that he has just developed. This alternative reading is especially attractive if it not only coheres with Kant's text, as I believe it does, but also renders his derivation more forceful than does the received interpretation.

V

Let me illustrate a way in which the derivation turns out to be a more interesting argument on the criterial reading than on the dominant view. Kant does not explicitly argue against utilitarianism. But let us consider a utilitarian principle, U: "Always perform a right action: one that yields just as great a sum total of well-being as would any alternative action available to you." Let us suppose, as it seems reasonable to do, that the utilitarian embraces this principle largely on the grounds of her being convinced of the following. First, the amount of goodness in the world depends solely on the sum total of individual well-being in it – the higher the sum total, the more goodness. Second, the rightness of an action depends solely on the goodness of its consequences. More precisely an action is right just in case that which results from it is at least as good as that which would have resulted from each of the alternative actions available to the agent.

Although U derives from these un-Kantian convictions, it would be precipitate to dismiss it as a candidate for the supreme principle of morality on the grounds of a manifest failure to conform to Kant's basic concept of this principle. U could, it seems, be a practical, absolutely necessary, universally binding, fundamental norm for moral evaluation of action. Moreover U is the sort of principle that illustrates the gigantic gap between the command "Conform your actions to universal law" and the FUL. In acting in accordance with U, an agent would (arguably) be conforming his action to a universal law, namely U. So, according to the dominant interpretation, Kant clearly fails to eliminate U as a candidate for the supreme principle of morality.

But the criterial reading suggests a simple but, in my view, powerful argument for eliminating U. For U runs afoul of some of the criteria for the supreme principle of morality that Kant develops in *Groundwork* I. The utilitarian might insist that an agent can, from duty, comply with U. After all, what would prevent her from performing a right action just because U commands her to do so? Yet she is committed to the following view: whether an agent's conforming to U from duty has moral worth depends solely on the action's effects, specifically its effects on well-being. For she holds that the amount of goodness in the world, including the "moral worth" of actions, depends solely on the amount of well-being in it. So the utilitarian cannot, rationally speaking, maintain that U fulfills Kant's second criterion, namely that the supreme principle of morality be such that the moral worth of conforming to it from duty stems not at all from that action's effects.

If we think of a consequentialist principle as one according to which the goodness of any action depends to some extent on the action's effects, in addition to the "effect" that the action has taken place, then it is easy to show that no consequentialist principle fulfills Kant's second criterion. For even the staunchest proponent of such a principle would have to acknowledge that he is committed to the view that the value of acting from duty depends at least in part on what that action produces.

Based ultimately on an appeal to the notion that, according to ordinary moral thinking, actions from duty have a special worth, Kant develops three criteria for the supreme principle of morality. Assuming these criteria are sound, Kant has solid grounds for dismissing some of the FUL's rivals for status as viable candidates for the supreme principle of morality.

VI

That is not to say that, even on the criterial reading, Kant's derivation of the FUL succeeds. Even if, employing Kant's criteria, we could eliminate all rivals that come to mind, it is not clear how we can be confident that we have not overlooked some rival. Kant claims to give an exhaustive classification of rival moral principles. But it is questionable whether he does so (Kerstein 2002: 140–4.) In any case, with the help of the criteria on the table, we are unable to dismiss rivals that, one would think, would have almost no chance of being the supreme principle of morality.

Consider the bizarre principle, BP: "Act only on that maxim such that you cannot, at the same time, will that it become a universal law." Assume that Kant is correct and the supreme principle of morality must be a universally valid, absolutely necessary, supreme practical principle. What argument does Kant have at his disposal that would show it to be impossible for BP to have these characteristics? Moreover, it seems that a proponent of BP would be able consistently to maintain that an action has moral worth if and only if it is done because BP requires it, that such an action's moral worth would not stem from its effects, and so forth. He would not be rationally compelled to acknowledge that BP runs afoul of the criteria implicit in Kant's three propositions.

Another, less provocative, example of a principle Kant would be unable to dismiss on the basis of his criteria is the following principle of weak universalization, WU: "Act only on that maxim which, when generalized, could be a universal law." WU is not equivalent to the FUL. Kant himself suggests that a maxim of nonbeneficence could, when generalized, constitute a universal law (G, 4.423). Since a world where no one acted beneficently is indeed a coherent possibility, acting on a maxim of nonbeneficence does not violate WU. On Kant's view, of course, acting on such a maxim does run afoul of the FUL because as a rational agent it is not possible to act on it and, at the same time, will that its generalization be a universal law. On the basis of the criteria discussed thus far Kant does not appear to have the tools to eliminate WU as a contender for the supreme principle of morality. For not only is it possible that WU satisfies Kant's basic concept of the supreme principle of morality, but there seems to be no reason to think that it couldn't fulfill the criteria suggested by his three propositions.

In my view, this difficulty prompts us to see that Kant actually suggests one further criterion for the supreme principle of morality. It must be such that a plausible set of duties, that is, plausible relative to ordinary moral thinking, would stem from the principle. Kant's starting point in *Groundwork* I is common rational moral cognition, which is a fancy term for ordinary moral thinking. Both BP and WU could be eliminated through an appeal to this criterion. According to ordinary moral thinking, contrary to BP and to WU, we have a duty of beneficence.

A textual basis for this criterion is not hard to discern. In *Groundwork* II, Kant offers a derivation of the FUL that parallels his derivation in *Groundwork* I. Right after he arrives at this formula, Kant says:

> Now, if all imperatives of duty can be derived from this single imperative as from their principle, then, even though we leave it undecided whether what is called duty is not as such an empty concept, we shall at least be able to show what we think by it and what the concept wants to say. (G, 4.421)

The derivation is not complete unless "all imperatives of duty" can be derived from the imperative Kant proposes as the only viable candidate for the supreme principle of morality. By "all imperatives of duty," Kant apparently means all imperatives that we, reflective rational agents, take to express our moral duties. Kant proceeds to try to show that four such imperatives, including, for example, a requirement not to make false promises for financial gain, follow from the FUL. He then says: "These are a few of the many actual duties, *or at least of what we take to be such*, whose derivation from the one principle cited above is clear" (G, 4.424, my emphasis). If these duties' derivation from the FUL were not clear, for example if it simply did not follow from the FUL that we had them, then, Kant implies, we could not accept the FUL as the only viable candidate for the supreme principle of morality. In the short paragraph (G, 4.420–1) following his statement of the FUL, Kant indicates an important criterion for any viable candidate for the supreme principle of morality. We must be able to see how it follows from this candidate that, if it were established, we would indeed have moral duties that we are convinced we do have. (For further textual evidence that Kant embraces this criterion, see Kerstein 2002: 87–9.)

With this additional criterion in place, Kant can advance towards eliminating rivals for status as viable candidates for the supreme principle of morality. But its addition brings up some difficult issues just one of which I am able to touch on here.

According to the criterial reading, in order for his derivation of the FUL to succeed, Kant would need not only to show that rivals are unfit to satisfy the criteria he indicates, but also that it remains viable to think that his candidate can satisfy them. Yet this latter task poses serious challenges when it comes to the criterion of generating moral prescriptions that square with common sense. It is very challenging to determine just which duties the FUL actually generates, but on each textually plausible interpretation I am acquainted with, the FUL yields at least some results that clash dramatically with ordinary moral thinking.

For example, suppose that Jack has the following maxim: "In order to earn a comfortable living, I will become a professor, rather than do physical labor." For him making a comfortable living amounts to making enough to have his own house, car, computer, and so forth. On a common interpretation of the FUL (see, for example, Korsgaard 1996b: 92–4), it turns out that it would be wrong for Jack to act on this maxim. According to this interpretation, Jack is to perform the following thought experiment. He is to imagine a world in which everyone acts on this maxim and then ask himself whether he can, rationally speaking, both act on this maxim and at the same time will this imagined world. It is not hard to see that he cannot do this. In acting on his maxim, Jack would be taking a certain means, namely that of becoming a professor, to his end of earning a comfortable living. But in willing a world in which everyone acted on his maxim, Jack would be willing one in which this means would be ineffective. For in the imagined world the institutional framework for salaried professors would not be in place. Universities do not function without support from people who earn a living through physical labor. So in this world it simply would not be possible for Jack to make a comfortable living through becoming a professor. In acting on his maxim and at the same time willing the imagined world, Jack would in effect be taking a means to an end and at the same time willing this means to be ineffective. He would thereby be acting irrationally.

Some maxims, such as Jack's, specify a means that is effective for attaining their end only in a context in which it is exceptional for agents to take this means to the end. These maxims take advantage of predictable regularities in agents' behavior. According to this common interpretation the FUL condemns as morally impermissible acting on such maxims. But this condemnation clashes with common sense morality, according to which acting on some of these maxims, for example Jack's, is not contrary to duty.

Of course it is possible that this common interpretation as well as the others with which I am familiar are misguided and that one exists according to which the FUL generates no moral prescriptions that clash dramatically with ordinary moral thinking. In my view this possibility is remote (Kerstein 2002: 168–74), so while I deny that Kant's *Groundwork* I derivation of the FUL contains the gap attributed to it by the received view, I nevertheless doubt whether it is successful. The interest of the derivation lies for me not so much in the principle it is designed to yield (the FUL), but rather in the criteria Kant develops for any viable candidate for the supreme principle of morality.

References and Further Reading

Allison, H. E. (1996). On a presumed gap in the derivation of the categorical imperative. In *Idealism and Freedom* (pp. 143–54). Cambridge: Cambridge University Press.

Aune, B. (1979). *Kant's Theory of Morals*. Princeton: Princeton University Press.

Herman, B. (1993). On the value of acting from the motive of duty. In *The Practice of Moral Judgment* (pp. 1–22). Cambridge, MA: Harvard University Press.

Hill, T. E., Jr. (1992). The rationality of moral conduct. In *Dignity and Practical Reason* (pp. 97–122). Ithaca, NY: Cornell University Press.

Kant, I. (1996a). *Critique of Practical Reason,* and *Groundwork of the Metaphysics of Morals*. In Immanuel Kant, *Practical Philosophy*, tr. M. J. Gregor. Cambridge: Cambridge University Press.

Kant, I. (1996b). *Religion within the Boundaries of mere Reason*. In Immanuel Kant, *Religion and Rational Theology*, tr. A. W. Wood and G. Di Giovanni. Cambridge: Cambridge University Press.

Kerstein, S. J. (2002). *Kant's Search for the Supreme Principle of Morality*. Cambridge: Cambridge University Press.

Kitcher, P. (2004). Kant's argument for the categorical imperative. *Noûs*, 38: 555–84.

Korsgaard, C. M. (1996a). Kant's analysis of obligation: The argument of *Groundwork* I. In *Creating the Kingdom of Ends*. Cambridge: Cambridge University Press.

Korsgaard, C. M. (1996b). Kant's formula of universal law. In *Creating the Kingdom of Ends*. Cambridge: Cambridge University Press.

Wood, A. W. (1999). *Kant's Ethical Thought*. Cambridge: Cambridge University Press.

21

Moral Motivation in Kant

PHILIP STRATTON-LAKE

In the *Groundwork* Kant proposes both a negative and a positive thesis about morally good acts. The negative thesis is that no action done from inclination can have moral worth. His positive thesis is that only actions done from duty (*aus Pflicht*) have moral worth. Since he holds that no action done from inclination can have moral worth, acting from duty cannot be acting from an inclination to do one's duty. So if one acts from this inclination, one is not acting from duty as Kant understands it. It seems then that acting from duty is acting from the belief that one's act is morally required. It is to φ because (one believes) φ-ing is right (where "right" does not mean "merely permissible," but "obligatory").

Like many other moral philosophers, Kant maintains that the moral value of one's action is determined not by what one does, but why one does it (*G*, 4.394). So his negative and positive thesis about morally good actions stems from parallel, but more fundamental, views about morally good motives: The parallel negative claim is that no motive of inclination is morally good; and the positive claim is that only the motive of duty has this distinctive form of value.

The Right and the Good in Kant

I shall clarify Kant's negative and positive theses, and present his argument for them, below. Before I begin, however, it is useful to outline a distinction in Kant between two questions. The first is: "What makes acts morally good (what gives them moral worth or value)?"; and the second is: "What makes acts morally right (obligatory, morally required)?" These are distinct questions in Kant. But although they are distinct, they are not independent of each other; for Kant attempts to answer the second question by answering the first. So in the order of knowledge, the question of moral goodness has priority. Starting from our knowledge of what has unconditional value, a good will, we can come to know what the ultimate criterion of right actions is, the categorical imperative.

But since morally good acts are done because they are morally right, moral goodness presupposes a distinct notion of moral rightness as well as being its ground. It is the moral rightness of an act that explains why it is morally good (when it is done for that reason). So moral rightness (duty or obligation) has priority in the order of explanation.

Although the right and the good are interdependent in Kant, they are clearly distinct notions. They must be distinct if moral goodness is to be explained with reference to moral rightness. This explanation would be empty if there were no distinction between moral rightness and moral goodness. It would be like trying to explain why someone is still a bachelor with reference to the fact that he is a man and has remained unmarried.

Furthermore, Kant's distinction between acting in accordance with duty and acting from duty shows that he distinguishes the right from the good. For an action that accords with duty which is not done from duty, will be morally right but not morally good; and if I mistakenly believe that I ought to φ, and I φ for that reason, then my act will not be morally right, although it will be morally good.

Kant's third proposition in *Groundwork* I – that "Duty is the *necessity to act out of reverence for the law*" (4.400) might be taken to suggest the view that he did not distinguish the right from the good; for this proposition might plausibly be interpreted as stating that our duty (the morally right act) is always to act from duty (to do morally good acts). But given Kant's distinction between acting in accordance with duty and acting from duty, this interpretation cannot be correct. Morally good actions are those that are done from duty. If duty were the requirement to act from duty, then acting in accordance with duty would be acting in accordance with the requirement to act from duty, and the distinction between acting in accordance with duty and from duty would collapse.

For Kant, then, morally good and morally right acts are distinct, but dependent. My act is morally right if its maxim can be conceived or willed as a universal law. It is morally good if it is done from duty. My focus here is on his account of morally good actions – that is, on his account of moral worth.

Clarifying the Negative Thesis

Kant begins the *Groundwork* with the bold claim that:

> It is impossible to conceive anything at all in the world, or even out of it, which can be taken as good without qualification, except a *good will*. (G. 4.393: translations from Kant 1960, 1964, 1985, 1991)

By a "good will" I take Kant to mean a disposition to act in certain ways from certain motives, rather than a particular act of will that manifests that disposition. Kant's strategy seems to be to argue from the idea of a good will, so understood, to an account of moral motivation. He does this first by claiming that what makes a good will good is not what it aims at – its objects – but its reasons for aiming at those objects – the motives (and principles) from which it is disposed to act. A good will, Kant claims, is not one that has certain ends, or goals, but is one that is disposed to act from morally good motives (G. 4.394). Having established this to his own satisfaction, he then considers which motives are morally good. He rejects the view that any motive of inclination can have moral value (his negative thesis), and maintains that only the motive of duty does. So a good will is one that is disposed to act from duty.

Kant's negative thesis is that no action done from inclination can have moral worth. To many philosophers this thesis has seemed excessive. They would accept that actions done from certain inclinations, such as hedonistic or self-interested inclinations, lack moral worth, or value. Nevertheless, actions done from other inclinations, such as a noninstrumental inclination to help others, or a desire to make the world a better place, seem to have inherent value. One might accept that it is better to act from duty than from some beneficent desire; but to insist that acting from a beneficent desire has no value at all seems to be to go too far.

There is no doubt that Kant's claim is bold, and at first sight, counter-intuitive. But we must be careful not to exaggerate what Kant is claiming with his negative thesis, for it is easily misunderstood. One common misunderstanding is that Kant's negative thesis implies that one's action cannot have moral worth if one is inclined to do it. Schiller assumes this when he satirizes what he takes to be Kant's view in the following lines:

> Gladly I serve my friends, but alas I do it with pleasure.
> Hence I am plagued with doubt that I am not a virtuous person.
> To this the answer is given:
> Surely, your only resource is to try to despise them entirely,
> And then with aversion do what your duty enjoins you.
>
> (Cited in Paton 1947: 249)

But the view Schiller satirizes is not Kant's. To see this we need to distinguish actions done with inclination from those done from inclination. The presence of an inclination to do a certain act does not mean that we will be caused to act from it. Even if I want to do what I should, I need not do it for that reason. I might do it just because it is right. In such a case I will act with, but not from inclination.

In *Religion Within the Limits of Reason Alone* Kant goes further. There he writes:

> If one asks, What is the *aesthetic* character, the *temperament*, so to speak, of *virtue*, whether courageous and hence *joyous* or fear-ridden and dejected, an answer is hardly necessary. This latter slavish frame of mind can never occur without a hidden *hatred* of the [moral] law. And a heart which is happy in the performance of its duty (not merely complacent in the *recognition* thereof) is a mark of genuineness in the virtuous disposition. (6.23n; Kant 1960: 19n)

This passage shows how distant Kant's view is from the one Schiller objects to.

The second thing to note about Kant's negative thesis is that he does not claim that all motives of inclination lack value. On the contrary, he describes the inclination to spread happiness as "amiable" and "right," as well as deserving "praise and encouragement" (*G*, 4.398; Kant 1964: 66). What he does claim is that this inclination lacks a distinctive type of value; namely, moral value. How, then, are we to understand the distinction between moral and nonmoral value in Kant?

Kant seems to assume that the value the motive of duty has is unconditional. This is suggested by the fact that the value of this motive is independent of any object of the will, and so independent of success in attaining any such object.

This interpretation may seem to conflict with the opening claim of the *Groundwork* that the only thing that is good without qualification is a good will. I do not think there is any serious difficulty here; for Kant defines a good will in terms of the motive of duty. Consequently, he may not have thought of a good will and the motive of duty as distinct things. If that is right, then the suggestion that the motive of duty is unconditionally good need not be incompatible with Kant's claim that the only thing that has unconditional value is a good will.

If morally good motives are unconditionally good, then the contrast between nonmoral and moral value may be understood in terms of a distinction between conditional and unconditional value. If X is unconditionally good, then its goodness cannot depend on context. Otherwise, it would be good only on the condition that certain contexts obtain. An unconditional good must, therefore, be good independently of context. This means that it must be good in every context.

Kant also maintains that an unconditional good is the condition of all other goods. One way in which a conditional good might depend on the unconditional value of a good will, is by being instrumental to a good will. I do not think it is plausible to understand Kant in this way. Kant thought that the value of happiness is conditional, and conditional on a good will. He did not, however, hold the implausible view that happiness is valuable only as a means to obtaining a good will. His view was, rather, that happiness is good only on the condition that it is deserved, and it is deserved only to the extent that the agent has a good will.

Given that the distinction between conditional (nonmoral) and unconditional (moral) value is not the same as that between instrumental and noninstrumental value, the claim that all motives of inclination lack moral value does not imply that such motives are only instrumentally good. Like happiness, such motives might have noninstrumental, conditional value.

But even if we do not identify conditional value with instrumental value, Kant's claim that all other values depend on a good will seems hard to accept. Knowledge seems to be worth seeking for its own sake, and this value does not seem to be conditional on the value of the will of the knower: furthermore, art seems to have a value that is independent of the value of the will of the artist or of the perceiver.

But Kant does not need to make this further claim about conditional value to get a distinction between unconditional and conditional value. All he needs is the idea of a context-independent value, and this idea does not imply that the value of all other things is conditional on this value.

We have seen that Kant does not claim that all motives of inclination lack value. He does not even claim that they lack noninstrumental value. All he claims is that they lack moral value. So far I have tried to clarify the distinction between moral and nonmoral value in terms of the distinction between unconditional and conditional value. But to get to the heart of the idea of moral value we need to look to Kant's *argument* for his negative and positive thesis. We will then see that what gives the motive of duty its distinctive form of value is its special relation to moral rightness. Before I move on to this, however, I shall say more about Kant's positive thesis.

Clarifying the Positive Thesis

Kant's positive thesis is that only actions done from duty have moral worth. So far I have been working with the standard account that to act from duty is to do some act because it is right, or because one believes it is right. But more needs to be said on this subject, for we have to fit this account of moral agency within Kant's broader account of practical agency.

Kant maintains that all actions are based on maxims. A maxim is a subjective principle of action. It is subjective in the sense that it is a principle on which the subject acts, and is contrasted with objective principles (practical laws) which are principles on which the subject ought to act. Kant sometimes says that subjective principles are valid only for the individual subject, whereas objective principles are valid for all agents (5.20–1; Kant 1985: 17). This makes it look as though subjective principles cannot also be object-ive ones, for one and the same principle cannot be valid only for the individual subject and, at the same time, valid for all subjects. But this cannot be Kant's real view, for he clearly allows the possibility that agents can act on the principles they ought to act on. In such cases their subjective principles (maxims, or principles on which they act) are also objective principles (practical laws, or principles on which they ought to act).

In the *Critique of Practical Reason* Kant makes it clear that only very general prin-ciples of action count as maxims. He calls more specific principles "rules" rather than "maxims." So, for example, I might have the maxim of being hospitable towards my guests and have various rules falling under this maxim which specify ways of being hospitable. I might have a rule that during the day I will offer tea, and another that during the evening I will offer wine to my guests (see O'Neill 1989).

Kant calls maxims based on inclination empirical, material, or a posteriori maxims, and contrasts them with a priori, formal maxims that make no reference to desired ends. Since he regards this classification as exhaustive, a good will must be one that acts either from a material or a formal maxim. Since a will is not good in virtue of producing some desired result, a will that acts from duty cannot be one that acts from a material maxim. It must, therefore, act on the basis of a formal maxim. This maxim cannot be "I will φ if I happen to have an inclination to φ," but must be something like "If φ-ing is morally required, I will φ" (Paton 1947: 62). This simple maxim expresses a great deal. In particular, it shows that the agent regards moral reasons as having a certain authority – that is, as being sufficient, unconditional and overriding.

If I have this maxim I must regard myself as having sufficient reason to φ simply insofar as I judge that I am obligated to φ. Otherwise, I would have to look for nonmoral reasons to act, say reasons of self-interest. But this would show that I have a very different maxim. My maxim would not be: "If φ-ing is morally required, I will φ," but "If φ-ing is morally required, and in my interest, I will."

The maxim of duty also expresses the fact that the agent regards moral reasons as unconditional. If I have this maxim I would not regard moral considerations as reason-giving under some specific condition, say, on the condition that I am inclined to do what they favor, or on the condition that compliance will benefit me. Rather, the maxim of duty shows that the agent regards moral reasons as unconditionally valid.

Finally, this maxim shows that the agent regards moral reasons as overriding. If the maxim were qualified in some way, the agent would have a different view about the normative force of moral reasons. If, for instance, my maxim were "If φ-ing is morally required, I will φ, unless φ-ing involves a significant sacrifice," this would show that I regard the normative force of morality as overridable. I will regard moral reasons as defeatable by considerations of self-interest. So the unqualified form of the maxim of duty expresses the agent's view that moral reasons are overriding.

A good will is not, therefore, simply exemplified by anyone who acts from the motive of duty. A good willed agent acts from this specific motive because, at a more general and fundamental level, she has made duty her maxim. A good will must act both from the *motive* and from the *maxim* of duty. This will be important in relation to Kant's argument for his positive thesis that only actions done from duty have moral worth. For as we shall see, his argument is only defensible if we focus on the maxim of duty rather than the motive of duty.

Why Motives of Inclination Lack Moral Worth

Now that we have got a clearer picture of Kant's positive and negative thesis, we can turn to their justification. Why should we agree with Kant that from a moral point of view all inclinations stand on the same footing – that in this respect the inclination to help others is no different from the inclination to benefit oneself?

I think the clue to Kant's argument is given by the following passage from the *Groundwork*.

> [acting from an immediate inclination to help others] has still no genuine moral worth. It stands on the same footing as other inclinations – for example, the inclination for honour, which if fortunate enough to hit on something beneficial and right and consequently honourable, deserves praise and encouragement, but not esteem . . . (G, 4.398; Kant 1964: 66)

Barbara Herman has argued that this passage suggests that if one does the right act from some inclination, it is just a matter of luck that one's act is right. As she understands Kant, all motives of inclination lack moral value because of their merely accidental relation to the rightness of the acts done from them. She considers Kant's example of the shopkeeper who is honest to his customers out of self-interest and the "friend of man" who helps others from an immediate inclination to do so. The relevant point in both examples, she argues, is that if the actions these motives give the agent reason to do are right, this will be because of an accidental alignment of the inclination and circumstances (Herman 1993: 3–6). If circumstances change so that it is in the shopkeeper's interest to lie to some of his customers his self-interested inclination would motivate him to act wrongly.

Herman uses the same line of argument in relation to Kant's example of the "friend of man." She states that if one helps others just because one wants to, then one will be motivated to help others even when what they are doing is wrong (Herman 1993: 5). But a morally good motive cannot be one that would motivate the agent to do what is wrong. Therefore, the immediate inclination to help others lacks moral value.

Herman thus concludes that Kant's examples imply that he held that actions motivated by inclinations, even the inclination to help others, have no moral worth because they are only accidentally connected with the rightness of the actions done from them. Consequently, they fail to provide the agent with an interest in the morality of her actions (ibid.). This suggests, she argues, that a morally good motive must be one that gives the agent an interest in the rightness of her act and "therefore makes its being a right action the nonaccidental effect of the agent's concern" (ibid. 6). Only the motive of duty does this.

I think this account of what it is for a motive to have moral value is along the right lines, but that Kant's argument can only be sustained if we focus on actions done from the maxim of duty rather than from the motive of duty. The problems arise when we try to clarify the notion of a motive's being nonaccidentally related to the rightness of the act done from it.

Although Herman does not distinguish them, she seems to work with two distinct conceptions of a nonaccidental relation to rightness. The first is that a morally good motive will guarantee that the action done from it will be right (ibid. 4). The second is that a morally good motive must be one that gives the agent an interest in the moral rightness of her actions. Neither conception supports both Kant's negative and positive thesis about moral worth. The moral guarantee account supports the negative thesis, but undermines the positive thesis; and whereas the moral interest account supports Kant's positive thesis, it undermines his negative thesis.

It is certainly true that no inclination is such that necessarily if one acts from it, one will do the right thing. Even the inclination to do one's duty cannot guarantee that one succeeds. But although it is true that someone who acts from some inclination will not necessarily do what she ought to, this seems to be equally true of someone who acts from duty. My belief that φ-ing is right might be mistaken. If it is, and I act from it, then I will not do the right act. Acting from the belief that φ-ing is right would guarantee that the action done is right only on the condition that this belief is infallible. Since such beliefs clearly are fallible, they cannot guarantee rightness.

The "moral guarantee" conception of moral worth is not only philosophically dubious, but is also exegetically suspect. Kant did not hold the implausible view that the motive of duty guarantees that one's act is right. What may lead some commentators to ascribe such a view to Kant is his view that the moral worth of an act is independent of any result of willing it, and hence is independent of successfully achieving that result. But this is to confuse views Kant held about moral worth, or goodness, with views he held about moral rightness. He clearly held that the moral value of an act is determined solely by the reasons and principles from which we act. It is also clear that he held that an action has moral value only if it is done from duty. But as we noted earlier, Kant held that moral rightness is quite distinct from moral goodness. Since he held that moral rightness and moral goodness are distinct concepts, the mere fact that he holds that an action can have moral worth simply in virtue of willing in a certain way in no way shows that he held the same to be true of morally right acts.

Perhaps Herman's second, "moral interest" account of a nonaccidental relation to rightness is more fruitful. According to this understanding, what is distinctive of the motive of duty and which every inclination lacks, is the ability to give the agent an interest in the morality of her actions. This interest would no more guarantee that we do the right thing, than an interest in being prudent would guarantee that we always promote our self interest. But on the moral interest understanding of a morally good motive what is important is not that the motive guarantee that the action is right, but that when it is right its being so is nonaccidental because the agent's motive gave her a nonderivative interest in the rightness of her actions.

328

But although this account of moral worth supports Kant's positive thesis, it is not clear that it supports his negative thesis. For although the immediate desire to help others fails to satisfy this criterion of moral worth, a nonderivative desire to do what is right seems to pass this test. To have a desire to do the right thing is to desire to do whatever one believes is the right thing in the circumstances. So when one's moral belief is correct and one does the right act, its being right does seem to be nonaccidentally related to the motive from which it is done. This is because if one is motivated by this desire then one will have a nonderivative concern for the rightness of one's actions. So at least this desire would be a suitable bearer of moral worth.

The Right Sort of Reasons

It seems, then, that neither of the ways in which Herman understands a nonaccidental relation to rightness supports Kant's positive and negative thesis. Is there some other way of understanding this relation that does better? One possibility rests on the idea of doing the right thing for the right reason. This idea can be illustrated in relation to epistemic reasons, i.e. reasons to believe. Suppose that p, and that I ought to believe that p. If I ought to believe that p, then there is a reason why I ought to believe this, and we may say that I believe that p for the right reason if I believe that p for that reason. For then the reason why I should believe that p and the reason why I believe that p will be the same.

Suppose, for instance, that I ought to believe that the Labour party will win the UK election tomorrow, and that the reason why I ought to believe this is that all the polls over the last two months have clearly indicated this result. If I believe that the Labour party will win the election tomorrow, not for that reason but because it is a leap-year, then I believe what I ought to believe, but for the wrong reason.

Because I come to have this belief for the wrong reason, it is just a matter of luck that I believe what I ought to believe. If all of the evidence indicated a Conservative victory I would still believe that Labour would win. If I held this belief for the right reason, for the reason why I should hold it, I would not only have the belief I ought to have, but my having it would not be a matter of luck.

We can apply this idea to moral oughts. If I ought morally to do some act there is some reason why I ought to do it – that is, some consideration that grounds this duty. If the reason why I ϕ is the same as the reason why I ought to ϕ, then it will be no accident that I have done the right thing. If, on the other hand I ϕ from some other reason, then it will be a matter luck that I did the right thing. Suppose, for instance, I ought to look after my neighbor's pet while he is on holiday, and the reason why I ought to do this is that I promised him that I would. If I look after his pet while he is away, then I have acted as I should. But if I do this for the wrong reason (because of some self-interested reason), the fact that I did the right thing would be a matter of luck. It would be like believing that the Labour party will win the election tomorrow because this is a leap-year. If, on the other hand, I look after his pet because I promised to, then I will not only have done the right thing, but will have done it for the right reason. Consequently, the fact that I did the right thing would be no accident.

Here, then, we have an alternative account of what it is for a motive to be non-accidentally related to the rightness of the act done from it. It is nonaccidentally related to the rightness of the act if the motive is the same as the reason why the act is right. Otherwise it is only accidentally related to the rightness of the act.

If we define morally good motives in terms of a nonaccidental relation to rightness, and accept that my motive is nonaccidentally related to the moral rightness of the act done from it only if I am motivated by the right sort of reason (as this has been defined), then we seem to have very good grounds for supposing that no motive of inclination could have moral worth. For it is very hard to accept that any of my inclinations could explain why I am obligated to do some act. I am never morally required to help others, or keep my promises, or to be honest, because I am inclined to, or because doing these acts subserves some other inclination I have. So the wrong-sort-of-reasons account supports Kant's negative thesis that no action done from inclination can have moral worth.

But although this criterion of moral worth supports Kant's negative thesis, it seems to undermine his positive thesis; for the fact that ϕ-ing is right cannot explain why ϕ-ing is right. My belief that ϕ-ing is right could explain why ϕ-ing is right, but this belief cannot plausibly be regarded as the ground of my duty; for it would imply that this belief has the magical power to make itself true, a power it clearly does not have.

At this stage things do not look good for Kant's argument. It seems as though we must do one of four things:

1. Accept either the "moral guarantee" or "right kind of reasons" account of a non-accidental relation to rightness, and reject Kant's positive thesis.
2. Accept the moral interest account, and reject the negative thesis.
3. Look for a better account of a nonaccidental relation to rightness.
4. Look for an alternative argument for Kant's negative and positive thesis.

None of these options looks particularly attractive. The first two lose what is distinctive of Kant's account of moral motivation, whereas the third and fourth do not look promising.

An Alternative Account of Acting from Duty

There is, however, a fifth response, which is to modify Kant's account of acting from duty in a way that retains what is distinctive of his view whilst making it fit better with its rationale. To act from duty for Kant is both to act from the motive of duty and from the maxim of duty. The problem we had with the right kind of reasons account of a nonaccidental relation to rightness was that it meant that the motive of duty is not related to the rightness of the acts done from it in such a way as to make it morally good. One way to respond to this is to propose an alternative account of acting from duty that involves acting from the maxim, but not the motive of duty.

Marcia Baron suggests something like this. Her account rests on a distinction between primary and secondary motives, rather than between motives and maxims, but this is a difference only in terminology. For what she means by a primary motive is what

I mean by a motive, and what she calls a secondary motive I (and Kant) would call a maxim. According to Baron one can act from duty even if one's primary motive is not duty (Baron 1995: 134). Moreover, she maintains that it is not duty as a primary motive, but the secondary motive of duty that is morally important. She writes:

> No premium is placed on the action being done from duty as a primary motive. What matters is that the action is in accord with duty and that it is no accident that it is: it accords with duty because the agent governs her conduct by a commitment to doing what is right. (ibid. 131)

If we accept Baron's suggestion, then one could act from duty even when the thought of duty does not figure among one's primary motives. One would be acting from duty if one is acting solely from the maxim (secondary motive) of duty.

Baron maintains that acting from duty as a secondary motive is consistent with the rationale for what I have called Kant's positive thesis. When I act from duty as a secondary motive, it will be no accident if I do the right thing. It will be no accident because, she claims, the action will be motivated, at the secondary level, by the agent's commitment to morality – that is, to doing what is right.

But this commitment does not seem to be sufficient to underpin a nonaccidental relation to rightness. The problem is that the agent's commitment to morality will make the rightness of her actions nonaccidental only if the agent does the right thing for the right reason. If she does the right act for the wrong reason, then the fact that she ends up doing the right thing will be accidental. It will be accidental for the same reason that the truth of some belief will be accidental if one does not hold it for the right reason.

But since duty has been replaced as a primary motive, this leaves room for the ground of duty to play this role. What I am suggesting is, then, that to φ from duty is to φ from a complex motivational structure according to which (a) one acts from the maxim of duty, and (b) one's primary motive is the ground of duty.

This raises the question of what it is that grounds our duties. The obvious place to look in Kant for an answer to this question is his principle of humanity. This principle tells us to act in such a way that we always treat humanity, whether in our own person or in the person of another, never simply as a means, but always at the same time as an end (G, 4.429). The fact that in φ-ing you would be treating someone as an end, or by not φ-ing you would be failing to treat that person as an end, presents us with a plausible, and distinctively Kantian, explanation of why we ought to φ. Since we treat others as ends when we are honest, keep our promises, help them when they are in need, etc. considerations such as these can ground duty. If this is right, then considerations of honesty, fidelity, beneficence, etc. will figure in the content of the (primary) motivating thoughts of a Kantian good-willed agent. The agent will still act from the maxim of duty, but her motive will not be duty, but rather the ground of duty, i.e. some specific way of treating others (or herself) as ends.

This account of acting from duty seems at last to get Kant what he wants – namely, a motivational structure that is nonaccidentally related to the moral rightness of the acts done from it, and as such has moral worth. This account also enables Kant to deal with certain criticisms, to which I now turn.

Kant's Critics

Some philosophers object to Kant's negative thesis. They are willing to accept that actions done from duty have moral worth, and even that the motive of duty is the best motive, but deny that it is the only morally good motive. Actions done from certain inclinations also have moral worth.

To have any force, this objection would have to engage with the argument for Kant's negative thesis. But those who criticize Kant's negative thesis never do this. This might be because they think that Kant had no decent argument for his view – that his negative thesis simply expresses a general antipathy towards inclination and desire. But I have argued that this is not the case. The argument for Kant's negative thesis rests on a principled account of what it is for a motive to have moral worth: it must be nonaccidentally related to the moral rightness of the act done from it. Until his critics engage with this argument, their objection has no force.

A more radical objection is that Kant's conception of moral motivation is alienating. It is alienating because it means that personal considerations, such as considerations of love and friendship, cannot motivate morally good individuals, and this leads to a certain detachment from our friends and loved ones.

Michael Stocker illustrates this line of objection with the example of a hospital patient who receives a visit from his friend, Smith:

> You are very bored and restless and at loose ends when Smith comes in once again. You are now convinced more than ever that he is a fine fellow and a real friend – taking so much time to cheer you up, travelling all the way across town, and so on. You are so effusive with your praise and thanks that he protests that he always tries to do what he thinks is his duty, what he thinks will be best. You at first think he is engaging in a polite form of self-deprecation, relieving the moral burden. But the more you two speak, the more clear it becomes that he was telling the literal truth: that it is not essentially because of you that he came to see you, not because you are friends, but because he thought it was his duty, perhaps as a fellow Christian or Communist or whatever, or simply because he knows of no one more in need of cheering up and no one easier to cheer up. (Stocker 1976: 462)

Bernard Williams makes the same point in a different way. He considers a situation in which a man can save either his wife, or a stranger, but cannot save both. Williams claims that the man should save his wife, simply because she is his wife, and that if he is motivated by a thought with explicitly moral content, such as the thought that it is morally permissible in this situation to save his wife in preference to a stranger, he will have had one thought too many.

> It might have been hoped by some (for instance, by his wife) that his motivating thought, fully spelled out, would be the thought that it was his wife, not that it was his wife and that in situations of this kind it is permissible to save his wife. (Williams 1999: 18)

Stocker and Williams express two related worries here. The first is that the motive of duty rules out other motives, such as love or friendship. The second is that a moral agent of the sort of which Kant would approve will be motivated by thoughts with explicitly moral content even in cases where such thoughts seem inappropriate, or objectionable.

On the account of acting from duty I favor, it is not clear that the first worry has any bite. What makes it seem as though it does is a failure to distinguish the motive of duty from the maxim of duty. The maxim of duty is a principle expressing the sort of actions the agent will do, and the conditions under which she will do them. The motive of duty is the reason why an agent does some particular act – because it is morally required. Many actions are not morally required, so could not be done from the motive of duty. They would, however, still be governed by the maxim of duty. They would be governed by this maxim if the agent would not have done them if she thought they were wrong. So if it is permissible to visit my friend in hospital, or to save my wife in preference to a stranger, but not morally required, then a Kantian agent could act from motives of friendship or love. The maxim of duty certainly does not rule out other motives.

But what about cases where some action is not merely permissible, but is morally required? Aren't nonmoral motives ruled out in such cases if one's action is morally good? I have argued that they are not. I think moral agents would not be motivated to do what they should by the deontic fact that they should do this act, but by the concrete considerations that ground this fact. What is important is that one act from the maxim of duty, and although someone who acts from duty in this sense will regard herself as having sufficient reason to φ simply insofar as she judges that she ought to φ, the thought that she ought to φ will not be one of the reasons which motivates her action. Rather, her motivating reasons will be those considerations on the basis of which she judges that she ought to φ – that is, her reasons for φ-ing will be identical with the reasons why she ought to φ. For Kant these reasons will be the specific ways of treating others as ends, such as considerations of beneficence, fidelity, honesty, etc. If the thought of these specific considerations is what motivates her to do what she ought, then it is not at all clear that she will be motivated by a thought with explicitly moral content. For instance, the fact that you need help may obligate me to help you and motivate me to do so. But when I am motivated solely by this fact I do not seem to be motivated by a thought with explicitly moral content.

This goes some way towards meeting Stocker's and Williams's objection to Kant theory of moral motivation. But it cannot capture Williams's view that the only thought a good husband should have for saving his wife in preference to a stranger is that she is his wife. For I think Williams would insist that the man should be motivated solely by the thought that she is his wife not only when saving her is permissible, but when it is required. But the fact that she is his wife is not a consideration that may be regarded as a specific way of treating her as an end.

The worry here is not so much with Kant's account of moral motivation, or my revised version of it, but with Kant's view that the ground of duty must always be some specific way of treating others or oneself as ends. The worry is that this omits the personal character of morality; the fact that various personal relations can ground duties. My revision to Kant's theory of moral motivation implies that if the fact that she is his wife is the reason why he ought (morally) to save her, then insofar as the husband has a good will he will be motivated solely by this fact. If there is an objection here it is not to Kant's theory of moral motivation, but to his view that only impersonal considerations can ground duty.

Perhaps Williams would still object on the ground that the agent's maxim of duty means that he has prioritized morality over love, and there may be something objectionable about that. But I do not see that there is anything objectionable here. It is true that the Kantian good-willed individual would not save his wife if doing so were morally wrong. If he could only save her by throwing a child off the lifeboat, he would not do so. But it is by no means clear that there is something objectionable about this. Indeed, if a man motivated solely by the loving thought of his wife threw the child off the boat to save his wife, without any thought at all about whether this is the right thing to do, then this man would have had one thought too few.

References

Baron, M. (1995). *Kantian Ethics Almost Without Apology*. Ithaca, NY: Cornell University Press.

Herman, B. (1993). *The Practice of Moral Judgment*. Cambridge, MA: Harvard University Press.

Kant, I. (1960). *Religion Within the Limits of Reason Alone*, tr. T. M. Greene and H. H. Hudson. New York: Harper Torchbooks. (Original work published 1793.)

Kant, I. (1964). *Groundwork of the Metaphysic of Morals*, tr. H. J. Paton. New York: Harper Torchbooks. (Original work published 1785.)

Kant, I. (1985). *Critique of Practical Reason*, tr. L. W. Beck. London: Macmillan. (Original work published 1788.)

Kant, I. (1991). *The Metaphysics of Morals*, ed. M. J. Gregor. Cambridge: Cambridge University Press. (Original work published 1797.)

O'Neill, O. (1989). *Constructions of Reason: Explorations of Kant's Practical Philosophy*. Cambridge: Cambridge University Press.

Paton, H. J. (1947). *The Categorical Imperative: A Study in Kant's Moral Philosophy*. New York: Hutchinson's University Library.

Stocker, M. (1976). The schizophrenia of modern ethical theories. *Journal of Philosophy*, 73: 453–66.

Williams, B. (1999). Persons, character and morality. In *Moral Luck: Philosophical Papers 1973–1980*. Cambridge: Cambridge University Press.

Further Reading

Allison, A. (1990). *Kant's Theory of Freedom*. Cambridge: Cambridge University Press.

Ameriks, K. (1993). Kant on the good will. In *Grundlegung zur Metaphysik der Sitten: Ein Kooperativer Kommentar* [*Groundwork of the Metaphysics of Morals: A Cooperative Commentary*] (pp. 45–65), ed. Otfried Hoffe. Frankfurt am Main: Vittorio Klostermann.

Beck, L. W. (1960). *A Commentary on Kant's Critique of Practical Reason*. Chicago: University of Chicago Press.

Benson, P. (1987). Moral worth. *Philosophical Studies*, 51: 365–82.

Blum, L. (1980). *Friendship, Altruism and Morality*. London: Routledge & Kegan Paul.

Hinman, L. (1983). On the purity of moral motives: A critique of Kant's account of the emotions and acting for the sake of duty. *Monist*, 66: 251–66.

Korsgaard, C. (1996). *Creating the Kingdom of Ends*. Cambridge: Cambridge University Press.

Nell (O'Neill), O. (1975). *Acting on Principle: An Essay on Kantian Ethics*. New York: Columbia University Press.

Ross, W. D. (2002). *The Right and the Good*, ed. P. Stratton-Lake. Oxford: Clarendon Press.

Stratton-Lake, P. (2000). *Kant, Duty and Moral Worth*. London: Routledge.

22

Moral Paragons and
the Metaphysics of Morals

MARCIA BARON

1.

This chapter focuses on a major work of Kant's that has until recently been neglected, *The Metaphysics of Morals*, and more specifically on Part II of that work, "The Doctrine of Virtue." *The Metaphysics of Morals* was first translated in its entirety into English in 1964, and still receives less attention than it deserves. Habits of teaching one classic rather than another die hard, so it is a safe bet that *The Metaphysics of Morals* is still not making a frequent appearance in Classics in Ethics courses, let alone in general introductory ethics courses. Lack of attention to this work is a pity not only because it is a major work of Kant's and is the culmination of his ethical writings, but also (and relatedly) because most of the widespread myths about Kant's ethics – e.g., that it concerns actions, not character or how to live; that it is all about applying a rule to generate a clear decision about how we should act; that it is rigid, leaving no room for hard cases; that it is not sensitive to the particulars of situations and to the nuanced character of moral life; that it does not take into account any feature of persons other than their rationality; that the Categorical Imperative not only is not based on anything empirical (true), but is supposed to be applied in such a way as to ignore empirical facts (false) – lose whatever semblance of plausibility they might otherwise have once one reads "The Doctrine of Virtue." So does the general picture some readers think they find of the ideal Kantian moral agent.

I will not try to demonstrate that all of the "myths" listed above are indeed only myths, but will focus instead on showing, mainly via *The Metaphysics of Morals*, that the picture of the ideal Kantian moral agent many readers come away with, after reading the *Groundwork*, is a distortion. More positively, I want to bring out the conception of moral excellence, or ideal moral agents, that *does* emerge from a careful reading of *The Metaphysics of Morals*.

2.

First I need to say a bit about the distorted view and its sources. One passage from the *Groundwork* in particular lends itself to the distorted view:

[I]f nature had put little sympathy in the heart of this or that man; if (in other respects an honest man) he is by temperament cold and indifferent to the sufferings of others, perhaps because he himself is provided with the special gift of patience and endurance towards his own sufferings and presupposes the same in every other or even requires it; if nature had not properly fashioned such a man . . . for a philanthropist, would he not still find within himself a source from which to give himself a far higher worth than what a mere good-natured temperament might have? By all means! It is just then that the worth of character comes out, which is moral and incomparably the highest, namely that he is beneficent not from inclination but from duty. (G, 4.398–9)

The picture of Kantian moral agents that many readers glean from this passage is not a pretty one. It is easy to get the impression (if one is looking for a sketch of an ideal agent) that Kant's model of a moral person is someone cold and indifferent to the suffering of others who forces himself to do his duty and (among other things) help others. That this should be anyone's model of moral excellence is jarring, to say the least. I and others have argued that the passage quoted above does not warrant the inference that Kant holds that the ideal agent is cold, indifferent to others, unmoved by their suffering. (See, among other works, Baron 2002; Herman 1993: ch. 1; Korsgaard 1996: ch. 2; Wood 1999: ch. 1.) Indeed, given the aim of the *Groundwork* – to search for and establish the supreme principle of morality (4.392) – we should not expect to find in that work an account of moral excellence or virtue, or an indication of what sort(s) of person is (are) morally ideal.

In this chapter I will not address the question of just how that passage should be understood except to mention that Kant's discussion in 4.397–401 is part of an attempt to draw out of an analysis of the good will the supreme principle of morality, and that it is a mistake to read it as a self-standing discussion, purporting to provide an account of the moral worth of actions (or of character) (see Baron 1995: ch. 5). But it is helpful to have the passage before us because it has contributed so much to the impression that Kant regards as morally ideal the person who lacks fellow-feeling and perhaps even has an antipathy to others, and acts from duty with, as it were, clenched teeth.

It is worth noting that although this is the passage in Kant's writings that most lends itself to the distorted view, readers already disposed to accept the interpretation may find some support for it elsewhere: in Kant's distinction between the practical and the pathological (see Mendus 1985), in his negative remarks on emotion and passion (which might lead some readers to think that he is equally negative about "affect" of all types; see Baron 1995: ch. 6; Denis 2000; and Sherman 1997), in the very fact that he is adamant that feeling should not serve in any way as the *foundation* of ethics, and perhaps even in his distinction between noumena and phenomena (see Allison 1990). None of these in fact provides support for the distorted view, but it is easy to regard them as supporting it if one is already convinced that the interpretation is correct. To locate more fully the sources of the distortion we should also keep in mind the fact that it was useful to some highly influential philosophers, most notably Hegel, to disseminate a caricature of Kant's ethics, a caricature which could then serve as a foil for their own work. They may not have willfully set out to do this; it can nonetheless happen that they overplay some points, or read passages in certain ways, in order to offer their own respective theory or approach as a fresh alternative, presenting it as more novel than it in fact is. (For discussion of Hegel's misunderstandings or misrepresentations of Kant's ethics, see Sedgwick 1988, and see chapter 30 below.)

3.

As we turn to *The Metaphysics of Morals* to consider what picture of an ideal moral agent is implied in that work, we need to give some attention to what sort of thing it is that we are looking for, or at any rate, what sort of thing there is some hope of finding. First of all, we need to bear in mind a distinction that will help us be clear on what Kant is offering and what he is not offering, a distinction he draws between character and temperament. What "nature makes of [one . . .] belongs to temperament (where the subject is for the most part passive); only by what man makes of himself can we recognize that he has character" (*APS*, 7.291). Insofar as Kant provides us with a sketch of what a good person – or good people – are like, his focus is on character, not on temperament. I mention this because it may be a point on which Kant's critics are looking for something rather different from what he offers. He is not interested in telling us, in *The Metaphysics of Morals*, what temperament is best; the interest lies in how we should shape our characters, not on what natural endowments it is best to have.

Second, as so often happens in philosophy, the questions we ask lead us to think of the issue in a certain way and to expect certain kinds of answers. It can be very helpful to ask, while reading a great classic in moral philosophy, "What sort of person does Kant/Mill/Hume think of as morally ideal?" but it should not be assumed that there will be one particular type of person who is the moral paragon for that particular philosopher. In the next three sections I will try to show that moral excellence, for Kant, admits of considerable variety. The remarkably altruistic person does not have the lofty moral position, on a Kantian picture, that he or she often enjoys in familiar conceptions of moral goodness and virtue.

In the context of Kantian ethics, the question "What sort of person is best?" is a little misleading, for three reasons. First, it may bring to mind personality or temperament rather than character, shifting the focus from how we should cultivate our characters – how we should "raise [ourselves] from the crude state of [our] nature . . . more and more towards humanity" (*MM*, 6.387) – to what sort of disposition it is (morally) best to have. Second, and relatedly, it may put the focus on rating people rather than on self-direction and self-cultivation (or put differently, on a third-person rather than a first-person inquiry or judgment). And third, it creates expectations of the wrong sort. It creates expectations that there will be a pinnacle, a certain type whom we all admire, maybe revere, as the best a person can be, when in fact there is no such pinnacle. There is no one best type of person (unless such a person is described highly abstractly, leaving room for a wide range of instantiations).

4.

To understand why there is no best type, we need to attend to the obligatory ends and the shape that they give to Kant's ethics. On Kant's view, whatever other ends we may have, there are two that are obligatory: self-perfection and the happiness of others. (It needs to be borne in mind that the perfection of others is not an obligatory end, nor is one's own happiness. For further discussion, and for an explanation of why these are obligatory ends, see Denis 2001.) That they are obligatory means that it is a duty to have these ends as one's ends. But what does that amount to?

The precise implications for conduct cannot be specified, the duties entailed by the obligatory ends being "wide" or "imperfect" (see Hill 1992: ch. 8 and Hill 2002: ch. 7). Nonetheless, having an end is not a hollow requirement. It entails adopting some ends that instantiate the obligatory end – though there will be leeway as to exactly which specific ends we adopt. For example, I might adopt as one of my ends learning to play the cello, and this would be an instantiation of the end of self-perfection. It is not obligatory to adopt the end of learning to play the cello, but is obligatory to adopt some ends that instantiate the end of self-perfection. More on this leeway shortly.

Adopting the obligatory ends entails acting accordingly, in the rather open-ended way just indicated. But in addition, having certain ends means noticing things one might not otherwise notice and seeing them in a certain way. Part of what it is to have an end is that one finds certain features of the world salient. This is true of ends in general, but the process of coming to find certain features salient may work differently with ends that are suggested by our inclinations than with obligatory ends. When the end is suggested by inclination, we are already inclined to perceive the world in the relevant way, but when the end is one that is prompted by reason, this might not be the case. (I draw in the preceding three sentences from Korsgaard 1996: 130.) We may therefore need to try to bring it about that certain things become salient for us. This will entail attuning ourselves more to the needs of others, to when we can help and how – whether to offer help, or simply to create an environment in which the other will feel comfortable requesting assistance, or alternatively to facilitate independence, possibly by refraining from (directly) helping. I am thinking in connection with the last disjunct of a poignant scene in *Ray*, a film about Ray Charles, in which the young boy, who has just recently become totally blind, trips and falls. Disoriented and upset, he calls for his mother's help. She stays where she is and says nothing, watching with great emotion as he slowly stands up and reorients himself by carefully listening to the sounds around him. She then tearfully embraces him, her emotion conveying her pride in him.

On the Kantian picture, this (sensitivity, proper attending, knowing how best to help) is something that even the virtuous person will have to work at. She may be extremely good at it, but it will not be second nature. It is worth noting here that someone for whom such things were always easy would lack moral depth, and would probably be rather unfeeling. It is a mark of her love for her son that Ray Charles's mother, as depicted in the film, did not find it easy to refrain from going to him when he called to her.

For some people, proper attending, knowing how best to help, and so on, will be very difficult indeed. But the fact that it is very hard for them does not excuse them from the duty, or even circumscribe it. "Ought implies can" is often recited as the Kantian principle that if you cannot do X, you cannot have a duty to do X (and "cannot do X" is then also understood rather expansively to cover instances where it is very hard to bring oneself to do X). Kant's point was not the contraposition of "Ought implies can" – that if you cannot do X, you cannot have a duty to do X – but rather that if you have a duty to do X, you *can* do it. "For if the moral law commands that we ought to be better human beings now, it inescapably follows that we must be capable of being better human beings" (*RBR*, 6.50). He was concerned to emphasize that we can do more than we might think we can do, not that duty has to be circumscribed by human frailty. That I am insensitive, or not very perceptive, is no excuse for not helping others. Adopting the obligatory end of others' happiness thus entails working to change, as needed, what is salient for us – more generally, changing our characters.

5.

The obligatory end of self-perfection has two parts to it: developing one's talents and perfecting oneself morally. Although there is little latitude in the latter part, there is a great deal in the former. I do not have a duty to develop all of my "gifts of nature"; I can choose which to develop, and if, as seems wise, I choose to develop several, I can prioritize as I wish. The other obligatory end, the happiness of others, likewise admits of some latitude, though exactly how much is a matter of some debate. This much is clear: we cannot promote everyone's happiness; we have to make some choices about whom to aid, when, and how. In addition, there is latitude in how much we do by way of helping others. There is no requirement that we do as much as possible. Nor, I would claim, does Kant hold that the more we help, the more virtuous we are; but on this there is room for debate. (On the issue of latitude, see Baron 1995: ch. 3; Baron and Seymour, forthcoming; Gregor 1963: ch. 7; Hill 1992: ch. 8; and Hill 2002: ch. 7.) Likewise, just how to go about developing one's talents is, as noted, for the individual to decide, though there are some parameters. Whatever else we do (learning foreign languages, learning to be excellent potters, striving to be better hockey players), we have a duty to diminish our ignorance and correct our errors.

> A human being has a duty to raise himself from the crude state of his nature, from his animality . . . more and more toward humanity, by which he alone is capable of setting himself ends; he has a duty to diminish his ignorance by instruction and to correct his errors. (*MM*, 6.387: translations from Kant 1996a and 1996b)

In addition to latitude in choosing which talents to develop, whom to help and how, and so on, there is latitude as to which of the two obligatory ends to regard as a higher priority (if indeed one gives either priority over the other). Kant makes no claims concerning which obligatory end is more important, so it appears that there is room for variation, as long as the agent really does adopt both ends. It is not morally permissible to excuse oneself from promoting others' happiness on the grounds that one is working so hard to develop one's talents; nor can one excuse oneself from self-perfection on the grounds that one does so much to promote others' happiness. But there is no barrier to putting more of one's energy into self-perfection than into promoting others' happiness – or vice versa. Nor is it necessary to see them as two competing ends, ends for which one can strive only one at a time. Talent development is understood broadly; self-improvement can encompass improvement of one's listening skills, of one's ability to offer helpful, noninvasive, noncondescending advice, of one's skills as a lifeguard . . . in short, talents that are directly related to helping other people. So the two ends will often be intertwined, and in more than one way. As noted above, we may need to work to be more perceptive, more attuned to others' needs; this is an instance of improving oneself so as better to promote others' happiness. But in addition, the development of artistic talents or technical skills will hopefully promote happiness, assuming that it is done in a way that is guided by moral considerations. As Kant says at the start of the first section of *Groundwork*, without the goodness of a good will, qualities that are generally good can be bad; and the same is true of skills and talents. (Consider the organizational skills of the most "successful" terrorists, or Hitler's oratorical talents.) It is to be hoped that any talent worth developing will, if developed and exercised in a morally permissible way, promote others' happiness (if not directly, indirectly, as when shocking new art, though infuriating many viewers, inspires others, and hopefully over time promotes human happiness).

I should note here that exactly how Kant understands happiness is somewhat unclear, and for that reason it is not obvious that the example in the previous sentence's parenthesis really is an example of something that over time is likely to promote human happiness. The case – more generally the case for claiming that developing talents will usually promote others' happiness – is easier to make out if we imagine a somewhat perfectionist, somewhat normative conception of happiness, of the sort that John Stuart Mill favored (despite its being in some tension with utilitarianism). The case is harder to make out if happiness is understood in a strongly nonnormative way, as the satisfaction of one's inclinations, as Kant sometimes suggests (*G*, 4.405; *CPrR*, 5.73).

6.

Even without exploring in more detail how much latitude the obligatory ends allow, we can discern some implications for what sort of person might count as morally excellent. Most notably: the person who excels as an artist, while at the same time embracing as an end the happiness of others (and of course taking seriously her own moral self-improvement, not only the development of her artistic talents), might count as just as morally excellent as the self-sacrificing, altruistic person. Indeed there are reasons why she might count as more excellent. That she is self-sacrificing might indicate a lack of self-respect and, more specifically, a failure to view herself as an equal. Self-sacrificing altruism need not involve failing to view oneself as an equal, but particular instances certainly call for scrutiny to ensure that they do not. Kant does not speak to this directly in *The Metaphysics of Morals*, and what he does say does not actually entail that self-sacrificing altruism is wrong. (Making oneself a worm is definitely out [*MM*, 6.437], but it would be a stretch to claim that self-sacrificing altruism entails making oneself a worm or, more generally, being servile.) A passage in the *Critique of Practical Reason* reflects some doubts about self-sacrificial altruism.

> The action by which someone tries with extreme danger to his life to rescue people from a shipwreck, finally losing his own life in the attempt, will indeed be reckoned, on one side, as duty but on the other and even for the most part as a meritorious action; but our

esteem for it will be greatly weakened by the concept of *duty to himself*, which seems in this case to suffer some infringement. (5.158)

Whether the self-sacrificing, altruistic person fails to qualify as morally excellent, it is at any rate clear that he or she does not have the lofty status of being *the* moral paragon, on a Kantian picture. In Kant's ethics there is no "pinnacle" – no Mother Teresa at the top, below which we find others who are also altruistic but not as remarkably so.

In mentioning Mother Teresa, I do not mean to endorse the view that if there were only one obligatory end, and if that end were others' happiness, she would undoubtedly be the "winner" in a "Who is morally best?" contest. I say that not only because there surely are morally magnificent people I have never heard of, and they might possibly be more remarkable than she, but because (as was pointed out to me years ago by William McBride when I blithely referred to Mother Teresa as a moral paragon) there is reason to hesitate to regard as a moral paragon someone who fervently – and publicly – opposed the use of "artificial" birth control, despite knowing the disastrous con-sequences to the health of many women if they do not use it (not to mention other predictable disasters when no such birth control is used). I mention her, rather, because she is so routinely cited as an undisputed moral paragon. That she is reflects the fact that extraordinary altruism and self-sacrifice are widely regarded as the hallmarks of moral excellence – indeed, as both necessary and sufficient conditions (assuming that the end for which the sacrifice is made is reasonably worthy). It seems that the willingness to accept, for the sake of altruistic goals, very harsh living conditions when one could live very comfortably, is regarded as so decisive a mark of moral excellence that doubts about the wisdom of the particular path to promote others' welfare do little to shake our assumption that the person is a moral paragon.

In her landmark piece "Moral Saints," Susan Wolf asks, "what, pretheoretically, would count for us – contemporary members of Western culture – as a moral saint?" She answers: "A necessary condition of moral sainthood would be that one's life be domin-ated by a commitment to improving the welfare of others or of society as a whole" (Wolf 1982: 420; see also Flanagan 1986: 52). The picture of moral excellence in Kant's ethics allows for more variation. The "necessary condition" is not a necessary condition for Kantian moral excellence, and as noted, there is plenty of room to ask questions about whether such altruism is even in accord with duty.

7.

What else can we ascertain from Kant's discussion in *The Metaphysics of Morals* about morally excellent persons besides the fact that their lives need not be dominated by a commitment to improving the welfare of others, that they are committed both to self-perfection and to promoting others' happiness (and need not give priority to the latter), that there is considerable latitude as to how they go about promoting others' happi-ness and developing their talents and, relatedly, considerable variety among morally excellent persons?

First, something that will probably come as no surprise to those who have read the *Groundwork* but are new to *The Metaphysics of Morals*: the Kantian agent helps others

341

in a nonpaternalistic manner. When S seeks to promote T's happiness, she (with only slight qualification) understands T's happiness as T does, rather than thinking that T does not know what will make him happy, and seeking to promote T's happiness as she, S, understands it (I am supposing here that T is an adult and mentally competent). The exceptions are that S is not to promote those ends of T's that are actually immoral (*MM*, 6.388 and 6.450) and, moreover, refrains from "doing anything that, considering the nature of a human being, could tempt him to do something for which his conscience could afterwards pain him" (6.394); in addition, S may choose from T's ends those that S endorses as part of T's happiness. She is under no obligation to choose to promote those that T most wants to promote (or most wants help in promoting).

Perhaps a little more surprising, though, is the level of sensitivity that is called for. Kant's discussion of the duties of love is noteworthy for its attention to the ways in which desires to aid may be tainted by superciliousness, wishes to feel superior to another, or wishes to put another in one's debt. The following passage is one of many that reflect sensitivity on Kant's part, sensitivity that belies those textbook depictions of Kant's ethics as concerned just with mechanically applying a principle, as contrasted with Aristotle's ethics, so rich with attention to the particulars. Kant writes:

> Someone who is *rich* (has abundant means for the happiness of others, i.e., means in excess of his own needs) should hardly even regard beneficence as a meritorious duty on his part, even though he also puts others under obligation by it. The satisfaction he derives from his beneficence, which costs him no sacrifice, is a way of reveling in moral feelings. He must also carefully avoid any appearance of intending to bind the other by it; for if he showed that he wanted to put the other under an obligation (which always humbles the other in his own eyes), it would not be a true benefit that he rendered him. Instead, he must show that he is himself put under obligation by the other's acceptance or honored by it, hence that the duty is merely something that he owes, unless (as is better) he can practice his beneficence in complete secrecy. (*MM*, 6.453)

This passage brings to mind the Aristotelian idea that acting virtuously involves not just doing a virtuous action, but doing it in the right way, and with the right tone and gesture. It is not enough that we render aid; we need to do it well. Indeed, we do not really aid at all – do not render a benefit – if we humiliate the person we are (supposedly) trying to aid. (See Baron 2001: 608–12.)

8.

For further insight into the morally excellent agent, I turn to Kant's conception of virtue. Virtue is "the strength of a human being's maxims in fulfilling his duty"; this of course involves self-constraint, "self-constraint in accordance with a principle of inner freedom" (*MM*, 6.394). A familiar contrast drawn between Aristotle's and Kant's conceptions of virtue is evident here: whereas the most virtuous man, on Aristotle's view, experiences no internal struggle (in Aristotelian lingo, he is not merely continent, but temperate), there is no suggestion of this in Kant's ethical theory. Virtue never becomes second nature. There is no notion that one might arrive at a point where moral effort is no longer needed; there is no notion, moreover, that one might reach a point where one could rightly be considered "fully virtuous," for virtue is "always in progress" (*MM*, 6.409).

All of this is just what the reader of the *Groundwork* would expect, given Kant's distinction between holy wills and our wills. But further details bring some surprises. One might think that Kantian virtuous persons will invariably have inclinations and, more generally, feelings at odds with duty, i.e., that whatever the duty, they will wish that they could be doing something different, or at least feel strongly ambivalent. Or one might think, more plausibly, that it is a matter of indifference to Kant what feelings and sentiments they have. After all, as I just mentioned, whereas Aristotle makes it clear that his temperate man is superior to the continent man, Kant does not draw a similar distinction and even indicates that internal constraint is part of the human (moral) condition. But we have to be careful here. The constraint that is inevitable need not be experienced all or much of the time as a clash between duty and affect; what is inevitable is that one has a sense of duty, and this is experienced as a constraint. Thus I have a sense of duty about reading my students' dissertation chapters, and this means that I recognize that whether or not I want to read them, I am obligated to do so. I need not, to have the sense of constraint, dislike reading them. As with so many activities, it is easy always to have something else I could do that at the time seems more appealing. The recognition that it is my duty motivates me when I might instead just repeatedly opt to read something else, to work on my own work, to take a walk, to meet a colleague for coffee, and so on. It may also happen with respect to certain duties that I always unambivalently want to embark on the activity they entail; perhaps, for instance, I love reading to my young child, and never feel tempted to do something else. (Note that this is unlikely. An old friend may phone, and it may feel easier to keep talking at length, calling out a quick "Goodnight!" to my child, than to ask if I can phone my friend back in half an hour; or I may be anxious to finish preparing tomorrow's lecture and be tempted to skip the nightly reading that my child loves.) Even so, if I did not feel like reading books to him, it would nevertheless be a duty to do so (and indeed it would be a duty to try to cultivate in myself some enthusiasm about reading to him). One may feel no internal resistance to doing what one sees to be one's duty; nonetheless one recognizes that it is a duty, that if it were contrary to one's interests and desires, one would still be morally required so to act.

In a section at the end of the *Metaphysics of Morals*, "Ethical Ascetics," Kant is explicit about the attitude that is to accompany duty, and makes it quite clear that the fact that duty is experienced as constraint does not mean that it is approached as something one would prefer not to have to do. "What is not done with pleasure but merely as compulsory service has no inner worth for one who attends to his duty in this way" (6.484). That duty is not to be approached as something one would prefer not to have to do receives further emphasis in the next paragraph where Kant registers his disagreements with the Stoics. They have it partly right, but only partly:

> With regard to the principle of a vigorous, spirited, and valiant practice of virtue, the cultivation of virtue, that is, moral *ascetics*, takes as its motto the *Stoic* saying: accustom yourself *to put up with* the misfortunes of life that may happen and *to do without* its superfluous pleasures . . . This is a kind of *regimen* for keeping a human being healthy. But *health* is only a negative kind of well-being: it cannot itself be felt. Something must

be added to it, something which, though it is only moral, affords an agreeable enjoyment to life. This is the ever-cheerful heart, according to the idea of the virtuous *Epicurus*. (*MM*, 6.484–5)

Someone wedded to the view that Kant's morally ideal person lacks fellow-feeling, or at least that it is a matter of indifference to Kant whether a person has or lacks fellow-feeling, will claim that the view (in either form) is consistent with the passages cited from "Ethical Ascetics." The passages, he might claim, show only that Kant holds that the virtuous person takes pleasure in doing his duty and that he has an "ever-cheerful" heart, not that he has fellow-feeling. Now, it is true that one could (perhaps priggishly) take pleasure in doing his duty simply because of a strong sense of moral rectitude, and without any sympathetic impulses/feelings of compassion. On the other hand, an absence of fellow-feeling would be a significant barrier to "an agreeable enjoyment" of life. It would be hard to enjoy life if one did not have any, or had very little, fellow-feeling. Thus, to suppose that virtuous people could lack fellow-feeling is in tension with "Ethical Ascetics."

Moreover, it should be evident from what has been said about obligatory ends that virtuous persons would not be cold and indifferent to others. To have others' happiness as one's end and act accordingly is more than simply saying "OK, I'll help people in need." One needs to be attuned to others' needs, to what will help and what will get in the way, to what will make the person feel even worse, to what will humiliate, and so on. That is incompatible with being indifferent.

Kant does seem to countenance the possibility that someone who has adopted the end of others' happiness might initially help others from duty without fellow-feeling (*Menschenliebe*) (*MM*, 6.401). But through acting beneficently, we are likely, Kant claims, to come to love the person we help. Kant says of beneficence "if someone practices it often and succeeds in realizing his beneficent intentions, he eventually comes actually to love the person he has helped" (6.402).

Significantly, the idea is not to leave such developments to chance. We have a duty (albeit only an indirect one) to cultivate our sympathetic impulses.

> But while it is not in itself a duty to share the sufferings (as well as the joys) of others, it is a duty to sympathize actively in their fate; and to this end it is therefore an indirect duty to cultivate the compassionate natural (aesthetic) feelings in us, and to make use of them as so many means to sympathy based on moral principles and the feeling appropriate to them. – It is therefore a duty not to avoid the places where the poor who lack the most basic necessities are to be found but rather to seek them out, and not to shun sickrooms or debtors' prisons and so forth in order to avoid sharing painful feelings one may not be able to resist. For this is still one of the impulses that nature has implanted in us to do what the representation of duty alone might not accomplish. (*MM*, 6.457)

It is worth noting that fellow-feeling ("love of one's neighbor") is one of the "moral endowments" that Kant says "lie at the basis of morality, as subjective conditions of receptiveness to the concept of duty" (not, of course, "as objective conditions of morality"). "Every human being has them, and it is by virtue of them that he can be put under obligation" (*MM*, 6.399). We cannot have a duty to have them, because without them we could not have any duties at all; but we can, and do, have a duty to cultivate them.

That Kant does not regard as a matter of indifference whether we feel compassion or malice, gratitude or indifference is evident from a number of other passages, in addition to the striking 6.457, quoted above. Kant holds that "human beings have a duty of friendship" (6.469) and mentions that friendship involves "each participating and sharing sympathetically in the other's well-being" (6.469). Moreover, implicit – and sometimes explicit – in his discussion of specific virtues and vices are duties to shape one's character so as to nurture certain affects and weaken others. Thus he speaks of a duty to cultivate a conciliatory spirit, duties of gratitude, duties not to be envious and not to take malicious joy in others' misfortunes, and a duty to be forgiving, all of which require that we shape our characters accordingly. (See 6.458–60; 6.469–74.) His discussion of vices that violate duties of respect for other human beings also implies duties of self-cultivation. We need, for instance, to weaken whatever propensity we have to wanton faultfinding and mockery (6.467).

It is time to take stock. What we do know thus far about Kantian moral paragons (morally excellent persons)? They embrace both the ends of self-perfection and others' happiness, and this entails adopting specific ends that instantiate the rather abstract obligatory ends. It also entails viewing the world in such a way that certain things are salient for one, e.g., others' needs. We also know that the morally excellent person will be sensitive, perceptive, attuned to moral considerations, yet need not be moralistic. Whereas it is common to guess, after reading only the *Groundwork*, that the Kantian moral paragon would be concerned only with doing his duty – acting for the sake of duty, not merely from duty – it is clear from *The Metaphysics of Morals* that good Kantians are attached to the particular ends (playing viola well; helping Joe) that they set for themselves as instantiations of the obligatory ends and not merely to the highly abstract notion of duty. To be sure, they adopt the obligatory ends from duty, and see themselves as morally constrained; but they are concerned not merely with doing their duty (which happens here to be X), but with doing X. It is not as if their purpose is to do their duty, rather than to do X. As Korsgaard explains, "Duty is not a different purpose, but a different ground for the adoption of a purpose" (Korsgaard 1996: 60). This is easier to discern in the *Groundwork* once one has read "The Doctrine of Virtue."

The virtuous person will have the virtues Kant mentions (e.g., moderation in one's demands, appreciativeness, being forgiving), and lack the vices (e.g., self-conceit, contemptuousness, arrogance, vengefulness, envy, malice, ingratitude) . . . but it is misleading to put it in precisely this way, for it may suggest that the virtuous person is, in effect, a finished product. Virtue is always in progress. The virtuous person will be striving not to engage in wanton fault-finding (*MM*, 6.467), not to be contemptuous of others, and never to deny to anyone, not even the most depraved person, the respect that is due to him as a human being (6.463). Some of what the virtuous person strives for involves fairly subtle distinctions. He must distinguish "from banter, from the familiarity among friends in which one makes fun of their peculiarities that only seem to be faults but are really marks of their pluck in sometimes departing from the rule of fashion (for this is not derision)" something that is to be avoided: "holding up to ridicule a person's real faults, or supposed faults as if they were real, in order to deprive him of the respect he deserves" (6.467). The virtuous person will not be complacent about his character, and will examine it. Kant writes that the "*First Command* of All Duties to Oneself" is "to *know* (scrutinize, fathom) *yourself*." "Only the descent into the hell of self-cognition can pave the way to godliness" (6.441). One will have to be probing to discern whether one is forgiving, as one should be, or whether one is instead meekly tolerating wrongs, or renouncing "rigorous means . . . for preventing the recurrence of wrongs by others" (6.461). Those familiar with the *Groundwork* will not be surprised to find this emphasis on self-scrutiny, for to apply the Categorical Imperative, one may sometimes need to engage in some soul-searching in order to discern what one's maxim is.

We should note that the virtuous person, on Kant's view, need not be especially smart; at least, Kant would be unhappy if it turned out that lurking in his account was an assumption that the person was of high intelligence, or was a scholar. "Only the teaching of M. R[ousseau]. can bring it about that even the most learned philosopher with his knowledge holds himself, uprightly and without the help of religion, no better than the common human being" (*R*, 20.176; see Wood 1999: 5–8). Kant recognizes his own earlier prejudice in a famous reflection:

> I am an inquirer by inclination. I feel a consuming thirst for knowledge, the unrest which goes with the desire to progress in it, and the satisfaction at every advance in it. There was a time when I believed this constituted the honor of humanity, and I despised the people, who know nothing. Rousseau set me right about this. This blinding prejudice disappeared. I learned to honor human beings. (*R*, 20.44)

Since I am focusing on *The Metaphysics of Morals*, I have skipped over some features of the morally excellent person that can be found in other works, e.g., in "What is Enlightenment?," which begins with the stirring, "Enlightenment is man's emergence from his self-imposed immaturity. Immaturity is the inability to use one's understanding without guidance from another" (8.35). It is worth noting that the virtuous person would be someone (learned or not) who is not afflicted with "self-imposed immaturity."

I have also not emphasized some of the features that are obvious and would not require any familiarity with *The Metaphysics of Morals*. It hardly needs to be mentioned that a morally excellent person would be honest, and would act in accordance with the Categorical Imperative. But what does deserve mention is that this is sometimes thought to entail rigidity – to imply, for example, that intentionally uttering an untruth is completely prohibited, that suicide is absolutely ruled out, and so on. It emerges in *The Metaphysics of Morals* that these things are not as cut and dried as they might have seemed. In a set of "Casuistical Questions," Kant raises such questions as the following:

> A man who had been bitten by a mad dog already felt hydrophobia coming on. He explained, in a letter he left, that, since as far as he knew the disease was incurable, he was taking his life lest he harm others as well in his madness (the onset of which he already felt). Did he do wrong? (*MM*, 6.423–4; for casuistical questions concerning lying, see 6.431)

Another very familiar feature of the morally excellent person that, despite its familiarity, needs to be mentioned, is that he acts from duty. As I have argued elsewhere (Baron 1995: chs. 4–5), this is best understood not as acting from duty as a primary motive as frequently as possible, but as acting in a way that is governed by a conception of duty and a commitment to living as one morally ought. The person who acts from duty is one who puts duty first, subordinating inclination to duty, and is committed to

346

so doing. (See 6.36.) We should note, though, that a commitment to doing whatever the moral law requires does not mean obsessing about every detail of one's life. Kant derides as "*fantastically virtuous*" the man who

> allows *nothing to be morally indifferent* . . . and strews all his steps with duties, as with mantraps. [It] is not indifferent to him whether I eat meat or fish, drink beer or wine, supposing that both agree with me. Fantastic virtue is a concern with petty details which, were it admitted into the doctrine of virtue, would turn the government of virtue into tyranny. (*MM*, 6.409)

Earlier I spoke of people qualifying, or not qualifying, as morally excellent. This is a somewhat misleading way to speak, and the reason why is instructive. It is misleading because it suggests that there is an elite, those people who qualify as morally excellent, the rest of us being either just morally decent, or worse than that. There is a tendency in many discussions of ethics to split people up into such groups, referring not just to performance but to aptitude; similarly, ever since Urmson's "Saints and Heroes" (Urmson 1958), it has been widely accepted that we need a category of "supereroga-tory" acts – acts that go beyond duty – in order to distinguish the saints and heroes from ordinary decent people. According to Urmson, it is vital that our "moral code" (a significant and not uncontroversial notion!) "distinguish between basic rules, summarily set forth in simple rules and binding on all, and the higher flights of morality of which saintliness and heroism are outstanding examples" (Urmson 1958: 211). I have argued elsewhere that this picture is at odds with Kant's view and that Kant's approach is in many ways more attractive than Urmson's (Baron 1995: chs. 1–2). Here I briefly sketch the contrast.

Whereas Urmson thinks it important that there be a line of duty, fairly clearly laid out ("in simple rules"), above which all is supererogatory, and that it be set "low" so as not to seem to the ordinary person to be beyond his reach, on Kant's view there is no concern to have our duties (or duty) be either crisply laid out or easily fulfilled. Kantian duty includes imperfect (or "wide") as well as perfect (or "narrow") duties, and as ethical duties do not entail the right to demand compliance, there is no particular reason why it needs to be easy to determine whether someone has met, or is fulfilling, his ethical duties. We are all capable of doing what morality asks of us. The fact that it is harder for some of us than for others does not raise the moral issues that it might raise if it were assumed (as it definitely is not in Kant's ethics) that failures to fulfill one's ethical duties merit moral censure (or even punishment). Another potential problem is avoided, or at least greatly ameliorated, by the latitude that the imperfect duties afford us: one might suspect, if duty is not set "low" as it is in Urmson's approach, that it will be far too demanding. It helps that while our responsibilities are, at a general level, the same (i.e., there is no "lower" standard for some than for others), there is considerable latitude as to how we instantiate our obligatory ends, and thus how much we sacrifice or jeopardize our own happiness or safety or comfort to promote these ends.

There is no room in Kant's ethics for the thought that for most (or many) of us, simply being decent ("rule-abiding") will have to do, while the "higher flights of morality" are for the morally gifted. Likewise, there is no room for the thought that the very virtuous need not continue striving to be morally better. We all have to strive to improve ourselves, and no one is a finished product. Thus "morally excellent" refers only to a standard we must all set for ourselves, rather than to a certain group who have achieved moral excellence.

Acknowledgments

I am indebted to Graham Bird and Justin Brown for very helpful comments on earlier drafts of this paper, and to Melissa Seymour for permitting me to draw some sentences from Baron and Seymour, forthcoming.

References and Further Reading

Allison, H. (1990). *Kant's Theory of Freedom*. Cambridge: Cambridge University Press.
Baron, M. (1995). *Kantian Ethics Almost Without Apology*. Ithaca, NY: Cornell University Press.
Baron, M. (2002). Acting from duty. In *Groundwork for the Metaphysics of Morals* (pp. 92–110), ed. and tr. Allen W. Wood. New Haven: Yale University Press.
Baron, M. (2005). *Grundlegung* 397–401: Acting from duty. In Kant's *Groundwork for the Metaphysics of Morals: New Interpretations*, eds. Christoph Horn and Dieter Schönecker. Berlin: Walter de Gruyter Verlag.
Baron, M. and Seymour, M. (forthcoming 2006). Beneficence and other duties of love in the *Metaphysics of Morals*. In *The Blackwell Companion to Kant's Ethics*, ed. Thomas E. Hill, Jr. Oxford: Blackwell.
Denis, L. (2000). Kant's cold sage and the sublimity of apathy. *Kantian Review*, 4: 48–73.
Denis, L. (2001). *Moral Self-Regard: Duties to Oneself in Kant's Moral Theory*. New York: Routledge.
Engstrom, S. and Whiting, J. (1996). *Aristotle, Kant and the Stoic: Rethinking Happiness and Duty*. Cambridge: Cambridge University Press.
Flanagan, O. (1986). Admirable immorality and admirable imperfection. *Journal of Philosophy*, 83: 41–60.
Gregor, M. (1963). *Laws of Freedom: A Study of Kant's Method of Applying the Categorical Imperative in the Metaphysik der Sitten*. New York: Barnes & Noble.
Guyer, P. (1993). *Kant and the Experience of Freedom: Essays on Aesthetics and Morality*. Cambridge: Cambridge University Press. (See esp. ch. 10).
Herman, B. (1993). *The Practice of Moral Judgment*. Cambridge, MA: Harvard University Press.
Herman, B. (2002). The scope of moral requirement. *Philosophy and Public Affairs*, 30: 227–56.
Hill, T. E., Jr. (1992). *Dignity and Practical Reason in Kant's Moral Theory*. Ithaca, NY&: Cornell University Press.
Hill, T. E., Jr. (2002). *Human Welfare and Moral Worth: Kantian Perspectives*. Oxford: Clarendon Press.
Kant, Immanuel (1996a). *Practical Philosophy*, ed. and tr. Mary J. Gregor. Cambridge: Cambridge University Press.
Kant, Immanuel (1996b). *Religion and Rational Theology*, ed. and tr. Allen W. Wood and George Di Giovanni. Cambridge: Cambridge University Press.
Korsgaard, C. (1996). *Creating the Kingdom of Ends*. Cambridge: Cambridge University Press.
Mendus, S. (1985). The practical and the pathological. *Journal of Value Inquiry*, 19: 235–43.
O'Neill, O. (1989). *Constructions of Reason: Explorations of Kant's Practical Philosophy*. Cambridge: Cambridge University Press.
Schiller, F. (1967). *Über Anmut und Würde, Schillers Werke*. Stuttgart: J. G. Cotta'schen Buchhandlung, Bd. 11, 238–96.

348

Sedgwick, S. (1988). On the relation of pure reason to content: A reply to Hegel's critique of formalism in Kant's ethics. *Philosophy and Phenomenological Research*, 49: 59–80.

Shapiro, T. (1999). What is a child? *Ethics*, 109: 715–38.

Sherman, N. (1997). *Making a Necessity of Virtue: Aristotle and Kant on Virtue*. Cambridge: Cambridge University Press.

Timmons, M., ed. (2002). *Kant's Metaphysics of Morals: Interpretative Essays*. Oxford: Oxford University Press.

Urmson, J. O. (1958). Saints and heroes. In *Essays in Moral Philosophy*, ed. A. I. Melden. Seattle: University of Washington Press. Rpr. in 1969 in *Moral Concepts*, ed. J. Feinberg. London: London University Press.

Wolf, S. (1982). Moral saints. *Journal of Philosophy*, 79: 419–39.

Wood, A. W. (1999). *Kant's Ethical Thought*. Cambridge: Cambridge University Press.

Wood, A. W. (2002). The final form of Kant's practical philosophy. In *Kant's Metaphysics of Morals: Interpretative Essays* (pp. 1–21), ed. M. Timmons. Oxford: Oxford University Press.

23

Applying Kant's Ethics:
The Role of Anthropology

ROBERT B. LOUDEN

The Second Part of Morals

For many readers Kant is the moral philosopher least likely to support the claim that anthropology and the empirical study of human nature have necessary and important contributions to make to ethics. As he declares in the Preface of his most famous work in ethics: there exists "the utmost necessity to work out for once a pure moral philosophy, completely cleansed of everything that may be only empirical and that belongs to anthropology," and that "all moral philosophy is based entirely on its pure part; . . . when it is applied to the human being it does not borrow the least thing from acquaintance with him (from anthropology)" (G, 4.389). Indeed, a long and varied line of critics from Hegel to Bernard Williams stand united in their condemnation of Kant's ethics for precisely this reason: it is charged with "empty formalism" and "abstract universality" (Hegel 1991: 162); an infatuation with a "purist" view of morality which rejects both a "biological perspective" as well as any "reasonable historical and psychological understanding of morality" (Williams 1995: 104). Even some contemporary commentators on Kant, who generally view themselves as friends rather than foes of the sage of Königsberg, also assert that anthropology has no necessary place in Kant's ethics, and so end up albeit unintentionally agreeing with Kant's critics on this point. We are told that "Kant did not believe that anthropological investigations were necessary for moral action," and that anthropology's "significance for Kant's general ethical theory may be quite limited" (Kitcher 2001: 250; Hill, Jr. and Zweig in Kant 2002: 180).

However, Kant's considered views on the importance of anthropology for ethics are quite different from what these critics and commentators maintain. Moral philosophy, like natural, does "have its empirical part" (G, 4.387), a part which Kant refers to variously as "practical anthropology" (G, 4.388), "moral anthropology" (MM, 6.217, *Moral Mrongovius II*, 29.599), "anthropology" (G, 4.412; *Moralphilosophie Collins*, 27.244; *Moral Mrongovius I*, 27.1398), "the counterpart of a metaphysics of morals" (MM, 6.217), and "the second part" of morals (*Moral Mrongovius II*, 29.599). In a 1785 ethics lecture – transcribed the same year the *Groundwork* was published – Kant states:

> The metaphysics of morals, or *metaphysica pura*, is only the first part of morals; the second
> part is *philosophia moralis applicata*, moral anthropology, to which the empirical principles

belong. . . . Moral anthropology is morals that are applied to human beings. *Moralia pura* is built on necessary laws, therefore it cannot ground itself on the particular constitution of a rational being, of the human being. The particular constitution of the human being, as well as the laws that are grounded on it, appear in moral anthropology under the name of "ethics." (*Moral Mrongovius II*, 29.599; translations from Kant 2002 and the author)

But what exactly is this mysterious second part of morals, a part that has somehow continuously managed to escape the notice of Kant critics and scholars? Where do we find it in the Kantian corpus? What is its relationship to the better-known first part of morals, and what is its overall significance for ethics? These are the questions that I shall attempt to answer in the present chapter.

Caution is necessary when discussing the relationship between Kant's ethics and anthropology, for at least two reasons. First and foremost, his views here are not static. Over the years, shifting conceptions of ethics, anthropology, and the relationship between the two are detectable (Kühn 2004). The most obvious example concerns Kant's pre-Critical work in ethics, which often has a marked empiricist tone. For instance, in his *Inquiry Concerning the Distinctness of the Principles of Natural Theology and Morals* (1764), he asserts confidently that "the faculty of experiencing the *good* is *feeling*" (2.299). The famous pure ethics project is announced as early as 1770.

I have resolved this winter to put in order and complete my investigations of pure moral philosophy, in which no empirical principles are to be found, as it were the metaphysics of morals. (Letter to Lambert, Sept. 2, 1770; 10.97)

But the actual carrying-out of this project took nearly thirty years. And by the time his work entitled *The Metaphysics of Morals* is published in 1797, the term "metaphysics of morals" appears to be used in a way that includes reference to "the particular *nature* of human beings, which is known only by experience" (6.217), whereas in the 1785 *Groundwork* a "metaphysics of morals" was strictly identified with pure, non-empirical ethics (Wood 1999: 193–6).

In what follows my aim is to articulate and defend Kant's most basic views about the significance of anthropology for ethics, views which I believe hold fairly constant from the time that he first conceptualizes the project of a pure moral philosophy until the end of his life, that is, from 1770 to 1804. The issues to be discussed below are not affected by possible changes in Kant's own conception of the precise contours of either a metaphysics of morals or of anthropology after 1770.

A second reason for caution is that some of Kant's most detailed and compelling remarks about the significance of anthropology for ethics are to be found in student lecture notes from his ethics and anthropology courses, which he taught together each winter semester from 1772 on, but whose accuracy, with respect to both content and date, is less than sure (Stark 2003: 23). Kant himself, in responding to former student Marcus Herz's request for a serviceable set of lecture notes from one of his metaphysics courses, sounded an appropriate warning against over-reliance on them when he remarked that those students "who are most thorough in note-taking are seldom capable of distinguishing the important from the unimportant. They pile a mass of misunderstood stuff under what they may possibly have grasped correctly"

(10.242). Kant's lecture notes are important documents, but they should be used conservatively as added support for claims made in his own published works but not as stand-alone indications of his position.

Defining Features of Pragmatic Anthology

In his anthropology lectures, Kant repeatedly emphasizes that his own approach to anthropology is *pragmatic*. However, he assigns several different meanings to the term "pragmatic," and it is important to familiarize oneself with these different meanings and intended contrasts before turning to the narrower issue of moral or practical anthropology (Louden 2000: 62–70; Wood 2003: 40–2; Frierson 2003: 53–6).

Pragmatic versus physiological

In a letter to Herz (10.145) written toward the end of 1773, in which he describes his anthropology course, Kant stresses that his approach is "quite different" from the physiological approach advocated by the physician Ernst Platner in his book, *Anthropologie für Ärzte und Weltweise* (Leipzig, 1772), which Herz had reviewed earlier for the journal *Allgemeine deutsche Bibliothek*. Twenty-five years later, in the Preface to his own published version of the anthropology lectures, Kant continues to contrast his approach to Platner's, noting that physiological anthropology "concerns the investigation of what *nature* makes of the human being; pragmatic, the investigation of what *he* as a free-acting being makes of himself, or can and should make of himself" (7.119; cf. Zammito 2002: 221–53). Essentially, the physiological approach championed by Platner and others is the predecessor of physical anthropology, while Kant's pragmatic anthropology, with its emphasis on free human action, is the progenitor of various philosophical and existentialist anthropologies. Max Scheler, an important voice in this latter tradition who also influenced Heidegger, notes that the human being is not only an animal being but also a "spiritual" being (*ein "geistiges" Wesen*) that is "no longer tied to its drives and environments, but rather 'free from the environment' [*umweltfrei*], or, as we shall say, 'open to the world' [*weltoffen*]" (Scheler 1989: 51; Heidegger 1962: iv, xii, 216).

Pragmatic versus scholastic

In the *Menschenkunde* lectures, probably transcribed in 1781–2, when the *Critique of Pure Reason* was first published, Kant again criticizes Platner for having merely "written a scholastic anthropology" (25.856). The scholastics, he adds, produced a "science for the school," but it was of "no use to the human being." Pragmatic anthropology, on the other hand, aims to promote "enlightenment for common life" (25.853; cf. *Mrongovius*, 25.1209). As Kant remarks in a note at the end of his 1775 essay, "On the Different Races of Human Beings," which also served as an advertisement for his companion course on physical geography for that year, his aim was "knowledge of the world" (*Weltkenntnis*), a type of knowledge which would

> provide the *pragmatic* to the otherwise acquired sciences and skills, so that they are useful not only for *school*, but also for *life*, and so that the accomplished student is introduced

to the stage of his destiny, namely, the *world*. (2.443n; cf. *Friedländer*, 25.469; *Pillau*, 25.733–4)

Knowledge of the world, he stresses later in his Preface to the 1798 *Anthropology*, "must come after our schooling," and is only properly called pragmatic "when it contains knowledge of the human being as a *citizen of the world*" (7.120). Accordingly, pragmatic anthropology must also be cosmopolitan in scope. The anthropology that concerns Kant "is not a local, but a general anthropology. In it one comes to know the nature of humanity, not the condition of human beings . . . [A]nthropology is not a description of human beings, but of human nature" (*Friedländer*, 25.471; cf. *Pillau*, 25.734).

Pragmatic as involving the use of others

As the contrast with scholastic implies, pragmatic anthropology is useful knowledge. But the main kind of usefulness stressed by Kant in the anthropology lectures involves the skillful use of other human beings. By means of our knowledge of human nature we acquire insight into how to use human beings for our own purposes. "Pragmatic," in this specific sense, refers to the ability "to use other human beings skillfully for one's purposes" (*APS*, 7.322). In the *Busolt* lectures (1788–9) Kant is particularly blunt:

> We must make an effort to form the way of thinking and the capacities of those with whom we have dealings, so that we do not become too difficult or offensive to them. Now anthropology teaches us this, it shows us how we can use people for our own ends. (25.1436)

Pragmatic anthropology is thus also "a knowledge of the art of how a human being has influence on others and can lead them according to his intention" (*Menschenkunde*, 25.855).

Pragmatic as prudential

Finally, pragmatic anthropology is also a doctrine of prudence, a *Klugheitslehre*. Kant sometimes uses "prudence" to refer to the skillful use of others (e.g., *Menschenkunde*, 25.855; *G*, 4.416n, 4.417n), but his primary use refers to the ability to use one's knowledge of human nature in order to promote the welfare and happiness of oneself as well as others. As he remarks in the *Groundwork*, "skill in the choice of means to one's own greatest well-being can be called *prudence*" (4.416). And in the *Parow* lectures (1772–3): "The capacity to choose the best means to happiness is prudence. Prudence consists in the satisfaction of all inclinations, and therefore to be able to choose happiness, one must be free" (25.413; cf. *CPR*, B 828). The *Friedländer* lectures open with a particularly strong emphasis on the prudential nature of pragmatic anthropology: "[A]ll pragmatic doctrines are doctrines of prudence, where for all our skills we also have the means to make a proper use of everything, for we study human beings in order to become more prudent" (25.471; cf. Kain 2003).

This is certainly not the whole story behind Kant's anthropology lectures. They comprise an unabashedly eclectic venture, one revealing various origins, competing concerns and aims, and multiple possibilities of application. Kant also strove to make

353

the lectures "entertaining and never dry" (letter to Herz, end of 1773, 10.146), and held that as a result "they can be read by everyone" (*Menschenkunde*, 25.856–7). But keeping these key features of pragmatic anthropology in mind, let us now turn to the issue of anthropology's significance for ethics.

Anthropology: Pragmatic versus Moral

Kant's anthropology course, from its commencement in 1772 until the last time he taught it in the winter semester of 1795–6, while often differing on important matters of detail, remained firmly pragmatic in its basic orientation. Nowhere in the lectures from this course does he change direction and offer a comprehensive practical or moral anthropology. To this extent, critics who hold that there is no connection between Kant's ethics and his anthropology are right: "Pragmatic anthropology is . . . not the discipline of practical anthropology, variously described by Kant, that was supposed to function as a complement to pure moral philosophy" (Brandt 2003: 92). But no one, least of all a philosopher who holds that we must always treat humanity always as an end, never merely as a means (cf. *G*, 4.429), has ever seriously maintained that practical or moral anthropology is *identical* to pragmatic anthropology. For the latter, as we have seen, is designed in part to show us how we can effectively use people for our own purposes – whatever these purposes may be. And it is clear that pragmatic anthropology can be put to many different purposes, some of which are blatantly immoral. People can and will choose to do different things with it. For instance, unscrupulous advertisers and businesspeople may use their knowledge of human nature to sell people things that they do not need and cannot afford, and shrewd politicians may exploit their knowledge of human nature to advance their own personal agenda for power and control. Thus any argument about whether pragmatic anthropology is or is not identical to "the counterpart of a metaphysics of morals, the other member of the division of practical philosophy as a whole, . . . moral anthropology" (*MM*, 6.217) is simply a red herring, a nonstarter.

But we can also choose to use our knowledge of human nature for *moral* purposes, and when we choose to do so, our anthropology becomes a moral anthropology. Moral anthropology is already potentially present within pragmatic anthropology, and we actualize this potential whenever we choose to apply it for moral purposes (cf. Jacobs 2003: 112–13). It is clear that Kant, throughout his twenty-four years of lecturing on anthropology, explicitly desired that people would choose to make moral use of anthropology. As he notes in the 1775–6 *Friedländer* anthropology lectures:

> the reason that morals and sermons, which are full of admonitions of which one never tires, have little effect, is lack of knowledge of the human being. Morals must be united with knowledge of humanity. . . . In order that morality and religion obtain their final purpose, knowledge of human beings must be combined with them. (25.471–2; cf. *Collins Moralphilosophie* 27.244; Stark 2004: 4–5, 402–4)

One chief advantage that anthropology offers to ethics is practical efficacy – the possibility of providing a priori moral principles with "access to the will of the human being and impetus for fulfilling them" (*G*, 4.389). As Kant remarks in several of his moral philosophy lectures, "consideration of the [moral] rule is useless, if one cannot make people prepared to fulfill it" (*Moral Mrongovius I*, 27.1398; cf. *Collins Moralphilosophie*, 27.244, Stark 2004: 6).

Defining Features of Moral Anthropology

Pragmatic anthropology becomes moral anthropology when we choose to make use of our knowledge of human nature for moral purposes. Thus in principle *all* aspects of pragmatic anthropology are potentially moral anthropology: all that is needed to turn any aspect of pragmatic anthropology into moral anthropology is the decision to apply it to moral rather than nonmoral ends. But Kant also speaks more specifically about what he believes are the most likely moral applications of pragmatic anthropology, and in the remainder of this essay I will focus on these more specific applications.

Hindrances and Helps

One specific application that is stressed repeatedly in both the ethics and anthropology texts is what Kant calls "hindrances and helps." One of moral anthropology's primary tasks is to point out "the subjective conditions in human nature that hinder people or help them in *carrying out* the laws of a metaphysics of morals" (*MM*, 6.217; cf. *G*, 4.387, 4.389). Similarly, in the *Powalski* ethics lectures, Kant emphasizes that we must study "not merely the object; that is, moral conduct, but also the subject; that is, the human being. This is necessary, one must see what sorts of hindrances to virtue are to be found in the human being" (27.97). In other words, what is it about the particular species of rational being Homo sapiens that makes it difficult for them to act on moral principle, and what aids for their specific moral development can the informed anthropologist offer?

Throughout his writing career, Kant appears to have held to the conviction that while each and every type of rational being is subject to the same universal moral principle, different types of rational being stand in different relationships to this moral principle (see *G*, 4.389). For instance, in his early work, *Universal Natural History and Theory of the Heavens* (1755), he notes that the inhabitants of earth "and perhaps also those of Mars" are "in the dangerous middle position, where temptations of sensible stirrings against the supremacy of spirit have a strong power of seduction," but whose spirit also "cannot deny that it has the capacity to put up resistance" to these temptations (1.366). Still, things could be far worse for those of us in this dangerous middle position. For instance, our ability to have thoughts that we do not at the same time utter (that is, to deceive one another) at least makes it easy to live in peace with one another. However, those rational beings "on some other planet, who could not think in any other way but aloud, would have an entirely different character from the human species, and unless they were all *pure as angels*, it is inconceivable how they could live in peace together" (*APS*, 7.332, 7.332n). Those who are concerned to make morality efficacious in human life need to learn more about the distinctive features of human nature.

355

Among the many hindrances to morality that human beings face and that come under Kant's scrutiny are our affects and passions (Frierson 2003: 59–61). This particular type of hindrance is substantial, since "both affect and passion shut out the sovereignty of reason" (*APS*, 7.251). Affect, however, involves merely a "lack of virtue," whereas passion is "*properly* evil, that is, a true *vice*" (*MM*, 6.408). These two kinds of emotion are thus "essentially different from each other, both with regard to the method of prevention and to that of the cure that the physician of souls would have to apply" (*APS*, 7.251; cf. *MM*, 6.408). Passion "can be conquered only with difficulty or not at all by the subject's reason," while affect refers to a "feeling of pleasure or displeasure in the subject's present state that does not let him rise to *reflection*" (7.251).

In his anthropology lectures, Kant discusses numerous affects and passions at length, showing both how and why they hinder moral conduct, and offering advice on how to treat and prevent these hindrances. In the case of passions, there often is no treatment – "passion is an *illness* that abhors all medicine," for someone in the grip of passion "does not want to be cured." (7.266). Here preventative measures, such as steering clear of them, are the best that can be hoped for. With respect to affects, the prospects for both treatment and prevention are better. Because affects are "rash" and unpremeditated as opposed to sustained and considered, they allow more room for self-treatment, for what an affect "does not accomplish quickly, it does not do at all; and it forgets easily" (*APS*, 7.252; *MM*, 6.407; *CJ*, 5.272n). Preventative measures also abound. For instance, one should steer clear of "novels, sentimental plays, shallow moral precepts, which make play with (falsely) so-called noble dispositions," not to mention religious sermons that preach "a groveling, base currying of favor and self-ingratiation" (*CJ*, 5.273).

As befits a philosopher who often doubts "whether any true virtue is to be found in the world" (*G*, 4.407), Kant devotes more attention to human hindrances to morality than he does to helps or aids. Morality is not easy for human beings (Louden 2005). But anthropology also teaches us that there are things we can do, given human nature, to promote the development of moral character.

One substantial aid to morality for human beings is politeness (Frierson 2003: 57–8). Because of our nature, we are susceptible to influence through politeness, and this influence can and should be used in cultivating moral character. Deception is also part of our nature, since our character "consists in the propensity to lie," but politeness manages to "deceive the deceiver in ourselves," and in order to "lead the human being to virtue, nature has wisely implanted in him the tendency to willingly allow himself to be deceived" (*APS*, 7.151–2, 7.331n). Politeness helps morality by cultivating self-restraint. The polite person refrains from satisfying illegitimate desires, and this self-restraint itself "betrays a self-mastery and is the beginning of self-overcoming. It is a step toward virtue, or at least a capacity thereto" (*Menschenkunde*, 25.930). In effect, we are fooled into virtue. Politeness itself is only moral *Schein* – an illusion or semblance, rather than true virtue. But it is also a "beautiful *Schein* resembling virtue" (*MM*, 6. 473), which in time will lead to the real thing. For "when people conduct themselves in company in a civilized fashion; they thereby become gentler and more refined, and practice goodness in small matters" (*Collins Moralphilosophie*, 27.456). The opportunity to practice goodness in small matters through civilized behavior is a mundane feature of daily life, but it has a cumulative effect on character, and eventually we are "won over to actually loving the good" (*Menschenkunde*, 25.931). Here too anthropology shows us how we can be fooled into virtue.

A second, related aid to morality is the civilizing impact that republican regimes bring to human life, that is, societies where the rule of law is practiced and where all citizens are involved in the process of making laws (Louden 2000, 144–52). In an important footnote to *Perpetual Peace* Kant argues that such regimes, by instilling non-violent behavior patterns, disciplining our emotions, and making us less partial toward our own interests, help establish a "moral veneer" over human society, and that in doing so, "a great step toward morality (although not yet a moral step) is made" (8.375–6n). Here as elsewhere, the strong influence of Rousseau on Kant's anthropology is detectable. As he remarks in the *Pillau* lectures: "Rousseau shows how a civil constitution must exist in order for human beings to reach their complete purpose" (25.847). (See chapters 24 and 25 below.)

These are just two examples of the many cultural and institutional practices discussed by Kant in his anthropology lectures that can serve as aids to humanity's moral transformation.

Moral *Weltkenntnis*

In the *Groundwork*, Kant asserts that while pure moral philosophy "does not borrow the least thing from acquaintance with the human being" in articulating and justifying its basic principles, it does "no doubt still require a judgment sharpened by experience, partly in order to distinguish in what cases they have their application . . ." (4.389). Here we find a second, fundamental contribution that anthropology makes to ethics (Louden 2003: 69–72). The *Weltkenntnis* aim of anthropology – its goal of imparting a "knowledge of the human being as a *citizen of the world*" (*APS*, 7.120; cf. *Pillau*, 25.734, *Geo*, 9.157, *Racen*, 2.443n) – provides us with an account of human nature by means of which we can better assess human conduct and character. As we saw earlier, this *Weltkenntnis* has multiple possibilities of application: It can be put to pragmatic, nonmoral uses as well as to moral ones. A businessman who uses his *Weltkenntnis* to expand his company's market share is using it for pragmatic purposes, but people who use *Weltkenntnis* in order more effectively and intelligently to apply pure moral principles to the human situation are using it for moral purposes.

Moral *Weltkenntnis* teaches us how to see a world with moral features; it provides us with the relevant empirical framework to which we are to apply pure moral principles. Human beings cannot simply jump unaided into pure ethics – informed knowledge of the empirical situation to which a priori principles are to be applied is necessary. By contributing to "the progress of the power of judgment," anthropology fills this gap (*CPrR*, 5.154). And it is a gap to which Kant explicitly draws attention in several of his lectures. For instance, in the Prolegomena to the *Collins* anthropology lectures, he remarks that it is because of "the lack of *Weltkenntnis* that so many practical sciences, for example moral philosophy, have remained unfruitful . . . Most moral philosophers and clergymen lack this knowledge of human nature" (25.9; cf. *Collins Moralphilosophie*, 27.244). The need for moral *Weltkenntnis* is one of the key reasons why pure moral philosophy "needs anthropology for its *application* to human beings" (*G*, 4.412).

Moral Education and Character Development

One of Kant's most radical claims concerning human nature is that it is not a given but rather something that must be self-produced by the species. As he notes near the beginning of his *Pedagogy* lectures: "The human being can only become human through education. He is nothing except what education makes of him" (9.443). In the anthropology lectures, humanity's specific need for *moral* education is stressed repeatedly (Louden 2000: 33–61, 74–82; Frierson 2003: 61–4). The human being needs "to *moralize* himself by means of the arts and sciences" (*APS*, 7.324); he must "be *educated* to the good*" (7.325). Kant's anthropology and ethics writings also abound in more specific recommendations concerning moral education. For instance, in the Doctrine of Method in the *Critique of Practical Reason*, which is concerned with finding a way "to provide the laws of pure practical reason with *entrance* into the human mind, [and] *influence* on its maxims," Kant encourages educators to search through "the biographies of ancient and modern times with the purpose of having examples at hand of the duties they lay down" (5.151, 5.154). By comparing and evaluating similar decisions made under different circumstances, students can thus develop their own capacities for moral judgment. And in the *Metaphysics of Morals*, he discusses at length an elementary method, the moral catechism, which he deems "the first and most essential *doctrinal* element of the doctrine of virtue" (6.478; cf. *Päd*, 9.490). Essentially a modified Socratic dialogue, the moral catechism involves an attempt on the teacher's part, in discussing popular cases drawn from ordinary life, to develop the student's judgment about morally right action (*Päd*, 9.448).

However, as the student matures more emphasis needs to be placed on self-reflection and the development of autonomy. First and foremost, the teacher "must keep students away from imitation" (*Mrongovius*, 25.1386). "The *imitator* (in moral matters) is without character; for character consists precisely in originality in the way of thinking. He who has character derives his conduct from a source that he has opened by himself" (*APS*, 7.293).

Educational institutions must be also be reformed. Above all, teachers must replace the vocational and careerist concerns that politicians and parents typically have for children by a cosmopolitan orientation:

> Parents usually care only that their children get on well in the world, and princes regard their subjects merely as instruments for their own designs. Parents care for the home, princes for the state. Neither have as their final purpose the best world [*das Weltbeste*] and the perfection to which humanity is destined, and for which it has the disposition. But the design for a plan of education must be made in a cosmopolitan manner. (*Päd*, 9.448)

While Kant discusses moral education in all versions of the anthropology lectures, the *Friedländer* lectures of 1775/6 contain the most extensive discussion. This particular set of lectures concludes with a six-page section entitled "On Education," and reflects both Kant's strong admiration for Basedow's *Philanthropin* Institute, founded in Dessau in 1774, as well as his own growing interests in pedagogy. In 1776/7, Kant taught for the first time a university course on pedagogy, and he also published two short essays in support of Basedow's school (2.445–52). The *Philanthropin* Institute, which combined Lockean and Rousseauian concerns with educational methods better suited to children's nature with a strong cosmopolitan orientation, is described by Kant in *Friedländer* as "the greatest phenomenon that has appeared in this century for the improvement of the perfection of humanity" (25.722–3; cf. *Moralphil. Collins*, 27.471).

The central task of moral education is the development of character, and the anthropology and ethics writings also contain extensive discussion of this topic. Moral character is "the distinguishing mark of the human being as a rational being endowed with freedom" (*APS*, 7.285; cf. *Friedländer*, 25.630), and thus the grounding of character must be "the first effort in moral education" (*Päd*, 9.481). At the early stages, "the acquisition of good character with the human being takes place through education" (*Menschenkunde*, 25.1172). Again though, as the student matures, external institutional influences on character recede into the background and self-reflection plays a stronger role. Accordingly, Kantian moral anthropology also contains practical advice on the self-development of character. The basic principles here are:

a. Not intentionally to say what is false . . .
b. Not to dissemble . . .
c. Not to break one's (legitimate) promise . . .
d. Not to enter into an association of taste with evil-minded human beings . . .
e. Not to pay attention to gossip derived from the shallow and malicious judgment of others . . . (*APS*, 7.294; cf. *Mrongovius* 25.1387–8, 1392)

Ultimately, we are responsible for our own character, and we are its chief architects. As he notes in *Friedländer*: "We all believe that we are educated in childhood, but we are not really educated. We must still lead ourselves to the result and form our character ourselves" (25.633).

The Vocation of the Human Species

Kant's anthropological investigations into human nature are also marked by a strong historical and teleological concern. He is keen "to discover an *aim of nature* in this nonsensical course of things human," and wants to trace humanity's "steps from crudity [*Rohigkeit*] toward culture" (*Idee*, 8.18, 8.21). In the Preamble to the *Friedländer* lectures, when Kant is articulating his own specific conception of anthropology, he complains that

> No one has yet written a world history, which was at the same time a history of humanity, but only of the state of affairs and of the change in kingdoms, which as a part was indeed major, but considered in the whole is a trifle. All histories of wars amount to the same thing, in that they contain nothing more than descriptions of battles. But whether a battle has been more or less won makes no difference in the whole. More attention thereby should be given to humanity. (25.472; cf. *Idee*, 8.29)

Part of anthropology's task, as Kant conceives it, is thus to contribute to a world history of humanity by articulating the steps in humanity's progress from crudity to culture and by describing our central vocation. In pursuing this task of a world history of humanity, anthropology also makes a fourth important contribution to ethics. For now Kant is also providing his audience with a much-needed moral map, one that describes both the long-term goal of humanity's efforts and the major steps by means of which this goal is to be reached (Louden 2002).

The final goal is a worldwide moral community that encompasses "the entire human race in its scope" (*RBR*, 6.94) and where all human beings are respected as ends in themselves. And the means? Here the story is not so pretty. First and foremost, there is our "unsocial sociability," a bidirectional inclination rooted in human nature that leads us both to form associations with others but also constantly to compete and quarrel against each other once we have done so. But as a result of our competitive, self-interested nature, our insatiable desire for status and power, our talents are developed and humanity progresses. Like Adam Smith's famous "invisible hand," social progress for Kant is often the unintended result of the behavior of self-interested individuals (Smith 1979: 456). However, in Kant's case the invisible hand is much bigger, for it is held to be the driving force behind the growth of the arts and sciences, political and international legal reform, and even the hoped-for transformation into a cosmopolitan moral whole:

> All culture and art that adorn humanity, and the most beautiful social order, are fruits of unsociability, which is compelled by itself to discipline itself, and thus, by an art extorted from it, to develop completely the germs of nature. (*Idee*, 8.22)

Even the destructive power of war is claimed by Kant to be part of "a secret plan of nature" (*Idee*, 8.27), for it too is just "one more incentive for developing in the highest degree all talents that serve culture" (*CJ*, 5.433). War is a spur to economic and technological development as well as an incentive for eventually compelling people "to enter into more or less lawful relations" with one another (*PP*, 8.363). But unlike other means of progress such as the arts and sciences, war is also programmed by "the great artist nature" (*PP*, 8.361) to eventually die out. At some future point,

> after many devastations, reversals, and even thoroughgoing exhaustion of their powers, nature drives human beings to what reason could have told them even without so much sad experience: namely, to go beyond a lawless condition of savages and enter into a federation of nations, where every state, even the smallest, could expect its security and rights . . . (*Idee*, 8.24)

Here we also see the strikingly different approaches to war found in a world history of humanity and standard histories of wars. The latter, again, "contain nothing more than descriptions of battles" (25.472), while the former analyzes the function and purpose of war within human life. (See also chapter 25 below.)

The German word *Bestimmung* can be translated variously as "vocation," "destiny," and "determination," and each of these meanings is present in Kant's use of the term. On the one hand, he is describing what he believes are inherent tendencies and dispositions within human nature. But we also pursue our *Bestimmung* as free beings and are not irrevocably fated or causally determined to reach it. Whether humanity will actually reach a stage where all human beings are "cosmopolitically united" depends ultimately on what we choose to do (*APS*, 7.333). Kant's assumption of progress is thus not as rigid as that of other Enlightenment authors. As he notes in the *Conflict of the Faculties*:

> No one can guarantee that now, this very moment, with regard to the physical disposition of our species, the epoch of its decline would not be liable to occur . . . For we are dealing with beings that act freely, to whom, it is true, what they *ought* to do may be *dictated* in advance, but of whom it may not be *predicted* what they will do. (7.83)

At the same time, the strong teleological undercurrent in Kant's analysis of humanity's *Bestimmung* is a clear sign that his anthropology, though intended as a science in which "the grounds of knowledge are taken from observation and experience," is not simply an empirical science (*Collins*, 25.7). For the concept of purposiveness itself, as he reminds us in the third *Critique*, while "indispensably necessary" for all investigations of nature, is also "a special *a priori* concept that has its origin solely in the reflecting power of judgment" (5.398, 5.181). Still less is Kant's anthropology intended to be a Weberian value-free social science (Weber 1978). From the start it is a deeply value-embedded and morally guided enterprise. As he notes in the *Collins* ethics lectures: "The sciences are *principia* for the improvement of morality" (27.462; cf. Kant's doctrine of the primacy of the practical in *CPrR*, 5.121; see also chapter 17 above). Theoretical (as well as pragmatic) inquiries ultimately serve the ends of morality.

Finally, yet another distinctive feature of Kant's analysis of humanity's *Bestimmung* is that he focuses exclusively on the species as a whole and across time rather than on individual members at specific times. This broader perspective too is one more implication of an anthropology that strives to be "not a *local* but a universal anthropology"; one concerned "not with the condition of human beings but with the nature of humanity" (*Friedländer*, 25.471; cf. *Pillau*, 25.734, *APS*, 7.120). As Kant writes in his published *Anthropology*:

> First of all, it must be noted that with all other animals left to themselves, each individual reaches its complete *Bestimmung*; however with human beings only the *species*, at best, reaches it; so that the human race can work its way up to its *Bestimmung* only through *progress* in a series of innumerably many generations. (7.324; cf. *Menschenkunde*, 25.1196, *Mrongovius*, 25.1417)

Assessing Kant's Moral Anthropology

Kant's moral anthropology is certainly not problem-free. On the theoretical side, as critics from Schleiermacher onward have pointed out, it is far from obvious how the concept of transcendental freedom that Kant develops in his Critical philosophy can make room for the empirical study of human beings as free-acting beings (Schleiermacher 1998). On the practical side, the project is infected by numerous ethnic, religious, racial, and sexist prejudices that continually threaten to undermine its core progressive principles.

But I hope I have shown both that there exists a distinct moral anthropology within Kant's pragmatic anthropology, and that this moral anthropology has a necessary and important role to play in his moral philosophy. Without moral anthropology, we are travelers without a map who know neither our destination nor our means of reaching it. We do not know how to make our moral principles and commitments efficacious, and we lack judgment concerning when, where, how, and why to apply them in daily life. Those of us today who aspire to construct humanly useful ethical theories need to consider more carefully Kant's conviction that "the metaphysics of morals, or *metaphysica pura*, is only the first part of morality; the second part is *philosophia moralis applicata*, to which the empirical principles belong." There are certainly some professors who are keen on "keeping philosophy pure" (Rorty 1982; 19–36), but thankfully Kant was not one of them.

Acknowledgments

Earlier versions of this paper were presented as keynote addresses at the Second UK Kant Society Graduate Conference on Kant (University of Hertfordshire, March 2005) and at a conference on "Kant, Morality and the Sciences" (University of Cambridge, March 2005). I would like to thank participants at both conferences for their stimulating questions and counterarguments, as well as my hosts, Isabell Ward and Alix Cohen, for the opportunity to present my work to audiences in England. Thanks also to Graham Bird for helpful editorial guidance and suggestions.

References and Further Reading

Brandt, Reinhard (2003). The guiding idea of Kant's anthropology and the vocation of the human being. In Brian Jacobs and Patrick Kain (eds.), *Essays on Kant's Anthropology* (pp. 85–104). Cambridge: Cambridge University Press.

Frierson, Patrick R. (2003). *Freedom and Anthropology in Kant's Moral Philosophy*. Cambridge: Cambridge University Press.

Hegel, G. W. F. (1991). *Elements of the Philosophy of Right*, tr. H. B. Nisbet. Cambridge: Cambridge University Press. (Original work published 1821.)

Heidegger, Martin (1962). *Kant and the Problem of Metaphysics*, tr. James Churchill. Bloomington: Indiana University Press. (Original work published 1929.)

Jacobs, Brian (2003). Kantian character and the problem of a science of humanity. In Brian Jacobs and Patrick Kain (eds.), *Essays on Kant's Anthropology* (pp. 105–34). Cambridge: Cambridge University Press.

Kain, Patrick (2003). Prudential reason in Kant's *Anthropology*. In Brian Jacobs and Patrick Kain (eds.), *Essays on Kant's Anthropology* (pp. 230–65). Cambridge: Cambridge University Press.

Kant, Immanuel (2002). *Groundwork for the Metaphysics of Morals*, tr. Arnulf Zweig, eds. Thomas E. Hill, Jr. and Arnulf Zweig. Oxford: Oxford University Press. (Original work published 1785.)

Kitcher, Patricia (2001). Kant. In Steven M. Emmanuel (ed.), *The Blackwell Guide to Modern Philosophers: From Descartes to Nietzsche* (pp. 223–58). Malden, MA: Blackwell Publishing.

Kühn, Manfred (2004). Einleitung [Introduction]. In Immanuel Kant, *Vorlesung zur Moralphilosophie* [*Lecture on Moral Philosophy*] (pp. vii–xxxv), ed. Werner Stark. Berlin: Walter de Gruyter.

Louden, Robert B. (2000). *Kant's Impure Ethics: From Rational Beings to Human Beings*. New York: Oxford University Press.

Louden, Robert B. (2002). *The Second Part of Morals: Kant's Moral Anthropology and its Relationship to his Metaphysics of Morals. Kant e-prints*, 1: 1–13; www.cle.unicamp.br/kant-e-prints.

Louden, Robert B. (2003). The second part of morals. In Brian Jacobs and Patrick Kain (eds.), *Essays on Kant's Anthropology* (pp. 60–84). Cambridge: Cambridge University Press.

Louden, Robert B. (2005). Moralische Stärke: Tugend als seine Pflicht gegen sich selbst. [Moral strength: Virtue as a duty to oneself]. In Mandfred Kühn, Heiner Klemme, and D. Schönecker (eds.), *Moralische Motivation: Kants Ethik in der Diskussion* [*Moral Motivation: The Place of Kant's Ethics in the Discussion*]. Hamburg: Felix Meiner.

Rorty, Richard (1982). *Consequences of Pragmatism*. Minneapolis: University of Minnesota Press.

Scheler, Max (1989). Die Stellung des Menschen im Kosmos [The place of the human being in the cosmos]. In Hans Dierkes (ed.), *Arbeitstexte für den Unterricht: Philosophische Anthropologie* [*Study-Texts for Teaching: Philosophical Anthropology*] (pp. 49–53). Stuttgart: Reclam. (Original work published 1928.)

Schleiermacher, Friedrich (1998). Review of Kant's *Anthropology*. In *Schleiermacher on the Workings of the Knowing Mind: New Translations, Resources, and Understandings*, ed. Ruth Drucilla Richardson. Lewiston, NY: Edwin Mellen Press. (Original work published 1799).

Smith, Adam (1979). *An Inquiry into the Nature and Causes of the Wealth of Nations*, 2 vols., eds. R. H. Campbell and A. S. Skinner. Oxford: Clarendon Press. (Original work published 1776.)

Stark, Werner (2003). Historical notes and interpretive questions about Kant's lectures on anthropology. In Brian Jabobs and Patrick Kain (eds.), *Essays on Kant's Anthropology* (pp. 15–37). Cambridge: Cambridge University Press.

Stark, Werner (2004). Einleitung [Introduction]. In Immanuel Kant, *Vorlesung zur Moralphilosophie* [*Lecture on Moral Philosophy*], ed. Werner Stark. Berlin: Walter de Gruyter.

Weber, Max (1978). Value-judgments in social science. In W. G. Runciman (ed.), *Max Weber: Texts in Translation* (pp. 69–98). Cambridge: Cambridge University Press. (Original work published 1917.)

Williams, Bernard (1995). *Making Sense of Humanity and Other Philosophical Papers, 1982–1993*. Cambridge: Cambridge University Press.

Wood. Allen W. (1999). *Kant's Ethical Thought*. Cambridge: Cambridge University Press.

Wood. Allen W. (2003). Kant and the problem of human nature. In Brian Jacobs and Patrick Kain (eds.), *Essays on Kant's Anthropology* (pp. 38–59). Cambridge: Cambridge University Press.

Zammito, John H. (2002). *Kant, Herder, and the Birth of Anthropology*. Chicago: University of Chicago Press.

24

Liberty, Equality, and Independence:
Core Concepts in Kant's Political Philosophy

HOWARD WILLIAMS

The notions of liberty, equality, and independence take us to the heart of Kant's political philosophy. At first it appears that he sets the three concepts in no particular hierarchical order, but closer examination reveals that although liberty and equality are fundamental properties of the modern citizen it is independence that sets the scene for the full-scale emancipation of human kind. Liberty and equality are first and foremost a priori concepts that can be imputed to human individuals as such; independence in contrast has an empirical element to it that only historical circumstances can provide. Independence is therefore the vital link between theory and practice in political life both at the domestic and international level.

Kant presents his political philosophy in a variety of writings. Predominantly those writings appear from 1784 onwards so that his political thinking is integral to his critical enterprise. The major systematic work in political philosophy that forms part of the Critical system, the metaphysical first principles of the "Doctrine of Right" (Part I of the *Metaphysics of Morals*) was first published in 1797 at the very end of Kant's active scholarly life. Though arguably Kant's intellectual powers were in decline when the volume was finally put together it nonetheless has a key place in the understanding and interpretation of Kant's political thinking. Probably equally important in understanding his thinking are, however, the good deal more lively shorter essays on political topics. The outstanding example of these essays is, of course, *Perpetual Peace*, published in 1795 as a short volume on its own. But Kant's many other essays which appeared in the *Berlinische Monatsschrift*, a quintessentially German Enlightenment journal edited by his friend Johann Biester, also play a very significant role in the development and presentation of his political philosophy. The focus is here on the article "On the Common Saying: That may be true in theory, but is of no use in Practice," published in 1793 in the journal. I shall use that article to delineate Kant's position on the major concepts of liberty, equality and independence in his political philosophy through a comparison with the views of other modern political theorists, in particular Hobbes and Rousseau. The object will be to show that Kant has a very cogent understanding of these concepts that challenges the orthodoxies of modern liberal political thinking, centered as it is on the nation state, and offers in its place through his notion of independence a persuasive cosmopolitan alternative.

A variety of issues seems to have prompted Kant to publish the article at the time, but one self-evident impulse was the course of political developments in France. Kant is reported to have responded with enthusiasm to first reports of the revolution in France and no doubt its rapid and violent progress had led him to the conclusion that he should outline his own political views in the light of these epoch-making events. Although not under the same kind of direct pressure that Edmund Burke had been in Britain (supporters of the revolution in France had written to Burke to solicit his response) to let the public know his reaction to the events, Kant nevertheless must have felt some prompting from a curious public anxious to know how the author of the famous Critical philosophy assessed these spectacular new developments. My suggestion is that it is helpful to regard this essay, written in the shadow of the French revolution, as an attempt by Kant to outline the main basis for his political outlook. Clearly in an essay intended for the public at large there was no opportunity to present in a fully systematic way the thinking lying behind all the conclusions he draws, but nonetheless Kant here gives a careful and precise outline of his decisive starting points.

For many reasons Kant would want the essay to give a highly accurate portrayal of his core political position. First, as his writing was at the time subject to close political censorship, he would not want to be interpreted as arguing for anything that was morally or politically subversive. Secondly, Kant was aware that he had a number of philosophical disciples and supporters who would follow his lead in political matters, so he would not wish to confuse or misdirect them. We can see something of the way in which Kant sees his role as a philosopher writing on political issues from the opening paragraphs of *Perpetual Peace* where he wants to "protect himself" from "any malicious interpretation" that may be made on behalf of the "worldly wise statesman" (Kant 1996: 317; 8.344). Thirdly, Kant conceived his task as an enlightener of a public that was anxious to learn. Above all, he would not wish to disappoint or deceive that public.

Liberty or Political Freedom

As those who are familiar with Kant's moral philosophy might expect, Kant's notion of political liberty or freedom is closely connected with his notion of autonomy. We can broadly state that Kant can regard no institutional framework or social relation incompatible with our autonomy as going together with our political freedom. Free political institutions and social relations are ones that accept and respect our potential to act in a way that is properly self-determined. But this is not to say that Kant regards autonomy as one and the same thing as political freedom. Above all, political freedom concerns our external sphere of action and does not, as does the idea of autonomy, reach into our internal considerations for acting or not acting. This opens up the possibility that we can act in a way that is compatible with liberty but does not necessarily demonstrate our autonomy. Thus from the standpoint of political freedom no institutions should frustrate our possible autonomy but they need not *require* that we act autonomously.

This is a complex distinction and one whose full implications will only become clear once we have looked more closely at how Kant conceives liberty. In "Theory and

Practice" Kant presents his key political views in the form of a critique of, and contrast with, Hobbes's political philosophy. Hobbes famously sees liberty as an absence of external constraint. For Hobbes a "free-man, is he, that in those things, which by his strength and wit he is able to do, is not hindered to do what he has a will to" (Hobbes 1991: 146). Liberty with Hobbes centers wholly upon the individual and is always exercised to the degree that others do not limit the individual's movements and actions. Because absolute liberty or the absolute lack of restraint upon the actions of human individuals is untenable – we are reduced to the ignominious war of all against all of the state of nature if we dispense with government or a common power – Hobbes argues for the liberty of subjects. The "liberty of subjects" is one that is formed under the overarching power and authority of the Leviathan, which through its might holds every member of the state in awe. So with Hobbes not only liberty and fear are consistent with one another but also liberty and necessity. He is prepared to formulate political freedom in such a way that it is not compatible with Kant's notion of autonomy.

This is not Kant's understanding of the matter. Although he greatly respects Hobbes's seminal contribution to political philosophy he sees the need to amend radically Hobbes's formulations. For Kant the freedom of the human being as a member of a state can be expressed "in the following formula: No one can coerce me to be happy in his way (as he thinks of the welfare of other human beings); instead, each may seek his happiness in the way that seems good to him, provided he does not infringe upon that freedom of others to strive for a like end which can coexist with the freedom of everyone in accordance with a possible universal law" (Kant 1996: 291; 8.290). In exercising our freedom we accord to others precisely those rights we enjoy ourselves. Kant is similar to Hobbes in thinking that the absence of external constraint must play a part in our freedom but this is not its sole focus. We have to see beyond our own needs and desires to the equally legitimate needs and desires of *other* human beings. Liberty is not simply a matter of excluding the influence of others upon us but also concerns the appropriate inclusion of the influence of others upon us. Liberty for Kant involves the reciprocal relations of human individuals to each other. It is a way of defining their fitting external form.

I want briefly now to give an account of how Kant sees autonomy. This account is seen not primarily as a contribution to understanding Kant's pure moral philosophy but more as an attempt to elucidate his applied moral philosophy in its political dimension. Kant defines autonomy as "the sole principle of morals" that stipulates "to choose only in such a way that the maxims of your choice are also included as a universal law in the same volition." So "autonomy of the will is the property of the will by which it is a law to itself (independently of any property of the objects of volition)" (Kant 1996: 89; 4.441). Autonomy of the will is contrasted with "heteronomy of the will" where the maxims that lie behind our action are determined by influences and causes *not* emanating from the will. Here we act according to a rule that comes not from ourselves but outside.

> Wherever an object of the will has to be laid down as the basis for prescribing the rule that determines the will, there the rule is none other than heteronomy; the imperative is conditional, namely: if or because one wills this object, one ought to act in such a way;

hence it can never command morally, that is, categorically. (Kant 1996: 92; 4.444; translations from Kant 1991 and 1996)

In order to be autonomous we have to act according to maxims that can be generalized for all rational beings. Autonomy consists therefore not solely in determining for ourselves the principles according to which we act. Rather those principles according to which we act must be ones that we can accept if we envisage that all others adopt them. I might for myself decide, for example, that it is all right to drive swiftly through a built up area when it is an emergency, but this action can only be seen as rooted in autonomy if I can agree to the rule being applied to all others in a similar situation. Being autonomous is therefore not simply a matter of something coming solely from the individual, but also of its compatibility with what all others might rationally will to be done. In other words the intentions underlying our actions must be measured against our potential existence in a moral community with others. Autonomy therefore goes well beyond the ideal of an absence from external constraints. It denies the influence of external factors on the grounds of our choice but it then requires that we take into account key external factors in exercising that choice. Our objectives have to be unequivocally our own, but they have nonetheless to be ones that are acceptable, in their underlying motives, with what all others might conceivably will. So with Kant duty and autonomy go together. No autonomous action can neglect our duty and in seeking to do our duty from the proper motives we are showing evidence of our autonomy.

We can turn now to the relation between autonomy and political freedom. Autonomy grounds political freedom but does not *fully determine* it. Kant's account of political freedom recognizes and takes forward the notion of liberty embedded in the American and French revolutions. Each individual should be free to dispose over their own lives and property in the way they see fit. Individuals should enjoy the full freedom of conscience and follow their own beliefs so long as this does not bring harm to others. Thus, political authorities should make no attempt to dictate to individuals of adult years what is good for them. Such individuals should be free to pursue happiness in their own ways. Here there is a something of a fit between Hobbes's notion of liberty and that of Kant. Hobbes's sees our individual choices as determined by desire. The tendency of every individual is therefore to seek felicity, which Hobbes defines as "continual success in obtaining those things which a man from time to time desireth, that is continual prospering" (Hobbes 1991: 46). The object of the liberty of subjects that the protection of the state offers is to provide the maximum latitude for the pursuit of felicity for each individual compatible with the maintenance of sovereign order. Kant's view of political liberty *includes* the possibility of the pursuit of felicity but it is not the moral point of view he himself recommends.

Political liberty can for Kant then lead to the realization of a rich diversity of choices. From the perspective of the state individuals should be encouraged to show the greatest possible independence in disposing over their lives and what is theirs. For the leaders of a state to attempt to decide for individuals what kind of lives they should lead and how they should attempt to fulfill their desires would "represent the greatest despotism thinkable" (Kant 1996: 291; 8.291). This latitude accorded to individuals in the pursuit of their aims does not come entirely without limitation and cost. There is the limitation, first, that we should not injure the equal right of others to pursue their own aims in

367

their own way but, secondly, and more distinctively Kantian, there is the stipulation that in acting out our freedom we accept that we are always subject to the possibility of reciprocal coercion. Kant is aware that when accorded the political right of liberty individuals will not always necessarily exercise their free choice morally or, more worryingly, legally. So in his understanding of political liberty the possibility of coercion is built in as an essential. Liberty rests on right.

> Right need not be conceived as made up of two elements, namely an obligation in accordance with a law and an authorization of him who by his choice puts another under obligation to coerce him to fulfil it. Instead, one can locate the concept of right directly in the possibility of connecting universal reciprocal coercion with the freedom of everyone. (Kant 1996: 388–9; 6.232)

Equality

Edmund Burke remarked in *Reflections on the Revolution in France* that certain occupations were a mark of very little honor to those employed in them and it was only natural therefore that their place in society was not so elevated as those of a different background and calling. Burke thought that in political standing "property" should play a role that was of greater significance than ability.

> Nothing is a due and adequate representation of a state, that does not represent its ability, as well as its property. But as ability is a vigorous and active principle, and as property is sluggish, inert, and timid, it never can be safe from the invasion of ability, unless it be, out of all proportion, predominant in the representation. (Burke 1969: 140)

Social and political inequalities consequently posed no difficulties for him, and if necessary they might well be stressed if this added to the stability and security of the state. Hereditary wealth Burke sees not as an obstacle to an individual playing a full part in the organization of society but as an asset. "Some decent regulated pre-eminence, some preference (not exclusive appropriation) given to birth, is neither unnatural, nor unjust, nor impolitic." In his account of civil society Kant follows a path that is markedly distinct from Burke's political vision. As Allen Wood aptly puts it, "Kant's commitment to the equal worth of all human beings pervades his ethical thought." In politics "by no reasonable standard can he be considered conservative in relation to the issues of his day" (Wood 1999: 6). Kant finds hereditary inequalities unacceptable and although he accepts some differences in individual's rights of representation he neither bases them on the amount of property an individual holds nor on hereditary qualities.

Kant chimes in far more with the view of Thomas Paine that "every generation is equal in rights to the generations which preceded it, by the same rule that every individual is born equal in rights with his contemporary." Kant provides a theoretical derivation for Paine's further claim concerning the "unity of man," by which Paine means "that all men are of one degree, and consequently that all men are born equal, and with equal natural rights" (Paine 1969: 42). The radical political philosophy of Paine approximates more closely to Kant's position than that of Burke but there is one radical of Kant's day he would have been certain to disappoint. Mary Wollstonecraft in her *Vindication of the Rights of Woman* strikes out in a direction Kant was not able to follow. He was not able to agree with her view that "let woman share the rights, and she will emulate the virtues of man; for she must grow more perfect when emancipated, or justify the authority that chains such a weak being to her duty" (Wollstonecraft 1982: 319). His progressivism does not run in this direction, much to the disgust of today's feminists. Here we can look at how Kant navigates through the competing views of equality that came to the fore in his time.

It is not nature that makes us equal for Kant but the rule of law. Ideally this is the rule of law safeguarded by republican institutions, or by a sovereign who rules in a republican spirit. We are in principle equal but it is not our biological make-up that puts is in this condition. For Kant human equality comes on the scene only once law is established. We are in his view equal as subjects under the law.

> The question which now arises is whether the sovereign is entitled to create a nobility as a hereditary class between himself and the rest of the citizens. The answer will not, however, depend upon whether it suits the sovereign's policies for furthering his own or the people's advantage, but simply upon whether it is in keeping with right that anyone should have above him a class of persons who, although themselves subjects, will in relation to the people be commanders by birth, or at least possess greater privileges than they do. (Kant 1991: 152; 1996: 470–1; 6.329)

The idea of the social contract lies at the basis of the rightness of an arrangement within a civil society.

> As before, the answer to this question will be found in the principle that anything which the people (i.e. the entire mass of subjects) cannot decide for themselves and their fellows cannot be decided for the people by the sovereign either. Now hereditary nobility is a distinction bestowed before it is earned, and since it gives no grounds for hoping that it will be earned, it is wholly unreal and fanciful. For if an ancestor has earned his position through merit, he still cannot pass on his merit to his descendants. On the contrary, members of the latter group must always earn it themselves, for nature is not such that the talent and will that enable a person to serve a state meritoriously can be inherited. Now since it cannot be assumed of anyone that he will throw his freedom away, it is impossible for the general will of the people to agree to so groundless a prerogative; thus the sovereign cannot make it valid either. (Kant 1991: 152–3; 1996: 470–1; 6.329)

In contrast then to Burke, for Kant the amount of an individual's property and inheritance should not play a significant role in the representation of the people. For Kant merit should be the principal guide and measure of public standing. Property does not for Kant entitle you of itself to play a more significant part than average in the ruling of a country. Ability should not only predominate, as Burke put it, in the determining of political weight and influence, but should for Kant be the key consideration. Kant was of course out of step not only with the social and political arrangements of Britain in claiming this, but also markedly so with the arrangements of his own country. He did not, however, want his views portrayed as recommending a bloodbath similar to that occurring in France. Kant recommends a gradual phasing out of feudal privileges, rather than their immediate complete overthrow.

It may be . . . that anomaly of this sort has crept into the mechanism of government in past ages (as with the feudal system, which was almost entirely geared to making war), so that some subjects claim that they are more than citizens and are entitled by birth to official posts (a hereditary professorship, let us say). In this case, the state can make good its mistake of unrightfully bestowing hereditary privileges only by a gradual process, by allowing the posts to fall vacant and omitting to fill them again. The state thus has a provisional right to allow such dignities to persist as titles until public opinion itself realizes that the hierarchy of sovereign, nobility and people should give way to the more natural division of sovereign and people. (Kant 1991: 152–3; 1996: 470–1; 6.329)

A fundamental issue in assessing Kant's attitude to equality is the distributional one. Does Kant have a theory of distributive justice similar to that of John Rawls which suggests who should get what, when, and how? The simplistic answer to this question would be to say no. Since Kant's concept of justice seems largely to be formal, spelling out how the relations among free individuals should be constituted, it would appear that it is of prime concern to the jurist and the lawmaker rather than the social theorist. Kant is firmly convinced that equality before the law should not be translated directly into material equality.

[The] . . . uniform equality of human beings as subjects of a state is, however, perfectly consistent with the utmost inequality of the mass in the degree of its possessions, whether these take the form of physical or mental superiority over others, or of fortuitous external property and of particular rights (of which there may be many) with respect to others. (Kant 1991: 75; 1996: 292; 6.291–2)

Kant seems to concur with inequalities which reflect different levels of culture. Where one person has more than another, this may be the product of greater desert that has the added benefit of spurring on others to emulate the achievements of the materially better off. Kant would have no plans to bring down the standard of life of each individual to a socially determined average. Indeed he thinks the existing distribution within a properly constituted civil society should be respected. Existing laws and the relations derived from them have to be respected. Political radicals cannot look to Kant for a justification for overthrowing present economic relations.

However, despite this appearance of quietude and acceptance of existing arrangements Kant's political philosophy does not sanction the persistence of *all* types of economic inequality. Individuals have to have the right to improve their own circumstances and ultimately property relations, and comparative wealth should alter to mirror ability and merit. Although Kant does not want to "expropriate the expropriators" in the manner of Marx (1970: 763) he does want to see inherited possession being replaced by rational possession. How does Kant bring about this reversal in his own apparent defense of the status quo? Here his republicanism comes into play. For Kant we should regard the laws of our society as ones that are, through our representatives, our own creation. In principle the laws embody the united will of the people. This is not a static state of affairs. Though we have absolutely to obey the laws that are in force they are nonetheless subject to change in accord with the will of the people. Thus, although Kant has no fully-fledged theory of distributional justice there are certain distributional parameters on which he does have a firm view.

370

In "Theory and Practice" Kant queries how it is possible "how anyone can have rightfully acquired more land than he can cultivate with his own hands" and how "it came about that numerous people who might otherwise have acquired permanent property were thereby reduced to serving someone else in order to live at all." He does not seem to sympathize here with the feudal system of land ownership and implies that he would support the breaking up of large inherited estates. By rejecting as unfeasible a law that allows the descendants of feudal landowners always to hold on to their familial property, and preventing its sale and re-distribution to others who are just as deserving, Kant indicates that he favors laws that encourage positive intervention by the state to redistribute. In his view it "should be left exclusively to the ability, industry and good fortune of each member of the commonwealth" at some point to gain an entitlement to a part of it and for each to gain an entitlement to the whole (Kant 1991: 78; 1996: 296; 6.296). Kant seems therefore to be very much opposed to anything that stands in the way of all men aspiring to the status of a property-holder in business or in land. As he put it in the *Metaphysics of Morals*: "within a state there can be no corporation, estate or order which, as owner of land, can pass it on in accordance with certain statutes to succeeding generations or their exclusive use in perpetuity" (Kant 1996: 467; 6.324). At the core of his understanding of equality is his conviction that an individual can

> be considered happy in any condition so long as he is aware that, if he does not reach the same level as others, the fault lies either with himself (i.e. lack of ability or serious endeavour) or with circumstances for he cannot blame others, and not with the irresistible will of any outside party. (Kant 1991: 76–7; 1996: 294; 6.293–4)

The sovereign should not stand in the way of my ambition to improve myself. This is at the heart of justice: no one is entitled to enjoy an unfair advantage over me in the pursuit of my legal goals.

Paul Guyer believes there is a close similarity between Kant's theory of right and John Rawls's theory of justice in its distributional implications. For Guyer,

> Kant is committed to the conclusion that there can be external or public legislation enforcing the right to property, but only under conditions of equality like those defined by Rawls's second principle of justice. Thus something like Rawls's second principle as well as his first is a necessary principle of justice in the Kantian sense of a coercibly enforceable principle of external freedom. (Guyer 2000: 285)

This is arguably too wide an interpretation of Kant's view of the reciprocity of property relations, since Kant seems to have no notion of the optimal distribution of goods implied by Rawls's difference principle, but it does permit us to stress how far Kant was from endorsing an economic free-for-all.

Independence as a Key Concept in Kant's Political Philosophy

Just as Hobbes's thinking represents a negative challenge to Kant in developing his own understanding of modern citizenship so Rousseau's political philosophy represents a positive challenge (Gulyga 1985: 58–9; Shell 1980: 20–32). For Kant Hobbes wanted too little public participation in the formation of laws and state policy, whereas with Rousseau Kant believed the demand for participation and popular sovereignty went too far. If anything Kant is more sympathetic to Rousseau's demands for public involvement and control, as can be seen by the extent to which Kant attempts to integrate the idea of the general will into his political philosophy, but Kant baulks at Rousseau's notion of an absolutely authoritative general will commanding the society from the bottom up (1968: 20–1). The people should for Kant see themselves as playing a part in the formation of the overall direction of their society, but they cannot see themselves, as some readings of Rousseau's political philosophy might imply, as always having the last say. Kant is drawn strongly to Rousseau's understanding of the social contract but he does not discard entirely Hobbes's interpretation of the emergence of the social covenant. Kant's positive appreciation of this aspect of Hobbes's political philosophy can be found in the *Critique of Pure Reason* (B 780) where Kant compares the role of his *Critique* in bringing an end to dispute in philosophy with Hobbes's view of the termination in the condition of war brought about by the social covenant. Onora O'Neill has examined more fully the role that political metaphor of this kind plays in the *Critique of Pure Reason* (O'Neill 1989: 3–27).

Citizenship for Kant involves a reciprocal relationship between authority and freedom. The authority of the society as a whole has to be embodied in the office of a ruler whose instructions cannot be resisted. Freedom implies the possibility of coercion, but it is a coercion that we respect as emanating from our own wills. Direct democracy does not work. Human individuals need a constituted authority to hold them in check. But although they cannot directly rule themselves, human beings can nevertheless sanction the authority that governs them by playing a part in creating the rules under which that authority functions and is effective. Through his notion of independence Kant presents the means by which the popular dimension in sovereignty, so strongly pressed by Rousseau, is incorporated into his republican account of the state.

Sovereignty and Independence

Kant thought hard before making independence into his third key political principle in "Theory and Practice" by altering the motto of the French revolution: "Liberty, Equality, and Fraternity" into "Liberty, Equality, and Independence." Kant evidently wanted to set some distance between himself and the uncritical enthusiasts for the events in France. Kant argues that the social contract institutes for the first time the independence of citizens. With Kant citizenship should be a legitimate aim of all male subjects of a civil society. Not everyone is qualified to become an independent citizen (Kant rules out automatically all women and minors), but no adult male can be ruled out from attaining the appropriate qualification (Kersting 1993: 381–3). The qualification is primarily an economic one, albeit with social and psychological dimensions. The person concerned should be his own master and therefore not owe his living to anyone else. In the *Metaphysics of Morals* Kant expresses this with the phrase that the individual must have a "civil personality." For Kant the citizen's independence is a right but also a duty. This right and duty is the responsibility for making the laws with fellow-citizens. "The independence (sibisufficientia) of a member of the commonwealth as a citizen, i.e. as a co-legislator" (Kant 1991: 77; 8.150). What marks our independence for Kant is our participation in the exercise of sovereign power through the shaping of laws. Kant does envisage that in principle all the qualified citizens will make the laws unanimously. This is how those laws should be seen from the standpoint of their interpretation and implementation. But many, of course, are passive citizens (like women and children) who enjoy the protection of the law but do not make it. Also it must prove impossible for unanimity to be achieved on all issues.

> An entire people cannot, however, be expected to reach unanimity, but only to show a majority of votes and not even of direct votes, but (in a large nation) simply the votes of those delegated to do so as the representatives of the people. (Kant 1991: 79; 8.152–3)

In principle the people as a whole is sovereign, but on a day to day basis a representative sovereign body that forms the legislature carries out their task. The sovereignty of the people as a whole is re-affirmed from time to time when the independent citizens elect the legislators who are to represent them.

Every individual within a commonwealth can be regarded as a protected partner, free and equal under the current public law. But only those who play a part in legislation, either directly or through electing their representatives may be regarded as independent. For Kant the right to vote is determined by a property qualification. Each individual is only allowed one vote no matter how large his or her property. "In this respect, craftsmen and large or small landowners are all equal, each is entitled to one vote only" (Kant 1991: 78; 8.151). Kant means by "property" in this instance, as we have seen, neither simply a piece of land nor fixed goods and money of any kind. What he has in mind is the capacity to regard oneself in the eyes of others as one's own master. You can regard yourself as your own master if you serve no one other than yourself in your occupation or calling. Kant has a great deal of difficulty in determining who precisely can be regarded as independent in their occupation but the principle he wants to put forward is significant. He suggests that those who shape the laws of a society should be beholden to no one other than themselves. In having control over their own livelihoods and enjoying a level of prosperity they owe to their own industry each is in a position socially to think and act for himself. What Kant seems to seek is an element of maturity and standing in a person that is of his own making. Kant's goal is admirable even if we acknowledge the difficulties in establishing empirically who can be counted as part of the independent citizenry (and the obvious anachronism that women are excluded). Everyone who makes the laws in a society, and ideally all those who select the lawmakers should be free of external political, economic and social pressure. Approving of this goal does not necessarily imply support for a limited franchise. In today's circumstances in the advanced democracies, where nearly everyone over the age of eighteen has the right to vote it might sensibly be taken to imply that every effort should be made to protect each voter from financial, social or political pressure to vote in any particular way.

Kant upholds popular sovereignty in the spirit of Rousseau and in the face of the authoritarian tendencies of both monarchs and peoples in his day. Each individual must agree with all others to subject themselves to a common authority that makes possible their freedom. This sovereign must be conceived as being incapable of doing anyone any harm through its enforcement of law. This is because its sovereign power emanates from the will of every individual, and no individual wills harm to himself. As Kant puts it,

> all right depends upon laws. A public law however, which defines for everyone that which is permitted and permitted by right, is the act of a public will, from which all right proceeds and which must not therefore be able to do an injustice to any one. (Kant 1991: 77; 8.294)

Kant turns the Hobbesian formula of the subordination of the people to the sovereign body on its head. Because we have all unconditionally to obey the sovereign, Hobbes makes the sovereign's laws the responsibility solely of the sovereign body, but with Kant the sovereign body is made to carry out the laws of the united will of the people. For a public law rightfully to come into existence requires "no other will than that of the entire people" (Kant 1991: 77; 8.294). The body that makes the laws cannot be the one individual, but rather the people that make up the body has to come from the entire nation. The sovereign body must conceive itself as always answerable to the public, which it represents. The individuals who make up the sovereign body can be replaced in a constitutional manner – through election – if they fail to meet the requirements of their post.

"Thus no particular will can make the laws for a commonwealth" (Kant 1991: 77; 8.295). The laws have to be made by the united will of the people. Here every one decides about every one and so each and everyone decides about himself as well (Kant 1991: 77; 8.295). Sovereignty should not created by individuals giving up their independence (or natural freedom and equality) and handing over to another individual or bodies of individuals their freedom to deliberate on matters of public concern. No such symbolic handing over or alienation occurs in Kant's conception of political authority in a civil society. Sovereign authority should emerge from our collective will to sustain peace and order. We are to understand ourselves as belonging to that collective will even if institutions of which we are *not* directly part, and maintained by individuals we have *not* directly chosen, sustain it. We cannot regard ourselves as having given up our interest and involvement in matters of public concern. The sovereign should not be depicted solely as another, but as another of which we as citizens are part.

The most obvious way of realizing this idea of participation in sovereign power is through voting in elections for representatives who make the law. In Kant's day very few states had reached this stage, but for him this is no justification for regarding sovereign power as alien to us as ordinary subjects. Where those who make the law are not the people's representatives they should nonetheless be regarded in principle as such. And where absolute rulers decide what is to be law, perhaps in consultation with certain classes and groups of people, they have a duty to regard themselves as the people's representatives. They are under an obligation to reform the political order in their state to the point where the people's representatives in fact make the law. Kant requires those who may historically enjoy such absolute authority to regard their sovereign role as provisional until such time as it proves possible to introduce peacefully a republican system.

Kant rejects the idea of individuals conferring all their power and strength on any one person or any assembly. He particularly rejects the idea of transferring all power and strength to one person. What individuals have to do instead is to see themselves as forming a common will that makes the law we all have to obey. Hobbes makes a similar point when he says the people "may reduce all their wills, by plurality of voices, unto one will" (Kant 1991: 120). The possibility of your becoming an independent citizen is tied up with the idea of creating a sovereign power. So no loss of personality can occur through the formation of a common will. As Kant sees it, the sovereign power both represents your person and preserves the possibility of your independence as a citizen. We all submit our wills and our judgment in matters of public concern to the will and judgment of the sovereign, but as it is we ourselves that form the sovereign this cannot be considered as a loss. Kant would agree with Hobbes's view that "this is more than consent, or concord; it is a real unity of them all in one and the same person" (Kant 1991: 120), but this real unity does not extinguish our independence. Our ability to create this "real unity" is for Kant the proof of our independence.

As Kant sees it, everyone must agree in principle that the law-making body of the society is constituted by the united will of all. Although in practice this is very difficult to attain we still approximate to it by assuming that the individuals we elect to make the law for us when they pass a law by majority vote are reflecting the unanimous view of us all. This assumption is the ultimate basis on which a civil constitution is formed.

This, then, is an original contract by means of which a civil and thus completely lawful constitution and commonwealth can alone be established. We should not imagine this contract as actually taking place "rather it is a mere idea of reason which however has its undoubted (practical) reality, namely to bind each law maker that he gives his laws in such way that they can have arisen from the united will of a whole people, and regards each subject, in so far as he wants to be a citizen, as though he had agreed together to such a will. For this is the touchstone of the justice of each public law" (Kant 1991: 79; 8.297).

Thus there are two aspects to Kant's views on independence. Independence has an economic and a political aspect. To enjoy economic independence an individual has to be an adult male who owes his existence to no one other than himself. This does not mean that the individual has always to be self-employed, nor does it mean for Kant that all self-employed people are independent. Kant appears to have in mind a kind of economic independence that allows the individual to choose who he works for and to determine for himself the conditions under which he works. Kant appears to believe, for example, that university professors and qualified teachers belong to the rank of the independent although they may all be employed by the state. The key condition seems to be that economically independent individuals can regard themselves as serving no one other than the state. Under such conditions higher state officials would doubtless also be regarded as independent. An independent individual must have some property with which to support himself. Kant defines this element of property very broadly to include "any skill, trade, fine art or science" so that very many people might aspire to the class (Kant 1991: 78; 8.295). But wage-workers are excluded because their ability to labor is wholly alienated and placed in the hands of another. To be independent you must be able, as we have seen, to exercise some freedom about the way in which you choose to exercise your skill.

The second respect in which you enjoy independence (and this for Kant is the crucial aspect) is that you play a part in making the laws of the commonwealth. Above all, an independent individual regards himself as a co-legislator within the commonwealth. Independence is the key feature of the kind of commonwealth that Kant recommends.

> Anyway to give us the idea of a commonwealth the ideas of external freedom, equality and the unity of the wills of all must come together. Independence is the precondition (if the first two, equality and liberty are taken together) to attain the latter, since voting is called for. This basic law which emanates only from the universal (united) will of the people/nation is called the original contract. (Kant 1991: 77; 8.295)

Independence for Kant confers responsibilities and obligations. We are not independent to do what we like; we are independent because we share the responsibility of devising rules which are to be binding for all in our community. Independence only comes within a framework of rules that we accept as our own. It is not itself a complete absence of restraint, but rather an acceptance of certain obligations which allows us to act without restraint in certain specified directions. Through independence we forge our own freedom.

If we take the two dimensions of Kant's notion of independence together what is most surprising about his understanding of it is his acceptance that there are certain historical and social prerequisites for the emergence of independence. He recognizes that there is an empirical dimension to independence. Unlike freedom which we possess a priori as rational beings the emergence of independence is tied to economic development. We might roughly express this empirical or economic dimension in this way: independence requires the existence in the society of a modern middle class. Although Kant defines his property requirement very broadly it seems evident that independent citizenship rests primarily on the emergence of a fairly substantial economic group which owes its living to its ability to produce, to buy and to sell commodities. Economically this group has to be separate from the state and also from the land. At the core of Kant's independent citizenry are the commercial, financial, and manufacturing classes. They set the scene for the growth of the professions such as the legal, medical, and artistic. These groups are in an economic position to develop and exercise independent judgment about the affairs of the society as a whole, and should therefore be allowed to deliberate both directly and indirectly upon them.

Kant's specifications for independence may look to us now in many respects elitist, discriminatory and snobbish. However, speaking historically they appear remarkably astute. He suggests that those who are "mere underlings of the commonwealth," such as the "tenant-farmer as compared to the leasehold farmer" who "have to be under the direction or protection of other individuals" should not be allowed to vote (Kant 1996: 458; 6.314–15). The step from an absolutist society to a modern republican society would not be conceivable without the prior emergence of the middle class. Genuine independence requires a literate, intelligent and reasonably well off social stratum. Independence does not flourish where there is poverty and ignorance. Moreover, Kant distinguishes between the potential to become an independent citizen which is open to us all (even minors and women may aspire to view the world from such a standpoint) and those who are in fact independent already. Those who empirically have gained independence are not an exclusive group; they set a standard to which all may aspire. They are at the forefront of social development, and by their responsible participation through their representatives in the process of law-making they set an example for others to follow. Thus, Kant is elitist and discriminatory in those who he chooses to call citizens but (with the sad exception of women) the elitism and discrimination is intended to encourage rather than disbar. Where the path to independent citizenship is blocked by distinctions of birth and caste it is an obligation upon the ruler to remove them. Even if our economic condition, age or sex prevents us from being active citizens we are still entitled to assume that perspective in judging the actions of the commonwealth. We must judge the actions of the commonwealth as co-legislators of its laws. This is the standpoint of independence.

Independence and Fraternity

In his philosophical estimation of the importance of the three principles "liberty, equality, and independence" Kant reverses the order of priority (see also the General Introduction above). For him independence comes before liberty and equality and even provides their basis (Kant 23.141). Judging by the evidence of Kant's published writings and, in particular, his essay on "Theory and Practice" it would appear that Kant altogether abandons the idea of fraternity. This seems odd as Kant's general moral philosophy places as much emphasis on the fellowship of human beings as their independence. Kant indeed regards all individuals as ends in themselves but he also sees them as sharing a common humanity and belonging to a potential dominion of ends. But we can gain a deeper understanding of Kant's views on independence and their relation to fraternity by looking at the notes he makes in the "Preparatory Work to the Common Saying."

In these notes Kant strikingly connects the idea of fraternity to the idea of independence. He links them together by means of a third idea of the cosmopolitan. Kant gives a full presentation of his idea of the cosmopolitan or cosmopolitan right in *Perpetual Peace* (1795) and later in the *Metaphysics of Morals*, Part I, "The Doctrine of Right" (1797). In these latter writings Kant develops the idea of cosmopolitan right which requires us to treat with hospitality all visitors to our territory. By hospitality Kant does not mean generosity but, rather, that we should greet visitors without hostility. Since we are common inhabitants of the earth's surface we should all be treated as though we have the right not to be harmed, and so until we have done wrong our liberty to engage in peaceful pursuits involving no injury to others should not be restricted. It may well be that in these preparatory notes Kant is pursuing for the first time the notion of cosmopolitan right. He says strikingly in the notes: "Freedom, equality and cosmopolitan unity [fraternization/*Verbrüderung*] – where independence is internally presupposed without contract" (23. 41). This makes evident that Kant links independence with fraternity but it is not absolutely clear how he comes to this apparently odd juxtaposition.

The formula of the French revolution was first applied within one state, although the implication was that it might apply to all states. The revolution also spread beyond the borders of France with the same formula leading to great disruption in the absolutist states of Europe. Because of his view that each sovereign body should reform

377

itself Kant will not have approved of this exportation of revolution. Sovereign states should improve themselves according to their own tempo and dispositions. The good intentions brought on by revolutionary enthusiasm provide no justification for trying to put in order the affairs of a neighbouring state. There is no doubt that in some respects Kant saw the French idea of universal brotherhood as too dangerous and overpowering. But he seems not to abandon it entirely. It appears for him that it has its rational essence in the idea of cosmopolitanism. Although there is an element of irony in the title of his later essay *Perpetual Peace* Kant is attracted by the idea of worldwide harmony; he genuinely believes in the moral reality of the project. This we can see in the "Preparatory Work to the Common Saying" where he identifies cosmopolitanism with the "good in the world [*Das Gute in der Welt*]" (23.140). He also separates the German term for cosmopolitan (*Weltbürger*) into its constituent parts "world" (*Welt*) and "citizen" (*Bürger*) to emphasize that the unity that comes about in the formula "liberty, equality and fraternity" should be seen as a unity amongst independent citizens.

Kant here empties the French revolutionary notion of brotherly solidarity of any of its collectivist connotations. Kant indeed asks us to think *together* but not to think together in the *same* way. The commonality should not in his view derive from consanguinity but from a shared self-sufficiency. The independent citizen helps shape the laws of his state through his representatives. He may even be one of those representatives who make those laws we regard as our own. These participants in law-making are the common authors of their public world. They share this characteristic with independent citizens of other states. This is the foundation of cosmopolitanism for Kant. Independence for him is not what it seems. The notion would seem to set individuals apart from each other and possibly in conflict. Independent people are notoriously willful and noncooperative. But this is not how Kant sees it. As the independent citizen derives his independence from a responsibility to shape the laws of his society he is in principle accommodating and honorable. In Hobbes's terms, the independent citizen is the kind of person who can be relied upon to observe natural laws. In exercising his independence he is all the while conscious of his dependence upon the rule of law and its effective implementation. This possibly explains why in *Perpetual Peace* Kant conspicuously does not list independence alongside freedom and equality as characteristics of people in a republic. Here the third quality he lists is "dependence" upon "a single common legislation" (Kant 1991: 99; 1996: 322; 8.350). Arguably he is not abandoning his concept of independence in doing this since he goes on to emphasize strongly that the legislators and the members of the executive in the republic should be the people's representatives. As he categorically rules out the principle of direct democracy we have to surmise that he holds to the position expressed in the essay on "Theory and Practice" that those representatives should be elected by the minority of independent individuals. They crucially help to provide the bridge between the national and the international.

This is what Kant appears to mean when he says fraternity in his sense of "cosmopolitan unity" "internally presupposes independence without contract" (23.139). Kant seeks peace not only *within* states but also *amongst* states on the basis of our independence. And unlike the French revolutionaries who sought to bring about world harmony by the imposition of a collective brotherhood creating one family of mankind, Kant attempts to bring about world harmony in the civil context of our independent citizenship. What is notable about this vision of worldwide harmony is that it is based on a voluntary arrangement. World peace cannot be instituted from above. This is in sharp contrast with domestic order which historically comes into being through "despotic occupation" (23.141). The social contract within the state cannot for Kant be a voluntary arrangement alone. Since no law comes into existence without the prior creation of a sovereign body, subjection may precede the rise of independent citizenship. But since in world politics citizenship already exists, although we lack a common sovereign, whatever steps toward world peace are made have to be taken under the presupposition of independence. We are bound to seek to attain universal citizenship not through a contract that we can regard as already forged but through an obligation we have to attain such an analogous position in world politics. The classical social contract has with Kant an obligatory foreign clause, which requires us to seek to bring about by voluntary means a world social contract for a universal civil society.

Kant takes a very firm stand about how this universal civil society is to be brought about. It cannot occur through intervention by one people in the affairs of another. Change has to come gradually from the top down:

> Should the good in the world (the cosmopolitan) start from the education (up-bringing) of the subjects i.e. from the people or from the government which first improves itself. The first principle begins from the clash of opinions as from the bottom up, from which nothing decent [*ordentlich*] can be established. Thus only from the top down. (23.140)

In other words "the old despotic possession [*Besitz*] remains and will gradually transform into a system of freedom only when the principles are well grasped/understood" (23.140). Cosmopolitanism has to be embraced by governments and then become a principle for their policies towards other states for it to take root and spread effectively. Republicanism replaces the old despotic possession of power at home and then turns outwards through its legislators and executive to law-like and peaceful relations with other states. Kant envisages this gradual change coming about through a continuous conflict between politics and morality. Historically political ascendancy has been gained by means we should no longer countenance as moral, yet political power when established is both necessary and moral. It provides the basis for the longterm reform of the human race. These inherited forms of the acquisition of power have continually to be transformed to bring them in line with the ideal of civil, republican government.

> In order to form a state (in the condition of peace as a juridical state of affairs) the founder and the law maker ought both to have a good will to submit themselves to the law (or to position themselves under the law). But where do we get these wills? They too have to be coerced. (23.141)

Here Kant seems to envisage a role for the social sciences, because he mentions "financial, police, and defense science" as a possible means of bridging the gap between the ideal of peace and the reality of human behavior. They are seen as alternatives to radical political measures. With events in France in mind Kant states categorically: "No revolution." Since the condition of perpetual peace as a juridical state of affairs is "a pure idea for which we do indeed have principles for carrying out the object, which is however supersensuous and can only be thought through by approximation according to a regulative principle" (23.141).

In developing his concept of independence Kant is adapting social contract theory in the light of the impact of the French revolution. Independence is portrayed not only as giving reality to the social contract but also as a counter to the French revolutionaries' uncritical call for universal brotherhood. Independence is seen as compatible with fraternity when the citizen's independence leads to informal links with citizens of other countries who are similarly independent. The independent citizen is the starting point for the cosmopolitan outlook. An independent citizen makes his own laws through his representatives and this shared responsibility brings together all independent citizens throughout the world. Kant develops this insight further in the first and second definitive articles of *Perpetual Peace*. In the first he requires that the "civil constitution in each state shall be republican" (Kant 1996: 322; 8.349) and in the second that "the law of nations be based on a federation of free states" (Kant 1996: 325; 8.354). The first can be realized only through the presence of independent individuals and the second presupposes that those independent individuals can work together at an international level.

Resistance and Publicity

Kant's rejection of resistance to the sovereign must be understood in the context of his concept of independence. Kant altogether rules out the rightfulness of resisting the sovereign's will.

> All resistance against the supreme legislative power, all incitement of the subjects to violent expressions of discontent, all defiance which breaks out into rebellion, is the greatest and most punishable crime in a commonwealth, for it destroys its very foundations. This prohibition is absolute. (Kant 1991: 81; 8.299)

This would seem to represent a paradox in an ostensibly social contract theory. On the surface Kant's sovereign derives its authority from the mutually related people and so when it acts wrongly it would seem as though the people could dismiss it. But this is not how Kant understands popular sovereignty since there is a greater respect and mutuality in the relationship of people and sovereign than a simple bargaining view of contract would imply. We should not even contemplate violent opposition where we as subjects judge that the legislative power or an agent who acts with its authority behaves in a tyrannical way. "The reason for this is that the people, under an already existing civil constitution, no longer has a continuous right of judgment about how the constitution should be administered" (Kant 1991: 81; 8.299). Under an existing civil constitution the sovereign is already the united will of the people, so any acts of policy which step beyond justice have to be regarded as errors of judgment on the part of the legislators and their agents. The legislators, because they act with the people's authority, cannot be regarded as wholly unjust or beyond improvement. They have misplaced their authority rather than permanently disqualified themselves from holding it.

Kant's notion of independence leads to a novel account of political sovereignty. He rules out resistance because it would represent resistance to ourselves as co-legislators who bring the commonwealth into being. We understand the sovereign to be created by an original contract which makes independent citizens into co-legislators. Although we are not all in fact co-legislators we regard those who legislate as our representatives who behave as the united will of the people. Thus, although we may not be direct participants in the exercise of sovereign authority, we should regard it always as though we were so, and therefore are unable to resist it. It is this participatory element in effective sovereignty that leads Kant to rule out resistance to it and not merely fear of the sovereign's loss of authority.

Kant acknowledges that one of the consequences of his doctrine is that monarchs under existing civil constitutions can be regarded as inviolable. He thinks the people in France who have overthrown their monarch are wrong, just as the people in Britain who did so in the previous century were wrong. He fears that the acts of the French revolutionaries will have very damaging consequences, and believes that they will not succeed in establishing as good a constitution as the one they have already destroyed. What has followed the revolution is not the legal rule of the united will of the people but the rule of faction (Kant 1991: 83; 8.302). France is, he thinks, being torn apart by aristocrats and clerics instead of developing greater equality in political obligations, as may have occurred under a head of state who enjoyed all the wide powers Hobbes envisaged for the sovereign. But although Kant's doctrine implies that the people should not overthrow monarchs, it does not imply that they are infallible or that their powers should not be altered:

> While I trust that no-one will accuse me of flattering monarchs too much by declaring them inviolable, I likewise hope that I shall be spared the reproach of claiming too much for the people if I maintain that the people too have inalienable rights against the head of state, even if these cannot be rights of coercion. (Kant 1991: 84; 8.303)

Not only do the people have the right to be heard, so that rulers should encourage them to speak their minds in order that defects in the political system can be remedied, but also the rulers have the duty to reform the constitution until it corresponds with its rational republican form. Just as "reason must subject itself to critique in all its undertakings, and cannot restrict the freedom of critique without damaging itself and drawing upon itself a disadvantageous suspicion" so a representative government must always be open to complaints and advice. Just as the "very existence of reason depends upon this freedom, which has no dictatorial authority, but whose claim is never anything more than the agreement of free citizens" (*CPR*, B 766) so the existence of a republic based on law depends upon the mutual respect of its independent members.

Conclusion

We have seen here how Kant presents his concepts freedom, equality, and independence as a challenge to the main premises of modern political philosophy, particularly as represented by Hobbes, and as a response to the major political developments of his day. Hobbes's political philosophy centers on the one political actor who has the sole right to act in a fully independent way. Hobbes even portrays this sovereign actor as independent of the laws of the society and the arbiter of what can be effective in international law. To this day this realist vision dominates domestic and international politics. Kant in contrast has a role for the independent individual under the law both within and outside the state. This is achieved by regarding the independent individual as the co-author of the law and, as such, a unifying factor in world politics. Admittedly Kant severely restricts the number of independent individuals he is prepared to accept within a civil society, and disappointingly offers no role for women as active citizens, but he considerably democraticizes the realist vision of politics. He also persuasively extends the boundaries of citizenship, seeing independent individuals as connected to each other in a worldwide civil society. They are connected through the role of law-making. This is a task that all genuinely modern polities have in common. A modern polity is for Kant representative and republican, and as modern polities extend to all parts of the globe so does the shared responsibility of devising just legislation. Independence is consequently one of the most interesting concepts of Kant's political philosophy. It is the keystone of his critique of Hobbesian political realism and provides the basis for his understanding of cosmopolitanism. Replacing as it does the third concept of fraternity in the French Revolution's trinity of liberty, equality, and fraternity, it preserves the progressive spirit of those times within a political program whose implementation is as necessary today as ever.

References and Further Reading

Burke, Edmund (1969). *Reflections on the Revolution in France*. Harmondsworth: Penguin.

Gulyga, A. (1985). *Immanuel Kant*. Frankfurt: Suhrkamp.

Guyer, Paul (2000). *Freedom, Law and Happiness*. Cambridge: Cambridge University Press.

Hobbes, Thomas (1991). *Leviathan*. Cambridge: Cambridge University Press.

Kant, Immanuel (1991). *Kant's Political Writings*. Cambridge: Cambridge University Press.

Kant, Immanuel (1996). *Practical Philosophy*. Cambridge: Cambridge University Press.

Kersting, W. (1993). *Wohlgeordnete Freiheit* [*Well Ordered Freedom*]. Frankfurt am Main: Suhrkamp.

Marx, Karl (1970). *Capital*. London: Lawrence & Wishart.

O'Neill, Onora (1989). *Constructions of Reason: Explorations of Kant's Practical Philosophy*. Cambridge: Cambridge University Press.

Paine, Thomas (1969). *The Rights of Man*. London: Dent.

Rousseau, Jean-Jacques (1968). *Social Contract*. London: Dent.

Shell, S. (1980). *The Rights of Reason: A Study of Kant's Philosophy and Politics*. Toronto: University of Toronto Press.

Williams, Howard (2003). *Kant's Critique of Hobbes*. Cardiff: University of Wales Press.

Wollstonecraft, Mary (1982). *Vindication of the Rights of Woman*. Harmondsworth: Penguin.

Wood, Allen (1999). *Kant's Ethical Thought*. Cambridge: Cambridge University Press.

25

Reason and Nature: Kant's Teleological Argument in *Perpetual Peace*

KATRIN FLIKSCHUH

I. Kant's Practical Political Teleology

How is one to understand Kant's "teleology of nature" argument – his claim that nature wills humanity's moral progress even against individuals' will – in the context of his philosophy of Right? In addressing this question, the present chapter takes as its focal point the famous First Supplement in *Perpetual Peace*, entitled "On the Guarantee of Perpetual Peace." The convoluted opening proposition of the First Supplement is crucial to the following interpretation, since it rules out as inappropriate both a speculative and a practically prudential reading of the ensuing teleological argument. In other words, the teleological passages in *Perpetual Peace* should not be read as pre-Hegelian exercises in the philosophy of history. Nor should they be read as a more or less implicit admission of moral defeat on Kant's part in the face of the acknowledged demands of political exigency. The teleological argument should be read, instead, from the perspective of one who acknowledges the concept of Right as a pure rational concept (*MM*, 6.229–30), and who is cognizant, in consequence, of the a priori obligation, in virtue of their freedom, to act in accordance with Right.

The suggested line of interpretation raises immediate questions. If the teleological passages are to be read from the perspective of one who acknowledges their a priori obligations of Right, what task is left for nature at all in this respect? Surely, one who acknowledges their juridical obligations will act on them and will not wait for nature to do the job in their stead. Secondly, how is one to make sense, on the proposed interpretation, of Kant's claim that nature ensures humanity's moral progress even against individual wills? Surely, if nature can and will achieve this task even against individual wills, then whether or not individual agents do acknowledge any juridical duties they might have makes no difference to the end result either way. The first objection might be voiced by one committed to a prudential reading of the teleological passages (see Schmitz 1990; Höffe 1992). On this reading, Kant introduces the argument from nature precisely in order to fill the gap created by his inability to offer a successful moral justification of agents' juridical as opposed to their ethical obligations. Nature, on this reading, does what Kant thinks human agents should do, but what he also acknowledges they will not do. They will not do it because, in the realm of politics as opposed to ethics, self-interest invariably trumps morality – a lesson Kant was forced to learn, on this account, in the course of his torturous teleological endeavors. The second question is one which might be raised by proponents of the philosophy of history reading, according to which the teleological passages represent an exercise on Kant's part in theoretical rather than practical reason: an interest in presenting a conjectural – or possibly even a predictive – history of the cultural development of the human race that abstracts from the issue of individual (moral) agency (see Yovel 1980).

I do not think that either of these well-known alternative interpretations are wholly mistaken. In the following I shall borrow from each of them. However, given my starting point – my contention that the teleological passages should be read from the perspective of one who already acknowledges their morally grounded obligations of Right – I shall give the content of both of these alternative accounts a somewhat different inflection. To the prudential reading I shall concede that, as a distinct branch of morality, the realm of law or politics presents Kant's practical philosophy with a set of difficulties that are encountered, if at all, in much more muted form in his ethics. This is the problem of the sensible, empirical, institutionalization of nonsensible laws of Right – a problem that arises in consequence of the external character of juridical obligation as opposed to the internal character of ethical obligation. While this does not mean that nature steps in to fill a gap left open by morality, the task of mediating between sensible nature and nonsensible moral laws presents itself more acutely in Kant's political writings. Kant's teleological appeal to the "means of nature" which can be employed to further the achievement of perpetual peace arguably represents, in part, such an attempt at sensible/nonsensible mediation. I will develop this point more fully in section II of this chapter.

To the historico-theoretical reading I shall concede that the final object, or end, of the teleological passages is "the Right of humanity itself," not individuals' particular interests or even their particular rights. Nonetheless, individual agents are indispensable contributors towards the eventual attainment of this final end. The teleological argument offers morally willing individual agents a perspective upon the nonindividualistic end of their endeavors towards peace. Kant's conjectural history of humanity's moral progress must therefore be read from a practical, agency perspective, not from a theoretical perspective. I shall elaborate on this point, albeit much more briefly, in section III. To begin with, I want to justify my insistence upon a moral reading of the teleological passages. The opening proposition of the First Supplement goes as follows:

> What affords this *guarantee* (surety) [of perpetual peace] is nothing less than the great artist *nature* (natura daedala rerum) from whose mechanical course purposiveness shines forth visibly, letting concord arise by means of the discord between human beings even against their will; and for this reason nature, regarded as necessitation by causal laws the ground of which is unknown to us, is called *fate*, but if we consider its purposiveness in the course of the world as the profound wisdom of a higher cause directed to the objective final end of the human race and predetermining this course of the world, it is called *providence*, which we do not, strictly speaking, *cognize* in these artifices of nature or even so much as *infer* from them but instead (as in all relations of the form of things to ends in general) only can and must *add in thought*, in order to make for ourselves a concept of their possibility by analogy with objects of human art; but the presentation of their relation to and harmony with the end that reason prescribes immediately to us (the moral end) is an idea, which is indeed transcendent for *theoretical* purposes but for practical

purposes (e.g. with respect to the concept of duty of *perpetual peace* and putting that mechanism of nature to use for it) is dogmatic and well founded as to its reality. (*PP*, 8.363; translations from Reiss 1970)

Kant distinguishes between "fate" and "providence" in relation to the "visible purposiveness" of nature's causal order. "Fate" is paired with the "mechanical" course of nature and juxtaposed with the contrasting pair "providence" and "higher cause/wisdom." Fate and providence are distinct yet plausible perspectives to adopt in relation to the observation of human nature and history. The fatalistic perspective notes and charts the law-like regularities discernible in human nature and history, but accepts their initiating causes as unknown to us. For the same reason this perspective posits no final end of nature's causal mechanism. Kant's admiring reference to the calculation of human birth and death rates in "Idea of a Universal History with Cosmopolitan Intent" might be viewed as an example of the "fatalistic" perspective (Reiss 1970: 41). However, although indispensable from a natural history perspective – from the perspective of studying humanity as an "animal class" (*PP*, 8.265) – the fatalistic perspective is insufficient, indeed, potentially disastrous, where nature is evaluated from the standpoint of its presumed purposiveness and related end. When evaluated from the latter standpoint, we require something akin to the providential perspective, which does postulate the ideas of a higher cause and of a final end. From this standpoint, events do not merely happen, but happen for a reason. Of course, the ideas of higher cause/final end may only be "added in thought," which is to say that we may employ them only for regulative, not for constitutive purposes. We cannot know either the causes or the ends of nature's necessitating laws, but if we are to go beyond mere mechanical explanation (or, in relation to human nature, beyond mere fatalistic explanation), we can and must render our intuitive perception of nature's "visible purposiveness" intelligible to ourselves by adding the thought or idea of a higher cause and final end.

For Kant, such a critically delimited providential perspective finds legitimate employment in both the theoretical and the practical interpretation of nature's purposiveness: we are constrained "in all relations of the form of things to ends in general" to adopt the regulative idea of a "higher cause." Up to this point, therefore, Kant appears to be neutral between either a theoretical or a practical standpoint upon nature's purposiveness in relation to perpetual peace. However, he then goes on to speak of the "presentation of their [i.e. 'the artifices of nature'] relation to and harmony with the end that reason prescribes immediately to us (the moral end)." At this juncture, the idea of nature's purposiveness is explicitly related to "the duty of perpetual peace." In invoking the ends of reason and the duty of perpetual peace Kant shifts from a neutral to a practical standpoint. Although he continues to deny the constitutive status of the postulated relation between nature's purposiveness and reason's end – we cannot *know* that such a relation obtains in fact – he asserts the practically "dogmatic validity" of thinking such a relation for practical purposes. We can and must relate our providential reading of nature's purposiveness to the end that reason immediately and independently prescribes to us. Finally, however, Kant issues the following qualifications:

The use of the word *nature* when, as here, we have to do only with theory (not with religion) is more befitting the limitations of human reason (which must confine itself

385

within the limits of possible experience with respect to the relation of effects to their causes) and more modest than is the expression of a *providence* cognizable for us, with which one presumptively puts on the wings of Icarus in order to approach more closely the secret of its inscrutable purpose. (*PP*, 8.362)

Given the immodesty of invoking the idea of providence in the context of a nonreligious inquiry, we should continue to use the term "nature" – presumably "mechanical nature." However, this does not take us back to the fatalistic perspective. Although we must acknowledge that the purposes of providence remain utterly "inscrutable" to us, our immediate consciousness of our moral duties and ends permits us to attempt a moral reading of nature's purposiveness in analogy with a providential reading of it. In other words, rather than appealing immodestly to providence and *its* (nonsensible) ends for nature, we are to interpret nature's purposiveness analogously in terms of *our* moral (nonsensible) duty to work towards perpetual peace.

II. Demands of Practical Reason and Nature's Will

II.1. *Nonsensible Right and the problem of its sensible realization*

I said in the section above that the prudential reading of Kant's teleological argument in *Perpetual Peace* rightly draws attention to the special difficulties Kant encounters in conceiving the empirical realization of a priori obligations of Right, but that it wrongly concludes from attention to these difficulties to Kant's inability to provide a moral justification of agents' juridical obligations. The claim is that Kant ultimately falls back upon an appeal to agents' sensible inclinations and enlightened self-interest, and that the justification of Right is therefore prudential rather than moral. The teleological argument, which asserts that nature brings about what individual agents morally should but will not do, is then averred in confirmation of the claim that Kant's attempted moral justification of Right fails.

In the "Metaphysical Elements of Justice" Kant speaks of the universal principle of Right as the law of external freedom, juxtaposing it with the laws of internal freedom, or virtue (*MM*, 6.218–21). An agent's internal freedom consists in a particular relation between *Willkür* (power of choice) and *Wille* (capacity for practical reason). That agent is internally free, hence virtuous, whose power of choice is in harmony with principles of pure practical reason, or to use Kant's terminology in the *Groundwork* and second *Critique*, whose subjective maxim of action is conceivable as a universally valid principle of action. Kant insists that agents are opaque to themselves: they can never be certain that *Willkür* is indeed in inner conformity with *Wille*. Even an outwardly virtuous act may, with regard to the agent's inner maxim of action, fail to qualify as a morally worthy action. Outwardly virtuous acts cannot then be regarded as empirical manifestations of agents' inner virtue. There are no possible empirical manifestations of agents' virtue of maxim, or inner freedom, and this does render problematic judgments concerning the moral worth of actions (*CPrR*, 5.68–71).

Matters are different with regard to agents' external freedom. Kant defines the concept of Right as specifying a law-governed formal relation between the *Willkür* of one and that of another: Right governs the form of external relations between agents' respective *Willküren* or powers of choice. According to the universal principle of Right, that agent is externally free who "so act(s) externally that the free use of [their] choice can coexist with the freedom of everyone in accordance with a universal law" (*MM*, 6.231). The intrapersonal *Willkür/Wille* relation is immaterial with regard to lawful external freedom because the latter concerns an interpersonal relation between the powers of choice of two or more agents. While Right, like virtue, has its a priori grounds in the idea of freedom, the interpersonal status of relations of lawful external freedom gives rise to two distinctive features that contrast sharply with Kant's more familiar account of internal freedom or virtue. The first is that, in contrast to internal freedom, agents can be externally compelled to act in outward conformity with laws of external freedom. This is not because in contrast to internal freedom the laws of external freedom derive from an appeal to agents' sensible inclinations or their enlightened self-interest. The fact of legitimate coercion in relation to the laws of external freedom is simply a corollary of these laws' interpersonal character. Given the intrapersonal relation between *Wille* and *Willkür*, only agents themselves can strive to be virtuous. By contrast, the interpersonal character of lawful external freedom means that agents can be compelled, on moral-juridical grounds, to act in outward conformity with the universal principle of Right. The second, related feature distinctive to Right concerns the requirement of the empirical manifestation or institutionalization of coercive laws of external freedom. While agents' judgments regarding the internal *Willkür/Wille* relation are necessarily introspective, remaining, in consequence, unavoidably opaque, it is crucial that "what rightfully belongs to each" in relation to all others be determined with "mathematical exactitude" (*MM*, 6.232–3). It is because of the external character of rightful interpersonal relations that the issue of their empirical institutionalization presents itself so acutely.

It is important to emphasize that, from Kant's perspective, the problem of the sensible institutionalization of nonsensible (rational) principles of Right cannot be regarded as insurmountable. Ought implies can: insofar as we do acknowledge our a priori obligations of Right, we must assume that it is possible for us to act on these obligations under given sensible conditions. In that sense the problem of empirical institutionalization is a technical problem, not a moral problem. This does not mean that the technical problem of sensible institutionalization is unimportant. Unless we do identify a way of empirically instituting external relations of Right, we cannot discharge our acknowledged juridical obligations. The point is simply to insist against prudential readings that the teleological argument adds nothing to the (a priori) justification of Right: it addresses, rather, the question of its sensible realization or institutionalization. In the remainder of this section I shall examine Kant's teleological argument in the First Supplement from the perspective of this technical problematic.

II.2. *Teleology as the sensible realization of nonsensible Right*

II.2.a. The retrospective argument

In the First Supplement Kant distinguishes between two tasks which he thinks arise in the context of assessing nature's contribution to the attainment of perpetual peace.

387

> Before we determine more closely [nature's] affording of the guarantee it will be necessary first to examine the condition that nature has prepared for the persons acting on its great stage, which finally makes its assurance of peace necessary; only then shall we examine the way it affords this guarantee. (*PP*, 8.362–3)

The first task is to identify those general conditions of nature that make peace necessary. The second task lies in specifying in more detail how nature makes peace possible. Note that Kant is not here claiming that nature brings peace about: he is only saying that nature makes peace both necessary and possible for "the persons acting on its great stage." Nature makes peace conditionally necessary and possible – the grounds of its unconditional necessity and possibility are not given in nature but lie in our immediate consciousness of our duty.

Kant approaches the practical task of inquiring into nature's conditionally necessitating and enabling conditions for peace from the perspective of one cognizant of their unconditional duty in this regard. Since in much of his discussion relating to this twofold inquiry Kant appears to be going over the same material twice, it may be helpful to distinguish between a retrospective and a prospective teleological perspective. Kant adopts a retrospective perspective in relation to the first task of his inquiry: in considering the empirical (conditional) necessity of peace, he offers a (conjectural) account of past human developments towards peace thus far. By contrast, the second task is considered from a prospective perspective: in considering the empirical (conditional) possibility of peace, he asks which means of nature human agents can deliberately employ in order to "accelerate" progress towards peace (TP, 8.311).

With regard to the first, "preparatory argument" Kant identifies three "conditions of nature." First, nature has made provisions to enable humans to live "in all regions of the earth" (*PP*, 8.363); second, nature has ensured, by means of war, that humans have indeed dispersed themselves "even into the most inhospitable regions"; and third, nature has compelled humans, again by means to war, "to enter into more or less lawful relations." Kant's exposition of these three conditions is organizationally inadequate: he does not always keep them distinct, though he does do so intermittently. In particular, condition three receives no separate treatment – Kant appears to subsume discussion of it under the first condition. Best known in relation to the first condition are the references to "reindeer," "camels (ships of the desert)," and "driftwood." While all of these "provisions" are deemed conducive to man's living anywhere on earth, the last of these arouses "most wonder in nature's foresight" when she brings this material to "the most barren regions," thus enabling humans to live even on the "shores of the Arctic Ocean." In a move that appears to incorporate both second and third conditions into the first Kant goes on to say that:

> What drove man into those regions, however, was presumably nothing other than war. But the first instrument of war, among all the animals the human being learned to tame, was the horse; so too, the art of cultivating certain kinds of grasses, called grain, . . . could arise only in the condition of already established states, where there was secured ownership of land, after human beings, previously in the lawless freedom of hunting, fishing, or pastoral life, had been driven to agricultural life; then salt and iron were discovered, perhaps the first articles, everywhere in demand, of a trade among various peoples, by which they were first brought into a peaceable relation to each other. (*PP*, 8.364)

This quite abrupt sketch of the gradual emergence of settled political communities through basic economic need and development echoes the reference to "more or less lawful relations" under condition three. It appears that fighting between nomadic hordes of individuals contributed towards the emergence of a prototype of states. The first instrument of war comes to be used for agriculture, and this is possible only under settled conditions with "secured ownership of land." Kant's account here is consistent with his view of the historical emergence of states in the "Metaphysical Elements of Justice." There the ("violent") institution of states and systems of positive law are deemed a necessary first condition to the emergence of rightful relations within them (*MM*, 6.318–19). However, "more or less lawful relations" are by no means synonymous with "rightful relations." More or less lawful relations of positive law may arise in consequence of material need and advantage: but although conducive to them, these considerations are not in themselves sufficient for relations of strict, a priori Right. They are insufficient because material considerations of the sort mentioned – agriculture and trade – can never provide the grounds of justification of Right as an a priori concept of pure practical reason. What these material needs and related natural developments nonetheless do indicate is the empirical necessity of entrance into rightful relations.

Having seemingly incorporated the third condition – entrance into more or less lawful relations – into the first, and having precipitately referred, in the course of so doing, to the phenomenon of war (a provision of nature initially specified separately under the second condition), Kant explicitly signals his official move from the first to the second condition:

> In taking care that people could live everywhere on earth, nature at the same time despotically willed that they should live everywhere, even if against their inclination, and without this "should" even presupposing a concept of duty. (*PP*, 8.364)

The rejection as irrelevant of people's inclinations is rather more difficult to make sense of than the qualification of the "should" in question as a nonmoral one. Even if people had not wanted war, nature made sure that war drove them apart nonetheless. Proof of this comes in the form of Kant's observation of linguistically related peoples and cultures which now live far apart from one another. These cultures must have been driven apart, Kant conjectures, by warring cultures that settled in-between these former neighbors. In contrast to the initial mention of war under the first condition – "what drove people into [even the Arctic] regions was presumably nothing but war" – the type of war described under the second condition is between established, "more or less lawful" (not rightful!) states. This second type of war, which occasions the dispersal of peoples, not of (hordes of) individuals, "needs no special motive but seems to be engrafted onto human nature and even to hold as something noble, to which the human being is impelled by the drive to honor without self-seeking incentives." The second type of warfare is not occasioned by material needs, but is conducted for its own sake. Kant speaks of individuals' growing capacity, in consequence of their subjection under more or less lawful conditions, to act "against their inclination" and "self-seeking incentives" for ends that are unrelated to immediate personal advantage. "Honor," "courage," "dignity": these are the epitaphs of state-warfare with which "philosophers have eulogized it as a certain ennoblement of humanity," forgetting, in so doing, "the saying of a certain Greek that "war is bad in that it makes more evil people than it takes away." Thus, while Kant does not endorse association of honor and dignity with the conduct of war, he does seem to perceive in the supposed "enno-blement" of the human race through interstate war indication of human agents' – albeit misconceived – capacity to act from grounds other than immediate, sensibly determined self-interest.

"So much for what nature does for its own end with respect to the human race as a class of animals." With this concluding remark Kant abruptly brings to an end his first set of considerations throughout *PP* 8.365: the formerly mentioned third condition receives, as I said, no separate discussion. The concluding reference to the human race as an animal class is somewhat confounding, complicated by Kant's failure to specify what nature's own ends might be, in contrast to the ends of reason. Given their focus on materially based considerations, the first two of the mentioned natural conditions – provision of means of survival and dispersal across the globe – may be consonant with a view upon the human race as an animal class. By contrast, entrance into more or less lawful conditions of positive law indicates the gradual emergence of reasoned relations and as such, the transition from animal to rational status. Again, however, the reminder is important that "more or less lawful relations" do not represent "rightful relations" in the strict sense. The "more or less" has an air of contingency about it, implying materially based developments towards statehood. Read this way, the materially grounded emergence of such regulated interaction can perhaps be classed as belonging to humanity as an animal class, though it sits, arguably, on the cusp of the sensible/rational distinction within man.

II.2.b. The prospective argument

In the second part of his teleological reflections Kant turns to

> the question concerning what is essential to the purpose of perpetual peace: what nature does for this purpose with reference to the end that the human being's own reason makes a duty for him, hence to the favouring of his moral purpose, and how it affords the guarantee that what man ought to do in accordance with laws of freedom but does not do, it is assured that he will do, without prejudice to his freedom, even by a constraint of nature, and this in terms of all three relations of public Right: the right of a state, the right of nations, and cosmopolitan right. (*PP*, 8.365)

Kant's contention here is not that nature brings about man's moral ends directly; rather, nature makes it possible for man to do that which he ought to do but does not do merely on the grounds of his acknowledged obligation so to act. The second part of the teleological argument thus abstracts from the (acknowledged) requirement of acting from duty and asks instead which specific features of (human) nature man can employ in order to act in outward conformity, at least, with the demands of Right even if not from the inner maxim of rightful action. In the course of this second line of argument, Kant refers back to the general conditions of nature mentioned in the first part of the argument. The discussion of the republican constitution builds upon the mentioned "more or less lawful" internal relations within existing (nonrepublican) states; the argument in behalf of instituting the right of nations has recourse to the cultural and linguistic diversity of peoples thematized under condition two of the first argument, and the phenomenon of "trade among various people" mentioned under the first condition is employed for the purposes of fostering the emergence of cosmopolitan right.

In contrast to the retrospective historical reflections of the first argument, Kant's prospective perspective – his account of a possible future history – introduces the idea of deliberate human agency: whilst an appeal to the demands of practical reason (*Vernunft*) is avoided, human understanding (*Verstand*) assumes a major role. This is nowhere more evident than in relation to Kant's notorious invocation, in the course of his republican argument, of a "nation of devils" – a turn of phrase which more than anything has served to bolster prudential interpretations of his philosophy of Right. The establishment of a republican constitution turns "more or less lawful" relations of positive Right into relations of strict Right – that is, relations of Right in accordance with principles of pure practical reason. Kant claims that "the republican constitution is the only one that is completely compatible with the rights of human beings." However,

> It is also the most difficult one to establish and even more so to maintain, so much so that many assert it would have to be a state of angels because human beings, with their self-seeking inclinations, would not be capable of such a sublime form of constitution. But now nature comes to the aid of the general will grounded in reason, revered but impotent in practice, and does so precisely through the self-seeking inclinations, so that it is a matter only of the good organization of the state (which is certainly within the capacity of human beings), of arranging those forces of nature in opposition to one another in such a way that one checks the destructive effect of the other or cancels it, so that the result for reason turns out as if neither of them existed at all and the human being is constrained to become a good citizen if not a morally good human being. The problem of establishing a state [*sic!*], no matter how hard it may sound, is soluble even for a nation of devils and goes like this: "Given a multitude of rational beings all of whom need universal laws for their preservation but each of whom is inclined covertly to exempt himself from them, so to order this multitude and to establish their constitution that, although in their private dispositions they strive against one another, these yet so check one another that in their public conduct the result is the same as if they had no such evil disposition." (*PP*, 8.366)

Many have taken this particular passage as proof of Kant's prudential justification of the establishment of relations of Right: they have read Kant as holding that the basis of Right lies in the (material) interest each has in their own preservation and more general advantage. Considered from the political perspective Kant is driven to concede, these commentators have argued, that humans basically behave like self-interested devils. Nothing could be further from the truth. The problem is not that humans are devils: the problem is that they are not angels. Quite unlike devils, humans "revere" the demands of pure practical reason yet, unlike angels, they routinely fail to act on these demands. It is in view of human moral frailty – the spirit is willing but the flesh is weak – that nature is called upon to assist in the empirical institution of relations of Right the moral validity of which humans (in contrast to devils) do acknowledge as grounded in pure practical reason. In contrast to the earlier, materially based and hence natural emergence of "more or less lawful" relations humans' now deliberate establishment of a republican constitution employs a targeted feature of human nature

– private inclination – in order to effect a result that accords outwardly with the demands of pure practical reason. Such a deliberate employment of sensible inclination for purposes of empirical institutionalization should not be confused with an argument that takes obligations of Right to be justified with reference to these inclinations. Nor should it be confused with an argument which regards the furtherance of individual interest as the motive for entrance into (republican) political society. For one thing, it is clear from the passage cited that constitution drafters are aware of human moral frailties. They are thus aware also of human agents' acknowledgement, in principle, of their a priori obligations. They employ the means of nature in order to effect an outcome that ensures outward conformity with these acknowledged principles even if individuals' wills should fail them. Secondly, Kant states quite unambiguously that the constitution is designed so as to effect a mutual cancellation of private incentives and thereby to make possible the rule of reason even against individuals' sensible inclinations. If what is to be effected is a cancellation of the political efficacy of private inclination, prudential interpretations are mistaken in making self-interest either the ground or the end of political obligation in Kant.

Kant's account of republican constitutional design involves a complex relation between reason, nature, and understanding. Reason dictates acknowledgement of a priori valid reciprocal obligations of Right. Yet given human moral frailty, constitution drafters abstract from this acknowledged duty of Right as direct incentive. Their understanding of nature's causal mechanism enables them to employ a specifically targeted aspect of human nature that makes possible the design of empirical constitutional arrangements that are in outward conformity, at least, with the demands of pure practical reason. The problem of human moral frailty is thus circumvented, via rational understanding of human nature, in relation to the empirical institutionalization of Right: a task that is nonetheless distinct from the moral justification of Right.

Similar strategies of argumentation are employed with regard to the two remaining levels of public Right – Right of nations and cosmopolitan Right. Each time Kant argues from the presumption of our acknowledged obligations of Right and each time he avoids direct appeal to these obligations when considering the issue of institutionalization, relying instead on specifically targeted "means of nature" which human agents may employ for the purpose of instituting relations of strict Right. With regard to the Right of nations, Kant refers, in apparent self-criticism, to the nonrightfulness of each individual state's aspiration towards attaining the status of a "universal monarchy" (*PP*, 8.367) – of growing in size and global power to the point where all other states are subsumed under it. It is "the craving of every state (or of its head) to attain a lasting condition of peace in this way, by ruling the whole world wherever possible." However, "nature wills it otherwise" ensuring a diversity of languages and religions (or cultures) which "accords with the idea of reason," namely a "federative union" of states. While these differences between peoples "do bring with them the propensity to mutual hatred and pretexts for war," they also make possible "the gradual approach of human beings to greater agreement in principles" and thus to a "peace that is produced and secured by means of [states] equilibrium in liveliest competition" (*PP*, 8.367). This "equilibrium in liveliest competition" is analogous to the constitution drafters' employment of "mutually cancelling" private inclinations at the intrastate level. Nature cannot bring about a federative union of states: this can only be brought about by those who acknowledge its requirement as an idea of reason. However, those who do acknowledge the requirements of reason can employ the means of nature in order to effect an empirical outcome that corresponds with a priori duty.

The "power of money" and the "spirit of commerce," finally, are those unifying elements of shared natural inclination among persons and peoples which constitute means to the emergence of cosmopolitan relations of Right. Here, too, "reciprocal self-interest" functions so as to "cancel destructive effects." The emphasis on reciprocity implies, however, a "freely governed" form of law-like interaction between persons. Cosmopolitan Right is the least institutionalized of Kant's three levels of public Right, though it presupposes the two lower-level forms of institutionalization of which the only first is explicitly coercive. Again, however, observation of the "mechanism of human nature" will not of itself bring about a form of rightful interaction based on reciprocal self-interest. The latter can merely be used as a natural means by humans "for practical purposes" insofar as they acknowledge it to be "a duty for [them] to work towards the end [of perpetual peace]," nature in itself will not bring it about, and it would be foolhardy of anyone to "predict this future" theoretically (*PP*, 8.368).

Let me summarize the argument of the present section. I have contested the well-established prudential reading of Kant's political teleology according to which Kant resorts to his "mechanism of nature" argument in a belated acknowledgement of the futility of any appeal to moral duty in the realm of politics. In opposition to this line of interpretation I have argued that the teleological argument must be read against a background understanding of systematic constraints that arise in the course of Kant's moral justification of the laws of external freedom in juxtaposition with the laws of internal freedom. More specifically, the problem of the empirical institutionalization of principles of Right arises in consequence of the external and interpersonal character of the a priori laws of Right in contrast to the internal and intrapersonal character of the a priori laws of virtue. Kant's teleological argument can be read, in part, as an attempt to mediate between nonsensibly grounded laws of external freedom and the requirement of their sensible institutionalization. Approaching the First Supplement of *Perpetual Peace* in this manner means presupposing the moral justification of Right as already given. The reason why it makes sense to do so is this: given his systematic division between nature and reason, Kant cannot get a moral argument out of nature. In the absence of a presupposed moral duty to advance perpetual peace he can either consider nature from a theoretical teleological perspective, asking what the ends of nature may be independently of the ends of pure practical reason. Alternatively, Kant can consider human nature fatalistically, registering the discernible regularities in human nature and developments (birth and death rates) independently of any conception of their ends at all. If, by contrast, he insists upon viewing nature from a practical teleological perspective, he must take reason's moral ends as given. He must do so because one cannot specify the means without having some idea of the ends. Kant could not have set out either the general conditions of nature in the first part of his teleological argument or the specific means of nature in the second part if he had not presumed the moral end of perpetual peace as given. Nature does not set moral ends and rational prudence does not ground relations of Right: though both nature and prudence can be employed as means by those seeking the empirical institutionaliza-tion of acknowledge a priori obligations of Right.

III. Perpetual Peace as the End of Right

In this final section I want very briefly to address the notion of perpetual peace or the Right of humanity as the nonsensible end of empirically instituted relations of Right between persons and states. Prudential readings tend to focus on Kant's remarks regarding the means employed by nature in behalf of the furtherance of peace. By contrast, those who approach the political teleology against the background of the account of theoretical teleological judgment set out in the *Critique of Judgment*, have tended to focus on the idea of perpetual peace as an end of a purposively judged nature (see Lindstedt 1999 for an alternative account). More recently such theoretically oriented readings of the political teleology have lost some of their former influence. This is partly a consequence of the ascendancy of Kant's political philosophy as an object of study in its own right. At the same time the austere character especially of Kant's mature political work – the "Metaphysical Elements of Justice" – has driven some interpreters to remobilize the resources of the third Critique's account of teleological judgment with regard to ascertaining the end or purpose of established relations of Right. There is thus a degree of continuity between earlier, theoretically oriented approaches to Kant's political teleology via the third *Critique*, and current, agency oriented accounts that seek to add moral substance to what they perceive as the excessive formalism of Kant's philosophy of Right.

Amongst these latter approaches, there is a tendency towards a highly individualistic reading of the supposed substantive ends of Kant's philosophy of Right. The end of Right, on these accounts, has to do with individual agents' status as purposive beings: as setters of self-chosen ends and thus as "ends-in-themselves." Through entrance into civil society and the establishment of reciprocal relations of Right individual agents are to be enabled to "realize their purposive agency," that is to say, they are to be enabled to realize or perfect the particular talents, aptitudes and interests they have in virtue of their individuality (see Kaufman 1999; Guyer 2000).

Kant's political teleology tells against the plausibility of such individualistic interpretations of the ends of Right. To see this it may help, first, to point out that the current tendency to interpret the ends of Right individualistically is not unrelated to the more established tendency to conflate Kant's references in his ethics to humanity as an end-in-itself with the – rather un-Kantian – conception of the intrinsic moral worth of individuals as beings endowed with capacity for choice. The *Groundwork* urges individual agents to respect the humanity in their own person and in that of everyone else as an end-in-itself (*G*, 4.429). Kant is not asking that agents treat the individuality of each person – that which sets each apart from the rest – as possessing intrinsic moral worth. To the contrary, agents are to respect that which they share with all others – their humanity – as morally sacred.

The idea of humanity as an end in itself is underdetermined in the *Groundwork* – hence, perhaps, the temptation among commentators to give it a more determinate interpretation by means of the notion of individuals' moral worth as individuals. These approaches barely avoid, at times, a kind of moral naturalism that is at odds with the arguably deliberate under-determination of Kant's notion of humanity as an end-in-itself. Arguably, the idea of humanity as an end-in-itself is to be regarded as morally sacred precisely because its content ultimately eludes our understanding. The idea of humanity as an end-in-itself is ultimately incomprehensible to us. We are conscious of this idea within us, and it is that which elevates us, morally, above the rest of nature. But we cannot know what it is or wherein precisely its moral worth lies. Like the idea of a "thing-in-itself" in his epistemology, that of humanity as an "end-in-itself" in Kant's moral philosophy falls within the negative realm of the noumenal and thus ultimately exceeds our rational and even our practical understanding, though filling us with a sense of the morally sublime.

It is true, of course that in his political philosophy capacity for choice is central to Kant's conception of external freedom and account of Right. What is less clear is whether Kant endows individual capacity for choice with any intrinsic moral significance. In Kant's justification of property rights – central to his account of political obligation more generally – individuals' claim to the exercise of their freedom of choice and action entails as a corollary of that claim their subjection to the laws of external freedom. In that sense what is morally significant is not capacity for choice as such but the fact that the claim to the exercise of this capacity is obligation-entailing (Ludwig 2002). Put differently, what is morally significant about capacity for choice is what follows from it – namely agents' obligations of Right. The moral significance, in turn, of individuals' acknowledgement of their obligations of Right lies in the fact that it makes possible realization of the end of Right. The end of Right is "the Right of humanity," or perpetual peace (Brandt 2003). We approximate the end of Right by means of the empirical institutionalization of relations of Right at the state, interstate and cosmopolitan levels. Strictly speaking, however, the "Right of humanity" is empirically nonrealizable. It is, again, a noumenal idea of reason that exceeds all possibility of its empirical manifestation or institutionalization.

Like the more general idea of humanity as an end-in-itself, then, the specifically juridical idea of the "Right of humanity" is a shared noumenal idea. It is precisely this idea which, according to Kant's political teleology, makes it possible for individual agents to act in furtherance of progress towards perpetual peace even in their knowledge of the fact that "they themselves will long be dead and gone when the fruits they helped to sow are harvested" (TP, 8.309; Reiss 1970: 89). Remarks such as this one are in direct conflict with a view of the end of Right as lying in agents' realization of their particular individual purposes, talents and projects. Individuals who have a conception of Right as to do with the realization of their particular ends and interests could not contribute towards a moral end the gradual approximation of which they know to exceed their own life time and know to require considerable sacrifices, in terms of their individual interests, on their own part. This is attested by the conceptual difficulties that more individualistically oriented contemporary conceptions especially of global or cosmopolitan justice encounter with regard to theorizing individuals' commitment to the task. Problems of "moral overload," of the "burdens of commitment," of the "moral unreasonableness" of our having to sacrifice our interests for the sake of others' interests – these problems that attend individualistically conceived accounts of justice especially at the supranational level are nonexistent in Kant's account of possible progress towards perpetual peace. In Kant's account we see individual agents persevere in their attempt to contribute to approximation towards perpetual peace even in the face of "many failed attempts" (TP, 8.313; Reiss 1970: 92). We see them express their disinterested moral approval in relation to distant events – such as the French revolution – which give indication of the actuality of progress towards peace, based on the understanding that "true enthusiasm is always directed exclusively towards the ideal, particularly towards that which is purely moral, such as the concept of Right, and that cannot be coupled with selfish interest" (*CF*, 7.86; Reiss 1970: 183).

References and Further Reading

Brandt, Reinhardt (2003). On the vocation of the human being. In Brian Jacobs and Patrick Kain (eds.), *Essays on Kant's Anthropology*. Cambridge: Cambridge University Press.

Guyer, Paul (2000). *Kant on Freedom, Law, and Happiness*. Cambridge: Cambridge University Press.

Höffe, Otfried (1992). Even a nation of devils needs a state: The dilemma of natural justice. In Howard Williams (ed.), *Kant's Political Philosophy*. Cardiff: University of Wales Press.

Kaufman, Alexander (1999). *Welfare in the Kantian State*. Oxford: Clarendon Press.

Lindstedt, David (1999). Kant: Progress in universal history as a postulate of practical reason. *Kantstudien*, 90: 129–47.

Ludwig, Bernd (2002). Whence public right? On the relation between theory and practice in Kant's doctrine of right. In Mark Timmons (ed.), *Kant's Metaphysics of Morals: Interpretative Essays*. Oxford: Oxford University Press.

Reiss, Hans (1970). *Kant's Political Writings*. Cambridge: Cambridge University Press.

Schmitz, Heinz-Gerd (1990). Moral oder Klugheit? *Kantstudien*, 81.

Yovel, Yirmiahu (1980). *Kant and the Philosophy of History*. Princeton: Princeton University Press.

Part IV

The Critique of the Power of Judgment

Introduction

GRAHAM BIRD

Kant regarded the transcendental concept of freedom as "the keystone of the Critical structure." It linked the first *Critique*'s account of knowledge in the speculative philosophy with the second *Critique*'s account of morality in practical philosophy, and has also a central role in the third *Critique of the Power of Judgment*. The third *Critique* addresses directly two new aspects of our experience, namely aesthetic responses to nature and to art, and teleology or purposiveness in biology and theology. The evident motive for this new development lies in the expectation that there should be a priori principles of judgment as there are a priori principles of understanding and reason. In the first *Critique* judgment figured as a means of connecting sensibility and understanding in the application of rules in experience. In the third *Critique* it links the understanding's cognitive exercise in science with respect to nature with reason's practical supervision of desire in our moral responses. There is an expectation that the discussion of aesthetics and teleology might finally unify these diverse aspects of our experience.

In the new context, however, Kant has the same goals and uses the same methods as in the earlier *Critiques*. The primary aim, to uncover the a priori structure of these new areas of our experience in aesthetics and teleology, is pursued in line with the earlier methods. There is little in the first *Critique* specifically about aesthetic responses (but see B 640, B 651–2). The Transcendental Aesthetic deals with speculative issues about space and time rather than our appreciation of beauty or of the sublime but even the first *Critique* contains accounts of purposes and goals in science, theology, and elsewhere (B 714). Kant's discussion of the new topics in the third *Critique* still uses the first *Critique*'s classification of categories in terms of quantity, quality, relation, and modality, and the discussion is similarly separated into an Analytic, Dialectic, and Methodology. The Analytic of aesthetic judgment offers detailed analyses of new notions such as the judgment of taste, genius, and the sublime. The Dialectic examines and resolves claimed antinomies or conflicts arising from these notions, and the same divisions are made for teleological judgment. The discussion generally carries the same warnings about misconstruing the character of the relevant claims, about their "subjectivity" or "objectivity," and about the temptations in them to "fly into the transcendent," that is to find in them constitutive references to supersensible noumena (First Introduction, 20.244–5).

Kant's most general requirements are first to establish the mediating link which the power of judgment provides between nature and freedom, and second to explain its partition into aesthetic and teleological judgments. The former echoes the first *Critique*'s discussion of the systematic unity of nature. (See also chapter 26 below.) In that context Kant recognized both the possibility and necessity of our taking speculative nature to be a unified system but placed major constraints on the status of that conception. Even if we are bound to conceive nature in a systematic way for the purpose of pursuing science we have also to recognize that such a system cannot be established immanently *by* science. Its principle can be only regulative and not constitutive; it cannot be presented as a fact or as an a priori truth, but it can, and necessarily does, guide us in the investigation of nature. The concept is a priori but its associated principles are not for us constitutive, establishable, truths. In the new context Kant similarly classifies such principles as "reflective" and not "determinant" in a restatement of the same restrictions. The speculative appeal to systematic unity, like the characterization of "reflective" rather than "determinant" judgment, results from what is called in the first *Critique* a "regressive" search for higher principles of experience and not from the "progressive" application of general principles to particular circumstances.

Kant has various ways of characterizing the appeal to such a higher systematic unity. In one he thinks that a correct recognition of the contingency of laws in our experience points us towards a conception of an underlying necessity. Even if we can never know that nature is systematic the need for us to believe it leads us to conceive of its truth in some underlying, inaccessible, realm. That conception, moreover, leads us to conceive of such an underlying unity as "purposive," as both holding in such a realm and possibly designed to do so. Kant connects these ideas by describing purposiveness as "the lawfulness of the contingent as such" (First Introduction, 20.217). It leads to a formulation for the transcendental principle of the power of judgment which regards the unity of the complex laws of nature as specifically suited for our understanding (*CJ*, 20.209; 5.180). All these claims, however, could hold only in transcendent realms inaccessible to human cognition, and are subject to the same restrictions placed generally on such noumenal references. Kant allows us, even recognizes a necessity for us, to *conceive* such things, but at the same time classifies such beliefs as only "regulative," "reflective," and "subjective." In this context they point towards conceptions of the "supersensible" but, with one addition noted later, cannot be regarded as constitutive truths.

It is a consequence of such an account that at the highest level these conceptions can be only "formal." Any particular regressive attempt to unify scientific theories, say physics and chemistry, must depend on empirical circumstances relating to our investigation of the physical and chemical properties of matter. The underlying regulative conceptions of nature as a systematic unity, and as purposive, consequently abstract from such a posteriori material, and provide only a formal transcendental principle of judgment. They appeal to concepts of systematic unity and of purposiveness *in general*. In a similar way Kant connects such a transcendental principle to its intended domain, namely that of pleasure and pain. The suggestions are that we feel pleasure and pain when our goals are, respectively, achieved or unsatisfied, and that pleasures and pains can be associated with the satisfaction of our purposes in attempting to unify theories. Pleasure is in this way linked to the appreciation of harmony and unity among our psychological faculties in our intellectual theorizing, and to the achievement of their goals or purposes. Such an account is itself formal in abstracting from any material pleasurable goals or harmonies that we might recognize.

These claims provide for Kant a guide towards the second requirement, namely that of outlining the domains over which the principle of judgment presides. On one side the principle already refers to the purposes or aims of particular branches of science and to the ultimate purposes we have in science in general. On the other it points to our appreciation of unity and harmony whether in unifying scientific theories or in appreciating beauty in nature or art. In the former scientific context it indicates the general domain of teleology, and in the latter that of aesthetics, but evidently the two areas overlap. Imagination, exercised in the creation of works of art, is exercised also in the reflective, regressive, unification or construction of theories. Kant suggests similarities, or analogies, in the exercise of judgment between a regressive art such as medical diagnosis, the production and appreciation of art, and the representation of nature as an art work with a purpose and an architect (B 655; 5.383). These connections partition the domain of the principle of judgment into its teleological and aesthetic contexts in what might otherwise seem a wholly arbitrary association.

Two features of that consequence deserve to be noted particularly for aesthetic judgment. (See also chapter 28 below.) Aesthetic responses are regarded as involving pleasure (or pain), but are not *derived* from pleasure (or pain) (5.182). Kant regards it as a typical empiricist error, committed by Burke, to derive aesthetic properties merely from the affective responses we have to objects (5.223). For Kant those responses are *consequent* upon our appreciation of aesthetic properties and not their antecedent *ground*. They are formal, a priori, and have other negative features such as being nonconceptual and nonobjective. For Kant an empiricist approach such as Burke's is "merely physiological (psychological)" and so misses the essential structure of aesthetic experience (5.227). A second feature in both contexts is the renewed appeal, under different descriptions, to the supersensible and transcendent. Not all such judgments make that reference, but at the highest level they do. Natural ends for living organisms in biology have their basis firmly rooted in our experience of such nature, but our beliefs in nature itself as purposive, or in an agency responsible for its design conformably with our cognitive powers, transcend any possible experience we can have.

Similarly in aesthetics our specific appreciation of works of art or natural beauty is rooted in the harmonies we associate with them in an immanent experience; but aesthetic properties do not belong properly to their objects and in some cases our appreciation, for example of the sublime, contains references to what is transcendent and so cannot be properly attached to any object of experience. Kant regards beauty as a natural representation of morality and of the transcendental freedom he had argued for in the first and second *Critiques*. In these cases there are inevitable references to the supersensible transcendent, and Kant's view, in making the added proviso noted earlier, is that these contexts provide us with a way of making it determinable. Even though these can be no more than "analogies" or "symbolic anthropomorphisms" (*Prol.*, §§57–8), they fulfill the role of making our thoughts about the transcendent rich enough to meet the requirements of aesthetics and teleology.

There is disagreement among commentators about the extent to which Kant merely reinforces, in the third *Critique*, the message of the earlier works, or makes a new departure from it. The third *Critique* undoubtedly employs some new vocabulary, and in some passages reviews the philosophy in earlier work as the second *Critique* had also done. Kant uses a new terminology in his distinction between "determinant" and "reflective" judgment, but it echoes what Kant had said in the first *Critique* of the difference between "progressive" and "regressive" enquiries. In both cases the contrast is between accepting a universal claim and applying it to particular circumstances ("progressive," "determinant"), and looking in a specific circumstance for a universal rule which might explain, or ground, it ("regressive," "reflective"). The appeal to goals and purposes in the later work is similarly an echo of what Kant had said earlier of the systematic unity of nature, and the need in science for completed theories with a clear understanding of their aims and goals.

It may be thought that Kant relaxes his earlier prohibition on claims about a supersensible realm of noumena in the later work, but this is at best controversial and arguably just an error. Transcendental freedom, the systematic unity of nature, and appeals to God's purposes all tempt a step towards the supersensible transcendent in the new context. But those temptations were outlined in earlier *Critiques*, and Kant continues to express the same reservations about them. Throughout the Critical project the transcendent is represented as necessarily thinkable, but it provides no possibility of knowledge and no possibility of serious, decidable, argument about its character. In the final pages of the third *Critique* Kant renews his earlier discussion of belief in God and theology from the fourth Antinomy and the Ideal of the *Critique of Pure Reason*, but there seems to be no major change in his views. In both contexts he regards the traditional proofs of God's existence as fallacious, but allows a moral appeal to the concept of a God as a vital part of that form of a necessarily thinkable transcendence.

There is nevertheless a natural expectation that the third *Critique* should be seen as a culmination of the whole Critical project. It is the concluding part of the three *Critiques*, and is represented as forging a central link within them between nature and freedom. The interconnections between science and purposes both in the general context of a belief in the systematic unity of nature and in the more specific area of biological adaptation, are reinforced in the third *Critique*. Kant recognizes again a temptation to invoke the supersensible realm of noumena without making the appropriate qualifications, and uses the same apparatus to issue warnings about its dangers. But for the most part Kant addresses the new issues in aesthetics and teleology without overt emphasis on the need to unify the diverse elements of the Critical structure. They add something to our understanding of the links between nature and freedom, but those links were already present in the earlier work. The suggestion that the third *Critique* should be regarded as authoritative for the whole project in virtue of that unifying role, like the comparable claim for the *Opus postumum*, should be regarded with suspicion.

1. Aesthetic Judgment

Judgment figured in the first *Critique* as a derivative faculty mediating between the contents of sensibility and understanding. It marked Kant's emphasis on judgment forms in identifying a priori categories in the Metaphysical Deduction, and on the Fregean priority attached to judgments over subjudgmental constituents. In the Analytic of Principles judgment's role was that of making possible the application of understanding's a priori categorial rules to sensory experience by means of the a priori intuitions of space and time. The first two *Critiques* had outlined a general scheme in which sensibility and understanding make possible our cognitive experience, and reason in its practical role governs desire and makes possible our moral responses under transcendental and practical freedom. Now the suggestion is that the a priori structure of our aesthetic responses to art and nature requires the faculty of judgment. In Kant's discussion it is important to distinguish two aspects: first an analysis of the responses made under the heading of aesthetic judgment, and second a reference to, and evaluation of, the supersensible transcendent in our understanding of beauty and the sublime (see chapter 28 below). The former topic qualifies as a transcendental but immanent enquiry; the second as a transcendental account of the role and limitations of appeal to the transcendent.

Kant divides aesthetic judgments into judgments of taste, which deal with beauty in art and nature, and judgments of the sublime. His analysis of both forms undoubtedly involves an appeal to our psychological faculties, but he rejects Burke's idea that empirical psychology is adequate to provide such an analysis. Feelings of pleasure and pain constitute the domain over which those judgments are exercised but the judgments are not themselves merely records of pleasure or pain in some artefact or in nature. Kant distinguishes between the *unqualified* subjective character of what we find personally pleasurable and the *qualified* subjectivity of judgments of taste. The former are personal likes and dislikes essentially independent of others' responses, but the latter make an essential claim to the assent of others. That general assent may not be forthcoming, and cannot be guaranteed, but to say "That is beautiful" is to make a claim to others' assent in a way in which to say "I like that" is not.

Kant denies that "That is beautiful" ascribes a genuine property to an object in the way that "That table is wooden" does, and as a consequence he denies that the former judgments are objectively valid. They are only reflective, subjective, judgments, but they essentially call for general agreement and are therefore not comparable to mere expressions of pleasure. In recent philosophy these features might be described by invoking the notion of "response-dependent" attributions (Johnston 1989). "I like that" is an assertion of a purely personal preference. "The table is wooden" ascribes an objective material property to an object, and is not response-dependent at all. "That is beautiful" is response-dependent, and so is a report neither of an objective property like "wooden" nor of a purely personal preference. It asserts some relation between an object, with its (nonaesthetic) properties, and a subject's apprehension of its aesthetic properties. Just as with some contemporary conceptions of response-dependence so Kant thinks of this classification as a priori, but he does not provide the logical detail offered in the current diverse accounts of the notion.

What Kant does provide is an account of the way in which such response-dependence relates to our fundamental, a priori, psychological powers and to our feelings of pleasure and pain. The leading idea is that the pleasure in aesthetic responses is provided by an apprehension of harmony in the "free play" of our cognitive faculties which invokes an appeal to imagination. At the formal, a priori, level at which Kant's transcendental enquiry works the idea is that personal likes and dislikes are derived from specific material features of some apprehended item, but aesthetic responses are not. There is, according to Kant, no simple observable property signified by "beautiful" and no adequate universal criterion for what is beautiful (*CJ*, §17). Aesthetic responses are in that way "disinterested," not targeted at any particular material property, but result from the pleasure we feel in recognizing the harmony elicited in our apprehension of the object. That harmony in the free play of our faculties can be elicited by any number of actual objects, in art or nature, with their distinctive material, objective, properties.

These distinctive, general and formal, aspects of judgments of taste lead to Kant's definition that "beauty is the form of purposiveness of an object so far as this is perceived in it without any representation of purpose" (§17). It leads him to regard aesthetic judgment as essentially "singular," "contemplative," and nonconceptual; and to postulate something like a "common sense" which accounts in part for the claims to universal validity in such responses. It leads also to his requirement for "exemplary models" for beauty, and to his primary identification of them in morality. The "true propaedeutic for the foundation of taste is the development of moral ideas, and the culture of moral feeling" (§60) (see also chapter 27 below). These are puzzling claims, and puzzling lines of argument, but they begin to capture something of what we intuitively recognize as distinctive about aesthetic claims.

Kant's second interest in mapping the links between such aesthetic judgments and appeals to a supersensible transcendent is more evident in his account of the sublime. These are distinguished from judgments of taste, or beauty, because they involve emotions where the latter do not, and because they mark what is formless rather than what has an aesthetic form. In this context two routes to the supersensible transcendent are open. In the first the central idea of purposiveness leads us to conceive of nature as in some way "designed," or in some way itself a work of creative art. Such a use for the concept of formal purposiveness is not one which we can exemplify in nature or in our experience, and it consequently immediately invites a reference to what is for us supersensible and transcendent. A similar move can be made, as Kant notes in his account of teleological judgments, with respect simply to the notion of purpose in nature, and which leads to a conception of God.

A second route to the transcendent leads from the sublime in nature to a recognition of a certain majesty or monstrosity which again cannot be exemplified in nature and is for us transcendent. Kant's central examples of the sublime echo his earlier references in the first *Critique* to the "abyss" we may feel when confronted with such magnitudes, or majesty (*CPR*, B 651–2). Kant's analysis of the complex of emotions which yield our recognition of the sublime involves both an awe, even terror, at the presentation of such power, and yet also a pride in the fact that we can cope with it, and not actually be terrified. Like the thrill of horror in the cinema we are both cowed by and proof against the apparent threat. In all these ways Kant allows us to think, imagine, or respond to, the transcendent, but only within the framework of a subjective response which has no objective validity. As in the earlier case it adds a richness to our conceptions of aesthetic appreciation and of the route from conventional, sensory, experience to the supersensible. It provides more "analogies" with which to provide a characterization, or determinability, of the transcendent, but as with the transcendent notion of freedom we can go so far but no further. The transcendent is an essential player in the aesthetic scheme, but its role is different from that of the immanent analysis of aesthetic judgment.

2. Teleological Judgment

Kant's discussion of teleological judgment addresses a new topic but follows the same pattern and deploys the same basic apparatus. At its center is an Antinomy between "blind mechanism" and "purposiveness," which is outlined and resolved using the earlier contrast between constitutive and regulative claims (see also chapter 29 below). The initial reference to teleology is secured by appealing again to the idea of a systematic unity of nature, and the recognition of contingency in nature's laws, which lead us to conceive an underlying but delusive necessity which might unify mechanism and purpose. Appeals are made again to analogies which permit such moves from sensible experience to a supersensible transcendent even though the latter remains only subjective and thinkable. We are drawn to conceive of nature as a work of art and then inevitably as a purposive product. In the same way as the earlier discussion of aesthetic judgment the new discussion contrasts an immanent, but transcendental, analysis of teleological judgments with deflationary warnings about overstepping the boundary between the immanent and transcendent. Kant describes the latter variously as "arbitrary" (*willkürlich*) (5.369), "presumptuous" (*vermessen*) (5.383), "unprovable" (*unerweislich*) (5.389), and "poetic enthusiasm" (*dichterisch zu schwärmen*) (5.410).

Kant places severe restrictions on what counts as a science (*MFNS*, Preface, 4.469–71), and does not think of chemistry or psychology or biology as genuine sciences. He nevertheless offers an analysis of immanent claims of purpose attached to living organisms in what we think of as a science of biology. He has two guiding principles in this context: First to outline and evaluate the connections between different, legitimate and illegitimate, purposive claims, and second to clarify the meaning of the legitimate claims. Under the former heading Kant indicates a variety of contexts for such purposive claims which deviate in various ways from a standard use located in the ascription of goals and intentions to human rational agents. Deviations from that standard include the ascription of aims to animals, which Kant does not regard as mere Cartesian mechanisms (5.464), to other living organisms, to other adaptive strategies in nature, to nature itself, and to some supernatural, supersensible, intelligent agency which might be responsible for those designs in nature. As that deviation from the standard human case becomes greater so the legitimacy of the associated claims becomes more dubious. Although Kant does not distinguish the ascription of evident aims to individual organisms from the ascription of implicit aims to their species that slide is an example of a move from a more understandable to a more dubious claim.

At some point in the slide from a core legitimacy to deviant error the claims fall into that class of "presumptuous, unprovable, poetical extravagances" noted above. Kant notes such slides, and implicitly separates such core and deviant cases, throughout the Critical philosophy. Kant rarely gets to the point of saying that the most suspect claims are strictly meaningless, though in a number of examples he gets close to this. He underlines the absurdities of supposing that deposits of sandy soil left by the receding sea exist for the purpose of nurturing pine trees, and of the idea that natural features exist just for the benefit of humans (5.367). More commonly he regards some such claims as having a restricted legitimacy, where the fundamental error is not that of expressing meaningless claims but of a failure to grasp their proper limitations. This is so, for example, of claims about the wisdom, economy, or foresight of nature (5.383). References to God, as architect of nature, are consequently treated as comprehensible and natural, but their status as easily misunderstood and their validity frequently overstated.

In the analysis of purpose in living organisms Kant identifies three criteria for such attributions and insists on the compatibility of our treatment of the associated claims in terms of mechanism and of teleology. That is supported by his resolution of the corresponding antinomy in which the alternatives are represented as non-exclusive injunctions. In the resolution we are enjoined, in investigating nature, to go as far as we can in appeal to mechanical causes, but to recognize that we may complete such explanations with an appeal to purpose. The criteria for the ascription of purposes to organisms are (1) reproduction, (2) maintenance, and (3) mutual interaction and dependence between parts and the whole (see chapter 27 below). In this analysis Kant opens a fruitful line of philosophical investigation but it is not pursued far in the third *Critique* and gives way to the more negative analysis of beliefs in God related to such purposiveness.

As with other approved references to the transcendent Kant accepts not only that we do, but even that we are bound to, regard God as an intelligent agent underlying the evident purposiveness and design naturally attributed to nature. Such references are qualified in several ways. They share in the general restrictions on references to the supersensible that they cannot be constitutive or objectively valid. At best they share the subjective character of reflective, regulative, judgments, but even in that case are further limited by the kind of support or proof which such a belief is capable of. Kant's central goal throughout the final parts of the third *Critique* reinforces his earlier discussions of theology and the belief in God from the first *Critique*'s fourth Antinomy and Ideal. In both contexts the traditional proofs are condemned and the sole legitimate ground for such beliefs lies in the appeal to morality. Kant consequently rejects what he calls a "physico-theology" in favor of an "ethico-theology." He strongly contrasts the latter with a "theological ethics" which he regards as unacceptable, and this points to a central concluding element in the whole discussion.

Theological ethics is unacceptable because it displaces the human rational agent in favor of a supernatural authority. Kant's moral philosophy has at its centre the idea of an autonomous, rational, free, self-legislating, human agent and not that of a divine command. Kant accepts a place for divine commands, but it is subordinate to the ethico-theological conception of God. Moral philosophy, in the shape of a categorical imperative, commands, but the commands are issued by the autonomous agent. In a similar way when Kant comes to rehearse the reference to the three standard metaphysical issues of God, freedom, and immortality it is "freedom" which provides the ground for the others (5.474). The second *Critique* and *Groundwork* provide the sole adequate basis for the other metaphysical concepts and provide the needed basis for theology and a genuine belief in God. Freedom is finally again represented as the keystone of the Critical structure. The appeal to morality provides also the proper ground for a belief in rational humanity as an ultimate, if not final, end in our experience. Kant connects this emphasis on morality both with teleology and aesthetics in his insistence on the basic moral models of aesthetic beauty. "[O]nly [in] the culture of moral feeling can genuine taste assume a determinate, unalterable, form" (5.356).

Reference

Johnston, Mark (1989). Dispositional theories of value. *Proceedings of the Aristotelian Society,* Supplementary Volume 63: 139–74.

26

The Demands of Systematicity: Rational Judgment and the Structure of Nature

PAUL ABELA

This unity of reason always presupposes an idea, namely that of the form of a whole of cognition, which precedes the determinate cognition of the parts and contains the conditions for determining a priori the place of each part and its relation to the others. (B 673)

Introduction

The demands of systematicity occupy a central place in the Kantian account of rational judgment. Reflected in both its content, and in its modus operandi – unrepentantly architectonic – Kant's Critical philosophy, in both the *Critique of Pure Reason* and in the *Critique of the Power of Judgment*, is deeply informed by the requirement for unity. Nowhere is this requirement more keenly felt, and yet interpreted more widely, than in the role Kant accords to systematicity in the first and third *Critiques*.

Assessing the precise status Kant assigns to this commitment is a tangled business. Kant himself offers the reader mixed signals. There are important sets of passages in both the *Critique of Pure Reason* and the *Critique of the Power of Judgment* in which Kant appears to oscillate between a subjectively oriented heuristic reading and a stronger objective characterization. This can invite in both the seasoned reader and the novitiate a nagging worry that perhaps Kant's claims overdetermine a stable interpretation. Couple this with the common view that Kant chose to "bury" his remarks in an appendix to the Doctrine of Elements and deep within the Transcendental Dialectic of the first *Critique*, and join this with the common refrain that highlights differences in aim and approach between the first and third *Critiques* concerning systematicity, and one might be tempted to view the consistency and significance of Kant's claims with some suspicion.

Nevertheless there are good reasons to resist this temptation. While acknowledging the range of Kant's statements on systematicity, it is possible to discern a common core of commitments. Unlike many other areas of Kant's philosophy, explicating the principles of systematicity is relatively straightforward. The more demanding task resides in assessing the precise status Kant assigns to these principles. In this chapter I offer an exposition of systematicity and suggest an alternative reading to dominant contemporary methodological interpretations.

The chapter is divided into four sections. In Section 1 I offer a sketch of the relation between rational judgment and the understanding, focusing on the regulative nature of the demand of systematicity and noting how Kant articulates its use. Section 2 details the tripartite division of principles that constitute systematicity, indicating both the logical modes of rational judgment and the corresponding transcendental principles that concern the deep structure of nature. In Section 3 I canvass, and reject, the not implausible contemporary interpretation that identifies the demand of systematicity with heuristic import. In particular, I suggest that the empiricist/pragmatic import of this methodological reading, while capturing important consequences of rational unity, ultimately fails to register appropriately the discursive linkages that underwrite this transcendental employment of reason. Section 4 presents a brief account of an alternative reading that posits a more objective cognitive role for systematicity. I suggest that the unity enforced by rational judgment serves as a final, and necessary, condition for the discrimination of objects and events. Much of the argument rests on claims Kant makes concerning the place rational unity occupies as the ground for supplying an empirical criterion for truth-conditional judgments. It is claimed that Kant's account of object-directed empirical judgments, from spontaneous representation (understanding) to rational judgment (reason), operates within a truth-conditional framework. Kant's objectivist assertion, in both *Critiques*, concerning the requirement of affirming an intrinsic structure in nature, is interpreted as an expression of this necessary involvement of truth considerations.

In the interests of a delimited discussion of the general demands of systematicity across the first and third *Critiques*, I have separated the following discussion from issues concerning purposiveness and teleology. I recognize that this separation is somewhat forced in terms of elements contained in the third *Critique*. These latter subjects are targeted for detailed discussion in other chapters of this anthology (see also chapters 27 and 29). Consistent with this strategy, I will use the notion of "rational judgment" to signify the discursive faculty (reason/reflecting judgment) that works upon the deliverances of the understanding.

Section 1: Rational Judgment and Understanding

> Concepts of reason serve for comprehension, just as concepts of the understanding serve for understanding (of perceptions). (B 367)

In its theoretical employment, the task of reason is to comprehend nature. Unlike the understanding which has constitutive principles of its own as it works upon the deliverances of sensibility, reason is an entirely dependent faculty. This limitation is at the heart of so much of what separates Kant from his rationalist predecessors. It also serves naturally as ground zero for his treatment of the conditions and cognitive structures necessary for knowledge of the empirical world.

Kant claims that reason "never relates directly to an object, but solely to the understanding and by means of it to reason's own empirical use" (B 671). It is important to discuss, at the outset, how this dependency bears on the status to be assigned to systematicity.

The most immediate consequence of the dependence of reason upon the deliverances of the understanding is the association of rational judgment with *structure* rather than *content*. As Kant emphasizes throughout the first *Critique*, reason "does not create any concepts [of objects] but only orders them and gives them that unity which they can have in their greatest possible extension" (B 671). This dominant theme is similarly expressed throughout the third *Critique*, reinforcing the arguments of the first *Critique* as well as enlarging the role of rational judgment to include teleology as an additional regulative contribution.

The activity of rational judgment is thus directed toward establishing a form of unity in the manifold contributed by understanding. Just as the understanding "unifies the manifold in the object by means of concepts, so reason on its side unites the manifold of concepts through ideas" (B 672). While rational judgment requires the deliverances of the understanding in order to have any legitimate employment, the unity that reason enforces originates entirely from itself, a *collective* unity different in type from the merely *distributive* unity of the understanding (B 672). The resulting parallel structures posited "in nature [of] a subordination of genera and species" (*CJ*, 5.185) are not merely extensions of the cognitive structures – appropriately cleaned up, filled in, and augmented – already supplied by the understanding. On the contrary:

> pure reason is in fact concerned with nothing but itself, and it can have no other concern, because what is given to it is not objects to be unified for the concept of experience, but cognitions of understanding to be unified for the concept of reason, i.e., to be connected in one principle. (B 708; translations from Kant 1998, 2000)

The particular structure(s) that constitute this collective unity are explored in section 2. What is important to stress at this stage is that reason's own cognitive structures are manifestations of a regulative function. Borrowing from the relation of concepts to intuitions, Kant claims that the transcendental principles of reason serve, by way of analogy, the same role as the schema does for a concept of the understanding; allowing for the application of a rule in conformity with the discursive function of the determining principle.

> Thus the idea of reason is an analogue of a schema of sensibility, but with this difference, that the application of concepts of the understanding to the schema of reason is not likewise a cognition of the object itself . . . but only a rule or principle . . . (B 693)

From the side of the understanding, Kant describes the effect of the demand of systematicity in terms of enforcing a projected unity:

> The hypothetical use of reason is therefore directed at the systematic unity of the understanding's cognitions, which, however, is the touchstone of truth for its rules. Conversely, systematic unity (as mere idea) is only a projected unity, which one must regard not as given in itself, but only as a problem [. . . helping] to find a principle for the manifold and particular uses of the understanding, thereby guiding it even in those cases that are not given and making it coherently connected. (B 675)

I leave for section 4 a discussion of the important, but neglected, connection between systematicity and truth. For present purposes it is sufficient to note how Kant, from the side of the understanding, identifies the contribution of the regulative role of systematicity with a maximally integrated domain.

Nonetheless, the import of the metaphor of a "projected unity," like that of the "focus imaginarius" at B 672, can easily mislead. It can seem attractive to view reason's contribution as little more than the mere extension of principles already suggested, or contained, in the deliverances of the understanding. While it is true that rational comprehension directs cognition beyond what the understanding can deliver, this extension is not realized by the mere augmentation of already given structures. If not augmentation, why not?

In terms of empirical knowledge, reason is a *dependent* faculty but it is not a *derivative* faculty. From the side of rational judgment, systematicity is fundamentally different, in origin and scope, from the unity of the understanding. This deep difference is rooted in the essential drive that constitutes reason; the task of realizing the unconditioned. As Kant states when describing pure reason early in the Dialectic:

> Now a transcendental concept of reason always goes to the absolute totality in the synthesis of conditions, and never ends except with the absolutely unconditioned . . . For pure reason leaves to the understanding everything that relates directly to objects of intuition or rather to their synthesis in imagination. It reserves for itself only the absolute totality in the use of concepts . . . Thus reason relates itself only to the use of the understanding, *not indeed insofar as the latter contains the ground of possible experience* (for the absolute totality of conditions is not a concept that is usable in an experience, because no experience is unconditioned), but rather in order to prescribe the direction toward a certain unity of which the understanding has no concept . . . (B 383, emphasis added)

The realization of this quest for unity thus involves cognitive structures not found among the categories of the understanding. The move from the aggregate manifold contributed by the understanding to a system of integrated belief reflects a cognitive shift in type, not degree.

Section 2: The Structure of Systematicity

Systematicity has a threefold structure. As in the Analytic of the first *Critique*, Kant offers a derivation of transcendental principles from pure forms of judgment (logic). Although Kant is, at times, guilty of varying the titles he assigns to these principles, in the main he designates the three logical principles as homogeneity, specification, and continuity. The corresponding transcendental expressions are genera, species and affinity (B 679ff).

In the most general sense, the governing rule of systematicity involves "the idea of the maximum of division and unification of the understanding's cognition in one principle" (B 693), requiring us to assert that "nature in its boundless multiplicity has hit upon a division of itself into genera and species that makes it possible for our power of judgment to find consensus in the comparison of natural forms" (*CJ*, 20.212n).

411

The first principle, of homogeneity, requires us to regard all given particulars as parts of larger possible wholes. The instantiation of this demand, as expressed in the transcendental principle of genera, imposes the task of recognizing shared conceptual features across the manifold of given particular objects and events. The structure of rational comprehension thus directs us to ever higher levels of conceptual organization in nature, so that "sameness of kind is necessarily presupposed in the manifold of a possible experience" (B 682). From the advanced theoretical quest in the natural sciences for a grand unifying theory to the pedestrian task of finding my way home – "as these roads run parallel, and that road is perpendicular to the first . . ." – it is the task of rational comprehension to push to higher levels of governing unity.

The principle of specification directs rational judgment in the opposing direction; viewing all particulars as embodying undiscovered diversity. In its transcendental expression, reason offers the concept of "species" as the basis in nature for the decomposition of any given particular; viewing nature as intrinsically suited to the "specification of the manifold under a given concept" progressing "from the highest genus to lower (subgenera or species) and from species to subspecies" (*CJ*, 20.215). Although Kant qualifies this rational mode of inquiry by noting that we cannot assume a truly infinite presence of natural kinds (B 684), his general point is that reason imposes a structure that requires us to view all conceptual application as, in principle, open to ever more fine-grained acts of discrimination. We can see this demand of reason at work in environments as varied as creating particle accelerators to shatter subatomic particles – a very expensive manifestation indeed – to the stay at home charge of coming to comprehend what the slight tonal variation in my infant daughter's cry really signals. In all such cases, we take the given as an object amenable to deeper investigation.

The final principle imposed by reason concerns the demand of continuity in the received manifold. As in the case of third categories of the understanding, continuity is a combination of the preceding two principles. Here reason frames the act of comprehension by constraining the domain of possible representation within a single and exhaustive order of unity and manifoldness.

The principle of continuity is, in this respect, systematicity simpliciter. At the conceptual level it asserts the principle of non datur vacuum – that there can be no original genera occupying a position that is independent of the ongoing disclosure of the highest concept. At the transcendental level it entails the principle of datur continuum formarum – that "all variety of species bound one another and permit no transition to one another by a leap, but only through every smaller degree of distinction" (B 687). Rational judgment therefore requires us to view all objects and events as flowing from an abiding single reality, "all manifolds [being] akin one to another, because they are all collectively descended, through every degree of extended determination, from a single highest genus" (B 686).

Section 3: Systematicity as Methodological Maxim?

Since Gerd Buchdahl's seminal contribution (Buchdahl 1969), English-language treatments of Kant's account of systematicity have tended to focus upon the link between the structure imposed by rational unity and important issues in the philosophy of science. That, in itself, is not unexpected. It is perhaps more surprising that the general importance of the role of systematicity in the first and third *Critiques* was for so long obscured by an overweening focus on the Analytic of the first *Critique*, and the account of aesthetics in the first book of the third *Critique*.

An influential reading initiated by Buchdahl, and developed in broadly the same spirit by Kitcher and Guyer, stresses the methodological import of Kant's approach to the regulative principle of systematicity. There are, of course, important and significant differences in the details supplied by these commentators, but what unites them is a general drive toward assimilating the regulative import of systematicity within the large tent of methodologically oriented approaches.

Buchdahl's reading connects the role of systematicity to the methodological context of scientific discovery and to the capacity of viewing experienced regularities in the context of causal laws. The structures of rational judgment are viewed as framing the representational assignments between experienced objects and their place within a single system of causal determination; in effect creating "the field in which the hypothesis is to be tested" (Buchdahl 1969: 510). More recently, commenting on systematicity and its link to purposiveness, Buchdahl has suggested that there is the requirement of a "supersensible substratum of things" to give a "necessary meaning to reason's methodologically-determined endless search for and projection of systematic unity" (Buchdahl 1992: 331).

The Kantian transcendental principles of genera, species and affinity seem a good fit for this methodological role. Rational judgment carries the burden of justifying the attribution of necessary causal relations since experience itself yields only inductively strong generalizations. If a condition for empirical knowledge and explanation requires a posited structure assigned to nature to sustain the attribution of necessary causal relations, then the invocation of reason's unity can be regarded as something of the closing chapter in Kant's extended response to Hume, supplying us with reasons for attributing necessity to causal regularities that garner inductive support only in experience. In this context, the varied set of empirical causal generalizations experience yields can be viewed as forming a hierarchical system of necessary empirical laws, with nomological force being preserved in the system as one moves from general covering laws to more particular instantiations.

Kitcher's approach is more radical than the model-theoretic approach suggested above and stresses the heuristic status of this principle. Systematicity is a "methodological principle that we are justified in following" where justification "does not rest on the correctness of Nature [a]s systematically unified" (Kitcher 1986: 211). Kant's regulative approach, on this reading, anticipates much of Kitcher's own view that patterns of explanation for phenomena require an abiding framing condition. That framing condition – viewing nature as an integrated whole, with definable features that are open to confirmation through hypothesis testing – supplies us with a kind of meta-methodological basis for employing particular empirical theories. While empirical investigation of nature would be impossible without such commitments, this does not entail that the framing conditions are themselves objective. Instead, the demand of unity acts as a kind of methodological limiting condition:

it is necessary that there should be a causal order of nature and that this causal order amounts to no more than the projection of the explanatory dependencies that would emerge in the limit as we strive to unify our system of beliefs. (Kitcher 1994: 263)

Unlike Buchdahl and Kitcher, who look to Kant's treatment largely with an eye to lessons for the philosophy of science, Guyer's analysis is situated in his larger project of offering an expansive and integrated interpretation of Kant's body of work. Separating a single strand from that body of work is difficult, but one can discern significant support for the methodological interpretation of systematicity. This support derives from a general strategy of infusing Kantian regulative principles with methodological import. This linkage is expressed in two related ways. First, Guyer associates the regulative principles of both the Analytic and Dialectic of the first *Critique* with structures that underwrite the confirmation, and integration (respectively), of causal judgments. In the Analytic Guyer claims that "the categories themselves, it seems, furnish both a guarantee that we can discover empirical laws applying to any empirical intuitions and all the method we need to discover these laws" (Guyer 1990: 224). On this reading, the task, for example, of the Second Analogy is to deliver the requisite objective succession by means of an appeal to discovered particular causal laws. The understanding thus provides knowledge of causal laws while rational judgment serves the comparatively minor role of providing a method for integrating the already determinate causal laws into a single hierarchy.

The second pertinent aspect of Guyer's reading flows from his suggestion that Kant fundamentally altered, when writing the third *Critique*, his conception of the roles assigned to the understanding and reason:

> In the first *Critique* Kant did not suppose that systematicity is necessary for the discovery of empirical laws, but instead treated it as an additional desideratum of reason, a hierarchy to be sought among laws already discovered. . . . In the third *Critique*, however, the reassignment of the search for systematicity from the faculty of reason to that of reflecting judgment indicates that systematicity is involved in the discovery of empirical laws themselves . . . (Guyer 2003: 201)

As many commentators have suggested, the third *Critique* does mark a contribution that Kant had not anticipated when writing the first *Critique*. Rational judgment must shoulder a burden not previously associated with reason in the first *Critique*. Nonetheless, interpretative charity places a substantial burden upon those who suggest, as Guyer does, that Kant radically altered his account of the interplay of the faculties of understanding and reason, as offered in the first *Critique*, when he introduced the additional regulative role of purposiveness in the third *Critique*. Assessing the merit of attributing this radical shift in Kant's approach between 1787 and 1790 is beyond the scope of this chapter. What is important to note is that even where one accepts the proposed revision, the same dominant pairing of regulative principles with methodological import remains:

> [T]hroughout this work [third *Critique*], Kant considers the idea of the purposiveness of nature and the systematicity that may be founded upon it, whether a systematicity of law

or of ends, to be a regulative and heuristic ideal, an aid for the discovery of mechanical explanations but not itself a piece of theoretical knowledge. (Guyer 2003: 204)

On this latter reading, the demands of systematicity are much more extensive, including both the identification of causal laws as well as their hierarchical integration. However, in both readings Guyer invests the regulative role of judgment with methodological significance.

Guyer is careful to temper the methodological characterization with an insistence that systematicity is not an optional extra. Commenting on the role of systematicity in connection with teleology in the third *Critique*, he notes that:

> the idea that nature as a whole is a single system only urges us to expand the scope of explanation in accordance with mechanical causation. Yet the heuristic status of the principle of universal teleology should not be mistaken for an optional status. (Guyer 2001: 389)

Note that although this passage is introduced in the context of teleology, Guyer directs the force of the claim to systematicity generally (B 699) (Guyer 2001: 389, note 23).

The methodological reading of systematicity is evidently not without its champions. The great virtue of this approach is that it appears to do justice to Kant's abiding caution against affirming any constitutive role for rational judgment. When we associate regulative principles with organizational structure, and identify the real of experience with what the constitutive principles render from sensibility, it is only natural to highlight the projective, subjectivist import of the demand of systematicity. Moreover, this strategy dovetails nicely with representative passages in the first and third *Critiques* where Kant stresses the heuristic element of systematicity:

> the idea is only a heuristic, and not an ostensive conception; and it shows not how an object is constituted but how, under the guidance of the concept, we ought to seek after the constitution and connection of objects of experience in general. (*CPR*, B 699)
>
> Now this transcendental concept of a purposiveness of nature is neither a concept of nature nor of freedom, since it attributes nothing at all to the object (of nature), but rather only represents the unique way in which we must proceed in reflection on the objects of nature . . . consequently it is a subjective principle [maxim], of the power of judgment. (*CJ*, 5.184)

Given these virtues, what, if anything, is defective in the methodological reading?

Most immediately, this reading is simply at odds with too many passages where Kant explicitly or implicitly denies merely heuristic value to systematicity. Consider the following passages from both the first and third *Critiques*:

> One might have believed that this is merely a device of reason for achieving economy, for saving as much trouble as possible. . . . Yet such a selfish aim can easily be distinguished from the idea, in accordance with which everyone presupposes that this unity of reason conforms to nature itself; and here reason does not beg but commands . . . (B 681)
>
> one can see clearly that the laws judge the parsimony of fundamental causes, the manifoldness of effects, and the consequent affinity of the members of nature in themselves

reasonably and in conformity with nature, and these principles therefore carry their recommendation directly in themselves, and not merely as methodological devices. (B 689)

in order to investigate these empirical so called laws, [judgment must] ground all reflection on nature on an a priori principle, the principle, namely, that in accordance with these laws a cognizable order of nature is possible – the sort of principle that is expressed in the following propositions: that there is in nature a subordination of genera and species that we can grasp . . . (CJ, 5.185)

When faced with what appear to be highly divergent commitments, it is tempting to retreat to Kitcher's view that "the interpretative difficulty is surely Kant's apparent wish to have things both ways; to dismiss the pretensions of reason and simultaneously to attribute to the search for unity some kind of 'objective validity' " (Kitcher 1986: 207).

The methodological reading overcomes this interpretative difficulty at the cost of discounting such conflicting passages, but this discounting is not arbitrary. It is motivated, I believe, by something of an empiricist bias in the interpretation of the significance of the Kantian constitutive/regulative dichotomy. Pausing to diagnose this bias is important for providing interpretative room to develop the objectivist interpretation below.

As we have seen, reason is a dependent faculty, never relating "directly to an object, but solely to the understanding and by means of it to reason's own empirical use" (B 671). It is tempting therefore to view the regulative use of reason as merely enforcing rational patterns of connection (inference patterns) laid over an already determinate representation of reality. Relevant background epistemological commitments that make this an attractive option include (empiricist) assumptions about the determinacy of the deliverances of receptivity, an association of objectivity with content against structure, and a general bias that results in separating the space of reasons from the cognitive activity responsible for object and event discrimination. I have elsewhere (Abela 2002: ch. 1) offered a detailed account of how the contours of Kant's transcendental idealist model of cognition are frequently miscast by common background empiricist assumptions.

For immediate purposes I wish to stress that there are deep reasons to resist the urge to deny objective import to principles merely because they enforce cognitive structure. The pairing of the real with experiential content, and the rational with order, is, of course, a plausible epistemological doctrine. But it is not Kant's. Modeling Kant's constitutive/regulative pairing on that basis is a mistake.

By returning to the constitutive/regulative pairing in the understanding we can gain some insight into how Kant's use departs from the received account. Recall that within the understanding, Kant associates the constitutive principles (Axioms of Intuition and the Anticipations of Perception) with the determination of intuitions (empirical and pure). The regulative principles (primarily the Analogies) supply the requisite temporal and causal structures necessary for the determinate representation of empirical objects and events by means of intuition. The discursive structures supplied by the Analogies, the subject/property relation, the successive causal structure, and the notion of causal reciprocity, are all elements of cognitive form. They add nothing to the content of the deliverances of receptivity. They serve instead as the necessary discursive structures required for the possibility of object and event discrimination.

416

Despite the fact that these regulative principles add no content to the deliverances of the constitutive principles, nonetheless, they are objective conditions, without which there would be no experience of objects at all by the understanding. In this sense the Analogies, although regulative and adding no content of their own, are constitutive of experience in toto:

> In the Transcendental Analytic we have distinguished among the principles of the understanding the dynamical ones, as merely regulative principles of intuition, from the mathematical ones, which are constitutive in regard to intuition. Despite this, the dynamical laws we are thinking of are still constitutive in regard to experience, since they make possible a priori the concepts without which there is no experience. (B 692)

Once we accept the general Kantian lesson that, as in moral deliberation, discursive structure reaches all the way down, making possible the determinate representation of objects and events by means of the intrinsically indeterminate deliverances of receptivity, then we are in a better position to appreciate the distorting effect of the empiricist influenced pairing of the constitutive with the real (objective), and the regulative with the merely rational (methodological). The Kantian model departs sharply from the broad empiricist view that associates the objective reality of experience with the supposedly determinate deliverances of receptivity. Consequently, a fully objective role for discursive structure remains a live interpretative option, not *in spite of* its form-giving rules, but *because* of this mode of engagement.

Now, of course, lessons drawn from the connection of constitutive and regulative principles of the understanding cannot be extended uncritically to the regulative role of reflective judgment. Understanding is concerned with the immediate conditions necessary for representing objects and events. Reason is directed to comprehending the deliverances of the understanding. Nonetheless, if we hold on to the general lesson – that regulative principles, while being rational, can also be connected to what is real and objective – we can open up some space for bringing Kant's apparently divergent remarks together. It may, in fact, point to a Kant who, while careful to deny a constitutive role for systematicity, is also directing the reader to the objective import of the regulative demand of systematicity.

Section 4: Nature and Rational Structure

Moving beyond the methodological reading requires a revisiting of how Kant licenses the shift from our cognitive modes of comprehension to the assertion of inherent, corresponding, structures in nature. In making this move toward an empirically real interpretation of systematicity one must be constantly alert to the danger of surreptitiously investing the regulative employment of this principle with constitutive force. Kant's prohibition on reading the employment of systematicity in terms of adding any content to the deliverances of the understanding is absolute. The weight of the argument must be borne by considerations aligned wholly to the role of rational structure. The challenge is to see how the investment of cognitive structure affirms a substantive, objective unity in nature.

417

Section 2 offered a review of the link between the logical principles of homogeneity, specification and continuity and the transcendental structures of genera, species, and affinity. One of the great virtues of the methodological approach is that it effectively avoids an otherwise obvious difficulty; how to justify the coordination of the demands of systematicity with the inherent structure of nature without introducing a questionable empirical coincidence of transcendent proportions. Paving over this empirical gap between mind and world requires more than bald assertion. The proposed objectivist reading of systematicity requires confronting this concern directly.

It is first worth recalling that Kant does not shy away from affirming this connection in both the first and third *Critiques*:

> The regulative principle demands that systematic unity be presupposed absolutely as a unity in nature that is recognized not only empirically but also a priori, though still indeterminately, and hence as following from the essence of things. (B 721)

> The power of judgment must assume it as an a priori principle for its own use that what is contingent for human insight in the particular empirical laws of nature nevertheless contains a lawful unity, not fathomable by us but still thinkable, in the combination of its manifold into one experience possible in itself. (*CJ*, 5.183–4; see also *CJ*, 5.179–80 and 5.185)

The "cosmic coincidence" charge garners its force from the otherwise common sense recognition of the empirical separation between thought and the world. Our thinking does not make the world, and it is the world that informs our thinking.

But it is a mistake to conflate the transcendental analysis of the conditions for empirical knowledge with the necessary empirical separation of mind and world. The issue of a primitive "gap" between mind and world is ill posed at the transcendental level. It presupposes an original bifurcation of comprehension and nature that, while comfortably at home at the empirical level, and within the empiricist epistemological framework generally, is nonetheless at odds with the transcendental idealist model of cognition.

The entire thrust of Kant's Copernican revolution is to locate the demands of determinate representation within a framework that builds in a secure bridge linking the discursive, structural, components of the cognizing subject with the objects of that mode of cognition. Objects, events and, by extension, nature itself must conform to the conditions under which representation and comprehension operate. Kant's familiar claim, that we "bring into the appearances that order and regularity in them that we call nature, and moreover we would not be able to find it there if we . . . had not originally put it there" (A 125), is no more than a reaffirmation of the abiding lesson of the Critical philosophy generally; that all objects of cognition must conform to the conditions of the possibility of experience. This general lesson applies with as much force when applied to rational comprehension as it does to the understanding.

Although the Kantian approach is not vulnerable to the notion of a primitive chasm between representation and the objects of representation, stopping here is to stop short. The original problem inevitably resurfaces, now transformed in terms of how transcendental idealism secures the discursive, formal, linkages between the deliverances of the understanding and the posited unity of rational judgment. On what basis can we calm the worry that the demands of rational systematicity, and its nonderivative rational unity, remain primitively external and in this sense foreign to the structures enforced by the understanding? What underwrites this required linkage?

Conditions of empirical truth, I believe, serve as the relevant discursive bond. What appropriately unites the demands of spontaneous representation (understanding) and the demands of systematicity (rational judgment) is that each is involved in supplying the discursive conditions for object-directed cognition; the spontaneous contribution of the understanding creates the implicit truth framework for object-directed judgments while reason contributes an explicit criterion for truth-claims upon the deliverances of the understanding. The two, working together, deliver determinate representation, ranging from navigating our common traffic with the world to the contribution of advanced scientific theory.

How is this accomplished?

Recalling the brief discussion of the Analogies in section 3 above, the central task of the understanding is to account for how the underdetermined manifold of intuitions rendered by the constitutive principles can form the basis for the determinate representation of objects and events by the regulative principles of the understanding. The rudimentary discursive structures of thing/property, causality, and mutual determination, along with the corresponding determinations of temporal structure (duration, succession and simultaneity) supply the necessary conditions for securing a determinate cognitive relation between the cognizing subject and a world of independent empirical objects. With these structures in place, object-directed beliefs are made possible.

Read in this way, the regulative principles of the understanding do not provide a method for identifying or confirming causal laws. Such a view would encourage the false idea that Kant is struggling in the Analytic to fashion an account of how we move from determinate inner representation to some (more) objective experience of corresponding objects. It is better to characterize the problem as one of establishing the necessary conditions for the discrimination of objects and events (truth-conditional judgments), given the underdetermination of receptivity (see Abela 2002; Bird 1962; Nagel 1983). Without these conditions of the understanding, sensibility would be literally "as good as nothing" to us (A 111, also see A 112, A 120). Instead, the regulative conditions of understanding are viewed as securing the object-bearing character of empirical judgments; making possible the deployment of truth-conditions that sustain this belief-informing relation with the empirical world.

The thought that truth-conditions are fundamental for the possibility of representation is a familiar modern epistemological project. The work of Quine in challenging the link empiricism enforces between receptivity and belief, the refinement of this challenge in Davidson's privileging of truth-conditions for fixing interpretation, and finally McDowell's invocation of the demands of reasons within the field of experiential judgments, all offer contemporary readers the promise of a powerful rejoinder to empiricism. It is not my intention here to detail the many relevant parallels between these thinkers and Kant's own assault on the empiricism of his day. What should be resisted is the not uncommon view that Kant is, in some sense, saving empiricism from itself. Hume may have awoken Kant from his rationalist slumber, but he did not plant the seed of empiricism in its place.

The general point is that Kant is not working, like empiricists, with a model where cognitive content is viewed as merely an artefact of receptivity. Concept application, and the discursive refinement we subject experience to, is always, for Kant, object-directed. As such, our judgments that things are thus and so implicitly, with understanding, and explicitly, in rational judgment, involves a general truth structure (see Abela 2002: chs. 2 and 3). In lieu of considerations of truth, on this reading, belief would have no object-directed character, and representation would fail. I return to this theme below.

I am suggesting, then, that the attribution of systematicity to nature by reflective judgment completes the task initiated by the understanding. Rational judgment offers the conditions for an explicit criterion for empirical truth. The implicit truth-conditions employed by the understanding that underwrite the object-directed character of spontaneous representation thus undergo refashioning, extension and correction as comprehension works upon the deliverances of the understanding and infuses it with its own collective unity.

Of course, the idea that systematicity makes a necessary contribution to the possibility of an empirical criterion for truth is not itself a departure from what one could glean from methodological interpretations. The methodological readings, as we saw in section 3, are at home stressing how the regulative unity of reason creates the conditions for hypothesis testing and the invocation of explanatory strategies.

Unlike these strategies which introduce considerations of empirical truth as the final chapter in empirical inquiry, I am suggesting that the unity supplied by rational judgment for the possibility of an empirical criterion for truth (B 675, B 679), is of more central importance as a condition for representation proper. If, as I am suggesting, reason infuses the implicit truth-structure of spontaneous representation with an explicit criterion for truth, then we ought to expect that reflective judgment offers a top-down component that informs, all the way down, how we discern our everyday engagements with nature. Common experiences such as mistaking the presence of a friend across the quad, falsely judging one's movement in a train as a neighboring train pulls out of the station or believing one has heard a noise downstairs on a dark and stormy night, all point to cases where the spontaneous truth-structure (of the understanding) that sustains original representation comes under pressure by the unity imposed by rational comprehension. In assessing what we are in fact experiencing we may realize that "I'm not seeing correctly because my friend is over six feet, and at that distance . . . ," or "I'm not really moving because that tree I can see through the window of the other train is stationary . . . ," or "I didn't really hear anything as I sleep with earplugs . . ." In each case, it is the explicit truth-conditions that provide for the discriminated character of the experience. Although such mundane encounters with the world do not garner the same attention as the more abstract items of reflective judgment, they are good, perhaps even better, examples of the regulative activity of rational judgment as it modulates the deliverances of the understanding under the demands for systematicity.

Instead of thinking of a firm boundary between the deliverances of the understanding and rational judgment, it would be better to view the interplay as occurring across a permeable boundary; rational judgment informing experience with its unique demands of systematicity, the understanding connecting reason with objects as it works upon the deliverances of sensibility.

This alternative reading places considerable stress on considerations of truth that I claim occupy the center of Kant's account of representation in general; viewing Kant's early strategy in the Analogies – beginning with the problem of the indeterminacy of receptivity and offering a response in terms of discriminating-conditions necessary for object-directed judgment – as emblematic of his approach simpliciter.

No doubt more needs to be said to make this case convincing. Nonetheless, it is profitable to note how the above approach offers a consistent strategy of interpretation for two important passages that remain a puzzle on alternative readings.

> For the law of reason to seek unity is necessary, since without it we would have no reason, and without that, no coherent use of the understanding, and, lacking that, no sufficient mark of empirical truth; thus in regard to the latter we simply have to presuppose the systematic unity of nature as objectively valid and necessary. (B 679)

> If among the appearances offering themselves to us there were such a great variety . . . that even the most acute human understanding, through comparison of one with another, could not detect the least similarity (a case which can at least be thought), then the logical law of genera would not obtain at all, no concept of a genus, nor any other universal concept, indeed no understanding at all would obtain, since it is the understanding that has to do with such concepts. (B 681–2)

Collectively, these passages enforce a twofold claim. Firstly, in each passage Kant asserts that lacking the top-down component of rational unity, the understanding has no employment. This is particularly clear in the second passage where Kant explicitly denies the possibility of concept application in toto where the assertion of a systematic order in nature is denied. Secondly, as is clear in the first passage, Kant connects the top-down component of rational unity with the conditions necessary for an empirical criterion for truth. Without an empirical criterion for truth, judgment, the discrimination of objects by the understanding, is not possible. Contra empiricist-minded commitments to the presence of determinate content given in receptivity independent of considerations of truth, Kant's treatment of representation appears to require considerations of empirical truth to be operative as a condition for the possibility of object-directed representation.

The passages above are not surprising on the proffered reading. They are, in fact, precisely what one would expect, if, as suggested, the understanding contributes implicit truth-conditions in the initial engagement with sensibility, and if, as is commonly agreed, the demand of systematicity creates the cognitive framework for an explicit criterion for empirical truth and, finally, if we refrain from viewing the determining role of the understanding as sequestered from the discursive contribution of rational judgment.

As with Kant's denial of the possibility of assigning cognitive content to sensibility independent of the discursive contributions of the understanding, so too we find, on the proposed reading, that the discursive structures contributed by the regulative principle of systematicity serve as objective principles necessary for establishing a discriminated field of objects and events. This puts the demands of systematicity near the center of Kant's account of cognition.

Acknowledgments

A special thanks to Antonio Franceschet, Andrew Graham, and Anna Wilks for their helpful comments on earlier drafts of this chapter.

References

Abela, P. (2002). *Kant's Empirical Realism*. Oxford: Clarendon Press.

Bird, G. (1962). *Kant's Theory of Knowledge: An Outline of One Central Argument in the Critique of Pure Reason*. London: Routledge & Kegan Paul.

Buchdahl, G. (1969). *Metaphysics and the Philosophy of Science*. Cambridge, MA: MIT Press.

Buchdahl, G. (1992). *Kant and the Dynamics of Reason: Essays on the Structure of Kant's Philosophy*. Oxford: Blackwell.

Guyer, P. (1990). Kant's conception of empirical law. *Aristotelian Society*, Supplementary Volume, 64: 221–42.

Guyer, P. (2001). From nature to morality: Kant's new argument in the Critique of Teleological Judgment. In H. F. Fulda and J. Stolzenberg (eds.), *Architektonik und System in der Philosophie Kant* (pp. 375–404). Hamburg: Felix Meiner Verlag.

Guyer, P. (2003). Beauty, systematicity, and the highest good: Eckart Förster's Kant's final synthesis. *Inquiry*, 46: 195–214.

Kant, I. (1998). *Critique of Pure Reason*, tr. P. Guyer and A. Wood. Cambridge: Cambridge University Press.

Kant, I. (2000). *Critique of the Power of Judgment*, tr. P. Guyer and E. Matthews. Cambridge: Cambridge University Press.

Kitcher, P. (1986). Projecting the order of nature. In R. Butts (ed.), *Kant's Philosophy of Science* (pp. 201–33). Dordrecht: Reidel.

Kitcher, P. (1994). The unity of science and nature. In P. Parrini (ed.), *Kant and Contemporary Epistemology* (pp. 253–72). Dordrecht: Kluwer Academic.

Nagel, G. (1983). *The Structure of Experience*. Chicago: Chicago University Press.

Further Reading

Allison, H. (2004). *Kant's Transcendental Idealism: An Interpretation and Defense*, rev. and enl. ed. New Haven and London: Yale University Press. See chs. 11 and 15.

Guyer, P. (1990). Reason and reflective judgment: Kant on the significance of systematicity. *Nous*, 24: 17–43.

Guyer, P. (2003). Two puzzles about Kant on the systematicity of nature. *History of Philosophy Quarterly*, 20: 277–95.

Wartenberg, T. E. (1992). Reason and the practice of science. In P. Guyer (ed.), *The Cambridge Companion to Kant* (pp. 228–48). Cambridge: Cambridge University Press.

27

Bridging the Gulf: Kant's Project in the Third *Critique*

PAUL GUYER

1. Why is there a Third *Critique*?

Although we take its existence for granted now, more than two centuries after its publication in 1790, Kant's *Critique of the Power of Judgment* could only have struck its original audience as a surprising and puzzling work. Surprising because neither the *Critique of Pure Reason*, not even the revised edition of 1787, nor the *Critique of Practical Reason* of 1788 had given any clue that a third *Critique* was to follow, let alone to follow so soon (see Guyer 2000, Introduction). Puzzling, because the book not only gives an extended treatment to one topic, namely aesthetic experience and judgment, which Kant had previously denied could be the subject of a science (*CPR*, B 35–6), but also links that topic with another, namely the teleological judgment of both organisms within nature and of nature as a whole, to which Kant had never before linked it, and which must at best have seemed to have a minor role in Kant's Critical thought. Clearly there must have been some fundamental revolution in Kant's conception of the tasks of philosophy as well in his assessment of the prospects of both aesthetics and teleology that both made it imperative for him and enabled him to write this book, linking two subjects that were not only disparate but that had also previously been problematic for him, so soon after having completed his exhausting labors on the first two *Critiques*.

Kant does not immediately reveal a profound motivation for the new book in either the first draft of its Introduction, the so-called First Introduction of 1789 (20.193–251), or in the Preface or first section of the published Introduction as well as several of its subsequent sections. These are focused on the distinctions among the several faculties of the mind and the divisions of philosophy, thereby making it seem as if Kant was moved primarily by a pedantic desire for completeness to find a place in his system for two disciplines, aesthetics and teleology, discussed by many of his German, British, and French predecessors but which had apparently not played a large role in his own thought heretofore. It seems that the main task of the third *Critique* will be to introduce the conception of a new class of judgments or new use of the power of judgment, "reflecting" (*reflektierend*) judgment, which will subsume the aesthetic and teleological judgment and demonstrate both their affinities with, and differences from, the theoretical judgments analyzed and grounded in the first *Critique* and the moral judgments treated in the second. Many interpretations of the unity behind Kant's puzzling connection of aesthetic and teleological judgment have focused on the introduction of the concept of "reflecting" judgment into Kant's system. Without downplaying the importance of this concept, however, I will argue here that Kant was driven to connect aesthetic and teleological judgment by a much more profound and powerful motivation than that of mere systematic housekeeping (see Guyer 2003). This deeper motivation is first revealed in the second section of the published Introduction. Here Kant claims that there is a substantive and important problem that calls for a third *Critique*, namely that

> Although there is an incalculable gulf fixed between the domain of the concept of nature, as the supersensible, and the domain of the concept of freedom, as the supersensible, so that from the former to the latter (thus by means of the theoretical use of reason) no transition is possible, just as if there were so many different worlds, the first of which can have no influence on the second: yet the latter should have an influence on the former, namely the concept of freedom should make the end that is imposed by its laws real in the sensible world; and nature must consequently also be able to be conceived in such a way that the lawfulness of its form is at least in agreement with the possibility of the ends that are to be realized in it in accordance with the laws of freedom. – Thus there must still be a ground of the unity of the supersensible that grounds nature with that which the concept of freedom contains practically, the concept of which, even if it does not suffice for cognition of it either theoretically or practically, and thus has no proper domain of its own, nevertheless makes possible the transition from the manner of thinking in accordance with the principles of the one to that in accordance with the principles of the other. (*CJ*, 5.174–5; translations from Kant 1996 and 2000)

The problem that has apparently not been solved by the earlier two *Critiques* is that of showing that our choice to act in accordance with the moral law, as the fundamental principle of all laws of freedom, a choice that can be free only if it is conceived of as taking place in a "supersensible" or noumenal realm that is not governed by the deterministic causal laws of "sensible" or phenomenal nature, must nevertheless be efficacious within that phenomenal world, and able to transform the natural world into a "moral world" where people really do act in accordance with the moral law, and ends imposed upon us by that law can be realized. And the reason for linking aesthetic and teleological judgment together in a third *Critique* apparently must be that these two forms of human experience and judgment together somehow offer a solution to this problem.

But what problem about the efficacy of the laws of freedom in the realm of nature could remain to be solved after the first two *Critiques*? The *Critique of Pure Reason* had argued that although we can disprove the possibility of any breach in the determinism of the natural world, and cannot have theoretical knowledge of the freedom of our will in the noumenal world, nevertheless we can coherently conceive of the latter. Then the *Critique of Practical Reason* argued that we can confidently infer the reality of our noumenal freedom to choose to do whatever morality requires of us from an immediate awareness of our obligation under the moral law combined with the principle that if we ought to do something then we must be able to do it (*CPrR*, 5.30; *RBR*, 6.62). The second *Critique* had also argued that since morality imposes an end upon us, namely that of realizing the highest good, the greatest happiness consistent with the greatest virtue, we must believe this to be possible, and thus must *postulate* "a supreme cause of nature having a causality in keeping with the moral disposition"

(*CPrR*, 5.125). If Kant has already established, on the basis of an awareness of our obligations under the moral law, that we can be confident of having free will, and that all the laws of nature are at least consistent with our realization of the ends commanded by the moral law, what more needs to be done in order to throw a bridge between the theoretical cognition of nature and the laws of freedom?

I propose the following approach to this fundamental question about the need for a third *Critique*. As both the second *Critique* and the preceding *Groundwork for the Metaphysics of Morals* (1785) make clear, Kant clearly recognizes that in order to act morally, we need to (i) understand the moral law and what it requires of us; (ii) believe that we are in fact free to choose to do what it requires of us rather than to do what all our other motives, which can be subsumed under the rubric of self-love (*CPrR*, 5.22), might suggest to us; (iii) believe that the objectives that morality imposes upon us can actually be achieved; and (iv) have an adequate motivation for our attempt to do what morality requires of us in lieu of the mere desirability of particular goals it might happen to license, or even impose, in particular circumstances. All of these together constitute the conditions of the possibility of morality.

Kant also thinks that at one level all these conditions are satisfied by pure practical reason itself: (i) the very form of pure practical reason gives us the moral law (*CPrR*, 5.27); (ii) the first "fact" of pure practical reason, namely a consciousness of our obligation under this law, implies the reality of our freedom to be moral by means of the principle that we must be able to do what we know we ought to do (*CPrR*, 5.30); (iii) we can postulate by pure practical reason alone that the laws of nature are compatible with the demands of morality because both laws ultimately have a common author (*CPrR*, 5.124–32); and finally (iv) pure respect for the moral law itself can be a sufficient motivation for us to attempt to carry it out (and attempts to do so have "moral worth" only when that is our motivation) (*G*, 5.400–1). But Kant also recognizes that we are sensuous as well as rational creatures, and need sensuous as well as rational presentation and confirmation of the conditions of the possibility of morality. He explicitly acknowledges this three years after the *Critique of the Power of Judgment*, when in *Religion within the Boundaries of Mere Reason* he asserts "the natural need of all human beings to demand for even the highest concepts and grounds of reason something that the senses can hold on to, some confirmation from experience or the like" (*RBR*, 6.109). The task of the third *Critique* will then be to show how both aesthetic and teleological experience and judgment provide sensuous confirmation of what we already know in an abstract way, but also need to *feel* or make *palpable* to ourselves, namely the efficacy of our free choice of the fundamental principle of morality in the natural world, and the realizability of the objectives which that choice imposes upon us, summed up in the concept of the highest good.

Specifically, Kant will argue the following:

i) First, the sensuous presentation of moral ideas, above all through the works of artistic genius, but perhaps also through the image of a maximally coherent character expressed by the beautiful human figure as the "ideal of beauty," offers a depiction of the moral law itself. This can be taken ultimately to represent the requirement of consistency among our own free choices and between them and the choices of others. It may also serve to represent other thoughts connected to morality, such as the blessedness that comes from fulfilling the demands of morality, or the contempt deserved by their rejection. Kant's specific examples of such moral ideas expressed in art can be understood in this way (*CJ*, 5.314).

ii) Second, the feeling of our freedom to choose to live up to the demands of morality in spite of all the threats of nature that we experience in the dynamical sublime, and the tendency to interpret the beautiful as a symbol of the morally good, are ways in which the freedom of will that we can intellectually infer from our consciousness of the moral law becomes palpable to us as sensory creatures. In the latter case, Kant explicitly argues that "to demonstrate the reality of our concepts, intuitions are always required," and that even ideas of pure reason that go beyond the limits of our sensibility need at least a symbolic "hypotyposis" or presentation that can make them sensible. It is our nature, in other words, to seek sensible symbols even of that which is too abstract to be fully grasped by the senses, and just as we may use the image of a handmill to represent the despotism of absolute monarchy, so we may use the sensuous experience of the freedom of the imagination to represent the indubitable but intangible fact of the freedom of our will (*CJ*, 5.351, 5.354).

iii) Third, the experience of beauty gives us a hint that nature is amenable to the realization of our objectives, and this hint can be interpreted as sensible evidence for what is otherwise only a *postulate* of pure practical reason, namely the consistency of the laws of nature and the law of freedom. Kant calls the pleasure that we take in such sensory evidence the basis of an "intellectual interest" in beauty, presumably because the fact that beauty confirms for us is of interest to us as agents with pure practical reason, but not in the merely empirical way that the possibility for agreeable socializing or disreputable self-aggrandizement through the possession of valuable works of art does. Nevertheless, the evidence for the amenability of nature to our objectives that the existence of beauty offers us is evidence for our senses, and thus *supplements* the postulate of pure practical reason. Further, it is the central thesis of the Critique of the Teleological Power of Judgment that the experience of the internal systematicity of organisms inevitably leads us to view the whole world as a moral system, but a moral system that we must create by the exercise of our own freedom (*CJ*, 5.425–36). Thus what ties the two halves of the third *Critique* together is precisely the idea that the experiences of natural beauty on the one hand and of the purposiveness of organisms on the other hand both offer us what we experience as *evidence* rather than a mere *postulate* of pure practical reason that the system of morality can be realized in nature (see Guyer 2005a, 2005b).

iv) Finally, Kant famously claims that the experience of *beauty* prepares us to love disinterestedly, and that of the *sublime* to esteem even contrary to our own interest, so that aesthetic experience may help bridge the gaps between the different classes and interest-groups that inevitably arise in any complex polity (*CJ*, 5.267, 5.355–6). In making these claims, he is suggesting that aesthetic experience can make a vital contribution to our disposition to act as morality requires. And while he does not explicitly make an analogous claim in the Critique of Teleological Judgment, in the Doctrine of Virtue of the *Metaphysics of Morals* he insists that abuse of the natural disposition to treat both inorganic and organic but nonhuman nature respectfully would damage our disposition to treat human beings themselves as duty requires, so conversely the care and cultivation of such feelings with regard to nonhuman nature provides a valuable condition for the successful implementation of our free choice to be moral.

426

In the sequel, I offer sketches of Kant's arguments in the critiques of aesthetic and teleological judgment designed to support these general claims about the underlying and unifying program of the third *Critique* as a whole.

2. The Critique of the Aesthetic Power of Judgment

Following the canonical model introduced into eighteenth-century aesthetics by Edmund Burke (Burke 1958), Kant divides the first half of the *Critique of the Power of Judgment*, the Critique of the Aesthetic Power of Judgment, into two main parts, the Analytic of the Beautiful and the Analytic of the Sublime. But Kant actually analyzes *three* main forms of aesthetic experience – the experience of beauty, paradigmatically natural beauty; the experience of the sublime, again paradigmatically of sublimity in nature; and the experience of fine art – and each of these forms of aesthetic experience ultimately reveals distinctive connections to morality. This suggests that there should have been at least three major sections in the *Critique*.

Kant begins his analysis of the judgment of taste, that is, our claim that a particular object is beautiful, from the premise that our pleasure in a beautiful object occurs independently of any interest in the existence of the object as physiologically agreeable or as good for some purpose expressed by a determinate concept of utility or morality (*CJ*, 5.205–7, 5.207–9). Yet, he insists, a judgment of taste does not express a merely idiosyncratic association of pleasure with an object: to call an object beautiful is to speak with a "universal voice," to assert that the pleasure one takes in the object is one that should be felt by anyone who responds to the object, at least under ideal or optimal circumstances, even though "there can also be no rule in accordance with which someone could be compelled to acknowledge something as beautiful" (see Rogerson 1986; *CJ*, 5.216). How can one's pleasure in an object be independent of its subsumption under any determinate concept and its satisfaction of any determinate interest and yet be valid for all who properly respond to the object? Kant's answer is that although our pleasure in a beautiful object is not a response to its subsumption under a determinate concept, it is an expression of the free play of the cognitive faculties of imagination and understanding that such an object induces, and that those cognitive faculties must work the same way in everyone. His underlying idea is that we experience a beautiful object as having a kind of unity ordinarily found in objects by subsuming them under a determinate concept but in this case separate from that subsumption. Beautiful objects *are* identified as objects of some kind, but their unity as beautiful is an additional consideration. Because finding such unity is our ultimate cognitive aim, we take pleasure in this discovery, especially since the unity we find must appear contingent, as it were unexpected, if it is not linked to any determinate concept (*CJ*, 5.186–7).

In this account, Kant makes two striking assumptions. First, he asserts that in "pure" judgments of taste our pleasure in beauty is a response only to the perceptible form of an object, not to any *matter* or *content* it may have – for example, in pictorial arts, "the *drawing* is what is essential," while the "colors that illuminate the outline . . . can . . . enliven the object in itself for sensation, but cannot make it . . . beautiful" (*CJ*, 5.225). Second, he assumes that the cognitive faculties of all human beings really do work the same way, respond to particular objects in the same way, even when they are in "free play" rather than at serious work. The second of these claims seems inde-fensible, but Kant never backs off from it, and the first claim also seems unjustifiable, but this time Kant modifies his claim almost as soon as he makes it (see Guyer 1997: chs. 6–9). While he continues to maintain that in pure judgments of taste our pleas-ure is in the unity of the form of the object alone, he quickly recognizes that there is a variety of impure forms of beauty where what we respond to with the free play of our imagination and understanding is harmony between an object's perceptible form and its matter, its content, or even its purpose. Thus, two sections after the assertion of formalism just cited, Kant introduces the category of "adherent beauty," which is the kind of harmony between an object's form and its intended function that pleases us in a beautiful summer-house or racehorse; and he will subsequently assume that success-ful works of fine art normally have intellectual content and please us in virtue of the harmony among their content, form, and material (see Guyer: 2002).

However, Kant interposes his analysis of the experience of the sublime between his initial analysis of pure beauty and his later analysis of fine art. Kant recognizes two forms of the sublime, the "mathematical" and the "dynamical." Our experience of both is a mixture of pain and pleasure, a moment of pain due to an initial sense of the limits of imagination followed by pleasure at the recognition that it is our own power of reason that reveals the limits of our imagination. The mathematical sublime involves the relationship between imagination and theoretical reason, which is the source of our idea of the infinite; our experience of this form of the sublime is triggered by the observation of natural vistas so vast that our effort to grasp them in a single image is bound to fail, but which then pleases us because this very effort of the imagination reminds us that we have a power of reason capable of formulating the idea of the infinite (*CJ*, 5.254–5). Kant holds that in this experience we do not just infer that we have such a faculty, but actually experience "a feeling that we have pure self-sufficient reason" (*CJ*, 5.258). In the case of the dynamical sublime, what we experience is a harmony between our imagination and practical reason. This experience is induced by natural objects that seem not just vast, but overwhelmingly powerful and threatening – volcanoes, raging seas, and the like. Here we experience fear at the thought of our own physical injury or destruction followed by the satisfying feeling that we have

> within ourselves a capacity for resistance of quite another kind, which gives us the cour-age to measure ourselves against the apparent all-powerfulness of nature, [namely] our power (which is not part of nature) to regard those things about which we are concerned (goods, health and life) as trivial, and hence to regard its power (to which, to be sure, we are subjected in regard to these things) as not the sort of dominion over ourselves and our authority to which we would have to bow if it came down to our highest principles and their affirmation or abandonment. (*CJ*, 5.262)

Now we can turn to Kant's analysis of fine art and our experience of it. For Kant, all art is intentional human production that requires skill or talent, yet fine or "beautiful" (*schöne*) art is produced with the intention of doing what anything beautiful does, namely, promoting the free play of the cognitive powers. That a work of fine art must be the product of intention and yet produce the free play of the mental powers seems like the paradox that "beautiful art, although it is certainly intentional, must nevertheless not seem intentional" (*CJ*, 5.306–7). Further, Kant also assumes that although our pleasure in beauty should be a response to the form of an object alone, fine art is paradigmatically mimetic, that is, has representational or semantic content (*CJ*, 5.311). This too seems like a paradox. Kant aims to resolve both of these apparent paradoxes through his theory that successful works of fine art are products of genius, a natural gift that gives the rule to art (*CJ*, 5.307). A work of genius must have "spirit," which it gets through its content, typically – as Kant assumes without argument, although perhaps in his time, long before the invention of nonobjective art, without any real need for argument – a rational idea, indeed an idea relevant specifically to morality. But in order to be beautiful, a work of art must still leave room for the freedom of the imagination, and therefore cannot present such ideas to us directly and didactically (indeed, such ideas cannot be directly and adequately presented in sensible form). Instead, a work of art succeeds when it presents an "aesthetic idea," a representation of the imagination that "at least strive[s] toward something lying beyond the bounds of experience, and thus seek[s] to approximate a presentation of the concepts of reason," but also "stimulates so much thinking," such a wealth of particular "attributes" or images and incidents, "that it can never be grasped in a determinate concept" (*CJ*, 5.314–15). It stimulates in this way a pleasurable feeling of free play among the imagination, understanding, and reason while at the same time satisfying the demand that a work of art have both a purpose and a content.

We can now see how Kant thinks that our aesthetic experiences and judgments can bridge the gulf between our abstract, intellectual understanding of the requirements and conditions of morality and a palpable, sensuous representation of those requirements and conditions. I will enumerate six such links, which together serve the four needs for a bridge between freedom and nature outlined above in section 1, (i)–(iv).

1) First, Kant evidently holds that objects of aesthetic experience can present morally significant ideas to us. This is obvious in the theory of aesthetic ideas, where Kant indeed assumes that works of art always have some morally relevant content. But this view takes other forms as well. In fact, Kant maintains that all forms of beauty, natural as well as artistic, can be regarded as expressions of aesthetic ideas: even natural objects can suggest moral ideas to us although such suggestion is not the product of any intentional human activity (*CJ*, 5.319). In The Ideal of Beauty, Kant also maintains that beauty in the human figure can be taken as "the visible expression of moral ideas, which inwardly govern human beings"; here he argues that only human beauty can be taken as a unique standard for beauty, because it is the only form of beauty that can express something absolutely and unconditionally valuable, namely the moral autonomy of which humans alone are capable. Nevertheless there is no determinate way in which this unique value can be expressed in the human form, so that there is always something free in the outward expression in the human figure of the inner moral value of the human character (*CJ*, 5.235–6).

2) The second link is Kant's claim that the experience of the dynamical sublime is nothing other than a feeling of the power of our own practical reason to accept the pure principle of morality and to act in accordance with it in spite of all the threats or inducements to do otherwise that nature might place in our way. Because the experience of the dynamical sublime so centrally involves an intimation of our own capacity to be moral, Kant actually insists that "the sublime in nature is only improperly so

called, and should properly be ascribed only to the manner of thinking, or rather its foundation in human nature" (*CJ*, 5.280). And while he does not want to claim that this experience is identical to explicit moral reasoning, but only a "disposition of the mind that is similar to the moral disposition" (*CJ*, 5.268), he does in at least one place argue that the complex character of the experience of the sublime makes it the best representation in our experience of our moral situation itself:

> The object of a pure and unconditioned intellectual satisfaction is the moral law in all its power . . . and, since this power actually makes itself aesthetically knowable only through sacrifices (which is a deprivation, although in behalf of inner freedom . . .), the satisfaction on the aesthetic side (in relation to sensibility) is negative . . . but considered from the intellectual side it is positive . . . From this it follows that the intellectual, intrinsically purposive (moral good), judged aesthetically, must not be represented so much as beautiful but rather as sublime, so that it arouses more the feeling of respect (which scorns charm) than that of love and intimate affection, since human nature does not agree with that good of its own accord, but only through the dominion that reason exercises over sensibility. (*CJ*, 5.271)

In spite of this emphatic statement, however, Kant elsewhere argues (3) that there are crucial aspects of our moral condition that are symbolized by the beautiful rather than the sublime. Here I refer to his claim that the beautiful is the symbol of the morally good because there are significant parallels between our experience of beauty and the structure of morality, and indeed that it is only insofar as the beautiful is the symbol of the morally good that we have any right not merely to predict that under ideal circumstances others agree with our appraisals of beauty but actually to *demand* that they do so (*CJ*, 5.53). Kant adduces "several aspects of this analogy," the most important of which is that

> The *freedom* of the imagination (thus of the sensibility of our faculty) is represented in the judging of the beautiful as in accord with the lawfulness of the understanding (in the moral judgment the freedom of the will is conceived as the agreement of the latter with itself in accordance with universal laws of reason). (*CJ*, 5.354)

Because the experience of beauty is an experience of the freedom of the imagination in its play with the understanding, it can be taken as a palpable symbol of the freedom of the will to determine itself by moral laws which is necessary for morality but not something that can be directly experienced (*CJ*, 5.29). In other words, it is the very independence of aesthetic response from direct determination by concepts, including moral concepts, that makes the experience of beauty an experience of freedom that can in turn symbolize moral freedom. Presumably this can be reconciled with Kant's earlier claim that the sublime is the most appropriate symbol of morality by observing that while the experience of beauty makes the freedom of the will palpable to us, it is only the mixed experience of the sublime that brings home to feeling that this freedom must often be exercised in the face of resistance offered by our own inclinations (see Guyer 1998).

4) Kant's fourth connection between the aesthetic and the ethical lies in his theory of the "intellectual interest" in the beautiful. Here Kant argues that although our basic

430

pleasure in a beautiful object must be independent of any antecedent interest in its existence, we may add a further layer of pleasure to that basic experience if the existence of beautiful objects suggests some more generally pleasing fact about our situation in the world. What Kant then argues is that since in the case of morality

> it also interests reason that the ideas (for which it produces an immediate interest in the moral feeling) also have objective reality, . . . reason must take an interest in every manifestation in nature of a correspondence similar to this; consequently the mind cannot reflect on the beauty of *nature* without finding itself at the same time to be interested in it. (*CJ*, 5.300)

Kant's claim is that since it is of interest to practical reason that nature be hospitable to its objectives, we take pleasure in any evidence that nature is amenable to our objectives, even when those are not specifically moral; and the natural existence of beauty is such evidence, because the experience of beauty is itself an unexpected fulfillment of our most basic cognitive objective.

5) Kant's fifth claim is that aesthetic experience is conducive to proper moral conduct itself. In his concluding comment on his analyses of both the beautiful and the sublime he states that "The beautiful prepares us to love something, even nature, without interest; the sublime, to esteem it, even contrary to our (sensible) interest," where being able to love without any personal interest and to esteem even contrary to our own interest are necessary preconditions of proper moral conduct (*CJ*, 5.267). Kant makes a similar point in his later *Metaphysics of Morals* when he argues that "a propensity to wanton destruction of what is beautiful in inanimate nature," even though we do not owe any moral duties directly to anything other than ourselves and other human beings, nevertheless

> weakens or uproots that feeling in [us] which, though not of itself moral, is still a disposition of sensibility that greatly promotes morality or at least prepares the way for it: the disposition, namely, to love something (e.g., beautiful crystal formations, the indescribable beauty of plants) even apart from any intention to use it. (*MM*, 6.643)

These claims that aesthetic experience can be conducive to proper moral conduct would be problematic for Kant if they meant that aesthetic experience can substitute for or even strengthen pure respect for the moral law as our fundamental motivation to be moral. Kant can argue only that aesthetic experiences can *prepare* us for successful moral conduct without *substituting* for pure moral motivation. Kant's idea has to be that naturally occurring feelings of attraction toward the beauty of nature can be considered, like naturally occurring feelings of sympathy and benevolence toward other human beings, as means that nature itself affords us, as creatures who are sensuous as well as rational, for the implementation of the moral law, although the latter can only be considered our own end freely chosen out of respect for the idea of duty or the moral law or humanity as an end in itself. And of course acting upon such feelings will not only be a means toward the end of implementing the moral law, but will also be subject to the condition that acting on such feelings in any particular circumstances is indeed consistent with the requirements of the moral law (*MM*, 6.456–7). Kant's injunction to cultivate compassion through aesthetic feelings requires conformity to moral principles and so excludes Barbara Herman's case, in which someone inadvertently helps to steal a work of art out of a sympathetic inclination toward anyone struggling to move a heavy object (see Herman 1993: 4–5).

6) Finally, in the brief Appendix on the Methodology of Taste, Kant suggests that the cultivation or realization of common standards of taste in a society can be conducive to the discovery of the more general "art of the reciprocal communication of the ideas of the most educated part" of a society "with the cruder, the coordination of the breadth and refinement of the former with the natural simplicity and originality of the latter" (CJ, 5.356), where this art is apparently necessary to the realization of the goal of "lawful sociability," or the establishment of a stable polity on the basis of principles of justice rather than sheer force. Thus, aesthetic experience can be conducive to the development of sound politics as well as personal ethics, although the two are of course not unconnected, since Kant is a political moralist who believes that we have a moral duty to establish a just state, not merely a prudential interest in doing so.

These six links between aesthetics and morality can be seen as satisfying the four conditions that need to be met in order to bridge the gulf between nature and freedom by making our abstract grasp of the contents and conditions of morality palpable to our sensuous nature: (i) the presentation of moral ideas in objects of natural and artistic beauty and especially in beautiful human form itself provides sensuous illustration of moral ideas and above all of the foundational idea of the unconditional value of human freedom itself; (ii) the experiences of the dynamical sublime and of the beautiful in their *different* ways confirm our abstract recognition of our own freedom always to choose to do as morality requires; (iii) the intellectual interest in the beautiful provides sensuous confirmation of nature's amenability to our objectives, which is otherwise only a *postulate* of pure practical reason; and (iv) the claims that the experiences of the beautiful and the sublime and the sharing of these feelings among different strata of highly diversified societies are conducive to the realization of morality reveal ways in which our natural sensuous dispositions can be used as means to the realization of the goal set by our purely rational disposition to be moral.

3. The Critique of the Teleological Power of Judgment

The second half of the third *Critique* is at least as intricate and in some ways even more obscure than the first half. Kant's discussion of teleology is often read as if his primary concern was to make a contribution to what we now regard as the philosophy of biology, by engaging with issues about the nature of organisms and their reproduction and evolution that were emerging in the life sciences of his time. Kant's interest in establishing the natural sciences on a firm philosophical footing, and where necessary using that foundation to resolve scientific controversies of his time was lifelong, evident from his earliest work *The True Estimation of Living Forces* (1747), to his last uncompleted work on the transition from the metaphysical foundations of natural science to physics, the so-called *Opus postumum*, on which he labored from about 1796 until the last years of his life. No doubt the Critique of Teleological Judgment was intended as an intervention in contemporary biological debates, but Kant's argument here is fundamentally structured by his concern about the relation between nature and morality (see also chapter 29 below). It culminates in a restatement of Kant's moral theology, that is, his argument for the determination of the concept of God and the postulation of his existence as the condition of the possibility of the realization of the highest good, but even before that it introduces a novel argument about the relation between nature and virtue. The argument is that while virtue always requires a free choice and enduring commitment that can never be considered natural, nevertheless we can and must *conceive* of nature as if it is aimed at making possible a natural condition necessary for the efficacy of virtuous choice, and we are led to do so by our experience of organisms in nature and of nature as a whole as a system to which our experience of organisms naturally leads us. It is this argument that provides the second support of Kant's bridge between nature and freedom and explains his connection of teleology to the aesthetic theory that provided the first support of the bridge.

This novel argument is the core of the Critique of Teleological Judgment, begun in its opening §§61–8 and then resumed, after an interruption to which I return below, in the key §§82–4. Kant begins this extended argument by initially rejecting the supposition of traditional teleologies that we can ever make an objective and determinate judgment that one thing in nature exists for the sake of another, or that there is "external purposiveness" in nature. Of course ocean currents may bring driftwood to the human beings who live in treeless arctic regions, but as soon as one asks why human beings should live in those hostile climes in the first place, any appearance of objective "external purposiveness" in this fact dissolves (*CJ*, 5.366–70). Kant then argues, however, that we experience some entities in nature, namely living organisms or as Kant calls them "organized beings," as having relations among their parts and between their parts and their whole that we at least can comprehend only as "internal purposiveness." We experience such beings as if in them each part is the cause and effect of every other, and as if the whole organism both depends upon and yet is the ground of each of its parts (*CJ*, 5.372–6). Specifically, organic processes such as reproduction, growth, and self-repair are processes that we experience but can comprehend only as involving the causal influence of the whole of such objects on the formation of their parts as well as the influence of the parts on their whole which we understand through our usual, "mechanical" concepts of causation. The only way in which we can *understand* the influence of the whole on its parts, Kant supposes, is through our own purposive creation, in which an antecedent concept of the whole determines the structure of its parts. But the wholes that we produce in this way do not have powers of growth, reproduction, and self-repair, so we must conceive of organisms both as if they were products of a purposive intellect like, but also more powerful than, our own, able to confer such powers and thus what Kant calls "internal purposiveness" or "inner natural perfection" on its products (*CJ*, 5.373–5). Kant insists, however, that this concept of "internal purposiveness" provides only a "maxim for the judging" of organisms, not any actual theoretical knowledge of them (*CJ*, 5.376), and that from the scientific point of view the only function of this teleological conception of organisms is to guide us in our continued search for further mechanical explanations of organic processes. Nevertheless, he also argues that once we come to look at some objects in nature as purposive in any way, it is inevitable for us to look at the whole of nature as if it were a purposive system (*CJ*, 5.378–81). Kant also observes that once we have been led to

433

PAUL GUYER

the thought of the purposive design of nature by our experience of organisms, we can also look back on our experience of beauty as further justification for conceiving of nature as if it were purposive, and so make a new connection between aesthetic and teleological judgment (*CJ*, 5.380).

Now, Kant does not spell out either the premise or the implications of this claim. The premise is presumably that human reason's fundamental interest in unity leads us to seek to extend a viewpoint that we have found necessary in order to comprehend *some* things in nature to *all* of nature. The implications are that once we have begun to look at nature as a whole as if it were a single system, then we can after all reintroduce at least an *analogue* of "external purposiveness." We can now think of those things previously regarded as separate entities that could be related only by arbitrary concepts of external purposiveness, such as driftwood and the inhabitants of the far north, as if they were parts of a single internally purposive system, and thus purposively related to one another after all. This step can be achieved only by introducing the idea of a unique and determinate goal or end for the system.

Kant's next step, however, is to argue that if once again we confine ourselves to a purely theoretical, scientific outlook on nature, we cannot find such an end:

> If we go through the whole of nature, we do not find in it, as nature, any being that can claim the privilege of being the final end of creation; and one can even prove a priori that whatever could be an ultimate end for nature could never, no matter with what conceivable determinations and properties it might be equipped, be, as a natural thing, a final end. (*CJ*, 5.426)

One certainly cannot judge empirically that human happiness is the final end of the system of nature: nature produces far too much human misery for us ever to think that (*CJ*, 5.430–1). However, from a moral point of view one can find something of unconditional value that could play the role of a final end of the system of nature: not happiness, of course, because that has no unconditional value in Kantian morality, but something that does have unconditional value, namely the human being, "considered as noumenon," that is, as possessing the "supersensible faculty" of freedom, and "of the human being . . . as a moral being." Kant claims,

> it cannot be further asked why (quem in finem) it exists. His existence contains the highest end itself, to which, as far as he is capable, he can subject the whole of nature, or against which at least he need not hold himself to be subjected by any influence from nature. (*CJ*, 5.435)

The experience of nature combined with the unifying urge of human reason sets us on a search for a final end of nature which science itself cannot satisfy. But the unique and unconditional moral value of human freedom allows us to see that as the unique and determinate goal of the system of nature, to which all else in nature can be subordinated as a means.

But how can human freedom be seen as the end of nature, when in Kant's own view freedom is necessarily noumenal rather than phenomenal, something perhaps *beyond* or beneath the fabric of nature but not *part* of it? In fact, Kant does not claim that the freedom of the human will itself can ever be seen as a product and therefore the goal of

434

nature; rather, what can be seen as a product and goal of nature is "the culture of training (discipline)," which

> consists in the liberation of the will from the despotism of desires, by which we are made, attached as we are to certain things of nature, incapable of choosing for ourselves, while we turn into fetters the drives that nature has given us merely for guidance. (*CJ*, 5.432)

That is, we can see nature as capable of producing the discipline or control over our desires that we need in order to be able to act on the virtuous decisions of our free will, but we cannot see nature as producing acts of free will itself. Therefore we can see nature as aimed at the development of a necessary condition for the implementation of virtue, but we cannot see nature as producing virtue itself.

I noted earlier that Kant's exposition of the argument just considered is interrupted and leaps from §68 to §82. Kant's central concern in the intervening discussion is the antinomy of teleological judgment. This antinomy is an apparent conflict between the thesis that "All generation of material things is possible in accordance with merely mechanical laws" and the antithesis that "Some generation of such things is not possible in accordance with merely mechanical laws" (*CJ*, 5.387). Kant observes that if these were to be interpreted as "constitutive principles of the possibility of the objects themselves," they would obviously be contradictory, but suggests that if they are interpreted as "maxims of a reflecting power of judgment," one enjoining us to seek to extend our mechanical explanations of natural phenomena as far as possible and the other to conceive of some objects in terms of intentional design or "final causes," they will not conflict. For then the second maxim will only assert that human reason "can never discover the least basis for what is specific in a natural end" through mechanical laws, not that there is any objective incompatibility between mechanical and final causation, but in the next section Kant labels this observation a mere "preparation for the resolution of the above antinomy" (*CJ*, 5.388). He then goes on to provide a solution to the antinomy that is more closely modeled on the solutions to the antinomies in the previous two *Critiques*, which rely on his characteristic distinction between the phenomenal and the noumenal. What Kant argues here is that in fact we can make room for the *conception* of final as well as mechanical causality only by a "theistic" conception of final causality, that is, one on which the designer and hence the design for the world is present in the noumenal or supersensible ground of the sensible world. This can be achieved only within the sensible or phenomenal world through the kinds of mechanical laws that apply throughout that world, whether or not we are capable of understanding how exactly this may be accomplished. Kant argues that this is the only alternative to an "idealism" of final causes, attributed to Epicurus and Spinoza, according to which there is nothing but a false appearance of purposiveness in the experienced world, or to "hylozoism," the view that matter itself can contain a purposiveness characteristic of living things, a view which he believes incompatible with the undeniable status of the principle of inertia as a principle for the physical world (*CJ*, 5.391–2). Kant's view is that we cannot simply dismiss our experience of purposiveness in organisms as a mere *appearance*, for then we have no way of comprehending this undeniable form of experience at all; but neither can we accept the contradiction inherent in hylozoism, so we must at least entertain the possibility of theism,

435

understood as the thought that "there is no other way of judging the generation of [nature's] products as natural ends," that is, organisms, "than through a supreme understanding as the cause of the world" (*CJ*, 5.395). But this is just the thought that underlies Kant's argument for the postulate of the existence of God as the condition of the possibility of the realizability of the highest good in the *Critique of Practical Reason*. In order to pursue the object which our virtuous commitment to the fundamental principle of reality sets for us, namely universal (not selfish) happiness, and in spite of the fact that virtue does not appear to cause happiness in the natural world at least through the exercise of our own merely natural powers, we must postulate a God as the author of nature who also has his eye on the moral law and writes the laws of nature so that they are compatible with the realization of the ends prescribed to us by morality (*CPrR*, 5.125–6). The argument of the antinomy of teleological judgment, then, is that our experience of organisms leads to the same conclusion as our reflection on the highest good must: we must be able to understand the laws of nature – mechanical laws in the language of the third *Critique* – as if they are the means through which purposiveness can be achieved. Our undeniable experience of organisms thus lends a kind of sensible confirmation to the same pattern of thought to which the abstract considerations of morality and the conditions of its possibility lead.

At the outset of this chapter, I suggested four ways in which arguments in the third *Critique* could be seen as bridging the incalculable gulf between nature and freedom: the forms of experience and judgment to be diagnosed in this critique could be shown (i) to confirm our comprehension of the moral law and the objectives it sets for us, (ii) to provide us with sensible confirmation of our freedom, which otherwise is only a fact of pure reason, (iii) to give us sensible evidence to supplement our purely rational postulation that the goals morality sets for us can actually be achieved, and (iv) in some way actually to prepare us to do as morality requires. The natural way to understand the arguments we have just found in the Critique of the Teleological Power of Judgment would be to see them as bearing directly on links (iii) and (iv): the latter, because the argument that we can see the development of the culture of discipline as the ultimate end of nature can be interpreted as an argument that although nature cannot itself give us the motivation to be moral, it can lead us to develop a capacity that is a necessary condition of acting on our free choice to be moral. The former, because the argument that we can only resolve the antinomy of teleological judgment by adopting a theistic point of view on which the sensible world is designed to achieve a rational purpose through natural mechanisms, although motivated by a problem in natural science rather than morality, in fact leads us to the same postulation about the authorship of nature to which we are also led by the necessity of postulating the conditions of the possibility of realizing the highest good.

But Kant's core argument at §§82–4 seems to presuppose the fact of our supersensible freedom rather than to provide any additional sensible confirmation of it, so we cannot read the Critique of the Teleological Power of Judgment as contributing anything further to (ii). While one could imagine that Kant might have suggested that the idea of a unitary system of nature can give us a sensible model of a realm of ends, thereby contributing to (i), he does not actually suggest that. However, this would hardly be to say that the contribution of the Critique of the Teleological Power of Judgment to the task of bridging the gulf between nature and freedom is less important than that of the Critique of Aesthetic Judgment. One could well argue that the *Critique of Practical Reason* had shown that every human being can readily recognize the content of the moral law and infer the fact of his freedom from his recognition of his obligation to adopt this law as his fundamental maxim. Then what really needs further *support* is the postulation of the possibility of realizing the object of morality, the highest good, while what really needs further *explanation* is how beings with our animal as well as rational psychology can actually come to *apply* the moral law to their own sensible desires. The central arguments of the Critique of the Teleological Power of Judgment bear precisely on these challenges, just as Kant's theory of the intellectual interest in the beautiful and his claim that the experience of the beautiful prepares us to love disinterestedly, and that of the sublime to love even against our sensible interest, do in the Critique of the Aesthetic Power of Judgment.

4. Conclusion

On first glance, Kant's project in the third *Critique* may seem to be one of compartmentalization rather than integration. Kant begins his Analytic of the Beautiful with the thesis that judgments of taste are disinterested, and thereby seems to separate the realm of the aesthetic from all concern with either cognition or morality. The teleological judgment of nature, however, seems to be of purely cognitive interest, a regulative ideal for our scientific image of nature to compensate for the limitations of our strictly constitutive knowledge of organisms. Thus the aesthetic seems to be separated not only from cognition and morality, but even from its stablemate in the third *Critique*, that is, from teleology, as well. But we have seen that beneath these superficial separations there are deeper affinities between the aesthetic and the teleological, and between them and the rest of Kant's philosophy, and above all, between them and Kant's conception of morality, the practical faith for which in many respects his theoretical philosophy exists to make room – "I had to deny knowledge in order to make room for faith" (*CPR*, B xxx).

While the experiences and judgments of the beautiful and sublime are *distinctive* forms of experience and judgment, they both depend upon the play of the same powers of the mind that are involved in cognition and moral reasoning, and they both turn out to have moral significance in spite of, and at least in the case of beauty even because of, their freedom from direct constraint by the concepts of morality. Both aesthetic and teleological experience turn out to offer *support* for our conviction that the goals morality sets for us can be achieved in the natural world in which we find ourselves, as well as *means* that we can use in attempting to fulfill the demand to be moral. So understanding what separates the aesthetic and the teleological from the cognitive and the moral turns out to be only a first step in the larger project of unifying our powers for the sake of what is ultimately our single overriding interest, namely, the interest of practical reason in creating a unitary system of nature and freedom (*CPrR*, 5.119–21, 5.134–41, 5.146–7).

Kant's grand vision of aesthetic and teleological support for the realization of human morality is very much a product of the eighteenth-century Enlightenment. Are any of Kant's ambitious claims on behalf of the ultimate value of aesthetic and teleological judgments still plausible? Here I offer only a few comments on the many issues Kant's arguments raise.

First, a general question that must be raised whenever Kant's argument for the highest good comes up: In order to make our pursuit of a goal mandated by morality rational, do we *need* an affirmative argument, whether an *a priori* argument from pure practical reason or any kind of *empirical* confirmation, that the realization of this goal is possible, or would absence of any argument or evidence that it is impossible suffice? Kant clearly assumes the former when he argues in the *Critique of Practical Reason* (*CPrR*, 5.125) that for it to be rational for us to seek to realize the highest good we must "postulate the possibility of the highest derived good (the best world)" as grounded in "the postulate of the reality of a highest original good, namely the existence of God," and when he suggests that we will see both natural beauty and teleological organization in nature as empirical confirmation of the realizability of our moral objective. But we might well think, especially in view of the overwhelming importance of striving to reach our moral objectives, that a reasonable belief simply in the absence of any evidence for the impossibility of realizing this goal would suffice to make our efforts rational. We might also think that this condition could easily be satisfied, first because we can know a priori that we can never have a proof of the non-existence of a God who could ground the compatibility of the laws of nature and of morality, and second because the empirical evidence of nature's hostility rather than hospitality to the realization of our moral objectives is, just as empirical evidence, never decisive. So, one could argue, we shouldn't actually *need* positive empirical evidence that nature is hospitable to our moral objectives as long as our evidence that it is hostile to them is inconclusive, just as we shouldn't actually need to postulate the actual existence of God as long as we cannot prove his non-existence a priori. To this extent, further support for the realizability of the highest good, whether from aesthetics or teleology, seems otiose.

The second question is whether Kant could succeed in showing that aesthetic and teleological experiences as he has described them are necessary in order to bridge the gap between nature and freedom. In the case of taste, Kant thought he could show that sensitivity to beauty as a symbol of the morally good, for example, can be "expected of everyone else as a duty" insofar as "it pleases with a claim to the assent of everyone else" (*CJ*, 5.353), and he might similarly have held that we have a duty to cultivate the teleological view of nature. But such claims could surely be sustained only if aesthetic experience and teleological judgment are both necessary and universally available means to moral ends, and that seems implausible on both counts. First, Kant clearly thought that he had shown that both aesthetic and teleological judgment rest on necessary features of the human mind, and thus can be proven to be necessary for every human being: the universal validity of aesthetic judgment, he argued, rests on the necessary similarity of the cognitive powers in every human being, and the necessity of teleological judgment rests on the limits to the power of mechanical explanation that are fixed by the structure of human thought; but he was clearly wrong on both these issues. The theses that the free play of imagination and understanding produces pleasure in beauty, and that the play between imagination and reason produce pleasure in the sublime, must surely be empirical rather than a priori claims about human psychology, and there will therefore no doubt be considerable variation in how susceptible individual human beings are to these feelings. Likewise, the claim that the

438

experience of beauty prepares one to love disinterestedly and that of the sublime to love even contrary to one's sensible interest must also be an empirical rather than a priori claim, so again there is likely to be variation among human beings in this regard. Similarly the claim that there are limits to our power to understand organic processes mechanically seems empirical rather than a priori, although Kant tries to make it seem otherwise, so an a priori claim that our experience of organisms can impel us all to adopt a teleological view of organisms and of nature as a whole seems implausible. The most that could be argued, one might well hold, is that some people at some times will have aesthetic and teleological experience and find them conducive to the fulfillment of their moral duties.

Even this would be no mean result, however. For at least on Kant's assumption that we all have an unremitting duty to fulfill the demands of morality, we would all also have the duty to make sufficient means to fulfilling these demands available to ourselves, and if aesthetic and/or teleological experience turn out to be helpful means to the fulfillment of our duties even for some of us some of the time, then we would certainly have good reason to preserve and cultivate these forms of experience. They would fall into the categories of means that nature has implanted in us – at least some of us, some of the time – for promoting our moral ends, "impulses that nature has implanted in us to do what the representation of duty alone might not accomplish," and as natural means to our moral end they should certainly be employed (*MM*, 6.457). Of course it is not very likely that these would be our only natural means to the realization of our moral ends, and Kant's example of natural duties of benevolence to other human beings in that section of the *Metaphysics of Morals* would belie this supposition. It is therefore not very likely that anyone could have anything approaching an unconditional duty to value and cultivate these forms of experience. But that may be more than is necessary in order to see these forms of experience and judgment as making a valuable contribution to our ultimate goal of bridging the gulf between nature and freedom. After all, each of the strands in the cables of a bridge helps to hold it up even if no one of them is unconditionally necessary for the bridge to stand.

References and Further Reading

Allison, Henry E. (2001). *Kant's Theory of Taste: A Reading of the Critique of Aesthetic Judgment*. Cambridge: Cambridge University Press.

Beck, Lewis White (1960). *A Commentary to Kant's Critique of Practical Reason*. Chicago: University of Chicago Press.

Burke, Edmund (1958). *A Philosophical Enquiry into the Origin of our Ideas of the Sublime and the Beautiful*, ed. Boulton. London: Routledge and Kegan Paul.

Guyer, Paul (1997). *Kant and the Claims of Taste*. Cambridge: Cambridge University Press.

Guyer, Paul (1998). The symbols of freedom in Kant's aesthetics. In Hermann Parret (ed.), *Kant's Ästhetik [Kant's Aesthetics]*, (pp. 338–55). Berlin: Walter de Gruyter.

Guyer, Paul (2000). Introduction. In *Critique of the Power of Judgement*, eds. and tr. Paul Guyer and Eric Mathews. Cambridge: Cambridge University Press.

Guyer, Paul (2003). Kant's principles of reflecting judgement. In *Critique of the Power of Judgement: Critical Essays* (pp. 1–60). Lanham, MD: Rowman and Littlefield.

Guyer, Paul (2005a). *Kant's System of Nature and Freedom*. Oxford: Clarendon Press.

439

Guyer, Paul (2005b). The ethical value of the aesthetic: Kant, Allison, and Santayana. In *The Values of Beauty: Historical Essays in Aesthetics* (pp. 190–221). Cambridge: Cambridge University Press.

Herman, Barbara (1993). *The Practice of Moral Judgment.* Cambridge, MA: Harvard University Press.

Kant, Immanuel (1996). *Practical Philosophy*, ed. and tr. Mary J. Gregor. Cambridge: Cambridge University Press.

Kant, Immanuel (2000). *Critique of the Power of Judgement*, eds. and tr. Paul Guyer and Eric Mathews. Cambridge: Cambridge University Press.

McLaughlin, Peter (1990). *Kant's Critique of Teleology in Biological Explanation: Antinomy and Teleology.* Lewisten: Edwin Mellen Press.

Rogerson, Kenneth (1986). *Kant's Aesthetics: The Roles of Form and Expression.* Lanham, MD: University Press of America.

Schönfeld, Martin (2000). *The Philosophy of the Young Kant: The Pre-Critical Project.* Oxford: Oxford University Press.

Timmons, Mark, ed. (2002). *Kant's Metaphysics of Morals: Interpretative Essays.* Oxford: Oxford University Press.

28

Kant's Aesthetic Theory

ANTHONY SAVILE

1.

The *Critique of Judgment*'s treatment of beauty and sublimity offers the fullest and richest treatment of aesthetic experience to be found in the philosophical canon. As obscure as anything else Kant wrote, it has nonetheless been immensely influential in the two centuries since its publication in 1790, although often in ways that have mistaken its true import. The central expository material lies between §§1–22 of that work and revolves around the questions of how judgments of taste, judgments that something is beautiful, that is, can be distinguished from others with a comparable structure, and under what conditions they can be properly entertained and rightly asserted. Since Kant holds that judgment is internal to experience itself, our experience being generally awareness of *something or other's being the case*, judgments of taste need not be thought of exclusively as articulated assertions. Consequently, his discussion may equally well be seen as providing illumination about aesthetic experience itself as we find this or that an object of beauty, whether in nature or in art.

Four conditions have to be satisfied by any uncontroversial instance of beauty: (a) experience of the object in question must evoke a response of pleasure in subjects who give it their disinterested attention; (b) that pleasure must be universal and not merely personal; (c) it will have its source in something Kant calls the "subjective form of purposiveness" that we find in our experience of the object; and (d) the pleasure is "necessary" in an exemplary way, one that we demand, or exact, of others. These points Kant confidently summarizes at the end of the various sections he devotes to them. Thus, more fully, and in his own words, (a) "*Taste is* the faculty of judging an object or a method of representing it by an *entirely disinterested* satisfaction or dissatisfaction. The object of such satisfaction is called *beautiful*" (§5); (b) "The beautiful is that which pleases universally without a concept" (§9); (c) "*Beauty* is the form of the *purposiveness* of an object, so far as this is perceived in it *without any representation of a purpose*" (§17); (d) "The beautiful is that which without any concept is cognized as the object of a *necessary* satisfaction" (§22).

Although they are all introduced specifically in elucidation of beauty, these four claims also hold of the other main aesthetic category Kant discusses, the sublime, which occupies §§23–9 of the *Critique*. Whether the satisfaction we take in something we experience signals its beauty or its sublimity is a matter of the different ways in which these points are realized, in particular the third of them. Save for an all-too-brief remark about the sublime at the very end, I shall attend here only to the beautiful.

2.

Kant sets out to secure a clear distinction between the purely personal judgment that something is aesthetically pleasant, or agreeable, and the interpersonally secure judgment that it is beautiful. Although not writing with it explicitly in mind, Kant develops his argument in a way that manages to bypass a number of notable difficulties that infect Hume's earlier reflection on the topic in his 1757 essay, "Of the Standard of Taste" (Hume 1875). The first of these arises directly from what Kant sees as the insufficiently thorough-going subjectivity of the Humean view. This may surprise anyone who recalls from Hume's essay primarily the claim that "beauty and deformity, more than sweet and bitter are not qualities in object, but belong entirely to the sentiment." What is easily forgotten though, and what might have stuck in Kant's mind, since he must have read that essay, is the continuation of that same sentence, where Hume says "it must be allowed that there are certain qualities in objects, which are fitted by nature to produce those particular feelings." Consequently, the Humean view of something's being beautiful is easily understood as being that the object in question is such as to provide wide-spread pleasure to the well-trained on account of possessing one or more of those particular qualities.

One does not have to suppose that Hume had gone so far as to identify an object's beauty with its possession of those specific features to understand why Kant should have found the suggestion unpalatable. It is enough to see that allusion to them is internal to the specification of the sentiment that Hume took be so central. It must be *those* particular qualities that make an object beautiful through generating those favored sentiments. Kant rightly finds that view unacceptable. Once we light on the putative feature or features to which the normal observer (Hume's "true judge") is supposedly responsive, we can always ask whether an object might be beautiful other than by way of possessing it or them. Experience suggests that no matter what qualities we ask this question about, the answer will be "yes," so it must be a mistake to build any identifying reference to them, no matter how obliquely, into the core of the elucidation.

Against this background we can hear Kant's first positive claim: the judgment of taste is *aesthetic*, that is, it is entirely subjective and quite uninformative about the object, even indirectly, other than as marking it out as one whose contemplation we find pleasing (or, in case it is ugly, displeasing). In particular, while Kant goes on to tell us rather more about the internal object of our pleasure in the beautiful, he repeatedly insists that the judgment of taste is not cognitive, and that it carries no implication of their being any particular recurring qualities fitted by nature to elicit that sentiment, which careful investigation might seek to isolate and identify. In this he is quite right and utterly at odds with Hume.

To say in this way, as Kant does, that the judgment of taste is not cognitive and does not bring its object under a concept (§1) only bears on the content of the judgment's predicate, "x is beautiful." We shall see later on that it must badly misrepresent his thought to suppose that in judging some object, a rose, say, to be beautiful, I am not even to bring the flower referred to by the subject term under the concept *rose*. Indeed, it may even be that to make that judgment correctly may oblige me to think of it, and to experience it, *as* a rose, and at the very least, it is important for Kant that in judging it so, we think of it as something in nature. Equally, in judging one of Redouté's roses to be beautiful, we need to judge it *as* art, not nature. In neither case, though, do we "bring the object under a concept" in the way Kant wants to exclude.

This noncognitive claim leaves ample room for Kant to suppose, reasonably enough, that the response of pleasure or satisfaction has its ultimate source in some feature or other of the object lying within a certain range, it being indeterminate which feature within that range will be in point in any particular case. And this he certainly does think, since, notoriously, he is inclined to say that we are essentially pleased by the beautiful object's having a certain form. This is entirely consistent with his emphasizing that the aesthetic character of our judgment rules out the possibility of there being any proof that something is beautiful (§57). That emphasis we can hear as the entirely correct thought that there is no sure criterion, no clear cut decision-procedure, that our command of the concept *beauty* enables us to bring to bear in the assessment of particular cases. The kind of form the beautiful object must have *qua* beautiful cannot be further specified except in reference to ourselves and our responses to it. This is what leads Kant to say that *beauty* is an "undeterminable concept and useless for knowledge" (*an sich unbestimmbar und zum Erkenntnis untauglich*) (§57). We shall return to the issue of form and, more fully, to the reference to ourselves in due course.

3.

To say that the judgment of taste is aesthetic and subjective does not yet distinguish the beautiful from the merely agreeable. Both judgments are aesthetic and neither is informative about its object on its own account, independently of its relation to the judging subject. So, Kant moves to refine his conception of the satisfaction we take in the beautiful by saying that it is *disinterested*, and as such independent of any concern for the existence of the object. What occupies us is the *representation* we have of the object, not its existence; how it appears to us in our experience, not just *that* it exists to be experienced and used for our practical ends. This is so even though the representation, or the experience, of the thing would, trivially, not be available unless the object existed. With the agreeable matters stand otherwise. There Kant does suppose that as we find something pleasant we are responding directly to the object and its existence rather than to the way in which we experientially represent it, and in that case our pleasure cannot be divorced from practical concerns in the way it is when we judge it to be beautiful. No one has ever found this aspect of Kant's discussion particularly compelling. Since it is complemented by other considerations, we can set it aside without further ado, other than to remark that Kant's determination to concentrate on how beautiful objects strike us in our experience of them is uncontroversial enough, even if he is mistaken in supposing that that might suffice to keep the beautiful and the agreeable apart.

4.

Beauty must occasion universal pleasure. Of course, those who are set against it from the very outset, or whose hostility derives from some purely utilitarian dissatisfaction, will not count against that universality. The satisfaction that is universal can only be that of those who are directly responsive to, and focused on, the representation, to the way the object appears in their experience, in a word, to the disinterested. By contrast, when something is found agreeable, there is no implication that anyone other than the judging subject will find it pleasing, though many others may in fact well do so. So while both satisfactions are aesthetic and noncognitive, that which we take in the beautiful is *essentially* universal, whereas that evoked by the agreeable need be no more than personally satisfying.

One could be forgiven for thinking that there is at this point a strong affinity between Kant's view and that of Hume, even that Hume's more nuanced stance comes closer to getting things right. However, Kant would strenuously resist that suggestion, and in doing so see himself as rectifying a second weakness in the Humean view. Pursuing an analogy with secondary quality judgments, Hume had taught that things of beauty are ones that are liable to occasion a uniformity of pleasurable sentiment among competent observers, namely among unprejudiced and well-schooled critics possessed of sound understanding and a capacity for fine discrimination. And just because strict universality is not to be expected, even among such a narrowly specified group, he had found it natural enough not to require anything quite so exigent, and had been content to demand no more than "a considerable uniformity of sentiment" among the group's members. We can well imagine him pointing out to Kant that that is quite enough to distinguish the beautiful from the agreeable, since a considerable uniformity of pleasurable response amongst competent observers is a perfectly satisfactory contrary of one that need be no more than personal. The mooted common-sense relaxation of the universality condition can easily seem a clear gain in Hume's favor.

5.

It is plain to Kant, however, that any such concession would be inconsistent with one fundamental feature of the judgment of taste, one that determines its very possibility. This is that the judgment of taste is a priori (§36). Evidently, it is not so in the usual sense that one may rightly judge an object to be beautiful without experiencing it, since, definitionally, a judgment of taste is made on the basis of the subject's own experience of and response to the thing in question. Rather, the judgment is a priori in that it is on the basis of the subject's own response alone that he legitimately commits himself to the responses of people other than himself. That is, in judging something beautiful, we impute a pleasure to others without needing to ascertain on the ground (by polling a large enough sample, say) how others do actually respond to it. The implicit content of a judgment of taste thus goes way beyond the particular experience of the person whose judgment it is, yet it is held in place by nothing more than that judging subject's own response.

444

To Kant's way of thinking, there is only one straightforward and unproblematic way for that to be possible. This is that our disinterested responses to the objects of aesthetic contemplation should be law-governed, where for him laws are rules that enjoy strict universality (see *CPR*, A 113). Consequently, as long as I am right in thinking that my pleasurable response to an object is indeed disinterested – focused on the representation it presents, and so not touched by my practical concerns and desires – then, if my judgments of taste are to have any real purchase on the world, all other disinterested subjects who come upon that same object must respond to it as I do. Anything less, such as general agreement, or Hume's considerable uniformity of response among the well-schooled, could be no more than an indication that the thing in question was generally agreeable. It could not possibly underwrite a judgment of taste proper, nor serve to keep the beautiful and the agreeable apart. Nor, of course, could it underpin the supposedly *a priori* nature of the judgment.

6.

At this point one might suspect that the obtaining of any strict law governing aesthetic response must involve there being some determinate features that beautiful things share, precisely the cognitivist idea that we have already seen Kant rejecting in his first anti-Humean move. However, in the difficult expository sections of §§10–16 Kant has it in mind to head off any such threat. The leading idea he pursues is reasonably straightforward, although its detail is certainly extremely murky. A beautiful object is one which in virtue of its particular form lends itself to engaging the two active cognitive faculties of mind – imagination and understanding – in such a way as to cooperate in a notably harmonious and satisfying fashion. It is fundamentally this harmonious mental activity itself that Kant takes to be the source of the pleasure enjoyed by anyone seized by the beauty of this thing or that. Kant calls this obscure harmony of our cognitive faculties the "subjective finality in the representation of an object," and the curious notion of finality (otherwise "purposiveness") that he invokes here just marks out the fact that a beautiful object invites being represented in this active way and that it serves the mind well thereby. It does that, Kant supposes, through stimulating and quickening our active powers of synthesis, strengthening our ability to employ our minds fruitfully elsewhere, notably in our cognitive endeavors, even while in our aesthetic engagements with the world that otherwise predominant concern is held in temporary abeyance. As he puts it later on in §49:

> Imagination is . . . aesthetically . . . free to furnish of its own account . . . a wealth of undeveloped material for the understanding to make use of, not so much objectively for cognition, as subjectively for quickening the cognitive faculties, and hence indirectly for cognition. (5.316–17; author's translations throughout)

I expand on this idea below.

How is this psychologizing move supposed to avoid the looming threat? First, even though Kant talks about the form of the (representation of the) beautiful object as that feature of it which generates the harmonious engagement of imagination and understanding, we can see that quite independently of any particular interpretation of what that might come to, there is nothing here like Hume's "certain qualities, fitted by nature to produce those particular feelings." Saying, as he did, that "amidst all the variety and caprice of taste, there are certain general principles of approbation or blame, whose influence a careful eye may trace in all operations of the mind," Hume had supposed that it should be possible to investigate the nature of objects that good critics view with marked favor and then to come up with something like a catalogue of those qualities. In Kant's view, however, there is no such expectation: what makes objects beautiful need not be the same formal qualities in different cases, nor need those qualities lie on some closed list. All we are told is that the crucial sense of harmonious cooperation between imagination and understanding ("the formal finality of the representation") is a response to *some* formal feature or other of a beautiful object's appearance. The putative laws that govern these matters will then not be ones that specify those features. They will not even bring them within the antecedents of those laws. That place is occupied by the purposive (harmonious) nature of those representations that are beautiful. Thus: a beautiful object is one which, on account of some or other of its formal features, is liable to elicit a harmonious interplay of imagination and understanding in the experience of anyone who comes to contemplate it disinterestedly, which interplay (*protasis*) is nomically productive of pleasure (*apodosis*).

7.

Incidentally, as far as the issue of Kant's alleged and much criticized "formalism" goes, that can be easily minimized once we notice that he introduces the idea of "form" to signal a contrast with the material or sensory features of things, features which he took to be interpersonally unstable, unstable in that what I see as, say, grey and is called "grey" by both you and me, might nonetheless systematically and undetectably appear to you in a way that it does not appear to me (cf. *CJ*, Introduction, VII, §3 and again at §14, 5.224). Unless such features are excluded from the properties of things and their representations that give rise to judgments of taste, we would have no ground for supposing that what you are responding with delight to, in the harmonious interplay of imagination and understanding as you experience a given thing, is the same as I do. Then the crucial universality requirement would be utterly inscrutable. However, since Kant's distrust of secondary quality experience is nowadays generally taken to be ill-founded, his stress on the formal (i.e. interpersonally communicable) character of the beautiful does nothing whatever to underpin a "formalist" aesthetic as that is usually understood. From the theoretical point of view then objects' so-called "material" and sensory features, that is, specifically their secondary and response-dependent qualities, are no less "formal" than their response-independent and primary ones.

8.

While my exposition glosses over it, Kant's own text displays a degree of uncertainty about the way the purposiveness of representations we judge beautiful meshes with the strict universality he is concerned to introduce. At moments he seems to suppose that there is a more or less open range of determinate features of things we experience which engage people's imagination and understanding harmoniously, where their feeling of harmony is itself the pleasure that characterizes the beautiful, and so features as the apodosis of the putative law. So, in §12 we find him saying: "The consciousness of mere formal finality in the play of the cognitive faculties of the subject attending a representation whereby an object is given *is the pleasure itself*..." (my emphasis). On the other hand, and avoiding any shadow of Humean cognitivism, no matter how open-ended and disjunctive, he supposes the feeling of formal finality to be distinct from the pleasure, and that the law that governs these matters is just that people cannot but respond with pleasure to objects that stimulate the mind in that way. Thus in §9 we are told:

> This purely subjective (aesthetic) estimating of the object, or of the representation through which it is given, is antecedent to the pleasure in it, and is the basis of this pleasure in the harmony of the cognitive faculties. (*CJ*, 5.218)

Clearly, it is the second of these alternatives that best answers to Kant's intentions, just because the interpersonally communicable character of the beautiful object does not fall within the scope of the putative universal law's antecedent, thereby laying the judgment of taste unacceptably open to proof. What is being claimed instead is just that there are objects, to wit, beautiful ones, whose inspectable character invites the fruitful engagement of imagination and understanding in our contemplation of them, which kind of engagement cannot but be found satisfying. Put in this way, there is no reason to think that any strict universality that there might be will bring with it some version of the unwanted cognitivist claim.

9.

The subjectivizing strategy here will evidently only be worth exploring as long as plausible sense can be made of it. Above all, it has to capture reasonably smoothly something that is salient in the phenomenology of our aesthetic experience. The most appealing construction of it, and one which Kant himself does more than a little to encourage, takes the cooperative interplay of imagination and understanding as alluding to what goes on as we come actively to fashion our experience of something, passively given to us in intuition, *as* being this or that for us. The imagination owes its allegiance to the passively given, of course, but it enriches and amplifies that by recruiting to it concepts supplied spontaneously by the understanding. It is here that we come to the reference to ourselves that I gave notice of earlier.

So, in contemplating this thing or that, and disinterested as we are to take ourselves to be, we seek to endow what is passively given with some significance for us (in understanding) and to find (via imagination) a perceptual anchor and embodiment for the significance that the object is represented as having. In a banal enough case that is what goes on as one finds one aspect of a landscape balancing, or answering to, another. I bring imagination to bear in seeing the balance in the various elements of the scene passively presented to me in intuition, and I do that by finding those elements are aptly conceptualized (by understanding) in terms of balance. It needs to be stressed here that this is not a matter of idle fancy; the object of our contemplation must exert a measure of control over the way in which imagination and understanding jointly operate. It was primarily for this reason that I insisted earlier on that it would misrepresent Kant to think that the "conceptlessness" of the judgment of taste involves abstraction from our recognition of the sort of thing we find beautiful. Were that the case, the satisfying interplay of the two faculties would be answerable to nothing and stand no chance of being reasonably imputed to others.

A more developed case of the same kind of thing is provided by Dante's account of coming to see Beatrice's face:

> the baits that nature and art use to capture first the eyes, and then the mind, by means of the human body [*carne umana*] and pictures of it, were as nothing compared with the divine delight that infused me as I turned to her radiant face – as she noticed my desire, she so smiled that her face was as God's own joy. (*Paradiso*, xxvii.88–106)

Here the thought that the poet brings to bear on his experience of his beloved saturates his perceptual experience of her, wherein, I take it, we have a paradigm of the harmony of imagination and understanding this lies at the heart of Kant's story. It is, I think, a way of understanding him that happily mirrors a recurrent feature of our aesthetic experience, though admittedly the glass will need a good polish before it can be definitively hung in place.

Another far from banal instance of the same phenomenon, but one that this time challenges the use to which Kant wants to put it, is again provided by Dante at the start of the poem as he recounts his experience in the dark wood. Looking back on that moment, it is difficult for him to express how savage, harsh and dense it was, so much so that even to think of it renewed the fear it had originally inspired (*Inferno*, i.4–6). In recalling the wood's fearful harshness, Dante is reporting the way his perception of the scene was infused with thought, just as his later encounter with Beatrice was to be. Thought saturates perception and thereby constitutes the experience itself, and once more, as Dante sees it, not by way of fancy or phantasy, but under the control of his external surroundings. The wood and the loved face both lend themselves to the conceptual richness that he brings to bear in his experience upon them. Yet, despite being entirely appropriate to its object, the interplay of imagination and understanding in the experience of the wood does not produce pleasure; as Dante emphasizes, his response was one of fear and distress. So, clearly, the committed Kantian will have to move away from satisfaction stemming from the apt (*scilicet* "harmonious") cooperation of imagination and understanding towards something more like an apt flooding of perception with *harmonious* thought, something we don't have in Dante's earlier experience, though in the later one we do. And that seems to be just right, for the wood was surely grim, not beautiful, and Beatrice beautiful, not grim, even though imagination and understanding worked aptly and productively together in both those cases.

It will be apparent that the ways the experience of these things are flooded by thought cannot be detached from the responses that Kant conceives of as generated in a law-governed fashion. In *Inferno*, seeing the wood as *selvaggia e aspra e forte* was itself to see it *as* fearful, not just in some way that was productive of fear in a law-governed manner. Similarly, in *Paradiso*, with the rapture occasioned by the radiance of Beatrice's face and smile. To see God's joy in that smile is itself to see it with rapture. The upshot of this must be that as we take on board the subjective purposiveness that lies at the heart of Kant's theory, we either find that there is no regular connection between the harmony of imagination and understanding and pleasure (witness the dark wood), or, if there is, it is a conceptual connection, not a law-governed one (witness Beatrice's smile). So either the vaunted subjective purposiveness of the representation does not bound the beautiful, or else it does do so, but only in a tautologous manner, whereby a beautiful object is one that anyone who sees it as beautiful (i.e. flooding their representation with harmonious thought in the way that I do) will find pleasing.

10.

At this delicate point Kant's elucidation appears to have broken down. And to the extent that it is the whole of his story, so it has. Only it isn't the whole story, for no notice has yet been taken of the fourth element of the account, nor any mention of a third acute difficulty that embarrasses Hume's discussion of the topic, and which Kant sought to overcome. The delight we take in the beautiful is a *necessary* delight, necessary in a nonapodeictic, nonconceptual, yet exemplary way. It does not imply that every disinterested viewer *will* in fact find satisfaction where I do (§18); instead it allows us to insist that "everyone *ought to* give the object in question their approval and follow suit in describing it as beautiful" (§19). Now, it might seem that in appealing to the idea of law-governed uniformity of response in accounting for the *a priori* character of taste, Kant has already implicitly introduced this necessity. For his idea is that on the basis of my own disinterested response I know how others must react to a comparable experience of what so moves me. As we have seen, that is indeed one important strand of Kant's theory. Only, to allow matters to rest there does not do justice to the richness of his thought. Nor does it do anything to overcome the breakdown just encountered.

Kant speaks of the judgment of taste as *exacting* agreement from everyone, where the claim that others ought to respond as I do is not merely an expression of expectation (as in "This cream ought to clear up that rash"), but rather a claim that there is a "kind of duty" to find contemplation of this particular thing rewarding, be it in nature or in art (§40). To make something of this it helps to return to Hume, bearing in mind as we do so how the failure of the governing-law model is likely to reinforce the allure of his "considerable uniformity" of response and make any appeal to necessity seem quite hopeless.

In his essay Hume had sought to show how disagreements about aesthetic matters may be reconciled by calling on the norm of the well-schooled judge. An issue that his proposal completely overlooks is why anyone whose preferences are not already fundamentally those of the well-schooled should be anxious to abandon their own attachments in favour of the critical standard that such alien judges recommend. Only if contending parties are prepared to do that will there be any prospect of reconciliation between them. Put in more Kantian language, Hume has no answer to the question why the preferences of true critics *ought* to be followed, no explanation why the truly beautiful demands our love, even the love of those who are, as it happens, insensitive to it. Now, this critical reflection provides a clear way in which Kant's claim about the exemplary necessity of our delight in the beautiful can be understood. Namely, it is a deep conceptual truth for him that anyone ought to find things of beauty rewarding, whether or not they do actually find them so. This is a genuinely novel contribution to the analysis, not simply a repetition of what Kant supposes has already been achieved, and it does face head-on the yawning defect in Hume's thought. Further, it enables one to see what Kant has in mind when he speaks of our *imputing* a pleasure to others, of *exacting* it, and of that positive response of pleasurable attachment to what is beautiful being "a kind of duty." Moreover – and for present purposes this is the important point – it opens up a second route to accounting for the *a priori* nature of the judgment of taste, one that is quite detached from the unwelcome appeal to natural psychological law that marks Kant's official position.

Of course, just by itself the novel claim does nothing to explain or ground the necessity it introduces, but since this part of Kant's discussion is concerned only with elucidation, that is no failing. Explanation and underpinning may be sought elsewhere. We may as well notice, though, that in Kant's mind this final element of his analysis is meant to complement the others, and in that way to provide a bridge from the theoretical to the moral that he thought of as crowning his whole Critical enterprise. The idea he is inclined to pursue is that the availability to us in our experience of beauty understood in the law-governed terms set out above gives us some otherwise distressingly wanting assurance that the moral law, enjoying an analogous structure, can genuinely be realized in our lives, and that it is fundamentally this that underpins the thought that we all ought to take pleasure in its instances. But for that we might be tempted to suppose it a merely illusory ideal. That strategy, however, cannot survive the present breakdown, and anyway there is far too much to be said against the Kantian conception of morality ultimately rooted as it is our supersensible, noumenal nature to make it inviting to pursue it. So let us just note it, and pass on.

11.

Notwithstanding his own large program, at the end of these purely analytic sections of his book Kant throws out an intriguing hint which invites exploration in a different direction than the one he took to be so clearly unproblematic. There, in §22, without answering it, he raises the question whether taste is

> a natural and original faculty, or only the idea of one that is artificial and to be acquired by us, so that a judgment of taste, with its demand for universal assent, is but a requirement of reason for generating such a consensus [or whether] the "ought" . . . only betokens the possibility of arriving at some sort of unanimity in these matters, and the judgment of taste only adduces an example of the application of this principle. (5.240)

This question immediately opens up the possibility of dropping the appeal to some inscrutable and noumenally anchored law in favor of general considerations about our shared psychological needs that we may see as normatively regulating feeling and behavior.

450

In a suggestive later passage (§42) Kant discusses what he calls our "intellectual interest" in natural beauty, where, contrasted with an interest that is merely empirical, the term "intellectual" carries with it the idea of being rationally mandatory, and intimates a second way of securing the apriority of the judgment of taste. He observes there that "to take an immediate interest in the beauty of nature is always the mark of a good soul" and that thought clearly picks up an earlier observation to the effect that "the beautiful prepares us to love something, even nature, apart from any interest" (§29, General Remark).

A man may turn to the beauty of nature, we are told, "so that he may there find as it were a feast for his soul in a train of thought that he can never completely evolve" (§42), and Kant makes plain that that feast for the soul has to take place under the guidance of the thought that it is nature that we are admiring. "It must be nature, or mistaken by us for nature, to enable us to take an immediate interest in the beautiful as such" (ibid.).

What is of interest here is less the attempt Kant makes to bolt this last element of the story onto the earlier ones, in the way just noted and set aside, than the way in which he is seeking to tie the novel necessity of the judgment of taste to our having reason for loving nature's beauties. In our affective responses to what lends itself to being experienced through saturation with harmonious thought, we find ourselves developing a loving disposition directed at things other than ourselves and doing so for reasons that are quite unmotivated. Since that loving attitude is one that we all need to acquire (it is, for Kant, a universal *a priori* human interest), it will be important to cultivate experience that can contribute to its growth and its psychological stabilization. With that thought in hand, we can then ground the demand implicit in the language of taste that anyone ought to (i.e., has reason to) take delight in natural beauty independently of all noumenal considerations and whether or not there are psychological laws governing these matters.

12.

It may be said, fairly enough, that this way of talking does not stretch much further than a general recommendation that people should cultivate an attachment to natural beauty. Yet it is only a short step from here to saying much the same about the individual case. As the particular mountain or landscape or bird, flower or insect lends itself to the rich train of thought that manifests itself in the wonder and attachment with which one greets it, the spiritual benefit that it is liable to make for is ground enough for thinking that particular thing worthy of attachment too (a demand that can extend to the sullen child, say, or the unfeeling adult), particularly since, as already emphasized, the attachment to be enjoyed is formed under the loose control of the object itself, and does not arise merely as a matter of arbitrary whim.

As we turn to the arts, a version of the same idea takes on rather sharper focus. Kant envisages the typical beautiful work of art (a poem, a statue, a painting) being structured around some large theme of significance for our inner lives. Examples he mentions are invisible beings, the kingdom of the blessed, hell, eternity, creation, etc., also love, fame, death, envy, the vices, and the like (all examples from §49). Under the artist's guidance, we are encouraged to find elaborated and apt ways of thinking and feeling about those themes, ways that are embodied and expressed in the particular representations that his work offers us. Imagination and understanding enrich each other in our sensitivity to and appreciation of the works we take into ourselves, and, as Kant puts it, "enable us to create a second nature out of the material supplied by actual nature" (ibid.). Naturally enough, there are ways of doing this which are coarse and barbarous, but in the case of beautiful art, we find images presented which are imbued with harmonious thought about their central themes, and to which we respond with delight, with potentially long-term benign effect. We are, of course, not moved to such contemplation with a view to such effect – our aesthetic response is after all not practically directed – but it is in the light of the prospective benefit that we can recommend to others that they should come to find those beautiful works as moving as do we. Therein lies the root of the exemplary necessity of the judgment we make about them, pursued once more along the second, more realistic pathway. In this case, we are not taking the common sense which Kant says is a presupposition of taste as a natural and original (lawbound) faculty, rather – as he very tentatively, and, as a lawyer might say, in the alternative, suggests – we are seeking to generate common agreement in pursuit of psychological goods which we can not reasonably decline.

13.

Three closing remarks. It has been said by one leading commentator, H. E. Allison (2001: 184), that any such attempt to interpret Kant's exemplary necessity as bearing on the individual case, be that natural object or work of art, is in direct conflict with his insisting that the judgment of taste is not cognitive and that it does not allow of proof. If that were really so, it would indeed be a serious objection. Only Kant's conception of "proof" is that of a determinate decision procedure applicable to the particular case by reference to some clear-cut criterion. That is almost laughably far from being the case here. The beautiful object is thought of as one that invites the active construction of a thought-saturated representation whose pleasurable internalization is beneficial for the sort of creatures that we are. That formula is as far removed from introducing a means of determinate proof as can be, but it does allow Kant to bring his emended theory to bear on the particular case as his concern with the singularity of the judgment of taste obliges him to do.

A different puzzle is that we have seen Kant introducing the harmonious interplay of imagination and understanding as benefiting us by strengthening and quickening our cognitive powers. It can look as if that crude idea has just been tactfully buried here, best forgotten. While this may display generosity to Kant, it does nonetheless distort his view. Now, his insistence that the judgment of taste is not cognitive and the tenuousness of the idea that our aesthetic enjoyment of the world ultimately and indirectly serves the progress of science certainly encourage that act of burial. Nevertheless, the distinction he draws between actual nature and second nature that is introduced in §49 offers a crutch with the help of which the possibly prematurely interred idea can reemerge. Of course, the active aesthetic engagement of imagination and understanding in our representations of nature and art are minimally answerable, even indirectly, to progress in the dispassionate investigation of actual nature. But it is a task for everyone in making sense of their lives what to make of actual nature and what to make of ourselves as parts of it. That is a question of how we may come to view it in ways that we can share with one another and which permit us to find ourselves tolerably well at home in the world. I see no very good reason to think that the idea of cognition cannot find a place here, in our exploration and construction of a common second nature, as well as in the investigation of actual nature. So possibly there is a happy continuum to be found between what Kant says in §9 (and elsewhere) about the operation and quickening of our cognitive faculties and our discussion of exemplary necessity along the second pathway he tentatively opens up. Kant himself describes the artistic fashioning of second nature more fully in terms of taste clipping the wings of raw genius and thus

> introducing clearness and order into the plenitude of thought, and in doing so giving a stability to the ideas, and qualifying them for permanent and universal approval, for being followed by others and for a continually progressive culture. (§50)

Anyone who thinks of the fruit of developed taste in terms like these could understandably view its attainment as a kind of inventive cognitive success.

Moreover, it is notable that in §59 Kant extends the term "knowledge" beyond "the theoretical determination of an object in respect of what it is in itself" to "the practical determination of what the ideas of it ought to be for us and for its final employment." This dovetails well with the construction of second nature that surfaces in §49 as well as with an earlier passage in which Kant speaks of beauty as

> giving a veritable extension, not, of course, to our knowledge of objects of nature, but to our conception of nature itself – nature as mere mechanism being enlarged to the conception of nature as art . . . (§23, 5.246)

Finally, this normatively focused reading of Kant's account of beauty can take some heart from what he has to say about the other main category of our aesthetic experience, the sublime, our satisfaction in which is also aesthetic, universal, purposive, and necessary, and about which our judgments are likewise idiosyncratically a priori. There are marked differences though. Crucially, while beauty prepares us to love, sublimity prepares us to respect, to admire and to esteem; beauty draws us in, sublimity keeps us at a distance; beauty is the product of the harmonious *interplay* of imagination and understanding, whereas the feeling of sublimity manifests the *opposition* of imagination and reason. Above all, the necessity of our pleasure in the sublime is rooted not in any obscure law supposedly anchored in the supersensible substrate of our humanity, but stems from the way in which our inability to find anything in actual nature that answers to the ideas of reason (absolute greatness, or absolute might) can serve to assure us of our spiritual invulnerability to the brute forces that bear down on the insignificant elements of first nature that we are. That is, in his discussion of the sublime Kant quite explicitly chooses not a nomic but a normative pathway to the grounding of the necessity of our satisfaction and to the a priori nature of the relevant judgments. His embracing it there should encourage us to make what we can of it in developing his

453

handling of the beautiful against the failure of the nomic model. Even though his own systematically motivated preference was clearly for the first line of attack, in the end it is surely the second constructive pathway that is the more fruitful, however lightly sketched in that may be. Moving along that line, we find Kant offering us something far richer than Hume had dreamt of, and something that is well in tune with the character of much of our deepest aesthetic experience.

References and Further Reading

Allison, Henry, E. (2001). *Kant's Theory of Taste*. Cambridge: Cambridge University Press.

Budd, Malcolm (2002). *The Aesthetic Appreciation of Nature*. Oxford: Oxford University Press.

Guyer, Paul (1979). *Kant and the Claims of Taste*. Cambridge, MA: Harvard University Press.

Hume, David (1875). On the standard of taste. In *Essays Moral, Political, and Literary*, eds. T. H. Green and T. Grose. New edition, ed. F. Miller (1985). Indianapolis: Liberty Fund.

Savile, Anthony (1987). *Aesthetic Reconstructions*. Oxford, Blackwell.

Savile, Anthony (1993). *Kantian Aesthetics Pursued*. Edinburgh: Edinburgh University Press.

Savile, Anthony (2003). Kant and the ideal of beauty. In J. Bermudez and S. Gardner (eds.), *Art and Morality*. London: Routledge.

29

Kant's Biological Teleology and its Philosophical Significance

HANNAH GINSBORG

Kant's Critique of Teleological Judgment, the second part of his *Critique of Judgment*, is concerned with the following question: to what extent is it legitimate to think of nature in teleological terms, that is, in terms of ends, goals, or purposes? The "new science" of the seventeenth century, associated with such figures as Galileo, Hobbes, Descartes, Boyle, and Newton, had constituted a significant break from Aristotelian science, in which the paradigm of natural explanation was teleological. The alternative explanatory paradigm offered by the new science was one on which all natural phenomena were to be explained "mechanically," that is, without appeal to guidance by ends or purposes. More specifically, the so-called "mechanical philosophy" aimed to explain all natural phenomena in terms of a few basic properties of matter: size, shape, motion, and (in some versions) solidity or impenetrability. This explanatory framework, especially when developed by Newton to allow attractive or gravitational force to matter, proved to be enormously fruitful for the development of physics and chemistry. But there was still much about nature which seemed to resist this kind of explanation: in particular, those natural phenomena which are now referred to as "biological." Take, for example, the formation of a chick embryo out of the apparently undifferentiated matter contained in a hen's egg. How could this be explained without supposing that the resulting chick was the end or purpose of the process of formation, or in other words, that the process took place in order to produce the chick?

For philosophers and scientists who were committed to the explanatory paradigm of the new science, such phenomena posed a challenge. One response to the challenge was to insist that biological phenomena could, appearances notwithstanding, be explained within the mechanical framework. Either gravitational force itself, or forces analogous to gravitational force, were sufficient to account for the production of organisms. Another, diametrically opposed, way was to deny that organisms were in fact naturally formed at all, and to ascribe them instead to a supernatural cause, namely God. This took the form, most commonly, of "preformationism." The apparent development of the chick embryo was merely an expansion of an organism which had been preformed in miniature by God, and this expansion was a purely mechanical process whose explanation required no appeal to purposes.

Debates among defenders of these, and related, positions were prevalent in the mid-eighteenth century, when Kant first started to write about the issue of natural teleology.

The Critique of Teleological Judgment contains Kant's most developed contribution to these debates, a contribution which differs radically from both positions described so far. Kant himself was, at least in the Critical period, a committed defender of Newtonian science. But he was also concerned throughout his career with the question of how to make sense of living things. Beginning with some of his earliest writings (in particular the *Universal Natural History* of 1755 and the *Only Possible Proof of the Existence of God* of 1763), Kant explicitly rejects the view that the fundamental forces of matter alone, which he understood as comprising both an attractive force responsible for gravitational phenomena, and a repulsive force responsible for matter's impenetrability, could account for the existence of plants and animals. But he also denies that we should treat plants and animals as though they were individually created by God as opposed to coming into existence through natural processes. These commitments led him to develop a third view, articulated most fully in the Critique of Teleological Judgment, which in effect reintroduces natural teleology. If the study of organisms is to constitute part of natural science, then organisms must be viewed, not as artefacts, but as products of nature. Yet they cannot be understood as existing merely in virtue of the fundamental forces of matter, and this implies that they must be regarded in teleological terms.

In what follows I try to explain Kant's view in the light of some of the more significant passages dealing with natural teleology in the *Critique of Judgment*, focusing, in the first section, on the Analytic of Teleological Judgment and, in the second section, on the Dialectic of Teleological Judgment. I also emphasize what I think is the central philosophical question raised by Kant's – or indeed any – defense of natural teleology: are the concepts of natural teleology, and the related concept of a "natural end," philosophically coherent, or do they represent a contradiction in terms? I claim that much of Kant's explicit discussion fails to get to the heart of this central question, but, in the third and final section, I propose a way of addressing it which I think is suggested by the argument of the *Critique of Judgment* as a whole. Many of the interpretative claims I make in explaining Kant's view are controversial. While there is not space to defend these claims here, aspects of the interpretation underlying them are presented more fully in Ginsborg 2001 and Ginsborg 2004.

I.

Kant's account of organisms in the Analytic is structured around the notion of a *Naturzweck*, a "natural purpose" or "natural end," which he discusses in detail in §§64–5. The notion of a natural end in turn derives from that of an end, which he defines in the Critique of Aesthetic Judgment as "the object of a concept insofar as the latter is regarded as the cause of the former" (§10, 5.220). It is clear that what Kant has in mind here is the example of artefacts such as a chair or a teacup. Such artefacts come into being in virtue of concepts in the minds of designers: for example, the concept of a wooden armchair upholstered in red velvet. When we encounter something falling under that concept, i.e. a wooden armchair upholstered in red velvet, we take it to have been produced in accordance with that concept, and so we regard the concept as playing an essential role in the causal history of the object. But it is a central theme of the Critique of Teleological Judgment that the application of the notion of end is not limited to artefacts. Products of nature too can qualify as ends, and these are entitled natural ends. This should strike us as paradoxical, and indeed Kant warns us that the concept of a natural end may contain a contradiction (§64, 5.370). We count something as an end if we regard it as produced by the causality of a concept, which implies that it was produced as a result of design. But something counts as natural, on the face of it, precisely to the extent that it is not the product of design, and hence, it would seem, not an end. One of the most important philosophical challenges for any sympathetic interpretation of Kant's views on organisms is to explain how this apparent contradiction is to be reconciled.

Kant's discussion of the notion of a natural end in §§64–5 centers on the conditions which an object has to meet in order to qualify as a natural end. At §64, he gives a "provisional" statement of what is required: a thing, he says, "exists as a natural end if it is cause and effect of itself" (5.370). He expands on this statement at §65 by distinguishing two conditions, one which is required for the things being an end *tout court*, the second for its being, in addition, a *natural* end as opposed to an artefact. The first condition, which applies to ends generally, is that "the parts . . . [be] possible only through their relation to the whole" (5.373). In the case of artefacts, this condition is satisfied in that the parts of the artefact, say the legs and the seat of the chair, or the handle of the teacup, can exist only in virtue of the designer's idea or concept of the whole. As Kant puts the condition in a subsequent formulation, each part exists "for the sake of the others and of the whole" (ibid.): the legs of the chair, or the handle of the cup, exist only in order that the chair or cup as a whole should exist. But in the more specific case of a natural end, this requirement is satisfied differently, in a way which is expressed by a second condition: "the parts [must] combine themselves into the unity of a whole by being reciprocally the cause and effect of one another's form" (ibid.). While in the case of an artefact the parts are produced and combined into a whole by an artisan working in accordance with a design, in the case of a natural product there is no artisan. If the object is still to qualify as an end, then, in accordance with the first condition, it must be the case that the parts of the organism are produced and combined into a whole *by one another*. As Kant puts it in a more detailed formulation, for something to be judged as a natural end "it is required that its parts altogether reciprocally produce one another, as far as both their form and combination is concerned, and thus produce a whole out of their own causality" (ibid.).

Does anything meet these conditions? According to Kant, plants and animals do; indeed they are the only things which do, and hence the only things which qualify as natural ends (§65, 5.375–6). Thus Kant illustrates his provisional statement of the overall condition on something's being a natural end, that the thing must be "cause and effect of itself," by citing three characteristics of a tree, which he presumably takes to exemplify characteristics of plants and animals more generally. First, a tree produces offspring of the same species, thus "producing itself with respect to the species" (§64, 5.371). Second, it produces itself "as an individual" (ibid.) by taking in nourishment from outside and converting it so that it forms part of the tree itself. Third, its parts stand in relations of reciprocal dependence on one another, in that, for example, the leaves are needed for the preservation of the trunk, but the trunk in turn is needed for the production of the leaves (ibid.). This last point is the one which is emphasized in the more detailed characterization of the two conditions in §65. But the three points

457

are related in that they all manifest the fundamental "formative force" (*bildende Kraft*) which is responsible for an organism's self-causing character and which distinguishes it from a complex artefact such as a watch. While a watch meets the first of the two conditions specified in §65, and hence counts as an end, it fails to qualify as a *natural* end because "one wheel in the watch does not produce another, and still less does one watch produce other watches" (§65, 5.374); relatedly, a watch cannot repair itself when damaged or replace parts which have been removed.

Kant goes on to say:

> An organized being is thus not a mere machine, because that has solely *moving* force [*bewegende Kraft*]; rather it possesses *formative* force . . . which cannot be explained through the capacity for movement (mechanism) alone. (Ibid.; author's translations throughout)

Kant presents his discussion of the "self-causing" character of organisms as though it addresses the threat of contradiction in the notion of a natural end (§64, 5.370–1). And the discussion does indeed suggest an indirect resolution of the conflict insofar as it points to a readily observable feature of organisms – their capacity to reproduce and maintain themselves – which seems to license our regarding them both as ends, and as products of nature. But the resolution is not definitive, in that worries about the coherence of the notion of a natural end might well lead us to doubt whether organisms really do have the kind of fundamental self-causing capacity which Kant ascribes to them. Such doubt might take one of two contrasting forms. One form would allow that organisms meet the first of Kant's two conditions at §65, that the parts are possible only in relation to the whole, but question whether they do so in the way specified in the second condition. Perhaps, it might be suggested, organisms and watches differ only with respect to complexity: while at the superficial level organisms appear to display a fundamental capacity for self-maintenance and reproduction, this can be seen at the microscopic level to reflect the operation of a highly complex mechanism no different in kind from that of a watch. Such a suggestion was indeed implicit in the eighteenth-century theory of preformationism, on which all plants and animals are in effect artefacts, directly created by God. On the popular "encasement" version of this view, the first organism of each species was created with all of its offspring, and their offspring in turn, encased in miniature form within it. Organisms, according to this and other versions of the view, lack the power to reproduce: what appears to be the generation of one organism by another is simply the unfolding or expansion of an organism which already existed at the microscopic level. (For discussion of the various kinds of preformationist theories, see McLaughlin 1990: ch. 1.)

The contrasting form of doubt would also question whether organisms have a fundamental capacity for self-maintenance and reproduction, but in a way which challenges their status as ends rather than their status as natural. Why couldn't organisms have come into existence, in the first instance, solely through the operation of basic forces present in all matter? Organisms, once formed in this way, might indeed exhibit self-producing and self-maintaining characteristics, but this would not imply their possession of a fundamental formative force. Rather, they might be compared to weather systems (tornadoes, say) which do indeed preserve and reproduce themselves to some extent, but where this self-preserving character is simply a reflection of the more basic

458

physical forces that were responsible for their formation in the first place. This suggestion was implicit in a view, developed in explicit opposition to preformation, according to which inorganic matter has a fundamental power to organize itself into complex plants and animals, in much the same way as it organizes itself into complex crystal formations such as snowflakes. This view was generally presented as Newtonian in principle. While gravitational force alone was not sufficient for the production of organisms, other basic forces, analogous to gravity, could be invoked to account for the emergence of organic complexity. (For references see Ginsborg 2004: 45.)

These doubts, and the availability of alternative hypotheses not requiring appeal to natural teleology, suggest the need for a more direct response to the threat of contradiction. Kant seems to offer just such a response towards the end of §65 when he says that the concept of a natural end is, as he puts it, "not a constitutive concept of the understanding or of reason" but rather "a regulative concept for reflective judgment, for guiding research into objects of this kind according to a distant analogy with our causality according to ends" (§65, 5.375). This amounts to the claim that the use of the concept of a natural end in application to organisms plays a merely heuristic role, and does not carry the implication that organisms *are* produced according to design as well as being the result of purely natural causes. Rather, in thinking of organisms as natural ends we think of them only *as if* they were produced in accordance with design. However, this consideration is, again, insufficient to remove the worry. For, we might ask, how can we coherently regard an object as a product of design, while at the same time regarding it as natural? Even if this does not imply the objective assertion that the object both is, and is not, a product of design, it still seems to imply a parallel conflict in our reflective stance on the object. And the appeal to analogy is empty unless it can be specified, without reference to the idea of design, what feature it is we are ascribing to the object, or how we are regarding it, when we are regarding it as if designed. Otherwise there is no such thing as regarding something *as if* designed, without regarding it as *in fact* designed, in which case we again seem committed to regarding the object as having two contradictory features, and hence adopting an attitude towards it which is apparently incoherent.

II.

I turn now to the Dialectic of Teleological Judgment, in which Kant takes up, at considerable length, an issue which seems closely related to the worry we have just been discussing. He does this by presenting an "antinomy" between two principles of reflective judgment which seem to contradict each other. The first principle, or thesis, states that "all production of material things and their forms must be judged as possible according to merely mechanical laws." The second principle, or antithesis, states that "some products of material nature cannot be judged as possible according to merely mechanical laws (the judging of them requires a quite different law of causality, namely that of final causes)" (§70, 5.387).

Kant's argument in the Dialectic is extremely hard to follow and has been the subject of much interpretative dispute, so my treatment of it will be brief and selective. I begin with a sketch of the main points. Immediately after introducing the two principles at

HANNAH GINSBORG

§70, Kant distinguishes them from a parallel pair of principles that are constitutive rather than regulative and belong to determining rather than reflective judgment. The constitutive principle which parallels the thesis of the antinomy is the principle that "all production of material things is possible according to merely mechanical laws" whereas the constitutive principle which parallels the antithesis is the principle that "some production of them [material things] is not possible according to merely mechanical laws" (5.387). The apparent implication in this and the following section (§71) is that the solution to the antinomy will lie in distinguishing the principles of the antinomy itself from these constitutive principles. When we see clearly that the principles belong only to reflective and not to determining judgment, that is, that they play only a heuristic role in our understanding of organisms, rather than making an objective assertion about how those organisms came to be, then we will see that the seeming contradiction is merely illusory.

To a large extent this implication is borne out in the continuation of the discussion. In §§72–3 Kant considers and rejects a number of metaphysical views about the origin of organisms to which philosophers have been led by adopting one or other of the constitutive principles: the Epicurean view on which they are due to blind chance; the Spinozistic view on which their existence follows by necessity from the nature of an original being; the "hylozoistic" view on which they are due to "living matter" (that is to say, matter endowed with animal life, which involves consciousness and desire); and finally the theistic view which ascribes them to divine intention. The error in defending these views seems to be just that which is, in effect, warned against in §71: that of confusing regulative principles with constitutive principles. §74 connects the merely regulative nature of the principles in the antinomy (in particular of the antithesis) with a point already mentioned in connection with §65, that is, the merely regulative character of the concept of a natural purpose. In §75, Kant again emphasizes that our need to invoke teleology in order to understand certain objects in nature does not imply that such objects are in fact possible only through design, this time, however, introducing the idea that the principle of teleology holds for us because of the "peculiar constitution" of our cognitive faculties (5.397). The requirement that we view organisms as teleological is necessary for us as human beings, but we cannot presuppose that this requirement is "necessary for every thinking and cognizing being, thus that it attaches to the object and not just to our own subject" (5.399).

This last idea is developed in what most commentators regard as the heart of the argument, namely §77, where Kant describes in detail the "peculiarity of the human understanding, by means of which the concept of a natural end is possible for us" (5.405). Here Kant introduces a distinction between our understanding, which is "discursive," and a hypothetical "intuitive" understanding which (although Kant does not say so explicitly) might be attributed to God. The discursive nature of our understanding consists in the fact that we can cognize a particular thing only by means of general concepts, or "analytic universals," which pick out features it has in common with other things. An intuitive understanding, on the other hand, can cognize things through intellectual intuitions, or "synthetic universals," which represent them in all their concrete individuality. For a discursive understanding, the particular is contingent with respect to the universal under which it is subsumed, since we cannot deduce all the characteristics of a particular thing solely from the general concepts which apply

460

to it. But for an intuitive understanding, there is no contingency in the relation between the universal and the particular: an intellectual intuition determines everything which is to be known about the object it represents. Kant uses this distinction to argue that our need to regard organisms as ends stems from the discursive character of our intellect, and so should not be taken to imply that organisms are in fact possible only by virtue of teleological causality. We regard organisms as ends only because we take them to be contingent with respect to the universal laws governing nature, in particular the laws of motion which express the fundamental nature of matter. The laws of matter do not determine that the parts of matter have to form themselves into precisely those arrangements that are required for the functioning of a plant or animal, so in order to make sense of the way matter is organized in a plant or animal we have to think of its arrangement as determined by a concept of the plant or animal, that is, as designed. But an intuitive understanding would not recognize this contingency, and so would have no need to regard organisms in teleological terms. Though Kant does not put it this way, we might say that an intuitive understanding comprehends the nature of matter not through general laws, as we do, but by representing the totality of matter as a completely determinate whole. For such an understanding it is not contingent with respect to the nature of matter that it comes to be arranged in the particular ways that it does: rather, all the arrangements, including those characteristic of organisms, are represented *a priori* in the synthetic universal through which the nature of matter is grasped.

So far Kant's discussion has followed the general line announced in §70 and §71, that of showing the principles opposed in the antinomy to be merely regulative as opposed to constitutive. But in the final section of the Dialectic, §78, the discussion introduces what is apparently a new element in the solution. We can explain this new element by noting that, even after it has been shown that the principles are regulative, the question still arises of how we are to pursue them both: how, in other words, we are to respect the thesis of the antinomy by seeking a mechanical explanation of organisms while at the same time acknowledging that mechanical explanations are insufficient and that instead we need to appeal to final causes. Kant addresses this by claiming that we must "subordinate" the principle of mechanism to that of teleology (5.414). The assumption of teleology on its own is not sufficient for understanding organisms; we must also consider the means by which the assumed ends are to be achieved, and these means must be understood as operating mechanically. While it is not obvious from the Dialectic itself what is meant by the subordination of mechanism to teleology, the immediately following Methodology of Teleological Judgment offers two examples which seem to shed light on what Kant has in mind. In §80, whose title specifically invokes the "necessary subordination of the principle of mechanism to the teleological principle," Kant describes with approval the way in which some researchers pursue the mechanistic principle in accounting for the origin of species (possibly he has Buffon in mind). The procedure he describes is one of attempting to trace different species back to a common ancestor by appealing to analogies of form, showing for example how one kind of skeletal structure could have been derived from another through "the shortening of one part and the lengthening of another" (5.418). But he notes that while this kind of procedure might eventually trace the origin of animal species all the way down to polyps, and indeed to mosses and lichens, it can never

461

attempt to derive organic things from inorganic matter. Rather, explanations of this kind must always assume as their starting-point organized matter, and indeed where the organization is "purposively arranged" (5.419) for the creatures which are produced by it. A second example is offered in §81, where Kant criticizes the preformationist view of the origin of individual organisms on the ground that it ascribes organisms to a supernatural cause, thus failing to do justice to mechanism. Here again, though, Kant denies the possibility that organisms can be accounted for by appealing to inorganic matter: instead, he defends the view, which he ascribes to Blumenbach, that all explanation of the formation of plants and animals begins with "organized matter" endowed with an irreducibly teleological "formative drive" (*Bildungstrieb*) (5.424).

In sketching the Dialectic, I have implicitly taken a stand on two interpretative issues which I now want to confront explicitly. The first issue is that of what Kant means by mechanism in the context of the antinomy, and in particular, why he thinks that organisms cannot be mechanically explained. Most recent commentators follow McLaughlin in holding that mechanical explanation is explanation in terms of parts which do not themselves depend on the whole (1990: 152–3). On this view, organisms are mechanically inexplicable because of what we might call the "nonmachine-like" character ascribed to them in §§64–5, for example when Kant contrasts organisms with watches. What makes organisms mechanically inexplicable, in other words, is their self-maintaining and self-reproducing character. (Versions of this view are held by Zumbach 1984: 79–80, Allison 1991: 26–7 and 35, Zanetti 1993: 347, and Guyer 2001: 264–5 and 2003: 45; I endorsed it myself in Ginsborg 1997: 333.)

I now think this is a mistake. As I have argued in Ginsborg 2004, organisms are mechanically inexplicable, not in virtue of what distinguishes them from machines, but rather in virtue of what they have in common with machines (or at any rate, complex machines such as watches): they possess a regular structure, and display regularities in functioning, which cannot be accounted for in terms of the basic physical and chemical powers of matter alone. To say that something is mechanically inexplicable is to deny that it can be explained in terms of the powers of the matter from which it comes to be, and this is true no less of watches than of organisms. Matter left to its own devices will no more spontaneously organize itself into a watch than it will into a caterpillar or a blade of grass. While it is important for Kant that organisms do indeed differ from machines in having a self-maintaining and self-reproducing character, this difference does not figure in his reasons for denying that they can be mechanically explained. On the contrary, as will become clearer at the end of this section, it allows us to see them as "mechanically explicable" in the qualified sense which Kant allows to organisms in contrast to artefacts: that is, by appeal to a kind of mechanism which is subordinated to teleology.

The second issue bears on the question of how, precisely, the antinomy is supposed to be resolved. McLaughlin criticizes a long line of distinguished commentators, including Hegel, Adickes, and Ernst Cassirer, for holding that the antinomy rests solely on a confusion of regulative with constitutive principles (1990: ch. 3). The most important difficulty for this view, which was pointed out by Hegel as an objection to Kant, is that, even when construed as regulative principles, the thesis and antithesis seem to contradict each other: the thesis implies that organisms must be judged as possible in accordance with mechanical laws, whereas the antithesis implies that they cannot be

(1990: 140ff). McLaughlin proposes instead that the contradiction is resolved by denying that we must be capable of explaining organisms. As he puts it: "[if] the presupposition that everything (all objects of experience) must be explainable for our mechanistic-reductionistic understanding is dispensed with, then the antinomy dissolves and both maxims can be true" (1990: 162).

Now I think that McLaughlin is right to emphasize that the principles contradict one another even when understood as regulative. But I draw a different conclusion with respect to the interpretation of Kant's argument, namely that the resolution to the antinomy requires a further step (on this point I agree with Quarfood 2004: 191, although my understanding of the second step differs from his). In addition to showing that the principles are regulative, so that they do not imply any contradiction from the point of view of an intuitive understanding, Kant must also show how they can be reconciled from the point of view of a discursive understanding applying these principles within the context of scientific enquiry. This second step, which begins in §78, invokes the "subordination" of mechanism to teleology. Specifically, we accord with the mechanical principle insofar as we explain the origin of organisms by appeal to the intrinsic powers of the "matter" out of which they come to be. But, as the examples at §§80–1 make clear, the matter to which we appeal is organized matter endowed with the kind of formative power which makes possible an organism's capacities of self-maintenance and reproduction, as described in §§64–5. And the possibility of this kind of matter is intelligible only on the assumption that it is teleologically directed towards the production of the organisms which it makes possible. In effect, then, this second step completes the resolution of the antinomy by allowing two different, although related, senses of mechanical explanation. On the narrower sense, on which the mechanical explanation of a thing involves accounting for its existence in terms of the fundamental powers of inorganic matter, organisms are indeed (as McLaughlin's view implies) inexplicable by us. But they can still be mechanically explained in a weaker sense which does not exclude teleology, namely in terms of the powers of organized matter.

III.

Does the argument of the Dialectic take us any further in addressing the worry left unresolved in section I, namely that the concept of a natural end involves a contradiction? As I have interpreted the Dialectic, its resolution of the antinomy between mechanism and teleology has two components. The first is the argument that the principles of the antinomy are merely regulative. The second is the appeal to the subordination of mechanism to teleology. But both of these components correspond to elements we already identified in the Analytic. Kant's argument for the regulative character of the principles of the antinomy can be seen as an extended defense of the view, expressed briefly at §65, that the concept of a natural purpose is regulative rather than constitutive. And his discussion of the subordination of mechanism to teleology, at least when understood in the light of the examples he gives in §§80–1, is of a piece with his discussion of the self-causing character of organisms in §§64–5: in both sets of passages he is expressing his commitment to a view of organisms, or of organized matter, as endowed with irreducible powers for self-development, self-maintenance and self-propagation.

If this reading is correct, then the Dialectic does not in fact get us any closer to the heart of the worry than the considerations raised in the Analytic. However successful Kant's argument for the regulative character of the principles of the antinomy, it does not resolve the question of how we can coherently adopt both of these principles in our scientific practice, and relatedly, how we can coherently regard an organism both as an end, and as a natural product. Nor is the question resolved by ascribing irreducible formative powers either to organisms themselves, or to "organized matter," for the question still arises of how we can take these powers both to be natural, and to be purposively directed. The fundamental difficulty remains of how to make sense of organisms in terms of natural teleology, given that the very idea of teleology or goal-directedness seems to assume the idea of production in accordance with design, which in turn seems to rule out the idea of production by natural causes.

In the remainder of this chapter, I want to suggest a solution to this difficulty which, while not offered by Kant in the Critique of Teleological Judgment itself, can, I think, be pieced together from the *Critique of Judgment* as a whole. The heart of the solution is an idea which I have argued for in Ginsborg 1997: that the notion of an end or purpose (*Zweck*), and the cognate notion of purposiveness (*Zweckmäßigkeit*), are essentially tied to the notion of normativity, and only incidentally to the notion of production by design. To regard something as an end is, in essence, to regard it as conforming to, and a fortiori as governed by, normative rules or constraints. This means that we can regard something as an end, without regarding it as in fact a product of design, simply by regarding its structure and behavior as governed by, normative constraints, but without taking those constraints to be represented in the mind of a designer. We regard the object, that is, as having (or failing to have) the structure it ought to have, and as behaving (or failing to behave) the way it ought to behave, but without any assumption that it was intended to be structured, or to behave, in those ways. This idea, if accepted, allows us to escape the threatened contradiction in the idea of a natural end because it separates the notion of an end from that of a particular causal history. It is not essential to something's being an end that its production be the result of intention. All that is essential is that it be governed by normative constraints, and that is compatible with its being the product of natural processes rather than design.

Here one might worry that, even if there is no direct contradiction in regarding a naturally produced object as governed by normative constraints, it is still unclear how we could be entitled to do so. Surely, it might be protested, natural objects and processes merely *are* or *happen*: how can we regard something both as natural, and as manifesting (or failing to manifest) how it *ought* to be, or what *ought* to happen? The answer to this question relies on a second idea, having to do with the need to recognize normativity in the natural psychological processes responsible for perception and empirical judgment. I take Kant to hold that, in order for empirical cognition to be possible, we must be able to regard the relation between our cognitive faculties on the one hand, and the objects presented to our senses on the other, not only as natural, but also as normative. We must be able to regard the sensory and imaginative responses which those objects elicit not only as natural psychological events, but as governed by normative rules, so that we can think of those responses as not merely caused by the objects, but also as appropriate to them. This is a condition of the responses qualifying as conceptual, and in particular as informed by empirical concepts. For concepts are, or signify, rules for the synthesis of imagination, and if we cannot regard our imaginative activity in response to objects as normatively constrained with respect to those objects, then we cannot regard it as rule-governed. Thus the possibility of empirical cognition, and more specifically experience, depends on the possibility of our taking the natural psychological processes involved in arriving at empirical judgments to be, at the same time, governed by normative constraints (see Ginsborg 1997a: sections II–III, and Ginsborg forthcoming).

If this second idea is accepted, it points the way to what we might call a "transcendental" legitimation for regarding nature in normative terms (see also chapter 8 above). We are entitled to regard nature in normative terms because we *must* do so if empirical cognition, and more specifically experience, is to be possible. Now this is not, of course, to say that we must apply normative notions to those aspects of nature that are not directly involved in the acquisition of empirical cognition. The requirement to regard nature in normative terms is limited to the natural psychological processes involved in cognition, and their relation to the objects which affect our senses. So it does not immediately license the application of normative notions to natural objects and processes over and above those involved in empirical cognition. In particular, it is not sufficient on its own to license our regarding specific objects in nature – notably plants and animals – as governed by normative constraints independently of their relation to our cognitive capacities. What it does do, however, is to remove what otherwise seems to be a conceptual obstacle to regarding plants and animals in normative terms: namely the thought that this is incompatible with regarding them as natural products rather than artefacts. It thus leaves the way open to a conception of organisms as displaying natural normativity, which in turn amounts – granted the first of the two ideas – to a conception of organisms as natural ends.

The solution I am proposing obviously requires more defense than I can provide here, but I take it to derive at least some textual basis from an important passage in section VI of the First Introduction (20.195–251), where Kant links the a priori principle of the faculty of judgment – that is, the principle of nature's (subjective) purposiveness for judgment – to the ascription of (objective) purposiveness to organisms. Kant points out that this principle

> by no means extends so far as to imply the production of natural forms that are purposive in themselves [but] because we already have a ground for ascribing to nature in its particular laws a principle of purposiveness, it is still possible and permitted, if experience shows us purposive forms in its products, to ascribe these to the same ground on which the first rests. (20.218)

Because we have this principle, as Kant goes on to put it, "ready in judgment," it is "permissible for us to apply such a special concept as that of purposiveness to nature and its lawfulness," and in particular to "natural forms which may be found in experience" (20.218). In other words, our entitlement to regard particular natural things as purposive, and hence as natural ends, derives from a more general principle belonging to the faculty of judgment, namely that of the purposiveness of nature for judgment.

While this principle alone does not imply that there are any natural ends, it does allow us to apply the concept of purposiveness, and thus the concept of an end, to natural objects which are revealed by experience as suiting that concept – that is, as we saw in section I, to plants and animals.

Whether this passage supports my proposal depends on how we understand the principle of nature's purposiveness to which Kant is referring, and this raises large and controversial issues. Kant often glosses the principle as that of the systematicity of laws and concepts under which natural phenomena can be subsumed, so that the principle of nature's purposiveness for judgment, or for our cognitive faculties, is the principle that we are capable of arriving at systematic scientific theories in which natural laws and concepts are hierarchically ordered. (See also chapter 26 above.) If we understand the principle in this way, then it is not a condition of the possibility of cognition, but simply of higher-order scientific theorizing. In that case, the key move that Kant is making in the passage is to link our entitlement to regard natural objects as ends, with the demands of scientific theorizing. We might, then, understand him as saying that scientific theorizing requires us to regard nature in general as if it were designed for the sake of our theorizing activities, and that this in turn entitles us to think of particular natural objects as if they were, themselves, products of design. But for the reasons explained in sections I and II above, I do not think that this gets to the heart of the philosophical difficulty involved in the idea of regarding something both as natural, and as a product of design.

There is, however, another way of understanding the principle of nature's purposiveness for judgment, on which the passage can be read as supporting the proposal I have offered, and hence, I would argue, as providing a deeper and more satisfying answer to the question of how natural teleology is possible. This way of understanding the principle is suggested by a number of passages, most importantly in section V of the First Introduction, in which Kant seems to regard the principle as a condition, not just of scientific theorizing, but of empirical cognition more generally. So understood, it implies not just that empirical laws and concepts are systematizable, but that nature is empirically conceptualizable *überhaupt*: that, as Kant puts it, "for all things in nature, empirically determinate concepts can be found" (5.211). If, as I have suggested, the possibility of bringing natural objects under empirical concepts depends on our being able to think of the cognitive activity elicited in us by those objects in normative terms, then the principle of nature's purposiveness for judgment amounts, in effect, to the principle that the relation between nature and our cognitive faculties is a normative one. In other words, it is the principle that the perceptual and imaginative activity with which we respond to nature outside of us, while itself a part of nature broadly construed, can also be regarded as *appropriate* (and, on occasion, *inappropriate*) to the natural objects which elicit it through their effects on our sense-organs. If the principle of nature's purposiveness for judgment is understood in this way, then we can read the passage as defending the legitimacy of natural teleology along the lines I have suggested. The idea of nature's purposiveness for judgment is the idea of a normative fit between nature outside of us, and the natural psychological processes through which we perceive and conceptualize it. It is ultimately our need to recognize this relation of normative fit which underwrites our entitlement to regard natural objects – now considered independently of these perceptual and cognitive processes – in normative terms.

I want to conclude by noting a contrast between the line of thought I have ascribed to Kant in this section, and a line of thought which has recently been defended by some naturalistic philosophers of mind, in particular Dretske (1995: ch. 1) and Millikan (1993: Introduction). This recent line of thought appeals to natural teleology, in particular biological teleology, to account for the representational or intentional character of mind. Our mental states count as representing, in the sense of being *about* or *of*, objects and properties external to us, in virtue of the fact that the perceptual and cognitive systems responsible for them have been designed, by natural selection, to respond to those objects and properties in certain specific ways. What is noteworthy about this line of thought for our purposes is that it takes natural teleology to be more secure than the representational character of the mind, and more specifically, the mind's capacity for empirical cognition. The capacity, not merely to respond to objects, but also to represent them – a capacity which is tied, at least by Millikan, to the possibility of misrepresenting them and hence to the existence of normative constraints governing their representation – is explained by appeal to a more general notion of natural teleology, or design in nature, which applies to all living things. For Kant, by contrast, the relation between natural teleology and the possibility of empirical cognition is the reverse. Kant takes as fundamental our capacity for empirical cognition, and derives from this our entitlement to regard nature in teleological terms. We are entitled, as a condition of the possibility of empirical cognition, to take our mental activity to be governed by normative constraints; and it is this entitlement which ultimately licenses our use of the notion of design in a biological context.

One might be tempted to suppose that this difference is due to the fact that Kant was writing before the development of the theory of evolution by natural selection. Unlike present-day naturalistic philosophers of mind, he did not have available to him a plausible account of how nature could work as a designer; so, if he was to defend the use of natural teleology, he had to find another source for our entitlement to think of nature in the normative terms which natural teleology seems to require. The theory of natural selection, it might thus be thought, removes the motivation for the kind of account which Kant proposes, and instead makes available the reverse strategy: that of explaining the normativity of cognition in biological terms.

But this, I think, would be to mistake the kind of problem which concerns Kant when he raises the question of how we are entitled to regard things as natural purposes: it would offer an empirical answer to what is, in effect, a conceptual problem. While the theory of evolution by natural selection certainly does constitute a conceptual advance, in that it allows us to understand how natural processes, unaided by conscious design, could have been responsible for the kind of complexity of organization that we see in plants and animals, it does so by providing an empirical hypothesis about how this complexity came about as a matter of historical fact. More specifically, it explains the various traits contributing to the organization of present-day organisms in terms of their causal influence on the capacity of previous organisms to survive and reproduce. However, the empirical fact that an organism displays such-and-such a trait because that trait increased its ancestors' capacity to produce offspring, does not on its own entitle us to think of the animal as *designed* to have that trait, or more specifically, to claim that it *ought* to have it. For that entitlement, according to Kant, is not simply an empirical matter.

467

> A teleological judgment compares the concept of a product of nature as it is, with one of what it *ought to be* . . . But to think of a product of nature that there is something which it *ought to be* . . . presupposes a principle which could not be drawn from experience (which teaches only what things are). (First Introduction, 20.240)

Since, according to Kant, we are in possession of the required principle, we are indeed entitled to think of natural things in normative terms. Moreover, there is nothing in Kant's view that would prevent us, once this entitlement is granted, from using the theory of natural selection to help us determine *which* are the norms governing the structure and behavior of this or that organism. What the theory of natural selection cannot do, however, is entitle us to think of nature in normative terms *überhaupt*: that is, to bridge the conceptual gap between a view of natural things and processes as simply *being* this or that way, and the view that some of these ways are ways in which they *ought* to be. As I see it, the question of how this gap is to be bridged is at the heart of the *Critique of Judgment* as a whole. And, to come finally to the issue adverted to in the title of this chapter, the philosophical significance of Kant's biological teleology lies primarily in the way it helps bring that question into focus.

Acknowledgments

I am grateful to Graham Bird and Peter McLaughlin for helpful comments. I also wish to acknowledge the support of the American Council of Learned Societies and the Max Planck Institute for the History of Science.

References and Further Reading

Allison, Henry (1991). Kant's antinomy of teleological judgment. *Southern Journal of Philosophy*, 30 (Supplement): 25–42.

Dretske, Fred (1995). *Naturalizing the Mind*. Cambridge, MA: MIT Press.

Ginsborg, Hannah (1997). Kant on aesthetic and biological purposiveness. In *Reclaiming the History of Ethics: Essays for John Rawls* (pp. 329–60), eds. Andrews Reath, Barbara Herman, and Christine Korsgaard. Cambridge: Cambridge University Press.

Ginsborg, Hannah (1997a). Lawfulness without a law. *Philosophical Topics*, 25(1): 37–81.

Ginsborg, Hannah (2001). Kant on understanding organisms as natural purposes. In *Kant and the Sciences* (pp. 231–58), ed. Eric Watkins. Oxford: Oxford University Press.

Ginsborg, Hannah (2004). Two kinds of mechanical inexplicability in Kant and Aristotle. *Journal of the History of Philosophy*, 42(1): 33–65.

Ginsborg, Hannah (forthcoming). Thinking the particular as contained under the universal. In *Aesthetics and Cognition in Kant's Critical Philosophy*, ed. Rebecca Kukla. Cambridge: Cambridge University Press.

Guyer, Paul (2001). Organisms and the unity of science. In *Kant and the Sciences* (pp. 259–81), ed. Eric Watkins. Oxford: Oxford University Press.

Guyer, Paul (2003). Kant's principles of reflecting judgment. In *Kant's Critique of the Power of Judgment: Critical Essays*. Lanham, MD: Rowman and Littlefield.

McLaughlin, Peter (1990). *Kant's Critique of Teleology in Biological Explanation*. Lewiston, NY: Edwin Mellen Press.

Millikan, Ruth Garrett (1993). *White Queen Psychology and Other Essays for Alice*. Cambridge, MA: MIT Press.

Quarfood, Marcel (2004). *Transcendental Idealism and the Organism*. Stockholm: Almqvist & Wiksell International.

Zanetti, Véronique (1993). Die Antinomie der teleologischen Urteilskraft. *Kant-Studien*, 83: 341–55.

Zumbach, Clark (1984). *The Transcendent Science*. The Hague: Martinus Nijhoff.

Part V

Kant's Influence

30

Hegel's Critique of Kant: An Overview

SALLY SEDGWICK

My title suggests that there is a single Hegelian critique of Kant, even though Hegel's discussions of Kant's various doctrines seem to indicate a wide variety of complaints. At least at first glance, there is no discernible connection between, for example, his critique of Kant's account of moral motivation and his claim that Kant failed to provide a satisfactory deduction of the categories of pure understanding. Nor is it obvious that Hegel's charge that the categorical imperative is an "empty formalism" shares anything in common with his objection to the question-begging nature of Kant's treatment of the antinomies. My reference to a (single) critique of Kant is in part a concession to economy. In so short a chapter, I cannot but do injustice to what is distinctive about Hegel's separate treatments of Kant's various doctrines. But I also believe that there is unity in the diversity – that underlying Hegel's apparently disconnected criticisms is a dissatisfaction with Kant's philosophical orientation overall, with his account of the conditions of philosophical reflection and what it can achieve, and with his commitment to a particular understanding of the activity we are engaged in when we perform critique.

My chief objective in this chapter is to cast Hegel's critique of Kant in a charitable light, and in doing so to identify points on which he and Kant substantively disagree. Commentators not uncommonly assume that Hegel directs this complaint at Kant's account of the role played, in our knowledge, by sensible affection and the a priori forms of intuition through which we are sensibly affected. They claim that Hegel discovers subjectivity in Kant's idealism only because he misunderstands the implications of Kant's restriction of human knowledge to objects given via our forms of intuition. I present this interpretation of Hegel's critique in section I and then go on, in section II, to suggest an alternative to it. The reading I defend in the remaining sections of the chapter redirects our focus. I argue that, for Hegel, the subjectivity of Kant's idealism has to do not with Kant's views about our reliance on sensible affection and on the a priori forms space and time, but with his account of the nature of human thought.

I.

Let's begin by considering some typical passages in which Hegel complains of the "subjectivity" of Kant's idealism. In his 1830 *Encyclopedia Logic* (*EL*), for example, he tells us that the

> Kantian objectivity of thinking is . . . only subjective insofar as, according to Kant, thoughts, although universal and necessary determinations, are *only our* thoughts and separated [*unterschieden*] by an unbridgeable gulf from what the thing is *in itself.* (EL, §41z2)

In his 1801 essay, "The Difference Between Fichte's and Schelling's System of Philosophy," he writes that the Kantian views nature from the limited standpoint of a "discursive human understanding," and that this "human perspective" is supposed to express nothing about the "reality of nature . . ." (1977a: 163; 1968: 69).

Not surprisingly, commentators rush to Kant's defense in response to these kinds of remarks. Kant does, of course, deny human cognition knowledge of things in themselves, but this does not mean that he denies us knowledge of "reality." For Kant, these commentators remind us, things in themselves are precisely those objects that *cannot* have reality for us. Things in themselves are not possible objects of our experience, according to Kant; they cannot be, for us, empirically real. They are not possible objects of our experience because, on his account, they are not given to us via our forms of intuition, space and time. For Kant, only objects that can be given to us in space and time are possible objects of our experience and as such possible objects of empirical knowledge. He calls these objects "appearances." He does not mean by "appearances" the empirically ideal (secondary or sensible) properties of things, the merely accidental effects of objects impinging upon our sense organs (*CPR*, A 29). In limiting our knowledge to appearances, then, Kant is not claiming that the objects we know are somehow less than real or mere illusions. (See also chapter 31 below.)

Critics thus charge that Hegel's interpretation of Kant as a subjective idealist is mistaken. Hegel's mistake, in essence, is to equate Kantian idealism with empirical idealism. Given this mistake, they argue, his interpretation of Kant does not merit serious consideration. Some critics take their attack on Hegel a step further. They react no more favorably to what they suppose is his proposed alternative to Kant. They take his insistence upon the knowability of things in themselves to imply that, in his view, our theoretical or scientific knowledge extends even to those objects, such as God, immortality, and freedom of the will, that transcend the limits of space and time. It is as if Hegel is convinced that dropping the intuitive constraint Kant places on the scope of our knowledge counts as an instance of philosophical progress. But if we drop the intuitive constraint, these Kantians point out, we essentially revive the dogmatic rationalist view that knowing an object is merely a matter of thinking it, of analyzing its concept. We reduce the conditions of knowability or "real possibility" to the conditions of mere thinkability or "logical possibility" (*CPR*, B xxvi [a]). We abandon the important Kantian distinction between objects of knowledge and objects of faith. If this is what Hegel has in mind in claiming for human cognition the capacity to know the "absolute" his alternative to Kant should be rejected.

At least on the face of it this reading of Hegel is not wholly groundless. The passages we considered above seem to support it, as do some of Hegel's further discussions of Kant's philosophy. A good case in point is his expression of admiration for Kant's idea of an intuitive mode of understanding. Kant's discussions of the intuitive intellect are intended to remind us of the limited nature of our cognitive powers. Our form of understanding, on his account, is not "intuitive" but rather "discursive" and "dependent" (*CPR*, B 72). In our efforts to know nature, we depend on being sensibly affected by an independently given manifold. For this reason, we are not entitled to claim, merely from the exercise of our capacity to think, that our concepts refer to anything real. Our concepts refer to real objects only if they apply to what is given in space and time, to appearances. The intuitive intellect, however, has the capacity to produce its objects merely by exercising its cognitive powers. In contrast to our mode of understanding, the intuitive intellect can therefore justifiably claim to be in immediate cognitive contact with its objects. What is for it logically possible is also really possible. As Kant notes in the *Critique of Judgment*, the intuitive intellect has no objects except actual ones (*CJ*, §76, 5.402; also *CPR*. B 139).

There can be no doubt that Hegel was intrigued by this intuitive model of cognition. In his 1802–3 essay, "Faith and Knowledge," he expresses his impatience with Kant's insistence upon the fact that, for our discursive understanding, the "universal and particular are inevitably and necessarily distinct," and that what must remain "transcendent" for us is "rational knowledge [*Vernunfterkenntniß*] for which . . . the universal and the particular are identical" (1968: 341f; 1977b: 89f). He criticizes Kant for denying us the powers of the intuitive intellect and for regarding discursivity as the "absolute fixed unsurpassable finitude of human reason" (1968: 333; 1977b: 77). Moreover, his fascination with the intuitive model is not only evident in his early Jena writings. He praises the idea of the intuitive intellect in his more mature works as well – for instance, in his 1813 *Science of Logic* (see the section "The Notion in General").

Critics derive from passages such as these the message that Hegel seeks to award human cognition God-like creative powers. Given that he seems to hold that the intuitive model captures the nature of our form of cognition, it must be the case, they argue, that he rejects Kant's account of the sense in which human understanding is dependent. He must be committed to the view, in other words, that we know objects without having to rely on the condition of sensible affection, since we are able to produce them simply by engaging in acts of representation.

The above, in rough outline, represents a typical reading of Hegel's critique of, and alternative to, the subjective idealism he discovers in Kant. Beginning in section II, I tell a very different story. In rejecting Kant's claim that we cannot know things in themselves, in charging that, for Kant, our knowledge of objects is "merely subjective," Hegel no doubt means to express his disapproval of the skeptical conclusions he takes to be implied by Kant's Critical philosophy. What I will argue, however, is that the skepticism he seeks to avoid is not, in his view, a consequence of Kant's insistence that, in our efforts to know, we have to rely on the impingements of an independently given sense content and on a priori forms of intuition. Hegel does not, in other words, take the subjectivity of Kant's idealism to follow from what has come to be referred to as Kant's restriction thesis. Instead, his objections are directed at Kant's account of the nature of our faculty of thought.

II.

To support this thesis I begin with a reconsideration of Hegel's interest in the idea of an intuitive intellect. He clearly holds that the intuitive intellect captures features that may be justifiably attributed to human cognition. But why is he convinced that this is so? If Hegel is not out to award us the capacity to bring the objects of our cognition into being, if he does not deny that in knowing nature we have to rely on an independently given sense content, what is it about the model of an intuitive understanding that accurately captures in his view the nature of our mode of cognition?

Hegel's early Jena writings contain his most informative reflections on this topic. In "Faith and Knowledge" he calls our attention to various features Kant associates with the intuitive intellect, relying on Kant's discussions especially in §§76 and 77 of the third *Critique*. For our purposes, one feature is of particular interest. Quoting from §77 (5.406), Hegel singles out Kant's claim that, for the intuitive intellect, there is no "contingency" in its "agreement" with "nature's products" (1968: 340; 1977b: 88). This passage is important because, as I shall argue, Hegel's critique of the subjectivity of Kant's idealism is essentially an attack on Kant's assumption that there *is* contingency in the relation of our discursive understanding to "nature's products."

What kind of contingency does Kant have in mind? In the above-mentioned sections of the Critique of Teleological Judgment, Kant in fact identifies *two* kinds of contingency with which our discursive intellect must contend. First, for our discursive form of understanding, he says, "the variety of ways in which [the given particulars] may come before our perception is contingent" (*CJ*, §77, 5.406; translations from Kant 1929, 1987, 1996, 1998). This contingency, in his view, is a consequence of the fact that a nonintuitive or discursive understanding must, in its efforts to know nature, rely on sensible affection. Its objects are not derived from or produced out of its concepts; rather, they are given to it in sensation. In Kant's words, the concepts of a discursive understanding do not "determine" anything regarding "the diversity of the particular" (*CJ*, §77, 5.407).

Kant is also convinced, however, that from this contingency in the way in which sensible intuitions "may come before our perception" follows another: namely, the contingency he refers to in the passage Hegel quotes. This is the contingency in the *relation* between "nature's products" (or "the particular in nature's diversity") and the "intellect." Since our mode of understanding lacks the intuitive intellect's power to give the existence of the object "through itself," Kant argues, it is not only incapable of determining the way in which the manifold presents itself to us in sensation; it can also cognize that independently given manifold only by means of concepts or universals (*CJ*, §77, 5.407). We must subsume sensible particulars under concepts, and we do this by dividing nature into species and genera. Since we cannot, however, determine how particulars may be given, we have no way of knowing that our classifications are in keeping with "nature's products." The fact that "our understanding has to proceed from the universal to the particular" thus has the "following consequence" according to Kant: "In terms of the universal [supplied by the understanding] the particular, as such, contains something contingent" (*CJ*, §76, 5.404). For the intellect that is intuitive, however, and "does not (by means of concepts) proceed from the universal to the particular . . . there would not be that contingency in the way nature's products . . . harmonize with the understanding" (*CJ*, §77, 5.406).

This is the skeptical gap Hegel is worried about, this gap that Kant discovers in the relation between our concepts and "nature's products." As Hegel puts it in the "Difference" essay, Kant derives from his reflections on the nature of human discursivity the conclusion that, for us, "concepts remain contingent with respect to nature just as nature does with respect to the concepts" (1968: 70; 1977a: 164). As we have just seen, Kant's view is that there is contingency not just in how sensible particulars are given; he is also convinced that it follows from the fact that we have to rely on an independently given content, that there is contingency in the relation between our concepts and that content. We can express the basis of Hegel's objection as follows: he finds unpersuasive this inference from the first form of contingency to the second.

Note that the thesis about the first form of contingency is one that even the Lockean realist could grant. It merely asserts that, in our efforts to know nature, we think about a sense content we do not make. But, again, Kant derives from this fact about our reliance on an independently given sense content the conclusion that any supposed harmony between our concepts and the given particulars has to remain, for us, a mere idea. Locke would not go along with this conclusion, and neither does Hegel.

I have been suggesting that, for Hegel, closing the gap between our concepts and nature's products is not a matter of rejecting Kant's view about our dependence, in cognition, on sensible affection. Hegel nowhere asserts, in opposition to Kant, that our understanding has the power to produce matter or content from its acts of representation. He does not attribute to our understanding, then, literally all of the cognitive powers of the intuitive intellect. What fascinates him about the intuitive intellect is the fact that it experiences no contingency in the relation of its representations to their objects. Hegel resists Kant's claim that a harmony between concepts and sensible particulars is unavailable to the experience of a discursive understanding such as ours. He is unconvinced by Kant's insistence that it follows from the fact that we must bring concepts to our cognition of an independently given sense content, that we have to conclude contingency in the relation between our concepts and that content. He urges us to raise the following kinds of questions: Why should it follow from our employment of concepts in our cognitions of an independently given sense content that we have no warrant in taking that content to be susceptible to our conceptual determinations? On what account of the faculty of thought and its forms does this inference depend – on what account of the subject doing the thinking?

III.

Relying on passages in which Hegel conveys his interest in the intuitive model of cognition, I have so far offered an interpretative suggestion as to how we should understand his charge that Kant's idealism is subjective. This charge, as I have portrayed it, does not call into question the assumption that we have to rely in cognition on an independently given sense content, nor does it call into question the Kantian thesis that the given sense content must appear to us via the a priori forms, space and time. Instead, Hegel's charge is directed at Kant's account of our faculty of thought. I turn now to provide further evidence in support of this interpretation. One piece of evidence is provided in the Introduction to Hegel's 1807 *Phenomenology*. This is an early work, but the themes I highlight are not unique to it. They reappear in some of Hegel's later writings as well, including his 1831 Preface to the *Science of Logic*, published in the final year of his life.

In the Introduction to the *Phenomenology* (PH), Hegel is once again preoccupied with the thesis of the unknowability of things. By "things," in this context, he means that content we suppose to be "on the other side" of cognition (*PH*, para. 74). He refers to this content in these paragraphs, alternatively, as: the "thing itself," "the true," "the absolute," "the in itself," "the absolute essence." He sets out to explain how it happens that the thesis of the unknowability of things comes to seem forced upon us. It seems forced upon us, he suggests, because of our commitment to a mistaken view about the nature of thought. Hegel tells us that the mistaken view he has in mind is held by "natural" consciousness. He mentions no philosopher by name in these pages, but there are indications in his discussion here and elsewhere that he includes Kant among those taken in by this mistaken conception (see, e.g., the 1831 Preface to his *Science of Logic*, and the section on Kant in his *Lectures on the History of Philosophy*).

The aim of natural consciousness, as Hegel characterizes it in these paragraphs, is to employ thought in the service of getting at the truth of things. Hegel never calls this aim into question; indeed, he seems to think it is the one thing natural consciousness gets right. What interests him, rather, is the assumption that prevents natural consciousness from achieving its aim. He tells us that the assumption in question is that thought is a "means" (*Mittel*).

On Hegel's account, natural consciousness takes thought to be a means in either of two ways. For some, he says, thought is a *tool* or *instrument* (*Werkzeug*) "by which to seize hold of the absolute essence." For others, thought is a *passive medium* (*passives Medium*) "which the light of truth passes through in order to reach us" (*PH*, para. 73). The problem with both of these versions of thought as a means, he suggests, is that neither in the end serves natural consciousness in achieving its aim. The aim of ordinary consciousness is to employ thought to get at the truth of things. If thought is an active instrument, however, thought reshapes or alters the thing; it does not let the thing be what it is for itself. If thought is a passive medium, on the other hand, our cognitive access to objects cannot be direct or immediate; we know objects, on this account, only through the medium.

Hegel goes on to argue that natural consciousness fares no better in achieving its aim by adopting the following strategy: by first informing itself about the rules or laws (*Wirkungsweise*) that govern the very functioning of the means. Here the hope is that once we are familiar with the nature of thought itself and with the concepts it contributes in the act of knowing, we will then be in a position to subtract (*abziehen*) that contribution away and thereby lay bare the thing itself. In Hegel's view, however, this strategy is equally unsuccessful in satisfying the aim of natural consciousness. Natural consciousness seeks knowledge of things. It is committed to the view that we only gain knowledge of things by employing thought as a means. It thus defeats its own purposes by subtracting away precisely what it deems to be its mode of access to things.

In a not so veiled reference to Kant, Hegel considers a possible response to this failure of natural consciousness to achieve its aim. Simply put, the response urges us to modify our ambitions. Rather than persist in the futile effort to know things, we should instead adopt the more modest project of acquainting ourselves with the subjective forms we put into them. The recommendation is that we undergo a kind of "Copernican revolution" in what we judge to be the proper objects of our knowledge. We are to redirect our attention away from the effort to know things and undertake instead an examination or critique of our cognitive faculties (*PH*, para. 73).

Hegel has no objection to the general effort to know the nature and limits of our cognitive powers. He is, however, suspicious of the motivation for critique in this particular case. In this case, critique begins where the effort to satisfy the aim of natural consciousness leaves off. It begins, that is, with an admission of defeat; it grants that the aim of natural consciousness cannot be satisfied. It does not consider the possibility that this skeptical result is based on a mistake. It fails to notice that, as Hegel puts it in the first paragraph of his Introduction, what is really "absurd" is that we employ thought as a means at all.

IV.

To summarize the main points of our discussion so far: I have been arguing that, when Hegel protests against the thesis of the unknowability of things, he puts the blame not on our reliance on sensible affection or on the a priori forms through which we are sensibly affected, but on the status we award thought in our cognitions of objects. On his account, it is only because Kant adheres to a mistaken view of the nature and role of thought that he discovers an inescapable contingency in the relation of our concepts to given particulars. I furthermore suggested that Hegel believes a mistaken conception of the nature and role of thought is to blame for Kant's decision to abandon the ambition of natural consciousness. It is what moves Kant to urge us to substitute for the effort to know things, the task of determining the subjective forms we put into them. It is why Kant tells us in the B-Preface to the first *Critique* that we are better off, in our attempt to secure certain material knowledge, if we give up the hope of establishing that our concepts conform to objects, and devote our efforts instead to demonstrating the necessary conformity of objects to our concepts (*CPR*, B xvii).

But even if I am right to suggest that what steers Kant off in the wrong direction is a mistaken conception of thought, in Hegel's view, we still do not know what that mistaken conception is. The label Hegel gives it, namely that thought is a "means," is not terribly illuminating. Hegel presumably intends to give us a clue when, in his Introduction to the *Phenomenology*, he tells us that there is a problem with what natural consciousness takes "for granted." It takes for granted, he says, that the "absolute" is "on one side" and thought or cognition (*das Erkennen*) is "on the other" (*PH*, para. 74). In his discussion of these issues in his Introduction to the *Science of Logic*, he repeats this diagnosis. There he writes that the problem is that natural consciousness assumes that "matter" and "form" occupy "separate spheres." These remarks should strike us as familiar. They are further formulations of the charge we encountered earlier when we reviewed his criticisms of Kant in the Jena writings. In the passages we considered, Hegel's objection was that, on Kant's understanding of the implications of our discursivity, the universal and the particular have to remain distinct. In these various discussions, Hegel's target is the same: he calls into question Kant's commitment to the dualism or heterogeneity of concepts and intuitions. But we still do not know precisely what he has in mind when he complains that, for Kant, thought is "on the other side" of content and inhabits a "separate sphere."

We can get some help if we probe more deeply into his account of how the mistaken conception of thought is responsible for additional features of Kant's philosophy. My

479

focus in section V will be passages in which Hegel voices his doubts about Kant's general philosophical methodology, the methodology he discusses under the heading of Kant's project of "critique." We have already seen that, on Hegel's reading, Kant's turn to critique is itself a consequence of the mistaken conception. The decision to trade the effort to know objects for the investigation of the contributions of the subject is motivated, he thinks, by Kant's acceptance of the following line of reasoning on the part of natural consciousness: that since thought is a means, we are not in the end entitled to our claims to know things. What I am now suggesting is that Hegel believes the mistaken conception also underlies Kant's expectations regarding what the project of critique can deliver. That is, Hegel seems convinced that at the basis of Kant's understanding of the kind of knowledge we can hope to get from critique are mistaken assumptions about, for example, the conditions of reflection, the degree of abstraction we can achieve as knowers, and the origin of our fundamental thought-forms or categories.

Our discussion of Hegel's attack on Kant's methodology will yield the following, perhaps unexpected, result: it will suggest that, far from rejecting Kant's claim that human cognition is a dependent form of cognition, Hegel is persuaded that Kant does not take this thesis about the dependent nature of human understanding far enough. It is not just that, in our efforts to know nature, we have to rely on an independently given sense content. Hegel believes it is also the case that human thought is *not* "on the other side of" content. By this he seems to mean that thought is incapable of the degree of autonomy or independence Kant awards it.

V.

When Kant uses the term "critique," it is usually with reference to his task in the *Critique of Pure Reason* of exposing the natural tendency of human reason to exceed its proper limits, to claim to know objects that lie outside the bounds of possible experience (*CPR*, A xii, B 763). It is by means of critique, he says, that we establish the "rules and limits" of reason's proper employment (A xvi). Kant recognizes, however, that we cannot successfully carry out a critique of pure reason without undertaking a more comprehensive investigation of our faculties of knowledge. The role and nature of pure reason needs to be carefully distinguished, for instance, from that of understanding and sensibility. Our critique of reason thus necessarily involves us in the larger enterprise of determining the nature of our various faculties and their respective roles. Since the role of our faculties will vary depending on the realm of inquiry in which they are engaged, our investigation will furthermore have to take into account the boundaries separating one domain of inquiry from another. We will arrive at different conclusions regarding the nature of pure reason, for example, depending on whether we are assessing its role for theoretical or for practical inquiry. From the standpoint of theoretical knowledge, reason's employment is quite limited, on Kant's account, since its objects are not strictly speaking possible objects of our experience. But if we turn our attention to the domains of faith or morality, we discover that the objects or ideas of pure reason have an extended and positive use.

Critique aims to discover the *subjective* conditions of a given realm of inquiry, conditions that reflect the employment of our faculties. But the subjective contributions

Kant is chiefly concerned to specify are of a particular kind: they are non-empirical or "a priori." A result of critique, then, is that we learn to identify reason's a priori ideas and maxims; we learn that the faculty of understanding is the source of a priori concepts or categories; and we discover that we intuit objects by means of the a priori forms, space and time. As a priori, these subjective conditions are more than merely contingently related to the form of inquiry they condition. They function as universal and necessary constraints on that domain of inquiry.

A further feature of critique is that it is carried out at a higher level of abstraction than any particular scientific investigation. This is because critique seeks to identify what we might refer to as the a priori framework or form of a science. Its objects, then, are not (directly) physical bodies in motion, divine nature, or the human will, but rather the a priori conditions of the possibility of the domains of physics, faith and morality. This is why Kant describes his objective in the *Critique of Pure Reason*, for example, as that of illuminating the "internal structure" of the science of metaphysics. Critique, he tells us, is a "treatise on method, not a system of the science itself" (B xxii ff.).

I mentioned in section IV that Hegel has reservations about Kant's methodological assumptions. I also said that these reservations are instructive in so far as they shed light on his charge that Kant is committed to a mistaken conception of thought. Hegel's reservations about Kant's methodology reveal themselves in his remarks on Kant's project of critique. He does not have kind words for the project of critique as I have just described it. In effect, he believes that critique rests on a certain illusion – an illusion about the nature of thought. In the section of the *Science of Logic* entitled "With What Must the Science Begin?," he writes: "[T]o want the nature of cognition clarified prior to the science is to demand that it be considered outside the science . . ." This, he notes, is something that cannot be accomplished. Hegel repeats this point in his *Encyclopedia Logic*. The "investigation of cognition cannot take place in any other way than cognitively," he says (*EL*, §10). It is thus a "mistake" to want to "have cognition before having any cognition . . ." (*EL*, §41 A1). Note that Hegel is not claiming in these passages that *any* effort to investigate our cognitive powers is ill-conceived. His point, rather, is that critique is impossible if we assume we can carry it out "prior to" or "outside" some particular form of inquiry or science. When he tells us that the "investigation of cognition cannot take place in any other way than cognitively," he seems to imply that our meta-investigations into the conditions of the possibility of a particular science invariably reflect, in some way, the actual practices and presuppositions of that science. What is incoherent or impossible, then, is not the attempt to abstract to the conditions of the possibility of a particular domain of inquiry, but the assumption that we are able to do so from a vantage point that is completely independent of, and so completely unaffected by, actual scientific practice.

But what evidence is there that Kantian critique is an instance of the effort to investigate cognition prior to having cognition, to know before we know? To answer this question, we need to consider more closely Kant's procedure for isolating the "internal structure" or a priori conditions of a given domain of inquiry. In rough outline, his strategy is this: He begins with some claim or set of claims he believes he has a right to take for granted – claims at least tacitly affirmed even by his chief philosophical opponent. So in the project to determine the internal structure or necessary conditions of theoretical knowledge, for example, he begins with an assumption he believes even

Hume cannot doubt: namely, the fact that we are conscious not just of having sensations in succession but also of perceiving or experiencing objects. His next step is to regress from this fact to the a priori conditions of its possibility. In the course of doing so, he takes himself to establish: first, that experience for us would not be possible without the reproducibility of impressions; second, that reproducibility is not itself given in sensation but is a product of the application to sensation of a priori rules or concepts; and third, that the application of a priori concepts presupposes the synthesizing activity of a transcendental subject identical through time.

The general features of this methodology are at work in Kant's practical philosophy as well. In a remark in his Preface to the *Groundwork*, he once again starts out by specifying an assumption he believes he is entitled to take for granted. He writes:

> Everyone must grant, that a law, if it is to hold morally, that is, as a ground of obligation, must carry with it absolute necessity; that, for example, the command, "thou shalt not lie," does not hold only for human beings, as if other rational beings did not have to heed it, and so with all other moral laws properly so called. (*G*, 4.389)

Regressing to the conditions of the possibility of this assumption, he then tells us he is warranted in claiming that

> therefore, the ground of obligation . . . must not be sought in the nature of the human being or in the circumstances of the world in which he is placed, but a priori simply in concepts of pure reason . . . (*G*, 4.389)

At what point in this procedure does Hegel discover evidence of fallacy or illusion? As is clear from his many discussions of the problem of making a beginning in philosophy, he believes that the suspicious step is the first one, the step in which Kant claims to identify assumptions "everyone must grant." Kant is not entitled to this claim, in Hegel's view, because it rests on a too generous estimation of our powers of abstraction. In effect, Kant awards himself powers of abstraction that no thinker has.

We can clarify Hegel's grounds for suspicion by considering this question: On what basis does Kant consider himself capable of identifying assumptions "everyone must grant"? One thing he assumes is that he is able to draw a clear boundary between the merely contingent assumptions commonly associated with a given domain of inquiry and the assumptions essential to it. He is confident that he can draw this boundary *with certainty*, because he is also convinced that he has the capacity to engage in special acts of reflection. He is convinced, in other words, that he can abstract to the universal and necessary conditions of the possibility of a particular science by engaging in a form of thinking that itself escapes the influence of particular scientific practices or philosophical objectives. He believes, then, that his performance of critique is uncompromised by presuppositions that may themselves turn out to be merely contingent. Critique, for him, is a form of inquiry free of the constraints of history.

Hegel's aim is to persuade us that this kind of critical exercise cannot be carried out. Critique of this nature cannot be carried out, in his view, for the reasons just mentioned: it overestimates the abstractive powers of human thought. Hegel's charge is not just that Kant failed to live up to the high standards of critique, failed to sufficiently scrutinize or make explicit his most fundamental presuppositions. Hegel directs this charge at Kant, but it is not his deepest criticism. The more serious error committed by Kant (and others) is that of supposing that the high standards of critique are standards human reason can meet. As far as Hegel is concerned, we deceive ourselves if we expect that, in undertaking critique, we achieve our starting point by liberating ourselves from assumptions that tie our thinking to some particular point in time, to what he refers to in the *Phenomenology* as some particular "shape [*Gestalt*] of consciousness" (*PH*, para. 87). This is the illusion of supposing that we can initiate critique from a place "outside" or "prior to" actual scientific and philosophical practice. As Hegel is fond of remarking, thought, rather than "on the other side" of content, is concrete from the start (*EL*, §55). Even our metareflections on the conditions of the possibility of a particular form of inquiry proceed from within and are therefore indebted to some shape of consciousness. Moreover, Hegel takes it to follow from the fact that we perform critique from within that our starting point is not one of perfect self-knowledge. The most basic assumptions that guide our critical investigations are not available to us via introspection; they are too close for us to see. Kant is mistaken, then, when he writes that, "what reason produces entirely out of itself cannot be concealed, but is brought to light by reason itself . . ." (*CPR*, A xx). We know or become aware of the most basic assumptions that guide our inquiries, Hegel suggests, only when they cease to serve their foundational function. We know a limit only when we are beyond it (*EL*, §60).

VI.

There is a real question whether Kant is in fact warranted in his claims to have articulated, via critique, the universal and necessary rules and principles governing our various forms of inquiry. It would be of great interest to know, once and for all, whether critique is capable of the degree of abstraction he awards it, and whether it is indeed possible for us to know before we know. I have not set out to settle these issues here, nor have I tried to defend Hegel's alternative vision of the conditions of reflection and of what critique can achieve. Instead, my aim has been to suggest the essential idea behind Hegel's critique of Kant. I have argued that his complaint about the "subjectivity" of Kant's idealism is not directed at Kant's thesis that human cognition is dependent, in its cognitions of nature, on an independent sense content given to us through forms of intuition. Rather, the subjectivity of Kant's idealism follows, for Hegel, from an overestimation of the abstractive powers of human thought. Hegel's worry (revealed, for instance, in his critique of the thesis that thought is a means) is that as long as we conceive of thought in this way, as on "the other side" of content, we have to live with the result that there can be for a discursive understanding such as ours no harmony between given sensible particulars and the concepts we employ in thinking and knowing them.

The account I have provided demystifies, at least to some extent, Hegel's more specific complaints about Kant's particular doctrines. There is a common theme running through his objections to, for example, Kant's derivation of the categories, his account in the Analogies of Experience of the nature of substance, his theory of human freedom, his formulation of the supreme practical law or categorical imperative. In Hegel's discussions of these various topics, he singles out Kant's "formalism" for attack. In each case, as I have been arguing, his complaint ultimately calls into question Kant's methodology, Kant's understanding of the conditions of philosophical reflection and of the vantage point he is able to achieve as the philosopher engaged in critique. Underlying Kant's claims to have articulated the formal or a priori principles without which we would have no experience of objects, the formal rules which govern the synthesis of intuitions, the formal law conditioning the possibility of imputations of moral responsibility, is in each case the presupposition that he has successfully purged his own reflections of everything contingent and empirical. He assumes, in addition, that his critical starting point is one of perfect self-knowledge.

The strategy Hegel enlists in exposing the illusion of this self-conception, and in deflating the pretensions of formalism, is always the same. In his discussions of the above topics, he draws our attention to assumptions that escape Kant's critical scrutiny. These are the questions Kant begs, the "content" he "presupposes" (the Newtonian context, for example, that frames his account of the nature of space and time, and the form of empiricism responsible for his conviction that we cannot derive laws of freedom from nature). Hegel's point is not the easily refutable one that Kant was entirely unaware of his intellectual inheritance. His point, rather, is that Kant *could* not have been sufficiently aware of the extent to which that inheritance shaped his very understanding of the problems he needed to solve and of the available options for solving them. The reason Hegel undertakes the exercise of exposing the assumptions that tie Kant's investigations to a particular moment in history is to impress upon us the general lesson that in *every* act of reflection questions are begged. "Every beginning," he writes, "is a presupposition" (*EL*, §1). The evidence he cites in support of this claim is simply inductive; he thinks its truth is revealed in any careful study of the history of ideas. What the evidence suggests so far, then, is that human thinking is *not* capable of acts of pure or unfettered spontaneity. Instead, thought owes a debt to the realm of the actual. This is another way of expressing the point with which we concluded section IV, namely, that the lesson Hegel wishes us to derive from his critique of Kant is that thought does not have the degree of independence Kant awards it.

References

Hegel, G. W. F. (1968–). *Gesammelte Werke* [*Collected Works*], eds. Hartmut Buchner and Otto Pöggler. Hamburg: Felix Meiner Verlag.

Hegel, G. W. F. (1977a). *The Difference between Fichte's and Schelling's System of Philosophy*, eds. and tr. Walter Cerf and H. S. Harris. Albany: State University of New York Press.

Hegel, G. W. F. (1977b). *Faith and Knowledge*, eds. and tr. Walter Cerf and H. S. Harris. Albany: State University of New York Press.

Hegel, G. W. F. (1989). *Hegel's Science of Logic*, ed. and tr. A. V. Miller. Atlantic Highlands, NJ: Humanities Press International.

Hegel, G. W. F. (1991). *The Encyclopaedia Logic: Part I of the Encyclopaedia of Philosophical Sciences with the Zusätze*, eds. and tr. T. F. Geraets, W. A. Suchting, and H. S. Harris. Indianapolis/Cambridge: Hackett Publishing.

Hegel, G. W. F. (2005). *Phenomenology of Spirit*, ed. and tr. Terry Pinkard. Cambridge: Cambridge University Press.

Kant, Immanuel (1929). *Critique of Pure Reason*, tr. Norman Kemp Smith. New York: St. Martin's Press.

Kant, Immanuel (1987). *Critique of Judgment*, tr. Werner S. Pluhar. Indianapolis/Cambridge: Hackett Publishing.

Kant, Immanuel (1996). *Practical Philosophy, Groundwork of the Metaphysics of Morals. The Cambridge Edition of the Works of Immanuel Kant*, ed. and tr. Mary J. Gregor. Cambridge: Cambridge University Press.

Kant, Immanuel (1998). *Critique of Pure Reason. The Cambridge Edition of the Works of Immanuel Kant*, ed. and tr. Paul Guyer and Allen W. Wood. Cambridge: Cambridge University Press.

Further Reading

Beiser, F. C., ed. (1993). *The Cambridge Companion to Hegel*. Cambridge: Cambridge University Press.

Bristow, W. (2002). Are Kant's categories subjective? *Review of Metaphysics*, 55(3): 551–80.

Forster, M. (2002). *Hegel and Skepticism*. Cambridge, MA: Harvard University Press.

Pinkard, T. (1994). *Hegel's Phenomenology: The Sociality of Reason*. Cambridge: Cambridge University Press.

Pippin, R. (1989). *Hegel's Idealism: The Satisfactions of Self-Consciousness*. Cambridge: Cambridge University Press.

Sedgwick, S., ed. (2000). *The Reception of Kant's Critical Philosophy: Fichte, Schelling, and Hegel*. Cambridge: Cambridge University Press.

31

The Neglected Alternative:
Trendelenburg, Fischer, and Kant

GRAHAM BIRD

The debate between Adolf Trendelenburg and Kuno Fischer was the most striking dispute among neo-Kantian German philosophers towards the end of the nineteenth century. During the decade 1860–70 the two engaged in a vigorous, not to say vituperative, polemic about issues of Kant interpretation and more generally about Trendelenburg's hostility to Hegel and to Fischer's Hegelianism. The quarrel seems to have arisen initially over Trendelenburg's comment that when Fischer confronted traditional idealism, "the most difficult problem that has ever engaged the Kantian epoch," he did not resolve the issue but only "mangled" it. Trendelenburg quoted and dismissed the following passage from Fischer:

> The proposition "Thought is" contains no pure being but the being of active thought and nothing else; and from the self knowledge "I am" to the universal assertion "I am being" is a jump in one bound from subject to object. . . . Thought declares its origin: I am being; and what thought says of itself is at the same time a universal concept, i.e. a declaration of the constitution of the world. (Quoted in Köhnke 1991: 171–2, from Trendelenburg's *Logical Investigations*)

The passage is unrepresentative of Fischer's usually plain and blunt style, but Trendelenburg was surely right to have serious reservations about this example.

The disagreement was pursued in Trendelenburg's *Logical Investigations* (2nd ed., 1865), *On a Gap in Kant's Proof of the Exclusive Subjectivity of Space and Time* (1867), and *Fischer and His Kant* (1869). Fischer offered his accounts of Kant in the *System of Logic and Metaphysics* (1865), and a four-volume *History of Modern Philosophy* (1860–7) and responded directly to Trendelenburg in the polemical *Anti-Trendelenburg* (1870). The debate focused on the interpretation of the *Critique of Pure Reason*, especially the argument in the Transcendental Aesthetic, but it ramified in many directions. It involved disputes about Kant's view of mathematics and his solution to the antinomies, both of which were associated with paradoxes arising from the infinity of space and time. Trendelenburg referred to the problem as "a monster untamed by myth or [Kantian] metaphysics," but Fischer believed that Kant's transcendental idealist therapy worked.

The dispute exhibited a level of acrimony which later commentators, such as Bratuschek (1870) and Vaihinger (1871) attempted to defuse. Although Fischer seems generally to have been criticized for the tone of the dispute Trendelenburg undoubtedly fueled the hostility with his patronizing title *Fischer and His Kant* and its cover motto from Terence "Veritas Odium Parit" (truth generates hatred). The disagreement has historical importance in its relation to the neo-Kantians and its two, "Marburg" and "South Western," schools of Kant interpretation, but I shall say nothing further of that historical development, or the polemical tone, or the wider issues of Hegelianism.

I consider only the central point in the dispute about the alleged gap in Kant's argument in the Transcendental Aesthetic about the "subjectivity" of space and time. That issue has more than historical significance, and represents even now a division among Kant commentators about the understanding of "transcendental idealism." Disagreements between Paul Guyer (1987) and Henry Allison (1983) over the substantive issues in the debate reflect again the disagreement between Trendelenburg and Fischer (see also chapters 7 and 9 above). In section 1 I outline the central points in the dispute about the Aesthetic, in section 2 I resolve the disagreement over Kant's *position*, and in section 3 consider the further issue of the alleged fallacy in Kant's *argument*. Despite the fact that most commentators, from Vaihinger to Guyer, have sided with Trendelenburg, I shall argue that Fischer was right.

1. Central Issues in the Historical Dispute

The central core of the dispute arises from Trendelenburg's criticism that Kant's argument in the Aesthetic has an alleged, and fundamental, "gap" – the neglected alternative. The criticism implies that a central inference in the Aesthetic about the character of space and time is a fallacy which undermines not only the Aesthetic but the whole Critical position. Fischer, by contrast, called the Aesthetic "a paradigm of scientific precision and method," and his response was to deny that there *is* any such gap, or that Kant *had* neglected the relevant alternative.

Trendelenburg's criticism has two related aspects: First the claim that Kant simply failed to *notice* the neglected alternative; and second that that failure *invalidates* the central inference in the Aesthetic to the exclusive "subjectivity" or "ideality" of space and time. Both criticisms are captured in the claim that while Kant successfully proved the "subjectivity/ideality" of space and time he failed to establish that they were *not* also, *could* not also be, "objective/real." The objection is that Kant wrongly *assumed* that if space and time were "subjective" then they *could not* also be "objective"; that "subjective" and "objective" strictly *excluded* each other. Kant consequently equivocated in his conclusion between saying that space and time were "subjective" and saying that they were "*exclusively* (or only) subjective." According to Trendelenburg Kant had established their "subjectivity" but not their "*exclusive* subjectivity." He had failed to notice that it was possible to be both subjective and objective at the same time, to be subjective but not *exclusively* subjective. Fischer's position by contrast was that Trendelenburg had failed properly to understand Kant's position and that Kant *had* noted and made room for the neglected alternative. According to Fischer Kant had argued quite properly from subjectivity to nonobjectivity *provided* that these terms were adequately understood.

That issue about Kant's unthinking assumptions and the consequent validity of the central inference in the Aesthetic involves three ambiguous contrasts (A) between Kant's *position* and the *arguments* for it; (B) between "subjective" and "objective," and (C) between "appearance" and "thing in itself."

(A) There is an ambiguity between Kant's *overlooking* an alternative in his *position*, and a consequent fallacious *inference* in his *arguments* for that position. The initial question is *whether* Kant noted the neglected alternative, but Trendelenburg's basic objection concerned the adequacy of the *inference* and *argument* supporting Kant's conclusions. The two points are connected but different. If Kant's position overlooked a relevant possibility in his argument, then any *inference* which requires it will be fallacious. If Kant did not overlook it, then the inference may still be fallacious in other ways, but at least it won't be vulnerable to *that* fallacy.

(B) There is perennial philosophical confusion over the terms "subjective" and "objective." They may be used to contrast, inter alia, what is *personal* (belongs to a subject) as opposed to what is *impersonal* (does not belong to a subject); or what is *mental* (inner) as opposed to what is *physical* (outer); or what is assessable as *publicly true/false* (matter of fact) as opposed to what is not so assessable (matter of *opinion/conjecture*).

(C) Finally there is a related unclarity about the "objects," appearances, or things in themselves for Kant, which space and time are variously supposed to belong to or not to belong to. This is inevitably related to (B) since it concerns the issue of Kant's "idealism" and the question whether (or in what sense) appearances are "subjective" and things in themselves "objective." Trendelenburg insisted that Kant held a strict, exclusive, opposition between "subjective" and "objective," but Fischer denied this.

2. Resolving Issues over Kant's Position

I first consider the issue in (A) whether Kant's position *did* overlook Trendelenburg's alternative, and how the two disputants interpreted Kant's conceptions of the "subjectivity" or "objectivity" of space and time in (B) and (C). This will enable me to provide an initial verdict about which of the disputants distorts, or more accurately represents, Kant's *actual* view. This won't end the discussion since it leaves out the further question, in (A), whether that view is properly *argued for*, or justified. Further clarification of the *inferences* in the Aesthetic and the character of Kant's "subjective" idealism will be considered in (3). The first question, then, is: How did Trendelenburg understand the neglected alternative?

Trendelenburg accepted that in the Aesthetic the inferences from space and time's "being a priori and intuitive" to their "being subjective" were *valid*, but he denied that this ruled out the possibility that what was a priori and intuitive might *also* be objective. He thought Kant wrongly *assumed* the step from "subjective" to "not objective" because it seemed obvious to him that what belonged (subjectively) to appearances could not also belong (objectively) to things in themselves. One natural way to understand such a position would be to regard appearances as subjective mental states, representations, and things in themselves as the real objects which those states represent. In those terms the objection would be that Kant both accepts a traditional subjective idealism, and commits himself to a resulting skepticism about our knowledge of real, outer, objects. Such a position gives traditional idealism's priority to inner representations, goes on to question an inference from those representations to an independent world, and then disallows genuine knowledge of such independent real things in themselves.

Trendelenburg commits himself to just such a view of Kant. He ascribes to Kant a sharp, exclusive, distinction between subjective *appearances* and objective *things in themselves*, associates the former with inner mental states and the latter with real objects. He consequently criticizes Kant's position for providing knowledge only of *ourselves*, of our minds, of what is subjective, and not of what we *want* to know, namely real things, that is, things as they really are in themselves.

> The central point in all knowledge is to reach the thing as it (really) is: We want the *thing*, not *us*; [according to Kant] we search for *things* but succeed only in capturing *ourselves*. This is a modesty which reduces science to beggary. (Trendelenburg 1865: 161; author's translations from Trendelenburg and Fischer throughout)

The knowledge Kant *licenses* is, according to Trendelenburg, only a second-best characterization of ourselves and our mental condition, while the hoped-for genuine knowledge of real things (in themselves), apart from ourselves and our minds, is beyond us and illusory. It is easy to see how such a position can be interpreted as a basic version of traditional idealism, perhaps even of Berkeley's idealism, with a consequent skepticism about objects beyond, apart from, outside, our own minds and ideas.

It may seem initially puzzling that Trendelenburg canvasses the idea that "subjective" and "objective" might *not* be exclusive, but when this is spelled out in Kantian terms the puzzle is partly resolved. For the issue is whether space and time (or spatiotemporal properties) belong *subjectively* to appearances (*Erscheinungen*) or *objectively* to things in themselves (*Dinge an sich*). The claim is that Kant rightly argued that such properties belong to subjective appearances but wrongly took it for granted that this excluded their belonging to things as they really are (in themselves). In that way according to Trendelenburg Kant never (seriously) considered the possibility that space and time might (also) belong to real things in themselves, that is might be both subjective and objective. He thus committed a fallacy, and at the same time committed himself to a skepticism which denied us *genuine* spatiotemporal knowledge of real things. According to Trendelenburg despite Kant's *intentions* and his explicit denials Kant effectively turns "*Erscheinung*" (appearance) into "*Schein*" (illusion).

> Kant counters the claim that his ideality of space and time transforms the whole sensible world into illusion, but I'm considering not what Kant *intended* but what results even if it is against his wishes . . . The anxiety remains that appearance [*Erscheinung*] is illusion [*Schein*]. (Trendelenburg 1865: 158–9)

At two obvious points Trendelenburg is correct. Kant evidently *did* hold that space and time in our experience belong to *appearances* and not to *things in themselves*, and he *does* deny us any genuine knowledge of things in themselves. Things in themselves are precisely understood as transcendent objects beyond our experience, and consequently as irremediably "problematic" for us. But Trendelenburg ascribes to Kant two *additional* claims which are not obviously correct: First that the subjectivity of appearances excludes any genuine knowledge of real objects and so is committed to skepticism; second that Kant deploys a univocal "subjective/objective" distinction *only* in order to make the contrast between appearances and things in themselves. I think that *both* of those added claims are mistaken and that Fischer understood this.

I consider first the position of things in themselves and their possible, especially spatiotemporal, properties. The issue is controversial but I am concerned here only with Kant's *position*, not yet with the *arguments*, or *justification*, for it. The central, uncontroversial, background is that Kant certainly denies us any genuine knowledge of things in themselves, that is of things accessible by reason alone and without the benefit of sensibility. According to Kant it is a major part of the required Dialectical therapy to recognize that we *cannot* properly claim to know that such transcendent things exist with specific properties, or indeed that they do *not* exist or *lack* those properties (see also chapter 13 above).

The Dialectic's therapy *requires* this since typically its problems, such as the antinomies, are resolved precisely by considering the ascription of properties to such things in themselves only to insist that we have no knowledge of them that could settle the dispute. The resolution claims that the dispute between those who accept and those who deny that such things have property P is spurious. Since neither side has any legitimate title to its claims the dispute is unresolvable at ground-floor level. To echo Quine's expression there is in these disputes no "fact of the matter" as far as we are concerned. For Kant the resolution of those disputes must consequently occur at a higher level; indeed at that higher level of his own consciously self-monitoring philosophy which he calls "transcendental," as opposed to "empirical" (B 25, B 80–1) (see also chapter 8 above).

One immediate conclusion can be drawn from this background. Kant evidently does *not* regard the denial of any genuine knowledge of *things in themselves* as a ban on genuine knowledge of ordinary immanent *objects of experience*, whether of inner sense (such as thoughts) or outer sense (such as tables). Those objects of experience are precisely objects accessed through sensibility, and *not* through reason alone; they are appearances. Kant's classification of those objects of experience as appearances does not entail that they are purely inner, like thoughts as opposed to tables. Appearances are not opposed to outer, spatial, objects of experience but include them. Consequently to deny knowledge of *things in themselves* is not to deny knowledge of ordinary outer, spatial, objects. Kant *is* skeptical about our knowledge of transcendent things in themselves, but he is *not* skeptical about our knowledge of immanent spatiotemporal objects of experience such as outer appearances.

Trendelenburg's immediate objection at this point is that Kant failed seriously to *consider* the possibility that *space and time* might belong to transcendent things in themselves *as well as* belonging to appearances. Even if, as Kant insists, things in themselves can never be *known* to us, such a possibility exists and should be at least considered for the argument's validity. Even if space and time in our experience belong *only* to appearances, and even if we can never know things in themselves, that does not strictly *exclude* the possibility that space and time may belong to things in themselves outside our experience. Trendelenburg talks ambiguously of ascribing spatiotemporal properties to "things" rather than to "things in themselves," but there is no doubt that the neglected alternative, which he thinks Kant overlooked, *is* the possibility of *things in themselves* having spatiotemporal properties. The earlier passages from Trendelenburg 1865 express the view that genuine objective knowledge has to be of things in themselves.

That claim provides an immediate test for the correctness of Trendelenburg's position, and a passage from the Transcendental Deduction (B) shows that he is wrong.

> Space and time as conditions under which alone objects can possibly be given to us, are valid no further than for objects of the senses and therefore only for experience. Beyond these limits they represent nothing; for they are only in the senses and beyond them have no reality. . . . If we suppose an object of a non-sensible intuition to be given we can indeed represent it through all the predicates implied in the presupposition that it has none of the characteristics proper to sensible intuition; that it is not extended in space or in time . . . But there is no proper knowledge if I merely indicate what the intuition of an object is *not* without being able to say what *is* contained in the intuition. (B 148–9; *CPR* translations from Kant 1929)

Kant's position is that we can meaningfully *characterize* supersensible things in themselves but that such characterization provides no *knowledge*. We can meaningfully say or suppose that things to which we have no cognitive access have, or lack, spatiotemporal properties, but, in line with the Dialectic's strategy, there is no way, no "fact of the matter," in which we can *establish* either assertion or denial. But there is a reason to opt for the denial rather than the assertion, since spatiotemporality in our experience is essentially connected to *our sensible* intuition while things in themselves are subject to a different and unknown intuition. In the passage Kant evidently seriously *considers* whether things in themselves are, can be represented as, spatiotemporal, and, subject to the Dialectic's provisos, characterizes them on balance as nonspatiotemporal. Whatever we opt to say or refrain from saying in this context at least those options are present and *not* neglected in Kant's text. In *Anti-Trendelenburg* Fischer muddies the water at this point since he cites Kant's *pre-Critical* consideration of things in themselves as spatiotemporal. This unfortunately encourages Trendelenburg's polemical, but correct, response that the issue concerned the *Critique* and *not* the pre-Critical works. But Fischer could have cited B 148–9.

Paul Guyer (1987: 363) holds another view; not that Kant never considered the possibility but deliberately *rejected* it. He consequently draws the conclusion that Kant was inconsistent in deliberately *denying* that things in themselves were spatiotemporal at the same time as saying that we know nothing of them. This is somewhat unfair to Trendelenburg for whom "considered" seems to have meant "seriously considered," but it also fails to admit the background from B 148–9 and the Dialectic in which Kant allows meaningful reference to, but no genuine knowledge of, transcendent things in themselves or their properties. Kant's view is evidently that we *know* nothing of them but on balance it is more plausible to say that they cannot be spatiotemporal than that they can. Kant is like one who wants to reject the claim that the King of France is bald, and carefully prefers to say "It is not the case that the King of France is bald" ("It is not the case [so far as we can tell] that things in themselves are spatiotemporal") rather than "The King of France is not bald" ("Things in themselves are [known to be] not spatiotemporal").

491

Trendelenburg can now also be seen to be inaccurate in his second view that Kant regards the "subjective/objective" distinction as strictly exclusive. The point can be put as Fischer put it; namely that *vis-à-vis* things in themselves appearances are "subjective," but that *vis-à-vis* our experience appearances are, or can be, "objective."

> Space and time are subjective and ideal compared with things in themselves; [but] as properties of objects of possible experience they are thoroughly objective and real. By the standards of things in themselves our experience is "subjective," but such a standard is transcendent and out of our reach. By the immanent standards of possible experience our ascription of spatiotemporal properties to appearances is as objective as it can possibly be. (Fischer 1860–70: vol. III, §2, pp. 315–16)

What Fischer points to is the fact that Kant has here *two* standards, *two* conceptions, of "subjectivity/objectivity," and that this makes it a distortion to regard the contrast as univocal and exclusive. Trendelenburg's belief that Kant has one univocal, strictly exclusive, distinction between "subjective" and "objective" is mistaken. Once it is recognized that there are *two* distinctions at issue, then it is easy to see that to call something subjective (in one sense) is not necessarily to deny that it is objective (in another sense). Let me try to clarify the two senses for each term (see Bird 1962).

In one sense, for Kant, transcendently "real" objects are, or would be if they exist, "objective." They are conceived as totally independent of us and our sensory capacities and accessible only through reason. They exist and have their properties without any reference to our senses, and as a consequence their properties are, or would be, a posteriori but cannot be known by us. In *that* sense all other nontranscendently, i.e. empirically, real objects of our possible experience are "subjective." These, according to Kant, are dependent on our sensibility and understanding, have some a priori properties, and can be known by us. That can be called Kant's "transcendental" use of the distinction and labeled "subjective$_1$/objective$_1$."

In another sense *within* the scope of an immanent possible experience we can use the "subjective/objective" distinction to separate what is mental from what is physical or what is (empirically) inner (thoughts) from what is (empirically) outer (tables). In that sense the outer, spatial, objects of our possible experience are empirically "objective" but not transcendentally objective as things in themselves are outside our possible experience. If the first contrast, "subjective$_1$/objective$_1$," defines Kant's "transcendental" distinction, the second defines his "empirical," "subjective$_2$/objective$_2$," distinction. Together they define Kant's "transcendental" and "empirical" conceptions of "real" and "ideal" in his complex classification of the philosophical doctrines empirical/transcendental *idealism* and empirical/transcendental *realism*. If we identify the "real/ideal" and the "subjective/objective" distinctions, then Kant identifies two (empirical/transcendental) subjective kinds of "ideality" and two (empirical/transcendental) objective kinds of "reality." The two cases match the two different kinds of "subjectivity/objectivity" and "dependence/independence" noted in 1(B) above. They are explicitly distinguished by Kant at A 373–5.

In those terms it is easy to see that Kant's "subjective/objective" contrast is neither univocal nor exclusive. Something can be empirically "objective$_2$," i.e. spatially outer, and yet transcendentally "subjective$_1$," i.e. to do not with transcendent things in themselves but with immanent experience. Trendelenburg's central question whether Kant seriously considers, or just overlooks, the possibility that space and time may be both sub-jective and objective can, however, be definitively answered for *both* uses. Kant seriously considers whether space and time belong to appearances or to things in themselves; he thinks they belong objectively$_2$ to appearances but, so far as we can tell, not object-ively$_1$ to things in themselves. Space and time are empirically objective$_2$, (empirically real), but transcendentally subjective$_1$, (not transcendentally real). Whether we focus on transcendental or empirical objectivity Kant cannot be said to overlook or fail to consider these possibilities. On the contrary Kant's account demonstrably makes room for, and responds consistently to, all of them. In recognizing these points Fischer is undoubtedly a more accurate reporter of Kant's position than Trendelenburg.

3. Kant's Arguments for his Claims

Although Fischer in this way represents Kant's position more accurately than Trendelenburg, we have to ask how Trendelenburg could *fail* to recognize the dualities in Kant's realism and idealism, or, if he did recognize them, why he dismisses (or neglects) the empirical contrast in favor of the transcendental. Trendelenburg's insist-ence on the exclusive character of the "subjective/objective" distinction *would* have been correct if he had concentrated on either *one* of the two contrasts. If his inten-tion was to focus on the philosophically important transcendental contrast between objectivity$_1$/subjectivity$_1$ the consequence is that he then *neglects* the empirical contrast, and *confuses* the two contrasts. It is Trendelenburg, rather than Kant, who neglects a salient alternative in the issue.

It would be of no use for Trendelenburg to say that it is only the transcendental distinction which has philosophical significance. Kant's transcendental idealism and its opposition to transcendental realism undoubtedly are at the centre of Kant's *philo-sophical* view, but the acceptance of *empirical* realism and rejection of *empirical* idealism are an integral part of that same view. Transcendental idealism is part of a Kantian package which *includes* empirical realism and *excludes* empirical idealism.

Trendelenburg would do better to say not that empirical realism, for space, time and appearances, is irrelevant to Kant's philosophical theory, but that the theory needs an argument to establish that empirical realism. Trendelenburg undoubtedly took the basic philosophical issue to be the *justification* for empirical realism in relation to exter-nal objects, and denied that this was provided by its mere assertion. Fischer's view might accurately represent Kant's *acceptance* of the empirical reality of our possible (inner and outer) experience, but that provides no *justification* for it. Its mere assertion would seem to Trendelenburg simply to beg the question in the way in which appeals to common sense or ordinary language were said to beg the question in their attempt to refute skepticism. In this context the question-begging is more pointedly targeted at the traditional idealist challenge of proving the existence of an outer, independent, world on the basis of prior representations of it. Trendelenburg's demand for a justification of empirical realism is part of his noted background assumption of such a traditional idealist theory.

Consequently once we move from the bare assertion of Kant's *position* to the *argu-ment* for it Fischer's case may seem less convincing, and this may in turn explain why so many commentators, from 1870 to the present, have accepted Trendelenburg's criticism and rejected Fischer's account. They may share the same assumptions of a traditional idealist background as Trendelenburg. They may recognize that Fischer represents Kant's position more accurately than Trendelenburg, but take the view that the latter was right to indicate a gap in Kant's *argument* for his position. I want finally to explain why I believe that Fischer is still right and Trendelenburg wrong even about the argument for empirical realism.

I first consider more exactly how Trendelenburg's objection is articulated, and then how it can be answered with an account of the Aesthetic argument. Trendelenburg's disregard of the contrast between empirical and transcendental subjectivity and his understanding of Kant's Aesthetic argument can be formalized as follows:

1) Our knowledge has to do *either* with appearances, that is empirically inner, mental, representations *or* with real (independent) things as they are in themselves.
2) Space and time are shown in the Expositions to belong to the former, that is, to subjective appearances.
3) Consequently space and time do *not* belong to the latter. They are not "objective" but "subjective."

Premise (1) represents Trendelenburg's insistence that Kant draws an exclusive contrast between subjective appearances and objective things in themselves. (2) constitutes the conclusion from the Aesthetic arguments which Trendelenburg accepts as correct. (3) is Kant's alleged immediate, unthinking, but fallacious, inference from (1) and (2) which, according to Trendelenburg, Kant never seriously considered. Its unthinking obviousness is evidently a consequence of the *assumption* in (1) of the exclusive alternative which marks the "gap" in the argument. The earlier quotation from Trendelenburg's *Logical Investigations* represents his view that Kant is committed, despite his caveats, to a further skeptical conclusion:

4) Objective knowledge of real independent things (in themselves) is out of our reach.

The suggestion is that if Kant had taken seriously the "gap" in the argument, and had recognized that space and time could belong *both* to appearances *and* to things in themselves, then he might have avoided (4)'s unwelcome, skeptical, conclusion.

That formal outline serves to clarify the noted objections to Trendelenburg's case. Premise (1) distorts Kant's position in three related ways. First it fails to recognize Kant's complex *fourfold* distinctions between empirical/transcendental objectivity (reality)/subjectivity (ideality). Second as a consequence it fails to notice that *some* forms of subjectivity (e.g. subjectivity$_1$) are compatible with *some* forms of objectivity (e.g. objectivity$_2$). Third it distorts Kant's position by opposing subjectivity$_2$ to objectivity$_1$ in what is a cross classification of Kant's scheme. Properly subjectivity$_1$ should be contrasted only with objectivity$_1$, and subjectivity$_2$ only with objectivity$_2$. By disregarding the complexity of Kant's classification Trendelenburg ascribes to Kant a traditional idealism. He effectively treats the subjective/objective distinction as an unambiguous opposition of what is empirically inner, and mental, to what is transcendentally outer, and real. He ascribes to Kant a simple duality of mental "ideas" and independent

494

things in themselves beyond our possible experience. That unequivocal duality between subjective inner experience and outer, independent, things (in themselves) is the hallmark of a traditional idealism which immediately poses the skeptical challenge of justifying our belief in such independent objects. The position which Trendelenburg ascribes to Kant is that combination of "empirical idealism with transcendental realism," which Kant explicitly rejects in the Aesthetic and at A 369–74.

It will still, rightly, be said that this does not indicate any *justification* for Kant's acceptance of the empirical contrast within possible experience of the (empirical) reality of inner states (thoughts) and outer objects (tables). By the same token it does not outline any alternative structure for Kant's Aesthetic argument once Trendelenburg's is discarded. Trendelenburg concedes that Kant's argument in the Aesthetic establishes the "subjectivity" of space and time, but he evidently oversimplifies and misconstrues the nature of that subjectivity. If we correct that misunderstanding how should we understand the Aesthetic's argument? I think that answers can be given in the following résumé.

To be an *a priori* contribution to experience excludes its being given a posteriori. Such an a priori contribution cannot be simply there to be detected, noted, and re-corded as an a posteriori feature. Similarly to be a contribution of an *intuitive* kind is to be essentially connected to sensibility with its individuating/presenting role in experi-ence. Both features, being intuitive and being a priori, demonstrated of both space and time in the Metaphysical and Transcendental Expositions, indicate a contribution which *cannot* be independent of us as cognizers in the way that a posteriori features are. The two together further indicate that their dependence on us is due to their dependence on the character and role of our psychological, sensory, powers. The two characteristics point to a necessary reference to those powers, and more generally to the minds which exercise them.

These twin appeals, to the a priori and intuitive character of space and time, are the basis for their subjectivity$_1$/ideality$_1$ and the rejection of objectivity$_1$/reality$_1$, that is, a necessary reference to those mental powers in giving a philosophical account of the character of our experience. That *philosophical* account is not part of our ordinary beliefs, and does not express a subjectivity$_2$ of the kinds we commonly understand in relation to those ordinary beliefs. In particular it does not, as the above classifications make clear, mark the distinction we recognize *within* experience between inner, mental, thoughts and outer, physical, tables. That latter distinction reflects Kant's empirical contrast between objectivity$_2$ and subjectivity$_2$, and not the philosophical, transcen-dental, contrast between objectivity$_1$ and subjectivity$_1$. Kant's appeals to subjectivity and to our mental, specifically sensory, powers neither are, nor entail, a *restriction* of the content of our beliefs to inner mental representations, and in that respect they differ substantially from traditional idealism. The necessary reference to our mental powers in ideality$_1$ identifies a distinctive, limited, and residual form of idealism which Kant calls transcendental idealism.

In the light of that account consider the two outstanding inferences. Is Kant entitled to infer either of the following?:

i) That things in themselves are not spatiotemporal.
ii) That our claims to spatiotemporal knowledge in immanent experience are justified.

495

With regard to (i): I have argued already on Kant's behalf that, on balance and with the outlined reservations, things in themselves *cannot* be spatiotemporal on his account of things in themselves, their properties, and our knowledge of them. His position could be expressed by saying that it is not the case, so far as we can tell, that things in themselves are spatiotemporal, rather than that things in themselves are definitely, known to be, *not* spatiotemporal. Understood in these terms with the required provisos the contested inference is valid, and Kant's argument neither neglects a relevant alternative nor contains a fallacious gap.

With regard to (ii): Can Kant infer that empirical realism is philosophically justified; that space and time provide justifiably known properties of empirical, inner and outer, objects of experience, that is, appearances? Here it seems to me that this *cannot* be inferred merely from the demonstrated classification of space and time as a priori and intuitive with all its consequences in Kant's distinctive form of idealism.

The arguments in the Aesthetic's Expositions which justify the classification of space and time as intuitive and a priori, *presuppose* that we make those ascriptions and do not question their justification, but they do not *establish* that they are philosophically justified. Kant's argument entitles us to infer that space and time belong to appearances and not to things in themselves if they justifiably belong to anything; but without establishing that antecedent we know only negatively that they *cannot* properly be ascribed to things in themselves. We cannot infer from their not belonging to things in themselves that they justifiably belong to appearances, for they might justifiably belong to neither. If there *is* a philosophical skeptical issue about the truth of, or justification for, our empirical spatiotemporal claims, then the classification argument in the Aesthetic does not resolve it. In particular it does not answer a traditional idealist doubt about our justification for claims about outer, spatial, objects. The argument makes an assumption *implicit* in the project of correctly classifying space and time as intuitive and a priori, but that assumption itself is not separately proved or justified in the Aesthetic.

So it might be said that Trendelenburg was right to identify a gap in the argument, and that Kant does *not* after all refute skepticism about our knowledge of an external, independent, world in the Aesthetic. Trendelenburg is correct in saying that Kant provides no such refutation in the Aesthetic, but he is wrong to think that Kant needs or intends to do so in that argument. In the light of what has been already said Trendelenburg's claim is open to two immediate objections. First even if the argument is not successful against skepticism about the external world its failure is not the one Trendelenburg identified. Trendelenburg's objection was that Kant did not justify spatiotemporal claims about transcendent things in themselves, but this objection is that he did not provide a justification for belief in immanent outer objects of experience, that is appearances. Kant is resolutely skeptical about our knowledge of things in themselves, but he does not think that that doubt has any relevance to our empirical experience of outer, spatial, objects. Second this objection to Kant's position *assumes* that his goal in the Aesthetic argument is that traditional idealist justification of belief in an external world. That assumption was undoubtedly made by Trendelenburg and ascribed by him to Kant, but it should be questioned and rejected.

Fischer's contrary view shows the inaccuracy of Trendelenburg's account of the subjective/objective distinction, but so long as the assumption of traditional idealism is maintained it is very difficult, and perhaps impossible, to see how Kant's position can be understood. The outline argument for the Aesthetic given above, however, dispenses with that assumption and shows that in the Aesthetic Kant does not attempt to prove or justify our beliefs about an external world on an idealist basis. His primary aim is to classify space and time correctly as they figure in our immanent experience, and to establish on the basis of their intuitive and a priori character a nontraditional, residual, version of idealism which does not *require* such a proof.

That project is outlined in the Prefaces and in the Amphiboly (B 316–49). In the former Kant's primary target is the identification of those elements in immanent experience, *if any* as he says at A 95, which are a priori. The goal is to locate them and then to understand their origin and role in experience. In the latter passage Kant refers to a "transcendental topic" which aims to allocate the central concepts in our experience to their rightful places. It takes our experience, ordinary and scientific, as a *datum* in order to disentangle its structure and disclose the relations between its principal elements. The central task of the Aesthetic is to carry out such a transcendental topic for space and time which results in the complex classifications of empirical and transcendental idealism and realism. It is a descriptive, and not a traditionally normative or justificatory idealism. It provides instead a "category-discipline" which classifies its central elements according to their locations in sensibility and understanding, and their consequent roles in experience. Kant's own account of a transcendental topic sets aside, at least initially, the normative, skeptical, challenges of traditional idealism in order to provide a correct map of those central features of our immanent experience. It fulfills Kant's promise of a reformed philosophy which renounces "windy metaphysics" in favor of enquiry into "the fruitful bathos of experience (*Prol. Anhang*, 4.373).

Kant's belief is that an accurate map of the structure of experience will show that some traditional problems are misplaced. They will be shown to be based on a misunderstanding, a misallocation, of the places properly assigned to the central concepts in that structure. In particular the suggestion is that this is true of the errors in such a doctrine as traditional idealism. The category discipline of the Aesthetic is designed to indicate a proper form of idealism which has none of the unwelcome consequences of its traditional predecessor. The intuitive and a priori character of space and time discloses a contribution to our experience from the senses, from our minds, and deserves for that reason to be called a nontraditional form of idealism, but it casts no doubt on our beliefs about spatiotemporal objects of experience. The classification of space and time leads in this way to an understanding of what *is* residually true in idealism, and then shows that that residue is *compatible* with empirical realism and properly casts no genuine doubt on our beliefs about the empirical reality of objects in inner or outer sense.

Transcendental idealism, properly understood, captures that minimal and residual truth in traditional idealism. It does not *prove* or *justify* our belief in an immanent external world, but shows that the residual truth in idealism does not challenge those beliefs and requires no such justification. In the two Aesthetic passages at B 43–4 and B 52 where Kant insists on the empirical reality of space and time within his own theory he says not that he has *proved* their empirical reality, but that his theory "asserts" or "teaches" it. Kemp Smith's translation glosses B 43–4 as "Our exposition therefore *establishes* the reality of space . . ." (my emphasis), and so gives the impression that a proof has been given, but the translation is an error. The text says only that the exposition *teaches* the reality of space, and later that "We *assert* the empirical reality of space . . ." (my emphasis). Kant speaks in a similar way elsewhere of outer objects requiring no idealist inference and being "immediately given," and of the truth of empirical realism as "beyond question" (A 375). Where Trendelenburg assumes that Kant's empirical realism needs justification in the face of a commitment to *empirical* idealism, Fischer's more accurate account indicates, in line with these texts, that *transcendental* idealism does not require it.

A more pointed form of such a correction, which confirms this account, is Kant's second-edition afterthought in the Refutation of Idealism (Preface B xl note; B 274–9; see also chapter 12 above). The refutation argues that the correct allocation of priority to inner and outer experience reverses the traditional idealist priority of inner over outer experience. Whether Kant's proof is valid or not its evident aim is to correct the traditional misplacing of that priority. That consequent line of argument is not the same as, and indeed presupposes, the category discipline of the Aesthetic in which space and time are correctly mapped in their places as intuitive a priori forms of sensibility. It confirms the idea that the Aesthetic classification of space and time does not even *attempt* a philosophical justification of an external world. If the Aesthetic were thought to have provided such a justification why would it be necessary to give a further argument in the Refutation?

That account of the central propaedeutic task of the *Critique* throws further light on the disagreement between Fischer and Trendelenburg. The choice is between Trendelenburg's view of Kant as a traditional idealist and Fischer's view of him as a radical reformer consciously deviating from that tradition. It is a choice between locating Kant within a firmly idealist tradition or as a revolutionary with a category discipline which demonstrates traditional error and points in a wholly new direction away from that idealism. The nineteenth century's persistent commitment to a traditional idealism made it virtually impossible to appreciate this contrast or to see the problems of what Trendelenburg called "the Kantian epoch" as anything other than those same idealist challenges. There is less excuse for twentieth century commentators who have followed Trendelenburg and failed to see the correct points that Fischer made. Even if Fischer's Hegelianism prevented him from fully developing the idea, he deserves every credit for correctly locating Kant's point of departure from that tradition.

Some commentators, such as Bird (1962) and Allison (1983), have followed Fischer's lead in taking seriously Kant's explicit repudiation of traditional idealism. Others regard such an account as uninteresting, trivial, or anodyne, and that will be the view of anyone dominated by the problematic of traditional idealism as Trendelenburg was. Those alternative views have ascribed to Kant either a traditional idealism with its skeptical challenge to the external world, or have used updated forms of idealism to understand his views, but all have serious drawbacks. They may be inadequately supported by Kant's text, or else ascribe to him anachronistic views which he could not have held. To see the Aesthetic as an answer to a Cartesian skeptical idealism (Stroud 1984), or as a form of phenomenalism or "virtual object" theory (Van Cleve 1999), has the drawback that such accounts represent Kant as closer to traditional idealism than is consistent with his vehement denials. The ascription of phenomenalism in particular is at odds with Kant's own text. Even if it is plausible to regard these doctrines as forms of idealism to treat Kant as a semantic externalist or a contemporary antirealist is an anachronism with no clear echo in Kant's text. Contemporary externalism and antirealism trade on doctrines in semantics and logic of which Kant had no conception (Bruckner 1983–4; Putnam 1983). These contemporary doctrines are less adequate as interpretations of Kant, and philosophically, than the position to which Fischer pointed in the mid-nineteenth century.

References and Further Reading

Allison, Henry (1983). *Kant's Transcendental Idealism: An Interpretation and Defense*. New Haven: Yale University Press.

Beck, Lewis White (1991). Introduction to Köhnke 1991.

Beck, Lewis White (1995). Neo-Kantianism. In *The Oxford Companion to Philosophy* (pp. 611–12), ed. T. Honderich. Oxford: Oxford University Press.

Bird, Graham (1962). *Kant's Theory of Knowledge*. London: Routledge & Kegan Paul.

Bratuschek, K. (1870). Kuno Fischer and Adolf Trendelenburg. *Philosophische Monatsheft*, May.

Bruckner, Anthony (1983–4). Transcendental arguments. *Nous*, I: 551–75; II: 197–225.

Fischer, Kuno (1860–70). *Geschichte der neueren Philosophie* [*History of Modern Philosophy*], 4 vols. Heidelbery: Bassermann.

Fischer, Kuno (1865). *System der Logik und Metaphysik* [*System of Logic and Metaphysics*], 2nd ed. Heidelberg: Bassermann.

Fischer, Kuno (1870). *Anti-Trendelenburg* [*Anti-Trendelenburg*]. Jena: Hermann Dabis.

Guyer, Paul (1987). *Kant and the Claims of Knowledge*. Cambridge: Cambridge University Press.

Kant, Immanuel (1929). *Critique of Pure Reason*, tr. Norman Kemp Smith. London: Macmillan.

Köhnke, Klaus (1991). *The Rise of Neo-Kantianism*. Cambridge: Cambridge University Press.

Putnam, Hilary (1983). *Realism and Reason*. Cambridge: Cambridge University Press.

Stroud, Barry (1984). *The Significance of Philosophical Scepticism*. Oxford: Clarendon Press.

Trendelenburg, Adolf (1865). *Logische Untersuchungen* [*Logical Investigations*], 2nd ed. Leipzig: S. Hirzel.

Trendelenburg, Adolf (1867). *Über eine Lücke in Kants Beweis von der ausschließeuden Subjectivitant des Raums und der Zeit* [*On a Gap in Kant's Proof of the Exclusively Subjective Nature of Space and Time*]. Leipzig: S. Hirzel.

Trendelenburg, Adolf (1869). *Fischer und sein Kant* [*Fischer and His Kant*]. Leipzig: S. Hirzel.

Vaihinger, Hans (1871). *Kommentar zu Kants Kritik der reinen Vernunft* [*Commentary to Kant's Critique of Pure Reason*]. Stuttgart: Union deutscher Verlagsgesellschaft.

Van Cleve, James (1999). *Problems from Kant*. Oxford: Oxford University Press.

32

Phenomenological Interpretations of Kant in Husserl and Heidegger

PAUL GORNER

Introduction

Edmund Husserl (1859–1938) and Martin Heidegger (188–1976) are two of the most influential "Continental" philosophers of the last century. Both were profoundly influenced by Kant and continued to study Kant, particularly his *Critique of Pure of Pure Reason*, throughout their philosophical careers. Husserl was the founder of phenomenology, and for a time at least Heidegger also regarded himself as a phenomenologist, although, as I suggest, their conceptions of phenomenology diverge. Husserl saw phenomenology as the final answer to the question of epistemology: How is knowledge possible? He sees Kant as representing a crucial stage on the way to the emergence of his own *transcendental* phenomenology, and provides interesting criticisms of Kant from that standpoint. Heidegger also approaches Kant from the standpoint of his own distinctive conception of philosophy, but he does not just use this conception as a yardstick against which Kant is to be measured. He produces an original interpretation of Kant but at the same time engages with the detail of Kant's text. He admitted that his interpretation did some violence to Kant's text but thought this inevitable in a "thinking dialogue" rather than an "historical philology" (Heidegger 1991: foreword to 2nd ed.).

Husserl and Kant

Kant's relation to Husserl is best brought out by sketching the latter's transcendental phenomenology.

The natural attitude

In what Husserl calls the "natural attitude" I am conscious of the world as endlessly extended in space and in time (Husserl 1950: §27). I experience the world as existing, as real. I experience things as being simply *there*, whether or not I specially attend to them or occupy myself with them. The objects which are there for me are not necessarily present in my perceptual field. Objects may be there for me, together with actually perceived objects, without themselves being perceived or even pictured in my imagination. At the present moment I see my computer. I am not currently perceiving the parts of the room behind my back, or the street outside. Nor am I picturing them in my mind, but they are nonetheless there for me. Consciousness of my unseen surroundings is inseparable from my perceptual consciousness of a particular object. They belong to what Husserl calls the *horizon* of my perception.

The horizon of my perception, however, is not exhausted by the objects of my immediate surroundings which, though not currently perceived, are co-present to my consciousness. The universal horizon of the consciousness of particular items is consciousness of the *world* as an all-embracing whole. The world as a whole is always already given as certainly existing. I may have doubts about a particular item in the world, whether it genuinely exists or has the properties I take it to have, but all such doubt takes place in a context of certainty regarding the existence of the world as a whole. The world is always already there for me. It is other than I suppose at most in particular circumstances. This unquestioning belief in the real existence of the world as a whole is what Husserl calls the *general thesis* of the *natural attitude*.

In the natural attitude my consciousness is directed toward objects in the world in what Husserl calls the *intentionality* of consciousness. For the most part I take these objects, and the world to which they belong, to be real and to have the properties they appear to have. An equally important feature of the natural attitude is how I regard *myself*. In the natural attitude I regard myself and all other persons as belonging to the one spatiotemporal reality which is always already given. Although I am the *subject* of consciousness I am also, as a psychophysical being, *in* the world, related causally and in other ways to other items in the world.

The transcendental reduction

What Husserl understands by *transcendental* phenomenology involves bringing about a radical change in the general thesis of the natural attitude, something he calls the phenomenological or transcendental *reduction* (Husserl 1950: chs. 1 and 4). In the natural attitude I posit particular things as existing, as *there*, and underlying all such positings of existence is the general thesis, the taken-for-granted belief in the existence of the world. Husserl's transcendental phenomenology involves a radical change in all such positings of real existence.

The transformation of the general thesis of the natural attitude brought about by the phenomenological reduction is *not* a transformation of the thesis into its antithesis. It is not a transformation of the general thesis into mere supposition, conjecture, undecidedness, or doubt. We as it were "put it out of action," "disconnect," or "bracket," it. The thesis remains but we "make no use of it." We perform what Husserl calls an *epoché* on the general thesis and all particular theses (Husserl 1950: §32). The purpose of this suspension, this inhibiting, of belief is to enable us to turn our attention away from things in the world and the world itself and to focus instead on *consciousness* of things in the world and of the world as a whole. This does not mean that things in the world and the world itself simply disappear. It means that rather than being interested in their reality we are interested in them simply as they appear, as objects of consciousness or *intentional* objects. Phenomenology, as Husserl understands it, is the description of the essential structures of consciousness, in virtue of which it *is* consciousness *of* the various types of object and of the world as a whole.

In the natural attitude I regard myself as a psychophysical reality belonging to the one spatiotemporal reality which is always already given. But in the phenomenological reduction I suspend the general thesis of the natural attitude. This means that the consciousness laid bare by the reduction is not consciousness understood as part of a psychophysical reality *in* the world, that is *mundane* consciousness. The consciousness we gain through the phenomenological reduction is *transcendental* consciousness. Transcendental phenomenology is the description of the essential structures of transcendental consciousness.

The life-world

Later versions of Husserl's phenomenology appeal to what is called the "life-world" (*Lebenswelt*). As the name suggests the life-world is the world in which we live as we experience it. It, or at least its basic stratum, is the spatiotemporal world of things as it is experienced in our prescientific and extrascientific life. The life-world is the world of perception. The perceptual life-world is the foundation or ground of the scientific world which may be taken to be the realm of the in-itself, of things as they objectively are, independently of subjectivity. The subjective and relative life-world is then thought to be something that must be overcome in favor of the being-in-itself which science purports to describe, but Husserl thinks this a mistake.

It is a mistake for Husserl because science, as he points out, is an historically late form of practice, which arises *within* the life-world and is ultimately intelligible only within that context (Husserl 1970a: §33). It is the life-world which gives rise to the questions of science and it is the life-world to which the scientist must ultimately appeal in answering such questions, and in verifying those answers. When physicists *see* their instruments they see them *in* the life-world and what they see are "life-worldly" objects. In conducting an experiment scientists experience such things as persons, equipment, or the laboratory. These objects, as they *experience* them, are quite different from things as described in scientific theories, but such scientific knowledge is inconceivable without the experience of life-worldly objects.

The life-world is the ultimate foundation of the objective world in the sense that the concepts science uses to describe the world refer back to the life-world. The key to this is what Husserl calls Galileo's *mathematization of nature*. Prescientifically, in everyday sense-experience, the world is given in a subjectively relative way. Galileo's idea was to overcome this subjectivity and relativity by applying pure geometry and the mathematics of the pure form of space-time to nature. In the intuitively given surrounding world we do not encounter the "pure" bodies, the straight lines and figures of geometry. The things of the life-world "fluctuate, in general and in all their properties, in the sphere of the merely typical" (Husserl 1970a: 23–5).

Those exact forms of geometry, Husserl argues, are the product of a process of *idealization* performed on the "inexact" and "vague" shapes of "life-worldly" objects. Prescientifically the world is already a spatiotemporal world, except that unlike the "objective" world, it does not contain ideal mathematical points, or "pure" straight lines and planes. Prescientifically the world is a world in which things are experienced as *causally* interrelated, but the causality of the physical sciences is an idealization of such life-worldly causality. Husserl's point is that, as the product of the idealization and mathematization of life-worldly structures, the concepts used to construct the "objective" world refer back in their sense to such structures, and that, consequently, it is absurd to dismiss the life-world, from the standpoint of the "objective" world, as *merely* subjective.

It is important, however, not to lose sight of the context of transcendental phenomenology in which Husserl develops the notion of the life-world. The life-world is a stage on the way to transcendental subjectivity. In order to secure the life-world as an object of study we must perform an *epoché* with respect to all the objective sciences, by putting "out of action" all their validity-claims so that scientific theories and science as a form of practice appear as cultural facts in the life-world. It is possible to study the life-world for its own sake, and laying bare the essential structures of the life-world is what Husserl calls the ontology of the life-world (Husserl 1970a: §51). Phenomenology can thus trace back the objective world to its "origin" in the life-world, but for Husserl this would not be the end of the phenomenological story. For the life-world itself has an origin, in the sense that it is constituted in transcendental subjectivity (or intersubjectivity). If the doctrine of constitution, with its idealistic implications, is thought to be problematic, then the introduction of the theme of the life-world does not resolve it; but it can be seen as a criticism of the kind of transcendentalism which takes natural-scientific knowledge as its starting point. In Husserl's view this is to start at too high a level; it overlooks the way in which such knowledge is grounded in prescientific experience of the life-world.

Kant as precursor of transcendental phenomenology

Husserl's transcendental phenomenology is the culmination of the turn to the subject that takes place in Descartes, but how does it relate to Kant? In Husserl's view Kant's significance lies in the fact that he succeeds in converting Descartes' subjectivism into philosophy which is genuinely transcendental. Descartes' subject remains an item in the world (Husserl 1960: §10). Kant's subject is transcendental in the sense that it is a subject in which the world as object is constituted. Such philosophy is the only one able to answer the epistemological question: How is knowledge possible?, and it does this by showing how the world is "constituted" in transcendental subjectivity. An inevitable consequence of Husserl's conception of transcendental phenomenology is transcendental idealism, and Husserl not only accepts this but enthusiastically proclaims it. He sees his own transcendental idealism as Kant's idealism rendered consistent.

Husserl's criticisms of Kant

1. Husserl does not *argue* that transcendental consciousness *must* have such and such structures if knowledge is to be possible. Phenomenology is essentially a form of *seeing*. The constitution of objects in transcendental subjectivity is something which can become the "object" of what Husserl calls transcendental experience. Access to the kinds of active and passive synthesis in which objects, and ultimately the whole world, are constituted requires the carrying out of the transcendental reduction. Lacking a proper conception of the phenomenological method Kant's account of the constitution of the

503

world by the transcendental subject operates with "mythical constructions" (Husserl 1970: §30, §12, §30).

2. Husserl thinks that because Kant never really appreciated the need for a transcendental reduction he was always in danger of falling back into psychologism (Husserl 1956: Foreword to *Kant und die Idee der transzendentalen Philosophie*). In the very earliest stages of his encounter with Kant Husserl thought that Kant was guilty of psychologism, trying to explain the necessity and universality of a priori truths by tracing them back to our psychological constitution which makes assent to them inevitable. By the time of *Logical Investigations* he had come to see that this view of Kant is false even though traces of psychologism remained (Husserl 1956: 369). Kant explains the possibility of a priori knowledge in terms of the faculties of sensibility, imagination and understanding, and these are human psychological faculties. But as items *in* the world human beings cannot fulfil a transcendental role. From the standpoint of Husserl's transcendental phenomenology human beings are entities in the world constituted in transcendental subjectivity which is not an entity in the world.

3. A genuinely transcendental philosophy cannot countenance things in themselves which cannot *themselves* be presented or given to consciousness. At the core of Husserl's phenomenology is the strict correlation between being (*Sein*) and consciousness (*Bewusstsein*) (Husserl 1950: §43). Given this correlation the idea of an unknowable thing in itself makes no sense. Although it is possible to interpret Kantian things in themselves in a way compatible with Husserl's transcendental philosophy there is still the strong suggestion that they have a causal role in Kant's epistemology, which Husserl thinks absurd. This explains why his transcendental idealism is more radical than Kant's and owes as much to Fichte as to Kant.

4. Kant starts at too high a level since he ignores the life-world and the constitution of the life-world (Husserl 1970a: 103–23). The synthetic a priori principles whose possibility Kant seeks to explain are supposed to be the fundamental principles of natural science. But in Husserl the concepts employed in the formulation of such knowledge refer back to experience of the life-world. So what is needed is *first* an account of the constitution of the life-world and its structures.

5. Kant does not subject his transcendental philosophy to transcendental self-criticism (Husserl 1956: 376; 1970: §63). We do not expect a natural scientist to be able to give an account of how natural-scientific knowledge is possible. If he or she should do so it is not qua scientist but qua philosopher. But we are right to expect a philosopher to be able to give an account of how philosophical knowledge is possible. This is because philosophy is *essentially* self-reflective. Husserl criticizes Kant on the grounds that his transcendental philosophy is not sufficiently self-reflective. It does not raise, let alone answer, the prior question of how transcendental philosophy is possible.

Despite these criticisms Husserl regarded himself as the heir to Kant's transcendental philosophy, but there are two fundamental respects in which this can be questioned. Firstly, there is something essentially *Cartesian* about Husserl's conception of transcendental philosophy. Phenomenological reflection is a kind of purified introspection. It is purified in being carried out on the basis of the phenomenological reduction, whereas "ordinary" introspection takes place within the natural attitude and on the basis of the general thesis. This is something quite alien to Kant's conception of philosophy.

Secondly, Husserl's conception of the a priori is really quite different from that of Kant. Kant's synthetic a priori judgments are characterized by necessity and strict universality. The synthetic a priori transcendental principles have these characteristics by virtue of being conditions of the possibility of experience. Husserl also uses the notion of synthetic a priori judgments but his conception of such judgments involves something which is entirely alien to Kant, namely the intuition of essences (*Wesensschau*, literally the viewing or seeing of an essence) (Husserl 1950: div. 1, ch. 1). For Husserl it is not only individuals but also universals which can be intuited. Every contingent something has an essence or "eidos." An individual object is not simply a "this, here" but has also an essential "what." Every specific sound, for example, has a universal essence "sound as such." Likewise every material thing has its essence. At a higher level of generality there is the essence "material thing as such" and, included in this, "temporal determination as such," "duration as such," "figure as such," and "materiality as such." Everything which belongs to the essence of an individual can also belong to another individual, and essences of the highest levels of generality demarcate "regions" or "categories" of individuals.

Every "what" of an individual can be separated from that individual and apprehended as an idea. Empirical or individual intuition can thus be converted into essential intuition, and what is then intuited is the pure essence or eidos. The essence is a new kind of object. Just as what is given in an individual or empirical intuition is an individual object so what is given in essential intuition (*Wesenserschauung*), is a pure essence. Husserl insists that the talk of *intuition* here is no mere analogy. Essential intuition is genuinely intuition and the eidetic object is genuinely an object. Essential intuition is a mode of consciousness of something in which the object, the essence, is itself given. The eidos, the pure essence, can be intuitively exemplified in what is given in experience, in perception, or memory, but it can equally well be exemplified in imagination. In order to apprehend an essence itself we can start out from either corresponding experiential intuitions or non-experiential intuitions in which existence is not apprehended, that is to say from intuitions in which something is merely *imagined*. For example essences of spatial forms, melodies, social processes, acts of experience, pleasure, displeasure, or willing can be intuited on the basis of purely imagined instances of such things. The positing and intuitive apprehension of essences does not imply the slightest positing of any individual existence. Pure essential truths do not contain the least assertion about facts. Consequently not even the most trivial factual truth can be inferred from them.

Essential truths (*Wesenswahrheiten*) are truths concerning relations between essences, such as those of exclusion and inclusion. Such relations, like the essences between which they obtain, can themselves be intuitively apprehended and not merely thought. An example of such an essential synthetic a priori truth would be that one and the same surface cannot be both red and green all over at the same time. They are necessarily true but cannot be converted into analytic truths. The latter can be reduced to purely formal truths by substituting formal concepts for the material concepts they contain. Formal concepts are concepts which apply to something simply as something. Truths of logic are true of anything regardless of content, but synthetic or material a priori truths are not reducible to formal truths.

Heidegger and Kant

Heidegger's conception of phenomenology

Whereas for Husserl phenomenology became inseparable from a certain kind of idealism, for Heidegger it is essentially only a method (Heidegger 1962: §7). Its subject-matter is not consciousness but being (*Sein*). Primarily and for the most part we are concerned with entities, with what is (*Seiendes*). But comportment (*Verhalten*) to entities, including that entity which I myself am, is only possible on the basis of the understanding of being. Being itself is not an entity, and normally remains hidden, while phenomenology is a method of gaining access to it. It is the letting be seen (*Sehenlassen*) of the being of entities (*Sein des Seienden*).

In *Being and Time* (1927), the work which established his reputation as a philosopher, Heidegger raises the question of the meaning or sense (*Sinn*) of being (*Sein*). This requires that we first focus on our own being, but not because of any absurd identification of human being with being as such. It is rather because what distinguishes our being from the being of other entities is that in our being we understand being, that of ourselves and that of entities other than ourselves. To designate the entity distinguished by the understanding of being (*Seinsverständnis*) he employs the term *Dasein*. The being of *Dasein* he calls "existence." Most of the published part of *Being and Time* is taken up with the laying bare, the "letting be seen," of the structures of the being of *Dasein*, which he calls "existentials." What lies at the base of all these structures and makes them possible is the *temporality* of *Dasein*. This is not time in the ordinary or common (*vulgär*) sense of a beginningless and endless sequence of "nows." The original temporality of *Dasein* is not being in time thus understood. The temporality which makes the being of *Dasein* possible is the unity of coming-toward-itself (future, *Zukunft*), coming-back-to-itself (having-been-ness, *Gewesenheit*), and enpresenting (present, *Gegenwärtigen*, *Gegenwart*). In each of these elements of its temporality *Dasein* is "outside itself," each of them is an *ecstasis* and Heidegger calls such temporality ecstatic temporality. Each of the ecstases creates a horizon from out of which entities are encountered. Time understood as ecstatic-horizonal temporality is the sense or meaning of being. This gives us some indication of how we should understand the title of the work. The relationship between being and time is not one of opposition but such that the latter is the key to the meaning of the former.

Kant and being

Heidegger lectured on the *Critique of Pure Reason* (hereafter the *Critique*) in the winter semester of 1927/8 in Marburg and subsequently in Riga and Davos. The Davos workshop, which included both Ernst Cassirer and Rudolf Carnap as participants, is discussed in Michael Friedman (2000). The essentials of Heidegger's Kant interpretation appeared in his *Kant and the Problem of Metaphysics*, which was published in 1929. The Marburg lectures were published in 1977, the year after his death, under the title *Phenomenological Interpretation of Kant's Critique of Pure Reason*. In the foreword to the first edition of *Kant and the Problem of Metaphysics* Heidegger states that his interpretation of the *Critique* arose in connection with work on Part Two of *Being and Time*, the subject of which was to have been the phenomenological destruction of the history of ontology. The first of three divisions of Part II was to have had the title "Kant's doctrine of schematism and time as a first stage in the problematic of temporality" (Heidegger 1962: §8).

In his interpretation of Kant Heidegger is not suggesting that Kant has a conception of *Dasein*. Nor is he suggesting that Kant consciously raises his *Seinsfrage*, that is, the question of being or, more precisely, the question concerning the meaning of being. Kant is concerned with the knowing *subject* but *Dasein* cannot be identified with the subject. The being of *Dasein* is being-in-the-world (*In-der-Welt-sein*) but this should not be equated with the relationship between a subject and an object. As regards being, Heidegger thinks that Kant, in common with other philosophers, equates being with "presence-at-hand" or "occurrentness" (*Vorhandenheit*). However, he sees Kant as groping towards an interpretation of being in terms of *time*. It is in this that he sees Kant's importance, rather than in any completion of the modern move, initiated by Descartes, from the object to the subject.

Heidegger thus interprets the *Critique* as *ontology*, understood as the study of *being*. With the collapse of German Idealism and its idea of philosophy as *absolute Wissenschaft* (absolute knowledge of the absolute), the view had come to dominate that knowledge of reality is provided by, and only by, science, so that the only thing left for philosophy to do is to analyze scientific knowledge and to try to explain how it is possible. Philosophy becomes theory of knowledge, more specifically theory of scientific knowledge. In line with this conception of the rather limited role of philosophy the *Critique* came to be seen as exclusively concerned with the theory of *natural* science. It asks: given the *fact* of natural scientific knowledge, what are the conditions of the possibility of such knowledge?

In Heidegger's view this is to get Kant completely wrong.

> The purpose of the *Critique of Pure Reason* is completely misunderstood . . . if this work is interpreted as a "theory of experience" or perhaps as a theory of the positive sciences. The *Critique of Pure Reason* has nothing to do with a "theory of knowledge." (Heidegger 1991: 16f)

The *Critique* is not epistemology but *ontology*. It belongs to *metaphysica generalis* (general metaphysics). Traditionally metaphysics has been understood as the fundamental knowledge of beings as such and as a whole. Beings as a whole, that is the totality of what is, is divided up into basic regions: God, nature and man. The rational sciences of these three regions – rational theology, rational cosmology, and rational psychology – together make up *metaphysica specialis* (special metaphysics). *Metaphysica generalis*, by contrast, is the study of beings as beings, being as such. That Kant is concerned with the possibility of *metaphysica specialis* would be agreed on all sides. But according to Heidegger's ontological reading of Kant his more fundamental concern is with *metaphysica generalis* and its possibility.

When the *Critique* asks: how are synthetic a priori judgments possible? Heidegger interprets such judgments as belonging to *metaphysica generalis* or ontology. Kant's synthetic a priori judgments are interpreted as *ontological* judgments, that is to say, they are not judgments about *entities* or *beings* (what Heidegger calls *ontic* judgments) but judgments about *being*, the being of entities (*das Sein des Seienden*). All comportment to entities presupposes an understanding of being, so that *knowledge* of entities, as a mode of comportment to entities, presupposes an understanding of the *being* of those entities. Ontic knowledge presupposes ontological knowledge. Kant's synthetic a priori principles represent the ontological knowledge required for knowledge of objects. They articulate the understanding of objectivity or objecthood (*Gegenständlichkeit*), the being of objects.

Interpreting synthetic a priori judgments as ontological judgments enables Heidegger to interpret Kant's Copernican revolution in a way that avoids absurdity. Given that we are finite beings it seems perverse to claim that objects must conform to our knowledge rather than our knowledge conform to objects. On Heidegger's interpretation of the Copernican Revolution, Kant is not saying that objects must conform to *empirical* or *ontic* knowledge, but that objects must conform to synthetic a priori knowledge, that entities must conform to *ontological* knowledge. Entities must conform to ontological knowledge in the sense that entities can only manifest themselves as entities on the basis of an understanding of their being. Far from dispensing with the traditional concept of truth as "correspondence" (*adaequatio*) the Copernican revolution presupposes it and for the first time shows how such ontic truth is possible (Heidegger 1991: 13).

Ontic knowledge can only correspond to entities if these entities are already manifest (*offenbar*) as entities, i.e. are known in the constitution of their being (*Seinsverfassung*). Objects, i.e. their ontic determinability, must conform to this ultimate knowledge. Manifestness of entities (ontic truth) revolves around the disclosedness of the constitution of the being of entities (ontological truth). But ontic knowledge can never *by itself* conform "to" objects because without ontological knowledge it cannot even have a possible thing to conform to (Heidegger 1991: 13).

The elements of ontological knowledge

According to Heidegger, Kant maintains that knowledge is primarily intuition (*Anschauung*). In support of this claim he quotes the opening sentence of the Transcendental Aesthetic:

> In whatever manner and by whatever means a mode of knowledge [a cognition, *eine Erkenntnis*] may relate to objects, *intuition* is that through which it is in immediate relation to them, and to which all thought as a means is directed. (B 33; translation from Kant 1961)

But although knowledge is *primarily* intuition, for finite knowers such as human beings intuition *by itself* can never be knowledge. In order to be knowledge finite intuition requires concepts or thought, for it needs to be determined as thus and so. Finite intuition of entities (empirical intuition) is dependent on the prior existence of its object. It cannot give its object to itself. Our intuition of entities is *intuitus derivatus* (Heidegger 1991: §5). This is contrasted with *intuitus originarius*, which of itself and through its intuiting first produces the intuited entity.

It is because human knowledge is finite that it requires *concepts*. Finite knowledge is thinking intuition (*denkendes Anschauen*) or intuiting thinking (*anschauendes Denken*). Representation through concepts (*begriffliches Vorstellen*) lacks the immediacy of even finite intuition. It relates to entities via the reference to something *general*. This circuitousness or discursivity (*Umwegigkeit*), which belongs to the essence of the *understanding* (*Verstand*), is, Heidegger says, the clearest mark of its finitude (Heidegger 1991: 30).

So the essential elements of finite knowledge are intuition and concepts. The first step towards explaining the possibility of *ontological* knowledge is to identify the essential elements of such knowledge. These are *pure* intuition and *pure* thought or concepts. In pure intuition what is intuited (*das Angeschaute*) is not an entity (*ein Seiendes*), but (an aspect of) the *being* (*Sein*) of entities. Concepts are general representations which "hold for many." They are formed by reflection, which is the focusing on the one in which the many agree. The origin of the content of empirical concepts is empirical intuition. A priori or pure concepts are not just a priori with respect to their *form* – this is true of all concepts – but also with respect to their *content*. Such concepts are not the product of reflection; rather they are representations of unity (*Einheit*) which belong to the essential structure of reflection as such.

Transcendental imagination and the unity of pure intuition and pure concepts

So far pure intuition and pure concepts have been dealt with in isolation. But there is a relationship of essential interdependence between them. Marburg neo-Kantians like Hermann Cohen recognized the artificiality of Kant's treatment of the pure intuitions of space and time in isolation from the Transcendental Logic but tried to overcome this by treating space and time as *categories* (Cohen 1885). In Heidegger's view this is totally misguided and runs counter to Kant's insistence on the primacy of intuition. Pure thought *essentially* relates to intuition and is the servant of intuition. But equally in a finite being pure intuition is essentially dependent on pure thought in the sense of being in need of determination (*bestimmungsbedürftig*).

What mediates between pure intuition and pure thought and makes their unity possible is the transcendental imagination. This synthesizes the manifold of pure intuition in accordance with those modes of unity represented in the pure concepts of the understanding. A priori knowledge of objects, that is knowledge of the objectivity or objecthood (*Gegenständlichkeit* or *Gegenständlichsein*) of objects, the being of objects requires, firstly, "the manifold of pure intuition," secondly, "the *synthesis* of the manifold by means of the imagination" and, thirdly, "the concepts which give *unity* to this pure synthesis" (*CPR*, B 104).

The product of this pure synthesis is what makes experience of objects possible. The modes of unity represented in the pure concepts in their interconnection constitute a horizon from within which objects are able to show themselves as objects. Or rather it is the manifold of pure intuition unified in these various ways which constitutes the horizon. This is not an entity nor a totality of entities but the *being* of entities. In all of this Heidegger consciously makes use of the literal meaning of the German word for "object," *Gegenstand*. The object is what "stands over against." The ontological synthesis "performed" by the transcendental (or productive) imagination is what makes this standing-over-against possible. That the transcendental imagination produces the horizon of objectivity does not mean that empirical objects are imaginary entities. Being is not itself an entity; objectivity is not itself an object.

Transcendence

But because such ontological knowledge involves a kind of "going beyond" objects, not to another realm of entities "behind" them, but to the being of objects, Heidegger also speaks of it as *transcendence*. Transcendence characterizes the *being* of the subject, the subjectivity of the subject. "Transcendent" does not mean being transcendent in the sense in which theologians speak of God as transcendent. Nor does it mean being transcendent in the Husserlian sense, according to which material objects are transcendent (in relation to consciousness) and such things as thoughts and sensations are immanent. It is to be understood in an active sense. *Dasein* is transcendent in the sense that it transcends. What does it transcend, go beyond? It transcends entities. To what does it go beyond? Being. This is not some mysterious superentity but the horizon of objectivity created by the transcendental imagination. Transcendence is not itself comportment to entities, what Husserl calls "intentionality," but the understanding of being which makes comportment to entities possible. Transcendence we might say is not an instance of intentionality but the condition of the possibility of intentionality.

The transcendental deduction of the categories

Such transcendence cannot be achieved by the pure concepts of the understanding considered simply as *notions*, as concepts derived from the logical forms of judgment. Notions must become *categories*. The task of the Transcendental Deduction is to exhibit the ontological character of the categories by uncovering their origin in pure imaginative time-related synthesis. Given that Kant's fundamental concern is to lay bare the essential content of these concepts the quasilegal conception of the Deduction is misleading. If metaphysics is thought of as the "ontic science of the super-sensible" then the question arises as to the *legitimacy* of the use of certain concepts. Dogmatic metaphysics (*metaphysica specialis*) seeks to provide knowledge of what lies beyond the bounds of sense by means of the most general concepts of the understanding without being able to show that the employment of such concepts is justified. But Kant's real concern is not with *metaphysica specialis* but with *metaphysica generalis* or ontology. For metaphysics as ontology the problem is quite different. What must the content of the categories be if they are to constitute the objectivity (*Gegenständlichkeit*) of objects? Or as Heidegger puts it: what must their ontological essence be? In the Transcendental Deduction Kant lays bare this essence – what constitutes a category as a category – in terms of time, the imagination and the logical function of concepts. However he does not do this for individual categories in the Transcendental Deduction.

Transcendental schematism

From Heidegger's perspective, the task of exhibiting the ontological essence of the categories is continued in the Transcendental Schematism (*CPR*, B 176–87) and in the presentation of the system of synthetic a priori principles (B 187–294). Of the former he says that these few pages of the *Critique* constitute the centerpiece (*Kernstück*) of the entire work (Heidegger 1991: 89). The transcendental schematism is not a "barock theory" but has been wrested (*geschöpft*) from the phenomena themselves (Heidegger 1991: 106). To become *categories* notions must be made sensible (*versinnlicht*). Schematism is the bringing into an image or picture (*in ein Bild bringen*) of a concept. But Kant says ". . . the schema of a *pure* concept of the understanding can never be brought into any image whatsoever" (B 181). In seeming contradiction to this he says that "The pure image . . . of all objects of the senses in general is time" (B 182). In fact the kinds of schema-images Kant means to exclude in the former quotation are those which belong to the schemata of empirical and mathematical concepts. Time as *pure* intuition is what, prior to all experience, furnishes an image for pure concepts of the understanding. This pure image is the pure succession of the sequence of "nows." Corresponding to the closed multiplicity of the pure concepts of the understanding is a multiplicity of ways in which this pure image can be formed (*gebildet*). The schemata of the pure concepts are nothing but a priori determinations of time in accordance with rules, or transcendental determinations of time. Such transcendental schemata are a "transcendental product of imagination."

Heidegger offers a brief interpretation of the transcendental schema of the category of substance. "The schema of substance is the permanence [*Beharrlichkeit*] of the real [*des Realen*] in time" (B 183). As a notion substance means simply: *Zugrundeliegen*, lying at the base, subsistence. Its schema must be the representation of subsistence in so far as this presents itself in the pure image of time. Now time as pure sequence of nows *is* always now; in every now it is now, and in this way time shows its own permanence. As such time is unchanging (*unwandelbar*) and abiding (*bleibend*), it does not pass away (*sie verläuft sich nicht*). Time is not one abiding thing among others, rather on the basis of this essential feature – that of being now in every now – it provides the pure image of abiding as such. As this pure image it presents subsistence in pure intuition.

However this function of presentation only becomes genuinely clear when we consider the full content of the notion of substance. Substance is a category of "relation" (between subsistence and inherence). Thus time is only the pure image of the notion substance if it presents precisely this relation in the pure image. But now time as the sequence of nows is such that, flowing in every now, it remains a now even while becoming another now. As the image of abiding it at the same time offers the image of pure change in abiding. In this way, the horizon of objectivity, in so far as substance belongs to it as a constitutive element, becomes a priori intuitable. It is the prior having in view of the pure image of permanence which makes possible the experience of entities as substances.

The "origin" of time

The transcendental schemata as determinations of time are the "transcendental product of imagination" but for Heidegger there is also a sense in which the transcendental imagination is responsible not just for the determination of time but for time itself (Heidegger 1991: 175f). Time as the sequence of nows is not original time. The transcendental imagination is what gives rise to time as the sequence of nows (*lässt die Zeit als Jetztfolge entspringen*) and is therefore original or primordial (*ursprünglich*) time. As the "origin" of time the transcendental imagination *is* time.

Ontology as the radicalization of epistemology

In his opposition to a *purely* epistemological interpretation of Kant, Heidegger somewhat overstates his case by suggesting that the *Critique* has *nothing* to do with epistemology, but his ontological interpretation of Kant is in fact compatible with recognition of an important epistemological dimension to Kant's work. Science, Heidegger would point out, can be viewed as a system of propositions, but can also be viewed *existentially*, as a distinctive mode of comportment to what is. Heidegger's ontological Kant can be seen as showing how such natural-scientific comportment to entities is possible by showing how it is grounded in the more basic comportment to entities as objects. The objectification of entities (beings, what is) is not the *result* of natural science but what makes natural science possible. Kant is then represented as providing an ontology of objects, an account of the being of objects, their objectivity or objecthood (*Gegenständlichkeit*), and as showing how the understanding of such being is grounded in the ontological constitution (*Seinsverfassung*) of the subject. This is a radicalization of epistemology rather than its rejection, which Heidegger, but not Kant, pursues further in his notion of "readiness-to-hand" or "availableness" (*Zuhandenheit*).

References and Further Reading

Bell, David (1990). *Husserl*. London: Routledge.

Cohen, Hermann (1885). *Kants Theorie der Erfahrung*, 2nd ed. Berlin: Dümmler.

Friedman, Michael (2000). *A Parting of the Ways: Carnap, Cassirer, and Heidegger*. Chicago: Open Court.

Heidegger, M. (1962). *Being and Time*, tr. J. Macquarrie and E. Robinson. Oxford: Blackwell.

Heidegger, M. (1977). *Phänomenologische Interpretation von Kants Kritik der reinen Vernunft* [*Phenomenological Interpretation of Kant's Critique of Pure Reason*], ed. Ingtraud Görland. Frankfurt am Main: Vittorio Klostermann.

Heidegger, M. (1991). *Kant und das Problem der Metaphysik* [*Kant and the Problem of Metaphysics*], 5th ed., ed. Friedrich-Wilhelm von Herrmann. Frankfurt am Main: Vittorio Klostermann.

Husserl, E. (1950). *Ideen zu einer reinen Phänomenologie und phänomenologischen Philosophie* [*Ideas for a pure Phenomenology and Phenomenological Philosophy*], ed. Walter Biemel. The Hague: Martinus Nijhoff.

Husserl, E. (1956). *Erste Philosophie* [*First Philosophy*], ed. Rudolf Boehm. The Hague: Martinus Nijhoff.

Husserl, E. (1970). *Cartesian Meditations*, tr. D. Cairns. The Hague: Martinus Nijhoff.

Husserl, E. (1970a). *The Crisis of European Sciences and Transcendental Phenomenology*, tr. D. Carr. Evanston, IL: Northwestern University Press.

Kant, Immanuel (1961). *Critique of Pure Reason*, tr. Norman Kemp Smith. London: Macmillan.

33

Conceptual Connections: Kant and the Twentieth-Century Analytic Tradition

JAMES O'SHEA

The founding figures and main movements of analytic philosophy, from Frege and the Cambridge analysts Russell, Moore, and Wittgenstein to the logical positivists and including the American pragmatist tradition, all frequently defined their own philosophical views in critical engagement with Kant's "Copernican revolution" in philosophy (see for example Coffa 1991, Friedman 2001, and Hanna 2001). Over the first half of the twentieth century the predominant tendency among analytic philosophers was to argue that while Kant had indeed raised important questions concerning the nature and possibility of our knowledge, subsequent developments in logic, mathematics, natural science, and philosophy entailed either the partial or complete rejection of Kant's transcendental philosophy. During the second half of the century, however, there was a revitalization of interest among analytic and neopragmatist philosophers not only in Kant's general approach to epistemological issues but in many of his substantive conclusions as well. This chapter presents a brief, nontechnical overview of some of these historical developments, by focusing on a representative sampling of certain key conceptual episodes in that history and relating them to the following well-known themes from Kant's *Critique of Pure Reason*.

Central Themes in Kant's Conceptual Revolution

In the second-edition Preface to the first *Critique* Kant formulated his proposed conceptual revolution in metaphysics by analogy with Copernicus's famous heliocentric hypothesis in astronomy:

> Up to now it has been assumed that all our cognition must conform to the objects; but all attempts to find out something about them a priori through concepts that would extend our cognition have, on this presupposition, come to nothing. Hence let us once try whether we do not get farther with the problems of metaphysics by assuming that the objects must conform to our cognition, which would agree better with the requested possibility of an a priori cognition of them, which is to establish something about objects before they are given to us. This would be just like the first thoughts of Copernicus, who . . . tried to see if he might not have greater success if he made the observer revolve and left the stars at rest. (B xvi; translations from Kant 1998)

Objects are given to us a posteriori, in Kant's familiar terminology, as a result of our having particular sensory encounters with them or "empirical intuitions" of them in experience. The disputed a priori cognitions in mathematics, natural science, and metaphysics are supposed to tell us something informative that is true of the objects themselves, thus "extending our cognition" in synthetic rather than merely analytic judgments (the latter merely unpack what is already contained in a given concept). And yet such synthetic cognitions also provide information that is in some sense known a priori, independently of any particular experiential encounters with those objects. They thus "establish something about objects before they are given to us," something which consequently holds necessarily of any object we may encounter in experience.

Since analytic philosophers throughout the twentieth century rejected or endorsed several closely related yet distinguishable aspects of Kant's basic revolutionary outlook, it will prove helpful to isolate the following four themes:

1) The problem of synthetic a priori judgments
2) The basic Copernican turn ("objects must conform to our cognition")
3) A priori conditions of the possibility of experience
4) Transcendental idealism (appearances vs. things in themselves), on both (a) traditional and (b) nontraditional interpretations.

First some brief comments on these Kantian themes, particularly the last:

(1) Kant indicates that in posing the problem of the *Critique of Pure Reason* as above he has sought to "bring a multitude of investigations under the formula of a single problem," for the "real problem of pure reason is now contained in the question: How are synthetic judgments a priori possible?" (B19). (2) The basic revolutionary suggestion or Copernican turn is the idea that, in complex ways carefully worked out in the *Critique* itself, "the objects must conform to our cognition" (B xvi), in particular, to the a priori forms of sensibility (space and time) and of understanding (the categories). (3) Kant argues that the epistemic legitimacy of our applying these a priori forms and principles to the experienced world as we do stems from their being necessary conditions of the possibility of experience itself:

> all a priori concepts . . . must be recognized as a priori conditions of the possibility of experiences. . . . Concepts that supply the objective ground of the possibility of experience are necessary just for that reason. (A B126; cp. B xvii)

Finally, (4) Kant presents his Copernican turn as inseparable from his transcendental idealism, which early on (B xviii–xx) receives two formulations that may be taken to illustrate two radically opposed scholarly interpretations in the analytic tradition of what Kant's "formal" or "critical" idealism, as he also calls it, amounts to (*Prol.*, 293, 375; B 518) (see also chapters 7 and 31 above). On the one hand, (a) Kant states that "our rational cognition a priori . . . reaches appearances only, leaving the thing [*Sache*] in itself as something actual for itself but uncognized by us" (B xx). This formulation might encourage the traditional interpretation according to which the ultimately real underlying realities that are responsible for the appearances are what Kant calls the "things in themselves," which we can think about and must postulate but which we cannot know or cognize as objects. On this reading, what we know are only the appearances of this unknown thing or things, whatever it or they may be, which affect us through sensation and to which we respond by constructing the phenomenal world of objects in space and time. On the other hand, (b) just two pages earlier Kant had introduced the same contrast between appearances and things in themselves in these terms:

> the same objects can be considered from two different sides, on the one side as objects of the senses and the understanding for experience, and on the other side as objects that are merely thought at most for isolated reason striving beyond the bounds of experience. (B xviii–xix note)

Highlighting the two standpoints or perspectives taken on "the same objects" in this passage, many nontraditional (b)-interpretations of Kant's references to "things in themselves" over the last four decades have contended that the heart of Kant's transcendental idealism is the idea that on his view "things are considered from this twofold standpoint" (B xix note). One of these gives us genuine cognition of the objects as phenomena in experience, while the other gives us only ideas of pure reason to which nothing corresponds. These ideas generate the errors of traditional metaphysics and the idea of our own freedom as a constitutive practical (moral) principle for our rational will (along with various other regulative principles of reason that govern our own rational conducts and inquiries).

These two opposed interpretations are often (arguably misleadingly) contrasted as the (a) "two-world" vs. (b) "two-aspect" interpretations of Kant's transcendental idealism. Traditional (a)-interpretations in the analytic tradition have generally found Kant's transcendental idealism to be implausible, but perhaps detachable from his more insightful contentions surrounding theme (3). Nontraditional (b)-interpretations have generally been articulated in defense of Kant's transcendental idealism as an essentially sound epistemological thesis that concerns the proper limits of our knowledge and is inseparable from themes (2) and (3) (e.g., Bird 1962 and Allison 1983). We shall return to this issue later, as we now examine the ways in which analytic philosophers have taken different stances toward these four fundamental themes in Kant's critical philosophy.

Frege, Russell, and the Synthetic A Priori

The turn from the nineteenth to the twentieth century witnessed logical and conceptual analysts such as G. E. Moore and Bertrand Russell in Britain, as well as pragmatists and realists in America, all making an emphatic break from the influential neo-Hegelian idealist systems of J. M. E. McTaggart and F. H. Bradley in Britain, and Josiah Royce in America. Accounts of what was called "transcendental" philosophy during this period often viewed Kant's own critical idealism through the transforming lens of post-Hegelian absolute idealist systems. In these accounts the Kantian "transcendental ego" tended to make its transitional appearance on the stage of history as an objectionably abstract and individualist spiritual ancestor of Hegel's Absolute Spirit. However, amid the distortions represented by the break away from the Hegelian Kant were some notable realist criticisms of Kant's own views by logical analysts such as Russell. We may take Russell's influential introductory book *The Problems of Philosophy* (1912) as a clear and representative example of an early analytic realist response to Kant's epistemology and metaphysics.

Although Frege and Russell are of course famous for their logicist project – roughly, the attempt to derive the truths of arithmetic from deductive logic as the latter had been revolutionized by mathematical logicians such as Frege and Russell themselves – neither thinker was opposed in principle to Kant's idea that we possess synthetic a priori knowledge in certain domains, as in theme (1). In fact they both endorsed it. It is well known, for example, that Frege in his *Foundations of Arithmetic* of 1884 wrote of Kant:

> I consider Kant did great service in drawing the distinction between synthetic and analytic judgements. In calling the truths of geometry synthetic and a priori, he revealed their true nature. And this is still worth repeating, since even today it is often not recognized. If Kant was wrong about arithmetic, that does not seriously detract, in my opinion, from the value of his work. His point was that there are such things as synthetic judgements a priori; whether they are to be found in geometry only, or in arithmetic as well is of less importance. (Frege 1953: 101–2)

Similarly, in his defense of the synthetic a priori Russell claimed that

> Kant undoubtedly deserves credit for two things: first, for having perceived that we have a priori knowledge which is not purely "analytic," i.e. such that the opposite would be self-contradictory; and secondly, for having made evident the philosophical importance of the theory of knowledge. (Russell 1912: 46)

However, Russell proceeded to firmly reject Kant's own theory of knowledge (as did Frege in important respects, though his relationship to Kant is a complex one). In particular Russell rejected Kant's transcendental account of the sources and justification of our synthetic a priori knowledge in terms of the above themes (2), (3), and (4), on Russell's very traditional (a)-interpretation of Kant's transcendental idealism.

Russell raised several objections to what he took to be Kant's view of our a priori knowledge in general. He protests, for example, that

> no fact about the constitution of our minds could make it true that two and two are four. Thus our a priori knowledge . . . is not merely knowledge about the constitution of our minds, but is applicable to whatever the world may contain . . . (Russell 1912: 50)

The Kantian synthetic a priori, according to Russell, would merely tell us what we must believe about things, given the particular mental make-up we happen to have. It would not give us genuine a priori principles that hold true of reality or the entities themselves. Furthermore, Russell objects, whatever is a priori necessary is supposed to be "constant" and "certain," whereas to "say that logic and arithmetic are contributed by us does not account for this. Our nature is as much a fact of the existing world as anything, and there can be no certainty that it will remain constant" (ibid. 49).

On Russell's own view at this time, by contrast, our synthetic a priori knowledge of what he calls the "general principles" involved in induction, arithmetic, geometry, morality, and logic itself must be based upon our direct acquaintance with relations among mind-independent, timelessly "subsisting" Platonic universals – "entities which do not, properly speaking, exist, either in the mental or in the physical world" (Russell 1912: 50 and ch. 10). From the perspective of Russell's own Platonic logical realism, Kant's critical idealist conception of our synthetic a priori knowledge is thus marred by psychologism, which in this case is the view that the laws of logic or mathematics are grounded in psychological laws concerning our mental processes.

Russell's Platonic realist approach to the synthetic a priori is an instance of a venerable non-Kantian line of metaphysical and rationalist approaches to the problem of our knowledge of a priori necessary truths. Kantians can respond, of course, by shifting the burden of argument and exploiting the well-known epistemological difficulties that immediately arise from the Platonist's positing of objects or properties that are (apparently) outside the spatiotemporal–causal fabric of nature. (See Kant's own severe criticism of Plato's account of mathematical cognition at B 371n.)

Important and familiar disputes concerning Platonism aside, however, Russell's basic criticisms of Kant's view would frequently resurface in new forms in the criticisms of later analytic realists. With respect to these criticisms much (but not all) hinges on how one interprets Kant's transcendental idealist conception of appearances or phenomena, and in particular how one handles Kant's frequent characterization of the latter as "mere representations" that are "in us." Many traditional (a)-interpretations of transcendental idealism have assimilated Kant's appearances to the empirically subjective "ideas" or "perceptions in the mind" of Descartes, Locke, Berkeley, or Hume (see Bird 1962 and Allison 1983 for detailed criticisms of these interpretations). In that case it is easy to assume, as Russell apparently has, that on Kant's view one's synthetic a priori cognitions are merely about the contents of one's own mind. For Kant, however, our synthetic a priori cognitions in mathematics, natural science, and the metaphysics of experience are cognitions of laws pertaining to persisting spatiotemporal material objects "outside us" in the empirically real world. The direct and necessary mathematizability of empirically mind-independent material reality is part of what Kant's nontraditional conception of idealism is meant to account for. The fact that the possibility of such cognitions depends upon certain a priori forms of sensibility and understanding "in us," as capacities of the knower, does not entail, contrary to Russell's characterization above, that those cognitions provide "knowledge about the constitution of our minds" rather than being knowledge that "is applicable to whatever the world may contain." To the contrary, the latter is precisely what Kant's view is intended to support.

Russell and subsequent analytic philosophers defending non-Kantian realist epistemologies have tended to be unimpressed by this sort of response (cf. Russell 1912: 49). The reply of such realists has generally been that even on what Kant calls his "empirical realism" the necessity of his synthetic a priori principles concerning the phenomenal realm nonetheless remains a necessity that would hold merely relative to the possibility of our exercising our human cognitive capacities for spatiotemporal sensible intuition and apperceptive conceptual synthesis in the ways Kant describes. The question is how exactly this elusive brand of relative necessity is different from the claim (as by Hume) that the relevant propositions are simply ones that human beings are by their contingent nature ineluctably compelled to believe. This objection has some force, and a later generation would find a related formulation in Stroud's well-known objections to Strawson on transcendental arguments (see below).

The important general dispute here arguably turns on questions concerning whether or not, and in what sense, the relevant a priori transcendental conditions succeed in being, in Russell's phrase, "applicable to whatever the world may contain." Russell and later like-minded realists hold that Kant has implausibly restricted the domain of the a priori to "the way we must think" (Russell 1912: 49) rather than to how things unrestrictedly are and must be in themselves. Kant, however, is contending, in accordance with theme (3) above, that there are certain extremely general (a priori) conditions concerning what any world of possible experience may contain, for any experiencing beings who are like us, not in our contingent and potentially variable psychological nature as Russell suggests, but rather in possessing a conceptual awareness of a sensorily encountered world of objects at all. Furthermore, Kant argues in the transcendental dialectic of the first *Critique* that the attempt by pure reason to grasp truths outside this carefully delimited domain of possible experience inevitably leads to the demonstrable systematic errors of traditional metaphysics. In Kant's eyes, then, the "restriction" to possible experience is only a restriction to "the land of truth (a charming name), surrounded by a broad and stormy ocean, the true seat of illusion" (B 295).

This fundamental debate concerning epistemological realism and idealism in relation to Kant's views, which bears generally on themes (2), (3), and (4), is an enduring one that would return to the fore in the final three decades of the last century and remains a heated source of controversy today. In the decades between the two World Wars, however, the nature of the objections to Kant's views shifted instead to a focus on theme (1) concerning the tenability of the entire notion of the synthetic a priori. Thanks in no small part to the systematic tools of logical analysis provided by Frege and Russell themselves, philosophers influenced by the logical positivists emigrating from Germany increasingly rejected the very idea of the synthetic a priori, and along with it whatever other Kantian doctrines were deemed to depend upon it.

The Rise and Fall of the Analytic A Priori and the Idea of a Relativized A Priori

Excellent work has recently been done on Kant's role in the historical development of logical empiricism or positivism, both by way of positive influence and as target of criticism (see e.g. Friedman 2001 and Coffa 1991). A deeply Kant-inspired conception of a "relativized a priori" can be found in the logical positivists' conceptions of the epistemology of science that were developed in reaction to the Einsteinian revolution in both mathematics and physics. (A noteworthy early contribution along these lines was Reichenbach's 1965 [i.e. 1920].) However, with respect to Kant's thesis concerning specifically synthetic, rather than analytic, a priori cognition, the basic positivist criticism was characteristically expressed in this passage from Reichenbach's later 1951:

> [W]e have seen physics enter a stage in which the Kantian frame of knowledge does break down. The axioms of Euclidean geometry, the principles of causality and substance, are no longer recognized by the physics of our day. We know that mathematics is analytic

and that all applications of mathematics to physical reality, including physical geometry, are of an empirical validity and subject to correction by further experience; in other words, that there is no synthetic a priori. (Reichenbach 1951: 48–9)

Put in Kant's terms, for Reichenbach and other logical empiricists all knowledge is either analytic a priori or synthetic a posteriori: the "program of empiricism," as Reichenbach puts it, is "the principle that all synthetic truth derives from observation and that all contributions of reason to knowledge are analytic" (Reichenbach 1951: 259). Analytic a priori truths for the logical empiricists in general are trivially necessary or "true by definition" in the sense that they are either themselves logical tautologies or they are deductive logical consequences of stipulated axioms or conventional definitions laid down within a given axiomatized theory. However, such a priori "coordinating definitions," to use Reichenbach's term, were far from trivial insofar as they functioned as meaning-constituting and application-enabling components of the new, conceptually revolutionary scientific theories (see Friedman for more on these issues). The various alternative non-Euclidean "pure" geometries developed during the nineteenth century were put to use in Einstein's relativity physics in the early twentieth century in a way which had involved (1) an a priori "stipulation," as Einstein put it, "which I can make of my own free-will in order to arrive at a definition of simultaneity" (quoted in Lewis 1929: 256); and this was followed (2) by the a posteriori experimental testing of the resulting theoretical framework against physical reality. Sense experience thus provides the data to be accounted for; logically constructed, formal systems of interpretation in mathematics and science "implicitly define" (as Schlick had put it) the terms in whatever theoretical hypotheses are put forward to account for the data; and these and any other predictively fruitful conceptual-linguistic theoretical frameworks are to be "logically reconstructed" by philosophical analysis along lines that were laid out with particular ingenuity in the writings of Rudolf Carnap.

In a succession of major works Carnap attempted impressively rigorous logical reconstructions of various alternative logico-linguistic conceptual frameworks. Once a given linguistic framework or theory is adopted, what Carnap (1950) called "internal questions" concerning the truth or falsity of claims formulated in accordance with the meaning rules of that particular framework can be answered by appeal either to those a priori meaning rules themselves, or by appeal to sense experience in the form of observation sentences. In accordance with the positivist verifiability criterion of meaningfulness, any such questions must be so answerable if they are to have genuine cognitive content. For Carnap external questions that concern which among alternative linguistic frameworks ought to be adopted are to be settled on pragmatic grounds of predictive efficiency, fruitfulness, simplicity, clarity, communicability, and so on, depending on the purposes for which the particular framework is to be adopted. Roughly speaking, for the logical positivists any remaining questions that are neither logical nor empirical nor pragmatic are either cognitively meaningless pseudo-questions of the disreputable sort characteristic of traditional metaphysics, or they are likely to be expressions of some noncognitive practical attitude or feeling (see also chapter 13 above).

Significantly, the central dispute above concerning realism and idealism, which seemed so pressing in our discussion of Russell on Kant, is now neatly handled by Carnap as merely reflecting an external question: that is, it is viewed as either a genuine but disguised pragmatic dispute concerning which of various linguistic frameworks is most convenient to adopt for any given purpose (e.g., the alternative sense-datum, physical thing, or microphysical linguistic frameworks); or it is viewed as a mere metaphysical pseudo-dispute. That this deceptively neat solution ultimately rested on Carnap's strong verificationist restriction on meaningfulness would not bode well for its future prospects. However, other Kant-inspired analytic philosophers later in the century would similarly attempt to argue on different grounds that the persistent "realism vs. antirealism" debates of this kind can be laid to rest or given therapeutic treatment, utilizing insights from Kant, without one's having to be drawn into the perennial contest of attempting to resolve such traditional disputes directly on their own terms (perhaps Bird, Putnam, and McDowell are cases in point; and see Stroud for criticisms of such approaches in general).

In the American pragmatist tradition, the Harvard philosopher C. I. Lewis had developed an account of the nature of knowledge in his influential 1929 book that paralleled many of these important developments in Reichenbach and Carnap. For Lewis all empirical knowledge, given some particular analytic a priori scheme of interpretation relative to which conceptual meanings are determined, is predictive, contingent, fallible, and hence revisable. Our a priori concepts determine what kinds of objects and what sorts of lawfulness we may expect to meet with in experience, and in this respect Lewis's epistemology had a strongly Kantian flavor to it. For Lewis as for Reichenbach and Carnap, however, the sensory "given" may prove resistant to any particular scheme of conceptual classification, in which case we must seek alternative analytic a priori conceptual frameworks for accommodating such experiences. Lewis, like Russell and the logical positivists, accordingly criticizes Kant for having held that his a priori forms of intuition and understanding are compulsory ways of sensing and thinking, and for having held that they constrain or legislate for all possible experience. What is a priori, as Lewis tended to put it, is not what is "inescapable by the mind," but what is "true no matter what" experience may bring, although open to pragmatic abandonment in light of it.

It should be noted, however, that when Lewis says in relation to theme (3) that his a priori categories, unlike Kant's, do not "legislate for possible experience," he is here taking "experience" in a very thin sense that pertains only to what he calls the sensory given. About the given, as Lewis sees it, nothing can be anticipated prior to experience, but also nothing can known about it without using concepts. And concepts for Lewis do indeed lawfully predict beyond the given and thus do legislate a priori for some real object of "experience" in the thick, conceptualized sense with which Kant is in fact concerned. For Lewis as for Kant, then, it is necessary for the possible cognition of any objects of experience at all that such objects conform to categorial laws that have their source a priori in the cognitive subject, in accordance with the Kantian themes (2) and (3).

The various conceptions of framework-relative analytic a priori principles discussed in this section came under particularly severe pressure from mid-century rejections of the entire analytic/synthetic distinction itself, most famously in Quine's "Two Dogmas of Empiricism" (1951). In a nutshell, Quine argued that the pragmatic considerations of predictive utility, simplicity, conservativeness, and so on, to which Carnap and Lewis had appealed in relation to the so-called "external" choices between the various alternative (allegedly) meaning-constituting a priori conceptual frameworks, are the factors that are in fact decisive in all of our knowledge claims whatsoever, whether they concern framework "internal" or framework "external" questions (a distinction which consequently loses the significance it was supposed to have). Any particular belief or principle in what Quine famously calls our overall "web of belief," whether it be in logic, mathematics, natural science, or in direct perceptual observation, may be subject to revision in the ongoing attempt (to use Quine's other lead metaphor borrowed from the positivist Otto Neurath) to keep the ship of science afloat and accommodate the flux of sensory experience. The entire set of allied distinctions between analytic "truths of meaning" vs. synthetic "truths of fact," between a priori vs. a posteriori judgments or knowledge, and between internal vs. external framework questions, are themselves argued to be at best pragmatic distinctions of degree concerning how willing or unwilling we are at any given time to give up particular strands in the web of belief or planks in the ship of science. As a result of such mid-century critiques, analytic philosophers who wished to defend the idea that there are a priori conceptual truths or categorial meaning principles of the sort that had been defended by Carnap and Lewis would now have to reckon with the fact that the analytic a priori had become as controversial post-1950 as the synthetic a priori had been pre-1950 (see also chapter 8 above).

Despite this, however, the estimation of Kant's Critical philosophy was soon to rise rather than fall in the eyes of many analytic philosophers.

Transcendental Arguments and the Resurgence of Kantian Analytic Philosophy

One major source of the increased influence of professedly Kantian views in analytic epistemology and metaphysics since the 1960s has been in Strawson 1959 and 1966. When considered together with Bird (1962) and Bennett (1966) in particular, major works on the first *Critique* were now appearing in which powerful arguments for substantively Kantian theses were expressed and evaluated using contemporary analytic insights and styles of argument.

Strawson 1959 introduced his well-known conception of descriptive metaphysics, which in contrast to "revisionary metaphysics" is "content to describe the actual structure of our thought about the world" and aims "to lay bare the most general features of our conceptual structure," "the indispensable core of the conceptual equipment" of human beings (Strawson 1959: 9). Strawson analyses the structure of our basic conception of the world as containing various particular things that are objective in the sense of persisting independently of our various encounters with them. For instance, we think that in general speakers and hearers are able to make successful identifying references to such objective particulars even when they are absent from the present scene. Strawson argues that within "the general structure of our thinking about identification" our concept of a single, unified "system of spatiotemporal relations has a peculiar comprehensiveness and pervasiveness, which qualify it uniquely to serve as the framework within which we can organize our individuating thought about particulars" (ibid. 21, 25). Furthermore, he argues, since as Kant correctly stressed space and time cannot themselves be perceived, our spatiotemporal concepts are able to play this uniquely comprehensive individuating role in our thought only because we conceive our world to be populated with reidentifiable and hence lawfully persisting material bodies:

> There is no doubt that we have the idea of a single spatiotemporal system of material things . . . Now I say that a condition of our having this conceptual scheme is the unquestioning acceptance of particular-identity in at least some cases of non-continuous observation. (Strawson 1959: 35)

Strawson in this way takes himself to have articulated a kind of Kantian transcendental argument (this phrase was not explicitly used by Kant) against the skeptic's contention that our beliefs in such independently persisting bodies cannot be epistemically justified (ibid. 32–40). For the possibility of even coherently raising the skeptical doubt about the existence of reidentifiable particulars presupposes, Strawson argues, the general idea that particulars are related within one spatiotemporal framework (as opposed to each stretch of experience constituting an isolated world, as it were); but we have just seen that this framework is itself impossible without "the condition that there should be satisfiable and commonly satisfied criteria for the identity of at least some items in one subsystem with some items in the other." In effect, then, the skeptic "pretends to accept a conceptual scheme, but at the same time quietly rejects one of the conditions of its employment" (ibid. 35). The complex concept of a single spatiotemporal system of persisting material bodies, therefore, forms the indispensable core or structure of our most basic and permanent conceptual scheme.

Strawson 1966 subsequently embedded many of the central arguments of *Individuals* within a deeper Kantian account of the connection between objectivity and the unity of consciousness. This account, which would further intensify interest among analytic philosophers in the possibility of transcendental arguments in epistemology, was based on Strawson's insightful analysis of "the role of the Transcendental Deduction as an argument" (Strawson 1966: 87). Put brusquely, from the premise that one's experiences "must somehow be united in a single consciousness capable of judgment," this transcendental argument attempts to show that such a unity is possible only if our experiences are so conceptualized as to "have the character of experience of a unified objective world" and hence as "capable of being articulated in objective empirical judgments" (ibid.). Fairly close descendents of Kant's synthetic a priori principles of the permanence of substance and of the law of causality then turn out to be necessary for achieving the latter conception of an objective empirical world. (See also chapters 10, 11, and 12 above.)

Strawson's conceptions of descriptive metaphysics and of transcendental arguments helped to revitalize not only Kant scholarship but also Kantian approaches to epistemology and metaphysics within the analytic tradition in general. However, much has remained elusive and controversial about the content and status of Strawson's arguments and conclusions themselves. This can be brought out by considering how Strawson's views stand in relation to the four fundamental Kantian themes distinguished at the outset.

With regard to transcendental idealism, theme (4), Strawson sought to preserve what he calls Kant's "analysis of experience" while rejecting what he regarded as "the chief obstacles to a sympathetic understanding of the *Critique*": namely, the "doctrines

522

of transcendental idealism, and the associated picture of the receiving and ordering apparatus of the mind producing Nature as we know it out of the unknowable reality of things as they are in themselves" (Strawson 1966: 22). Given Strawson's strongly traditional (a)-interpretation of Kant's transcendental idealism, most analytic philosophers have agreed that philosophical progress will not be achieved by traveling down that muddy road (and few have found the phenomenalist interpretation of Kant's idealism offered in Bennett 1966 to be enticing either – although Bennett's Kantian modification of Wittgenstein's antiprivate language was a vital contribution to the ensuing debates). The plausibility of the more sanguine (b)-interpretations of Kant's transcendental idealism offered by Bird and Allison, on the other hand, continues to remain a matter of heated dispute among interpreters of Kant.

Strawson's aversion to Kant's alleged model of the "mind producing nature" not surprisingly also leads him to largely negative assessments of what he takes to be Kant's "doctrine of synthesis," which turns out to consist in a transcendental drama starring the "understanding, the active faculty, with the help of its no less active lieutenant, imagination . . ." as players in the misguided performance that Strawson (at least at this stage) dubbed "the imaginary subject of transcendental psychology" (1966: 97). In contrast Kitcher (1990) provides a recent defense of Kant's transcendental psychology with its multilayered account of our various cognitive syntheses, from the perspective of recent theories of cognition. Similarly, to the extent that themes (2) and (3) are likewise taken to be infected by those same mistaken transcendental doctrines, Strawson's "austere" analytic Kant primarily leaves us with Strawson's own descriptive metaphysics and reconstructed transcendental arguments pertaining to theme (3).

Strawson's various attempts to reconstruct Kantian transcendental arguments stimulated lively subsequent debates (see e.g. Stern 1999). It has remained unclear, however, whether Strawson's central transcendental argument in chapter 1 of *Individuals* really succeeds in generating an antiskeptical conclusion. For the skeptic of Hume's stripe can grant that we do indeed ineluctably believe ourselves to possess "adequate criteria" of various familiar kinds for reidentifying material bodies, and concede that such beliefs are basic to the conceptual framework in terms of which we do in fact think about things. But the skeptic's question is whether we can know that it is true that the satisfaction of the criteria we take ourselves to possess is in fact an adequate indicator of the corresponding facts concerning existing material bodies. Stroud (1968) on "Transcendental Arguments" in effect echoed Russell's critique of Kant's alleged psychologism but added Stroud's own critique of transcendental arguments as plagued by antirealism and semantic verificationism. In general it is also not clear what the status is supposed to be of the various nontrivial conceptual connections that Strawson claims to unearth, which Kant would have characterized as synthetic a priori necessities. To suggest as he does that "the argument of the Deduction establishes the most general features of any conception of experience which we can make intelligible to ourselves" (1966: 108) does not appear to advance beyond the original appeal to the ordinary criteria of intelligibility we take ourselves to possess. If that is the case then it remains unclear, for all that Strawson has said, why non-Kantians, whether skeptics, naturalists, or common sense realists, *must* grant that our beliefs are structured by any substantive conceptual necessities having genuine existential import, rather than simply being a web of contingent empirical hypotheses of varying degrees of entrenchment or explanatory plausibility. Debates of this kind concerning the nature and possibility of transcendental arguments constitute one of the most fascinating areas of contemporary analytic epistemology.

More generally in relation to the Copernican theme (2), however, Strawson has subsequently argued "that Kant's Copernican revolution can plausibly be seen as having substantially prevailed in the philosophical tradition to which I belong," that is, in "modern analytical philosophy" (in Strawson 1997: 232). If we set aside the traditional (a)-aspects of Kant's transcendental idealism, Strawson argues that Kant's Copernican thesis that "there are highly general formal conditions which objects must satisfy in order to become possible objects of human knowledge," so that any "attempt to establish how things really are in total abstraction from those conditions will be doomed to failure" (ibid. 232–3), is in different ways sustained in the views of Wittgenstein, Putnam, Quine, Davidson, and Dummett. Despite their differences, Strawson suggests, each of these thinkers in some sense embraces what Putnam (1981) has called internal realism, or pragmatic, commonsense, human realism. For Putnam himself, at any rate, his internal realism is comparable to Kant's empirical realism in its defense of a kind of "objectivity for us" (Putnam 1981: 55), which is relative to the value-laden and pragmatically successful conceptual schemes in terms of which we apprehend the encountered world. This is in contrast to a traditional "God's Eye point of view" or metaphysical realism that is based, as Strawson puts it, on "the conviction that the nature of things as they are in themselves" may and probably does in fact go beyond "all that human beings can, or could, discover or even conceive of" (Strawson 1997: 236; see Moran 2000 for a detailed discussion of the Putnam/Kant comparison).

Putnam's internal realism contends that once we see our way past the subtly misconstrued dichotomies that come in train with the traditional metaphysical realist picture (inner vs. outer, subjective vs. objective, fact vs. value, correspondence to reality vs. warranted assertibility, things in themselves vs. appearances-to-us), we can embrace Kant's Copernican restriction to essentially humanly knowable reality without collapsing into either subjectivism or cultural relativism, and also without subscribing to transcendental idealism on its traditional (a)-interpretation. From this perspective, Russell's and Stroud's criticisms of the anthropocentric character of Kant's descriptive metaphysics can be diagnosed as gaining their seeming plausibility only from the illusory but tempting perspective of metaphysical (i.e., transcendental) realism.

In these ways both appeals to and criticisms of Kant's Copernican revolution continue to occupy center stage not only in current realism vs. antirealism debates but more broadly in discussions concerning the fundamental nature of philosophical inquiry itself. There is, however, a further significant line of Kantian influence among recent analytic philosophers that was not mentioned above by Strawson but which has recently received much discussion and so merits at least a mention in closing.

Two highly influential books that appeared recently, McDowell 1994 and Brandom 1994, were explicitly presented as developing certain related ideas from Kant's theory of conceptual cognition in light of Wilfrid Sellars's conception of the "logical space of reasons" and his critique of the "myth of the given," as indeed had Rosenberg's 1980. Perhaps less well known is that Sellars himself had regarded his own philosophical system as developing analytic versions of all four of the central Kantian themes discussed above.

In Sellars 1953 he defended a framework-relativized conception of the synthetic a priori, thus explicitly resurrecting theme (1). According to Sellars, "every conceptual frame involves propositions which, though synthetic, are true ex vi terminorum, [but] every conceptual frame is also but one among many which compete for adoption in the market-place of experience" (Sellars 1963: 320). One crucial notion in this account is the idea, later developed in detail by Brandom and by Rosenberg, that our concepts have the content or meaning that they do entirely in virtue of their normatively rule-governed role in our inferences, actions, and responses, as implicitly governed by substantive (i.e., not merely formal-logical) material inference principles. Brandom and Rosenberg highlight in particular Kant's own conception of concepts as rules, which they enrich with insights from Wittgenstein and Sellars. Crucially, while empiricists such as Carnap have tended to hold that the meaning of such basic observational beliefs as "This is red" is simply "given" in experience, the Kantian upshot of Sellars's holistic critique of the myth of the given is that no one possesses the concept of red in the first place who has not already been initiated, in the spirit of Kant's themes (2) and (3), into a wider pattern or "logical space" of inferential reason-giving that reflects a communally inherited conception of the causal law-governed nature of things within a given linguistic framework (see also Bird 1962: 101–2). John McDowell in particular has emphasized the Kantian constitutive role of this conceptual "space of reasons" in our grasp, without any appeal to "the given," of the facts that directly manifest themselves to us in the empirically real world.

Finally, and more controversially, Sellars also defended a robust interpretation of theme (4), Kant's transcendental idealism. Similar in some ways to the nontraditional (b)-interpretations in Bird and Allison, Sellars offered a subtle account of Kant's "appearances" according to which they are the ordinary denizens of the objective empirical world, yet they also have the essential status of being possible intentional objects of our forms of representation. In addition, however, Sellars also holds that Kant never doubted – and rightly so, Sellars thinks – that such appearances are due to our being affected by ultimately real things in themselves, about the nature of which Kant held that we must remain agnostic (as on the traditional (b)-interpretation). It is in his scientific reinterpretation of the role of "things in themselves" that Sellars famously diverges from Kant's own views. On his scientific realist construal of the revolutionary changes in fundamental conceptual frameworks involved in the advancing "scientific image" of the world, Sellars ultimately holds that Kant's quasi-theologically conceived domain of things in themselves is ultimately to be reconceived in terms of the projected regulative ideal of a fully comprehensive scientific categorization of the ultimate microphysical nature of things. In the end this provides for Sellars the best explanation of the "manifest image" or Kantian-phenomenal world of appearances-to-us. On this systematic Sellarsian view, Aristotle, Kant, and Strawson turn out to be the heroes of the perceptually manifest image of persons and the world, the correct conceptual articulation of which is the primary task of the perennial philosophy as well as being the fundamental precondition of its successful synoptic integration with the scientific image of the world.

Although only briefly mentioned here, the recent works by Brandom and McDowell are in their very different ways explicitly indebted to these Sellarsian-Kantian views on conceptual cognition, the logical space of reasons, and the myth of the given. Like Strawson and Putnam, however, Brandom and McDowell follow Kant's Copernican revolution primarily in relation to themes (2) and (3) alone. These they see as offering vital clues as to how to correctly reorient our understanding of our own cognitive relationship to the ordinary manifest world of experience, while seeing no bar to accepting the latter as in principle a revelation of how things are in themselves. Whether these last approaches really succeed in avoiding any idealist consequences is at present the subject of much lively debate.

References and Further Reading

Allison, Henry E. (1983). *Kant's Transcendental Idealism*. New Haven: Yale University Press.

Bennett, Jonathan (1966). *Kant's Analytic*. Cambridge: Cambridge University Press.

Bird, Graham (1962). *Kant's Theory of Knowledge*. London: Routledge & Kegan Paul.

Brandom, Robert (1994). *Making it Explicit*. Cambridge, MA: Harvard University Press.

Carnap, Rudolf (1950). Empiricism, semantics, and ontology. *Revue internationale de philosophie*, 4: 20–40.

Coffa, J. Alberto (1991). *The Semantic Tradition from Kant to Carnap*, ed. L. Wessels. Cambridge: Cambridge University Press.

Frege, Gottlob (1953). *The Foundations of Arithmetic*, 2nd ed., tr. J. L. Austin. Evanston, IL: Northwestern University Press. Work originally published in 1884.

Friedman, Michael (2001). *The Dynamics of Reason*. Stanford: CLSI Publications.

Glock, Hans-Johann, ed. (2003). *Strawson and Kant*. Oxford: Clarendon Press.

Hanna, Robert (2001). *Kant and the Foundations of Analytic Philosophy*. Oxford: Oxford University Press.

Kitcher, Patricia (1990). *Kant's Transcendental Psychology*. Oxford: Oxford University Press.

Lewis, Clarence Irving (1929). *Mind and the World Order*. New York: Dover.

McDowell, John (1994). *Mind and World*. Cambridge, MA: Harvard University Press.

Moran, Dermot (2000). Hilary Putnam and Immanuel Kant: Two "internal realists"? *Synthese*, 123: 65–104.

Putnam, Hilary (1981). *Realism, Truth and History*. Cambridge: Cambridge University Press.

Quine, Willard Van Orman (1951). Two dogmas of empiricism. In *From a Logical Point of View*. New York: Harper & Row.

Reichenbach, Hans (1951). *The Rise of Scientific Philosophy*. Los Angeles: University of California Press.

Reichenbach, Hans (1965). *Relativitätstheorie und Erkenntnis Apriori* [*The Theory of Relativity and A Priori Knowledge*]. Berlin: Springer. Originally published in 1920.

Rosenberg, Jay F. (1980). *One World and Our Knowledge of It*. Dordrecht: D. Reidel.

Russell, Bertrand (1912). *The Problems of Philosophy*. Oxford: Oxford University Press, 1998.

Sellars, Wilfrid (1963). *Science, Perception and Reality*. Atascadero, CA: Ridgeview Publishing.

Sellars, Wilfrid (2002). *Kant's Transcendental Metaphysics: Sellars' Cassirer Lectures Notes and Other Essays*, ed. Jeffrey F. Sicha. Atascadero, CA: Ridgeview Publishing.

Stern, Robert, ed. (1999). *Transcendental Arguments: Problems and Prospects*. Oxford: Clarendon Press.

Strawson, P. F. (1959). *Individuals*. London: Methuen.

Strawson, P. F. (1966). *The Bounds of Sense*. London: Methuen.

Strawson, P. F. (1997). *Entity and Identity and Other Essays*. Oxford: Oxford University Press.

Stroud, Barry (1968). Transcendental arguments. *Journal of Philosophy*, 65: 241–56. Reprinted in Ralph C. S. Walker (ed.), *Kant on Pure Reason* (pp. 117–31). Oxford: Oxford University Press, 1982.

Index

Lightning Source UK Ltd.
Milton Keynes UK
UKOW05f0126170917

309286UK00002B/6/P